Faithfully yours,

Marshall Stringfield

A HISTORY

... of ...

CAROLINE COUNTY

VIRGINIA

From its Formation in 1727 to 1924.

*Compiled from Original Records and
Authoritative Sources and Profusely
Illustrated.*

By

MARSHALL WINGFIELD

To which is Appended

"A DISCOURSE OF VIRGINIA"

By EDWARD MARIA WINGFIELD

*First Governor of the Colony of Virginia, which 'Discourse'
constitutes Virginia's first written History.*

Baltimore

REGIONAL PUBLISHING COMPANY

1975

Originally Published
Richmond, 1924

Reprinted
Regional Publishing Company
Baltimore, 1969

Baltimore, 1975

Library of Congress Catalogue Card Number 70-88162
International Standard Book Number 0-8063-7975-8

PREFACE

Four years have been spent in the writing of this book, but, notwithstanding the time and labour devoted to the enterprise, imperfections will no doubt appear. There are no perfect histories—or men either, for that matter—in this world. Accuracy, rather than literary excellency, has been the constant aim of the author, and, while errors will no doubt appear, it is believed that these have been reduced to the minimum and are of a minor nature.

No mercenary motive has entered into the writing. The very warmest friends of the author have advised against the enterprise as a ruinous proposition financially, but he has persevered in the belief that a sufficient number of men and women may be found who will be so appreciative of this effort to preserve the history of their native county that they will purchase the very limited edition being issued and thus reimburse the cost of publication. If a sufficient number of copies are sold to repay the actual cost of printing and engraving the author will be content, and will find, in the appreciation of lovers of this kind of history, and in the consciousness of work honestly done, an ample reward for the time, money and energy spent in the writing.

It is regrettable that the work was not undertaken by some one years before the author was born, for then many valuable facts could have been preserved which have now passed from the realm of history into the mists of tradition. Many men, women, and places, well-known in a former day, have been forgotten, and in many instances little or nothing remains to give them "a local habitation and a name."

The old Order Books of the county were not sent to Richmond for preservation at the outbreak of the Civil War, as were most of the other court records, and so were preserved, while those sent away for safe-keeping were lost. These ancient Order Books contain much of the history of the county, and are of inestimable value to the genealogist, but they do not have as large a place in this volume as one could wish, for the reason that other and more important matter required space. The Will Books, Deed Books and Marriage Registers have but small place in this volume for the same reason. No doubt the reader will agree that there is enough detail in the book without them.

There is enough left-over material, if added to abstracts from
Order, Deed, Will and Marriage Books, to make another volume
equally as large as this, and, from many standpoints more
valuable, but the financial risk involved in such a publication is
greater than the author wishes to assume and so the matter must
rest. However, should as many as two or three hundred persons
express a desire for a second volume the book might be brought
out by subscription.

The indifference on the part of those who should have been
most keenly interested in the preservation of Caroline's history
has been the most disappointing thing in connection with this
work, but, on the other hand, a lively interest has been manifested
by a great number of persons but slightly connected with the
county, if at all. These latter have lent valuable assistance and
the recollection of their sympathetic co-operation and courtesy
will offset any memories of the indifferent.

Grateful acknowledgments are extended to the following,
without whose assistance and encouragement this book had never
been written: Dr. H. R. McIlwaine, State Librarian of Virginia;
Wilmer L. Hall, Assistant Librarian; Morgan P. Robinson, State
Archivist; E. G. Swem, Librarian of William and Mary; W. G.
Stanard, Secretary of Virginia Historical Society; Officials of the
Congressional Library at Washington; Captain J. B. Baylor,
Washington; Hon. Rosewell Page, Hanover; Mrs. Frank Page,
Bridgeport, Conn.; M. G. Willis, Fredericksburg; Rev. E. L.
Goodwin, Ashland; Bishop D. J. O'Connell, Richmond; Rev.
George Stuart Fitzhugh, Fredericksburg; Rev. John A. Callahan,
Fredericksburg; Miss Margaret Crenshaw, Richmond; Judge J.
Hoge Ricks, Richmond; Judge Wm. Moncure, Richmond; General
Jo. Lane Stern, Richmond; Miss Helen La B. Huntley, Richmond;
Rev. E. H. Rowe, Milford; Mrs. Pickett A. Timmins, Chicago;
President A. B. Chandler, Jr., Fredericksburg; President J. A. C.
Chandler, Williamsburg; C. W. Bransford, Owensboro, Kentucky;
Miss Lula C. Redd, Ashland; Rev. Andrew Broaddus, Sparta;
Miss Anne Maury White, Richmond; Miss Sally Nelson Gravatt,
Fredericksburg; Mrs. A. F. Turner, Fredericksburg; Hon. George
P. Lyon, Woodford; Rev. R. C. Gilmore, Fredericksburg; Hon.
James B. Wood, Richmond; Mrs. A. L. Martin, Naulakla;
W. H. Pittman, Raleigh, N. C.; Mrs. J. E. Warren, Newport
News; L. D. George, Penola; H. H. George, Richmond; Francis

W. Scott, Deltaville; Mrs. W. W. Sale, Vinita; Mrs. W. E. Williams, Berwick, Pa.; Prof. Algar Woolfolk, Richmond; Rev. H. T. Louthan, Staunton; Mrs. J. H. Rives, Richmond; Miss Ida Birkenhead Smith, Brandywine; Hon. Warner Peatross, Norfolk; Prof. A. M. Walker, Bowling Green; Prof. L. L. Davis, Bowling Green; Clerk E. R. Coghill, Bowling Green; L. D. Vincent, Bowling Green; Miss Laura Christian, Point Eastern; Prof. John Roy Baylor, Chattanooga, Tennessee; Gurney C. Gue, Merrick, N. Y.; Eppa Hunton, Jr., Richmond; Mrs. L. D. Scott, Atlanta, Ga.; William Dickinson Buckner, New York City; Mrs. J. Fulton Williams, Charlottesville; Dr. Hermon B. Anderson, Noel; Horace A. Hawkins, Richmond; Charles H. Callahan, Alexandria; Charles A. Nesbitt, Richmond; Prof. W. A. Vaughan, Bowling Green; Rev. L. M. Ritter, Bowling Green; Rev. W. D. Bremner, Penola; Mrs. T. B. Gill, Bowling Green; Mrs. Daniel Coleman DeJarnette, Milford; Willing Bowie, Bowling Green; Thomas C. Valentine, Bowling Green, and the Hon. Otis Bland, of Washington.

MARSHALL WINGFIELD.

Bowling Green, Va., February 27, 1924.

CONTENTS

LIST OF ILLUSTRATIONS

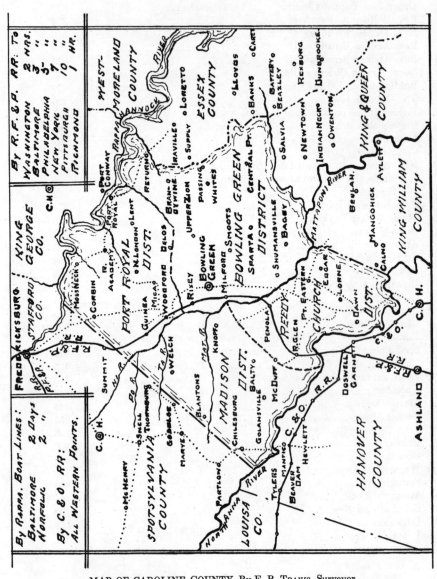

MAP OF CAROLINE COUNTY, By E. B. TRAVIS, Surveyor.

SCALE: 10 miles to the inch.

History of Caroline County, Va.

THE ERECTION OF CAROLINE COUNTY

Caroline county, Virginia, was formed in 1727, the first year of the reign of George II, and derived its name from the new Sovereign's wife, Queen Caroline. The story of the legislation incident to its establishment is set forth in the following extracts from the Legislative Journals of the Colonial Council of Virginia, Volume 2, which were edited by H. R. McIlwaine, State Librarian of Virginia:

"*Saturday, March the 9th, 1727.* Present Robert Carter, James Blair, Mann Page, Peter Beverly, John Robinson, John Grymes & John Custis, Esqrs.

"A message from the Burgesses by Mr. Clayton & others, that the House has passed a Bill entitled, An act for erecting a new County on the heads of Essex, King & Queen, and King William Counties, and for calling the same Caroline County, to which they desire the concurrence of the Council.

"An Engrossed Bill from the Burgesses Ent'd *An Act for Erecting A New County on the Heads of Essex, King aud Queen and King William Counties and for Calling the Same Caroline County* read the first time. Ordered, That the Bill be read a second time. Adjourned till Monday ten o'clock.

"*Monday, March the 11th, 1727.* Present same as above save Custis. A bill entitled *An Act for Erecting A New County Etc.*, read the second time and Ordered to be committed for amendments.

"*Tuesday, March the 12th, 1727.* Present as yesterday. A bill ent'd *An Act for Erecting A New County Etc* read the third time with the amendments. Resolved, that the Bill with the Amendments be agreed to. Ordered, That the Clerk of the General Assembly carry the said Bill to the Burgesses and desire their concurrence to the said Amendments."

Thus was formed the twenty-ninth county of the Commonwealth (twenty-first, if original shires are omitted), which was destined to make, through her sons, an inestimable contribution to the state and nation. Probably no political unit of the same area has contributed more to the sum of human thought and action since the golden days of Athens.

In the Council Journals above referred to, Vol. 2, p. 914, it is recorded that on Wednesday, May 26, 1742, the Council received a Message from the House of Burgesses that they had passed a Bill entitled, "An Act for dividing the County of King and Queen, and adding the upper part thereof to the County of Caroline, to which they desire the concurrence of the Council." This Bill was read the first time when presented, the second time on the following day and a third time on June 7th, and at the third reading was amended, agreed to, and referred back to the House for their concurrence to the amendment. The House amended the amendment of the Council and referred the Bill back to the Council which resolved, "That the said amendment be agreed to." Thus were the boundaries of Caroline enlarged and fixed.

COLONIAL GOVERNMENT OF CAROLINE COUNTY

EARLIEST DIVISIONS

The earliest groups in Colonial Virginia were known as Plantations, Congregations, Hundreds and Cities. These several names signified very nearly the same thing. As to the origin of these first divisions, or groups, but little is known, save that the hostility of the Indians made it safer for the colonists to maintain such local organizations for purposes of defense, and the social and religious life of the people was better served by such grouping, which gave to every settlement its own house of worship. The civil and political life also functioned through these divisions, each group having representation in the General Assembly. As early as 1619, burgesses were sent to the General Assembly from "James City," "Captain Ward's Plantation," "Stanley Hundred," and other units of the colony, eleven places all told.

In "The List of the Living on February 16, 1623," as preserved in the Colonial Records of Virginia, we learn that the colony contained twenty-four settlements after the fearful massacre of 1622. The list of burgesses elected to the Assembly of 1629, discloses the fact that each of the twenty-four settlements had representation in that body. Immediately after 1629, the Plantations began to consolidate, and in the next General Assembly only thirteen groups or Plantations were represented.

LATER DIVISIONS

The Parish, County, and Precinct, succeeded the Plantation, Congregation, Hundred and City. In the list of burgesses of 1631, the word "parish" first occurs as referring to a politico-ecclesiastical division of the colony, it being used here in connection with the localities of Waters Creek and Elizabeth City and the return of a burgess from "Upper Parish of Elizabeth City."

As early as 1618, the Governor and Council had been ordered to divide the colony into Counties (see Hening's Statutes at Large), but, for some reason, this was not done until 1634, in which year the colony was "divided into eight shires (Counties) which were to be governed as the shires in England, with lieutenants appointed as in England, and in a more especial manner to take care of the war against the Indians; Sheriffs were to be elected as in England, to have the same powers as there, and Sergeants and Bailiffs where need required." (Hening Vol. I, p. 224.)

The county was a territorial division, in which justice was administered by eight, or more, men sitting as a county court, and in which the citizens were members of one body of county militia, commanded by the county lieutenant.

THE COUNTY LIEUTENANT

The County Lieutenant corresponded to the Lord Lieutenant of England, and was one of the most important men in the county. He received his appointment from the Governor and the Council, commanded the county militia, and was empowered to place all male, white, persons, above the age of eighteen, in the militia, and under such captains as he wished to appoint. He could order private drills whenever and wherever he pleased, and was under compulsion to hold four general musters annually. W. W. Scott, in his History of Orange, says: "These musters constituted a distinctly social feature *   *   *   * The companies had their places of assembly for drill, and the contrast between the flamboyant and gorgeous uniforms of the officers and the homespun drab of the privates was very striking. The officers would be assembled for 'training' for several days prior to each General Muster, and when the great occasion came the people flocked to see it as they do now to a circus. The appearance of the field and staff mounted on prancing steeds was a triumphal pageant, and when the music struck up the martial spirit became intense, and the maneuvres much involved." The County Lieutenant also presided over courts martial and exercises much authority in time of war.

THE MONTHLY COURT

In 1623, the Governor and Council ordered that courts of record be kept monthly in each corporate unit of the colony, and that the commanders of these places, and such others as the Governor and Council might appoint should be the Judges, with reservation of appeal after sentence to the Governor and Council. "The commanders were to be of the quorum and sentence was to be given by the major parties." (Hening, Vol. I.) The quorum consisted of a select number of justices of the peace, chosen for their superior knowledge and discretion, one or two of whom had to be included in the number of justices necessary to constitute a court. The commissioners of the Monthly Court had jurisdiction over all civil cases not involving more than ten pounds, and one member of the Council had to sit with such commissioner at all hearings.

THE COUNTY COURT

An enactment of 1642, provided that the Monthly Court be reduced to six courts annually, and that these be called County Courts, instead of Monthly, and that the commissioners be styled Commissioners of County Courts. (Hening, Vol. I). These bi-monthly courts were held for about twenty-five years, or till 1769, after which time they were held monthly. The County Court consisted of eight or more citizens of the county who were commissioned by the Governor and Council and called justices of the peace. Four justices, if one were of the quorum, constituted a court. These courts had jurisdiction over all cases in common law, or in chancery, provided the amount involved was over twenty-five shillings, and the penalty for the alleged crime less than loss of life or outlawry. Matters under twenty-five shillings were adjusted by a single justice, while all greater crimes were adjudicated by the Governor and Council in the General Court.

The County Court had, in addition to its judicial functions, the authority to erect and repair the county court-house, to contract for the construction of roads and bridges, or, in the absence of such contract, to procure labour for the construction of the same by drafting all able-bodied, tithable males, to perform a certain amount of work under the direction of a surveyor. These courts also had the authority to clear the rivers of obstructions, to beat the bounds of parishes, to license taverns, to recommend inspectors of tobacco, to designate places for tobacco warehouses, to designate "landings," to appoint constables, and to nominate for sheriff three of its own members, one of whom the Governor invariably appointed for the ensuing year.

THE SHERIFF

The sheriffs were the ministerial officers of the County Court, and performed the duties pertaining to that office as they were understood in England, so far as applicable to Virginia; they collected the "quit rents," the public and county levies, the parish levy, and also held the election for burgesses, and summoned the juries for both County and General Courts. Trial by jury was given the colony in 1621, and was confirmed and established by the Act of 1642. The juries which tried capital offenses in the General Court were summoned from the county in which the crime was alleged to have been committed, but no juror could serve if challenged by the accused.

THE CONSTABLE

The sheriffs were assisted by officers, called constables, who were appointed by the County Courts and set over certain bounds, within the county, termed precincts. Their authority was, to a great extent, co-ordinate with the sheriffs, but in many cases they had certain authority peculiarly their own. They collected fines for small offenses, whipped criminals, arrested violators of the revenue laws, accompanied those who searched places suspected of containing smuggled goods, and had sole charge of runaway sailors, servants and slaves. To these were added the duties of visiting tobacco fields and destroying all inferior growths, such as "seconds" or "suckers," the killing of stray dogs, and superfluous dogs about the "quarters," and the execution of the game laws. The constable's fees, like the fees of many other officers of that period, were paid in tobacco. For serving a warrant he received ten pounds of tobacco, for summoning a witness, five; for summoning coroner's jury and witnesses, fifty; for putting person in the stocks, ten; for whipping a person, ten; and for removing from the parish any person suspected of becoming a public charge, two pounds for every mile traveled going and returning. He also received one pound of tobacco out of the county levy for each tithable in his precinct, and was exempt from payment of taxes, and from jury service, while in office.

THE PARISH

The parish was a politico-ecclesiastical division of the colony, which was coexistent with the county, as a rule, but not always coterminous. Some counties contained several parishes, and some parishes embraced more than one county. The law required that Churches be so situated that all inhabitants might attend them without any great inconvenience, and as a result Churches were to be found on an average of from ten to fifteen miles apart, according to density of population.

As the population moved upward from the "lower counties" new Churches were erected to accommodate the people, and new parishes were formed on the heads of the old, by the General Assembly, and thus the number of parishes grew in proportion to the number of new counties. Indeed it frequently happened that the parish preceded the county, and Churches were built in new sections before the county court-house or the jail.

THE VESTRY

The parish vestry consisted of twelve of the most prominent and substantial men of the parish, and divided with the court the responsibility for the public welfare of their respective communities. They exercised considerable civil authority, such as processioning the bounds, or beating the bounds, of all farms and plantations, and the making levies for the support of paupers and unfortunate children. Every fourth year the vestry divided the parish into precincts and appointed two honest and intelligent freeholders of each precinct to see that the bounds of each farm or plantation were processioned, and that the reports of such surveying, or processioning, were registered with the parish clerk. This was the only method of recording land titles in Virginia before the war of the Revolution.

Each year the vestry laid the parish levy of a certain number of pounds of tobacco upon each "tithable"—that is, every male white person, and every negro or Indian servant above sixteen years of age, the taxes of the family, and of the servants being paid by the master, or head of the household. From these levies the vestry paid for the building and repairing of Churches, the purchase of glebes, salaries of ministers, salaries of sextons, and support of indigent persons and illegitimate children.

Thus the county government of colonial Virginia was ·divided into five branches—namely, executive, legislative, judicial, ecclesiastical and military. The Governor, or executive, was appointed by the Crown; the General Assembly, or legislative, was elected by the people; the justices of the peace constituting the County Court, or judicial, were appointed by the Governor; the twelve men constituting the vestry, or ecclesiastical, were appointed by their predecessors (a close corporation); and the county lieutenant, or military, was appointed by the Governor.

It frequently happened that the county lieutenant, and the justices of the peace were also members of the vestry, thus centering all local authority in the hands of twelve men, none of whom were elected by the people. Thus it was that the common people, except when casting a ballot for a member of the House of Burgesses, frequently found themselves as powerless to correct irregularities of the local government under which they lived, as the subjects of an absolute monarchy.

VIRGINIA COUNTIES IN THE ORDER OF THEIR FORMATION AND TERRITORY FROM WHICH FORMED

Charles City	1634	Original Shire.
Elizabeth City	1634	Original Shire.
Henrico	1634	Original Shire.
James City	1634	Original Shire.
Isle of Wight	1637	Formerly Warrosquyoake.
Nansemond	1642	Formerly Upper Norfolk.
Northampton	1642	Formerly Accomack.
Warwick	1642	Formerly Warwick River.
York	1642	Formerly Charles River.
Northumberland	1648	From Chickacoan.
Gloucester	1651	From York.
Lancaster	1651	From Northumberland and York.
Surry	1652	From James City.
Westmoreland	1653	From Northumberland and King George.
New Kent	1654	From York.
Accomack	1663	From Northampton.
Stafford	1664	From Westmoreland.
Middlesex	1673	Lancaster.
King and Queen	1691	From New Kent.
Norfolk	1691	From Lower Norfolk.
Princess Anne	1691	From Lower Norfolk.

Essex	1692	From Rappahannock (Old).
Richmond	1692	From Rappahannock (Old).
King William	1702	From King and Queen.
Prince George	1703	From Charles City.
King George	1721	From Richmond and Westmoreland.
Hanover	1721	From New Kent.
Spotsylvania	1721	From Essex, King William and King and Queen.
Caroline	1727	From Essex, King William and King and Queen.
Goochland	1728	From Henrico.
Prince William	1731	From Stafford and King George.
Brunswick	1732	Prince George, Surry and Isle of Wight.
Orange	1734	From Spotsylvania.
Amelia	1735	From Prince George and Brunswick.
Fairfax	1742	From Prince William. (Part of Loudon added afterward).
Louisa	1742	From Hanover.
Frederick	1743	From Orange and part of Augusta.
Albemarle	1744	From Goochland and part of Louisa.
Augusta	1745	From Orange.
Lunenburg	1746	From Brunswick.
Culpeper	1749	From Orange.
Cumberland	1749	From Goochland. (Part of Buckingham added afterward).
Southampton	1749	From Isle of Wight and part of Nansemond.
Chesterfield	1749	From Henrico.
Dinwiddie	1752	From Prince George.
Halifax	1752	From Lunenburg.
Prince Edward	1754	From Amelia.
Sussex	1754	From Surry.
Bedford	1754	From Lunenburg and part of Albemarle.
Loudon	1757	From Fairfax.
Fauquier	1759	From Prince William.
Amherst	1761	From Albemarle.
Buckingham	1761	From Albemarle. (Part of Appomattox added afterward).
Charlotte	1765	From Lunenburg.
Mecklenburg	1765	From Lunenburg.
Pittsylvania	1767	From Halifax.
Botetourt	1770	From Augusta.
Henry	1777	From Pittsylvania.
Montgomery	1777	From Fincastle which became extinct in 1777.
Washington	1777	From Fincastle and part of Montgomery.
Powhatan	1777	From Cumberland and part of Chesterfield.
Fluvanna	1777	From Albemarle.
Rockbridge	1778	From Augusta and Botetourt.
Rockingham	1778	From Augusta.
Shenandoah	1778	Formerly Dunmore County.

Greenville	1781	From Brunswick and part of Sussex.
Campbell	1782	From Bedford.
Franklin	1786	From Bedford and Henry (Part of Patrick added afterward).
Russell	1786	From Washington.
Nottoway	1789	From Amelia.
Wythe	1790	From Montgomery.
Patrick	1791	From Henry.
Bath	1791	From Augusta, Botetourt and Greenbrier.
Mathews	1791	From Gloucester.
Lee	1793	From Russell.
Grayson	1793	From Wythe and part of Patrick.
Madison	1793	From Culpeper.
Tazewell	1800	From Wythe and Russell.
Giles	1806	From Montgomery, Monroe, Tazewell, Wythe, Mercer and Craig.
Nelson	1808	From Amherst.
Scott	1814	From Lee, Russell and Washington.
Alleghany	1822	From Bath, Botetourt and Monroe.
Floyd	1831	From Montgomery and Franklin.
Page	1831	From Rockingham and Shenandoah.
Smyth	1832	From Washington and Wythe.
Rappahannock	1833	From Culpeper.
Clarke	1836	From Frederick and part of Warren.
Warren	1836	From Shenandoah and Frederick.
Greene	1838	From Orange.
Roanoke	1838	From Botetourt and Montgomery.
Pulaski	1839	From Montgomery and Wythe.
Carroll	1842	From Grayson and Patrick.
Appomattox	1845	From Buckingham, Prince Edward, Charlotte and Campbell.
Highland	1847	From Bath and Pendleton.
Craig	1851	Botetourt, Roanoke, Giles, Monroe, Montgomery and Alleghany.
Wise	1856	From Lee, Scott and Russell.
Buchanan	1858	From Tazewell and Russell.
Bland	1861	From Giles, Tazewell and Wythe.
Dickenson	1880	From Russell, Wise and Buchanan.
Arlington	1920	From Alexandria County (name changed).

EXTINCT COUNTIES WHOSE AREA IS NOW IN VIRGINIA

Warwick River	1634	Original Shire. Became Warwick in 1642.
Warrosquyoake	1634	Original Shire. Became Isle of Wight in 1637.
Charles River	1634	Original Shire. Became York in 1642.
Accawmack	1634	Original Shire. Became Northampton in 1642.

New Norfolk	1636	Divided into Upper Norfolk and Lower Norfolk in 1637.
Lower Norfolk	1637	Became Norfolk in 1691.
Upper Norfolk	1637	Became Nansemond in 1642.
Rappahannock	1656	Divided into Essex and Richmond Counties in 1692.
Fincastle	1772	Divided into Montgomery and Washington in 1777.
Dunmore	1772	Became Shenandoah County in 1778.
Alexandria	1846	Became Arlington County in 1920.

EXTINCT COUNTY WHOSE AREA IS NOW ON THE WESTERN SIDE OF THE OHIO RIVER

Illinois County formed from Augusta in 1778. Became State of Illinois in 1784.

EXTINCT COUNTY WHOSE AREA IS NOW IN WESTERN PENNSYLVANIA

Yohogania County formed from Augusta in 1776. Became part of Pennsylvania in 1786.

EXTINCT COUNTY WHOSE AREA IS NOW IN KENTUCKY

Kentucky County formed from Fincastle County in 1777. Became State of Kentucky in 1780.

OLD VIRGINIA COUNTIES NOW IN KENTUCKY

Fayette	Formed	1780	From	Kentucky County.
Jefferson	"	1780	"	Kentucky County.
Lincoln	"	1780	"	Kentucky County.
Nelson	"	1785	"	Jefferson County.
Mercer	"	1786	"	Lincoln County.
Madison	"	1786	"	Lincoln County.
Bourbon	"	1786	"	Fayette County.
Woodford	"	1789	"	Fayette County.
Mason	"	1789	"	Bourbon County.

OLD VIRGINIA COUNTIES WHICH BECAME WEST VIRGINIA UPON THE RENDING OF VIRGINIA IN 1862

Hampshire	Formed	1754	From	Augusta and Frederick.
Berkley	"	1772	"	Frederick.
Monongalia	"	1776	"	Augusta.
Ohio	"	1776	"	Augusta and Yohogania.
Greenbrier	"	1778	"	Botetourt and Montgomery.
Jefferson	"	1780	"	Kentucky County.
Harrison	"	1784	"	Monongalia.
Hardy	"	1786	"	Hampshire.
Randolph	"	1787	"	Harrison.

Pendleton....	Formed	1788	From Augusta, Hardy, Rockingham and Bath.
Kanawha....	"	1789	" Greenbrier and Montgomery.
Woodford....	"	1789	" Fayette.
Brooke......	"	1797	" Ohio County.
Wood.......	"	1798	" Harrison and Kanawha.
Monroe.....	"	1799	" Greenbrier and Botetourt.
Mason......	"	1804	" Kanawha.
Cabell......	"	1809	" Kanawha.
Tyler.......	"	1814	" Ohio County.
Lewis......	"	1816	" Harrison and Randolph Counties.
Preston.....	"	1818	" Monongalia and Randolph.
Nicholas.....	"	1818	" Greenbrier, Kanawha and Randolph.
Morgan.....	"	1820	" Berkley and Hampshire.
Pocahontas..	"	1821	" Bath, Pendleton, Randolph and Greenbrier.
Logan.......	"	1824	" Giles, Cabell, Tazewell and Kanawha.
Fayette.....	"	1831	" Logan, Greenbrier, Nicholas and Kanawha.
Jackson.....	"	1831	" Mason, Wood and Kanawha.
Marshall....	"	1835	" Ohio County.
Braxton.....	"	1836	" Lewis, Nicholas, Randolph and Kanawha.
Mercer......	"	1837	" Giles and Tazewell.
Marion......	"	1842	" Monongalia and Harrison.
Barbour.....	"	1843	" Harrison, Lewis and Randolph.
Ritchie......	"	1843	" Harrison, Lewis and Wood.
Taylor......	"	1844	" Harrison, Barbour and Marion.
Gilmer......	"	1845	" Lewis and Kanawha.
Doddridge...	"	1845	" Harrison, Tyler, Ritchie and Lewis.
Wetzel......	"	1846	" Tyler.
Boone.......	"	1847	" Logan, Cabell and Kanawha.
Wirt........	"	1848	" Wood and Jackson.
Hancock....	"	1848	" Brooke.
Putnam.....	"	1848	" Mason, Cabell and Kanawha.
Raleigh.....	"	1850	" Fayette.
Upshur......	"	1851	" Randolph, Barbour and Lewis.
Pleasants....	"	1851	" Wood, Tyler and Ritchie.
Calhoun.....	"	1856	" Gilmer.
Roane.......	"	1856	" Gilmer, Jackson and Kanawha.
Tucker......	"	1856	" Randolph County.
McDowell...	"	1858	" Tazewell.
Clay........	"	1858	" Braxton and Nicholas.
Webster.....	"	1860	" Braxton, Nicholas and Randolph.

NOTE.—Kentucky has a county named for General William Woodford, of Caroline; West Virginia has counties named for General Woodford, Edmund Pendleton, and John Taylor, of Caroline; Virginia and Missouri have counties named for Caroline men.

CLERICAL SIDELIGHTS ON COLONIAL CAROLINE

The Reverend Jonathan Boucher was born in England, "at Blencogo, in Cumberland, England, a small hamlet on the road between Wigton and Allonby," March 12, 1738. He came to America in the year 1757, and in 1761 was nominated by the vestry of Hanover Parish, King George County, for the rectorship. Not being in orders he went to England, where, on March 26, 1762, he was ordained. On returning to America he took charge of the parish to which he had been nominated and here he remained until he removed to St. Mary's Parish in Caroline County, which lay across the Rappahannock river, opposite Hanover Parish.

Mr. Boucher was married three times; his first wife being a niece of the great Addison of The Spectator. She was a woman of rare beauty, and the story of their first meeting is both singular and interesting. Mr. Boucher was visiting a certain community in Caroline for the first time, and, while here, he called on a man with whom he had no previous acquaintance. This man's daughter had dreamed on the night before of the arrival of a strange young man who should become her husband. On answering the knock at the door the young lady swooned, for before her was the face she had seen in her dream.

During those troubled and trying days just before the outbreak of the Revolution, when many of the most pronounced Tories weakened, Boucher remained an ardent Royalist and persisted in preaching loyalty and adherence to the mother country. This led to intense opposition to his ministry in St. Mary's Parish, and even to attempted violence. On one occasion he was warned before the morning Service in Old Mount Church (now Rappahannock Academy) that if he dared to read one word of the loyal Bidding-prayer he would be instantly shot dead in his pulpit. Nevertheless he appeared in his pulpit, on the moment, with two ominous horse pistols which he placed on his pulpit cushion, and thereupon proceeded to read the forbidden prayer distinctly. When he had finished he calmly descended the pulpit stairs to his vestry.

It appears that Mr. Boucher conceived the notion that for some unaccountable reason—possibly his intimacy with Washington—he had been singled out from all others who held similar political sentiments, and persecuted and punished beyond reason.

His deep grief and strong indignation found expression in a letter to Washington under date of August 6, 1775, which letter is reproduced in full in *Notes and Queries* (London) Volume six of the fifth series, and which is in part, as follows:

" *To Colonel George Washington,*
    "*The Lodge, August 6th, 1775:*

"Dear Sir,—I thought it far from the least pleasing circumstance attending my removal hither that it placed me in your immediate neighborhood.   For having now been happy in your acquaintance several years, I could not help considering myself, nor indeed help hoping that I was considered by you, as an old friend; and of course I counted on our living together in the pleasing intercourse of giving and receiving the mutual good offices of neighborhood and friendship.

"That things have turned out much otherwise I need not inform you.   Mortified and grieved as I confess myself to be at this disappointment, I am by no means prepared to say that you are wholly to be blamed for it; nor, as I would fain hope you in your turn will own, is it entirely owing to any fault of mine. I can easily suppose at least that neither of us think ourselves to blame; and yet I cannot help thinking that had I been in your place I should have taken a different part from that which you have chosen.   Permit me, sir, as one who was once your friend, freely to expostulate with you.   If I am still in the wrong, I am about to suffer such punishment as might satisfy the malice of even the most vindictive enemy.

"On the great points so long debated between us it is not my design to again to solicit your attention.   We have now each of us taken and avowed our side, and with such ardour as becomes men who are earnest in their convictions.   That we should both be right is impossible, but that we both think we are must in common candour be allowed.   And this extreme difference of opinion between ourselves, where we have no grounds for charging each other with being influenced by any sinister or unworthy motives, should teach us no less candour in judging of and dealing by others in a similar predicament.   *   *   *   * The true plan is for each party to defend his own side as well as he can by fair argument, and also, if possible, to convince his adversary; but everything that savours of, or approaches to, coercion or compulsion is persecution and tyranny.

"It is on this ground that I complain of you and those with whom you side. How large a proportion of the people in general think with you or think with me it is not in our power to ascertain here. * * * * But there is this difference between us. No Tory has yet in a single instance misused or injured a Whig merely for being a Whig. And whatever may be the boasted superiority of your party, it will not be denied that in some instances at least this has been in our power. With respect to Whig, however, the case has been exactly the reverse: A Tory at all in the power of a Whig never escaped ill treatment merely because of his being a Tory. How contrary all this is to that liberty which Whigs are ever so forward to profess need not be insisted on here; it is so contrary to all justice and honour, that were there no other reasons, I would not be a Whig, because their principle as exemplified in practice, lead to that which is so mean and unmanly.

"It is a general fault to charge all the errors of a party on every individual of that party. I wish to avoid the disgrace of so indiscriminate a judgment by acknowledging that I know many Whigs who are not tyrants. In this number it is but doing you common justice to place you. I wish I could go on and also declare that you have been careful to discourage others from persecution; but, scorning to flatter, as much as I scorn to tax you wrongfully, I am bold to tell you that you have much to answer for in this way. It is not a little that you have to answer for with respect to myself.

"You know you have acknowledged the sincerity and the purity of my principles; and have been so candid as to lament that you could not think on the great points that agitate our common country as I do. Now, sir, it is impossible I should sometimes avow one kind of principles and sometimes another. I have at least the merit of consistency; and neither in any private or public conversation, in anything I have written, nor in anything I have delivered from the pulpit, have I ever asserted any other opinions or doctrines than you have repeatedly heard me assert, both in my own house and yours. You cannot say that I deserve to be run down, vilified, and injured in the manner you know has fallen to my lot, merely because I cannot bring myself to think on some political points just as you and your party would have me think. And yet you have borne to look on, at least as an unconcerned spectator, whilst, like the frogs in the fable, I have in a manner been pelted to death. I do not ask if such conduct in you was friendly: was it either just, manly or generous? * *."

It is fitting to remark here that twenty-two years later, on publishing *A View of the Causes and Consequences of the American Revolution*, Mr. Boucher dedicated his volume to the very man whom he thought had played so mean a part, and who was no longer worthy of his friendship. The dedication was in the following words:

"To George Washington, Esquire, of Mount Vernon, in Fairfax County, Virginia. Sir, In prefixing your name to a work avowedly hostile to that Revolution in which you bore a ·distinguished part, I am not conscious that I deserve to be charged with inconsistency. I do not address myself to the General of a Conventional Army, but to the late dignified President of the United States, the friend of rational and sober freedom.

"As a British subject I have observed with pleasure that the form of Government, under which you and your fellow-citizens now hope to find peace and happiness, however defective in many respects, has, in the unity of its executive, and the division of its legislative, powers, been formed after a British model. That, in the discharge of your duties as head of this Government, you have resisted those anarchical doctrines, which are hardly less dangerous to America than to Europe, is not more an eulogium on the wisdom of our forefathers, than honourable to your individual wisdom and integrity.

"As a Minister of Religion I am equally bound to tender you my respects for having (in your valedictory addressed to your countrymen) asserted your opinion that 'the only firm supports of political prosperity, are religion and morality,' and that, 'morality can be maintained only by religion.' Those best friends of mankind, who, amidst all the din and uproar and Utopian reforms, persist to think that the affairs of this world can never be well administered by men trained to disregard the God who made it, must ever thank you for this decided protest against the fundamental maxim of modern revolutionist, that religion is no concern of the State.

"It is on these grounds, Sir, that I now presume (and I hope not impertinently) to add my name to the list of those who have dedicated their works to you. One of them, not inconsiderable in fame, from having been your fulsome flatterer, has become your foul calmuniator: to such dedicators I am willing to persuade myself I have no resemblance.   I bring no incense to your shrine even in a Dedication.   Having never paid court to you whilst you shone in an exalted station, I am not so weak as to steer my little bark across the Atlantic in search of patronage and preferment; or so vain as to imagine that, now, in the evening of my life, I may yet be warmed by your setting sun.   My utmost ambition will be abundantly gratified by your condescending, as a private Gentleman in America, to receive with candour and kindness this disinterested testimony of regard from a private Clergyman in England.   I was once your neighbor and your friend: the unhappy dispute, which terminated in the disunion of our respective countries, also broke off our personal connexion: but I never was more than your political enemy; and every sentiment even of political animosity has, on my part, long ago subsided.   Permit me then, to hope that this tender of renewed amity between us may be received and regarded as giving some promise of that perfect reconciliation between our two countries which it is the sincere aim of this publication to promote.   If, on this topic, there be another wish still nearer to my heart, it is that you would not think it beneath you to co-operate with so humble an effort to produce that reconciliation.

"You have shown great prudence (and, in my estimation, greater patrotism) in resolving to terminate your days in retirement.   To become, however, even at Mount Vernon, a mere private man, by divesting yourself of all public influence, is not in your power.   I hope it is not your wish.   Unincumbered with the distracting cares of public life, you may now, by the force of a still powerful example, gradually train the people around you to a love of order and subordination; and above all, to a love of peace.   *Hae tibi erunt artes.*   That you possess talents eminently well adapted for the high post you lately held, friends and foes have concurred in testifying; be it my pleasing task thus publicly to declare that you carry back to your paternal fields virtues equally calculated to bloom in the shade.   To resemble Cincinnatus is but small praise; be it yours, Sir, to enjoy the calm repose and holy serenity of a Christian hero; and may 'the Lord bless your latter end more than your beginning!'

"I have the honour to be, Sir, your sincere Friend and most obedient humble Servant,

"JONATHAN BOUCHER.

"Epsom, Surrey, 4th Nov. 1797."

Rev. E. D. Neill, in his *Notes on the Virginia Colonial Clergy* (Philadelphia 1877), says Washington replied from Mount Vernon under date of August 15, 1798, in part as follows:

"For the honour of its dedication, and for the friendly and favourable sentiments therein expressed, I pray you to accept my acknowledgements and thanks. Not having read the book, it follows of course that I can express no opinion with respect to its political contents; but I can venture to assert beforehand, and with confidence, that there is no man in either country more zealously devoted to peace and good understanding between the nations than I am; no one who is more disposed to bury in oblivion all animosities which have subsided between them and the individuals of each."

The autobiography of the Reverend Jonathan Boucher appeared in *Notes and Queries* (London) during the years 1885–1886, having been contributed by his grandson Jonathan Boucher, and may now be found in Volumes 1, 5, 6 and 9 of the Fifth Series in several of the better American libraries. The following extracts, bearing mainly on Boucher's life in Caroline, are taken from these volumes:

"I went to Workington to learn mathematics and boarded at the Rev. Mr. Ritson's, who was to instruct me, paying for board and education at the rate of a guinea a month. Here I went through all the practical branches of navigation, and also land surveying, in which I had much practice. I remember our diet was both ordinary and scanty. For a time I surveyed land every day, working in severe weather from sun to sun, without eating or drinking; and I do not remember ever to have dined at his house when there was not salmon and mashed potatoes, or when there was anything else. In 1759, Mr. Younger, a respectable merchant in Whitehaven, wanted a young man to go out as a private tutor to a gentleman's sons in Virginia. I was to enter into pay on the day of my leaving England; to have my passage gratis; to have my board and sixty pounds sterling a year for teaching four boys, with liberty to take four more on such terms as I could agree for on my arrival. On the 12th of July I landed at Urbanna and soon after got up to the place of my destination which was Captain Dixon's, at Port Royal in Caroline county. Here I met with a cordial reception. Being hospitable as well as wealthy, Captain Dixon's house was much resorted to, but chiefly by the toddy drinking company. Port Royal was inhabited by factors from Scotland and their dependents, and the circumjacent country by planters in middling circumstances. There was not a literary man, for aught I could find, nearer than the country I had left behind, nor were literary attainments, beyond mere reading and writing, at all in vogue or repute. In all the years I lived at Port Royal I did not form a single friendship on which I can now look back with approbation, though I had numerous acquaintances and many intimacies. In such society my thoughts which had long been withdrawn from the Church turned back, and a train of unforeseen circumstances made me an ecclesiastic.

"A Mr. Giberne, Rector of Hanover Parish across the River, opposite Port Royal, was now engaged to marry a rich widow in Richmond county, and a parish there being vacant, and offered to him, it was natural he should accept it, which he did. Thereupon Hanover Parish was offered to me. I accepted it and arranged to sail to England for Orders the week after. Captain Stanley, of 'The Christian,' offered me passage home and back again gratis. I embarked on board 'The Christian' about the middle of December and the middle of the following month arrived at Whitehaven, after a tempestuous voyage. I went from Whiteheaven to London for Ordination, and Bishop Osbaldston being then just come to that see, I was long detained and much plagued before I succeeded. It was a remarkable coincidence, though perfectly accidental, that I again landed at Urbanna on the 12th of July.

"Soon after my return the Rev. Mr. Dawson, of St. Mary's parish in Caroline county, died and my friends of that parish, among whom I had formerly lived, solicited me to succeed him. I consented and in the spring removed thither. St. Mary's was not a pleasant place, neither had it good water, but there was a good house, and another old one, which at a little expense was made into such an one as I wanted. I now added largely to the furniture of my house and bought stocks of cattle and horses and slaves.

"But my industry and exertions were extraordinary. I had the care of a large parish, and my Church was eleven miles distance from me; neither had I as yet any great stock of

Sermons. My first overseer soon turned out good for nothing and I soon parted with him, so that all the care of the plantation devolved upon me; and although it was my first attempt in that way, I made a good crop. I had now increased the number of my boys to nearly thirty, most of them the sons of persons of the first condition in the colony. They all boarded with me, and I wholly superintended them for two years without any usher. Among my boys I had the stepson of the since so celebrated General Washington; and this laid the foundation of a very particular intimacy and friendship, which lasted until we, taking different sides in the late trouble, separated never to unite again.

"On the 24th of November, 1765, I baptized in St. Mary's Church one hundred and fifteen negro adults, and on the 31st of March, 1766, being Easter Monday, I baptized three hundred and thirteen negro adults, and lectured extempore to upwards of a thousand. I question whether so extraordinary an accession to the Church of Christ, by one man and in one day, can be parallelled even in the journals of a Popish missionary. They are so numerous because my predecessors, shrinking, I suppose, from the great fatigue and disagreeableness of the duty, had in general omitted it, on the pretense that the poor creatures were extremely ignorant and wholly uninstructed, and could get no proper sponsors. These did not appear to me to be sufficient objections. All knowledge, as well as everything else, is to be judged of by comparisons. Negroes, when compared with any other class of people in a Christian country, are no doubt lamentably ignorant, yet I saw no reason to think they were more so than many of the first converts to Christianity must needs have been, and particularly those made and baptized by St. Thomas in Africa, nor is great knowledge and much regular instruction absolutely necessary to baptism. The injunction to go and teach is ill translated; it should be, 'Go and disciple, or make disciples of all nations.' And negroes are not indocile; nor is it hard even in a few conversations and lectures, to give them all necessary instructions in the elements of our religion, and in my humble opinion it is injudicious to attempt to instruct them or Indians in its mysterious doctrines. I may add, moreover, and with strict truth, that I had under my care many Negroes as well informed, as orderly, and as regularly pious, as country people usually are,

even in England. Corresponding with the society called The
Associates of Doctor Bray, I had set up two or three serious
and sensible black men as school masters to teach the children
around them merely to read at their leisure hours, and chiefly
on Sunday afternoons, something as Sunday schools now are
here in England. I had in consequence almost every Sunday
twenty or thirty who could use their Prayer Books and make the
responses, and I had towards the last of my ministry there thirteen
black communicants. I continued this attention to the care of the
blacks of my parish, who amounted to upwards of a thousand
taxables, all the time I remained in St. Mary's.

"During the period of my residence in St. Mary's, Virginia
was overrun with sectarians. They had in a manner taken
possession of two neighbouring parishes, in one of which there
was no minister, and in the other a minister of a bad life. In
my own parish I remember with pride and comfort I had not a
single dissenter of any denomination. Some of the thoughtful
people of those unhappy parishes applied to me to go amongst
them, and endeavour to check the delusion. Accordingly, I
prepared some sermons, which I delivered among them, and by
the blessing of God with such effect that many who had been
decoyed from the Church returned to it; and so, finding their
congregations fall off, the sectarian leaders soon left them. I
attributed much of my success in this to my avoiding all disputa-
tions with their ministers, whom as I spoke of as beneath such
condescension, on the score of their ignorance and impudence.
And when one of them publicly challenged me to a public debate
I declined it but at the same time set up one Daniel Barksdale,
a carpenter in my parish, who had a good front and voluble tongue,
and whom therefore I easily qualified to defeat his opponent, as
he effectually did. And I am still persuaded that this method
of treating sectarian preachers with well judged ridicule and
contempt, and their followers with gentleness, persuasion, and
attention, is a good one.

"While traveling through Caroline I met a Mr. Swift, of
Maryland, to whom I gave some small assistance, with the result
that the next year four boys from his neighborhood applied to me
and were received into my school. This led to such friendships
in Maryland that I was soon invited to take charge of a parish
there, and, after debating the matter for two or three years, I

decided to remove to that neighborhood. After these views as to Maryland I declined to take boys but two of them insisted on accompanying me into Maryland, Mr. Custis, General Washington's stepson, and Mr. Carr, who afterward married the sister of my wife. My parishioners of St. Mary's, on my leaving them, gave me such testimonies of their regard as I still feel with lively gratitude. They not only elected Mr. Abner Waugh, on my sole recommendation, to be my successor, but over-paid me half a year's salary and wrote me a letter full of the kindest expressions.

"On my finally quitting them I made a sale of all my stocks of corn, tobacco, cattle, and horses, and such of my furniture as I did not choose to carry with me. To my slaves I gave the option either to go with me or to choose themselves masters in Virginia. All the unmarried ones chose the former; and the others I sold by their own desire chiefly to gentlemen who, having been my pupils, had lived with me. It affords me more comfort than I can express to recollect that I have nothing bad to charge myself with on the score of severity to my slaves. No compliment ever paid me went so near to my heart as when a gentleman was one day coming to my home, and, having overtaken a slave, asked him, as is common, to whom he belonged, to which the slave replied, 'To Parson Boucher, thank God.'

"Virginians in general I have thought eminently endowed with a knack of talking; they seem to be born orators. I remember a whole family, in Hanover county, of the name of Winslow, who were all distinguished as speakers; and so were the Lees and many others. And there is also this peculiarity observable in that country, that the first settlers having usually taken up large tracts of land, these have since from time to time been divided among and allotted to their descendants in small portions; so that by this means, and by intermarrying, as is common among them, with one another, certain districts come to be settled by certain families; and different places are there known and spoken of, not as here, by any difference of dialect (for there is no dialect in all America); but by their being inhabited by the Fitzhughs, Randolphs, Washingtons, Carys, Grimeses, or Thorntons. This circumstance used to furnish me with a scope for many remarks, such as do not so often occur here. The family character, both of body and mind, may be traced through many generations: as for instance, the Fitzhughs have bad eyes; the

Thorntons hear badly; Winslows and Lees talk well; Carters are proud and imperious; Taliaferros are avaricious; and Fowkses are cruel.

"I did not much like Philadelphia. The city is disgusting from its uniformity and sameness; one street has nothing to distinguish it from another, there are no squares, no public edifices of any dignity; the situation is flat and level, and, in short, everything about it has a Republican aspect. The people, too, are like their town, all very well, but nothing more. One is as good as another, and no better; and it is in vain to look for anything like character among them. In one point, not contented with being not agreeable, they are almost disagreeable: the almost universal topic of conversation among them is the superiority of Philadelphia over every other spot of the globe. All their geese are swans: and it is a fact not to be denied that by thus forever trumpeting their own praise they have in some degree prevailed on their neighbours to acquiesce in their claim to it; just as the French have made all the world agree in giving preference to the French language.

"I used to consider the two colleges of Philadelphia and Princeton in the Jersies, as the chief nurseries of the frivolous and mischievous kind of knowledge which passed for learning in America. Like some of the Academies in and around London, they pretend to teach everything, without really being competent to the teaching of anything as it ought to have been taught. But their chief and peculiar merit was thought to be in rhetoric and Belles Lettres, a term not easily defined or understood. Hence in no country were there so many orators, or so many smatterers. Two or three years spent at one of these seminaries were in general deemed sufficient to qualify a person for the gown; and persons so qualified had now pretty generally gotten the Churches, which in Virginia were immediately in the gift of the people. It is surprising what indecent contentions these popular elections occasioned. I have oftener than once known half a dozen candidates all trying for a vacant parish, and preaching alternately, to give their electors an opportunity of determining which they liked best. These two colleges of Prince-town and Philadelphia manufactured physicians also with equal facility. I have known many a young man come and set up as a doctor in the neighbourhood in all due form, and with all requisite authority, after a winter or two spent in the 'University' of Philadelphia. As for lawyers, they seemed to grow up spontaneously; many of the first name and note in their profession were men without any education and totally illiterate. Such a state of society was peculiar, and could not but have peculiar effects, for no other body of men, nor all the other bodies of men put together, had half so much influence as the lawyers."

Upon his removal to Maryland, Mr. Boucher's real troubles with the Whigs began. He was as ardent a Royalist as ever, and, in the face of the growing sentiment for independence, he continued to preach his convictions respecting loyalty as faithfully as before. The first offence given to the Maryland patriots was the calling of a convention of the clergy which petitioned for a bishop. This so incensed the Governor and other leading citizens that they declined for a time to speak to the intense Royalist. The Annapolis charge became so unpleasant that Mr. Boucher removed to Queene Anne parish in Maryland, but here also he had a very unpleasant reception, even finding the Church doors shut against him on his arrival. Soon afterward one of his parishioners paid a man eight dollars for as many loads of rocks to drive Boucher and his friends away. He preached for a time under the protection of a brace of pistols lying on his pulpit, but even these were unable to protect him much longer, On arriving at Church one day he found it nearly filled with armed and determined men, twenty of whom had been picked out for the purpose of firing on him when he ascended his pulpit. One of his friends, Mr. David Cranford, seized him and by sheer physical force deterred him from his purpose. Mr. Boucher then seized Mr. Osborne Sprigg, head of the armed band, and cocking his pistol forced him to conduct him in safety back to the rectory. This Mr. Sprigg did, but retaliated by having his men play The Rogue's March as they escorted the rector home. It was while living at Castle Magruder in Queene Anne parish that Mr. Boucher administered a threshing to the blacksmith, and accepted the challenge of Mr. Sprigg to a duel. Mr. Sprigg, however, showed the white feather and was ever after branded as a coward in that community. This is interesting by way of showing that it was not considered wholly improper for a clergyman of that day and place to resort to "the field of honour."

Mr. Boucher removed to the parish of Rev. Mr. Addison, his

wife's uncle, in 1775, where he officiated as Mr. Addison's curate, but the time was near at hand for the bursting of the war clouds and so he resolved to return to England for a year or two until the storm blew over, leaving his wife to care for the estate, but she, being unequal to the ordeal of separation, determined to go with him. Accordingly on the 10th day of September, the last day of intercourse between America and Britain before the beginning of hostilities, he and his wife, amidst the tears and cries of their slaves, went aboard the Nell Gwynne, leaving all their possessions behind save bills of exchange to the amount of 400 pounds. On September 20th they sailed out of the Chesapeake Bay and out of sight of the shores of Virginia, which they were to see nevermore. They arrived in Dover October 28th and soon thereafter Mr. Boucher was made Vicar of Epsom Parish, where he lived the life of a scholar, producing many volumes, and where he died April 27, 1804.

PHYSICAL FEATURES

Caroline county is almost at the head of tidewater and is thus to some extent the dividing line between the Tidewater and Piedmont sections of the State. The county is thirty miles long and twenty miles wide and contains approximately three hundred and fifty thousand acres. The Rappahannock river flows on its Northern boundary, the counties of King George and Stafford being on the opposite side of the river. The Pamunkey and North Anna rivers flow on the Southern boundary, Hanover county being opposite. Essex, King and Queen and King William counties constitute the Eastern boundary and Spotsylvania county the Western. The county is drained by the Rappahannock, the Mattaponi, the North Anna and Pamunkey rivers and their tributaries, which are numerous; therefore the county is both well drained and well watered. It is estimated that there are not above ten thousand acres of unimprovable or waste land in the county.

RESOURCES, NATURAL AND OTHERWISE

Transportation facilities are unusually good in Caroline, both by rail and water. The Richmond Fredericksburg and Potomac Railroad passes through the entire length of the county, and almost through the centre of it, from north to south. There are five freight and passenger stations—namely, Guinea, Woodford, Milford, Penola and Ruther Glen. Besides these there are numerous sidings and flag stops. The Rappahannock river affords direct steamer connection with Baltimore and Norfolk and the entire Atlantic seaboard. The Southern portion of the county has easy access to the Chesapeake and Ohio Railroad, which connects the Seaboard with the Mississippi and the West. No station in Caroline is over two hours from the National Capitol or over one hour from the State Capitol.

The Richmond Fredericksburg and Potomac Railroad crosses and runs along three rivers in passing through Caroline. The soil on the second elevation from these rivers and on the intervening ridges is of light loamy character, easily cultivated, more easily drained, responds to improvement and, having a stratum of clay lying not far from the surface, holds improvement. The rich lowlands lying along the Mattaponi, Rappahannock and North Anna rivers are highly productive and on these may be seen crops of corn, wheat and oats, which compare favorably with the fields of the West. The mild climate and the adaptibility of this land to grass, makes good grazing nearly all the year, hence cattle raising and dairying grow more popular every year.

The soil of Caroline is especially adapted to the growth of fine tobacco. There is much land which may be made to produce a large, heavy tobacco, suitable for export trade, and there is more land adapted to the growth of sun-cured and flue-cured tobacco. The county has long been famous for the quality of its sun-cured tobacco and the remark has often been made on the Richmond markets, under the old regime of marketing, that tobacco from other sections having the same texture and appearance seldom had the same quality. The tobacco lands cannot be said to occupy the whole surface of the county, but is so interspersed that on a farm of ordinary size in any section of the county sufficient fine tobacco land may be found. All fruits and vegetables common to Virginia and the Southeast may be found in Caroline. Many carloads of strawberries are shipped from the county every year. The value of the tobacco crop of the county is in excess of one million dollars annually.

INDUSTRIES

EXCELSIOR MANUFACTURING

If we exclude farming the manufacture of excelsior easily becomes the outstanding industry of Caroline. The introduction and establishment of this industry in the county by George P. Lyon, of Woodford, in 1896, was indeed the first introduction of this business to the entire South.

Mr. Lyon, in 1896, was residing at Woodford, and operating a small general merchandise store, from which he was deriving a comfortable living; but seeing no probability of accumulating anything for the proverbial rainy day, he began to take an inventory of the resources around him with a view to developing other business and adding to his slender income. In this he differed from the vast majority of men who, when incomes are unsatisfactory, seek the golden fleece in another country. It is a trite observation that the best land, best pastures, greatest opportunities are all over in another country—far, far away. There is an old Persian tradition to the effect that one Ali Hafed sold his farm by the River Indus and went away to search for wealth and died in poverty in a distant land, while his successor discovered diamonds on the farm Ali Hafed had left behind and so became as rich as Croesus. The greatest gold mine in California was found on a farm which had been sold to enable the former owner to go to Southern California to search for gold. The greatest oil field in Pennsylvania was discovered on a farm which had been sold for less than one thousand dollars in order that the former owner might go farther north and engage in the oil business with a kinsman. The greatest coal mines in West Virginia were sold "for a song" to enable the man who had owned the "good-for-nothing hills" for years to go to the "Golden West" and make his fortune.

The founder and developer of what has proven to be the greatest manufacturing industry in the county might have sought his fortune elsewhere and failed, as many men have done before, but, taking inventory of the resources around him, he decided that the excelsior business, of which he had learned something from friends at the North, could be established to advantage in Caroline, where material was plentiful and labor prices reasonable.

Accordingly, Mr. Lyon set about establishing his first excelsior mill with no experience and little capital; but the information he had gathered from the North stood him in good stead and his enterprise was successful from the beginning. Through a Baltimore friend advantageous marketing arrangements were made and soon the business was making splendid returns, considering the capital invested. The returns from the first mill were so pleasing that other mills followed in rapid succession and the output, which at first was one car load per week of the manufactured product, soon increased to thirty car loads per week on daylight run alone.

When the excelsior industry was first established in Caroline, it was thought, by all men engaged in the business, that the raw material consisted of poplar wood only, but Mr. Lyon, seeing the need of a cheaper grade of excelsior for rough packing, began to manufacture excelsior from pine wood, and was soon successful in creating a market for this product. As time passed on the pine product became the leading excelsior on the market and is now in demand not only for packing, but for all purposes for which any other type of excelsior may be used.

Thus the excelsior industry has created a demand for the small pine timber of the county, which prior to the establishment of the industry, was used for fuel only and was of little value, stumpage being bought freely at that time for ten cents per cord. Since that time, especially during the World War, young pine timber has sold for as much as five dollars per cord on the stump, and the increased value of the pine timber, added to the profitable employment given many men in the manufacture of the same, has added much wealth and prosperity to the county.

There are now more than a score of excelsior mills in Virginia, the larger number of these being in Caroline county along the R., F. and P. Railroad.

Mr. Lyon served as Supervisor in Port Royal District for many years and in 1923 was elected to represent Caroline in the House of Delegates.

LUMBER MANUFACTURING

The first sawed lumber in Caroline was manufactured by the pit and whipsaw method. It took two men to operate those primitive machines. A hole was dug in the ground, over which a crude scaffold was built. The log was then put on the scaffold and one man stood in the pit below the log while the other stood on the scaffold. The log was first hewn to a square with a broad-ax and then "lined" on the upper and lower sides at every place where it was to be sawed. This was sometimes done with poke-berry juice. The men then drew the saw up and down through the log, sawing off a board about every hour. Two able-bodied men could hardly saw more than two hundred feet per day in this way. This method was assisted later by water power mills, using an up-and-down sliding frame with straight saw in the center with the log fed to the saw on rollers, later by the log fed to the saw on a carriage and using headblocks to set the log out to cut off each board, the carriage being gigged back by hand. Later the circular saw was introduced. Captain Henry H. George built "Thornberry" in Caroline County, making the bricks for his house on the premises and sawing the timbers and the lumber for his house with a whipsaw, using one man in the pit below the saw-log and one or two men on the scaffold above the pit, sawing all of the lumber for his home and the various buildings on his farm of Thornberry by man power.

Sometimes in the later fifties Captain H. H. George purchased a steam engine and boiler and a circular sawmill and planted this mill on his farm "Thornberry"—sawed lumber for himself and for his neighbors, which business was carried on until the beginning of the Civil War. During the latter part of the War, Captain George was detailed to saw timbers and lumber for the Confederate Government to use in building the fortifications around Richmond and other Government uses. He went back to his regiment after this was done and returned to his home after Lee's surrender at Appomattox.

On reaching "Thornberry" he found it stripped of every-thing movable, by the Union troops who had visited that section many times during the return of the Northern Army to Washing-ton, but found the troops had not destroyed the saw mill. He got to work as soon as possible and began sawing lumber and continued in this business of manufacturing and selling lumber until within a few years of his death, which occurred at his home on June 26, 1902, in his seventy-ninth year.

Archie S. George went into the saw mill and lumber business with his father, Captain H. H. George, in the year 1882 and they continued the business for several years and finally sold their mill to Joseph and Cecil L. Baker and Captain H. H. George retired from the lumber business, having been engaged in it about forty years.

Lewis D. George engaged in the lumber business in June, 1879, with his father, Henry H. George, and Mr. John George Coleman and this firm continued actively in the business of manufacturing lumber until October 1, 1881, at which time H. H. George, Jr., second son of Captain H. H. George, bought out the interest of John G. Coleman, in the same business and then L. D. George and H. H. George, Jr., traded their father H. H. George, Sr., two farms for the saw mill and logging outfit and they ran the business as George Brothers from October 1, 1881, to April, 1887, at which time L. D. George bought his brother's interest in the business.

L. D. George has been in the business continuously from June 1879, at which time he bought an interest in the business with his father and John G. Coleman, until the present time. Having no children and being desirous of perpetuating the business that he had been years in building up, he incorporated the L. D. George Lumber Company, in 1911 and later in 1915 he incorporated the Rose Hill Lumber Co., Inc., a close corporation, all of the stock being held by L. D. George, his wife, Carrie L. George, and John W. Clarke, who is secretary of the company. They have an up-to-date planing mill, a large woodworking shop, well equipped machine shop and do all of their machinery and other repairing, except casting. They make anything in wood-work that is used in building, besides many specialties for the Northern markets. They manufacture every specie of lumber from native Virginia hardwoods and Virginia pine in every shape, from framing lumber to the smallest moulding or turning.

When the George family began in the lumber business there was no other in Caroline, or, so far as is known, in any adjoining county. There has not been a time since 1850 that there has not been one or more of this family in the business. When the present head of the firm began sawing in 1879 there were only a few mills in Caroline county, but within ten years after he began in the business there were over forty mills sawing lumber in Caroline and there are many mills in the county cutting lumber today. Some of the men who have been in the business longest have cut over the same tracts three to five times and there is still timber to cut. During the past fifty years there has been an immense quantity of pine and hardwood timber cut and shipped from this county; possibly as much or more than from any county in this section of the country.

There has, in former years, been great waste of material by the crude manner of harvesting the timber and fitting it for market. Millions of dollars of wealth have year after year gone up in smoke from the slabs, edgings and trimmings made at the saw mills, as well as tops of trees and large branches that have been left to rot and go to waste, after the logs have been taken from the trees.

THE MANUFACTURE OF SUMAC EXTRACT

Sumac is indigeneous to many sections of this country. That which grows in the Eastern part of Virginia and the Carolinas produces a larger percentage of tannin than the sumac of any other section. In fact there is no sumac of any country finer than this, save that which is imported from Sicily, and the Sicilian sumac is only superior because of the superior methods of gathering, drying, baling, etc. The sumac shipped from Palermo is carefully picked, only the small twigs on which the leaves grow being gathered, while in Caroline county much of the stem is broken with the leaves and there is little or no tannin in the stems. The Sicilian sumac is carefully cured in the shade, although called sun-cured and is bright and strong, while in Caroline county the green product is frequently dumped in piles in sheds, or allowed to lie on the ground, until it has molded to a dark color, thus destroying fifty per cent. of the tannin. A chemist from the Agricultural Department (Mr. Veitch) visited Caroline in the interest of the sumac industry and while in the county prepared some sumac as nearly after the Sicilian method as possible, and this Caroline sumac, when tested and compared with the Sicilian product, proved superior. The Government has issued bulletins on the cultivation, gathering and curing of sumac, which, if followed, would probably make it unnecessary to import the raw material from Europe.

Sumac was used in Virginia nearly a century since in the tanning of light leathers and nearly one-half century ago the extract was manufactured by the Knox Brothers in Fredericksburg. This plant was moved to Milford, in Caroline county, in 1913, and was operated for a time by Thomas Haigh. Mr.

Haigh sold the plant to William Pettus Miller, of Kentucky, who now operates it. It is said to be the largest plant of its kind in the United States. The sumac extract is used extensively in the tanning of light leathers and as a mordant to fasten colors in all textile fabrics.

THE STAGE COACH ROAD THROUGH CAROLINE

The road which passes through the entire length of Caroline county, and which is commonly called the Bowling Green-Hanover Highway, is one of the oldest roads in Virginia. Just when it was first surveyed cannot be definitely determined, but it is certain that this road was used by through traffic from North to South before the end of the seventeenth century.

The stage coaches which passed over this road over two hundred years ago ran on a fixed schedule and many notables passed this way in the colonial times. Over this road passed John Penn, en-route from the Province of North Carolina to the Continental Congress in Philadelphia; Edmund Pendleton, General William Woodford, George Washington, LaFayette and a host of others, whose names are writ large in the nation's life.

Of course, there were other and less frequented roads between the North and South, but the stages on such routes were irregular and the inns or taverns along the way were often kept by disreputable and vicious persons. Many of them indeed were veritable robber's dens. It was in one of these frontier taverns that Meriwether Lewis, of the famous Lewis and Clark Expedition, was robbed and murdered. He was enroute to Philadelphia at the time to arrange for the publication of his Journal of the great expedition.

The taverns along the road through Caroline were at intervals of from five to ten miles and were also relay stations where the tired horses were replaced by fresh ones, thus giving to travel both uniform and rapid speed. These taverns were rude structures at first, but were kept by reputable persons and as time passed the log structure gave way to commodious brick or frame buildings which gave to the traveler many comforts. As a rule the main door opened into a large room corresponding to the lobby or foyer of our modern hotels and here the travelers and others gathered during the long evenings and recounted the experiences of travel, discussed politics and religion—mainly politics—and

played cards. The taverns were the resorts of the social element
of the surrounding community and here the people assembled on
Saturdays to spend the time in scientific, literary and political
discussion, wrestling, racing, target practice, shooting-matches,
"raffles" and other amusements. Near these taverns the petit
musters were held, as were the barbecues, beef-shootings, etc.

The prices charged by the taverns in Caroline and other counties were regulated by the county courts every year and thus we
find among the old records of Caroline, Orange, Hanover and
adjoining counties, that as early as 1735 such orders as the following were entered:

"The Court doth set and rate liquors: Rum, the gallon, eight
shillings; Virginia brandy, six shillings; Punch, or Flipp, the
quart, with white sugar, one and three pence, with brown sugar,
one shilling; French brandy, sixteen shillings; Punch of same,
two and six pence; Frill or Maderia wine, quart, two shillings;
a hot dyet one shilling; a cold dyet six pence; a lodging with
clean sheets six pence; Oats, the gallon, six pence; Pasturage,
the day, six pence per head."

"Ordered that the several tavern keepers in this county sell
and retail liquors at the above rates and that they presume not
to sell at any other rates, and that if any person do not pay
immediately that he pay for the same at the Fall in tobacco
at ten shillings the hundred weight."

A bar was always kept in connection with the taverns and,
if we may believe the stories which have been handed down to us,
they were liberally patronized. Perhaps the bar contributed
something to the warmth of the political discussions of the time.

Traveling showmen frequently came to the taverns and gave
their plays. Bishop Meade, in his "Old Churches and Families
of Virginia," relates that several of these strolling players came
to "White Chimneys" in Caroline, and there arranged for an
exhibition. The neighbors came in and joined the guests to
witness the performance. For some reason one of the troupe
could not fill his role and a clergyman stopping there, one Rev.
Mr. Weems, better known to history as "Parson Weems,"
volunteered to take the part and so the play went on very satis-
factorily. This versatile clergyman was at the time a traveling
.book-seller for Matthew Carey, of Philadelphia, and later
wrote a "Life of Washington." Bishop Meade's characterizes

Weems as "one of nature's oddities," and says of him that he
never preached or prayed but that he created uproarious merriment, many of his prayers being entirely broken up by the uproar
created.

There were five taverns in colonial times and long afterward,
on this historic Caroline road.   The first one approached by the
traveler coming from the North was called Tod's Tavern, afterward Vilboro, and was located about six miles from the Caroline-
Spotsylvania line.   A school was maintained in the old building
after it ceased to be used as a tavern.   Part of the building still
stands.   Mrs. W. R. W. Garrett relates that she attended a
school here taught by Prof. Moore Boulware.   Eight miles South
of Vilboro stood New Hope tavern on the site now occupied by
the Lawn Hotel, of Bowling Green.   Ten miles South of Bowling
Green stood Union tavern, at the junction of the Penola road
with the Bowling Green-Hanover Highway, and four miles to
the South of Union tavern was White Chimneys tavern.   Two
miles to the South of White Chimneys and five miles North of
Page's Bridge, the Southern boundary of the county, stood
Needwood tavern.   This was a large three-story brick building
and the best tavern on the road.   The building stood until 1920
and was occupied for many years by an old woman and her
hogs.   The people for the most part called her "the Witch."
When Mr. J. C. Haley razed the old building, that he might use
the material in erecting his garage and other out-buildings, the
names of many men well-known to history were found carved
in the bricks.

Mr. Jourdan Woolfolk, of Caroline, operated the stage coach
line over this road as late as 1836, for a time table of the Richmond, Fredericksburg and Potomac Railroad of that year, which
is reproduced elsewhere in this volume, states that, "The stage
traveling (in connection with this road) is conducted by J.
Woolfolk & Co., in the handsomest manner."   The old stage
line records are still in the possession of his descendants who
reside at "Mulberry Place" in Caroline.

THE RICHMOND, FREDERICKSBURG AND POTOMAC RAILROAD

The Richmond, Fredericksburg and Potomac Railroad is a grand trunk line connecting the transportation lines of the North with the South. It is operated in connection with the Pennsylvania system to the North and all of the great passenger trains of the Atlantic Coast Line Railroad and the Seaboard Air Line Railroad pass over the entire length of its trackage. This road passes through the entire length of the county from North to South, a distance of about thirty miles and more than a score of passenger trains pass over it daily. No station in Caroline is more than two hours from Washington or four hours from Baltimore. Richmond is one hour, Philadelphia five hours, and New York seven hours from the heart of the county. Fruit and vegetables may be gathered ripe in the late afternoon and put on the early markets in New York City fresh the next morning. By the Rappahannock River Boat Lines Caroline is two days from Baltimore and two days from Norfolk. The Chesapeake and Ohio Railroad which traverses the Southern and Southwestern boundaries of the county gives convenient shipping facilities to all Western points.

The stations on the Richmond, Fredericksburg and Potomac Railroad in Caroline are, reading from South to North, as follows: Chandler, Ruther Glen, Coleman's Mill, George, Penola, Kenbrook Dairy Farm, Milford, Bowling Green Park, Rixey, Collins, Woodford and Guinea. Chandler was named for A. B. Chandler, who was for many years attorney for the road; Ruther Glen, formerly Chesterfield Station, was named for an ancient town in Scotland; Coleman's Mill was named for a mill near the station owned by Emmett M. Coleman, of Penola; George was named for the George family of Penola; Penola was named for the celebrated John Penn; Bowling Green Park was named for the county seat; Rixey was named for the Rixey family which had its seat near by; Collins was named for the Collins family of the county; Woodford was named for the distinguished revolutionary general; and Guinea was named for a colonial family of the name of Guiney, which lived near where the station now stands.

The President of the Richmond, Fredericksburg and Potomac Railroad, Mr. Eppa Hunton, Jr., under date of June 28, 1923, wrote the author as follows: "Our records give the following dates as to the opening of the several sections of line in Caroline county:

"Line opened to North Anna River, February 5, 1836.

" Line opened to Ruther Glen, June 15, 1836.
" Line opened to Mattaponi River, August 2, 1836.
" Line opened to Milford, September 15, 1836.
" Line opened to Woodford (formerly Woodslane), Oct. 26, 1836.
" Line opened to Hazel Run, December 23, 1836."

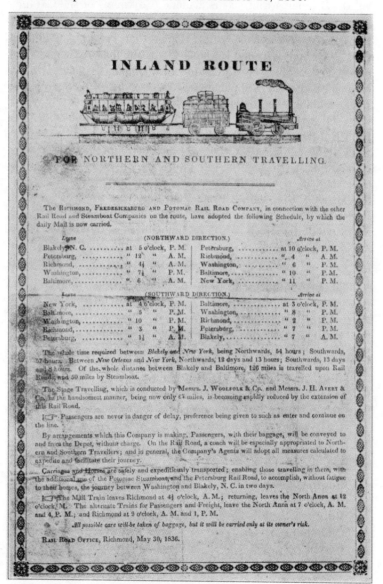

INLAND ROUTE

FOR NORTHERN AND SOUTHERN TRAVELLING.

The RICHMOND, FREDERICKSBURG AND POTOMAC RAIL ROAD COMPANY, in connection with the other Rail Road and Steamboat Companies on the route, have adopted the following Schedule, by which the daily Mail is now carried.

Leave				(NORTHWARD DIRECTION.)		Arrive at		
Blakely, N. C.	at	5 o'clock, P. M.		Petersburg,	at	10 o'clock, P. M.		
Petersburg,	"	12	" A. M.	Richmond,	"	4	" A. M.	
Richmond,	"	4½	" A. M.	Washington,	"	6	" P. M.	
Washington,	"	7½	" P. M.	Baltimore,	"	10	" P. M.	
Baltimore,	"	6	" A. M.	New York,	"	11	" P. M.	

Leave				(SOUTHWARD DIRECTION.)		Arrive at		
New York,	at	4 o'clock, P. M.		Baltimore,	at	3 o'clock, P. M.		
Baltimore,	"	5	" P. M.	Washington,	"	8	" P. M.	
Washington,	"	10	" P. M.	Richmond,	"	2	" P. M.	
Richmond,	"	3	" P. M.	Petersburg,	"	7	" P. M.	
Petersburg,	"	1½	" A. M.	Blakely,	"	7	" A. M.	

The whole time required between *Blakely* and *New York*, being Northwards, 54 hours ; Southwards, 57 hours. Between *New Orleans* and *New York*, Northwards, 12 days and 13 hours ; Southwards, 13 days and 8 hours. Of the whole distance between Blakely and Baltimore, 126 miles is travelled upon Rail Roads, and 50 miles by Steamboat.

The Stage Travelling, which is conducted by Messrs. J. WOOLFOLK & CO. and Messrs. J. H. AVERY & CO. in the handsomest manner, being now only 6¾ miles, is becoming rapidly reduced by the extension of this Rail Road.

☞ Passengers are never in danger of delay, preference being given to such as enter and continue on the line.

By arrangements which this Company is making, Passengers, with their baggage, will be conveyed to and from the Depot, without charge. On the Rail Road, a coach will be especially appropriated to Northern and Southern Travellers ; and in general, the Company's Agents will adopt all measures calculated to expedite and facilitate their journey.

Carriages and Horses are safely and expeditiously transported ; enabling those travelling in them, with the additional use of the Potomac Steamboat, and the Petersburg Rail Road, to accomplish, without fatigue to their horses, the journey between Washington and Blakely, N. C. in two days.

☞ The Mail Train leaves Richmond at 4½ o'clock, A. M. ; returning, leaves the North Anna at 12 o'clock, M. The alternate Trains for Passengers and Freight, leave the North Anna at 7 o'clock, A. M. and 4, P. M. ; and Richmond at 9 o'clock, A. M. and 1, P. M.

All possible care will be taken of baggage, but it will be carried only at its owner's risk.

RAIL ROAD OFFICE, Richmond, May 30, 1836.

Fac simile of first Time Table of R., F. & P. R. R.

SOME LOCAL NAMES AND THEIR ORIGIN

PEUMANSEND

Rollins Creek, which forms the dividing line between Port Royal and Bowling Green Magisterial Districts, was originally called "Peuman's End," as is evidenced by many of the Caroline land surveys and plats, several of which are in the possession of the Motley family, of Upper Zion. The name—"Peuman's End"—became attached to the creek in the following manner: A pirate and robber, by the name of Peuman, frequently made incursions into the Rappahannock river country, by way of the river, robbing the colonists and the craft that plied the river, until he was generally dreaded. Finally, a number of men formed a searching party and went out to capture the marauder. They sighted him on the river and pursued him up the stream so closely that he turned off into the creek to escape, but he was overtaken at a point in the creek where his boat could go no further and was slain. From that day the creek was called Peuman's End, the two words finally becoming one. Like the Mattaponi, this creek was large enough to accommodate boats in colonial times.

HAWES' LANE

This road branches off from the old Stage Road, about two or three hundred yards from the corporate limits of Bowling Green on the North, and leads in a westerly direction to Page. The road was named for the Hawes family, of Caroline.

THE CHASE

This was an immense tract of land owned by Robert Beverly, of "Blandfield," in Essex, and was so called, it is said, because over this territory the great deer and fox chases took place.

POSTOFFICES	ORIGIN OF NAME
Bagby	Bagby Family.
Blantons	Blanton Family.
Bowling Green	Hoomes Estate.
Brandywine	Boutwell Estate.
Burruss	Burruss Family.
Chilesburg	Chiles Family.
Corbin	Corbin Family.
Croxton	Thomas Croxton, M. C.

FOST-OFFICE	ORIGIN OF NAME
DeJarnetts...............	DeJarnette Family.
Guinea (or Guiney's)........	Guiney Family.
Kidd's Fork..............	Kidd's Family.
Knopf...................	Knopf Family.
McDuff..................	McDuff Family.
Penola...................	John Penn.
Point Eastern............	Location.
Port Royal...............	Thomas Roy.
Rappahannock Academy....	School.
Ruther Glen.............	Ruther Glen in Scotland.
Shumansville.............	Shuman Family.
Smoots..................	Smoot Family.
Upper Zion..............	Church.

THE CAROLINE COUNTY COMMITTEE OF SAFETY
1774-75

On May 24, 1774, the Virginia House of Burgesses adopted resolutions deploring the action of Great Britain relative to the Boston Port Bill and set apart June 1st "as a day of prayer, fasting and humiliation, for Divine interposition in averting the calamity which threatens destruction to our civil rights and the evils of civil war."

On being informed of this resolution Governor Dunmore commanded the House of Burgesses to attend him in the Council Chamber and when the House had assembled, on May 26, 1774, in obedience to the summons, his Excellency addressed them in the following words:

"Mr. Speaker, and Gentlemen of the House of Burgesses: I have in my hand a paper, published by order of your House, conceived in such terms as reflect highly upon His Majesty and the Parliament of Great Britain, which makes it necessary for me to dissolve you; and you are dissolved accordingly."

On the day following the dissolution of the House of Burgesses eighty-nine men who had been members of the disbanded House met and formed an "Association for promoting the principles of representative government, and for securing their dearest rights and liberty from destruction by the heavy hand of power * * * lifted against North America."

Shortly after the formation of this Association the news came that the colonists of Philadelphia and New York purposed to hold a Continental Congress, whereupon the ex-burgesses, who still remained in the vicinity, issued a call to "the late representatives of Virginia to meet in Williamsburg on the 1st day of August next, to conclude finally on these important questions." The assembly thus called was duly held and is known to history as the Virginia Convention of August, 1774.

On September 5, 1774, delegates from the twelve colonies met in Philadelphia in the first Continental Congress. Edmund Pendleton, of Caroline, was a delegate from Virginia to this first Congress and during the following year, 1775, John Penn, also a son of Caroline county, was elected a delegate to the Continental Congress by the Provincial Congress of North Carolina, to which State he had removed from Caroline in 1774.

The first Continental Congress formed another "Association," the constitution of which contained the following articles of agreement: (1) Not to import into the colony any British merchandise. (2) Not to engage further in the slave trade. (3) Not to purchase tea on account of the East India Company. (4) Not to export any goods to Great Britain. (5) To direct that all merchants of the colony inform their British mercantile houses not to ship goods to them under any pretence. (6) To instruct all ship owners to give orders to captains and masters of vessels not to receive on board any British goods. (7) To increase the number and improve the breed of sheep and cattle. (8) To discourage extravagance, dissipation, gaming and so-called "gentlemanly sports" and to promote industry, agriculture, art and manufacturing. (9) To instruct merchants not to take advantage of the scarcity of goods to charge exorbitant prices. (10) To have all British goods received between December 1, 1774 and February 1, 1775, returned to shipper or delivered to the County Committee of Safety, hereinafter mentioned, which Committee would store until cessation of non-importation agreement, or else sell and reimburse the owner the first cost and charges; turning all possible profits to "relieving and employing such poor inhabitants of the town of Boston as are immediate sufferers by the Boston Port Bill." (11) That a Committee be chosen in every county, city, and town, by those who are qualified to vote for Representatives in the Legislature whose business it shall be attentively to observe the conduct of all persons touching this Association; and when it shall be made to appear, to the satisfaction of a majority of any such Committee, that any person within the limits of their appointment has violated this Association, that such majority do forthwith cause the truth of the case to be published in the *Gazette*, to the end that all such foes to the rights of British America may be publicly known, and universally contemned as the enemies of American liberty; and thenceforth we, respectively, will break off all dealings with him or her.   (12) To have the Committee of Correspondence in the various colonies inspect entries of custom houses and report to each other all findings of interest to the Association.   (13) To have all manufactures of this county sold at reasonable prices regardless of the scarcity of the article.   (14) To have no dealings with any colony not acceding to, or hereafter violating, this agreement.   (15) To continue the Association until the repeal of all acts of Parliament inimical to the rights and liberties of North America.

Under the Eleventh Article of the Agreement the voters of each county elected the Committee of Safety for their county. Caroline's Committee, as elected on November 10, 1774, consisted of twenty of her leading citizens, whose names are as follows:

Edmund Pendleton, Chairman.	Sam'l Hawes, Jr., Clerk
James Upshaw	Wm. Nelson
William Woodford	George Baylor
Richard Johnston	George Taylor
Thomas Lowry	John Jones
Benjamin Hubbard (or Hubard)	Anthony Thornton
Thomas Lomax	John Tennant
John Minor	George Guy
John Armistead	Samuel Hawes
Edmund Pendleton, Jr.	Walker Taliaferro.

Col. Edmund Pendleton, on being appointed Chairman of the Committee of Safety for the entire colony, resigned the chairmanship of the County Committee, and was succeeded by Col. James Taylor.   The Committee also appointed Col. Anthony Thornton to be the presiding officer in Col. Taylor's absence.

Col. James Taylor was one of Caroline's most distinguished

sons. He was elected County Lieutenant of Caroline in 1775, was a member of the Conventions of 1775 and 1776, with Pendleton and Woodford as associates, member of the Ratification Convention of 1788, and also a member of the State Senate from Caroline, both before and after 1788.

CAROLINE REPRESENTATIVES IN THE HOUSE OF BURGESSES FROM THE FORMATION OF THE COUNTY IN 1727 TO THE FORMATION OF THE COMMONWEALTH IN 1776

Henry Armistead, 1727–1735.
Robert Fleming and Jonathan Gibson, 1736–1737.
Jonathan Gibson and John Martin, 1738–1741.
Lunsford Lomax and John Baylor, 1742–1751.
Lunsford Lomax and Edmund Pendleton, 1752–1755.
Edmund Pendleton and John Baylor, 1756–1765.
Edmund Pendleton and Walker Taliaferro, 1766–1768.
Edmund Pendleton and Francis Coleman, 1769.
Edmund Pendleton and Walker Taliaferro, 1770–1773.
Edmund Pendleton and James Taylor, 1774–1776.

CAROLINE REPRESENTATIVES IN THE HOUSE OF DELEGATES, FROM THE FORMATION OF THE COMMONWEALTH, 1776, TO THE PRESENT, 1924. ALPHABETICALLY ARRANGED

Gibbons Allensworth, 1887–88.
Walter J. Anderson, 1881–82.
Hay Battaile, 1815–20.
Lawrence Battaile, 1788, 1814–15.
R. L. Beale, 1916–17.
John H. Bernard, 1815–17, 1822–23.
W. L. Blanton, 1895–96.
Andrew S. Broaddus, 1844–45.
George Buckner, 1796–1800.
Richard Buckner, Jr., 1829–30.
William A. Buckner, 1849–53.
Thomas Burke, 1791–92, 1802–04.
John D. Butler, 1863–65, 1871–73.
Samuel Childs, 1824–29.
Daniel Coleman, 1800–1815.

Henry C. Coleman, 1808–09.

Thomas B. Coleman, Jr., 1825–27.

C. B. Conway, 1918–19.

Robert B. Corbin, 1838–41.

Daniel C. DeJarnette, 1853–58.

John Dickinson, 1832–33.

James M. G. Dickinson, 1845–47.

William W. Dickinson, 1819–24, 1831–32.

S. H. Evans, 1912–13.

Robert Gilchrist, 1782–83.

John W. Guerrant, 1920–21.

Richard Hawes, 1806–08.

Samuel Hawes, Jr., 1784–88.

William Holmes, 1812–13.

John Hoomes, 1791–95.

William Hoomes, 1808–11, 1813–14.

Robert Hord, 1834–35.

John M. Hudgins, 1869–71, 1874–76, 1889–92.

William Jones, 1808–12.

George P. Lyon, 1923——

Thomas Lomax, 1778–79, 1881–82.

Thomas Lowry, 1777, 1780–81.

E. C. Moncure, 1904–05.

William A. Moncure, 1847–49.

Anthony New, 1785–90.

John Page, Jr., 1782–83.

Stafford H. Parker, 1818–25, 1828–29.

R. O. Peatross, 1869–71, 1876–77.

Edmund Pendleton, 1776–77.

Samuel E. Pitts, 1899–1900.

David B. Powers, Jr., 1901–02, 1906–07, 1908–09, 1910–11,
    1914–15.

Richard T. Pratt, 1922–23.

William D. Quisenberry, 1897–98.

R. A. Ricks, 1893–94.

Robert Gilchrist Robb, 1800–02.

Thomas R. Rootes, 1793–1795.

Archibald Samuel, 1829–30, 1833–37, 1841–43.

Cornelius T. Smith, 1885–87.

Norborne E. Sutton, 1827–28.

Samuel E. Swann, 1871–77.
James Taylor, 1776.
John Taylor, 1779–85, 1796–1800.
William P. Taylor, 1830–31.
Charles Todd, 1831–32.
George Tyler, 1859–63.
James Upshaw, 1778, 1789–90.
John Washington, 1843–44.
S. J. R. White, 1875–80, 1883–84.
John T. Woodford, 1802–06, 1817–18.
Charles Wright, 1877–78.
W. R. B. Wyatt, 1865–67.

CAROLINE REPRESENTATIVES IN THE STATE SENATE FROM THE FORMATION OF THE COMMONWEALTH, 1776, TO THE PRESENT TIME, 1924

DISTRICT COMPOSED OF CAROLINE AND HANOVER COUNTIES

Thomas Lomax, 1776.
James Taylor, 1777–1783.
John Syme, (of Hanover) 1784–1787.
John Page, 1788.
James Taylor, 1789–1791.
Samuel Temple, 1792–1795.
John Hoomes, 1796–1803.
Robert G. Robb, 1804–1808.
George Washington, 1809–1815.
Armistead Hoomes, 1816–1820.

DISTRICT COMPOSED OF CAROLINE, HANOVER, KING WILLIAM, KING AND QUEEN AND ESSEX

Charles Hill, 1821–1824.
William Armistead, 1825–1827.
John H. Bernard, 1828–1830.

DISTRICT COMPOSED OF CAROLINE, SPOTSYLVANIA AND ESSEX

John H. Bernard, 1831.
Stafford H. Parker, 1832–1839.
James B. Thornton, 1840.
James B. Thornton, Jr., 1841–1843.
Norborne E. Sutton, 1844–1847.
Austin M. Tribble, (of Essex) 1848–1851.

DISTRICT COMPOSED OF CAROLINE AND SPOTSYLVANIA

William A. Moncure, (of Spotsylvania) 1852–1854.

William A. Moncure and Frederick William Coleman, 1855–1856.

Frederick William Coleman, 1857–1858.

William D. Quesenberry and Frederick Wm. Coleman, 1859–1861.

William D. Quesenberry, 1862–1867.

DISTRICT COMPOSED OF CAROLINE, KING GEORGE, WESTMORELAND, RICHMOND, NORTHUMBERLAND AND LANCASTER

Lawrence Washington (of Westmoreland), 1868.

DISTRICT COMPOSED OF CAROLINE, ESSEX AND KING WILLIAM

Edmund W. Massie (of King William), 1869–1870.

DISTRICT COMPOSED OF CAROLINE AND HANOVER

William D. Quesenberry, 1871–1878.

Joseph A. Wingfield (of Hanover), 1879–1882.

Williams C. Wickham, 1883–1888.

Henry T. Wickham, 1889–1904.

DISTRICT COMPOSED OF CAROLINE, HANOVER AND KING WILLIAM

Henry T. Wickham, 1904–1906.

Charles U. Gravatt, 1908–1922.

DISTRICT COMPOSED OF CAROLINE, HANOVER, KING WILLIAM AND GOOCHLAND

Henry T. Wickham, 1923——

NOTE.—Several Caroline men have served as President of the Senate.

CAROLINE DELEGATES IN VIRGINIA CONVENTIONS

August 1, 1774—This Convention met in Williamsburg, Va. Peyton Randolph was chosen President. There is no record of the election of a Secretary. This Convention passed resolutions similar to those passed by the first Continental Congress which was held during the following month. (See chapter on Committee of Safety). The Convention appointed Hon. Peyton Randolph, Richard Henry Lee, George Washington, Patrick Henry, Richard Bland, Benjamin Harrison and Edmund Pendleton to represent the colony in the General Congress at Philadelphia, September 5, 1774. Edmund Pendleton and James Taylor represented Caroline in this Convention of August 1, 1774.

March 20, 1775—This Convention met at Richmond, Va., in St. John's Church. Peyton Randolph was elected President and John Tazewell Clerk. Edmund Pendleton and James Taylor represented Caroline. In this Convention Patrick Henry made his immortal speech. Thomas Jefferson was appointed a Deputy to represent the colony in the General Congress, in the room of the Hon. Peyton Randolph, in case of the non-attendance of the said Peyton Randolph.

July 17, 1775—This Convention met in Richmond, with Peyton Randolph in the Chair and John Tazewell at the Clerk's desk. James Taylor and William Woodford represented Caroline. This Convention approved the proceedings of the March Convention, and made plans for "putting the country into a posture of defense."

December 1, 1775—This Convention met in Richmond on December 1, 1775, and adjourned the same day to meet in Williamsburg on the following Monday, where the remainder of the sessions were held. Edmund Pendleton was elected President and John Tazewell Clerk. Edmund Pendleton and James Taylor represented Caroline. The Convention elected Carter Braxton a delegate to the General Congress in place of Peyton Randolph, who died September 22, 1775; adopted two declarations condemning Lord Dunmore's tyranny; and adopted ordinances for raising additional forces for defense.

May 6, 1776—This Convention met in Williamsburg on May 6, 1776, and "framed the first written constitution of a free State in the annals of the world." This quotation is from an address of Prof. Washington before the Virginia Historical Society in 1852, and of it Prof. Hugh Blair Grigsby declares, "And he has said truly." The Great Seal of Virginia was adopted in this Convention (George Mason, of the Committee, reported the device prepared by the Committee); adopted the Declaration of Rights; elected Patrick Henry Governor of the Commonwealth; fixed Governor's salary at 1,000 pounds per annum; reduced the number of delegates to the General Congress from seven to five, and honored the following five men with commissions as delegates to the General Congress: George Wythe, Thomas Nelson, Richard Henry Lee, Thomas Jefferson and Francis Lightfoot Lee. Edmund Pendleton was elected President and John Tazewell Clerk. Edmund Pendleton and James Taylor were Caroline's representatives.

1788—This Convention met in the State House at Richmond to ratify or reject the Constitution which had been recommended to the States by the Federal Convention held in Philadelphia in September, 1787. Edmund Pendleton was elected President and John Beckley Secretary. Edmund Pendleton and James Taylor represented Caroline.

1829–'30—Assembled in Richmond. Purpose: To revise State Constitution. James Monroe elected President, but resigned his seat on account of ill health and was succeeded by Philip P. Barbour, of Orange. George W. Munford was elected Secretary, but, on being re-elected Clerk of the House of Delegates, resigned and was succeeded by D. Briggs. The Fourteenth District, in which Caroline was included, was represented by John Roane, William P. Taylor, Richard Morris and James M. Garnett.

1850–'51—Known as "The Reform Convention." John Y. Mason was elected President and Stephen D. Whittle Clerk. The District, comprising Caroline, Spotsylvania, King William and Hanover, was represented by Francis W. Scott, Corbin Braxton, Eustace Conway, Beverly B. Douglas and Edward W. Morris. This Convention made many changes in the Constitution, chief among which were in the qualifications of voters and method of electing the Governor. This Convention gave the people the right to elect the Governor, who, prior to that time, was elected by the General Assembly.

1861—Known as the Secession Convention. John Janney was elected President and John L. Eubank Secretary. Caroline was represented in this Convention by Edmund T. Morris. Mr. Janney resigned as President of the Convention on November

14, 1861, and was succeeded by R. L. Montague, representative of Matthews and Middlesex and popularly and affectionately known as "The Red Fox of Middlesex." A son of President Montague of the Secession Convention has since served the Old Dominion as Governor and Congressman. Alexander H. Stephens, Vice-President of the Confederacy; Captain Matthew Fontaine Maury and Major General Robert E. Lee were introduced to this Convention and addressed the delegates. Many commissions, among them those of Lee and Jackson, were given in this Convention.

1864—This Convention met in Alexandria, Va., on February 13, 1864. LeRoy G. Edwards was elected President and W. J. Cowing Secretary. Only seventeen delegates attended this Convention and fewer than twenty counties were represented, the greater portion of the State, after West Virginia was taken off, being within the Confederate lines. This Convention adopted the Bill of Rights, as contained in the Constitution of 1850-'51. The nearest county to Caroline having representation in this Convention was New Kent.

1867-'68—This Convention is known as The Reconstruction, or Underwood Convention. Met in Richmond on December 3d. All acts and proceedings of the political, military and civil organizations in Virginia had been declared null and void by the Federal Government. Virginia was under military rule, being Military District No. 1. *President Johnson had proclaimed that the "insurrection" was at an end, and was, henceforth, to be so regarded, but in the face of this proclamation an act was passed by Congress on March 3, 1867, "To provide a more efficient government for the Rebel States."* (See U. S. Stat., Vol. 14, p. 248). Thus the Convention of 1867-68, was brought about without any action whatsoever on the part of the people of Virginia. General Order No. 65, issued September 12, 1867, by Brigadier and Brevet Major-General J. M. Schofield from Headquarters First Military District, State of Virginia, Richmond, states that "in pursuance of the Act of Congress of March 23, 1867, an election will be held for delegates to a State Convention and to take the sense of the registered voters upon the question whether such Convention shall be held, for the purpose of establishing a constitution and civil government for the State of Virginia, loyal to the Union." The vote showed a majority of 46,000 in favour of Convention. The delegates assembled on December 3d. Of the 105, 35 were

Conservative, 65 were Radical, and the remainder doubtful. Of the 65 Radical 24 were negroes, 14 native white Virginians, 13 New Yorkers, 1 Pennsylvanian, 1 Ohioan, 1 from Maine, 1 from Vermont, 1 from Connecticut, 1 from South Carolina, one from Maryland, 1 from the District of Columbia, 2 from England, 1 from Ireland, 1 from Scotland, 1 from Nova Scotia and 1 from Canada. A large proportion of the Northern men and foreigners, came into the State in some non-combatant capacity during, or immediately following the war. The Convention elected John C. Underwood, of New York, President, and George Rye, of Maryland, Secretary. A Marylander was elected Sergeant-at-Arms, and an Irshman of Baltimore was elected stenographer. The assistant clerk was from New Jersey, the two doorkeepers were negroes and the pages, with one or two exceptions, were negroes, or sons of Northern men or foreigners. The clerks of the twenty standing committees, with two or three exceptions, were also negroes or Northern men.

The Reconstruction Convention is without a parallel in all history. Never before were different nationalities and different races, carpet baggers and adventurers, illiterates and half savage people set over the task of framing a constitution for the government of a cultured and highly civilized people like the Virginia Cavalier. Many members of the Convention expressed their disgust with the entire proceedings and for such expressions were expelled from membership in that heterogeneous body. Street brawls and fights were common occurrences among the baser element of the Convention (which was the larger element) and many went armed on the floor of the Convention. One hundred thousand dollars were appropriated for the expenses of the Convention and this sum was spent long before the day of adjournment. During the sessions sixteen resolutions and amendments were proposed providing an additional sum to pay the expenses of the body. The Convention adjourned in debt, no provision having been made for paying the expenses during the last ten days of its session and so far as the records go there is no evidence that this indebtedness was ever liquidated. On the 17th day of April, 1868, which was the seventh anniversary of the adoption of the ordinance of secession, the Convention adjourned, subject to the call of a committee appointed for that purpose, but the Convention never reassembled. John L. Marye, Jr., Frederick

S. C. Hunter and John J. Gravatt, represented Spotsylvania, King George and Caroline Counties in this Convention.

1901-'02—This Convention was held for the purpose of revising and amending the Constitution. The Hon. John Goode, of Bedford county, was President and Mr. Joseph Button, of Appomattox, Secretary. Mr. W. L. Cobb represented Caroline in this Constitutional Convention.

THE CONGRESSIONAL DISTRICTS OF VIRGINIA WHICH HAVE INCLUDED CAROLINE COUNTY AT VARIOUS PERIODS SINCE THE BEGINNING OF THE REPUBLIC AND NAMES OF REPRESEN-TATIVES THEREFROM

Hening's Statutes, V. 13, p. 331–335, contains "An Act for arranging the counties of this Commonwealth into districts to choose Representatives to Congress," passed December 26, 1792. The districts as arranged under this Act are not specifically numbered, but the provision for the sixteenth of the districts as arranged for reads: "The counties of King & Queen, King William, Essex, Middlesex, and Caroline, shall compose another district."

In the division of counties into districts under the Act passed January 24, 1823, the same counties are made to "compose another district." In this instance, too, the districts are not specifically numbered, but this particular district is the twelfth one named in the statute as enacted. See Virginia Acts, 1822–1823, p. 41–42.

In the "Act for arranging the counties and towns of this commonwealth into districts for the choice of representatives to congress," passed February 27, 1833, the same counties are made to "compose another district," and the marginal reading is *Ninth*. See Virginia Acts, 1832–1833, p. 29–30.

In the Act passed March 7, 1843, the reading is: "The counties of Essex, Middlesex, King & Queen, Richmond, Westmoreland, Caroline, Spottsylvania, King George and King William shall compose the eighth district." See Virginia Acts, 1842–1843, p. 30–31.

In the Act passed April 6, 1853, the reading is: "Richmond city, Henrico, Chesterfield, Louisa, Goochland, Hanover, King William and Caroline shall be the third district." See Virginia Acts, 1852–1853, p. 3–7.

In the Act approved March 13, 1872, the reading is: "Richmond city and the counties of Henrico, Chesterfield, Hanover, Caroline, and Louisa shall form the third congressional district." See Virginia Acts, 1871–1872, p. 258–259.

In the Act passed February 22, 1884, the reading is: "The counties of Accomac, Northampton, Lancaster, Richmond, Northumberland, Westmoreland, Gloucester, Middlesex, Mathews, Essex, King & Queen, Caroline, Spotsylvania, and the city of Fredericksburg, shall form the first congressional district." See Virginia Acts, 1883–1884, p. 183.

In the Act approved February 15, 1892, the arrangement is the same, the district remaining the first. See Virginia Acts, 1891–1892, p. 348–349.

In the Act approved March 5, 1912, the arrangement of counties is the same while the cities named are—Newport News, Hampton and Fredericksburg, and the district is constituted as the first. See Virginia Acts, 1912, p. 156–157.

Caroline's Congressmen are as follows:

James Madison, 1st and 2d Congresses.

Anthony New, 3d, 4th, 5th, 6th, 7th and 8th Congresses.

James M. Garnett, 9th and 10th Congresses.

John J. Roane, 11th, 12th and 13th Congresses.

William H. Roane, 14th Congress.

Richard S. Garnett, 15th, 16th, 17th, 18th and 19th Congresses.

John J. Roane, 20th, 21st, 22d Congresses.

William P. Taylor, 23d Congress.

John J. Roane, 24th Congress.

Robert M. T. Hunter, 25th, 26th and 27th Congresses.

Willoughby Newton, 28th Congress.

Richard L. T. Beale, 30th Congress.

Alexander Holladay, 31st and 32d Congresses.

John S. Caskie, 33d, 34th and 35th Congresses.

Daniel Coleman DeJarnette, 36th and 37th Congresses.

Civil War: No Representatives from Virginia in 38th, 39th and 40th Congresses.

Richard S. Ayer, 41st Congress.

John Critcher, 42d Congress.

John Ambler Smith, 43d Congress.

Gilbert Carlton Walker, 44th Congress..

Richard L. T. Beale, 45th and 46th Congresses.

George D. Wise, 47th and 48th Congresses.

Thomas Croxton, 49th Congress.

Thomas H. Bayly Brown, 50th and 51st Congresses.

William A. Jones, 52d, 53d, 54th, 55th, 56th, 57th, 58th, 59th, 60th, 61st, 62d, 63d, 64th, and 65th Congresses.

Schuyler Otis Bland, 66th, 67th and 68th Congresses.

NOTES

James Madison became the fourth President of the United States.

Anthony New was a native of Gloucester. He removed to Kentucky after serving six terms in Congress from Virginia, and became a Congressman from Kentucky. He is named one of the trustees in an Act passed by the Virginia Assembly, November 2, 1792, "To establish a town and Inspection of tobacco on the land of John Hoomes in the county of Caroline." This town was Milford. (See Hening's Statutes, Vol. 3, page 576). He was a half brother of Dr. Wm. Baynham. (See Wyatt genealogy).

James M. Garnett was a native of Essex.

John J. Roane was a native of King William.

Wm. H. Roane was a native of King and Queen.

Richard S. Garnett was a native of Essex.

William P. Taylor was a native of Caroline.

Robert M. T. Hunter was a native of Essex. After three terms in Congress he served in the United States Senate from March 4, 1847 to March 28, 1861.

Willoughby Newton was a native of Westmoreland.

Richard L. T. Beale was a native of Westmoreland and was the grandfather of Col. Richard L. Beale who has practiced law in Bowling Green since 1908 and has been otherwise prominent in the life of the county. (See Glassel genealogy).

Alexander Holladay was a native of Louisa county and connected with the Holladays of Richmond.

John S. Caskie was a native of Richmond.

Daniel Coleman DeJarnette was a native of Caroline, father of the present Daniel Coleman DeJarnette of "Spring Grove," and grandfather of Joe Willis DeJarnette, of Bowling Green, who married Alice, daughter of Mr. and Mrs. James T. Richards, of Bowling Green. (See DeJarnette genealogy).

Richard S. Ayer was a native of Richmond county.

John Critcher was a native of King George county.

John Ambler Smith was a native of Essex.

Gilbert Carlton Walker was a native of Richmond.

George D. Wise was a native of Richmond.

Thomas Croxton was a native of Essex. A postoffice in Caroline is named for him.

Thomas H. Bayly Brown was a native of Accomac.

William Atkinson Jones was a native of Richmond county.

Schuyler Otis Bland is a native of Gloucester.

ABSTRACTS OF ALL CAROLINE COUNTY LEGISLATIVE PETITIONS NOW IN ARCHIVES OF STATE LIBRARY

No. 168. Dated November 21, 1777—Prays House of Delegates to declare fishing rights along Rappahannock river common to all. About one hundred signatures.

No. 181. Dated December 5, 1777—Prays House of Delegates to fix "one certain annual sum" to be paid by all tithables for the support of ministers and the upkeep of the Churches. Signed by 118 citizens.

No. 324. Dated May 25, 1779—Prays the House of Delegates to dissolve the vestry of Drysdale Parish and grant right to elect a new vestry by the suffrage of the people. 167 signatures.

No. 361. Dated October 15, 1779—Prays for a division of Drysdale Parish into two parishes, and for sale of property and division of proceeds between the two parishes thus formed. Approximately 50 names.

No. 367. Dated October 16, 1779—A counter petition protesting against the division of Drysdale parish. 300 signatures.

No. 380. Dated October 22, 1779— Two petitions: one praying for a division of Drysdale parish, and the other protesting against such division. The former signed by 35 citizens, and the latter by about 300.

No. 417. Dated November 4, 1779—Sarah Bowie, widow of James Bowie, the younger, prays House of Delegates to repeal that portion of Act of 1776 which required James Bowie, or heirs of his public ferry, to set foot-passengers aross the Rappahannock free.

No. 571. Dated November 22, 1780—Richard Roy and John Catlett pray for "an increase in their salary, and of the reward for prizing transfer tobacco, and finding nails."

No. 602. Dated December 12, 1780—Prays that the vestry of St. Margaret's Parish be dissolved, basing petition on the declaration that the vestry was not elected by the suffrage of the people at large. Signed by about 75 parishioners.

No. 634. Dated June 1, 1781—Edmund Pendleton and John Taylor pray House of Delegates to assist said Pendleton in the recovery of 3000 acres of land which was granted him by the Crown in 1765, as being in Augusta county, but which proved to be in North Carolina, and which that State had confirmed to her citizens.

No. 1199. Dated November 16, 1784—Prays "that whatever tax shall be found necessary to be laid on suitors shall be allowed in the Bill of costs, if the party recovers." This petition also refers to the "emigration to the western country taking place this fall." 70 signatures.

No. 1233. Dated November 30, 1784—Prays House of Delegates to pass a Bill requiring all land owners adjoining the Mattaponi river to clear away all obstructions in the river opposite their lands, to the middle of the stream, and keep same clear so there may be a free passage for boats and fish. This petition recites that by an Act of 1753 a considerable sum was appropriated and trustees appointed for clearing the Mattaponi, "to so good purpose that Boats could pass from Burk's bridge in this county with great ease and expedition and a more plentiful supply of fish was experienced by the people up the river." 41 signatures.

No. 1299. Dated October 27, 1785—A petition declaring against a Bill published by the House of Delegates obliging all inhabitants of the commonwealth to pay the teachers of the Christian Religion. There are 143 signatures, that of John Young, Baptist preacher of Caroline, heading the list. A significant religio-legislative document. 143 signatures.

No. 1382. November 18, 1785—The petition of John Lewis in behalf of his daughter Mildred, and of Thornton Washington in behalf of himself, praying that the Act of October 1788, relative to lands of John Thornton, be repealed, and the lands be re-vested in the hands of trustees, so that petitioners may receive their just share of the estate.

No. 1390.   November 22, 1785—William Evans petitions House of Delegates for eighty pounds, same being value of Sancho, a Negro belonging to petitioner, who was executed by court martial for giving intelligence to, and acting in the capacity of pilot for the British forces.

No. 1437.   December 9, 1785—Charlotte Dalton, wife of Samuel Dalton, prays for an Act enabling her to sell tract of land on the Rappahannock river and give title to same in order that she may the better care for her husband who had, "had the misfortune to lose his understanding, and who, to her great grief and trouble, hath continued in a state of insanity for many years."

No. 1737.   November 1, 1787—Richard Towner and John Woolfolk volunteer to take over the stage lines between Richmond and Hampton and between Richmond and Norfolk for a period of three years.   The petition recites that Act of 1784 gave John Hoomes exclusive privilege over these lines.   Nearly 200 signatures.

No. 1944.   Dated November 7, 1788—A protest against the removal of Page's Inspection down to Newcastle.   Proclaims the superiority of Page's Inspection to Meriwether's.   Several signatures.

No. 1981.   Dated November 21, 1788—Protest against the tax imposed on Clerks of Courts by Act of Assembly of 1787.   125 names.

No. 2223.   Dated November 16, 1789—James Upshaw, late Sheriff of Caroline county, "humbly sheweth that from the peculiar distresses of the people and the burthen of the taxes in the years 1785 and 1786," his deputies were unable to collect tax in full, in consequence of which judgment was obtained against him.   Prays remission of costs assessed against him.

No. 2299.   Dated October 30, 1790—Memorial of the Clerks of the several Courts of Justice in Virginia protesting against Act of 1786 imposing tax on Clerks in sums of one-third of fees received for services performed.   30 signatures.

No. 2319.   Dated November 4, 1790—Sets forth that second Thursday of each month, fixed by law as date for holding Caroline court, "interferes with the court days in some of the adjacent counties" and prays that the date be changed to second Tuesday of each month.   30 names.

No. 2452. December 2, 1790—Resolution stating that the petition of James Upshaw (see File No. 2223) is reasonable.

No. 2533. Dated October 31, 1791—Charles Anderson sets forth that in April, 1785, he received a military certificate as a soldier in the First Virginia Regiment, on Continental estalishment, in the sum of thirty-six pounds which certificate he lost. Prays that the House will direct the issuance of a duplicate.

No. 2710. Dated October 3, 1792—Prays House of Delegates to have an Inspection of Tobacco established at the head of navigation on the Mattaponi river, on " the land of John Hoomes at Dogue Town Bridge, on the Mattaponi river, and a Town laid out adjacent thereto." 175 signatures.

No. 2584. October 13, 1792—Petition that two duplicate warrants in the sum of twenty-four pounds each be issued to James Powell Edmondson upon his giving bond and security according to the law in such cases.

No. 2857. October 13, 1792—George Guy, late Sheriff of Caroline, explains why his deputies did not turn in taxes "so soon as the law required," and prays remission of fine assessed against him for their tardiness.

No. 2939. October 16, 1792—Prays House of Delegates to pass an Act empowering tobacco growers to carry condemned tobacco to another Inspection, or to export it at the growers "risque" that they might at least get some advantage from the sweat of their brow. 50 signatures.

No. 2941. Dated October 16, 1792—John Rogers represents that he entered the service of the State in the spring of 1776, was promoted to the command of a regiment immediately in the service of the State, continued in such service until February, 1782, when he was deprived of his captaincy by a supernumerary officer, and that he was never re-instated although he held himself in readiness until the end of the war. Prays House of Delegates to allow him half pay for life.

No. 3051. Dated October 29, 1793—A lengthy document protesting against "the dismemberment of Caroline county" "to patch up a new county," and naming seven reasons on which the protest is based, one of them being that "in answer to the generous proposition of an individual (William Streshley) to erect public buildings at his private expense, we observe that Court Houses should be made for Counties and not Counties for Court Houses." There are about 500 signatures to this petition.

No. 3053.   October 29, 1793—A petition for the establishment of a new county from Caroline, King and Queen and Essex, representing that if such county were formed "the county of Caroline would then contain 16,700 souls and 650 freeholders; the county of King and Queen 8,152 souls and 370 freeholders; the county of Essex 7,976 souls and 370 free holders and the new county 4,776 souls and 250 freeholders." About 450 signatures.

No. 3054.   Dated October 29, 1793—Petition against "the dismemberment of Caroline county in order to patch up a new county." 38 signatures.

No. 3090.   Dated November 2, 1793—Elizabeth Trainham shews by certificates of Captain Johnson Faulkner, Anthony New and Captain Beverly Stubblefield, that her husband, Joshua Trainham, served 18 months in the army and died in the service, and prays House of Delegates to grant her some relief from her poverty.

No. 3109-A.   Dated November 4, 1793—Samuel Hargrave states that he is seized of a tract of land lying on the north side of the Pamunkey at Cook's Ford in Caroline, and that it is advantageously situated for a town, being at the head of navigation. Prays House of Delegates to pass an Act to "lay off 15 acres and establish a town thereon."

No. 3256.   Dated November 24, 1794—Peyton Stern and Thomas Alcock, Inspectors at Roy's Warehouse, shew theft of one hhd. of tobacco and ask House of Delegates to "make such redress as your Honours may conceive just."

No. 3284-D.   October 26, 1794—Joseph Temple and Benjamin Johnson, Inspectors at Todd's and Aylett's Inspection, set forth, "That by an Act of the last session of Assembly establishing an Inspection of Tobacco at the town of Milford, on the Mattaponi river in the county of Caroline, by the name of York Warehouse, the Inspectors of Todd's Warehouse are directed and required to receive all tobacco brought down from York warehouse and store same without compensation. This Act the petitioners conceive to be unjust and pray for relief.

No. 3288.   November 26, 1794—Cornelius Beazley shews by certificates of John Taylor and Samuel Coleman that he enlisted in a Caroline company on February 17, 1777, and served three years in a regiment of which Moses Hazen was colonel and he the major and prays for his depreciation in money or bounty of land.

No. 3701. December 8, 1797—Charles Vivian petitions for compensation for "waggon and team impressed and taken into public use" in 1781.

No. 3892. December 8, 1798—A remonstrance against oppressive measures of the new government made by the citizens of Caroline in mass meeting and signed by Edmund Pendleton, Jr., Chairman.

No. 3897. December 10, 1798—Anna Swinton prays House of Delegates to grant to her certain lands in Caroline which were willed to aliens by her late husband, George Swinton.

No. 3899. December 10, 1798—James Swinton, of Scotland, nephew of George Swinton, deceased, prays House of Delegates to confirm to him certain lands asked for by Anna Swinton, widow of George Swinton deceased.

No. 4032. December 6, 1799—"The Justices, Bar and sundry Inhabitants" of Caroline shew that the March and May courts conflict with neighbouring courts and pray that the second Tuesdays of April and June be substituted. 25 signatures.

No. 4128. December 19, 1799—A petition from citizens of Caroline, Hanover and King William for the annulment or repeal of an Act relative to the obstruction of rivers, etc., so that they may erect hedges in the Pamunkey at certain seasons when the river is not navigable, so they may catch fish.

No. 4191-A. December 6, 1800—A petition representing that since the division of Drysdale parish the large and commodious old church in the original parish has not been much used and is falling to ruin, and prays for an Act enabling the trustees to sell or repair the old building so that at any rate it may be opened "to all Christians of every persuasion and denomination whatsoever." About 100 signatures.

No. 4412. December 23, 1801—James Upshaw, William Lyne and Edward Hill, Trustees of Drysdale and St. Stephen's Parishes, and numerous others with them, remonstrate against a petition (see No. 4941-A) which had been circulated to the end that old Drysdale parish Church may be sold or repaired and opened to all religious bodies.

No. 4421. December 24, 1801—Sarah Bowie, of Port Royal, prays for authorization to increase ferriage rates from Port Royal to Port Conway on opposite bank of the Rappahannock.

No. 4617.   Dated December 16, 1803—John Hoomes represents that in the year 1794 one Mr. James Johnston owned the lands on which the Court House of Caroline stood, (2) that the said Johnston came to him and offered to sell the seat of justice, (3) that application was then made to the County Court which consented and advised him (Hoomes) to pay 700 pounds for the removal of it to Bowling Green, (4) that petition was made to the General Assembly, asking that the people be placed on the same footing at the Bowling Green that they were on at the former Court House, (5) that this petition was universally signed by all to whom it was presented, (6) that an Act was passed in 1794 for the removal of the seat of justice to a House in Bowling Green founded by the petitioner as a temporary Court House, (7) that this house was received by the Court until one could be built of the same size and material as the former one, (8) that bounds for debtors were laid out and upwards of four acres laid out for public purposes, (9) that the petitioner bound himself in the sum of five thousand dollars to make a deed to the Justices of this land, (10) that the petitioner has thus placed the county on a much better footing at the Bowling Green than it was at the former place where it did not own a foot of land and where there was far less comfort, (11) that one Mr. Kenner has presented to the General Assembly a petition asking that two acres more of the petitioner's land be condemned for public use, saying to the people that as soon as this is done other taverns will be built thereon giving the people what they want 100 per cent. cheaper, notwithstanding that tavern rates are fixed by court, (12) that the court has already voted for the removal of the Clerk's Office to the Bowling Green, (13) that the petitioner being unwilling to accede to the proposal contained in Mr. Kenner's petition, and not being eager to continue the Court House at Bowling Green, having an opportunity to sell it to be carried back to its former place, therefore prays the House of Delegates to post pone the condemning of two more acres of his land that he (the petitioner) may have time to arrange his business and come forward at the next session with a petition for the removal of the Court House back to its former place.   This petition is accompanied by certificates from Thomas Hicks, William Nelson, John Pendleton, Wm C. Woodford, verifying the statements of the petitioner, and also the petitioner's bond in the sum of five thousand dollars agreeing to build the Court House and deed the lands afore-mentioned free.

No. 4618.   December 16, 1803—Petition for an Act condemning two acres of land at Caroline Court House, etc.   300 signatures.

No. 4629.   December 20, 1803—Henry Burruss and Thomas Oliver, security for the good behaviour of one Aaron Estes, who forfeited his bond and went to jail, pray the House of Delegates for remission of fines imposed on them, inasmuch as Estes was imprisoned.

No. 4686-A.   December 18, 1804—Abner Waugh, rector, and about 70 others with him, pray for an Act enabling them to sell the glebe of St. Mary's parish and place the proceeds of same at interest which shall be paid to the said Abner Waugh so long as he is the incumbent of the parish.

No. 5102-A.   December 9, 1807—Petition for the passage of an Act directing payment of tolls at Littlepage's bridge for the benefit of the counties of Caroline and Hanover which it connects. About 65 signatures.

No. 5130.   December 11, 1807—Sarah Hewlett, administratrix for Wm. Hewlett, prays for an Act enabling her to sell a tract of her late husband's land in order to discharge his debts.

No. 5250.   December 8, 1808—Represents that proceeds of sale of St. Mary's glebe, now that Rev. Abner Waugh is dead, will go to establish an academy in the parish and asks for con-stitution for same, etc.   About 100 signatures.   (This was Rappahannock Academy).

No. 5409-C.   December 8, 1809—Prays that the jail at Fred-ericksburg, which was built by Caroline and surrounding counties under the District Court system and abandoned when that system was discontinued be sold and divided among the counties which built it.   About 100 signatures.

No. 5641.   December 11, 1810—Petition for an Act to establish an academy in Mount Church (the parish Church) of St. Mary's parish, and for calling the same Rappahannock Academy.   61 signatures.

No. 6147.   December 16, 1812—The Trustees of Rappahannock Academy petition for an Act to punish adults for selling intoxicants to the students, and for power to use a part of the capital of the school in furnishing buildings, and for power to appropriate a fund for the enlargement of the library.

No. 6148. December 16, 1812—William Atkinson who was disabled in the Revolutionary War asks that the legislature increase his pay from $40.00 to $60.00 per year.

No. 5888-C. December 13, 1811—William P. Napier, executor of Dangerfield Graves, deceased, and guardian of his five children, petitions for an Act enabling him to sell a certain tract of land in Caroline which belonged to the said Graves.

No. 6213-A. December 13, 1815—Praying for the establishment of a District Court of Chancery in Fredericksburg for Caroline and surrounding counties. Above 200 signatures.

No. 6249. December 17, 1813—The inhabitants of St. Margaret's parish in Caroline pray for an Act empowering the overseers of the poor to sell the books, ornaments and plate which belonged to the late Church in that parish, and to apply the proceeds to the establishment of a free school "on the Lancasterian plan." About 115 signatures.

No. 6403. December 16, 1814—A number of the citizens of Caroline legally exempt from military service on the score of age pray to be moulded by law into a form enabling them to render any military service of which they may be capable.

No. 6640. December 21, 1815—A number of citizens of Caroline and Hanover counties pray the General Assembly to provide relief in the form of tolls for Benjamin Kidd who is represented as "having ruined himself financially in building Littlepage's Bridge at a price far below costs."

No. 6688-B. November 12, 1816—Clerk of Caroline Court joins other Clerks in petitioning the General Assembly for an Act increasing fees.

No. 6820. December 9, 1816—The residents of Port Royal state that the increase of free negroes and mulattoes in said town causeth sundry inconveniences, among these being that many hogs owned by these persons run at large, making conditions unsanitary, and they, therefore, pray for an Act incorporating the town so that certain regulations may be established and a public officer employed to enforce the same. 50 signatures.

No. 6829. December 11, 1816—Citizens of Port Royal and adjacent community petition for the right to establish a bank. 60 signatures.

No. 7211. December 14, 1818—Citizens of Caroline, King William and King and Queen petition for an Act incorporating a company for raising funds to open the Mattaponi river to its highest point of improvement. About 60 signatures.

No. 7517. December 8, 1820—Memorial of Dover Baptist Association signed by R. B. Semple and James Webb praying the General Assembly to enact a law which will protect all religious bodies from interruption or disturbance when engaged in worship, or in the transaction of business.

No. 7570. December 19, 1820—F. W. Taliaferro prays for an Act enabling him to discontinue Capon's Ferry.

No. 7596. December 21, 1820—Richard Turner, George W. Tennent and Benjamin Sedgwick represent that they were appointed Superintending Committee to erect a house of worship at Port Royal and as such entered into contract with the workmen to pay for construction upon the completion of the work, it being understood that they (the Committee) were to be secured by public subscriptions made to the cause. Inasmuch as they have not been reimbursed they pray the House of Delegates to authorize John G. Catlett to turn over to them the proceeds from the sale of an old school-house, which occupied the public square and which was sold to William George White, Junior.

No. 7681. December 11, 1821—Citizens of Caroline pray House of Delegates to reconsider the petition made by Joseph Tyree, a a freeman of colour, at the last session of the legislature asking that he and his wife and seven children might be permitted to remain in Virginia, which petition was rejected. 60 signatures.

No. 7715. December 15, 1821—Citizens of Caroline, Stafford and King George counties pray House of Delegates to repeal Act of last session discontinuing Capon's Ferry. About 450 signatures.

No. 7720. December 17, 1821—Freeholders and housekeepers of St. Margaret's Parish represent that there are two Churches in said Parish—Reedy Church and Bull Church—and pray for authority to sell Churches, glebes and parish houses under Acts of January 24, 1799, and January 12, 1802. About 115 signatures.

No. 7775. December 4, 1822—Elizabeth Dudley, widow of William Dudley, prays for authority to sell 341 acres of land in Caroline in order to discharge debts of her late husband.

No. 8104. January 6, 1824—John T. Rawlins, jailer of Caroline county, represents that he was compelled to receive into his jail a runaway negro who was confined for a considerable length of time and when sold brought only $78.40 (being crippled and infirm) and that this amount was far short of the actual cost of keep. Prays House of Delegates for relief.

No. 8735.   December 18, 1826—Caroline M. Carson, widow of George Carson, deceased, and Theophilus R., Augustus E., Egbert W., Emily G., Melvina W., and Alonza B. Carson, children of the aforesaid, represent that 200 acres of land in Harrison county has escheated to the commonwealth and pray for an Act restoring said lands to petitioners.

No. 8972.   December 17, 1827—Moses Green represents that he served in the Revoluntary Army and prays the Legislature for a pension. His representation is certified to be true by John L. Pendleton, Clerk of Caroline; Gray Samuel, George D. Baylor and others.

No. 9192.   December 15, 1828—A petition for the establishment of a voting precinct at Golansville.   55 signatures.

No. 9380.   December 28, 1829—William Southworth represents that he served in the Revolutionary War until disabled and prays for pension.

No. 9401.   December 24, 1829—Moses Stanley represents that he served in the Revolutionary War and prays for pension. Representation endorsed by certificates of George Alsop, Francis Brooke, Walter D. Blair, Thomas G. Thornton and others.

No. 9550.   December 10, 1830—The citizens of Port Royal represent that they are too far from the Court House to vote there with convenience and pray for the establishment of a voting precinct in their own village.   100 signatures.

No. 9637.   December 22, 1830—A memorial remonstrating against separate elections being held at Port Royal and praying that the petition for a precinct at that place be rejected.   120 signatures.

No. 9639.   December 22, 1830—A memorial praying relief for Robert T. Pendleton and Hiram Chiles, Deputy Sheriffs of Caroline, for extra services rendered in connection with the trial and execution of Charles Young, who murdered Thomas Griffin Thornton, Sheriff of Caroline.   54 signatures.

No. 9640.   December 22, 1830—Citizens of the Bowling Green represent that their town has grown to that extent that it is necessary to have special laws for governing the same, and therefore pray for an act of incorporation.   About 50 signatures.

No. 9883.   December 22, 1831—A petition for an Act relieving James C. Luck and Sarah, his wife, from the operation of the judgment entered against them in 1827 for violations of the law against incestuous marriage, the said Luck having married Sarah Chiles, widow of his uncle, Pleasant Chiles.   Over 300 signatures.

No. 7884.   December 22, 1831—Lawrence Battaile represents that he was High Sheriff of Caroline in 1805 and 1806, and also a part of 1804, in which year he served out the unexpired term of John Hipkins, that he had five deputies in as many districts of the county, that seventeen years after retiring from office large militia fines were assessed against him and also a small balance of the revenue tax, and that judgments were entered upon these in General Court.   Believing such treatment unjust he prays the House of Delegates for relief for himself and his deputies, Reuben Turner, William Saunders, William Jones, Daniel Turner, Jr., and Philip Samuel.

No. 9979.   January 20, 1832—This file contains two petitions setting forth the rapid increase of the Negro population in Caroline and praying for the removal of all free Negroes from the State of Virginia, and for the purchase, deportation, and maintenance at public expense, of a few hundred slaves annually.   About 100 signatures.

No. 10012.   February 2, 1832—This file contains petitions for and against the establishment of voting precincts in various parts of the county.   There are several hundred signatures on each side of the question.

No. 10275.   January 26, 1833—Mordecai Broaddus, on behalf of the Board of Overseers of the Poor, represents that the poor-house lands have worn out and that the wood has been cut therefrom and prays for authority to sell these lands and buy a fresh situation.

No. 10350.   December 4, 1833—Petition for the establishment of an election precinct at Needwood.   73 signatures.

No. 10648.   December 5, 1834—A petition for a change in the laws relative to enclosures (the fence law).   About 115 signatures.

No. 11032.   December 21, 1835—A petition for the erection of a new county from the counties of Caroline, Essex and King and Queen.   Approximately 500 signatures of citizens of these three counties.

No. 11033. December 21, 1835—A petition remonstrating against the formation of a new county from Caroline, Essex, and King and Queen. 300 signatures.

No. 11287. December 6, 1836—A petition for an Act making the North Anna river from Oxford to the junction of the South Anna and thence the Pamunkey to Tidewater a lawful fence. 40 signatures.

No. 11505. January 10, 1837—A petition for an Act incorporating the town of Bowling Green. 20 signatures.

No. 11578. January 24, 1837—Petition of the Justices of Caroline, M. H. Jones, Thos. Rowe, A. C. Coleman, Geo. D. Baylor, Wm. W. Dickinson, Richard Buckner, Jr., John P. Miller, S. C. Dickinson, praying to be reimbursed a sum of money spent in line of duty.

No. 11671. February 16, 1837—Petition for the establishment of a voting precinct at Central Point. 55 signatures.

No. 11672. February 16, 1837—A petition for the establishment of a voting precinct at Sparta. 34 signatures.

No. 11717. March 8, 1837—Citizens of Caroline and other counties pray for the establishment of a bank at Tappahannock. Approximately 100 signatures.

No. 12477. February 13, 1839—A memorial praying the aid of the Legislature in promoting the culture of silk. 70 signatures.

No. 12732. December 17, 1839—A petition for an election precinct at Sparta. 83 signatures.

No. 12974. December 1, 1840—Memorial of Col. Archibald Samuel contesting the election of Robert B. Corbin as a delegate to the Legislature.

No. 13790. February 10, 1843—Benjamin T. Taliaferro and John Taylor, Jr., on behalf of Rappahannock Academy, pray for authority to sell part of the lands of the said Academy and use proceeds in making certain improvements.

No. 13891. December 16, 1843—Thomas B. Taylor prays remission of a fine assessed against him by a jury composed of George T. Rose, Robert Cunningham, William H. Farish, Peter D. Goodwin, Daniel Lefoe, William H. Bullard, Aylett Boulware, Robert DeJarnette, Samuel Terrell, German Goodloe, Edmund Pendleton and William Chapman. His offence was an assault on Robert Sale. A large number of citizens joined in his petition, the jury among them.

No. 14723. January 2, 1846—A petition of citizens of Caroline, Essex and King and Queen praying the establishment of a new county to be called Union county and to have its Court House "located at the village of Central Point." About 500 signatures.

No. 14771. January 6, 1846—Petition remonstrating against the formation of a new county from Caroline, Essex, and King and Queen. About 60 signatures.

No. 14879. January 21, 1846—Petition of 44 citizens of Caroline praying remission of certain expenses and costs incident to the prosecution of William Norment, whose crime against his own daughter so aroused the people of Caroline that there was a change of venire to the county of Hanover.

No. 14911. January 29, 1846—Citizens of Caroline and adjacent counties pray for repeal of Act of February 21, 1845, which prohibited non-residents of Virginia to seine in any of its waters. Approximately 200 signatures.

No. 15533. February 11, 1847—Wesley Wright and Woodson Wright, deputies of Pichegru Woolfolk, Sheriff of Caroline, pray to have refunded to them certain damages assessed because of their delay in remitting funds accruing from merchants licenses.

No. 15645. December 8, 1847—Same as File No. 15533.

No. 15885. January 13, 1848—Petition from citizens in northwest part of Caroline praying an Act for the extension of the Louisa railroad to or near the dock in Richmond. 32 signatures.

No. 16165. March 10, 1848—Petition of the citizens of Bowling Green praying that the corporate limits of the town may be extended. Signed by R. B. Tunstall, Wm. P. Roper, A. M. Glassell, John L. Pendleton, J. G. Parrish, Wm. Maury, Samuel C. Scott and others.

No. 16367. January 4, 1849—Petition of Anthony Thornton, Commissioner of Revenue, for repeal of portion of Act of March, 1848 relative to the duties of his office.

No. 16521. January 29, 1849—The voters in the northwestern part of Caroline county petition for a voting precinct in their section, the same to be called "Sycamore's." 66 signatures.

No. 16921. January 10, 1850—George Fitzhugh prays for privilege of rebuilding a wharf at Port Royal.

No. 16982. January 16, 1850—A petition for the establishment of a "Branch Bank" in Port Royal. 75 signatures.

No. 16998. January 21, 1850—Remonstrance against George Fitzhugh's petition relative to rebuilding a wharf at Port Royal. About 65 signatures.

No. 16999. January 21, 1850—Petition of Elizabeth Quesenberry and 24 others against George Fitzhugh's wharf petition.

No. 17877. January 22, 1852—A petition for the establishment of an election precinct at Oakley in the house of F. C. Phillips. 24 signatures.

No. 18390. November 27, 1852—A petition for the establishment of a bank at Port Royal. Many signatures.

No. 18461. December 22, 1852—A petition for the establishment of a bank at Port Royal with a capitalization of not less than two hundred thousand dollars. Many signatures.

No. 18534. January 21, 1853—Petition for a plank road from Milford to Port Royal, and another from Sparta to intersect the Milford-Port Royal road. 52 signatures.

No. 18687. December 14, 1853—Petition of Henry R. Carter, J. Fontaine, B. F. Johnson, S. Gouldin, J. F. Redd, Thos. B. Anderson and others for an Act declaring the North Anna river from Oxford to Dabney's Mill a lawful fence.

No. 18695. December 17, 1853—Petition for the charter of a company to build a railroad or a plank road from Milford to Port Royal. 31 signatures.

No. 18706. December 20, 1853—Remonstrance of Isaac Butler and 19 others against making North Anna a lawful fence.

No. 18752. January 5, 1854—Petition of James Lowry, J. A. Matthews, Thos. B. Anderson that the North Anna be declared a lawful fence.

No. 18864. January 18, 1854—Petition for the suppression of the traffic in ardent spirits. 300 signatures.

No. 18999. February 6, 1854—Petition that the North Anna River be made a lawful fence. 7 signatures.

No. 19443. December 17, 1857—Petition to amend Act of 1856-7 relative to the tax on hawkers and peddlers, exempting the deaf, dumb and blind. About 50 signatures.

No. 19595. January 18, 1858—Petition for a reduction of the tax on merchants, and that property and capital employed in mercantile pursuits be taxed at the same rate of property employed in manufacturing and agriculture. 31 signatures.

No. 19908. January 12, 1861—Petition to amend the charter of the town of Port Royal. 23 signatures.

In the Executive Papers in the Archives of the State Library may be found the certificates of elections in Caroline, Recommendations for Sheriffs, Officers of the Militia, etc., etc. These papers have not yet been classified and to locate the Caroline papers would entail a search through nearly 150,000 pieces of matter.

ANCIENT CAROLINE MARRIAGE BONDS

Thomas Allen and Margaret Fields, January 16, 1787.

Thomas Ayres and Molly Noell, January 16, 1787.

James Andrews and Molly Broaddus, January 30, 1789.

Thomas Allen and Jenny Hackney, July 7, 1789.

William Allen and Mary Collier, February 21, 1795.

William Bridgford and Lucy Long, October 12, 1786.

John Baxter and Jane Tiller, August 17, 1787.

William Bush and Nancy Kee, August 17, 1787.

William Bell and Sally Doggett, August 17, 1787.

Samuel Butler and Patty Douglass, August 17, 1787.

George Burchell and Elizabeth Pemberton, September 8, 1790.

Carter Blanton and Susannah Snead, August 17, 1787.

David Bibb and Mary Chandler, October 16, 1789.

James Berry and Nancy Buckner, January —, 1790.

Lewis Ballard and Sukey Miller, March 6, 1791.

John G. Brown and Frances Eubank, January 29, 1792.

Thomas Barlow and Nancy West, March 31, 1792.

John Bond and Molly Sale, ——, 1789.

William Brown and Susannah Dyamett, January 28, 1792.

Anthony Baber and Rhoda Carlton, September 1, 1797.

John Bocock and Lucy Norment, October 22, 1788.

Thomas Burrows (Burruss) and Nelly Bibb, December 25, 1793.

Lewis Bell and Netty Dillard, December 30, 1793.

William Bullock and Lucy Timberlake, December 30, 1793.

Joseph Brame and Elizabeth Thomas, January 9, 1794.

John Broaddus and America Broaddus, January 13, 1794.

Andrew Broaddus and Fanny Temple, November 10, 1794.

Adam Beaseley and Fanny Vawter, May 15, 1799.

Richard Boulware and Elizabeth Skinner, May 26, 1795.

James Brown and Mary Farmer, December 22, 1795.

Richard Boulware and Mary Narrett, June 11, 1796.

Frederick Bourne and Jenny Sampson, February 1, 1796.

William E. Bowers and Fanny Jones, December 27, 1796.

David Baylor and Peggy Page, October 4, 1798.

Walke Bowler (Boulware?) and Elizabeth Self, June 4, 1797.

Edwin Broaddus and Frances Jerdon (Jordan) November 26, 1798.

Thomas Belle and Sarah Grafton, December 24, 1798.

Thomas Blackburn and Sally Daniel, March 13, 1794.

John Barlow and Ursula Southworth, March 5, 1796.

Hawes Barbee and Polly Jones, December 13, 1799.

Thomas Blackburn and Nancy Green, May 25, 1799.

John Carter and Nancy Carter, May 19, 1786.

Thomas Crenshaw and Elizabeth Saunders, March 22, 1787.

Reuben Clift and Sally Stevens, July 14, 1787.

William Cannon and Elizabeth Brown, December 17, 1787.

John Courts and Fanny Winn, March 5, 1788.

Lewis Collins and Martha Emerson, March 5, 1788.

John Croucher and Martha Long, March 5, 1788.

John Cox and Patty Bush, March 5, 1788.

William Crawford and Milly Chewning, December 16, 1788.

John Clark and Nancy Byrd, August 17, 1789.

Isaac Croucher and Nancy Blanton, September 8, 1790.

John Chandler and Jenny McKee, September 8, 1790.

James Coleburn and Mary Crudle, January 22, 1792.

James Collier and Nancy Pitts, —, 1792.

Ambrose Carlton and Nancy Slaughter, December 22, 1792.

Thomas Terry Cook and Elizabeth Richeson, May 20, 1793.

Samuel Chenault and Brune Pitts, July 10, 1793.

Reuben Crenshaw and Fanny Hundley, January 3, 1795.

William Collins and Elizabeth Pitts, January 6, 1795.

Edmund Carson and Sally Mourning, July 18, 1795.

John Carpenter and Polly DuVal, July 18, 1795.

Presley Carter and Elizabeth Pettus, December 3, 1794.

John Cox and Polly Holloway, May 13, 1794.

Elijah Chenault and Molly Graves, November 5, 1796.

James Clark and Susan Jeter, June 28, 1797.

Elijah Camall (Campbell) and Jane Yarbrough, June 28, 1797.

Thomas Camall (Campbell) and Elizabeth Harris, June 28, 1797.

James Camall (Campbell) and Anna Hatcher, January 17, 1798.

Richmond Camall (Campbell) and Phoebe Jones, April 10, 1798.

Thomas B. Coleman and Elizabeth Coghill, December 9, 1798.

Edmund Clark and Sally Boulware, December 26, 1799.

Joel Dunn and Lucia Page. (No date given).

Thos. Docotes and Elizabeth Sandland. (No date given).

William Davenport and Milly Blackhall, April 18, 1789.

Garland Duke and Jane Roy Coleman, September 19, 1789.

Benjamin Daniel and Peggy Brown, September 8, 1790.

William Durrett and Sarah Conner, January 2, 1790.

Joseph Duerson and Jenny Bowie (no date).

Thomas Donahoe and Patty Umbreckhouse (no date).

John Dodd and Lucy Poe (no date).

Jonathan Dickerson and Croshe Seizer, February 9, 1792.

Reuben Dear and Jenny Vawter (no date).

David Dillard and Susannah Stevens (no date).

William Dunn and Sarah Coghill, June 30, 1797.

William Douglass and Eliza Miller, March 12, 1798.

William DuVal and Lucy DuVal, July 12, 1798.

Henry Dunn and Ann Dunn, October 5, 1798.

John Dye and Delphia Alsop, November 1, 1799.

Daniel Esmond and Catherine Miller (no date).

George Estes and Ann Samuel, December 14, 1788.

—— Edwards and Kate Boulware (no date)

George Estes and Sarah Anderson (no date).

William Elliott and Elizabeth Edwards, May 12, 1793.

Daniel Esmonds and Ann Murry (Maury), May 20, 1794.

John Fletcher and Flower Seizer, August 9, 1792.

John Farish and Ann Rogers, June 14, 1796

John Farmer and Betsy Wright, September 10, 1796.

Edmund Gatewood and Judith Gatewood, February 1, 1787.

Richard Gatewood and Elizabeth Bowcock, December 27, 1787.

Spilsby Gregor and Caroline Muse (no date).

Reuben Gaunt and Sally Sullenger (no date).

Charles Gervis and Sarah Cissell (no date).

Edmund Gaines and Sukey Broaddus, ——, 1790.

John Gayle and Betsy Pitts, February 23, 1792.

Leonard Gatewood and Clara Gatewood, September 20, 1793.

William Gadberry and Mary Barlow, January 7, 1794.

William Garnett and Lucy Garnett, October 10, 1793.

Joseph Graves and Rachael Hay, January 12, 1796.

William Gayle and Lucy Dillard, November 10, 1797.

James Gray and Sally Merritt, September 19, 1799.

John Hall and Frances Wright, December 8, 1796.

William Hudson and Mary Guilmore (no date).

James Hughes and Sarah Seizer, November 6, 1790.

John Hopkins and Mary Ann Luck (no date).

George Henedge and Sally Buckner (no date).

Thomas Hawes and Hannah Wright, January 2, 1792.

James Houston and Molly Page, January 7, 1792.

Benjamin Hall and Elizabeth Hargrove, May 28, 1792.

——— Hudgins and Nancy Johnston, December 26, 1793.

Benjamin Hurt and Frances Richeson, January 10, 1795.

William Hudson and Frances Holloway, October 5, 1794.

Robert Hill and Phoebe Royster, December 14, 1797.

James Harris and Nancy Rains, September 20, 1798.

Epaphroditus Howle and Mary Jones, March 15, 1798.

Bloxton Howard and Rosy Samuel, February 22, 1799.

John Hopkins and Eliza Vawter, January 14, 1799.

F. C. L. Irish and Ancy Susannah Pierce, September 7, 1786.

Asa Ireland and Euland Toombs, January 2, 1790.

Littleton Jeter and Jane Alsop, September 7, 1786.

Horatio Jeter and Elizabeth Roland, September 7, 1786.

Thomas Johnston and Millicent Hargrove, March 6, 1791.

Fauntley Johnston and Sarah Farish, January 2, 1790.

Jonathan Jones and Milly Coleman, April 18, 1792.

Washington Jones and Fanny Kidd, November 6, 1793.

Lee Jones and Katy Bloxton, May 22, 1796.

Robert Jones and Elizabeth Wright, November 20, 1796.

John Jones and Nancy Dew, December 6, 1798.

Elijah Jeter and Rebecca Martin, October 12, 1797.

Richard Johnston and Elizabeth Tribble, November 16, 1799.

George Kelly and Caty Baley, January 12, 1792.

Edmund Kidd and Sally Jones, ———, 1792.

Garnett Keeton and Nancy McDonald, January 23, 1792.

Joel Kidd and Sally Saunders, November 15, 1797.

Lee Lewis and Caty Covington (no date).

Benjamin Long and Ann Beray, September 15, 1787.

James Laughlin and Sarah Coleman, December 18, 1788.

Andrew Monroe and Sarah Roberts, December 21, 1786.

James Maylain and Betty Dismukes, October 24, 1787.

William Marshall and Dorothy Griffin, (no date).
George Marshall and Sally Saunders (no date).
Benjamin Murrah and Molly Carter (no date).
Obediah Martin and Ann Turner (no date).
William Murrah (Maury) and Elizabeth Alsop (no date).
James Mason and Fanny Chewning, November 27, 1788.
William Molin and Margaret Tinsley, September 18, 1790.
Thomas McKee and Ellis Cornall (no date).
Larkin Miller and Frances Wright, July 9, 1790.
William Miller and Mary Durrett, January 2, 1791.
John Morgan and Eleanor McDonald (no date).
Henry Mayfield and Milly Davy (no date).
William Miller and Nannie Jeter, December 20, 1792.
James Merritt and Lucy Page, February 27, 1792.
Frederick Moore and Jane Russell, April 23, 1793.
John McGraw and Mary Burks, November 23, 1793.
Henry Motley and Ann Segar, December 13, 1794.
Edwin Motley and Elizabeth Kidd, December 13, 1794.
James Martin and Ann Houston, November 5, 1794.
William Martin and Caty Hargrove, September 5, 1794.
Simeon Morgan and Sarah Claytor, May 7, 1796.
William Mason and Sally Kelly, February 2, 1797.
Joel Mason and Jenny Kelly, December 14, 1798.
Hickman Mitchell and Letty Wright, December 22, 1797.
William Martin and Letty Turner, November 18, 1798.
Younger Martin, of "Clay Hill," and Betty Bowler (Boulware),
October 24, 1798.
Simeon Morgan and Polly Hutson, May 10, 1798.
William Mullin and Nancy Chenault, January 1, 1798.
Richard Mahon and Eliza Gardner, February 21, 1799.
Harrison Monday and Patsy Sneed, September 19, 1799.
Gray Nutgrass and Edna Pugh, September 8, 1790.
Alexander Noell and Sarah Ayres (no date).
Samuel Noell and Elizabeth Timberlake, November 23, 1793.
Gilbert Nokes and Caty Tignor, March 6, 1794.
James Noell and Judith Bowie, March 9, 1798.
John Norment and Sally Gunnells, November 24, 1798.
Nathaniel E. Norment and Amelia Bridges, October 27, 1798.
John Oliphant and Fanny Long (no date).
Thomas Oliver and Mary Ann Berry, October 24, 1793.
Thomas Oliver and Lucy Eastin, October 5, 1797.

Daniel Powers and Elizabeth Lambeth, May 28, 1786.
Reuben Pembroke and Betty Croucher, December 21, 1786.
John Page and Rebecca Crutchfield, December 16, 1786.
William Pitts and Sally Ingram, ——, 1788.
Coleman Pitts and Sally Graves (no date).
John Philippe and Elizabeth Emerson (no date).
Richard Pope and Jenny Collins, December 11, 1790.
Thomas Payne and Fanny Fortune, December 5, 1788.
Moses Pruett and Frances Elington (no date).
John Parish and Polly Hewlett, August 9, 1792.
Joseph Pitts and Sally Daniel (no date).
John Pattee and Sally Daniel, January 3, 1794.
Levi Pitts and Elizabeth Taylor, November 23, 1793.
John Page and Sally White, December 4, 1794.
Elijah Pruett and Elizabeth Williams, December 20, 1795.
Joseph E. Payne and Peggy Pruett, October 20, 1795.
Fred'k Pilcher and Margaret Alsop, September 9, 1796.
Moses Pruett and Amy Hall, May 23, 1797.
Uriah Pruett and Alice Credle, August 1, 1798.
William Page and Peggy Vaughan, May 15, 1797.
William Poltney and Betsy Vaughan, September 13, 1799.
Coleman Pitts and Lily Vaughan, February 3, 1798.
Nehemiah Rozel and Ann Goodloe (no date).
Robert Rennolds and Dolly Robinson, November 3, 1786.
Hugh Roy and Elizabeth Marshall, June 19, 1788.
Reuben Roeve and Sukey Wright (no date).
William Rollins and Sally Brame, November 27, 1788.
George Robinson and Elizabeth Dishman (no date).
Thomas Royston and Susannah Holloway (no date).
John Reynolds and Molly Pemberton (no date).
Jacob Rennolds and Martha Burruss, November 15, 1793.
Thomas Rennolds and Lucy Carter, December 25, 1794.
John Robinson and Elizabeth Houston, November 18, 1796.
David Robinson and Margaret Houston, November 18, 1796.
Turner Redd and Nancy Floyd, September 29, 1797.
Giles Rains and Dorothy Austin, January 10, 1799.
James Smith and Sally Waters, July 20, 1786.
Richard Sampson and Nancy Stevens, March 8, 1787.
Jesse Slaughter and Lucy Thornton Slaughter, November 25, 1787.

John Scott and Patty Woolfolk, December 27, 1787.
Thomas Shirley and Molly Yates, April 5, 1788.
James Sampson and Molly Stevens, September 8, 1790.
Oliver Sutton and Elizabeth Douglass, June 20, 1790.
Alex. Stuart and Lucy Aylett, January 2, 1790.
John Ship and Lucy Farish (no date).
George Southworth and Molly Gleason, December 20, 1792.
John Scandland and Ruth Taylor, October 29, 1792.
Robert Sale and Anne Broaddus, Novmber 27, 1794.
James Scanland and Tabitha Jones, July 18, 1794.
Isaac Seysil (Cecil) and Betty Page Dillard, September 28, 1794.
Alexander Sneed and Sukey Sneed, January 11, 1793.
Sam Schooler and Anne Williams, January 14, 1796.
Henry Stuart and Betty Richeson, February 26, 1796.
Samuel Sneed and Polly Daniel, September 30, 1797.
James Samuel and Betsy Samuel, February 25, 1799.
John Self and Aggy Bowler (Boulware), ——, 1798.
Thornton Seal and Molly Bell, October 9, 1795.
Francis Self and Sally Boulware, December 22, 1796.
Gabriel Slaughter and Sally Hord, ——, 1797.
Thomas Southworth and Betty Barlow, October 19, 1797.
—— Thurston and Caty Reynolds, April 18, 1797.
William Tinsley and Dolly Estis, April 30, 1789.
Edward Thacker and Priscilla Yarbrough, October 31, 1789.
John Turner and Fanny Davis, ——, 1790.
William Taylor and Barbara Allen, ——, 1792.
Bartholomew Taylor and Frances Loving, March 24, 1794.
William Tignor and Frances Covington, September 17, 1794.
John Traynham and Mary Daniel, June 14, 1796.
Lewis Tarrant and Elizabeth Redd, February 26, 1797.
Wilson Turner and Polly Hurt, May 3, 1797.
George Tiller (Tyler) and Lucy Mills, July 28, 1799.
Christopher Terrell and Mary Collins, December 26, 1798.
Daniel Tiller (Tyler) and Rebecca Camall (Campbell), December 28, 1798.
Godfrey Toler and Charity Barnes, September 27, 1799.
William Tucker and Margaret Scanland, January 12, 1798.
John Traynham and Fanny Richeson, December 11, 1799.
Lewis Tennant and Sally Clark, December 18, 1799.

Jacob Umbreckhouse and Patsy Dismukes, November 27, 1787.

Boulware Vawter and Sally Berry, November 2, 1786.

Richard Vawter and Sally Vaughan, July 12, 1787.

Lewis Vaughan and Mary Lee, October 23, 1787.

Abraham Venable and Amy Hundley, January 21, 1790.

William Vaughan and Patty Vaughan, December 5, 1793.

William Venablé and Rebecca Hurt, December 14, 1794.

James Wilson and Agnes Pickett, October 16, 1786.

William Wright and Fanny Riddle, January 7, 1789.

William Wayt and Mary Ann Hedges, February 5, 1789.

Roy Webster and Sarah Scanland, September 8, 1790.

Elijah White and Susannah Brame, December 1, 1789.

William White and Eliza Durrett, May 22, 1790.

Willis Wright and Leah Hewlett, January 2, 1790.

Henry Willy (Wiley) and Elizabeth Tinsley, January 2, 1790.

Achilles Webster and Sarah Webster, January 2, 1790.

Benjamin Waller and Joana Thompson, May 8, 1782.

George White and Anne Jeter, October 21, 1792.

Benjamin Whitlock and Polly Richeson, May 19, 1793.

John Willmore and Patty Taylor, July 19, 1794.

William Webster and Agnes Jones, January 10, 1795.

William Willson and Delphia Foster, February 11, 1795.

John Wright and Elizabeth Durrett, January 14, 1796.

Nathan Winston and Ann Yarbrough, January 14, 1796.

Richard Walden and Polly Isbell, September 21, 1798.

James White and Elizabeth Green, December 26, 1798.

Francis Wyatt and Fanny Austin, December 23, 1799.

James Young and Sally Jeter, December 15, 1792.

John Yeatman and Lucy Patty, December 15, 1792.

Many of the foregoing marriages, if not most of them, were celebrated by the following clergymen: John Sorrell, Theodrick Noell, Henry Goodloe, John Self, Thomas Mastin, Archer Moody, Abner Waugh, Archibald Dick and Samuel Shield.

CAROLINE COUNTY LAND GRANTS OF RECORD IN LAND OFFICE

COLONIAL GRANTS

John Cheadle and Thomas Hackett, 400 acres, September 2, 1728. Book 13, page 276.

John Sutton, 175 acres, September 2, 1728. Book 13, page 388.

Robert Holmes (Hoomes), 317 acres, September 28, 1728. Book 13, page 323.

Edward Yarbrough, 200 acres, September 27, 1729. Book 13, page 400.

Daniel Henry White, 500 acres, September 27, 1729. Book 13, page 400.

Isaac Allen, 50 acres, September 27, 1729. Book 13, page 400.

John Partle, 250 acres, September 27, 1730. Book 13, page 415.

Henry Raines, 250 acres, June 2, 1730. Book 13, page 445.

Henry Raines, 436 acres, June 2, 1730. Book 13, page 445.

Thomas Ham, Sr., 580 acres, September 28, 1730. Book 13, page 488.

Micajah Chiles, 379 acres, September 28, 1730. Book 13, page 489.

John Clark, 207 acres, September 28, 1730. Book 13, page 489.

Thomas Carr, 570 acres, September 28, 1730. Book 13, page 490.

John Harris, 162 acres, September 28, 1730. Book 13, page 490.

Richard and Francis Fowler, 137½ acres, September 28, 1730. Book 13, page 491.

Robert Beverly, 4,254 acres, February 14, 1730. Book 14, page 151.

Robert Chandler, 357 acres, June 26, 1731. Book 14, page 159.

John Ellis, 530 acres, June 26, 1731. Book 14, page 162.

William Marshall, 150 acres, August 25, 1731. Book 14, page 286.

Zacharias Martin, 306 acres, August 25, 1731. Book 14, page 287.

John Sandland, 400 acres, January 25, 1731. Book 14, page 373.

Richard Maulding, 387 acres, April 11 ,1732.   Book 14, page 400.

Thomas Carr, 2,530 acres, April 11, 1732.   Book 14, page 432.

Thomas Carr, 400 acres, July 1, 1732.   Book 14, page 457.

Thomas Catlett, 66 acres, September 28, 1732.   Book 14, page 512.

Robert Beverly, 929 acres, September 28, 1732.   Book 14, page 529.

Henry Raines, 436 acres, June 2, 1730.   Book 14, page 445.

William Bell, 162 acres, June 20, 1733.   Book 15, page 50.

John Sutton, 400 acres, June 20, 1733.   Book 15, page 66.

Lewis Burwell, 400 acres, June 20, 1733.   Book 15, page 76.

Charles Gooddal, 915 acres, June 20, 1733.   Book 15, page 126.

William Beverly, 4,254 acres, October 26, 1733.   Book 15, page 126.

Thomas Catlett, 1,376 acres, March 23, 1733.   Book 15, page 176.

Richard Long, 1,165 acres, August 20, 1734.   Book 15, page 286.

Benjamin Walker, 200 acres, August 9, 1735.   Book 16, page 144.

George Wilson and John Clark, 277 acres, January 10, 1735. Book 16, page 490.

George Woodroof, 400 acres, March 15, 1735.   Book 17, page 18.

Hugh Rea, 118 acres, October 3, 1737.   Book 17, page 421.

Robert Baber, 10 acres, July 20, 1738.   Book 18, page 34.

Samuel Coleman, 100 acres, July 20, 1738.   Book 18, page 36.

Thomas Collins, 90 acres, August 20, 1740.   Book 19, page 714.

Joseph Berry, 286 acres, December 1, 1740.   Book 19, page 814.

William Crutchfield, 596 acres, October 15, 1741.   Book 20, page 25.

William Pemberton and Easter Bell, 83 acres, July 30, 1742. Book 20, page 430.

William Trigg, 157 acres, March 30, 1743.   Book 20, page 480.

William Stayton, 167 acres, August 30, 1743.   Book 21, page 518.

Henry Bartlett, 68 acres, August 30, 1743.   Book 21, page 520.

William Woodford, 36 acres, August 30, 1744. Book 22, page 199.

William Beverly, 70 acres, March 5, 1745. Book 24, page 169.

Lawrence Taliaferro, 162 acres, January 12, 1747. Book 28, page 357.

Richard Davenport, 396 acres, September 15, 1752. Book 31, page 201.

William Burdett, 81½ acres, July 10, 1755. Book 31, page 503.

William Daniel, Jr., 1,000 acres, October 17, 1754. Book 32, page 405.

Edmund Pendleton, 96 acres, August 19, 1758. Book 33, page 475.

Henry Terrell, 379 acres, September 26, 1760. Book 33, page 936.

William Lindsey, 294 acres, August 10, 1759. Book 34, page 335.

John Sutton, 400 acres, February 14, 1761. Book 34, page 806.

Duncan Graham, 72 acres, August 7, 1761. Book 34, page 936.

James Murry (Maury), 95 acres, July 12, 1762. Book 34, page 1,033.

William Boutwell, 18 acres, July 12, 1762. Book 34, page 1,035.

Lawrence Taliaferro, 12 acres, August 30, 1763. Book 35, page 461.

William Quarles, 15 acres, June 27, 1764. Book 36, page 562.

John Phillips, 32 acres, October 31, 1765. Book 36, page 913.

Lawrence Taliaferro, 12 acres, July 10, 1767. Book 36, page 1,056.

John Micou, 138 acres, September 10, 1767. Book 37, page 194.

Lawrence Battaile, 20 acres, July 20, 1768. Book 37, page 250.

Ignatius Rains, 47 acres, October 24, 1768. Book 38, page 489.

John Chiles, 255 acres, April 6, 1769. Book 38, page 524.

David Chivis, 6½ acres, May 12, 1770. Book 39, page 55.

George Turner, 63 acres, August 27, 1770. Book 39, page 180.

Anthony Thornton, Jr., 65 acres, June 15, 1773. Book 41, page 450.

COMMONWEALTH GRANTS AND PATENTS

John Minor, 200 acres, December 11, 1780.   Book D, page 325.

John Pickett, 400 acres, December 11, 1780.   Book D, page 326.

Mace Pickett, 339 acres, December 11, 1780.   Book D, page 327.

Robert Gilchrist, ½ acre, December 11, 1780.   Book E, page 841.

John Hord, 53 acres, July 18, 1787.   Book 9, page 673.

James Miller, 78 acres, December 13, 1787.   Book 14, page 391.

Thomas Lomax, 58 acres, April 17, 1788.   Book 15, page 708.
Thomas Lomax, 13 acres, April 17, 1788.   Book 15, page 709.
Robert Beverly, 114 acres, April 17, 1788.   Book 15, page 728.
William Peatross, 18 acres, July 26, 1793.   Book 28, page 624.

NOTE.—Many of the historic plantations of Caroline are not included in the foregoing grants and patents because same were colonial grants, made before the formation of Caroline county. Only lands granted after the establishment of the county appear in this list.

CAROLINE COUNTY'S FIRST SURVEY BOOK

The nineteenth volume of the William and Mary College *Quarterly* contains a communication from Lewis Beckner. of Winchester, Kentucky, which is, in part, as follows:

"While at work in the office of the county clerk of Campbell county at Alexandria, in this State, I ran across an old record book which was brought from Caroline county, Virginia, about the beginning of the nineteenth century. It is a part of the records of the Surveyor's Office of Caroline county, but was also used for a time as a deed book of Campbell county, Kentucky. It is a large book, about a half sheet in size, and is covered with vellum.   On the inside of the covers is written, "James B. Taliaferro's book, November 24, 1814.' and 'James T. Taliaferro,' while on the back is "John N. Taliaferro, Newport, Ky., July 7, 1821," also 'James Taylor, C. C. C. C.'   Inside in several places there are 'James Taylor, Jr.' and 'John N. Taliaferro,' who, by his signature, shows that he is deputy for James Taylor, Clerk of Campbell county court.

The Campbell county deeds are written in the back of the book, and do not interfere with the Caroline county surveys, which take up the front. The first Caroline county survey entered in it is dated the 22d of May, 1729, and the last the 26th of January, 1762; and the first Campbell county entry is dated the 11th of July, 1821, and the last the 16th of May, 1821. In the Campbell county end of the book there are twenty deeds, two surveys and one sale bill, while the Caroline part of the book contains forty-seven surveys, all made by R. O. Brooke, S. C. C. C.

Between the Caroline county surveys and the Campbell county deeds there is a large section of the book unused, except a few pages, which have been used by James B. Taliaferro to state and work a number of problems in physics, surveying and arithmetic.

The first survey is for 137 acres, on the 22d of May, 1729, in the parish of St. Margaret's and is for Richard and Francis Fowler. (2) For William Marshall, 150 acres, of the same date, in the same parish. (3) For Henry Rains, 250 acres on May 28, in Drysdale parish. (4) For Henry Dillion and Thomas Coleman, 600 acres on the Mattapony, on the 10th of June, 1729. (5) For the prison bounds, 9 acres and 8 poles on the 3d of June, 1729. (6) For Richard Long, 340 acres and 70 poles, near Solomon's Garden, in St. Margaret's parish, on the 13th of June, 1729. (7) For Thomas Carr, 2,530 acres in St. Margaret's Parish on the 28th of October, 1729. (8) For Major Thomas Carr, 575 acres in St. Margaret's parish near Thomas Dickerson, October 5, 1729. (9) For Captain Richard Maulding, 387 acres in St. Margaret's parish, on the 9th of September, 1729. (10) For Micajah Chiles, 379 acres in St. Margaret's parish, on the 11th day of December, 1729. (11) For Robert Beverley, Esq., 4,775 acres, on the same date as above. (12) For Robert Chandler, 357 acres in St. Margaret's parish, on the 2d of February, 1730. (13) For John Ellis, 530 acres in St. Margaret's parish on the 26th of February, 1730. (14) For John Ellis, 533 acres in St. Margaret's parish, same date as above. (15) For Zach. Martin, 306 acres in St. Margaret's parish, near Paul Pigg, Robert Powell, William Marshall and Mr. Baylor, same date. (16) For Robert Faldo vs. Ralph Wormeley, William Taliaferro claims 600 acres of the

Henry Berry patent, 1664, and survey made April 29, 1730.
(17) For Major Thomas Catlett, 66 acres in St. Margaret's parish,
near Messrs. Robert Taliaferro, Grymes, Thomas Corbin and
White, March 22, 1730. (18) For Major William Woodford, 630
acres in the Edward Wrackley patent, 1662, on Abe Moor's Creek,
November 19, 1730. (19) For Robert Beverly, Esq., 929 acres
in St. Margaret's parish, on February 24, 1730. (20) For Mr.
Charles Goodloe, both sides of Long Beach in St. Margaret's
parish, on May 14, 1731. (21) For William Perry, 162 acres
beginning at Francis Anthony Thornton's corner, February 18,
1731. (22) For Major Thomas Catlett, 1376 acres in St. Mary's
parish bounding on Taliaferro and Royston's outside line and
the Golden Hole Swamp, on March 23, 1730. (23) For Richard
Long, 1,165 acres in St. Mary's parish near Nicholas Battaile's,
near Solomon's Garden and adjoining Francis and John Taliaferro,
April 26, 1733. (24) For Charles Morgan vs. William Daniel,
122 acres near Port Tobago, May 6, 1734. (25) For George
Marsh, 68 acres in St. Mary's parish near John Ellis and ———
Martin, May 30, 1737. (26) For Hugh Redd, 118 acres in St.
Mary's parish bounding on lands of Durrett and Richard Maulding,
on June 1, 1737. (27) For Crutchfield vs. Baber, 2,920 acres of
the Bray survey, not dated. (28) For same, 596 acres on Herring
Creek, Bray survey, on June 27, 1738. (29) For Henry Bowcock
vs. Henry Ball, 557 acres in Peumansend Swamp, on March
11, 1730. (30) For William Trigg, 157 acres in St. Margaret's
parish, near William Eubanks, on April 23, 1731. For same,
162 acres, near John Hurt and Reedy Swamp, April 23, 1741.
(31) For George Marsh, 68 acres near John Ellis and ———
Martin, May 31, 1737. (32) For Hugh Redd, 110 acres in St.
Margaret's parish, near Richard Maulding's, June 1, 1737. (33)
For Wormeley vs. Beverley, the edge of a percorson in Sir Thomas
Lunsford's patent near Peumansend Swamp. The names appearing are Hon. John Grymes, Esq., executor of his father, Mr.
William Taliaferro; Col. Lunsford Lomax. Survey made on
September 18, 1738. (34) For Capt. Joseph Berry, 286 acres
in Drysdale parish, near Col. William Beverley, Thacker, Baylor
and Taylor, on January 4, 1739. (35) For prison bounds, 10
acres on March 14, 1752. (36) For William Coune, 1,165 acres
on February 9, 1754. (37) For 96 acres lapsed from William
Morris by Edmund Pendleton, February 28, 1757. (38) For Adam
Lindsey, 290 acres on July 11, 1755. (39) For William Boutwell,

18 acres on December 31, 1759. (40) For Absalom Davis, 72 acres on May 7, 1759. (41) For John Micou, 138 acres in the sunken ground, or percorson, on November 29, 1760. (42) For the executor of Henry Terrell, deceased, 255 acres lapsed of John Chiles, this survey made by Edward Vauter, assistant, not dated. (43) For Lawrence Taliaferro, 12 acres and 42 poles of sunken land on March 17, 1761. (44) For Robert Goodloe, of Spotsylvania, 190 acres of January 22, 1762. (45) For Samuel Hargrave, 15 acres on Fleming Island January 26, 1762.

These notes were not taken with a view to form the basis of this article, else they would have been made more complete, and would have given every name mentioned in each survey. The book captured my attention because I was on the chase of some elusive Taliaferro ancestor, and it looked like it would repay an investigation. Seeing it was so full of Taliaferro names, I made the above abstract. It will be noticed that the entries in which the Taliaferro name appears have been more fully noted by me. My mother, Betty Taliaferro, was a daughter of Major John Taliaferro, of Winchester, Ky. He was the son of Hay Taliaferro who came to Clark county, Ky., from Caroline county, Va., about 1812. Hay Taliaferro was the son of William Taliaferro, of Caroline, and Margaret Aylett. It was my search for the ancestors of the last-named persons that led me to make discovery of this curious relic. Since then it has occurred to me several times that it ought to be brought to the notice of someone in Virginia; and I can think of no one to whom the notice would be of more interest than the readers of the *William and Mary Quarterly*. Surmising upon that part of the history of the old book, which is shown on its pages, I would say that one of the Taliaferros was assistant to Surveyor Brooke, or married into his family, and so became possessed of the book, and by some mistake carried it to Kentucky at the time of the Taliaferro migration. James Taylor, of Caroline county, Va., father of the James Taylor, Clerk of the Campbell county, Ky., court, married for his wife a Taliaferro, daughter of Colonel John Taliaferro, of Dissington, and his wife, who was a Thornton. This will doubtless account for the fact that John N. Taliaferro was Deputy Clerk, and why this book was used for a Deed Book. This (Clark) county was the seat of a large settlement of Caroline county people—Battailes, Taylors, Taliaferros, Thorntons, Willises, Lanes and others, and among them were Hubbard and Reuben Taylor, brothers of

James, the Campbell county clerk; and Hay Taliaferro, their ancestor. They were my ancestors and one can imagine the thrill of interest with which I went through the old book . . ''

NOTE.—Through the generosity of Fairfax Harrison, President of the Southern Railway System, and Judge Embrey, of Fredericksburg, a photostat copy of the foregoing book—page by page—was made and presented to Caroline county and is now on file in the clerk's office.

NAMES OF CAROLINE CITIZENS WHOSE OBITUARY NOTICES APPEARED IN THE RICHMOND "ENQUIRER" FROM THE YEAR 1800 TO 1828

Mrs. Frances C. Battaile..........August 12, 1828.
William Bernard.................February 9, 1822.
Joseph Brame...................November 17, 1820.
Richard Bridges..................April 18, 1826.
Mrs. Martha Brown..............December 20, 1823.
Capt. Thomas Burruss............March 19, 1824.
Thomas Burke...................February 6, 1807.
Dwight Backers Chandler.........September 18, 1821.
Timothy Chandler...............March 30, 1831.
Mrs. Eliza Dabney...............May 4, 1827.
William Dickinson...............October 7, 1823.
Thomas Dickinson...............July 24, 1826.
A. G. Dickinson.................December 1, 1826.
Reuben Garnett.................August 26, 1825.
William Guy....................March 17, 1807.
Mrs. Mary Guy ....June 29, 1819.
Mrs. Ann Guy...................September 27, 1815.
Hannah M. Hill.................October 8, 1828.
Richard Hoomes.................December 27, 1823.
Mrs. Lucy Mary Hoomes.........August 13, 1814.
Mrs. Judith Hoomes.............August 16, 1822.
Capt. John Hoomes..............December 27, 1805.
Major John Hoomes..............March 23, 1824.
Col. Armistead Hoomes..........February 6, 1827.
Mrs. Annie C. Hoomes...........March 27, 1810.
Col. Reuben Lowkersley.........September 30, 1823.
Mrs. Nancy D. Minor............October 9, 1821.

Edmund Pendleton...............July 10, 1827.

Mrs. Sarah Rawlins..............January 20, 1824.

John Scott.....................February 28, 1822.

Mrs. Patsy Scott................January 26, 1813.

Thomas Streshley...............April 26, 1825.

Mrs. Anna Swinton..............September 1, 1820.

Geo. Lawrence Taliaferro.........February 23, 1826.

Robert H. Taliaferro............July 1, 1807.

Col. John Taylor................March 18, 1828.

Col. John Taylor, of Caroline......August 27, 1824.

Capt. William Taylor............October 13, 1809.

Elizabeth Thomas...............January 6, 1824.

Mrs. Elizabeth M. Todd..........December 12, 1826.

Mrs. Mary Toler................November 26, 1813.

Col. James Upshaw..............July 22, 1806.

Mrs. Ann Watson................May 28, 1822.

Mrs. Mary Ann White............January 24, 1822.

Mrs. Sarah C. Woodford..........April 27, 1827.

John G. Woolfolk...............April 23, 1819.

Richard Woolfolk...............May 30, 1820.

Joseph M. Wyatt................August 12, 1823.

NAMES OF CAROLINE CITIZENS WHOSE OBITUARY NOTICES APPEARED IN THE RICHMOND "WHIG" FROM 1825 TO 1838

Robert W. Allen.................March 26, 1836.

John M. Blondell ....July 27, 1838.

James Blunt....................January 26, 1832.

George Buckner.................November 28, 1828.

Patrick Clopton................July 23, 1829.

T. T Dickinson.................February 11, 1825.

Dr. B. F. Doswell...............November 1, 1828.

Mrs. Judith Page Harrison.......July 25, 1834.

Elizabeth D. Hill................November 17, 1835.

Josiah Hotchkiss...............September 7, 1832.

Mrs. Caroline M. Kean..........September 22, 1831.

Samuel Luck...................January 23, 1838.

William B. McGruder...........September 24, 1833.

Mrs. Mary O. Meaux............September 30, 1825.

Robert C. Pendleton.............April 15, 1836.

John Roy......................May 16, 1834.
Eliza Taliaferro.................January 9, 1838.
Peter Thornton..................October 11, 1833.
Thomas Griffin Thornton.........November 2, 1830.
Thomas Trevilian...............December 2, 1825.
William Turner.................October 17, 1829.
Mrs. Mary Ann Motley...........April 10, 1835.

GLEANINGS FROM OLD NEWSPAPERS

Digest of the *Virginia Herald and Fredericksburg Advertiser*, published in Fredericksburg, Va., in the latter years of the eighteenth century, files of which may be seen in the Library of Congress.

June 24, 1790—In this issue Robert Beverly advertises, "8000 acres of the lower part of my Chace lands in the county of Caroline......also about fifty women and children in families."

September 30, 1790—In this issue appears an advertisement that "The Virginia Jockey Club Races will commence at Bowling Green, Caroline county, on the second Tuesday in October next and will continue three days." This advertisement is signed "John Hoomes, S. C."

September 30, 1790—Gideon Bosher, tavern keeper at the Bowling Green, Caroline county, announces in this issue that special building arrangements have been made in order to accommodate the attendants on the Virginia Jockey Club Races.

December 16, 1790—In this issue Thomas Lomax, of "Port Tobago," in Caroline, offers for sale twenty negroes, and for rent the greater part of "Port Tobago" plantation.

November 25, 1790—Anthony Thornton, Trustee, advertises "sale of slaves belonging to the late Joseph Robinson, to be held at Tod's Ordinary in the upper part of Caroline, eleven miles from Fredericksburg, on December 14, 1790." Tod's Ordinary or tavern afterward became Villboro.

December 2, 1790—Edmund Pendleton, Jun., John Hoomes and James Robb, executors, advertises for sale at the plantation of Robert Gilchrist, deceased, on the Mattaponi river, four miles above the Bowling Green, "All the crop of corn, fodder, stocks of all kinds, utensils, eighty likely slaves and the above plantation of fifteen hundred acres. Also corn, fodder stocks of all kinds and furniture at the dwelling of the deceased at Port Royal."

January 6, 1791—Joseph Timberlake, Jun., of Port Royal, gives notice that John Taylor, of Caroline has resigned into his hands the business of Mr. James Dunlop, and that he has legal authority to receive moneys, settle claims, etc. (NOTE.—The author believe that this Joseph Timberlake was the progenitor of Joseph Timberlake, City Attorney, of Gastonia, N. C., Mrs. John D. Cave, of Louisa, and Mrs. Callahan, of Seattle, Washington).

January 6, 1791—This issue contains notice of mare strayed from, "The plantation of Captain William Marshall in the upper end of Caroline."

March 10, 1791—William C. Woodford offers reward of twenty dollars for slave who ran away from him "last Christmas was twelve months."

April 7, 1791—In this issue is an item reading as follows: "The members of the Loyal Company are requested to meet at the Bowling Green in Caroline county on the 27th of April next to consider some important business." The item is signed "Thomas Walker, Agt."

July 7, 1791—Anthony Thornton, of "Ormesby," advertises in this issue that Captain Charles Thornton has made him a deed of trust of his whole estate, and asks that all of the said Captain Thornton's creditors furnish him with a written statement of their claims.

July 28, 1791—Lawrence Battaile, of "Prospect Hill," advertises for sale four hundred acres.

August 4, 1791—The ship *Williamson*, for London, is advertised as "Now lading at Port Royal and is intended to sail this month. For freight and passage apply to Messrs. Hipkins and Bernard, Port Royal, or to the master on board."

August 18, 1791—William A. Buckner, of Port Royal advertises for sale, for cash or wheat, "West India and Continental rum by the hogshead, molasses, sugar, limes and oranges."

September 8, 1791—Joseph Valentine, of the "lower end of Caroline county," offers ten dollars reward for the return of a runaway salve named Jerry.

October 6, 1791—John Hipkins, of Port Royal, advertises that the brigatine *Ann and Mary* has just brought in "A very large and general assortment of merchandise from London."

January 7, 1970—George Turner, of "Moss Neck," in Caroline, advertises for sale "Fifty likely Virginia-born negroes."

March 25, 1790—John Taliaferro advertises "Hayes"—a plantation of twenty-one hundred acres on the Rappahannock, in Caroline, encumbered by mortgages to the extent of fifty-four hundred pounds.

FROM OLD NEWSPAPERS AND MAGAZINES

Digest of *The Virginia Herald* (Fredericksburg, Va.), now in the Library of Congress:

January 25, 1799—Robert C. Bruce, of Caroline, advertises for sale, "Fifteen likely young negroes."

January 25, 1799—Anthony Thornton, Administrator of Reuben Thornton, offers for sale to the highest bidder on March 5, 1799, at Todd's Tavern in Caroline, three negroes.

February 1, 1799—Edmund Pendleton, Jun., attorney-in-fact for J. Dunlop, of Port Royal, offers for sale at Bowling Green on February 15, 1799, twenty-five negroes.

February 5, 1799—Reuben Turner, deputy for George Terrill, late Sheriff of Caroline, advertises, "Eighteen likely negroes of the estate of the late Joseph Timberlake, to be sold by order of the County Court."

February 5, 1799—The tavern known as The Half-Way House, located between Fredericksburg and Port Royal, and operated by Mrs. Boulware, is advertised for rent in this issue by George Turner.

February 8, 1799—William C. Woodford, of "White Hall," Caroline county, advertises for service his famous horse, Democrat, in this issue.

March 8, 1799—Thomas Minor in this issue advertises for service his famous horse "Silverheels." "Fearnaught," celebrated horse of John Baylor, is mentioned in this advertisement.

March 8, 1799—Anthony Thornton, of "Ormesby," advertises his horse "Flimnap" in this issue.

March 12, 1799—John Tayloe, of "Mt. Airy," advertises "Stirling," a famous horse, imported from England by John Hoomes, of Bowling Green.

March 15, 1799—"Cormorant," celebrated horse of John Baylor's Newmarket stud, is advertised for service in this issue.

March 19, 1799—Catesby Young, of "near Mount Church" in Caroline, advertises for "my mulatto man named James, who has run away."

April 2, 1799—John Tayloe, of "Mt. Airy" advertises for sale his celebrated running horse, "Gabriel."

April 26, 1799—Sarah Beazely, administratrix of John Beazely, deceased, of Caroline, advertises for sale at auction "one negro man named Davy."

July 2, 1799—In this issue is record of a case in the Court of Quarterly Sessions in Caroline involving Thomas Miller, Plaintiff and James Frazer.

September 24, 1799—In this issue is an advertisement of John Baylor, of Newmarket plantation in Caroline, stating that he "Will give liberal encouragement to a good classical Tutor, for two Boys only."

October 22, 1799—John Hipkins, of Port Royal, advertises, "An elegant coachee, with placed mouldings, and harness for two horses."

October 25, 1799—William Dunlop & Company, of Port Royal, advertises in this issue a shipment of merchandise just received from Liverpool.

EXTRACTS FROM THE GAZETTE (Williamsburg)

Issue of February 10, 1737–38—"Captain Robert Fleming, of Caroline county, one of the representatives in Assembly, died last week."

September 8, 1738—"Last Monday was se'ennight died, of the gout, at his home in Caroline county, Mr. Benjamin Walker, who had practiced in law several years in the County Courts, in which he arrived to a degree of eminence and at the last General Court was admitted to plead there."

——— *1766*—Lawrence Taliaferro advertised for sale in the *Williamsburg Gazette* of 1766, "A plantation on the Rappahannock near Port Royal, upon which is a house with four rooms on the first floor and two above, a twelve foot porch in front; and at the rear, facing the river, a portico fifty-two feet long and eight wide."

KILWINNING-CROSSE LODGE, No. 2-237, OF BOWLING GREEN, CAROLINE COUNTY

(Originally Port Royal Kilwinning-Crosse Lodge, No. 2)

In the Proceedings of the Grand Lodge of Virginia for 1910, pages 28 and 29, Joseph W. Eggleston, Grand Master of Masons in Virginia for that year, says:

"While in Philadelphia in June I found the Secretary's old record books, two in number, stolen during the Civil War from Kilwinning Crosse Lodge, No. 2, Port Royal, Virginia. They were being offered for sale at the price of two hundred and fifty dollars. I asked that they be held until I could consult our Past Grand Masters, which was agreed to. The negotiations were held in the Museum of the Temple, and at this point that splendid man and Mason, Bro. Julius F. Sachse, Grand Librarian, took me aside and offered to pay for them for us and wait any necessary time. It was a generous offer, because I knew that but for his consideration for us he would have bought them for their Museum, even at a far greater price. His act deserves your recognition and gratitude.

"These books go back from 1859 to 1754, and are, so far as I know, the oldest Secretary's Records in America, except those owned by Fredericksburg Lodge, No. 4. The oldest one was evidently made here in the Colony, and is covered with rawhide and sewed with rawhide thongs. Right Worshipful Brother Andrews has prepared for you a review of their contents at the request of the Most Worshipful Brother Quinn, Chairman of your History Committee. I have read them carefully myself, but will not spoil his report by saying more."

Turning to W. L. Andrews' review of the ancient records of Port Royal Kilwinning Crosse Lodge, No. 2, which review is bound with the Grand Lodge Proceedings for 1910, we find the following record, quoted from the ancient minutes: •

"*April 12th, 1754*—At a Lodge begun and held at Port Royal of Free and Accepted Masons there were present the following members—viz:

"Patrick Coutts, Robert Gilchrist, John Cross, John Gray, James Miller, William Fox, Gideon Johnston, Alex Rose, Andrew Crawford, John Crawford, John Miller, Collin Riddick, and Thomas Landrum and John Douglass visiting brethren.

Fac simile of Original Charter of Kilwinning-Crosse Lodge of Masons. Reduced to One-Fourth Size of Original.

"The Lodge then proceeded to an election of Master, Wardens and other Officers, which was as follows:

Patrick Coutts............................*Master*
Robert Gilchrist..................*Senior Warden*
John Cross:......................*Junior Warden*
John Gray............................*Treasurer*
James Miller..........................*Secretary*
William Fox and Gideon Johnston........*Stewards*

and each member having taken his proper place in the Lodge, the Master presented the Lodge with a set of Laws compiled for the use & better regulations of this Lodge, which, by his order being read by the Secretary, were agreed to, and ordered to be copyd into the Secretary's book, which was done and signed by the Lodge.

"Then the Master set the Brethren to work and the business of the Lodge being ended, which was carried on with the greatest harmony, unanimity, & alacrity, as is usual among Masons, the Master closed the Lodge & adjourned it to Lodge in course.

" (Signed)   PATR. COUTTS."

From the foregoing minutes, the first of record in this Lodge, it will be observed that neither name nor number were attached to the Masonic body at Port Royal, and it is quite likely that the Lodge was nameless and numberless at the time these first minutes were recorded. It is interesting to note the manner in which the Kilwinning Port Royal Crosse Lodge received its name. The first part of the name—"Kilwinning"—was derived from the ancient seat of the Grand Lodge of Scotland to which the Masons of Caroline applied for a charter. It is quite likely that the applicants, Robert Gilchrist, John Gray, James Miller, John Cross, feeling more kindly toward Scotland than they did toward England, preferred a recognition of Scottish authority, and a name indicative of their sympathies. It should be borne in mind that the Grand Lodges of England, Scotland and Ireland exercised the right of chartering other Lodges in the several British Provinces. Thus Fredericksburg Lodge, Fredericksburg, Va., was charted by the Grand Lodge of Scotland, July 21, 1758; Williamsburg Lodge, No. 6, by the Grand Lodge of England on November 6, 1773. The middle part of the name—"Port Royal"— indicated the location of the Lodge, and the last part of the

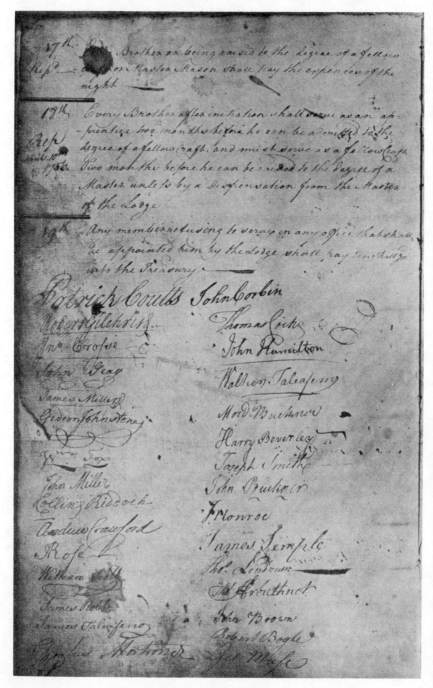

Fac simile of Ancient By-Laws of Kilwinning-Crosse Lodge of Masons.

name—"Crosse"—was taken in honour of David Cross, a staunch friend of the Lodge, who presented it with a set of Lodge Jewels and Aprons.   David Cross is supposedly the father of John Cross, one of the petitioners for the Scottish charter, and the first Junior Warden of the Lodge.

In the minutes of June 8, 1754, it is recorded that by vote of Port Royal Cross Lodge (not Crosse) it was "Ordered that the Secretary write a letter of thanks to our worthy Brother David Cross for his generous present to the Lodge of proper Jewels and Aprons for the Master and Wardens, and that the Junior Warden do assist him therein.   The Lodge also returned thanks to our worthy Brother Wm. Gray for his care in bringing them over the sea."

The ancient charter of the Lodge is no less interesting than the name, and was secured by a petition based on authorization given by Port Royal Cross Lodge under date of May 10, 1755, at which time, "On motion made for a Charter from Kilwinning being put to the vote, was agreed that the Right Worshipful will be pleased to write to some Brethren for that purpose, the charge not to exceed Ten Pounds, and to be called The Kilwinning Port Royal Cross Lodge."

On presentation of the petition of Port Royal Cross Lodge the Grand Lodge of Scotland on the first day of December, 1755, issued a Charter, which is now in possession of the Lodge, and which reads as follows:

"*To All and Sundry*—To whose knowledge these prefents shall come—*Greeting: Whereas*, upon Application to the Grand Lodge of Scotland at their Anniversary Meeting held in St. Mary's Chappel in Edinburgh the First day of December in the year of our Lord One Thousand Seven Hundred and Fifty-Five.   By the Worshipful Robert Gilchrist, John Gray, James Miller and John Crosse, for themselves and in name of sundry other Brethren Free and Accepted Masons residing in Virginia Praying the Grand Lodge would be pleased to grant Warrant for issuing a Patent under their Seal Constituting and Erecting the Petitioners into a Regular Lodge of Free and Accepted Masons under the Title and Designation of Kilwinning Port Royal Crosse Lodge. The Grand Lodge granted Warrant for expeding the underwritten Patent of Constitution and Erection in their favours.   *Know Ye Therefore*, That The Most Worshipful The Grand Master of Scotland and the Grand Lodge aforesaid Have Constituted

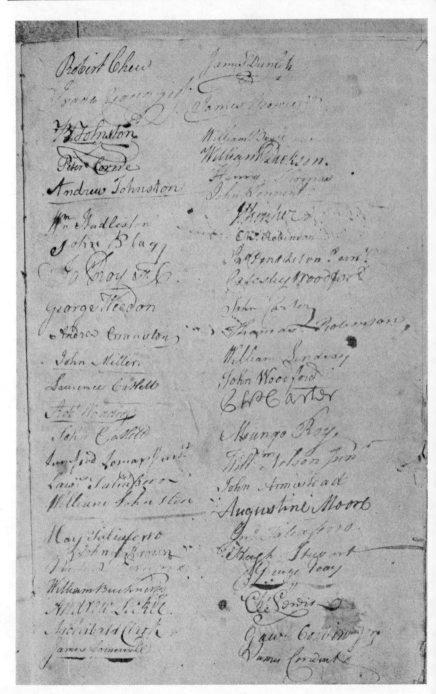

Fac simile of Ancient Records of Kilwinning-Crosse Lodge of Masons.

Erected and Appointed hereby Constitute Erect and Appoint,
The Worshipful Brethren aforesaid and their successors to be
in all time coming, a just, true and regular Lodge of Free and
Accepted Masons under the Title and Designation of Killwinning
Port Royal Crosse Lodge and Appoint and Ordain all regular
Lodges to Hold Acknowledge and Respect them as such. Hereby
Granting and Commiting to them and their successors full power
and authority to assemble and conveen as a Regular Lodge, and
to enter and receive Apprentices, pass Fellow Crafts, raise Master
Masons; and confer upon their deserving Brethren all other
Honours Dignity and Pre-eminencys known and practised in
any Regular Lodge; And to Elect and Chuse Masters Wardens
and other Officers annually or otherways as they shall think proper.
And to exact from their Intrant Members such Compositions as
they shall judge necessary for the Relief of their Brethren in
distress. Recommending to the Brethren aforesaid to Reverence
and obey their Superiors in all things Lawfull and Honest as
becomes the Honour and Harmony of Masonry. And to record
in their Books this present Charter with their own private Regulations and By-laws and their whole acts and proceedings from
time to time as they occur. And not to desert their said Lodge
hereby constituted nor form themselves into separate meetings
without the Consent and Approbation of their Master and
Wardens for the time being; *All Which* by acceptation hereof
they are holden and engaged to observe *and Further*, the Brethren
aforesaid by accepting hereof Acknowledge the Grand Master
and Grand Lodge of Scotland as their Superiors and shall pay
due Regard to all such Instructions and Recommendations as
they shall receive from thence, And pay all due Honour and
Obedience to such Provincial Grand Master as shall be vested
with a commission from them and they are hereby invited to
correspond with the Grand Lodge, and to attend the Meetings
thereof by their proxys being Master Masons or Fellow Crafts
of some Established Lodge holding of the Grand Lodge of
Scotland. And for the more effectual preservation of these
presents the same are hereby appointed to be recorded in the
Books of the Grand Lodge. Given at the Grand Lodge at
Edinburgh the First day of December in the year One Thousand
Seven Hundred and Fifty-Five By the Right Honourable and
Most Worshipful Sholto Charles Lord Aberdour, Grand Master,
George Frazer, Esqr., Deputy Grand Master, Richard Tod

Fac simile of Ancient Records of Kilwinning-Crosse Lodge of Masons.

Esqr Substitute Grand Master, Doctor Henry Cunningham and
William Budge Esqr Grand Wardens and the Seal of the Grand
Lodge Appended hereunto Witnessing to these presents: Alexander
McDougal Grand Secretary James Ewart Grand Treasurer
James Allison Grand Clerk.

Apud Edinburgum unum Decembris 1775

Recorded in the Books of the Grand Lodge and the Seal
appended hereunto by

> Alex. McDougall G. Secretary
> James Alison Gr. Clerk.
> James Ewart Gr. Treas.
> Henry Cunninghame S. G. W.
> Will Budge J. G. W.
> Aberdour G. M.
> Geo. Frazer D. G. M.
> Rich'd Tod Sub. G. M.

The foregoing charter (see fac simile herein), still in the possession
of Kilwinning-Crosse Lodge, is conceded to be the oldest charter now
in possession of any Masonic Lodge in the United State.   At the
Communication of the Grand Lodge of Virginia in 1785, the
question of rank among the Lodges was brought up, and Kilwinning Crosse was conceded to, "Rank as first Lodge in the
State of Virginia, and this seniority was awarded them both on
account of the seniority of their charter and full and explicit terms
in which it was worded."   See Minutes of Kilwinning Crosse
Lodge of November 24, 1785, and also page 180 of 1910 Proceedings
of Grand Lodge of Virginia.

Representatives from Kilwinning Crosse Lodge were present
when the Grand Lodge of Virginia was formed in Williamsburg
in 1777, and regularly thereafter until 1786, and it is significant
that at the meeting of 1786 Kilwinning Crosse was assigned to
second place in the list of Virginia Lodges.

From the Introduction of John Dove's Reprint of "Proceedings
of the Grand Lodge of Virginia from 1777 to 1823" we learn that
Masonry was practiced in Virginia under chartered privileges
derived directly from the mother Grand Lodge of Scotland as
early as 1733.   The Grand Lodge of Scotland is said to have
chartered the Royal Exchange Lodge, No. 172, in the borough
of Norfolk in 1733, which Lodge is accredited with being the

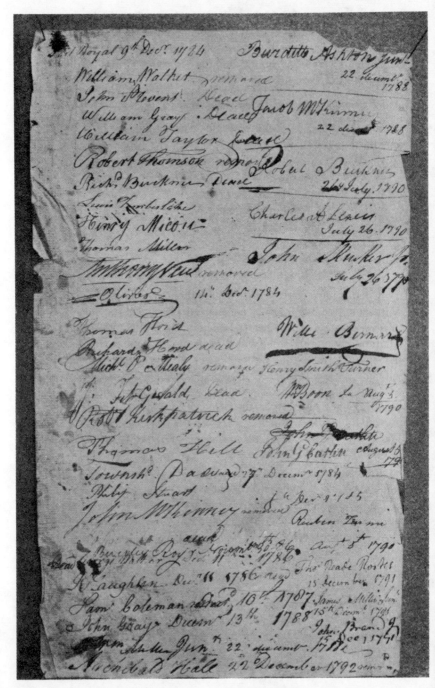

Fac simile of Ancient Records of Kilwinning-Crosse Lodge of Masons.

first Lodge chartered for America by that or any other Grand Lodge. This Lodge evidently became extinct, for forty-four years after its institution, when the Grand Lodge of Virginia was formed, the borough of Norfolk was represented by Lodge No. 141, which, in 1786, was given Kilwinning Crosse's place as No. 1 in the register. The Lodge at Yorktown, which is said to have been chartered by the Grand Lodge of Scotland in 1755, was not reported at the Convention or Grand Lodge of Virginia Masons in 1777, but received a charter from the Grand Lodge as Lodge No. 9, in 1780.

On the twenty-third day of June, 1777, Blandford Lodge of Petersburg, Kilwinning Port Royal Crosse Lodge of Caroline, Fredericksburg Lodge, Cabin Point Royal Arch Lodge of Surry County and the Lodge of Williamsburg, met in convention at Williamsburg for the purpose of forming a Grand Lodge just as four Lodges of England had organized the Grand Lodge in 1717, and four Scottish Lodges had organized the Grand Lodge of Scotland in 1736. At this Convention James Mercer, Master of Fredericksburg Lodge, presided, and James Kemp, a Master Mason of Kilwinning Port Royal Crosse Lodge of Caroline, was Secretary. Owing to the small number of Lodges represented on this occasion no Grand Master was elected, but another Convention was called and met at Williamsburg October 13, 1778, and elected Warner Lewis, of Botetourt Lodge as Grand Master, but, upon his declining to serve, John Blair, of Williamsburg Lodge, was elected the first Grand Master of Masons in Virginia. He was installed in office on October 30, 1778. In addition to being first Grand Master of Masons in Virginia, John Blair was also one of the first Associate Justices of the Supreme Court of the United States and Governor of Virginia.

Eight Lodges were given rank in the Grand Lodge of Virginia at its session in Richmond in 1786, and shown to have had legal Masonic existence prior to the election of a Grand Master on October 13, 1778. These were Norfolk, No. 1; Kilwinning Port Royal Crosse, No. 2; Blandford, No. 3; Fredericksburg, No. 4; St. Tammany, No. 5; Williamsburg, No. 6; Botetourt, No. 7; and Cabin Point Royal Arch, No. 8. The original charter of six of these ancient Lodges are preserved in their own archives or in the archives of the Grand Lodge at Richmond. These six charters are as follows: Kilwinning Port Royal Crosse, No. 2;

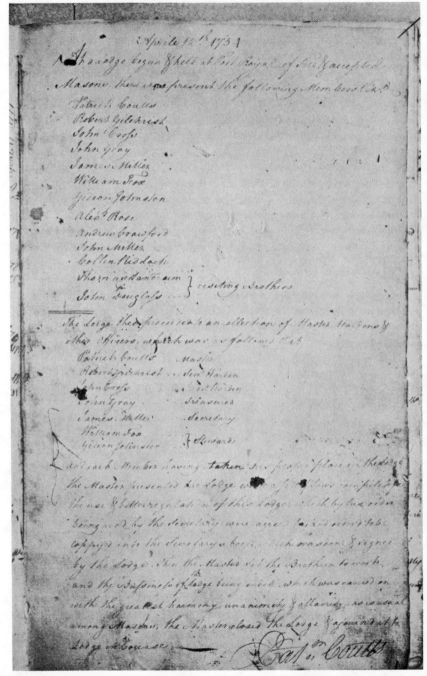

Fac simile of Ancient Records of Kilwinning-Crosse Lodge of Masons.

December 1, 1755; Blandford, No. 3, September 9, 1757; Fredericksburg, No. 4, July 21, 1758; Williamsburg, No. 6, November 6, 1773; Botetourt, No. 7, November 6, 1773; and Cabin Point Royal Arch, No. 8, April 13, 1775. The last-named Lodge was suspended in 1796, and was never revived, but its old charter is in the archives of the Grand Lodge, as are the charters of several others, which are active. It is certain that no other Grand Jurisdiction in America, and probably no other in the world, can produce so many old original charters as the Grand Lodge of Virginia, which traces its Masonic title by this unquestioned evidence back to the middle of the eighteenth century.

It is quite interesting to note that these early Virginia Lodges, by virtue of their English or Scottish charters, organized and chartered other Lodges in the surrounding territory. Lodge No. 4 at Fredericksburg, according to its old records, held a meeting on October 10, 1770, at which time the following was adopted:

"A motion was made by Brother Page and seconded by Brother Yates, that a deputation should be given Brother Fontaine and some other members of this Lodge, who live in Gloucester, to constitute a Lodge there, being attended with the greatest inconvenience for some of these members to attend the Lodge as often as they could wish.

"*Resolved*, That Brothers James Maury Fontaine, Arthur Hamilton, Mann Page, Sr., Mann Page, Jr., Robert Andrews and Warner Lewis, shall be properly authorized and warranted by the Lodge to hold regular Lodges in the county of Gloucester, and that the Secretary, as soon as he can, make out a proper warrant for that purpose."

Warner Lewis, mentioned in the foregoing minutes, was the first chosen Master of this Lodge. He was no doubt made a Mason in Fredericksburg Lodge, but on the establishing of Botetourt Lodge at Gloucester Court-House, of which he was a warrant member, he seldom visited Fredericksburg Lodge, although he did not cease to be a member.

Thus it will be seen that the Virginia law of dual membership, to which a number of Grand Lodges object, is honourable with age, having existed for more than ten years before the establishment of the Grand Lodge of Virginia.

In the charter granted Kilwinning Port Royal Crosse Lodge

by the Grand Lodge of Scotland, and in most of the Scottish charters of that period, appeared a clause providing that the members of a Lodge under such charter should,

"Not desert their said Lodge hereby constituted nor form themselves into separate meetings without the consent and approbation of their Master and Wardens for the time being."

The inference was, of course, that the brethren, with the approbation of Master and Wardens, could constitute and form themselves into separate meetings, which was accordingly so done. It was by virtue of this clause that Fredericksburg Lodge granted warrant for the establishment of Botetourt Lodge in Gloucester, before mentioned, and that Kilwinning Port Royal Crosse Lodge on August 14, 1756, issued authority to institute and hold a Lodge at Hobbs' Hole, now Tappahannock.

EXTRACTS FROM THE ANCIENT MINUTES OF KILWINNING PORT ROYAL CROSSE LODGE

December 27, 1756—First Masonic sermon preached by the Rev. Brother Robert Innis.

May 3, 1757—George Weedon (afterward General Weedon), made a Mason.

December 10, 1760—"Ordered that Brother Gray be payd one pound one shilling which he expended for the relief of an indigent and decrepit soldier."

March 3, 1758—" William Miller, an indigent Brother, who has met with many misfortunes and suffered much by our implacable enemy, the French, having applyd to the Right Worshipful, the Master, he, with the advice of several members of this Lodge, thought proper to give him forty shillings out of the treasury."

December 28, 1758—"Peter Corne, on his humble petition to the Lodge, is initiated an Entered Apprentice according to the usual form and solemnity, on paying the accustomed dues, and the Lodge taking into their consideration the disadvantage the sd. Peter Corne layd under as being a seafaring man and obliged to sail the next day and consequently not having time or opportunity of learning the mysteries of the Art requisite to make himself known among Masons and considering that a Certificate from this worshipful Lodge of his being regularly admitted an initiated as an Entered Apprentice therein, might in some measure supply that defect and be of singular service to him in case by the fortune of war he should fall into the hands of the enemy, ordered that a Secretary prepare and draw up such a Certificate to be signed by the Master, Wardens and Secretary and the Seal of the Lodge appended thereto."

January 10, 1767—"*Resolved*, unanimously to attend (as much as their business will permit) every month on the second Thursday according to the law formerly made in this Lodge."   An election of officers was held at this meeting with the result that Robert Gilchrist was chosen Master, James Miller Senior Warden and James Gray Junior Warden.   The office of Deacon does not appear in this Lodge for many years.   The officers elected on this occasion were present on April 12, 1754, the first recorded meeting of the Lodge.

February, 1767—"Present, Robert Gilchrist, Master; James Miller, Senior Warden; John Gray, Junior Warden; Wm. Fox, George Weedon and others.   This being a Master's Lodge a Petition was presented from the Secretary of our Lodge, Brother Brown, praying that he might be by us raised to the degree of a Master, which being agreed to he was accordingly raised in the usual manner and the business of the Lodge of Masters being gone through, the Worshipful the Master opened a Fellow Craft Lodge with the same members.

"On the humble petition of Brothers John Miller, William Buckner, William Johnston, Andrew Leckie and Archibald Clark, that they might by this Lodge be passed as Fellow Crafts, the question was put for each severally and the Lodge having agreed to their request, they were severally passed accordingly.   This Lodge having finished their business and the Lodge being shutt as usual a petition from Brothers James Somerell (Sorrell) and Henry Thomas was presented to the Master and praying that they might be passed as Fellow Crafts, on which the Master again opened a Fellow Craft Lodge (the same members present as in the last) and the vote being put and the petitions agreed to by the Lodge, the said James Somerell and Henry Thomas were accordingly passed as Fellow Crafts in the usual manner, after which the Worshipful, the Master, having closed the Fellow Craft Lodge and opened an Entered Apprentice Lodge &c. * * "

"Brother George Weedon (afterward General), setting forth that he is an inhabitant of Fredericksburg, has become a member of that Lodge there and, finding it inconvenient to attend this

Lodge, desires to be excused attending here as a member, the question being put, the said petition was agreed to and he is discharged his attendance as a member.

"Ordered that our Brother, William Fox, be requested to bring from London or send in, to be here before next December, four Dozen good aprons, together with a Master's and Officers' aprons and four Dozen pair white gloves to be paid for out of our Treasury.

"Ordered that the Secretary do provide a proper Jewel for himself as Secretary at the expense of this Lodge."

March 16, 1767—Six petitions were presented at this meeting and accepted. The By-Laws provided that no more than five could be initiated at one time, but the resourcefulness of the Worshipful Master, Robert Gilchrist, surmounted this obstacle. At the end of Secretary John Brown's minutes is the following entry made and signed by the Worshipful Master:

"NOTE:—The Lodge was closed after initating John Skinker and afterwards another Lodge opened when the remaining gentlemen were initiated.

" (Signed)   ROBERT GILCHRIST."

April, 1767—Following an ancient Masonic custom in England and Scotland, the Kilwinning Port Royal Crosse Lodge at its organization provided in its By-laws that "Every new member, at his making, shall decently cloathe the Lodge (that is, the Master and other officers) and pay the expenses of the night and shall pay into the treasury one pound one shilling and six pence," but at this communication, held on the second Thursday of April, this section of the By-Laws was revoked in the following words:

"A motion being made that the expense attending Initiation, Passing as Fellow Crafts, or Raising to a Master is too high as our Lodge becomes numerous; the Question being put,

"*It Is Enacted* from this Time all new members shall pay Two pounds three shillings and Entrance Money and the Tyle for the Night, and no more than their Club of the expence of the night—And that no member Passed as a Fellow Craft or Raised to the Degree of a Master, shall pay more than one pistole and the charges of the Tyle for the evening and equal Club with other members."

April 28, 1768—"R. W. James Robb, Master for the night——opened an Entered Apprentice Lodge and after going through our Lecture and singing a cheerful song, as is common among Masons, the Lodge was adjourned to Lodge in course."

December 28, 1767—"Our Worshipful Master congregated the Lodge about 11 A. M., and immediately after sent a deputation of our Brothers Skinker and Carter to our Sister Lodge of Fredericksburg, intimating that our Lodge was convened and would be glad to join them.

"Our brethren returned with answer it would be extremely agreeable to them, upon which the Lodges joined and some time after walked in procession to Church where our Brother Mildrum gave us an excellent discourse upon the Benefits arising from Masonry, and from Church we walked back to the Lodge Room where the Lodge was shut and we all adjourned to Brother Weedon's to dinner and from thence to the Market House where there was a most Brilliant Assembly."

(NOTE.—George Weedon was tavern keeper and postmaster in Fredericksburg at this time).

The late Judge J. B. Sener, in his History of Kilwinning Crosse Lodge, says:

"It is recorded in the history of Alexandria Lodge, No. 22, that on September 19, 1783, a delegation from that Lodge attended at Fredericksburg and assisted Kilwinning and Fredericksburg Lodges in the ceremony of 'fixing at the market-house a grand keystone and plate of silver inscribed in testimony of the revival of Masonry and our intention to fix our covenant there.' At that time in Fredericksburg the Lodge building of Lodge, No. 4, as well as the time Washington was made a Mason was located at Market-House Square. Major-General George Weedon, member of Kilwinning Port Royal Crosse Lodge and of Fredericksburg Lodge, was master of ceremonies at the 'fixing' of the keystone."

1769—Kilwinning Port Royal Crosse Lodge appointed committees to visit Lodges at Fredericksburg, Tappahannock and Falmouth to solicit subscriptions to aid in "building a ball-room, the Lodge to be over it." The building was never erected.

December 27, 1769—"At 11 o'clock A. M. the Right Worshipful Master opened the Lodge and from the Chair delivered a most pathetic charge to the brethren, recommending Brotherly Love &c and concluded with a general Charge to the Officers,

Stewards and Brethren to regulate their conduct for the approaching Assembly and, after settling everything necessary for carrying on the Assembly that evening, the Lodge duly formed in the following procession: Walked out of the Lodge Room towards the Cross and from that to the East, then to the South and from that to the West and in like order returned to the Lodge. Sword Bearer, Andrew Loggie; Two Past Masters, Robt. Gilchrist & Jas. Miller; Right Worshipful, Andrew Leckie; Secretary, Jas. Dunlop; Treasurer, John Miller; Senior Warden, William Bogle; Master Masons; Junior Warden, John Skinker, Fellow Crafts; Entered Apprentices; Two Stewards, Wm. Linsay & Geo. Gray.

"Then, after singing social songs &c, the Lodge was closed and adjourned to dinner and after drinking a few Toasts rose to get ready for the Assembly.

"At Five O'clock P. M. the Assembly began and continued till Twelve O'clock at Night with the greatest Brilliancy, Unanimity and Decorum, which is never separate from the Assemblyes of the Accepted."

February 22, 1770—Under this date is recorded the first rejection of a petition in the history of the Lodge. The same petition was presented at the next regular meeting and was again rejected. Since that time it has become a Masonic law that a rejected petitioner shall wait one year before renewing his petition.

March 24, 1770—On this date the first Masonic funeral, according to the minutes, was conducted by Kilwinning Port Royal Crosse Lodge, the funeral being that of John Miller, whose name appears in the first minutes of the Lodge. The order of the Lodge procession at that time was as follows: The Tiler was followed by Past Masters, Worshipful Master, Master Masons, Senior Warden, Fellow Crafts, Junior Warden, Entered Apprentices. The Stewards had supervision of the entire procession, and assigned the members to places in their respective bodies, according to seniority of membership.

March 26, 1772—Under this date the By-Laws of the Lodge were amended as follows: "*Resolved*, That every Officer in this Lodge shall serve but one year in each Office at one time. That each Officer shall be a Master Mason." The former was evidently enacted out of deference to the wishes of Worshipful Robert Gilchrist, who had served the Lodge as Master almost continuously from its beginning. This By-Law failed of its purpose, for it was ignored in 1776, and Gilchrist was re-elected.   The reason for the enactment of the latter—"That each Officer shall be a Master Mason"—does not appear, but the wisdom of it will be apparent to all Master Masons.   This latter By-Law, like the former, was disregarded, and in 1774, James Kemp was elected Secretary. Kemp was Provisional Grand Secretary of the Grand Lodge of Virginia at its organization, and was a Fellow Craft.

November 24, 1774—At a meeting of the Lodge on this date it was "Ordered that the Treasurer apply to every stranger that is initiated or made in this Lodge for what is customary to pay for Initiation of Raising, the morning following."

May 2, 1776—Under this date is recorded the passage of a motion, "That no person shall for the time to come be made a Mason in this Lodge, or no brother be passed or raised until the fees due the Lodge on such occasions, are first paid to the Treasurer."

April 14, 1777—Rt. Worshipful Robert Gilchrist "Proposed to have a Sermon preached by our Brother, the Rev. Mr. Waugh, to the memory of our late worthy Brother General Hugh Mercer— which being unanimously agreed to, all members were desired to meet at the Lodge Room at Nine O'clock on that day."   (March 22, 1777).

"The Master having laid before the Lodge a letter from the Williamsburg Lodge desiring the attendance of the Master and Wardens of this Lodge, or their deputies, on a certain day to choose a Grand Master for this State.

"*Resolved*, That Brother Lomax and Brother Kemp be deputed to represent this Lodge."

February 25, 1778—"The petition of Thomas Paul was received, and he was accordingly initiated in the usual form."

(NOTE.—Thomas Paul, mentioned in the foregoing extract from the ancient minutes, was a brother to John Paul, who took the name Jones and became famous as Commander in the American Navy during the Revolution).

November 24, 1785—"The deputation being returned from the Grand Lodge at Richmond, they made report that this Lodge, agreeable to their Charter, held rank as first Lodge in the State of Virginia and this seniority was awarded them, both on account of the seniority of their Charter, and the full and explicit terms in which it was worded, and the deputies, finding it unnecessary to make any donation to the Grand Lodge, the money given them for that purpose, after deducting their expenses, was returned into the Treasury."

November 30, 1786—"Whereas, Bro. Richard Dixon has made a practice of getting drunk at every Lodge he has attended for a considerable time past, and has behaved himself in a manner unbecoming a Mason as well as in direct opposition to the By-Laws of this Lodge, and having this evening got so very much intoxicated as to prevent the Lodge from going on the business now before them; Brother McKinney in the Chair, the Brethren being called to order, they all obeyed but Brother Dixon, who still continued to be noisy and, being again called to order, he, in a very disrespectful manner, said that he would not be commanded, and went on cursing and swearing in a manner unprecedented in a Regular Lodge of Free Masons.

"Brother Taylor, Senior Warden, taking the Chair, Brother McKinney made complaint of the contempt that had been shown the Chair by Bro. Dixon.

"A motion was then made by the R. W. that as B. Dixon has been often admonished without any alteration in his conduct, that he should be excluded from the Society as a person altogether unfit for setting there or in the Company of Gentlemen. The Ballot being put round he was unanimously voted out of the Lodge and the Tyler ordered to forbid him admittance in future.

"After drinking a few cheerful glasses and singing a few songs, the Lodge was Shut til Monday evening the 11th Dec. next a Call Lodge for considering the mode of celebrating the anniversary of St. John ensuing."

December, 1805—Under this date a resolution was passed providing that, "All Brethren who are indebted to the Lodge for as much as Five Dollars shall be suspended six months, and if the debt be not discharged at the expiration of that time they shall be expelled."

December 21, 1803—In the minutes of this date, the number assigned Kilwinning Port Royal Crosse Lodge, by the Grand Lodge in 1786, is recorded for the first time.

December 27, 1803—"A Resolution was brought forward and seconded—that Brother John Mason be directed to make an escutcheon for our worthy Brother Clack Row and that the Treasurer be directed to apply to some relative of Brother Row's to defray the expense and, if the relative so applied to will not pay the expense, then such charge must be paid out of the Treasury."

(NOTE.—At this meeting the custom of "reading the minutes" was adopted).

January 5, 1804—On this date the Lodge buried "Brother Clack Row," mentioned in the preceding extract from the minutes, and it is likely that there is some connection between the "escutcheon" ordered and his burial, i. e. it was, probably ordered for his coffin, he being "in extremis" at the time the "resolution was brought forward."

September 2, 1804—"The R. W. Master * * * entered into a Lecture on the First Degree of Masonry for the first time for many years."

November 27, 1804—Under this date is the first record of deacons in the Lodge, it having existed nearly half century without this office.

November 3, 1806—"The Petition of Bro. Taliaferro Hunter praying to be passed to the Degree of Fellow Craft and raised to the Sublime Degree of Master was read, whereupon he was admitted without a decenting voice & received the benefit of both Degrees accordingly "

December 23, 1806—At a meeting held on this date the practice of reading "the By-Laws and Charges" to the new initiates was inaugurated.

Autumn of 1807—Kilwinning Port Royal Crosse Lodge donated One Hundred Dollars to the citizens of Fredericksburg who were in distress because of a fire which had devastated the town.

September 27, 1810—"A. Hodge was expelled from the benefits for contempt and non-payment of dues. C. I. Dade was suspended by this Lodge for 12 months except he comes forth, and pays his dues. George Washington, John Hoover and Edd Pendleton, Jr. be suspended as C. I. Dade.

"Resolved that notice be given to Brother Robert Baylor, that if he does not come forward before the next Lodge in course, and shew cause why he has paid his fees and dues, that he will be expelled from the benefits of Masonry."

(NOTE.—The omission of the "not" in the foregoing order indicates that these minutes were not read for the approval of the Lodge).

December 18, 1818—On this date the custom of "drinking a few cheerful glasses" in the Lodge was abolished by a vote of the members.

December 26, 1818—Under this date "Brother William D. Pope" was cited for un-Masonic conduct.

February 5, 1819—On this date "Brother William D. Pope" was fined one cent, but, on his promise to reform, the fine was remitted.

December 11, 1819—In the minutes of this date certain members are "Cited to appear before the next Lodge in course to answer Charges which will then be made known." As a result of not obeying this order one of the members was expelled.

February 5, 1820—The minutes of this date disclose that three members were "Cited to appear at our Lodge Room on the night of the 7th instant, to answer Charges to be then preferred." At the hearing two of the three were excused and one was "expelled the Lodge for refusing to pay his fees and dues and speaking contemptuously of the Lodge."

December 27, 1820—On this date the Lodge celebrated the Festival of St. John the Evangelist, and the menu of the banquet was as follows: "*Tea, Coffee, Bread, Butter, Cake, Raisins, Almonds, and Sangaree for the Ladies. Bread, Cold Meats of every description which the season may afford, with Fr. Brandy, Rum and Whiskey for the Gentlemen.*" The banquet and the ball on this occasion were provided for at an expense of forty dollars.

November 29, 1821—The minutes of this date show that Kilwinning Port Royal Crosse Lodge voted to ask the Grand Lodge of Virginia for dispensation to establish their Lodge at Bowling Green, the county seat. The dispensation was granted, but the Lodge was not established in Bowling Green until 1881.

January 30, 1823—According to the old minutes on this date twenty-nine members were expelled and suspended for non-payment of dues and fees, their total indebtedness amounting to seven hundred and twenty-nine dollars.

May 14, 1825—On this date the Grand Lecturer, James Cushman, "gave a very appropriate lecture in the first degree of Masonry."

November 27, 1828—An annual election of officers was held on this date, and after this there is a period of about twenty-five years without minutes or other local record.

1840—The last return to the Grand Lodge was made in this year, and this report showed officers as follows: Charles Urquhart, Master; William Gray, Senior Warden; P. C. Robb, Past Master; John Taylor, Past Master; Charles Urquhart, Past Master; and A. W. Tennent, Past Master. There were reported fifteen members, but their names are not given.

1848—Because of its failure to report to the Grand Lodge of Virginia, and for non-payment of Grand Lodge fees, Kilwinning Crosse Lodge was suspended on December 12, 1848.

1850—A dispensation was granted by the Grand Master in 1850, but if the Lodge resumed work there is no record of it.

1854—No return was made to the Grand Lodge from the granting of the dispensation in 1850 to 1854, when the Lodge was again suspended.

1855—The Lodge was re-chartered by the Grand Lodge of Virginia in 1855, with the following officers: Charles Urquhart, Master; Philip Marshall, Senior Warden; P. H. Pendleton, Junior Warden.

December 24, 1855—On this date the first initiate was received into the re-chartered Lodge, one Colin B. Catlett by name. He died August 12, 1856, and the Lodge made his daughter, Anna Gordon Catlett, their beneficiary for the years 1859 and 1860.

June 19, 1857—Charles Urquhart was succeeded as Master by Randolph Peyton, and the retiring Master's address is recorded in the minutes of this meeting.

1857—In 1857, the Lodge, which had celebrated the Festival of St. John the Evangelist for more than a century, began to celebrate the Anniversary of St. John the Baptist.

1858—During the year 1858, the Lodge appointed a committee to secure a subscription of one dollar from each member of the Lodge, to be placed in the hands of the "Mt. Vernon Ladies Association of the Union" for the purpose of aiding in the purchase of the "Home and Grave of Washington." The contribution of the members to this cause totaled twenty-three dollars.

1859—The last report to the Grand Lodge, under the Charter of 1855, was made in 1859, and was as follows: Randolph Peyton, Master; G. Washington Catlett, Senior Warden; William P. Snider, Junior Warden; Carter B. Page, Secretary; Philip Marshall, Treasurer; A. J. Kendrick, Senior Deacon; Thomas D. Lumpkin, Junior Deacon; E. Ambold and Mark Boulware, Stewards; Thomas

O. Burrows, Tyler; Randolph Peyton and Charles Urquhart, Past Masters; and Mark L. Boulware, John T. Boutwell, Apollos Boutwell, R. L. Pendleton, Brockenbrough Peyton, E. F. Foster, George W. Upshaw, J. E. Clemm, John O. Sale, James S. Mc-Kenney, Gray Boulware, R. V. Tiffey, Joseph H. Selecman, E. Ambold, members. Not long after this return was made to the Grand Lodge the Kilwinning Crosse Lodge again became dormant.

1881—On December 14, 1881, the Grand Lodge of Virginia again issued a Charter to the Masons of Caroline, designating the body as Kilwinning Crosse Lodge, No. 237, at Bowling Green, Va. Shortly afterward the number of the Lodge under the Charter of 1796 amd 1855 was added, and the Lodge officially became No. 2-237, which number it holds to this day. The Lodge was chartered in 1881, with R. O. Peatross, Master; Charles Wright, Senior Warden; and W. O. Thompson, Junior Warden.

1881-1924—In the Proceedings of the Grand Lodge of Virginia from 1881 to 1923 are recorded the following names of members who were lost to the Lodge during this period by death, dimit, and suspension:

R. O. Peatross, Charles Wright, W. S. Thompson, J. T. Mastin, W. T. Chandler, J. T. Lawless, Roderick Vincent, A. B. Chandler, W. R. Broaddus, Travis Bagby, M. W. Cole, W. E. Evans, Maurice Evans, L. T. Fuller, T. E. Henshaw, R. S. Jones, Moses Rolph, J. A. Scott, George H. Saunders, John P. Taylor, E. W. Woolfolk, Watson Walker, E. C. Moncure, J. H. DeJarnette, A. A. Taliaferro, T. H. Stiff, W. E. Ennis, J. P. Gayle, K. R. Farrish, James O. Fox, F. M. Travis, George Robert Collins, G. H. Boggs, Mercer A. Nunn, Purcell Rowe, G. F. Stringfellow, W. A. Rountree, R. W. Wright, Andrew Broaddus, II, St. Ledger Moncure, J. W. McCown, J. B. Sener, C. R. Collins, H. L. Quarles, R. A. Watkins, O. H. Gresham, T. H. Phelps, George Turner, C. T. Jesse, E. L. Pearlman, W. E. Tyler, George Turner, Jr., W. L. Broaddus, J. M. McManaway, George Gwiner, Granville Burruss, I. O. Abbitt, G. E. Brock, W. B. Boulware, H. B. Coghill, Clarence Chewning, T. H. Chewning, C. R. Cruikshank, J. N. Harris, B. C. Nelson, G. L. Reid, M. T. Beazeley, P. M. Mills, C. K. Milligan, J. S. Ryland, W. H. Coates, J. R. Collins, R. L. Parker, M. G. Wright, R. D. Dickinson, J. H. Donohue, J. B. Meyer, W. L. Barlow, J. R. Blanton, R. L. Brooks, Jr., F. Q. Tompkins, W. F. Donahoe, J. C. Hoskins, C. A. Nunn, T. E. Barlow, S. B. Jeter, Jr., C. R. Cosby, H. E. Johnson, E. M. White, T. W. Poyner, J. K. M. Lee, J. W. Beazeley, W. L. Burruss, J. G. Shackleford, S. W.. Broaddus, C. R. Cruikshank.

In the "Proceedings of the Grand Lodge of Virginia From 1777 to 1823"—commonly called "Dove's Digest"—we find the following deaths in Kilwinning Crosse Lodge between the years 1800 and 1823. From 1802 to 1805: Andrew Gray, J. L. Alexander and Abner Waugh. From 1805 to 1810: John B. Brown, Stewart Bankhead, Charles Stewart, Hugh Quinland, James Miller, Sr., Townsend Dade, Sr., Thomas Hord, Reuben Saunders, John Skinker, Leroy Hopkins. From 1810 to 1814: Thomas Slaughter, Sr. From 1814 to 1816: Philip Henshaw, Robert Baylor, Ralph Lomax, Simon Miller, J. D. Dishman, John S. Massey, Jeremiah B. Scott, James D. Jameson, and Richard Phillips. From 1816 to 1819: Charles Browne, Henry L. Letzur, Taliaferro Hunter, A. B. Armistead, Robert Boyten, Hawkins Howard, James Bowie, and George Tebbs. From 1819 to 1823: Thomas M. Stiff, William Bernard, Jr., and C. Brockenbrough.

Following is a roster of the present membership of Kilwinning Crosse Lodge. There being but one Lodge of Masons in the county practically every section of Caroline is represented in this list:

T. R. Aaron, A. H. Allen, Joseph Baker, P. M. Barlow, V. M. Barlow, W. L. Barlow, T. E. Barlow, R. L. Barlow, R. L. Beale, Roland J. Beasley, J. W. Beazeley, Thomas H. Blanton, J. A. Blatt, T. B. Blatt, A. V. Borkey, F. H. Borkey, H. V. Borkey, J. E. Borkey, W. R. Boulware, Willing Bowie, Walter N. Bowie, W. D. Bremner, Andrew Broaddus, C. A. Broaddus, J. P. Broaddus, M. G. Broaddus, Sr., M. G. Broaddus, Jr., R. L. Brooks, C. L. Bullard, E. C. Bullock, W. L. Burruss, E. E. Butler, Sr., E. E. Butler, Jr., C. W. Butterworth, A. E. Carter, John W. Clark, E. C. Cobb, E. S. Coghill, T. D. Coghill, W. G. Coghill, E. Burke Collins, J. C. Collins, J. T. Cosby, A. G. Dalton, F. E. Derby, W. F. Donahoe, G. R. Dorsey, B. A. Dratt, J. W. Dratt, L. R. Dunn, J. W. DeJarnette, J. W. Elliott, Sr., J. W. Elliott, Jr., E. J. Eubank, S. H. Evans, Wm. Flegenheimer, N. M. Fox, L. D. George, T. B. Gill, R. T. Glassel, W. D. Gravatt, W. J. B. Hall, C. M. Harris, P. L. Haymond, L. J. Head, C. A.

Hite, R. F. Holberton, J. C. Hoskins, T. B. Jeter, G. R. Jeter, J. L. Jordan, O. D. Kean, C. E. Knopf, George P. Lyon, L. E. Martin, J. B. Meyer, B. W. Mahon, O. S. Moncure, A. C. Monroe, H. D. McWhirt, Ray L. Parker, E. B. Peatross, H. M. Pegg, W. E. Poyner, J. T. Richards, R. C. Richardson, Robert Ritchie, W. A. Rountree, E. H. Rowe, E. V. Russell, W. E. Sale, C. M. Saunders, Charles Seal, J. G. Shackelford, C. T. Smith, R. L. Smith, W. B. Smith, George W. Swain, L. E. Southworth, F. Q. Tompkins, J. B. Toombs, F. M. Travis, A. L. Taliaferro, E. B. Travis, J. R. Travis, R. C. Travis, W. A. Vaughan, L. D. Vincent, J. W. Voss, G. M. Washburn, E. A. White, E. May White, Marshall Wingfield, Robert Woolfolk, M. G. Wright.

On page 161 of the Proceedings of the Grand Lodge of Virginia from 1777 to 1823 is the following entry relative to the first Charter granted to Kilwinning-Crosse by the Grand Lodge of Virginia:

"In consequence of the representation of Brother McGruder, of the Port Royal Kilwinning Crosse Lodge, No. 2, that their Lodge had never received the Charter heretofore issued for them from the Grand Lodge of Virginia, but since that period and previous thereto, they have continued to work under the Grand Lodge of Scotland, they now pray the Most Worshipful Grand Lodge of Virginia to grant them a Charter under their jurisdiction.

"*Ordered*, That the prayer of the petition be complied with, and that a Charter do issue to them, appointing Thomas Miller, Master; William Bernard, Senior Warden, and Benjamin Hazlegrove, Junior Warden, to hold a regular Lodge in the town of Port Royal, in the county of Caroline, designated and to be known by the name of the Port Royal Kilwinning Crosse Lodge, No. 2, and this Grand Lodge considering the peculiar situation under which said Lodge, No. 2, has laboured, they also order that the above Charter do issue upon the payment of forty dollars in lieu of all delinquencies."

Thus it appears that from the organization of the Grand Lodge of Virginia in 1777 to 1796, Kilwinning Port Royal Crosse Lodge was under the jurisdiction of and rendered allegiance to both the Grand Lodge of Scotland and the Grand Lodge of Virginia. It is doubtful if any other Lodge in the world has existed under two different Grand Lodges at the same time, and it is equally doubtful if any other Lodge can produce four Charters from two Grand Lodges. The four Charters in the possession of Kilwinning Crosse Lodge are as follows: From the Grand Lodge of Scotland December 1, 1755; from the Grand Lodge of Virginia December 3, 1796; December 12, 1855, and December 14, 1881.

Kilwinning-Crosse Lodge building was raided by the Federal Army during the Civil War, and many of its belongings taken away, but notwithstanding this, misfortune the Lodge still possesses many of its old Jewels and much of the old regalia. District Deputy Grand Master Leake reported in 1885 the surrender from Catlett Burrus and others the following property belonging to Kilwinning Crosse Lodge: One large silver square, one silver compass, one silver plumb, one pair silver cross keys, one pair silver quills, a secretary's jewel, one silver star, and three charters bearing dates 1755, 1796 and 1855 respectively.

R. O. Peatross, District Deputy Grand Master, in his report to the Grand Lodge in 1887, says:

"The recovery by Kilwinning-Crosse Lodge of a second installment of the jewels and regalia, taken from the Lodge room in Port Royal during the late war by raiding Federal soldiers, through the efforts of Brother Emory Packard, of Paul Dean Lodge, Easton, Massachusetts, affords a pleasing illustration of the value of Masonic principles. The correspondence had in effecting this restoration led to the interchange of Masonic courtesies and of fraternal and personal intercourse between the brethren of these two Lodges mutually pleasant and beneficial."

"The jewels and regalia, on account of their antiquity and association, are exceedingly interesting and valuable, having been brought over from Scotland along with the original Charter of Kilwinning Crosse Lodge, under which it was established, as the second Lodge in the Colony of Virginia. They are among the oldest Masonic emblems in this country."

Joseph W. Eggleston, Grand Master of Masons of Virginia, in his address to the Grand Lodge of Virginia, on February 8, 1910, said in part:

"I was personally presented with the old "G," which hung in the East in that same old Lodge (Kilwinning Crosse) at Port Royal more than a century and a half ago, and that it might be preserved, I gave it to Dove Lodge, No. 51, on the promise that it would be put in a glass case. Richmond Lodge, No. 10, has in this building a corner-stone and it silver plate, laid by that historic Lodge in 1816."

Kilwinning Crosse Lodge had the By-Laws of 1881, 1903 and 1914, printed in booklet form, and copies of all of these are now in the possession of Mr. L. D. Vincent, a member of the Lodge. The published By-Laws of 1903 and 1914 each contains a roll of the members at the time of publication, but otherwise are not unusual in any respect. But the more ancient By-Laws are unusual in many respects, as will be noted from the following quotations and statements from them:

"No man shall be admitted a member of this Lodge without his being balloted, and in balloting should there happen to be two negatives it shall not be required whose they are and the petitioner shall be declared rejected, but should there be one nay, the member who gives the negative shall also declare his reasons, and the Lodge, after considering the same, must unanimously receive him, otherwise he shall not be admitted, but the member giving the negative shall have no vote in such case."

"Every Brother after initiation shall serve as an apprentice two months before he can be admitted to the degree of a Fellow Craft, and must serve as a Fellow Craft two months before he can be raised to the degree of a Master, unless by a Dispensation from the Master of the Lodge."

"No more than five new brethren can be initiated at one time, *and at no time a servant or bondsman.*"

"Every new member at his making shall decently cloathe the Lodge (that is the Master and other Officers) and pay the expences of the night &c."

"No member shall absent himself from the Lodge one night, under the penalty of seven pence half penny and no officer under the penalty of one shilling and three pence unless lawfully detained."

"After the Lodge is over the brethren may enjoy themselves with innocent mirth, treating one another according to ability, but avoiding all excess, or forcing a brother to drink beyond his inclination, or hindering him to leave the company when his occasions call him. No pique or quarrels of any kind must be brought within the doors of the Lodge, whether religious, national, political or commercial."

"Every Officer in this Lodge shall serve but one year in each Office at one time."

"Before the Election of Officers, the list of delinquents shall be called in order to ascertain whether any member has forfeited his right to vote or to hold office."

"Each visitor, after his first visit, shall pay to the Lodge the sum of fifty cents."

RECAPITULATION OF INTERESTING FACTS

Kilwinning Crosse Lodge in the beginning was nameless and numberless.

The members were called "Free and Accepted Masons" instead of Ancient Free and Accepted Masons, by which name they are known today.

The Kilwinning Crosse Lodge chartered other Lodges by virtue of its Scottish Charter.

The ancient minutes are written on vellum paper and bound in raw-hide.

All meetings were held in the Entered Apprentice Degree until 1843, as were the meeting of all other Masonic Lodges in Virginia.

Petitions were acted on at the very time they were presented.

All officers, except Master and Wardens, were chosen indiscriminately from Apprentices and Fellow Crafts up to 1773.

For more than fifty years the office of Deacon was unknown in Kilwinning Crosse Lodge.

The Master of the Lodge was styled "Right Worshipful" instead of "Worshipful" as today.

Members elected to office in the Lodge were fined upon refusal to serve.

The Master signed all minutes of the Lodge up to December 19, 1768.

All members were required to sign the By-Laws, which requirement has given to history many famous names.

The Lodge was closed by being "Adjourned to Lodge in Course," "Continued" or "Shutt."

A committee of three was appointed by the Lodge to investigate every petitioner.

The only disturbance during the first century of the Lodge's existence was that caused by a member in Essex county, preferring charges against a member who lived in Westmoreland county, in which he claimed that his "brother" sold him a watch which would not keep time. The disturbance was settled by the dismissal of the complaining member.

DOCTORS AND DISEASES

DR. THOMAS BATES ANDERSON

Dr. Thomas Bates Anderson was born of Caroline parentage at "Pleasant Level," in Hanover county, January 14, 1792. He received his preparatory training in Humanity Hall Academy, in Hanover, and, in 1809, entered the medical department of the University of Pennsylvania, from which he was graduated in 1811. After two years' study in the Philadelphia Lyceum of Sciences and Medicine, and one year in the office of the famous Dr. Berkeley, he located at Jericho, Caroline county, Va., making his home in the home of Mr. John McLaughlin on the North Anna river. He married the daughter of Mr. McLaughlin on September 18, 1815, and purchased a farm from one Mr. Guiney at Landau, in the upper part of Caroline, about three or four miles from the eastern border of Spotsylvania, and settled here, where he lived and practiced medicine for over fifty years. Harriett McLaughlin, his wife, was a granddaughter of Vivian Minor, of "Springfield" in Caroline, and a grandniece of Major John Minor of "Topping Castle." (For Minor genealogy see elsewhere in this volume.)

Dr. Anderson was intimately associated with Mr. Burbage Coleman, founder of the famous Concord Academy in Caroline, of which see chapter on Education and Educators. The Rev. James D. Coleman, son of Burbage Coleman, wrote a beautiful tribute to Dr. Anderson soon after his death, which was published in "Brief Biographies of Virginia Physicians" by Dr. L. B. Anderson, of Norfolk, Va. This volume was published in Richmond in 1889 by the Southern Clinic Press, and a copy is now in possession of Dr. Herman B. Anderson, Noel, Hanover county, Va.

The diary of Dr. Anderson sheds much light on the early history of Caroline, both political and religious. Many allusions are made to the efforts put forth to revive "true and undefiled religion," in Caroline and adjoining counties. The Fork Church in Hanover was an old Colonial Church (Episcopal) which, after the disestablishment, was possessed and used as a preaching place by all denominations. Here Dr. Anderson heard Rev. Mr. Meade, afterward Bishop; Bishop Moore, Rev. Messrs. Boggs, Rowzie, Andrew Broaddus, I., Kirkpatrick, and Rush, the last three of whom Dr. Anderson characterized as the finest orators he had ever heard.

The diary relates that Mr. Thomas Nelson, after he united with the Baptists, preached at Fork Church on one occasion in the presence of his brother "Billy" Nelson, a rather morose, cynical and bitter-natured person. As the two brothers rode homeward the preacher said, "I felt so cold and inanimate today that I couldn't half preach," to which "Billy" replied, "No, and by —— you never could half preach." Among other references in Dr. Anderson's diary to religious matters are the following:

"Landau, Caroline county, Va., March 23, 1818.

"Two preachers from Kentucky, Hudgins and Warden by name, of the Society called Baptists, are preaching about here. They are extremely warm in their sermons, denouncing wickedness in very strong terms. Their preaching is having considerable effect on the people. Four of my negroes have applied to me for notes to go to the meetings and relate their experiences and be baptized, provided the Church will receive them. I should be pleased if this attention to religion among them should be well grounded in a proper faith in our Lord and Saviour, Jesus Christ, and not be from over-persuasion, hurrying them, without proper consideration, into the arms of the earthly Church, relying on membership therein for salvation. This fear and doubt of mine arises from the short time many of them spend in meditation before beoming Church-members. I am afraid that when the enthusiasm of the moment passes they, not being grounded, will fall back slowly or violently into the old habits thereby bringing dishonour upon religion."

Landau, Caroline county, Virginia,——1816.

" * * * A very bitter religious controversy between Mr. William Guiney, of the Christian Church, and Mr. Stith, of the Methodist Church, has ended. Guiney is a man of much learning, fluency, sarcasm and wit. He closed the controversy with the following lines:

> Poor Stith is dead and here he lies,
> Nobody laughs and nobody cries;
> Where he's gone and how he fares,
> Nobody knows and nobody cares."

Dr. Anderson cared for a territory embracing four counties

and which since has given ample practice to more than a score of physicians. He rarely saw his patients oftener than every third day during the "sickly season" and many were unable to secure his service at all except through prescriptions based on a report of the case by a careful observer, and by the character of the prevailing epidemic.

He carried a large and varied assortment of medicines in his saddle-bags, but his patients frequently had to send to his office for such as he could not dispense at their homes. These office calls were made in the early morning hours because for many years he never reached home until very late at night. He would, nevertheless, rise early, and it is said that he frequently compounded medicines for a dozen cases by sunrise. During the spring and early summer the prevalent bilious disorders were treated by an active purgation with calomel and jalap, fifteen grains of the former and twenty-five or thirty of the latter being the usual dosage for adults. The patient was not permitted to use any intoxicating beverage the next day, nor any food save corn meal gruel. On the second day he drank a julep, ate breakfast, and went to work. During the summer the bilious fevers and dysenteries so prevalent were treated with a mercurial purge and salts. For the bilious fevers, calomel, ipecac and nitrate of potash, with an occasional bleeding, were relied upon to produce an intermission, which was embraced as a favourable opportunity to administer Peruvian bark freely.

Dr. Anderson says, "The winter diseases were generally of an active inflammatory character. Nearly all pulmonary troubles were located in the pleura. There was great heat, headache, pains in the muscles and joints and side, and a hard, bounding pulse. Bleeding would make the pulse soft and compressible, whereupon the pain would cease, a free perspiration would appear, and the patient usually needed nothing more to complete the cure. But in the winter of 1814 the disease assumed a different character and the inflammation, in pulmonary troubles, was no longer located in the pleura, but in the pulmonary tissue proper. The intensity of the pain, the difficulty of breathing, the apparent volume of the pulse would seem to indicate bleeding; but the great debility and rapid prostration which followed blood-letting or purging would clearly contradict this method of treatment. The pulse, apparently full, was easily compressible, and was what might be called a gaseous pulse, and a resort to the lancet was almost uniformly fatal.   My plan was to give an emetic of tartrate antimony, then a mercurial purge, followed by James' powder, seneka and nitrate of potash with free blistering.   If the circulation was feeble I gave whiskey freely, and, occasionally camphor and serpentaria were used with happy effect.   Occasionally the pulmonary oppression became very great, the breathing short and laboured, the pulse feeble and frequent, or what Dr. Rush would call a typhoid pulse.   I tried many modes of treatment in these cases without avail.   Stimulants produced no impression whatever.   I then determined upon a course of treatment as follows: Pulvis antimorialis, grs. 2; opium, gr. ½; calomel, gr. ½; to be given every two or four hours, and the whole thorax, except a narrow space on each side of the spine, to be enveloped in a blistering plaster.   Spirits of nitre was given while the blister was drawing.   This plan was usually successful."

"In 1819 a fever appeared in Caroline of an obstinate character. It was called nervous fever, typhus fever, &c., but I think it might with more propriety be called typhoid bilious fever.   The symptoms varied much.   In some cases the nervous system was seriously affected, in others but very little; the pulse in some cases was full, in others small and frequent; in some instances the skin was moist, in others dry; some were costive, others were affected with diarrhoea; in some the mind was clear, in others there was wild delirium.   The tongue was read and dry, sometimes cracked, and the teeth, gums and fauces coated with dark sordes.   It lasted from fourteen to thirty days, and sometimes longer, and prevailed in Caroline through 1820–1824."·

Among the many Caroline families treated for this malady, during this period, were the Buckners, Catletts, Lomaxes, Dixons, Conways and Chandlers, and the Motleys, Tylers and Thorntons on the Mattaponi.   The treatment used by Dr. Anderson was small doses of calomel and opium, spirits of nitre, camphor and blisters.   In advanced cases, when the fever had declined, he says he "used whiskey, Peruvian bark, serpentaria, chamomile, &c."

Dr. Anderson was not a slave to the medical routine of the times, but, on the contrary, he made many startling innovations and departures.   It is said that he freely used cold drinks and crushed ice in fevers many years before he saw such treatment recommended in any medical work.   Especially effective was the use of crushed ice in the treatment of the congestive chills which frequently appeared along the Mattaponi. In these cases the skin would be bathed in sweat, the extremities cold, the pulse feeble, the breathing short and hurried, the heart quick and feeble, and the thirst insatiable, while consciousness remained. Instead of stimulants, which only increased the internal fires, Dr. Anderson gave crushed ice until the sweat dried, extremities became warm, pulse reappeared, and reaction was established. The record is that he never lost a congestive fever patient unless the collapse was so profound as to incapacitate for swallowing.

In bilious fevers Dr. Anderson prescribed watermelon juice and buttermilk as the sole article of diet. An amusing incident in his experience is told by his son, Dr. L. B. Anderson, in "Brief Biographies of Virginia Physicians." While visiting a patient in the home of Judge Stanard, an elderly gentleman of convivial habits, who was also a guest of the Judge, asked Dr. Anderson to prescribe for a swelling in his feet and legs. The Doctor, believing that at best he could only relieve a man possessed of such habits, prescribed a compound jalap powder every other night for three nights, whereupon the gentleman responded, "I can't take it, sir; I can't take it." After a pause the Doctor said, "Well, Sir, what is your objection to taking what I prescribe?" To which the gentleman made reply, "Sir, when I was a boy my mother thought I needed some medicine, and sent me to Dr. Bankhead for a prescription. He wrote my mother to give me a dose of jalap. She weighed it out and tried to put it in a tablespoon but it could not hold it. She then put it in my grandmother's ladle, but before she had put enough honey in to mix, it ran over and then she mixed it in a plate, and I ate it as one would eat milk and mush." After a pause, as if in deep thought, the Doctor asked, "Will you be kind enough to tell me, sir; what effect it had on you." "Why, sir," responded the gouty gentleman, "it acted for eight consecutive days and night, and has been acting off and on ever since, and I have sworn never to take another grain of jalap as long as I live." Amid great laughter the Doctor withdrew his prescription, and expressed his entire approval of the oath.

Among the physicians with whom Dr. Anderson was associated in the practice of medicine, during the earlier years of his career were Doctors Berkeley, Honeyman (father and son), Lewis, Holliday, Curtis, Morris, Carmichael, Browne, Durrett, Meux, Wolford, Coleman, Pendleton, Sheppard, Minor, and French.

Among those with whom he was associated in his later life may be mentioned Doctors Urquhart, Gravatt, Glassel, Benjamin Anderson, Thornton, Scott, Morris, Tyler, Taylor, Pendleton, George Carmichael, Waller, DeJarnette, Smith, Nicholas, Terrell, Rowzie, Fleming, Swann and Flippo.

Dr. J. A. Flippo attended Dr. Anderson in his last illness. He died on May 3, 1872, aged eighty years, and on May 5, was laid to rest in the old burying ground of "Topping Castle." The study of medicine seems to have had a peculiar fascination for both paternal and maternal branches of the Anderson family. He had a son, Dr. L. B. Anderson, who was born in Caroline and who practiced in Norfolk many years, a grandson; Dr. Herman B. Anderson, of Hanover county; two brothers, Dr. John M. Anderson who settled in Texas, and Dr. Horace F. Anderson who settled in Tennessee; three nephews, Dr. Monroe W. Anderson, of Clarkesville, Ky., Dr. Zebulon M. P. Anderson, of Texas, and Dr. Clopton Anderson, of Tennessee. The following were among his cousins who followed the profession of medicine: Doctors Archibald Anderson, Benjamin Anderson, Matthew T. Anderson, Matt. Archy Anderson, John B. Anderson (of Louisa) and A. W. Clopton and John G. Trevilian, of Richmond.

EDUCATION AND EDUCATORS

FREDERICK WILLIAM COLEMAN

Frederick William Coleman, third son of Thomas Burbage Coleman and Elizabeth Lindsey Coghill, was born on his father's estate—"Concord"—in Caroline county on August 3, 1811. He was sprung from the best English blood in Virginia, and from an ancestry noted for intellectuality. His grandfather, Daniel Coleman, who had been an officer in the Revolution, presided for many years over a school at Concord, and was succeeded by his son Thomas Coleman, father of Frederick William, who, in turn, was succeeded by his sons Atwell and James.

Frederick William Coleman received his preparatory training in his father's school, and, when twenty-one years old, entered the University of Virginia. At that time he was described as "an almost perfect type of Herculean young manhood—six feet, two inches in height, deep of chest and long of limb—a fellow of infinite jest, the soul of every company with his quaint flahes of merriment, yet withal possessed of a strong passion for scholarship." Before matriculation in the University, he had settled upon teaching as his profession, and it was to better qualify himself for his chosen calling that he went to the University. So assiduous was he in his studies that within a short time he was in all his classes a man of mark, and, after three years of unbroken success, was graduated Master of Arts.

During his residence at the University political excitement was running high in Virginia, and, although eager student that he was, Frederick Coleman, like the majority of Virginians, was borne along on the crest of the wave. His father, Thomas Coleman, who represented Caroline for years in the Virginia Assembly, was a "Jeffersonian Democrat" of the strictest sort, and a firm believer in John Taylor's "strict construction" of the Constitution, and naturally the son had been bred in the faith of "States Rights doctrine." "Nullification," "the Force Bill," "Compromise Tariff," and "the Removal of Deposits" were among the great questions which threatened to rend asunder the nation in '32 and '33, and not even in 1860 was there fiercer contention in Congress or more bitter animosity in humble debate than everywhere prevailed at this time.

Professor John A. G. Davis, a man of notable ability, was the head of the Law School during these times, and taught law as a code of principles rather than a line of precedents. Davis was an ardent States Rights advocate and in his classes in Constitutional Law argued eloquently, on historical premises, that the United States Courts had no right to fix by construction the rights of a State. As in the stirring autumn of 1860 students "cut" their lectures in the Academic Department to throng the lecture-room of James P. Holcombe, so, in the exciting days of '33, was Davis's lecture room crowded with eager students, who came to hear him discuss the question which Calhoun and Webster were debating on a larger field—namely, whether the Constitution were a simple compact or a fundamental law; and, among all his enthusiastic listeners there was no keener listener than Frederick Coleman. At that time he became what he remained to the end of his days—an enthusiastic politician and States Right advocate.

On graduating, in 1835, he joined his brother, Atwell Coleman, in the conduct of the school in Caroline, and called it "Concord Academy," the name by which it afterward became so famous throughout the entire South.

When, a year or two later, Atwell Coleman removed to Alabama, Frederick Coleman became the sole proprietor of Concord Academy, a new order was at once inaugurated. In his extreme iconoclasm every vestige of the traditional methods was swept away. His experience at the University of the evils resulting from multiplicity of rules and regulations, added to his inbred impatience of all conventionality and restraint, determined him to try the bold experiment of giving his pupils such freedom as no school boys had ever known before, and to make the unwritten law of personal honour, and not the fear of punishment, the controlling power of the school.

This honour system was as new as it was bold. The Yankee school masters who had come down in swarms from New England to Virginia between 1810 and 1830 brought with them all of the traditions of the colleges in which they had been trained. They prided themselves on their slyness in espionage, and put a premium on lying by attempting to compel a boy when "caught in a scrape" to "peach" on his comrades. They delivered themselves of long homilies on the sinfulness of fighting and other boyish mischief, to which the boys listened demurely but with inward rebellion and contempt. These were the days of "barring out" and "cold water traps" cleverly set for the deluging of the teacher in his sudden nightly raids into dormitories, whereby they made wretched the hapless New England pedagogue, who commonly revenged himself for the contemptuous insubordination of the older boys by unmercifully thrashing the smaller ones.

The late Professor Edward S. Joynes, M. A., LL. D., of the University of South Carolina, in a sketch of his schoolboy life at Concord Academy, says:

"Concord Academy was a massive brick building, surrounded by a few log cabins, situated absolutely in the 'old fields'—no enclosure—no flowery walks—no attractions for the eye, such as I had been accustomed to in the academies I had attended at the North. Within, all was rude and rough, the barest necessities of decent furniture—the table abundant, but coarsely served— the rooms devoid of all luxury or grace—no trace of feminine art— nor sound of woman's voice to relieve the first attacks of homesickness—everything rough, severe, masculine.

"I looked and inquired after the 'Rules and Regulations' of the School. I found there were none! To my horror I felt deserted even by the eye of discipline. It seemed to me the reign of lawlessness with utter desolation and loneliness.

"But I soon found that there reigned at Concord the one higher law—*Be a man!* That what I thought solitude and helplessness was the lesson of individuality: *Be yourself.* As for discipline there was none in the usual sense of the term. *Be a man—be a gentleman*—nothing more. Far too little, indeed nothing at all of those rules, those proprieties, those methods that belong to the well-regulated school.

"*Obedience and truthfulness* were the only virtues recognized or inculcated at Concord—*obedience absolute* to Frederick Coleman—his will was law, was gospel, was Concord. There was not a boy, even those who loved him most, who did not fear him absolutely. And *truthfulness with courage.* All else was forgiven but lying and cowardice. These were *not forgiven,* for they were impossible at Concord."

Not less extraordinary was the absence of all rules in regard to the preparation of tasks and hours of recitation. The boys studied when and where they chose, and the length of time given to a class varied from thirty minutes to three hours, according to the judgment of the instructor. The boys were often aroused in the night, sometimes long after midnight, and summoned to the recitation room by "Old Ben," the fathful negro janitor, who equally feared and worshipped his master. A sharp rap at the door, and the familiar cry, "Sophocles, with your candles, young gentlemen," would send the youngsters tumbling out of bed in the long winter nights, and each fellow, with his tallow dip, would sit until the small hours of the morning, and never a sleepy eye, while "Old Fred" expounded Antigones or Ajax.

Professor Gray Carroll, who took a brilliant Master's degree at the University of Virginia in 1855, relates the following: "On one occasion, Coleman, in giving out the lesson, inadvertently announced the wrong day for the next recitation. The class determined to take advantage of his absent-mindedness and go fishing. Silently and swiftly they sped away to the fishing hole, two miles distant, and were just casting their line, with many a chuckle over their prospective holiday, when their blood was frozen by the terribly familiar cry: "Ripides, young gentlemen, right away; Mars Fred is waitin'."

The law of place, continues Professor Carroll, was as uncertain as that of time, and in the long summer days, "Old Fred," in shockingly scanty attire, surrounded by his eager pupils in like scanty raiment, would lie on the soft sward under the great trees and "hold high converse with the mighty dead."

Governor John L. Marye, who entered Concord in 1838, writing to W. Gordon McCabe, said: "My schooling, up to the time I entered Concord, had been under the tuition of old-fashioned teachers, chiefly imported from the North. Going from a town and having been for five years under the instruction of what was dubbed 'The Classical and Mathematical Academy of Fredericksburg,' I entered Concord with some complacent idea as to my comparative scholarship with that of the average boy. You will not doubt that my first experience as a pupil under Mr. Coleman was a startling and humbling revelation to my young and callow mind. My recollection is that he succeeded on the very first day of my appearing in class before him in convincing me that much which I valued as my acquirements had to be summarily unlearned. Then followed day by day that exhibition by him of the elevated, enlightened and philosophical method of instruction, which marked his teaching and made his school the pioneer in the grand line of academies, which followed in Virginia."

Professor Edward Joynes further says: "I cannot analyze or describe Frederick Coleman's teaching. I only know that I have seen no such teaching since, and I have sat at the feet of Harrison and Courtney and McGuffey at home, and Haupt and Boeckh and Bopp abroad. It was just the immeasurable force of supreme intellect and will, that entered into you and possessed you, until it seemed that every fibre of your brain obeyed his impulse. Like 'The Ancient Mariner' he 'held you with his glittering eye' and like him 'he had his will' with you. If I should try to define its spirit, it would be by the word of self-forgetfulness. If I should try in a word to define its method, it would be concentration. But, indeed, Frederick Coleman's teaching cannot be analyzed except by saying that it was Frederick Coleman himself. He was a man of massive power of body, mind, will. Through this power he dominated his boys—impressed himself upon them—wrought himself into them—controlled them by his mighty will-power—roused them by his mighty sympathy. As a teacher, he was the greatest of his age—there has been no other like him."

Coleman's temper, says McCabe, was furious when aroused, and the stoutest lad quailed before it. Against anything that savoured of baseness or meanness, his indignation knew no bounds. Two things he would never forgive—lying and cowardice. He accepted a boys word implicity, and if he deceived him he must go. Fighting he allowed, but he was always ready to mediate, and, if that failed, he was equally ready to see that the fight was a fair one. Bullying he would not tolerate. If, after the fight, anything remained unforgiven, he would adjudicate, and the boys were required to shake hands.

The whole nature of the man was instinct with honesty and truth, and his high personal courage was proverbial. One of the traditions gloried in by Concord boys was of the day, famous in the annals of Caroline, when he vanquished single-handed six strapping bullies who had long been the terror of the court green.

Lewis Coleman, a nephew of Frederick Coleman, came to Concord in 1846 as Assistant Master, and, under his guidance, regularity, method and conventionality, with which the Master was so impatient, came to have a larger place in the school.

In 1849, after fifteen years of phenomenal success, he suddenly decided to close the school. He urged many reasons for the step to his intimates, who remonstrated against his purpose, chief among which was his plan to further the fortunes of his nephew, Lewis Coleman, who had determined to establish a school of like grade in Hanover. In this plan he was successful, for the year in which Concord closed its doors, saw the establishment of Hanover Academy, which was simply a removal of Concord to Hanover. This new institution flourished, as had Concord. In 1859, Lewis Minor Coleman accepted the chair of Latin in the University of Virginia. His service in the University was brief. He entered the Confederate Army as captain of a light battery and rose to be Lt. Colonel of Artillery. He was killed on the historic field of Fredericksburg. Upon the retirement of Coleman, Hillary P. Jones became Head Master of Hanover Academy and remained in this position until Virginia seceded and actively entered the Civil War, when he, and the majority of the students, joined the Confederate forces.

The Old Master of Concord Academy retired with an easy competence, but after a brief period of leisure his energetic spirit called him again into action. He entered the political arena and was elected a member of the State Senate, but at the end of his first term he declined to stand for re-election. Being an ardent

State Rights advocate he championed the cause of the South and confidently believed in success of her cause.   He did not live to see that cause lost at Appomattox for he died in Fredericksburg, Va., in November, 1860.

Bowling Green Female Seminary

MRS. W. T. CHANDLER

Alice Scott, the daughter of Mr. Francis Woolfolk Scott (1799–1863) and Ann Maria Minor (1804–1889), was born in Caroline county, Va., on the 31st day of August, 1839. She was educated in the old Buckingham Female Institute in Buckingham county, then presided over by Dr. John C. Blackwell, a well-known edu-

Student Body of Bowling Green Female Seminary 1908

cator, who married a sister of Governor Letcher, and was one of the ripest scholars of his day. She was united in marriage to William T. Chandler, of Caroline, born May 17, 1832, a young lawyer and Civil War veteran, in 1858, and they established their home at "Sherwood," near the husband's birthplace. Mr. Chandler now entered upon the active practice of law, driving

Campus Scene Bowling Green Female Seminary

from "Sherwood" to the county seat each morning and back to his home each evening. It was not long, before fire destroyed

"Sherwood" and all their personal effects, leaving them without shelter in those tragic, poverty-filled days which came to the South in the wake of the Civil War.

Shortly after the burning of their home Mr. and Mrs. Chandler settled in Bowling Green, the county seat, Mr. Chandler continuing the practice of law, and Mrs. Chandler establishing a private school in a part of their residence which came to be known as the Home School. Possessing rare gifts of personality and intellect, and having a genius for the work of teaching and administration, Mrs. Chandler found no difficulty in gathering around her a splendid group of students—the daughters of the representative families of the community. The name "Home School" was soon changed to Bowling Green Female Seminary, and a commodius and beautiful building was erected to house the rapidly growing institution. The faculty was enlarged from time to time, the school having all the departments usually found in a high-class female academy, and the institution gradually took its place among that splendid group of schools which undergirded the South in the dark days of Reconstruction.

Upon the marriage of Miss Emma B. Scott, Mrs. Chandler's sister, to the Rev. E. H. Rowe, Mrs. Chandler gradually retired as head of the seminary and Rev. Mr. Rowe became principal. Mrs. Chandler purchased the Washington Female Seminary in Atlanta, Ga., in 1891, and continued the work of education until her death in July, 1904. Mrs. Chandler's dust sleeps in Lakewood Cemetery, Bowling Green, where rests also the dust of her husband. There were no children. The Washington Seminary in Atlanta still flourishes under the direction of her nephew, Llewellyn Davis Scott, and her niece, Emma B. Scott, associate principals.

The Rev. Mr. Rowe moved the Bowling Green Female Seminary to Buena Vista, Va., in 1901, changing the name to Southern Seminary, and there the institution founded by this brave and brilliant woman in the soul-testing days of Reconstruction continues to flourish—a monument to courageous Southern womanhood.

Riding Class in Bowling Green Female Seminary 1908

SAMUEL SCHOOLER

Samuel Schooler was born in Caroline county, Va., in the year 1827.

After a very thorough preparatory education, under the direction of his father, Rice Schooler, and his maternal uncle, Professor Nelson, of Louisa and Hanover, he entered the University of Virginia in 1844, and after two years graduated from that institution, at the head of his class, with the degree of Master of Arts.

Shortly after graduation he entered upon the profession of teaching, locating at Millwood, Clarke county, Va. He continued his work as principal of the school at Millwood until 1850, at which time he became Assistant Master of Hanover Academy in Hanover county, Va.

This Academy was established in 1850 by Lewis Minor Coleman, a nephew of Frederick William Coleman, celebrated educator of Caroline, and was, in many respects, the successor of Concord Academy, for it is a well-established fact that Frederick William Coleman closed Concord in order to advance the fortunes of this, his favorite nephew who wished to establish an academy of his own. Lewis Minor Coleman fashioned this academy along the same lines as old Concord in Caroline, with the additional improvements incident to the development of higher education. So successful was he in his endeavors that the new academy won instant favour at the University of Virginia, and soon became widely known as "The Rugby of the South."

After a brief period of service here, Schooler established a preparatory school of his own at Edge Hill in Caroline county, following to a great extent the methods so successfully pursued by the Colemans.

While conducting the Edge Hill Academy Mr. Schooler wrote and published a Descriptive Geometry, which won instant recognition and was widely acclaimed as being the finest treatise of descriptive science which had appeared up to that time. Many other works on that branch of science found their origin in Schooler's book, but none ever equaled his treatise, which, for many years, was used as a text book in the University of Virginia.

When the Civil War broke out Schooler closed Edge Hill Academy and entered the Confederate Army. He was soon commissioned Captain of Artillery for Ordnance duty, and was assigned to duty at the Richmond Arsenal, where he remained until April, 1864, when he was ordered to take charge of the Reserve Ordnance Train of the Army of Northern Virginia under Lt. Colonel Briscoe G. Baldwin, Chief of Ordnance of the Confederate Army. He remained in this position until October, 1864, when he was ordered back to duty at the Richmond Arsenal.

Joseph Packard, a promient attorney of Baltimore, says: "I was his (Schooler's) assistant, and messed with him during all the period he was with the train, and derived great benefit from his conversation, which covered a wide range of accurate knowledge. I was preparing to take the examination for Captain in the Ordnance Service and needed to brush up on my mathematics. I had no text books accessible and he dictated to me from memory all of the algebraic formulae which I needed to study. His knowledge of mathematics has seldom, if ever, been equaled. I often heard him speak of Lewis Minor Coleman (at that time Colonel), whose half-sister, Mary E. Fleming, he married, and of the days at Hanover Academy."

Many ideas and suggestions made by Captain Schooler were adopted by the Ordnance Department, and were acknowledged as great factors in promoting the efficiency of the Artillery service. He was also one of the Examining Board before whom all aspirants to commissions in the Ordnance and Artillery service appeared.

Captain Schooler, in collaboration with his brother-in-law, Colonel W. L. Broun, head of the Ordnance Department, originated and worked out a system of Civil Service in the Confederate Army, from which was taken and applied the first Civil Service in the United States. Thus Civil Service, as well as the Honour System in schools and colleges, had its birth in the mind of one of Caroline's sons.

Schooler possessed marked literary ability and could have made his mark in the world of letters had he closely applied himself in that direction. Early in his life he wrote and published an article entitled: "Wrinkles on the Horns of Toby, or Confession of an Ugly Man," which won much favourable notice. Thackeray on his visit to America attended a literary club at

Hanover Academy, of which John R. Thompson, editor of the *Southern Literary Messenger*, was a member and during this visit Thompson called the attention of the celebrated author to Schooler's article, which had just appeared. Thackeray was delighted with the production and pronounced it "the finest piece of humorous literature ever written by an American."

He frequently wrote verse of a high order; but few, if any, of his poems ever appeared in print, nor, indeed, were they preserved in any form. A few lines of verse entitled "Thoughts of Other Days," and written for his friend, Mr. Thomas W. Valentine, Clerk of the Circuit Court of Caroline, are in the possession of Mr. T. C. Valentine, Deputy Clerk of the Circuit Court of Caroline, are hereto appended.

After an eventful but not long life, Samuel Schooler died quite suddenly in Richmond, Va., in 1873 and was buried at "Locust Grove" (also known as the Fitzhugh Catlett place), near Guinea, Va. His grave is marked by a stone erected by his oldest son, George Fleming Schooler, who died in 1907. Samuel Schooler was married to Mary E. Fleming, half-sister of Lewis Minor Coleman, and to this union were born five children, two sons and three daughters. Willa S. Page (Mrs. Frank Page) is the only surviving child. A granddaughter, Mary A. Ambler, is now teaching English in the High School of Fredericksburg, Va.

> Soft as rays of sunlight stealing
>   O'er the dying day;
> Sweet as chimes of low bells pealing
>   When evening fades away.
> Sad as winds at night that moan
>   Through the heath o'er mountains lone,
> Come the thoughts of days now gone
>   Over manhoods memory.
>
> As the sunbeams from the heavens,
>   Hide at e'en their light,
> As the bells when fades the even,
>   Peal not on the night;
> As the winds cease to sigh,
>   When the rain falls from the sky,
> So pass the thots of days gone by
>   Over age's memory.

But the sunlight, in the morning,
   Forth again shall break;
And the bells give sweetest warning
   To the world to wake;
Soon again the winds shall breathe
   Thru the mountains purple heath;
But man's path is lost in death—
   He hath no memory

NOTE —This poem is used in Professor Schooler's "Wrinkles on the Horns of Toby," which appears in Volume 19 of the *Southern Literary Messenger.*

Caroline County Court-House as it Appeared 100 Years Ago.
See Legislative Petition No. 4617, Page 57.

Dr. H. T. Anderson

DR. H. T. ANDERSON

The Andersons have been prominent in American life for nearly three centuries. The first members of this family to come to America were Richard Anderson, Sr., and Richard Anderson, Jr., who sailed from England in July, 1635. Land Office Book VII, page 272, shows that Robert Anderson, I, was granted 727 acres of land in New Kent county, Va., in 1683 for the importation of 15 persons. He married Cecilia Massie, of New Kent, and was vestryman of St. Peter's parish until the parish of St. Paul was cut off in 1704. He died in 1712. Robert Anderson, II, married Mary Overton and had issue as follows: Richard, James, Garland, Matthew, David, Robert III, and three others whose names are not known. Garland Anderson owned much property in New Kent, Caroline, Hanover and adjoining counties, and was a member of the Richmond Convention of 1775, by which legislation was enacted placing Virginia on a war basis. Garland Anderson married Marcia Burbage, of Caroline, and to this union was born John Burbage Anderson, who married Martha Tompkins, of Caroline, to whom were born six sons and three daughters. Henry Tompkins Anderson, the subject of this biography, was the sixth son of John Burbage Anderson and Martha Tompkins, and was born on January 27, 1812. He was brought up in a home of culture and refinement. His mother was an unusually brilliant woman and taught all of her sons Latin and Greek. When barely twenty-one H. T. Anderson united with the Christian Church (Disciples) and was baptized by his elder brother, Dr. Benjamin Anderson, a widely known physician, who for many years was an elder in the Antioch Christian Church at Bowling Green. Within ten months after his baptism he began to preach the Gospel, and in his twenty-fifth year removed to Kentucky to accept the pastorate of the Christian Church of Hopkinsville. Here he met and married Henriette Ducker, a lady of great beauty and brilliancy. The Church at Hopkinsville flourished under his leadership and his labours there are commemorated by a beautiful window placed in the Church and dedicated to him.

Through the influence of his life-long friend, John Augustine Williams, President of Daughters College, Harrodsburg, Ky., Anderson turned his brilliant mind into educational channels and for a time, after retiring from the Hopkinsville pastorate, presided over a classical school in Northern Kentucky.

In 1847 he became the pastor of First Christian Church, of Louisville (which Church has since been served nearly forty years by E. L. Powell, another Virginian) and continued in this capacity for six years. Upon retiring from the Louisville pastorate Anderson re-entered the field of education as instructor in Daughters College at Harrodsburg, Ky., and here he lived and taught and preached for several years. Later he presided over a classical school at Midway, Ky., where he was assisted by his son, Henry T. Anderson, Jr., and his daughter Jessie, both of whom were brilliant Greek and Latin scholars.

Writing his friend, John Augustine Williams, regarding the school at Midway, he says:

"Seventy-two pupils give me as much as I can do. * * * There is a vast amount of work to be done, to which I am addressing myself with all diligence. There is much good material on which I shall bestow abundant labour. It is a saying of the Wise Man that 'one sinner destroyeth much good.' I will ever keep this in mind, and my course will be to keep the school free from such."

Anderson also presided over a classical school at Flemingsburg, Ky., and while in this position wrote to his friend, President Williams, in the following words:

"The people here are a substantial set. They have looked more to their bodily than to their mental and spiritual well-being. The field is a great one for labour and much may be accomplished if the people can be taught that grand secret—the habit of thinking. It falls to the lot of but few to learn this secret. * * * To look on the events of life and see them working out one grand result, the glory of God and the happiness of the race, is the lot of fewer still. * * * * I know not what will take place on the morrow, but this I know, that He who put forth his hand and upheld the sinking Apostle from the depths, can so guide my footsteps as to save me from all evil. * * * * * If we commit our ways to Him he will so order our steps that we shall enjoy the greatest amount of good, for 'no good thing will he withhold from them who walk uprightly.'"

The labours of an educator seem to have grown irksome to Dr. Anderson, for in one of his letters to President Williams he says:

"Give me a few acres, with a good garden, a small forest and lasting spring, and I shall be content. The Lord made man upright but he hath "sought out many inventions," boarding schools being one of them." * * * I would go to my little place in the country, read Hebrew and Greek, translate, write notes and essays, and beautify the little thirty-acre plot with trees, flowers, shrubbery, and whatsoever is pleasant to the eyes and good for food. This nervous affection is my 'thorn in the flesh'—a messenger of satan surely—that will allow me no rest on earth save that which I find in study, translating, and writing."

In December, 1861, he began to translate the New Testament from the original Greek and, in a letter to President Williams about this time, says:

"If I succeed in translating the New Testament will it not give a reason for my past retired labours in the study of the Holy Oracles? Surely such a result would be worth a life of labour! Whatsoever the result one thing is certain: I shall have filled my own mind and heart with the knowledge of His truth. * * * I am here, 'like a sparrow on the housetop,' to use one of David's figures. I have always thought this simile one of the most apt and striking in the Bible. Did you ever see a sparrow upon a housetop? Of all lonely and insignificant looking things surely this is the most lonely. * * * * * I am better this morning and attribute my improvement to a glass of lemonade. Acids are good for nervousness; if you are unbelieving, try it. I know you will here exclaim, 'What a descent!—From Hebrew and Greek, and David's similes, to lemonade!' Oh, well, 'Variety is the spice of life.'"

When the Civil War broke out, and young men laid down their books and took up the sword, Anderson gave up his school work and devoted his time to translating, preaching and lecturing. Writing to President Williams about this time he says:

"Tell me what it is within the mind, which sees that a thing will not be; or, on the other hand, pierces the veil of the future and lights up some spot, and says we shall be there—sometime? Benjamin Franklin (a noted Disciple preacher and publicist of Anderson's day) would have me come to Cincinnati in a short time, but this 'inward something' has told me, and yet tells me, that I shall not be there. When I look in the direction of Mercer that 'something' seems to say to me that I shall be there—and that I ought to be there. Is this an illusion? Or is it that a ray from a better world flashes upon the future and lights it up for the lonely soul that is to sail out upon an uncertain sea? The latter, let us believe, for, as the poet said, "We are not all clay." * * * * .

So the next year finds him in Mercer, as the "inward something" had foretold. Here he was near President Williams, between whom and himself existed a friendship like that between David and Jonathan of old, and here he gave himself wholly to the work of translating. From Mercer he wrote to President Williams in these words:

"I have finished the Acts. Have re-written Matthew, Mark and Luke. I took the Acts next to Luke that I might not have a change of writers by translating John. I knew I would have but little difficulty with John, so left this for the warm weather. The translation is such as satisfies me. I have no fear for Robinson, Bloomfield and the rest of the critics, as their views, collected by Trollope, of Cambridge, in his Analytics, sustain me. Pendleton and Loos—like Aaron and Hur with Moses—will hold up my hands. I have sent Pendleton two chapters of

Romans, and he and Loos gave them fulsome praise—almost as extravagant as that given by Pendleton in his notice of my version of Matthew. Favourable notice from such scholars as these adds to my joy. How could I ask for more?"

In July, 1862, he writes to President Williams as follows:

"I am now translating the Second Epistle to the Corinthians, and intend to finished the New Testament by the first of September, if health lasts, and publish the whole this fall. You will say this is doing the work in too great haste, but my work is the result of nearly thirty years study, and I find that all I have read and studied has not been lost, but has been in a somewhat dormant state ready for being used in my present work."

Dr. Robert Richardson, the brilliant President of Bethany College, said, "H. T. Anderson's knowledge of the Scriptures is greater than Mr. Campbell's at his best years."

Benjamin Franklin, noted Disciple minister and publicist, wrote:

"I am pleased with Brother Anderson. He has a mighty fund of learning and knowledge. He is a great man."

The "great man's" opinion of himself may be learned from the following extract from a letter to President Williams regarding certain complimentary notices which had appeared concerning his translation:

"Whatever merit it may possess is only the reflection of the image of my Master, to whom be all the glory and honour. * * * I am poor and weak, and in my weakness and poverty I have taken refuge under His wing. I have felt His power and, apart from men, I have lived in His presence."

Dr. Anderson, while of a deeply spiritual nature, was not without his humourous side. Referring to some complimentary review of his Translation, by one Dr. Rice, he writes as follows to his friend, President Williams:

"If others think as Dr. Rice thinks then my work will enable me to buy a horse and ride around some. Don't you think that a man who has made such a Translation, as you know mine to be, ought to have a horse?"

Again he writers in the same vein to President Williams:

"Double thanks for your wonderful essay on 'To Be and to Live.' I know of nothing that excels it save my Translation."

In 1864, he completed and published his Translation, which, he said, was intended to open and illuminate the Scriptures for the masses, and the work found instant favour in both America and Europe.   Writing from Louisville, Ky., in 1865 he says:

"But now *I am*, and that is about all of me.   I am in the right place, no doubt, for my mind must rest for future motion and life.   A new world opens before me for a full play of all my powers, whatever they are.   Isaac Errett wishes me to deliver lectures on the Greek Testament—principles of interpretation—and this will suit me very well, but the presidency of a college in Iowa has been offered me, and my wife is inclined to that region.   *   *   *   The presidency of a college presents no pleasing anticipation to me.   *   *   *   *   I have no desire to accept.   *   *   *   *

Contemporaneous with Dr. Anderson's labours of translation was Tischendorf's discovery of the Codex Sinaiticus.   Writing to Dr. Williams, regarding this discovery, he says:

"I feel as if my fortune was made.   I have the Codex Sinaiticus, the most ancient of the Codices.   This crowns my joy.   I know of nothing I wanted so much.   *   *   *   *.   It is wonderful how works flow to my hand—the very works I want.   The Lord is surely with me in this, and sends me what I want, both in books and in a friend to help me."

From Washington, D. C., he wrote to Dr. Williams in August, 1868, in the following words:

"I have made a version for the masses which, I believe, will illumine and make plain many obscure passages, heretofore hidden to the multitudes; and now, here in the East, I shall make a version for scholars which will defy all the efforts of fault-finders."

Writing again from Washington, in 1869, he says:

"Do you know a sound man?   If you do let me hear from you. I believe in God, the Father Almighty, maker of heaven and earth; and in Jesus Christ, His only begotten Son, our Lord: and also, I am persuaded that all who so believe, and live righteous lives will be saved.   I believe in one Baptism for the remission of sins, *to all who have sufficient knowledge;* but I think man's obligation is limited by his knowledge.   'To him that knoweth to do good, and doeth it not, to him it is sin.'   Well, I want to see a man who has a soul, a large soul, a soul full of the love of God and of man.   I am sick, John Augustine, of small souls, of cold, narrow souls. I want to see a man with a soul that burns with divine fire, a man who soars to heaven like an eagle, and who can guide me in my solitary way. * * * Daniel was a great man, better than kings, yet he was in Babylon and lived and loved God, without a temple, an altar, or a sacrifice. I tell you, "J. A." that I am of the Scribe's opinion, that to love God with the whole soul, heart, mind and strength, and one's neighbor as himself, is better than all burnt offerings and sacrifices. There is salvation in the love of God, and the love of God is the supreme law."

This letter was probably called forth by certain strictures of the "legalistic" and "ceremonially minded" leaders in Dr. Anderson's communion, who thought that he did not place enough emphasis on Church ordinances, and did not sufficiently stress the dogma, then held by a few leaders among the Disciples, of the absolute necessity of immersion for the remission of sins.

Dr. Anderson preached for the Disciples in Washington during the year 1868 and the early part of 1869, after which he returned to Caroline and spent two or three years at the old home, near where his brother, Dr. Benjamin Anderson, lived, and here for a short time his wish for "a few acres of land—a forest—and a lasting spring" was realized to some extent. Here, amid the scenes of his childhood and youth, he spent many hours in translating and other literary pursuits.

After this brief sojourn in Caroline he returned to Washington, where he died on September 19, 1872. The "dust and ashes" of this distinguished son of Caroline rests in Glenwood Cemetery near the National Capitol.

REV. E. H. ROWE

Rev. E. H. Rowe, son of Rev. John G. Rowe and Margaret Ann Purcell, his wife, was born on September 17, 1857, in Westmoreland county, his father at that time being pastor of the Methodist Churches of that county. Shortly after the Civil War the family returned to Bowling Green and here the subject of this sketch grew to manhood.

Rev. E. H. Rowe received his preparatory training in private schools of Caroline, after which he attended Randolph-Macon College, the University of Virginia, and Princeton University. He attended the last named institution after he had entered the ministry of the Methodist Episcopal Church, South, withdrawing temporarily from the active pastorate for this purpose. The following quotation from a letter written by Professor Thomas R. Price, M. A., LL. D., Professor of Greek in the University of Virginia and sometime Professor of English in Columbia, of New York City, which letter was for some time in the possession of the author, indicates the high standing of Mr. Rowe in the University of Virginia.

UNIVERSITY, VA., 2 February, 1880

" My dear Rowe:

" It was a grief to me to learn that you had made up your mind not to return to us. I shall miss you from your place in my class, and, as I had hoped, in my list of graduates. But I do not doubt that you have acted wisely: and your education is already ample for you to make of yourself whatever you wish to become. If, as you propose, you go into the Church, your excellent English style, accurate and simple, will be your best outfit: and your knowledge of Greek, and, as I believe, of Latin, will enable you to carry on your professional studies to any extent, and to become a distinct force in giving to our somewhat narrow and degraded forms of religion a wider, truer and nobler development. One man now who is capable of dealing with the sacred texts of Christianity and with the early records of the primitive Church, as an accurate and scholarly interpreter of what they mean, is worth an hundred who in their blind ignorance go on narrowing and degrading the faith into erroneous perversions.   *   *   *

" (Signed)   THOS. R. PRICE."

In 1879, Mr. Rowe was licensed to preach by the Bowling Green Quarterly Conference, Rev. L. Rosser, Presiding Elder, and became a member of the Virginia Conference in 1884. His first appointment, as pastor, was to the Church in Murfreesboro, N. C., where he served for two years, resigning at the end of the second year to enter Princeton University for special courses.

On returning from Princeton Mr. Rowe was appointed to the Boydton (Virginia) Church, but after one year of service he retired from the itineracy, on account of increasing ill health, and was given an educational appointment, by his Conference, to the Bowling Green Seminary, Bowling Green, Va., of which institution he became principal in 1888.

In 1894, Mr. Rowe was elected President of Wesleyan Female College at Macon, Ga., the oldest female college in the South, and served in this capacity for two years. On his acceptance of the presidency of this school Bishop A. G. Haygood, a member of the Board of Trustees, said, "I believe you are the providential man for our college." Upon his retirement from the presidency, Rev. W. P. Lovejoy, also a member of the Board of Trustees, wrote, "I believe you have proved to be the providential man for us," and the Board of Trustees, as a body, passed resolutions in "appreciation of the able, faithful, and successful services" rendered to the institution. While President of Wesleyan Female College Mr. Rowe was a member of the South Georgia Conference of the Methodist Episcopal Church, South.

Mr. Rowe was elected President of Martha Washington College, Abingdon, Va., upon his retirement from Wesleyan in 1896, but before entering upon his duties resigned the position to take up again the presidency of Bowling Green Seminary. Upon returning to Bowling Green larger plans were made for the Seminary, and, in keeping with the enlarged plans, the name of the institution was changed to Southern Seminary.

The Southern Seminary prospered in Bowling Green until 1901, when it was moved to Buena Vista, Va., where it still flourishes. An editorial in the *Baltimore and Richmond Christian Advocate* of June 4, 1914, said in part: "We most cordially congratulate Rev. E. H. Rowe upon the completion of twenty-five years as the head of the Southern Seminary. During that period Dr. Rowe has rendered faithful and efficient service in the field of education, and so wisely administered the affairs of the institution over which he presides that it has grown to be one of the largest and most prosperous schools for young ladies in the State.

"The pupils of the Southern Seminary come from every section of the country, and its patrons render most unqualified endorsement of its work. The commencement exercises of this year (1914) were of special interest, marking the closing of the forty-seventh session and commemorating the twenty-fifth year of Dr. Rowe's administration. Addresses were delivered by Dr. Joshua Stansfield, pastor of the Meridian-Street Methodist Church of Indianapolis, and by Senator Robert M. LaFollette of Wisconsin."

In 1922, Dr. Rowe sold Southern Seminary, and, at the Annual Conference of Virginia in 1922, addressed the presiding Bishop (W. A. Candler, of Georgia) as follows:

"Though I have severed my connection with Southern Seminary, I have not retired from the field of education. I have mapped out work enough to fill my time even though I shall live to the green old age of my mother, who died in her eighty-fourth year; and, whether so or not, it has seemed to me more important than any other work of the Church."

The Bishop accordingly appointed Dr. Rowe to such a relationship in the Conference as would enable him to continue his work of education in a new field, whereupon he (Dr. Rowe) retired to his plantation—"Holly Hill"—to give himself to the task of working out the principles of his proposed reforms in education, and for the publication of the same under the title "A New System of Complete Education."

The proposed reforms embraced in the "New System of Complete Education" were first definitely set forth by Dr. Rowe at the Annual Virginia Conference of the Methodist Episcopal Church, South, in 1916, in the following resolutions:

"While rejoicing in the inauguration of a Conference-wide evangelistic movement, which we heartily endorse, * * we are coming, at the same time, to see more and more clearly that Christ came not simply to 'pluck brands from the burning,' but rather to build up an order of spiritual life and character that will exemplify the spirit and ideals of the Sermon on the Mount * * * . And since the chief hope for such a type of character is out of the first and unspoiled life of childhood and youth * * * ; therefore,

"*Resolved*, First, That we will give ourselves to the spiritual education of the young life of the Church through all of the Church organizations, especially through the Sunday school.

"Second, That we will endeavor to influence all institutions of learning to establish a distinct department of spiritual education * * * which shall have for its great aim the systematic development and training of the spiritual nature * * * using the same definite, sustained and philosophic methods which are being used by our modern educational system for the development of the physical and intellectual nature * * * that the faculties of the soul may thus be given an equal chance with the mental and physical to come to their full perfection."

(See Virginia Conference Annual of 1916).

H. C.-10

No further action was taken on this matter by the Virginia Conference during the next four or five years, notwithstanding the fact that the question was constantly kept to the front by Mr. Rowe, who regularly presented resolutions and memorials touching the matter to Annual and General Conferences. The idea made progress, however, and won the approval of many leading educators and churchmen.

In 1921, the Virginia Conference definitely placed its approval on Mr. Rowe's proposed reforms, and memorialized the General Conference of 1922, in the following words:

"The Virginia Conference memorializes the General Conference to create a commission of five or more, for investigations and recommendation for such a reform in the existing system of education as will give to the spiritual nature of man a place of as much prominence at least as the intellectual, and will provide that the education of the spiritual nature shall begin at the same time as that of the intellectual, and shall continue co-ordinate to the end of the course of education. Second, that the Methodist Episcopal Church, and other denominations, be requested to co-operate by the appointment of like commissions."

A still more notable advance of this educational idea was made in the Annual Virginia Conference of the Methodist Episcopal Church, South, held in Norfolk in 1922, when this Conference created the commission for which Dr. Rowe had so long contended, placing thereon such eminent educators as Dr. R. E. Blackwell, President of Randolph-Macon College; Dr. Dice Anderson, President of Randolph-Macon Woman's College, and Dr. J. W. Moore.

Dr. Rowe married (1) Miss Emma B. Scott, of Bowling Green, in 1861, who died in 1884, leaving one child, Scott Rowe; (2) Mary Winslow Shaw, of Massachusetts in 1888, by whom he had four children, two of whom—Orra Curtis (Mrs. F. E. Coyne, Jr.,) and Edgar H., Jr.—still survive; and (3) Frances Walker Hunter, of Tennessee, in 1908, by whom he has a son and daughter, John Rufus and Frances Hunter. Dr. Rowe has one brother, Mr. Purcell Rowe, who lives in California, and three sisters, Mesdames J. T. Richards, B. F. Smoot and A. A. Anderson, who reside in Caroline.

HENRY WISE TRIBBLE

Henry Wise Tribble was born in Caroline county on February 8, 1862, and was educated in Richmond College and in the Southern Baptist Theological Seminary, Louisville, Ky. He won the Frances Gwin Philosophy Medal at Richmond College at the time of his graduation in 1884, and on June 15, 1885, he was ordained to the Gospel ministry in Carmel Church, Caroline county.

His first charge was in Appomattox county, Va., where he served Liberty and Hebron Churches for one year before his graduation from the Seminary. Upon graduation he became pastor at Jackson, Tenn. where he remained until 1895 when he became the pastor of First Baptist Church, Charlottesville, Va. Here at the seat of the University he duplicated the splendid work he had done in the college town of Jackson.

After five successful years at First Church, of Charlottesville, Dr. Tribble led in the organization of High-Street Baptist Church which he subsequently served as pastor for eight years. During this period High-Street Church grew from a congregation of fifty to three hundred and fifty, and acquired an excellent house of worship. During the High Street pastorate Dr. Tribble had upon his shoulders the additional burden of the presidency of Rawlings Institute, which school he kept full of students and in flourishing condition. While in Charlottesville he frequently preached in the University Chapel, whose pulpit is filled from Sunday to Sunday by distingushed men of all States and all denominations, and was regarded by the University community as the peer of the ablest visitors.

After thirteen years in Charlottesville Dr. Tribble became President of Columbia College, Lake City, Florida. While serving in this capacity he attended the Florida Baptist Association at Ocala, and, returning home by way of Rodman, Florida, where he was preaching in connection with his college work, he met with the tragic accident which resulted in his death. An auto truck, using the tracks of a logging road, crashed into the rear of a logging train which had no lights, and crushed Dr. Tribble's leg from which injury he died on February 6, 1912. He was buried on the campus of Columbia College, Lake City, Florida, on February 8, 1912. His wife was Miss Belle Estelle Rawlings, of Augusta county, who, with six children, survived him.

Dr. J. A. C. Chandler

J. A. C. CHANDLER

The son of Dr. Joseph A. Chandler and Emuella Josephine White, was born at Guineys in Caroline county on October 29, 1872. He was educated in the College of William and Mary and in Johns-Hopkins University, receiving the degrees of A. B. and A. M. from the former and Ph. D. from the latter. Richmond College, now University of Richmond, conferred the honorary degree of LL. D. upon him in 1904.

Dr. Chandler's life has been devoted to the cause of education. On graduating from the College of William and Mary he became principal of the public schools of Houston, Va., from which position he was called to a professorship in Morgan College, Baltimore. Here his superior talents were quickly recognized and he was made dean of the faculty and a little later acting president. Returning to his native State in 1900, Dr. Chandler became an instructor in Richmond Woman's College, from which position he was called to a professorship in Richmond College. In 1909 Dr. Chandler was made superintendent of the public school system of the city of Richmond, which position he held until he was called to the presidency of his alma mater in 1919.

In the midst of his busy educational career Dr. Chandler has found time to write and the product of his mind and pen has been of a high order. Among his books may be mentioned, Representation in Virginia (1896), History of Suffrage in Virginia (1899), Geography of Virginia (1902), Makers of Virginia History (1904), Makers of American History (joint author) 1904, Our Republic (joint author), 1910. Dr. Chandler also has the distinction of having been editor for Silver, Burdett & Co., editor of *The Virginia Journal of Education*, Director of History for the Jamestown Exposition in 1907, and Chief of the Rehabilitation Division for Disabled Soldiers under the Federal Board for Vocational Education.

Dr. Chandler was married to Lenore Burton Duke, of Churchland, Va., on July 10, 1897 and had issue three sons. His wife died in 1920. He is a member of the Virginia Historical Society, American Historical Association, Society for Preservation of Virginia Antiquities, National Education Association, Kappa Alpha, Phi Beta Kappa, Westmoreland Club of Richmond and other distinguished societies.

In every educational movement in Virginia during the past twenty-five years Dr. Chandler has been an acknowledged leader. His experience as the head of a great public school system, as professor, as editor of school text books, as editor of the *Virginia Journal of Education*, and as President of the College of William and Mary have phases of the educational life of the State. The development combined to give him an unusually wide acquaintance with all of the public school system of Richmond under his guidance was an outstanding achievement, and marked him for the high honor of the presidency of William and Mary. As the head of this ancient institution his labours have been as fruitful as were his efforts in the Capitol City of the State. From an enrollment of 130 in 1919 to nearly one thousand in 1924 is but one item in the story of the remarkable progress of the college under his guidance. Finances, faculty, and standards have kept pace with the growth of the student body.   His enthusiasm has inspired all with whom he has been associated.

Believing in progressive ideals and methods, he has been among the first to sense the deficiencies of the old regime and lead in a reform.   As a result his influence has been felt far and wide in the United States, and as an officer of the National Educational Association, his counsel has been sought in the questions vitally affecting the educational policies of the country.

Dr. Chandler was one of the few who, two or three decades ago, took an active interest in the preservation and study of Virginia history.   He is one of the leading authorities on the constitutional history of Virginia, and his treatises on the History of Suffrage in Virginia, and Representation in Virginia are most comprehensive and exhaustive.   As Director of History at the Jamestown Exposition in 1907 he prepared one of the most attractive exhibitions on the grounds, due to his familiarity with the history of the State.   It is not too much to say that he has been as great a factor in the upbuilding and development of education in Virginia as any other man of his time.

A. B. CHANDLER, JR.

Algernon Bertrand Chandler, Jr., the eldest son of Algernon Bertrand Chandler, Sr., and Julia Yates (Callahan) Chandler, was born at Bowling Green, Va., May 12, 1870.

His elementary education was received in the public schools of Bowling Green; the Bowling Green Academy, under the direction of Professors Coleman, Rowe and others; the private school of Prof. J. P. Downing, Bowling Green; the Virginia Midland Academy, Culpeper, Va., under the direction of R. R. Powell and John Hart, Sr., and John Hart, Jr., and the Bowling Green Academy, under the direction of Professors Hart and Bain.

Thus, with thorough preparatory training, he entered the University of Virginia in 1889, and was soon a man of mark in all of his classes.   He retired from the University at the end of four years, having won brilliant B. A. and M. A. degrees.   During his residence at the University he won the Orator's Medal in the Washington Literary Society and otherwise distinguished himself on the platform.

Following his graduation from the University of Virginia Mr. Chandler entered upon the profession of teaching (in Locust

A. B. Chandler, Jr.

Dale Academy), but after a brief period he took a course in law in Washington and Lee University, under John Randolph Tucker and Charles A. Groves, noted professors of law, and was licensed to practice in 1895. Upon his admission to the bar he formed a partnership with his brother, John W. Chandler, also a graduate from the University of Virginia, and together they practiced in Atlanta, Ga., for a few years.

While practicing law in Atlanta, Mr. Chandler, upon invitation of the Virginia Society of Atlanta, delivered the Annual

Oration (on the Life and Character of Robert E. Lee) before that Society, being at that time only twenty-six years of age and the youngest man ever accorded that honor.   During the same year he delivered the commencement address before the Georgia State Normal School at Milledgeville, an unusual honor for a man of his years, and an eloquent testimonal to his ability on the platform.

The call of the school soon proved stronger than the call of the bar, and after a few years he returned to the profession of teaching, becoming principal of the elementary schools of Richmond, and later State School Examiner.   While principal of the elementary schools in Richmond Mr. Chandler edited the School Page of the *News Leader* and also served as Professor of English in the Virginia Mechanics Institute, a night school which has given many a poor young man an opportunity to equip himself for greater usefulness in the world.

When the Fredericksburg State Teachers' College was established, Mr. Chandler retired from his position as State School Examiner to become Professor of Latin in the new institution, and so largely did he contribute to the growth and development of the school that, after three years, he was made dean of the institution.   His service in this capacity further demonstrated his ability as an educator and executive, and marked him for further promotion.   So when the office of president became vacant in 1919, he was chosen to preside over the destinies of the institution.

The school, under his direction as president, entered upon an unusual period of prosperity, and the first three years of his administration brought remarkable expansion and development. A 50,000 gallon steel water tank was constructed; an independent gas line was laid to the kitchens and Home Economics Department; a moving picture machine was installed, new seats added to the auditorium; a Faculty Home Annex was erected; many concrete walkways and asphalt driveways were built; a cold storage and ice manufacturing plant added; a central program clock, auxiliary clock and gong system were installed, and the most beautiful open air theatre in Virginia was constructed.

The educational standard of the school kept pace with the external improvements.   All high school studies were eliminated and the school placed on a strict professional basis; a commercial teacher training course was added—the only institution of its

Birthplace and Old Home of A. B. Chandler, Jr.

kind in Virginia offering such a course; four differentiated four-
year degree courses were added, summer school extended to
12 weeks, a full quarter, with both junior and senior courses;
four differentiated practice schools were secured; several new
professors were added to the faculty; a splendid athletic program

was inaugurated; the enrollment doubled, and a distinctive school spirit built up.

In his work as President of the Fredericksburg institution, and in other fields of endeavor as well, Mr. Chandler has been ably assisted and encouraged by his wife, a woman of rare grace and charm, fitted by birth and training to adorn any circle of society, and who, before her marriage, was Miss Blanche Montgomery, of Warsaw, Va.

In addition to his outstanding work as educator, Mr. Chandler has made splendid contributions to the life of Virginia, both on the platform and with the pen.   He is the author of the Virginia Supplement to Frye's Higher Geography, "Rappahannock River Country," a monograph published by Fredericksburg State Normal (1915), "An Appreciation of Matthew Fontaine Maury," "Christian Education the Hope of the World," "The Philosophy of Reading," and numerous articles in various educational journals.

Possessing unusual oratorical powers Mr. Chandler is much sought after by schools, churches, clubs and civic organizations, and frequently addresses meetings held under the auspices of such bodies.   His lectures on "Robert E. Lee," "Woman in History," and "Mother and Home," have been delivered in many places in Virginia, and in other States, and have been enthusiastically received wherever heard.   His address at the laying of the cornerstone of the Matthew Fontaine Maury monument in Richmond, Va., won wide and favorable notice, and was published, with other addresses, in 1923.

Mr. Chandler is a member of Antioch Church (Disciples) of Bowling Green, Va., of which his father was elder for over one-half century, and is in great demand as a speaker by the churches and general conventions of his communion.   He is also a member of the Westmoreland Club of Richmond, and the Rotary Club of Fredericksburg.   As an indication that his fame is more than local, it may be pointed out that he is one of the two men of his city whose names appear in *Who's Who in America*.

CHARLES PICHEGRU WILLIAMSON

Charles Pichegru Williamson, son of Gabriel Galt Williamson and Gabriella Winston Woolfolk, was born in Caroline county at "Holly Hill," the home of his maternal grandfather, Pichegru Woolfolk, on August 6, 1848.

His father, at the time of his birth, was a lieutenant in the United States Navy, and shortly before the outbreak of the Civil War, was promoted to the office of Commander and placed in charge of the S. S. *Fulton* and ordered to Cuba to watch for "Slavers." While serving in this capacity he was shipwrecked off Santa Rosa in 1859, during an equinoctial gale, and one month later died of yellow fever at Pensacola, Fla.

The family of Commander Williamson had residence in the historic Wythe house at Williamsburg, Va., at the time of his death, but at the outbreak of the war returned to "Holly Hill," in Caroline. On returning to "Holly Hill" John, the eldest son of the family, then sixteen years of age, was commissioned midshipman in the Confederate Navy, and Charles Pichegru, who was four years younger than his brother John, was sent to a school in the lower part of Caroline which was taught by his uncle James Woolfolk.

"Holly Hill" was sold in 1863, upon which the Williamson family removed to Richmond. Here Charles Pichegru, though barely past fifteen, was given a position in the Ordnance section of the Confederate War Department. During the last months of the war he enlisted in the Confederate Army and served until the evacuation of Richmond.

After the close of the war he, with his mother, lived for a few months at Elk Hill, Goochland county, Va., in the home of his brother-in-law, Randolph Harrison, who had been a distinguished Colonel in the Confederate Army. In the fall of 1865, the family returned to Williamsburg, where Charles Pichegru attended the College of William and Mary for two years. After leaving William and Mary he decided to enter the ministry in the Christian Church (Disciples) and so, after working for Dean & Somerville, of Richmond, and others, until he had accumulated sufficient funds, he matriculated in the Bible College of Transylvania University, Lexington, Ky., from which institution he graduated with second honors of his class.

While a student in Transylvania University he met and married Betty Johnson, granddaughter of John T. Johnson, a famous pioneer preacher of the Disciples, and a great niece of Richard M. Johnson, at one time Vice-President of the United States.

Upon graduation the Rev. Mr. Williamson accepted the editorship of *The Apostolic Guide*—a church paper of the Disciples—and also the presidency of the Madison Female In-

stitute, of Richmond, Ky. He served this school as president
for ten years and while here became known as one of the foremost
educators of Kentucky. He also preached frequently during his
presidency of the school. Mrs. Daniel Coleman DeJarnette (nee
Willis), of "Spring Grove"—the ancestral home of the DeJarnettes
of Caroline—was a student of the Madison Female Institute during
Mr. Williamson's presidency.

After ten successful years as an educator President Williamson,
upon the advice of his physician, retired from the presidency of
the Madison Institute for rest and recuperation, his health having
become impaired, but after a very brief rest he accepted the
pastorate of First Christian Church, Atlanta, Ga., and in connection with the pastorate, the editorship of *The Southern
Christian*, which was at that time the official organ of the
Disciples of Georgia and adjoining States. Here he served for
ten years in the dual office of pastor and editor, winning for
himself a large place in the life of the city. A physical breakdown
made it necessary for him to retire from the Atlanta pastorate,
and he returned to his native State once more for recuperation.
While in the State he purposed to re-enter the field of education
and so, after sufficiently regaining his health, he became the
head of the old Powell School of Richmond, Va., in which position
he remained for two years. At the end of the second session of
the Powell School under his presidency, Doctor Williamson (he
had received a doctorate at this time) went to New York to
consult a specialist, and caught a severe cold on the boat between
Norfolk and New York which developed into pneumonia, from
which he died on July 16, 1903.

In recognition of his scholastic ability, and his splendid contribution to the cause of education, both Bethany and William
and Mary colleges conferred honorary degrees upon him. He
was a member of the parent chapter of Phi Beta Kappa, and owned
a very superior library, which was loaned indefinitely to his
alma mater, Transylvania University.

Dr. Williamson was survived by his widow, and three children:
Clarence Linden, attorney-at-law; Sadie Gabriella (afterward
Mrs. Robert M. Kent) and Elizabeth Cary, and one adopted
daughter, Gay Braxton, the child of his only sister, Mary Gay
Williamson, who married Charles Braxton.

His widow, Betty Johnson Williamson, still survives and has

seven grandsons, four of whom are the children of her son
Clarence, and three the sons of her daughter, Mrs. Robert Meredith
Kent, of Richmond.

JOHN VAUGHAN KEAN

John Vaughan Kean was the son of the famous Dr. Andrew
Kean, of Goochland county. His mother was Kitty Vaughan.
He was born in 1802, and was educated at the University of Virginia. His father was offered the Chair of Medicine in the
University of Virginia by Thomas Jefferson, but, high as the
honor was, he declined it, and kept the offer such a secret that no
one knew of it until the Jefferson letter was found among his
papers after his death.

John Vaughan Kean married Caroline Hill, of Caroline
county, and established "Olney," in Caroline, and entered upon the
profession of teaching. Dr. L. B. Anderson, of Caroline, who
practiced medicine in Norfolk for many years, published in
Richmond a volume, entitled "Brief Biographies of Virginia
Physicians," in which he writes in part as follows: "When seven
years of age I was sent to school to Mr. John Vaughan Kean at
Olney, Caroline county, Va., about two miles from my father's
residence. Mr. Kean had recently lost his wife, Caroline Hill,
leaving him with two sons, Lancelot Minor and Robert Garlick.
Lancelot Minor Kean died of typhoid fever while a medical
student in Philadelphia, and Robert Garlick Hill Kean became a
distinguished barrister in Lynchburg. * * * In John Vaughan
Kean, my first preceptor, were strongly blended *suaviter in modo,*
fortiter in re. I have seen him weep like a female in reading a
little poem in my spelling book, entitled "A Mother's Gift to Her
Only Boy." Under other circumstances, though it was never my
misfortune to feel its impress, I have had my little heart to bound
and flutter and pause and tremble as his ponderous hand would
fall with sharp concussions on the ears of truant boys. He would
preserve a stern dignity in school hours, and in 'play time'
would mingle with the boys in playing marbles, cat, bandy, and
a favorite game called in our school vernacular 'chumny.'
During these social hours he would relate anecdotes, grave, sad,
and amusing, some of which were illustrative of the life and
character of his distinguished father, Dr. Andrew Kean."

LEE-MAURY HIGH SCHOOL

Lee-Maury High School is located at Bowling Green, the county-seat of Caroline. It was established in 1913 and was named in honor of two of Virginia's most distinguished and beloved sons—Robert E. Lee and Matthew Fontaine Maury. The grounds on which the building stands were donated to the school authorities by Dr. C. S. Webb and Mr. O. P. Smoot, of Bowling Green. Mr. John Washington, County Superintendent of Public Instruction for Caroline, Col. R. L. Beale, Dr. C. S. Webb and Mr. E. B. Travis conducted the campaign through which the funds were subscribed for the erection of the building. One of Caroline's native sons, Rev. Granville Burruss, was Lee-Maury's first principal. He served in this capacity until his death in 1918. The school made great progress under his wise and efficient leadership, and his untiring efforts and splendid spirit greatly endeared him to the community. A bronze memorial tablet was placed in the main entrace hall of the building shortly after his death to commemorate his unselfish life and services.

There were only two graduates the first year of the school's existence, and only one the second year, but since that time there have been not less than five in any graduating class. There were over fifty graduates in the first nine years of the school's history, and all of these, with one or two exceptions, have continued their scholastic work in colleges. Among Lee-Maury graduates are lawyers, dentists, teachers, nurses, bankers and professors.

The school has a fair laboratory equipment for Domestic Science, General Science and Chemistry, and a library of six or seven hundred volumes. Other improvements, chiefly on building, will give Lee-Maury one of the best equipments in the county.

The first year of the school's history the enrollment was approximately 150 with a faculty of six teachers. The number has steadily increased until the beginning of the tenth session found approximately 275 enrolled, of whom about 80 were in the high school department.

GRADUATES OF LEE-MAURY HIGH SCHOOL FROM ITS INSTITUTION
TO DATE (1924)

1914

Frances D. Glassell,   Frank Smoot.

1915

Hermine Coghill.

1916

Thomas H. Blanton,	Louisa Glassell,
Joseph Willis DeJarnette,	Nellie J. Carter,
Bernard Mahon,	Mary Martin.

1917

Lola Bruce,	Charlotte Taliaferro,
Dorothy Cave,	Mary Dudley Williams,
Madge Rixey,	Recer Farmer,

Mary Elliott.

1918

Blanche Broaddus,	John Julius Dratt,
Pattie Martin,	James Pelham Broaddus,

1919

Mary Cook	Maude Boulware Motley,
Gladys Bruce,	Mason Sale,
Agnes Butterworth,	Lee Scripture,
Mary Burt,	Marion Smoot,
Elizabeth Jordan,	Alice Dunnington,
Marion Motley,	Mary Lyell Smoot.

1920

Florence Finch,	Marion Walker Glassell,
Theresa Bruce,	Louise Gill,
Richard Moncure,	Ruby Chenault.

1921

Frances Henderson,	Lucille Jones,
Helen Scripture,	Cordie Lee Moncure,
Charles Webb,	Louise Dunnington,
Heloise Finch,	Charles Brooks,

Virginia Wright.

1922

Elliott Campbell,	Elizabeth Sottesz,
Doris Barlow,	Ada Smith,
Margaret Brooks,	Fannie Taliaferro,
Mae Campbell,	Margarett Webb,
Eugenia Coghill,	Thelma Woolfolk,
Margaret Comfort Dorsey,	Betty Wright,
Elsie Gray,	Russell Wright.

1923

Walter Dunnington,	Esther Eagle,
Perry Penny,	Bessie Motley,
John Smoot,	Louise Motley,
Esther Campbell,	William Webb.

1924

Garnett Martin,	Nettie Taliaferro,
Gwen Martin,	Arlie Borkey,
Susie Broaddus,	Corbin Ridgely Dorsey,
Gladys Andrews,	Joe Leonard McKenney,
Linda Broaddus,	Robert Holberton,
Laura Jordan,	Jean Broaddus.

EDMUND PENDLETON HIGH SCHOOL

Edmund Pendleton High School was established at Doggett's Fork in 1914, with Mr. Henry T. Louthan as the first principal. The school was first named for its location, but shortly afterward the name was changed to Reedy Church High School, after the name of the magisterial and school district in which it was located. Later the patrons set all other schools in Carolina good example by naming the school in honor of Edmund Pendleton, Caroline's most distinguished son (See chapter on Statesmen of Caroline).

The building originally consisted of that part of the present structure which faces the Bowling Green-Richmond Highway, a three-story structure with two rooms on each floor, the top floor being a double class-room, capable of being converted into an auditorium.

In 1916 an addition was built back of the original, and with it, formed an L facing the South. The addition was also three stories high, with one room on each floor. The basement room of the addition was later completed by the students and fitted up as a Science Laboratory.

In 1921 an auditorium was erected back of the main building. The two dressing-rooms back of the stage, being quite large, are used for class-rooms, thus giving the school altogether eleven class-rooms. Below the auditorium is a concrete basement 90 x 30 which may be used for many social festivities. There is a small music room in the school yard where piano is taught.

In 1920 there was erected, about 200 yards from the school buildings, a commodious and modern eight-room house as a home for the teachers. This building is known as the Teacherage and is the only building of this kind owned by any school in the county.

The buildings, lands, desks, pianos, and other equipment represent a value of approximately $25,000. The school opened with four teachers and a small enrollment, but so prospered that within seven years the faculty had doubled and the enrollment increased to 200, of whom over 50 were in the high school department. Twenty-nine were graduated from the school during the first five years, the greater number of whom have continued their education in higher institutions of learning. Much of the success of this school has been due to the efficient administration of Mr. H. T. Louthan and Rev. W. D. Bremner who presided over the school for many years; and also to Messrs. L. J. Head, J. R. Blanton, George Burruss and J. C. Haley of the local school board.

A LIST OF THE GRADUATES OF EDMUND PENDLETON HIGH SCHOOL
FROM ITS INSTITUTION TO THE PRESENT (1924)

1917
Halbert Covington.

1918
Ivy Dale Andrews,
Ellis Bowers,
Ashton Carneal,
Mabel Chiles,
Julian Coleman,
Hilda Green,
Hattie Robinson,
Clyde Southworth,
Gladys Southworth,
Janie Young.

1919
Benjamin Jeter,
George Jeter,
Wheeler Simpkins,
Emma Burruss.

1920
Pauline Bowers,
Lucy May Freeman,
Robert Freeman,
Eugene Jeter,
Lillian Sanford,
Franklin Southworth.

1921
Eula Andrews,
Madeline Allport,
Edith Chiles,
Kester Freeman,
Edith Gibson,
Early Peatross,
Horace Taylor,
Clarice Coleman.

1922
Durward Campbell,
Estelle Campbell,
Floy Head,
Ruth Hutcheson,
Alma Green,
Bernice Pitts,
Boyd Samuel,
Eugene Southworth,
Alberta Taylor,
Estelle Young.

1923

Wesley Freeman,	Thelma Andrews,
Henry Jeter,	Margaret Bremner,
Albert Long,	Gladys Dyson,
Claude Thomas,	Dorothy Head,
Maggie Adams,	Ethel Thomas,
Pearl Adams,	Madge Thomas,

Evelyn Peatross.

1924

Lillian Beasley,	Oswald Covington,
Berlyn Blanton,	Arthur Gravatt,
Gertrude Bowers,	William Hobbs,
Roper Bowers,	Irma Peatross,
Dorothy Campbell,	Marvin Peatross,
Henry Carneal,	Louise Taylor,
Henry Chinault,	Hawes Terry,
Lois Chiles,	Charles Tribble,
Laura Christian,	Mary Tribble,
Wickham Coleman,	Annie Williams.

MICA HIGH SCHOOL

Mica High School is located at Mica in the Port Royal District. This school building was erected in 1918 at a cost of approximately ten thousand dollars. To Mr. W. H. Vaughan belong much credit for supervising the work of erecting the building. It is seldom that a school building of the proportions of Mica school is erected in shorter space of time. It was not decided until June of 1918 that a high school should be erected in the Port Royal District. The specifications were received, the lot surveyed and the work begun late in August, and the building was completed and occupied November 1, 1918.

Mr. R. L. Rosenbaum, of Southwest Virginia, was the first principal. The school opened with 70 pupils and 4 teachers. Of the 70 pupils 23 were in the high school department. There was only one graduate the first year of the school's history—a young lady, Miss Estelle Sale, who came to this school from the junior class of Lee-Maury at Bowling Green. The second year there were 8 in the graduating class, the third year there were 6, and the fourth year there were 18. Within four years the enrollment of the school increased from 70 to 173 of whom there were over 70 in the high school department. Over one-half of the graduates of Mica have sought higher education in colleges.

Laboratory equipment has been installed and the school is prepared to do laboratory work in three of the sciences. A library of no mean proportions has been added and the school made a fully accredited high school.

GRADUATES OF MICA HIGH SCHOOL FROM ITS ORGANIZATION TO 1924

1919–20
Estelle Sale.

1920–21

O'Neal Broaddus,	Madge Klock,
Gladys Gray,	Theresa Vaughan,
Louise Bullock,	Eugene Vaughan,
Minnie Samuel,	Henry Buckner,

1921–22

Lucille Lewis,	Eloise Garth,
Ruth Klock,	Mary Denson,
Ruby Dratt,	William Denson.

1922–23

Ursula Kay,	Alvin Vaughan,
Lucy Ellen Kay,	Emma Vaughan,
Victorine Garth,	Erwin Pepmeier,
Mattie Bullock,	Jack Palmer,
Lucy Hearn,	Arthur Douglass,
Evelyn Mothershead,	Haley Taylor,
Ruby Lee Blaydes,	Everett Sale,
Anna Vaughan,	Milton Sale.

1923–24

Gordon Beazley	Hazel Colbert,
John Brooks,	Alma Dillard,
Judson Dillard,	Ella Marshall,
A. D. Sale,	Nina Marshall,
Elliott Vaughan,	Irene Pepmeier,
Billy Vaughan,	Dorothy Smith,

Mary Kay Vaughan.

SPARTA HIGH SCHOOL

The Sparta High School has the distinction of being the oldest high school in Caroline. This school is located at Sparta, ten miles east of the county-seat, and was established in 1909. An interesting fact in connection with this school is that the building was erected by the citizens of the community, without any outside help whatever, completely furnished with desks and stoves, and presented as a gift to the school board.   The school board added two rooms to the building four years later, making it large enough to meet the rapidly increasing attendance.

In December, 1917, the building was completely destroyed by fire and the remainder of the session held in Salem Baptist church. The old building was replaced at once by a large, modern, twelve-room building, costing $12,000.   One-half of this amount was raised by the patrons.   The session of 1918–19 opened in the new building

In January, 1919, the Board of Education established in the school, under the Smith-Hughes provision, departments of vocational agriculture and home economics.   The basement of the school was fitted up for the installation of these departments, and an adequate agricultural laboratory, equipped with all necessary apparatus for the teaching of practical agriculture was installed.   A separate shop, equipped with all tools essential to the teaching of practical construction and repair of farm implements, and conveniences of iron, wood, leather and concrete was also added to the equipment.   Two large rooms in the basement were equipped for the teaching of home economics.   One of these rooms was fitted up as modern kitchen in which domestic science students are taught how to plan, prepare and serve appetizing and wholesome meals.   The other room is equipped with sewing-machines, cutting tables and fitting closets.   Here girls are taught how to design, cut and make their own clothing, and many other articles which are indispensable to every well ordered home. The equipment in these two departments cost $3,000, of which the State contributed $2,000 and the patrons $1,000.

This school has a faculty of 10 and a student body of about 150, of whom approximately 50 are in the high school department. In an essentially agricultural county, such as is Caroline, the value of such an high school as this cannot be estimated.

GRADUATES OF SPARTA HIGH SCHOOL FROM ITS ORGANIZATION

TO 1924

1912–13

Henry Garnett,	Everett Jordan,
Mattie Carter,	Latimer Beazley,
Aubrey Carter,	Roland Beazley,
Bernice Jordan,	Mabel Kay.

1913–14

Percy Fox,
Reuben Rolph,
Ashby Kay,
Mamie Carter,

Annie Broaddus,
Bessie Brooks,
Alma Brooks,
Ida Kay.

1914–15

Ethel Kay,
Mary Kidd,
Margarett Collins,

Estelle Harris,
Clement Harris,
Ben Carter,
Butler Wright.

1915–16

Nelson Fox,
Frederick Sirles,
Frank Beazley,

Calvin Phippins,
Lottie Kay,
Bowie White.

1916–17

Annie Kay,

Rogers Harris,
Overton Brooks.

1917–18

Eugenia Pitts,
Mary Wright,
Edith White,
Hilda Brooks,

Frank Broaddus,
William Gravatt,
George Collins,
Walker Pollard.

1918–19

Elizabeth Head,
Bettie Broaddus,
Maxie Broaddus,

Harvey Seal,
Floyd Kay,
Louise Fraughnaugh.

1919–20

Hilda Faughnaugh,
Aubrey Harris,
George White,
Lucy Farmer,

Herbert Adams,
Linda Brooks,
Sallie Chinault,
Lucile Broaddus,

1920–21

Margaret White,
Everett Puller,

Phoebe Broaddus,
Clarice Kelley,
Gladys Beazley.

1921–22

Rebecca Collins,
Marion Derieux,
Kate Fraughnaugh,
Virginia Harris,

Elizabeth White,
Louise Moore,
Edward Trice,
Olive Parr.

1922–23

Malcolm Andrews,   Gladys Chenault,
Vera Wright.

1923–24

Helen Moore,   Mildred White,
Myrtle Wright,   Alma Taylor,
Annie Shaddock,   Lucy Motley,
Virginia Fraughnaugh,   Lucy Faulkner,
Wilburn Fuller.

CHESTERFIELD JUNIOR HIGH SCHOOL

Chesterfield Junior High School was established in 1920, and thus has the distinction at this time (1923) of being the youngest high school in Caroline. It also has the distinction of being the only junior high school in the county.

The citizens of Ruther Glen and McDuff communities had felt the need of a high school for a long time prior to 1920, so when the matter of consolidating the Ruther Glen and McDuff schools, and building a high school, was actively taken up by Mrs. J. R. Blanton, of McDuff, the patrons responded generously and soon five thousand dollars were pledged to the enterprise. Other funds were secured from the State, and from local "benefits" and an adequate building was erected near old Chesterfield, from which place the school derived its name.

Mr. A. B. Chandler, Jr., President of the State Normal School for Women at Fredericksburg, upon being consulted regarding teachers for the new school, visited the community and placed before the local School and Civic League a plan for organizing the school as a junior high school under the supervision of the Normal School over which he presided.

Then plan was accepted, President Chandler organizing the school and supplying teachers, in return for which his school was given the privilege of sending its seniors to Chesterfield for practice teaching and observation.

The school opened with approximately ninety pupils. Miss Margaret Jeffries was the first principal. The school has prospered, and with the establishment of a school truck system and the closing of one-room schools, as in other sections of the county, the enrollment will be sufficiently increased as to enable the school to qualify as an accredited high school.

THE COLORED CITIZENS OF CAROLINE

When the Civil War closed Caroline's colored population was as large as that of the white race. Aside from a very few who had lived on rented lands, and who were designated as "free," these people began their career as an independent race with no material possessions. Under slavery the Negro race was free from those cares and problems which attend the struggles for independent social and economic existence, and thus there were grave fears in the hearts of black and white alike as these people, wholly untrained, set about the task of establishing homes, educating the young, and seeking productive labor.

During the first few years following the war nearly all of the Negroes in the South lives in rented houses, and many of them worked as "share-croppers" on the lands of their former masters. Farming, however, offered but little at this period to the newly emancipated people who were desirous of owning their homes, schools and churches, and thus it came about that many of them sought the "public works," as every industry, save agriculture, was commonly called. At this period the railroad passing through Caroline bought large quantities of wood, all engines being wood-burners, and so the cutting of cord-wood and railroad ties gave much work to the colored people of the county, and enabled them to acquire homes far more rapidly than they could have done otherwise.

In securing homes, schools and churches the Negro race in Caroline was, in many instances, greatly aided and encouraged by the white people, while, on the other hand, there were those whose attitude was discouraging. The results of their efforts in Caroline, as elsewhere in the South, have been remarkable, when considered in the light of their economic background. At present (1924) there are nearly seventeen hundred home-owners among the Negroes of Caroline, nearly half of which are un-encumbered. They own approximately sixty thousand acres of land, nearly half of which is improved. There are about one thousand colored farmers in the county. Their land holdings in the county, with the buildings thereon, may be conservatively valued at one million dollars. There are now (1924) about seventeen thousand people in Caroline, the population being quite evenly divided between the two races. In no section of the country do the two races live together in more harmony, peace and co-operation.

The effort to secure homes was no greater than the effort to secure places of worship, for the colored race possesses a remarkable religious sense. Under slavery many of them attended the churches of their masters, and after the war many continued to do so. However, the new status made a continuation of the pre-war custom undesirable. The first attempt of the colored people of Caroline to have a separate and distinct place of worship ante-dates the war. The records show that as early as 1850 the white people of Port Royal aided those who had belonged to Enon Baptist Church (white) to build for themselves. Dr. Charles Urquhart gave the land for the building, and Philip Lightfoot and others gave the material. The servants around Port Royal were given time to work on the building. George Smith, servant of Philip Lightfoot, was made the first leader of this congregation. White ministers preached for them occasionally. Ministers of the colored race were always in charge, and prom'nent among these was one Tolson Johnson, "who could read the Bible."

In 1867, the colored people around Port Royal united and formed Shiloh Baptist Church. Tolson Johnson was made the first pastor and C. G. Jackson, J. H. Satterwhite, Morton Jefferson, Henry Turner and William Johnson the first deacons. This church was burned in 1869 and rebuilt in 1871. Following the death of Rev. Tolson Johnson in 1888, Rev. J. H. A. Cyrus became pastor, and he, in turn, was succeeded by Rev. L. A. Goodloe, under whose pastorate two churches were built, the first one being destroyed by a cyclone. Upon the death of Rev. L. A. Goodloe in 1912, Rev. L. L. Davis, a professor in the Caroline Training School, became pastor and still continues in this office. This church has a membership of 214 and property valued at $4,000.

The next church organization among the colored people of Caroline was the Bethlehem Baptist Church near Mica post-office. This organization was effected the year after the war by Burrell Toler, Elmo Taylor, Charles Barnett, E. J. Roy and fifteen others. This church has been served successively by Rev. J. W. Pendleton (1865–97), Rev. J. H. A. Cyrus (1898–07), Rev. T. M. Allen (1907–22), Rev. E. L. R. Guss (1922—). Beginning in a brush arbour this church has erected four buildings, the present one valued at five thousand dollars, and having gas lights, iron fence around grounds and other improvements. The membership is nearly three hundred.

In 1866, a number of the colored members of Salem Baptist

Church (white) at Sparta, met and formed Jerusalem Baptist Church near Sparta. Four of the charter members of this organization survive (1924), one of them Wilson Young, having been the leading spirit in the organization. For two years Jerusalem Church met from house to house and in 1868 a plot of land was secured and a log building erected thereon. Gabriel Winston, Henry Young, Richard Banks, Spencer Todd, Washington Young, James Pollard, Nelson Garner, Washington Banks, Randall Montague, and others, descendants of the founders, are the leading spirits in the church today. Rev. Gabriel Winston, Rev. Herod Johnson, Rev. H. L. Young, Rev. Spencer Todd and Rev. R. W. Young, have served this church as pastors. The membership is 395 and the property valuation is five thousand dollars.

First Mt. Zion Church, located on the road from Upper Zion to Sparta, was organized in 1870 by James Carter, Virginia Carter, Malinda Lee, Humphrey Latane, Martha Latane, Philip Johnson, Lucy Johnson and others. The first place of worship was a brush arbour, the next a rented building. The present house of worship was erected in 1899 and is valued at ten thousand dollars. Rev. R. W. Young, son of a former pastor, has served this church for many years and has accomplished much in the educational and spiritual life of the community. Probably no colored minister has made a more valuable contribution to the county.

Mt. Dew Baptist Church was organized in 1869 by Rev. Elmore Taylor, Rev. Burwell Toler and Rev. Spencer Kay. The latter became the first pastor. The church was first named Moss Neck Church, from the location and later named Mt. Dew for Captain Dew, who gave an acre of land to the congregation. Rev. Spencer Kay, Rev. John Pendleton, Rev. J. H. A. Cyrus and Rev. L. L. Davis have served this church. The membership is 169 and the property valuation two thousand dollars.

Zion Grove Baptist Church was organized in 1880 by Rev. John Pendleton, and has since been served by Rev. —— Clair, Rev. —— Osborne, Rev. —— Samuel, Rev. —— Barton, and the present pastor, Rev. L. M. Stephens. This congregation worships in one of the most beautiful buildings in the county, which is valued at ten thousand dollars and which was erected in 1917 under the leadership of the present pastor. The membership is two hundred.

Mt. Tabor Baptist Church was organized in 1872 by a council

of white Baptist ministers and the Rev.—— Hart, a white minister, served the church as pastor for some time, having an assistant in the person of Rev. Harrison Smith, a licensed colored minister, who also preached occasionally. In 1876 Rev. L. A. Goodloe became pastor and served twelve years. Suceeding him were Rev.—— Bias, Rev.—— Yates, Rev. R. W. Young, who served twelve years; Rev. T. M. Allen, who served thirteen years, and the present pastor, Rev. R. N. Lawson. The membership is 340 and the property valuation eleven thousand dollars.

St. Stephen's Baptist Church, at Central Point, was organized in 1872 by Rev. Spencer Todd and Rev. H. L. Young, with the assistance of Rev. Andrew Broaddus (white), of Salem Church, Sparta. Like most of the churches, this congregation has had two buildings, the second and present one being the largest and most costly house of worship in Caroline, white or colored. The property is worth about twenty thousand dollars and the membership is nearly three hundred. The following ministers have served this church. Rev. A. Goode, nine years; Rev. E. Freeman, five years; Rev. A. G. Bundy, one year; Rev. E. A. Johnson, thirty-one years; Rev. L. L. Davis, present pastor, since 1917 There are few members of this congregation who have as much as one-half negro blood The people of the church and community are, as a whole, very nearly white and, out of their community, could not be recognized or distinguished as colored people. It is said that the predominating blood in them is that of the Indian and white races. M. W. Byrd has served St. Stephen's Church as clerk for over forty years.

Jericho Baptist Church, near McDuff, was organized in 1877, with Henry Carter, Isaac Johnson and Harvey Nelson leading. Rev. J. M. Hines and Rev. W. M. Washington have served the congregation since it formation. The membership is 146 and the property valuation $5,000.

First Baptist Church, at Guinea, was organized by Rev. Willis Robinson, Rev. J. J. Coates and Rev. George McGowan in 1892 and has been served since by Rev. George McGowan, William Washington, Rev. W. P. Carter, Rev. W. Johnson, Rev. W. L. Hancock and Rev. J. M. Boswell. This church owns and occupies the building formerly owned and occupied by a white congregation known as Bithynia Church (Disciples), which was disbanded about twenty-five years ago.

St. James' Baptist Church was formed in 1867 from the

colored members of Providence Church (white) and is located on the road from Bowling Green to Sparta. This congregation has built one brush arbour, two log-houses and two frame buildings. Rev. L. A. Goodloe, Rev. E. A. Johnson, Rev. C. A. Lindsey and Rev. E. L. R. Guss have served. The membership is about 150 and the property valuation $3,500.

Shiloh Baptist Church, located in the town of Bowling Green, was formed in 1866 with sixty members, under the leadership of Rev. Burrell Toler and Rev. Herod Johnson. There are three members now living who were present at the organization. These are: London Myers, James Baylor and William Fortune. A plot of ground was bought for the erection of a building, but, owing to a defect in the title, was about to be lost when Robert Hudgin (white), who was clerk of the court of Caroline, came to the rescue and saved the lots to them. This church has erected or improved three buildings. The present house of worship and the land owned by the church on which a parsonage will be erected, are valued at fifteen thousand dollars. The membership of this church is 325 and the Sunday school is the largest in the Mattaponi Baptist Association.

St. John's Baptist Church, near Balty, was organized in 1866, under the leadership of Rev. J. F. Wright, who was its first pastor. He was succeeded by Rev. Spencer Todd, Rev. C. W. Berkeley and Rev. C. A. Lindsey. The last named is the present pastor. This church has a membership of 750, the largest in Caroline, and holds property to the value of five thousand dollars.

Mt. Calvary Church, near Milford, was organized in 1899 by W. M. Paige, W. L. Smith, Ralph Coleman, Robert Tyler and Paul Waytes. Rev. Washington Young was the first pastor and was succeeded by Rev. C. W. Berkeley and Rev. M. L. Johnson. The membership is 130 and the property valuation $3,000

Second Mt. Zion, near Dawn, has a membership of 314. Rev. H. Debricks is pastor.

Third Mt. Zion, near Woodford, has a membership of 135. Rev. M. L. Johnson is pastor

Oxford Mt Zion, near Doswell, has a membership of 184 Rev. G. G. McGhee is pastor.

Mt. Olivet, near Lent, has a membership of 96. Rev. W. H. Ford is pastor.

Ebenezer Church, near Chilesburg, has a membership of 257. Rev. W. H. Ford is pastor.

First Mt. Calvary, near Dawn, has 74 members. Rev. J. B. Braxton is pastor.

Mt. Salem, near Penola, has 130 members. Rev. M. C. Ruffin is pastor.

St. Paul's, near Delos, has 73 members. Rev. R. L. Harrison is pastor.

Second Baptist, near Ruther Glen, has —— members. Rev. J. R. West is pastor.

St. Luke's, near Dawn, has 88 members. Rev. A. Williams is pastor.

Rappahannock-Liberty Church, near Return, has 31 members.

Reedy Church, near Penola, has a membership of 100.

THE CAROLINE COUNTY SUNDAY SCHOOL UNION

After twenty-five years of experience in group organization, through the church and Sunday school, and after a few of the younger coloured people had received training in Hampton and Petersburg, another organization was effected which was destined to play a larger part in the developing life of the colored people than any other institution in the county, save the church. This was the Caroline Sunday School Union, which was formed in 1893 under the leadership of Rev. W. J. (?) Turner. The purpose of the organization was to bring the scattered groups of young colored people together to study the Sunday school lessons together and to better prepare this selected group for Christian leadership. Little progress was made prior to 1896, there being at that date only $3.36 in the treasury and only two Sunday schools holding on to the Union. Under the care of Rev. R. W. Young, who took charge of the Union in 1896, a period of growth ensued and in six years, twelve new organizations were added and property valued at five hundred dollars was acquired.

THE CAROLINE COUNTY TRAINING SCHOOL

The Caroline Sunday School Union definitely decided as early as 1902 to build a high school for the colored youth of the county. A tract of land was purchased two miles south of Bowling Green, on the highway, and on October 1, 1903, an eight-months school, under the name Champlain and Bowling Green Industrial Academy was opened.   After one year the word Champlain was dropped and the Bowling Green Industrial Academy operated as a private institution for the next eleven years, under the direction of a board of trustees.   Rev. L. L. Davis was for eleven years the principal of this school and also instructor in vocational agriculture.   During this period many of the leading colored people of the county attended this school and from it went out many young men and women who presided over the smaller schools of the county.   It is conservative to say that Rev. L. L. Davis has contributed more to the intellectual, cultural and spiritual life

Caroline County Training School

of the colored people of Caroline than any other man.   Under the leadership of Rev. L. L. Davis and Rev. R. W. Young the school bought 35 acres of land during the eleven years, erected two buildings and increased the faculty to four teachers.   The people of the county contributed over seven thousand dollars to the school during the eleven years it operated as a private institution.   A few white people in the county lent some aid. Rev. L. L. Davis interested Miss Frances E. Wright, a white lady, who had assisted him during his student days at Hampton Institute and upon her death she left the school five thousand dollars.

In 1914, when sentiment was rising in favor of establishing rural high schools in Virginia for colored youth, John Washington (white), then Division Superintendent of Schools in Caroline, made application for the Bowling Green Academy to be accepted into the public school system and to receive aid from the Slater Fund. Thus the school came to be the Caroline County Training School, operating under the local school authorities. Prof. G. Hays Buchanan was appointed principal and remained at the head of the school two years, retiring in 1916.

Prof. A. M. Walker, of the Colored State Normal, Petersburg, Virginia Union University, and Howard University, was elected principal in 1916 and has presided with ability since that time. The school has added an agricultural building, a dormitory for boys and an administration building of six rooms with auditorium, within the past six years, at a cost of about seventeen thousand dollars. Of this amount the local school board was not asked to contribute a cent.

The growth of the school in material value, great as it has been, has not kept pace with the growth of the school in importance to the cultural and spiritual life of a rapidly developing people. The school fosters the ideal of service, and fully one-half of the eighty-seven graduates of the school have served as teachers within Caroline county. Many have pursued their studies in higher institutions of learning and are now holding responsible positions. One of the graduates, Rev. E. L. R. Guss, is pastor of two churches in the county. For earnestness of purpose and a desire to help humanity a more serious set of workers would be hard to find. That the school is touching the entire life of the colored population of the county is shown by the fact that pupils from twenty-eight public schools in Caroline attend here and in 1922 there was a pupil or a teacher from every community in the county.

The Caroline Training School offers, in addition to ten grades of work as set down by the State Department of Education, courses in agriculture and home economics. In 1922 the high school department stood second in reading and first and second in writing among the eleven colored high schools of the State of Virginia. Graduates are entered without examination in Hampton Institute, Hampton, Va., Virginia Normal and Industrial Institute, Howard University and other like institutions.

COLORED PUBLIC SCHOOLS IN CAROLINE

In the organization and support of school improvement leagues and in the fostering of education among their people, the colored citizens of Caroline challenge comparison with any section of Virginia. For the past twelve years there has been a supervisor for colored schools and much progress has been made during this period, especially in the school buildings and grounds. Practically all of the thirteen two-room schools and the twenty-two one-room schools in Caroline have been remodeled so as to conform to the State requirements. The work in this connection and the cost attached thereto has been cared for in most cases by the patrons of the schools. In some instances aid has been received from the Julius Rosenwald Fund, but in all cases the patrons, under the leadership of the pastor of the neighborhood church, or the supervisor of colored school, have cheerfully contributed to the limit of their ability. Education and religion are the chief interests of the colored people of Caroline. In 1915 the colored school leagues of the county contributed eight thousand dollars to school work within the county. There are now in the county one high school, one three-room school, thirteen two-room schools, and twenty-two one-room schools.

THE MATTAPONI BAPTIST ASSOCIATION

In 1879, under the leadership of Rev. R. C. Kemp, Rev. L. A. Goodloe, Rev. B. F. Robinson and others, the Mattaponi Association was formed at Shiloh Baptist Church in Bowling Green. This body is not confined exclusively to Caroline, but it is a striking fact that Caroline has thirty of the seventy-three churches embraced in the Association. The purpose of this Association of colored churches is "to promote the cause of Christ by fraternal intercourse, mutual counsel and by fostering Christian education, home and foreign missions, and evangelistic work." The seventy-three churches of the Association raised much money for the purposes outlined in the constitution and also contributed to needy ministers and supports a number of boys and girls in the higher institutions of learning. Rev. C. A. Lindsey, a native of Caroline, has been moderator of the Association for many years.

POLITICAL LIFE

The colored people of Caroline, while using the political privileges granted them, have not made politics and political ambitions the important things in life. Two colored men, William E. Crockett and Philip Pendleton, have made the race for membership in the House of Delegates, but both were defeated.

Rev. L. A. Goodloe was appointed postmaster of Bowling

Green under Grant's administration and held the office for several years.   Isaac Morton, Philip Pendleton and J. H. A. Cyrus each served as postmaster of Port Royal.   M. F. Byrd and Wilson Young are at present (1924) postmasters respectively at Central Point and File.   In 1923 there were 450 colored voters in Caroline.

THE CAROLINE COUNTY NEGRO AGRICULTURAL AND SCHOOL FAIR

In 1905, there was formed at the Bowling Green Academy a Farmers' Conference.   This organization had for its aim the improvement of farming conditions among the colored people of the county.   This Conference has met regularly and increased in importance steadily since that time.   Under its auspices a county fair is held annually.   At this fair the several farm clubs of the county place on exhibition their best products.   The county fair was begun in 1914 under the direction of W. G. Young, colored farm demonstrator, and is being continued under the leadership of W. H. Craighead who holds the same office and who is a very capable instructor.

Thus it will be seen that the colored people of the county have made remarkable progress during the past half century. They have learned thrift and economy and have taken on all of the responsibilities of good citizenship.   The two races live in peace and harmony and in an industrious manner the colored people are working out their own salvation along the line laid out by their fathers who formed the present church and school organizations.

William Clark

WILLIAM CLARK

SOLDIER—EXPLORER—STATESMAN

The first member of the Clark family to settle in Virginia was one John Clark, of England, who settled in King and Queen county in the year 1630. He married a Scottish lady from the neighboring colony of Maryland by whom he had two sons— John and Jonathan—supposed to have been twins. The latter was married in 1725, to Elizabeth Wilson, of an English Quaker family in King and Queen and to this union were born two sons and two daughters, the oldest of whom was John 3d. In 1749, John Clark 3d, married his cousin, Ann Rogers (who on her mother's side was related to the Byrds, of Westover,) and settled on "the western frontier" in what afterward became a part of Albemarle county. Here were born the first four of their ten children— Jonathan in 1750, George Rogers in 1752, Ann 1755 and *John IV. in 1757. After seven years of residence on the frontier, John Clark III., inherited the large estate of his uncle John II., situated

---

*Settled in Orange county in "Clark's Mountain" and became the progenitor of the Clark family of Orange county. Two of his grandsons— John W. Clark and Frank Clark—are now living at Unionville at an advanced age.

in the southwestern part of Caroline county and thus returned to the old family seat, where the last six of the ten children were born—Richard 1760, Edmund 1762, Lucy 1765, Elizabeth 1768, William 1770 and Frances 1773.

William Clark, the ninth of the ten children, was born in Caroline county August 1, 1770. At the time of his birth his brother, George Rogers Clark, was twenty years of age, and a surveyor west of the Alleghanies, in the Kentucky colony. Shortly before William Clark reached his majority his parents and several of his brothers and sisters left Caroline county for the newer settlement of Kentucky and here on Bear Grass creek—three miles from Louisville—the Clark family established a new home which they called "Mulberry Hill."

The life at "Mulberry Hill" was similar to that in Caroline, save that frontier conditions were more evident. The "old Virginia hospitality" was transplanted to this new region and in the hospitable Clark home the pioneers and immigrants of the Kentucky movement were frequently entertained.

Soon after reaching the new colony William Clark enlisted under his brother, George Rogers Clark, then General Clark, in the Wabash Expedition and shortly afterward joined Colonel John Hardin's unfortunate expedition against the Indians north of the Ohio.

On reaching his majority, William Clark was commissioned ensign and acting lieutenant and served with distinction in the Wabash Indian campaign under Generals Scott and Wilkinson. Of this particular incident in his career Dr. James O'Fallon, writing under date of May 30, 1791, to General Jonathan Clark (William Clark's oldest brother), says: "Your brother William is gone out as a cadet with General Scott, on the expedition. He is a youth of solid and promising parts and as brave as Caesar." This reference to his bravery was, no doubt, based upon the very dangerous missions to the Creeks and Cherokees, which had just been executed by Clark for the Federal Government. This mission to the Southern Indians was not more perilous than the expedition up the Wabash late in 1793, during which he and his comrades were for several weeks forced to depend solely upon their rifles for food, while for three weeks of this period their progress was blocked by ice, thus adding the terrors of cold to the pangs of hunger.

In the spring following the perilous expedition up the Wabash,

Clark, who prior to the expedition had been commissioned first lieutenant of riflemen in General Wayne's Western Army, was ordered to escort seven hundred pack-horses laden with supplies to Fort Greenville. During this expedition he gallantly repulsed an attack of the Indians on the supply train, with the loss of only six men killed and two wounded. During the same year he commanded a company of riflemen in the battle of Fallen Timbers and in this engagement won further distinction.

Clark's last service in the Western Army was as bearer of a message from General Wayne to the Spanish authorities at New Madrid, protesting against the erection of a fort at Chicasaw Bluffs. The Spanish were much impressed by the dignity and soldierly bearing of this young Virginian. On account of ill health Clark resigned his commission on July 1, 1796, and retired from the army with the brevet rank of captain. Immediately after his retirement he assumed active charge of "Mulberry Hill," which on the death of his aged father passed into his possession. To the management of the estate was soon added the tangled affairs of his famous brother, George Rogers Clark—"the Hero of Vincennes"—against whom numerous suits were being brought for supplies furnished to his troops during the Revolutionary War. To meet these claims, William Clark's loyalty to his brother led him to part with the greater portion of his possessions, including the family seat—"Mulberry Hill." In recognition of his brother's self-sacrificing loyalty, General Clark conveyed to him sixty-five thousand acres of land below the mouth of the Tennessee river, and William Clark in later years, when this tract became valuable, generously shared it with other members of his family.

On July 16, 1803, William Clark received a letter from his old friend and comrade in arms in Wayne's Army, Captain Meriwether Lewis, lately private secretary to President Jefferson, inviting him to "participate in the fatigues, dangers and honors" of an exploring expedition through Spanish territory to the Pacific ocean and assuring him that "there is no man on earth with whom I should feel equal pleasure in sharing them as with yourself." This letter, after one month, reached Clark and was enthusiastically received, Clark replying that, "This is an immense undertaking, freighted with numerous difficulties, but, my friend, I can assure you that no man lives with whom I would sooner undertake and share the difficulties of such a trip than yourself."

Congress, agreeable to the wishes of Jefferson, who had long dreamed of exploring the Far West, appropriated a sum of money to carry the project into effect, and permits were obtained from both French and Spanish officials who had but little knowledge of what the expedition meant—the enterprise having been cloaked as "a literary pursuit."

Clark enlisted a number of young Kentucky riflemen for the expedition, and Lewis assembled boats and supplies at Pittsburg, from which point he descended the Ohio river about mid-summer with his little flotilla and joined Clark and his Kentuckians at Louisville. The winter of 1803, was spent in camp near the mouth of the Dubois river, opposite the entrance of the Missouri.

During this winter Lewis spent much time in the village of St. Louis, consulting French fur traders and others conversant with the new country, while Clark was occupied at camp preparing suitable craft for the long journey, accumulating stores, and organizing and disciplining the volunteers.

On May 14, 1804, Clark started from camp on the Dubois and proceeded up the Missouri, picking up Lewis at St. Charles six days later. The entire summer and fall were spent in the tedious voyage up the Missouri and the winter of 1804 was six days later. The entire summer and fall were spent in the tedious voyage up the Missouri and the winter of 1804 was spent in log-huts among the Mandan Indians not far from the place where the city of Bismarck, North Dakota, now stands.

On April 7, 1805, the expedition left Fort Mandan for the head-spring of the Jefferson fork of the Missouri, not far from the Montana-Idaho line, arriving there August 12, 1805. The rugged, snow clad Bitter Root mountains, which here constitute the divide, were crossed, after which the expedition descended the Columbia river, reaching the Pacific in November.

The winter of 1805, which was spent in Fort Clatsop on the coast, was filled with distress, for, owing to the absence of trading vessels on the Northwest coast at that season, the general letter of credit given by Jefferson could not be presented for funds for relief, and the explorers being in dire straits were reduced to the necessity of making trinkets, practicing medicine and the like, in order to obtain scant supplies from the avaricious natives.

The expedition left Fort Clatsop on March 23, 1806, but heavy snows on the mountainous divide hindered their progress until June and caused intense suffering. The explorers reached St. Louis on September 23, 1806, after an absence of two years, four months, and nine days, during which time they had made one of the most romantic, exciting and significant chapters in all history.

Soon after returning to St. Louis both Lewis and Clark were called to high office—Lewis being made Governor of the territory of Louisiana, and Clark the Superintendent of Indian Affairs in the territory, and brigadier-general of the territorial militia. Lewis is said to have been murdered at a tavern in Tennessee where he was stopping en route to Washington and Philadelphia for the purpose of arranging for the publication of the journals of the great expedition.

Shortly after the death of Meriwether Lewis the name of the Louisiana territory, or a part of it, was changed to Missouri, and General Clark was appointed by President Madison as the first Governor of the new territory, which office he ably administered until 1821, when Missouri entered the Union as a State.

Upon the admission of Missouri to the Union, Clark became a candidate for Governor of the new commonwealth, but was defeated by his old Colonel, Alexander McNair. After his defeat Clark was appointed by President Monroe to be Federal Superintendent of Indian Affairs—an office newly created by Congress—which office he filled continuously until the time of his death, save a brief period in which he held the office of Surveyor General of Illinois and Missouri and Arkansas.

As Federal Superintendent of Indian Affairs Clark exercised sympathy and diplomacy and by his affable and conciliatory manner inspired the confidence of many tribes by whom he was affectionately known as "Red Head."

William Clark's private life was as upright as his public life was prominent and around the St. Louis of other days clustered many traditions of his stern integrity, his deep sympathy with the unfortunate and his advocacy of the rights of the downtrodden.

On January 5, 1808, he was married to Miss Julia Hancock, daughter of Colonel George Hancock, of Fincastle, Va., of whom he had for some time been an ardent admirer and for whom during the great expedition, he named one of the principal tributaries of the Missouri—"Julia's River"—now called the Big Horn. She died in June 1820, leaving him four sons and one daughter and about two years afterward he was married to the cousin of his first wife, Mrs. Harriett Kennerly Radford, who bore him two sons.   Three of his children, the daughter and two of the sons, died while quite young and the others lived to mature years and became the progenitors of many of the most prominent families of Missouri, Kentucky, New York and elsewhere, while from his brothers and sisters left behind in Virginia are sprung the Clark families of Culpeper, Orange and other Virginia counties.

Clark was prominent in the commercial life of St. Louis and was possessed of considerable means.   The brick mansion which he built on the corner of Main and Vine streets in 1818–19, was one of the most imposing of early St. Louis residences.   He was also one of the founders of the Protestant Episcopal communion west of the Mississippi, assisting liberally in the establishment of Christ Church in St. Louis, the oldest Protestant Episcopal Church in the West.   In Christ Church Cathedral, an outgrowth of that early church, there may be seen today a beautiful memorial window on the left side of the chancel, placed there by his daughter-in-law, in memory of his son and her husband, George Rogers Hancock Clark.

Thomas Jefferson was greatly interested in the publication of the Lewis and Clark journals and after the death of Lewis, induced Clark to assume charge of the undertaking.   Nicholas Biddle, of Philadelphia, was engaged to edit the journals and prepare from them a popular narrative.   This publication appeared in 1814, and has become an American and geographical classic.   But it was not sufficiently detailed from a scientific standpoint to satisfy Mr. Jefferson, so he set about to collect the original note books for the use of some future historian.   Such as were collected were placed in the care of the American Philosophical Society at Philadelphia; but Clark, unknown to Jefferson, retained at St. Louis the larger part of his own notes and maps.   These original journals and maps were removed to New York about one-half century after Clark's death, and were discovered there, in the possession of Clark's descendants, at the opening of the twentieth century, by the eminent authority on western history, Reuben Gold Thwaites, LL. D., from whose works the author has freely drawn for the facts contained in this biography.   Through the labors of this eminent historian the "Original Journals of the Lewis and Clark Expedition" with maps were published in full, in seven volumes, one century after they were written and drawn on the long trail.

On September 22, 1906, the one hundredth anniversary of

the return of the Lewis and Clark Expedition, there was unveiled in St. Louis a bronze tablet to the memory of William Clark. The tablet was a gift of the National Bank of Commerce in St. Louis and was placed upon the Broadway front of the bank building, which occupies the site of the dwelling of Meriwether Lewis Clark, which house was the home of Governor Clark in his later years.

The designing and erection of the tablet was done under the direction of the Civic League of St. Louis, which inspired the gift. The safe keeping of the tablet is committed to the Missouri Historical Society. The inscripton on the tablet is as follows:

Here lived and died
WILLIAM CLARK
1770–1838
of the
LEWIS AND CLARK EXPEDITION
Soldier, Explorer, Territorial Governor,
Superintendent of Indian Affairs.
Erected September 23, 1906, The One Hundredth
Anniversary of The Return of The Expedition.

A tall monument in Indianapolis honors the memory of William Clark and both he and his famous brother, George Rogers Clark, have been honored with monuments in the city of Charlottesville, Va.

General George Rogers Clark, known to history as "The Hannibal of the West" and "The Hero of Vincennes" was the most famous of all the distinguished sons of John and Ann Rogers Clark, of Caroline county, and so occupies the foremost place in history; but, rightly considered, William Clark was as great a man as his more noted brother.

George Rogers Clark's conquest of the Illinois country, from which was formed the States of Illinois, Indiana, Ohio, Michigan and Wisconsin, is easily one of the most splendid deeds of the Revolution and indeed, one of the greatest achievements in all the annals of time. And while it is frequently said that "comparisons are odious," it must nevertheless be pointed out that William Clark's last years closed in brightness and splendor, while the closing years of George Rogers Clark were shadowed with gloom. Excessive drinking weakened his last years and poverty embittered them. The Legislature of Virginia voted him a jeweled sword in recognition of his distinguished services to the State and nation, but the token was not graciously received, Clark complaining that the State for which he had cheerfully drawn the sword, mocked him in his poverty by sending a jeweled sword when he needed bread. His dust sleeps in an unmarked grave in Louisville, Ky., the State of his adoption and the State which would have given him the highest honors in its possession had not the habits of his later years disqualified him for the acceptance of them.

The Clark Arms are thus described: On a chev. betw. three dragons' heads erased az.

Crest: A dragon's head as in the Arms.

Motto: Fortitudo.

GENERAL WILLIAM WOODFORD

PATRIOT—SOLDIER—GENTLEMAN

About the close of the seventeenth century Major William Woodford came from England to Virginia and settled in Caroline county on the Rappahannock River. Major Woodford was of the best English blood and bore an ancient coat of arms, described as follows: Sa. three leopard's heads reversed gu. jessant-de-lis ar. Crest: A woodman holding a club in the dexter hand and a palm branch in the sinister, in bend, all ppr. Motto: Libertate quietem.

On September 2, 1722, Major Woodford married Anne Cocke, daughter of Dr. William Cocke, Secretary of the Colony in 1709 and member of the King's Council in 1713, and Elizabeth Catesby, daughter of Mark Catesby, the distinguished naturalist.

Upon his marriage to Anne Cocke, Major Woodford established his home on the estate called "Windsor"—now the property of Mrs. Minnie W. Dew—on the Rappahannock, about ten miles below Fredericksburg. Here the delightful country life of an English gentleman of the period was reproduced. In John Fon taine's Journal of the expedition of the Knights of the Golden Horseshoe are entries indicating that Governor Spotswood and his merry party rested and refreshed themselves here, both as they journeyed to, and returned from the mountains. The entries are as follows:

"22nd. (Aug. 22, 1716) At nine in the morning, we set out from Mr. Beverley's. The Governor left his chaise here, and mounted his horse. The weather fair, we continued on our journey until we came to Mr. Woodford's where we lay, and were well entertained. This house lies on Rappahannock river, ten miles below the falls."

"23d. Here we remained all this day, and diverted ourselves, and rested our horses."

"13th. (Sept. 13)   About eight of the clock we mounted our horses, and went to the mine, where we took several pieces of ore; and at nine we set out from the mine, our servants having gone before; and about three we overtook them in the woods, and there the Governor and I dined. We mounted afterwards, and continued on our road. I killed a black snake about five feet long. We arrived at Mr. Woodford's on Rappahannock river, about six, and remained there all night."

Into this delightful and hospitable home, surrounded by an atmosphere of culture and refinement such as only the best Virginia society could give, William Woodford was born on October 6, 1734. He was trained from early youth in the manly arts of riding, shooting and carving, for without these accomplishments a man was not prepared to move in the best circles of society of that period. Young Woodford also was blest with those educational advantages which only young men of wealth and social standing enjoyed.

On June 26, 1762, William Woodford was married to Mary Thornton, daughter of Col. John Thornton and Mildred Gregory Thornton, of the celebrated Thornton family of Caroline. She (Woodford's wife) was the granddaughter of Mildred Washington, the sister of Augustine Washington and the aunt and godmother of the Father of His Country. It was her grandmother, Mildred Washington, who married Roger Gregory who deeded Mount Vernon estate to Augustine Washington. There were only two years difference in the ages of Woodford and George Washington, whose cousin he (Woodford) married, and it is said that they were the most intimate of friends.

William Woodford's ancestors, for generations before him, had been distinguished soldiers in the British Army, and he seemed to inherit their love of military life, an heritage which he passed on to his son, John Thornton Woodford, who was a Lieutenant-Colonel in the War of 1812.

Woodford had distinguished himself as a soldier in the French and Indian War, therefore it was quite natural that, upon the assembling of Virginia troops at Williamsburg in 1775, his ability and bravery were recognized and rewarded. The names of the three men who commanded the three regiments which were formed consequent to Lord Dunmore's hostile attitude, are high names in American history. William Woodford, who was Colonel of the Second Regiment; Patrick Henry, Colonel of the First, and Hugh Mercer, Colonel of the Third.

Upon the assembling of Virginia troops at Williamsburg, Lord Dunmore, the colonial Governor, fled from the city to an English warship and establishing himself at Norfolk began to terrorize the inhabitants along the coast. The Virginia Committe of Safety in October, 1775, sent Woodford and his Second Regiment, in which John Marshall was a lieutenant, and a battalion of Culpeper Minute Men, to relieve the colonists who were suffering from Dunmore's persecution. Woodford made his way to the vicinity of Norfolk, which Dunmore was further endeavoring to defend by an out-post stationed at Great Bridge. Here the colonial troops were attacked on December 9, 1775, but repelled the assault with the loss of one hundred and twenty men killed and wounded. This engagement caused Dunmore to evacuate Norfolk and seek safety on board a British warship in the Chesapeake Bay.

The correspondence of William Woodford as it is preserved in "The Woodford-Howe-Lee Letters," and in "Miscellaneous Papers 1775–1776" reveals the soul of a great man as well as a great soldier. Many of these letters, especially those written during the latter part of 1775, are addressed to Edmund Pendleton, who was at that time head of the Government at Williamsburg and are in the nature of reports to the Government. Immediately after the Battle of Great Bridge he wrote to Pendleton, then President of the Convention, as follows:

" * * * None marched up but his Majesty's soldiers who behaved like Englishmen. We have found of their dead Capt. Fordyce and twelve privates, and have Lieut. Batut, wounded in the leg, and seventeen privates prisoners, all wounded. They carried their cannon back under cover of the guns of the fort, and also a number of their dead. * * * Lieut. Batut having an inclination to inform the King's Troops of the humane treatment he has met with here, I dispatched Ensign Hoomes (a Caroline man) with a flag of truce, and ye Lieut. Lre, who returned with the enclosed answer from the commander of the fort. The unfortunate Capt. Fordyce was a Capt. of ye Grenadiers of ye 14th Regiment—most of the soldiers were Grenadiers of that regiment—and as the Capt. was a gallant and brave officer, I promised to inter him with all the military honor due his great merit, which I hope will meet with the approbation of the Honourable Convention."

Again on the next day, December 10, 1775, he writes:
" * * * Lieut. Batut commanded the advanced party,

and Capt. Fordyce of the Grenadiers led the van with his company, who, for coolness and bravery, deserved a better fate, as well as the brave fellows who fell with him. All of them behaved like heroes. They marched up to our breast-works with fixed bayonets, and perhaps a hotter fire never happened, or a greater carnage for the number of troops. I have the pleasure to inform you that the victory was complete."

After the battle of Great Bridge, and the flight of Dunmore from Norfolk, Woodford issued the following proclamation:

"*To the Inhabitants of Frincess Anne and Norfolk Counties:*

"The late action at this place it is hoped will convince you that we are able to give you that protection which we were sent down to afford you; and this is to inform all persons that notwithstanding you have taken the Oath prescribed by Lord Dunmore, and some of you have actually taken arms against your country, still, it is not my design to injure any of your persons or properties; on the contrary, I mean to protect them and to afford you all the assistance in my power. For these reasons, I expect you to behave well to all my parties &c.

"Given at Great Bridge, this 11th day of December 1775.

"WILLIAM WOODFORD."

While occupying Norfolk and adjacent territory the colonial troops made no attempt to disturb the British warships which were at anchor a short distance from shore. On the contrary Woodford gave the wives and children of the Tories, who had fled to the ships at the news of the battle of Great Bridge, permission to come ashore in order that they might escape the almost unbearable living conditions existing on the vessels.

Shortly after the battle of Great Bridge, Colonel Robert Howe, of North Carolina, whom Congress had made a brigadier-general, joined the Virginia forces at Norfolk and commanded jointly with Woodford. In a letter to the Virginia Convention, under date of December 15, 1775, Howe wrote:

"The course of service necessarily inducing an inquiry between Col. Woodford and myself respecting our commissions, we found that mine, from the nature of it, had the precedent of his. He conducted himself upon this occasion in that manner which his knowledge of discipline could not but dictate, and with that gentility which never forsakes him. It is with diffidence, sir, that I undertake this charge; and I must add, however honourable, with reluctance, as I supersede a gentleman I so much esteem, whose abilities I know to be equal to the duties of the station, and who hath so amply filled the measure of his duty. * * * I am promised the assistance of my friend, Col. Woodford, whose advice I shall upon every occasion ask, and whose aid I am certain never will be denied me."

Colonel Woodford was active in all military achievements of 1776 and early in that year was promoted to the command of the First Virginia Brigade, which was composed of the "Third, Seventh, Eleventh and Fifteenth Regiments." Among the military orders of the Revolutionary War is one reading as follows:

"Camp at Middle Brook, May 26, 1777—1 sergeant, 1 corporal, and 12 privates to mount immediately as a Guard at General Woodford's Quarters. The Brigade Major will not receive any soldiers for this guard, or any other, except those who are clean and dressed in a soldier-like manner."

The Seventh Virginia Regiment was subjected to a galling fire at the battle of Brandywine (September, 1777) and was literally cut to pieces. In this engagement General Woodford was severely wounded and the command devolved upon Colonel Cropper, who himself was also severely wounded and who, when the American Army was ordered to retreat, could not muster over two hundred men of his Regiment, the others having been killed or wounded.

It was during this engagement that Col. Cropper immortalized his name in American history, by drawing a ram-rod from a musket and tying his red bandanna handkerchief to the end, hoisted it for a flag, the regimental colors having been captured. On the following day Cropper and his sadly decimated regiment, hungry and exhausted, marched to Chester, and on Chester Bridge met Generals Washington and Woodford. Recognizing Cropper, Woodford dismounted and pressing Cropper to his bosom exclaimed, "The boy we thought lost is found." Washington publicly commended Cropper for his gallantry.

During the year 1778, Woodford served as Brigadier-General in LaFayette's Division and the roll-call of officers at White Plains also discloses that John Marshall, afterwards Chief Justice of the Supreme Court of the United States, had been promoted to a captaincy.

At the siege of Charleston, General Woodford was made a

prisoner of war, and was taken on Board a British war ship to New York harbor, where he died in captivity, on November 13, 1780. He was buried in Trinity Church yard, New York City.

From an address delivered in Bowling Green, Va., by Mr. B. P. Willis, of Fredericksburg, on the occasion of the unveiling of the portrait of General Woodford, which was presented to the county by Mrs. Lucy Woodford Herndon, Marion Gordon Willis and Benjamin P. Willis, his descendants, we learn that many original letters and the miniature from which the above mentioned portrait was made, are in the possession of Dr. T. Madison Taylor, of New York City, and that Mrs. Herndon has in her possession a portrait of Woodford as a youth of fourteen years of age. We also learn from this address, which was published in *The Free Lance*, of Fredericksburg, that General Woodford's family Bible and his carnelian studs with gold rivets are in possession of M. G. Willis, ex-mayor of Fredericksburg; that his knee-buckles were made into tiny tea-spoons for his great granddaughter, Mary Catesby Thornton Woodford, who married the Rev. John Churchill Willis, and whose grand-daughters now own these spoons; that the General's rosewood box which he inherited from his great grand-father, Mark Catesby the famous naturalist, is now in the possession of Miss Irene Woodford Gordon, of Spotsylvania county; and that Mildred Gregory's silver puff-box, with her name engraved thereon, which descended the General's wife, Mary Thornton Woodford, is now the property of Benjamin P. Willis, of Fredericksburg.

JOHN TAYLOR "OF CAROLINE"

John Taylor, "of Caroline," was born at "Mill Hill" in Caroline county in the year 1754. W. W. Scott, State Law Librarian, member of the State Historical Society, and for ten years State Librarian of Virginia, in his admirable "History of Orange County, Virginia," says: "Nearly all the encyclopædias allege that this eminent statesman was born in Orange. This statement is, after most careful inquiry, ascertained to be an error. The Taylor family of Orange was a distinguished one from the beginning, which probably gave rise to the statement. A letter from his grand-daughter, Mrs. Hubard, confirmed by his great-grandson, Mr. Henry T. Wickham, seems to establish the fact that his birthplace was at 'Mill Hill Farm' in Caroline; so Orange will have to resign this distinction."

He was orphaned at the early age of ten years and was adopted by his maternal uncle, Edmund Pendleton, who at that time had already become a famous man in the affairs of the nation.

Taylor was privately tutored in the home of his uncle, and afterward entered the College of William and Mary, from which institution he was graduated in 1770.   Soon after graduation he began the study of law in the office of Edmund Pendleton in

John Taylor "of Caroline"

Bowling Green, and so closely did he apply himself to reading and study that he passed the bar examinations and was licensed to practice in 1774.

The public career of Taylor began during the political reformation which was inaugurated by Patrick Henry and Richard Henry Lee, in 1766, when these reformers exposed the corruption then existing in the political life of Virginia, which *expose* was instrumental in launching the campaign which finally broke down the political dynasty which had existed in Virginia for a score of years.

When Taylor had barely attained his majority his ardent patriotism led him to enlist in the first brigade of Virginia troops, under the command of Patrick Henry, whom he greatly admired. Here he served acceptably for a time, and when Henry was relieved of his command in favor of William Woodford, of Caroline, a subordinate officer in the First Brigade, and a more experienced soldier, Taylor, notwithstanding his resentment at the change, remained loyal to the cause of American freedom and saw service at the battle of Great Bridge in December, 1775, under the where the combined forces of Virginia and North Carolina, under the command of Woodford, won a brilliant victory over the British.

Shortly after the battle of Great Bridge Taylor was elected a Major by the Continental Congress and as such saw service in the campaigns around the cities of Philadelphia and New York.

Under the influence of Patrick Henry and Richard Henry Lee, who sincerely believed Washington unfit for the command of the Continental Army, Taylor became greatly dissatisfied with the conduct of military affairs, resigned his commission as major, returned to Caroline and entered the political life of the county, with the result that he was almost immediately chosen to represent the county in the House of Delegates.

Taylor's re-entry upon military life indicates that his attitude toward Washington as a leader underwent a great change. In 1780, while LaFayette was in Virginia watching Cornwallis, who was then in North Carolina, Taylor formed a regiment, or part of a regiment, of volunteers which was sent to join LaFayette's forces. Taylor was made Lieutenant.Colonel of this regiment and was stationed in Gloucester county to resist the attacks of foragers who were working havoc in that section. While stationed here Cornwallis surrendered and the Revolution came to an end.

The war nearly depleted Taylor's fortune and the Government partially recompensed him for his services by granting him five thousand acres of land, but whether he accepted the grant is not of record. On the establishment of peace he turned to the practice of law, for which he had fitted himself in the years immediately following his graduation from William and Mary and was eminently successful in this profession; so much so, that he retired from active practice in 1792, with a fortune larger than that which had been dissipated by the war.

From 1776 to 1781 Taylor was a member of the Virginia Legislature and, as such, added his strength to that of Richard Henry Lee, Patrick Henry, James Monroe and George Mason in firmly opposing the plans of Washington for a more perfect union and a more compact nation. For to understand the life and activities of John Taylor it must be constantly borne in mind that he was a Virginian first and an American second. When the

The Present House on Mill Hill Farm.
On this plantation John Taylor was born. The place passed from the Taylors into the hands of the Buckners.

plan for a National Government was submitted to Virginia, Taylor was one of the very first to take up the pen against its acceptance. George Mason quickly followed with a pamphlet setting forth the dangers of acceptance of the plan; Patrick Henry turned his eloquence against what he termed the "menace of centralization" and Richard Henry Lee shrewdly planned to defeat the "innovation of government"—as he termed it—but all in vain. The new scheme of government looking to a stronger national authority, and championed by Washington and the conservative party, gradually made its way over all obstacles and Virginia became a part of the American nation.

The position of Caroline county in those times, respecting "nationalism" or "federalism" can hardly be definitely stated. It would appear from her action in choosing Edmund Pendleton, rather than Taylor, to represent her in the Richmond Convention of 1788, that she was in favor of the new scheme of government, but, on the other hand, it may be as strongly argued that Pendleton's advocacy of the new scheme was not fully known, or definitely stated, until after he was chosen. Many conservative historians state that all Virginia was carried into the Federalist movement, against her wishes, through a sense of loyalty and gratitude to Washington, who was Federalism's chief champion.

After Taylor's retirement from the Virginia Legislature he bought a large estate—"Hazelwood"—on the Rappahannock river, near Port Royal and devoted all of his time and energies to agriculture. In 1803 he published a volume, entitled *Arator*, which was one of the first books on agriculture ever written in this country. In this volume were suggestions for the improvement of soils, housing of slaves, rotation of crops and conservation of forests, and other live agricultural questions of the time.

Because of this deep interest in agriculture Taylor was chosen the first president of the Virginia Agricultural Society, which organization had for its object the promulgation of such information as would better the conditions of plantation life in the State.

Taylor's retirement from the political arena was short lived. His heart was set against the Federal Constitution, which Virginia had adopted at the behest of Washington, and so he again took up the pen in behalf of the candidacy of William Grayson and Richard Henry Lee, who were aspirants to Congress on a States Rights platform and who were in entire accord with Patrick Henry rather than Washington. So unanimously were the common people in favor of States rights that Grayson and Lee were overwhelmingly chosen the first Senators of Virginia, despite the efforts of the "nationalists" who had the leadership and the wealth of the State on their side.

After four years service in the Senate, Richard Henry Lee, being incapacitated from tuberculosis, resigned his high office and John Taylor was appointed by the Governor of Virginia to serve out the unexpired term. Taylor accepted the appointment and before the expiration of the term, he was regularly chosen by the Virginia Legislature for the office. He declined this honor, we are told, "because he was averse to a prolonged residence at the national capitol." During his brief term in the Senate Taylor was active in his opposition to Hamilton's National bank scheme and also to the meeting of the Senate behind closed doors. He supported a proposal for an investigation of the Treasury Department and heartily opposed every gesture of the Federalist wing of the Senate which looked to closer relations between England and the United States. In this latter contention he was strongly supported by the Virginia Assembly, which not only endorsed his general attitude, but went a step further and specifically instructed him to move a bill in the Senate ordering the sequestration of British debts due from America, as retaliation for England's unfaithfulness in her observance of the treaty of 1783 and also for the unwarranted search of American ships, by British authorities. on the high seas.

It is recorded in Gaillard Hunt's pamphlet, "Disunion Sentiment in Congress, 1794," that two New England Senators—King and Ellsworth—knowing of the opposition in Virginia and the South generally, to Washington's administration, invited Taylor to a conference to consider the question of a quiet and peaceable dissolution of the Union—the East from the South—with a boundary line to be drawn between the Potomac and the Hudson rivers. Although Taylor had learned to think of the South and Southern interests as separate and apart from the nation, he was not prepared for this definite proposal for a separation and so counseled that the Union be given further trial. Shortly after this conference he committed the proposals to paper and this document, in the handwriting of Taylor himself, composed a part of the Madison Papers until 1835, when Mrs. Madison removed it from the collection on turning the papers over to the government. Nearly seventy years later this remarkable document came to light once more and was published, with *fac similes*, in Washington by Gaillard Hunt in 1905.

Upon the expiration of his term as Senator, Taylor returned to his plantation in Caroline and began a systematic campaign, through the press, to further the fortunes of the "radicals" of Democratic party, of which Jefferson, Madison and Monroe were the outstanding leaders. Under Taylor's fostering publicity Jefferson and his Democratic party gained great strength in Virginia and the South generally and won votes enough in New York and Pennsylvania to secure control of the National administration, which control they held for a quarter of a century.

Taylor, however, was not always in accord with the party whose fortunes he had so signally advanced; but, notwithstanding his disposition at times to break away, he was appointed in 1803 to fill a vacancy in the Senate, and during this second term in that body he rendered valuable service to the Administration, especially in the acquisition of Louisiana. He declined to remain in the Senate and although he headed the Jefferson electoral ticket in 1804, it was not long before he withdrew his support from the "Sage of Monticello" because he believed that Jefferson had set his heart on making Madison his successor, rather than Monroe; while, as a matter of fact, Jefferson had long since purposed to make both Madison and Monroe Presidents of the United States, but had chosen to make Madison President first.

Taylor declined to support Madison on the grounds of Madison's "tendency toward Federalism" and bent all of his energies to the furtherance of the political fortunes of Monroe, who, for years, had been his bosom friend. In this effort to elect Monroe over Madison, Taylor was supported by Macon, Randolph, Nicholson, Standford and others, comprising a group known to history as "The Quids." All of their efforts were unavailing and Madison was elected to "the first office" in 1809.

Deciding, however, that it would be "politically unwise" for the defeated aspirant to oppose the new President, Taylor counseled Monroe to "accept the olive branch" when it should be proffered, and so the beginning of the Madison Administration found both Taylor and Monroe "supporting the interests of the party." However, the change of attitude toward Madison's Administration did not deter Taylor from continuing to press the claims of his friend Monroe for the presidency. Rather these things strengthened his cause, for the change of attitude toward the Administration won the support of the new President and also the support of Jefferson who had, on account of the Taylor-Monroe opposition to Madison's candidacy, withdrawn his support to some extent from Monroe. Thus Monroe's political fortunes, began to rise. The Legislature of Virginia, honoring the wishes of the "Sage of Monticello," chose Monroe for Governor and shortly afterward, Madison, noting the enthusiasm with which the people of Virginia received the new Governor, decided to strengthen his own administration by making Monroe a member of his Cabinet. Accordingly Robert Smith, Secretary of State, who was both incapable and displeasing to the Administration, was relived of his position and Monroe invited to fill the vacancy. Monroe accepted this "olive branch" and so safely embarked on his voyage to the presidency. Taylor had written Monroe sometime prior to this that it would be wise to make friends with the President in view of a probable change in the Cabinet, significantly adding, "Our Bureau of State has been accustomed to contain the Presidential ermine." In this he was not mistaken, for in 1816, the end of which he had been working was realized and Monroe was safely elected to the "first office." Thus Taylor's wise counsel, shrewd political planning and unceasing propaganda through pamphlets and newspapers, were more largely instrumental in making Monroe President than any other, or all other, forces combined.

Monroe's election to the presidency having been accomplished, Taylor set about to deliver his State from "the thralldom of Federalism." States Rights had become with him a sort of religion. He could not bear Marshall's "intensely nationalistic opinions" from the bench, nor the "nationalistic teachings" of Clay and Calhoun and John Quincy Adams in the political arena. Hence he again took the pen in an effort to counteract the teachings of "these new political gods" who, it seemed to him, were "trying to pull down the altars of the ancient faith."

His first effort in this direction was the publication, in 1814, of his "Inquiry Into the Principles and Policy of the Government of the United States," which was intended as an answer to John Adams' intensely nationalistic book, entitled "A Defense of the American Constitution." The "Inquiry" had a wide reading in Virginia and the South and ranked him with Jefferson and Madison as a publicist.

Five years after the publication of the "Inquiry" he published another volume, entitled "Construction Construed," which was an answer to John Marshall's nationalistic opinions from the Supreme bench. So favorably was Jefferson impressed with this work that he wrote: "A copy of it ought to be put into the hands of every member of Congress as a standing instruction."

"Construction Construed" was shortly followed by a book entitled: "Tyranny Unmasked," the same being intended as a reply to the report of the "Committee of Congress on Manufactures of January 15, 1821." This volume did not have the reading which the preceding volumes had received.

Taylor's last book came from the press in November, 1823, just as he was about to return to his seat in the United States Senate. This volume, entitled "New Views of the Constitution," was of the same general tenor as his prior works and was intended to discredit the Supreme Court by attempting to show how the purposes of that body had been perverted under the leadership of Chief Justice Marshall. Jefferson and many other States Rights advocates, endorsed the "New Views" and commended the book to the public. This volume was intended to influence Congress touching several amendments then pending and to a small extent served its purpose.

Among the political activities of Taylor's closing years was his proposal to inaugurate a campaign of publicity in behalf of the candidacy of John C. Calhoun, or John Quincy Adams, both Federalists, for Monroe's successor. He explained that he would advocate the candidacy of either of these men, though they were Federalists, "on the principle of choosing the lesser of two evils." Of the manner in which this proposal was received by the great triumvirate—Jefferson, Madison and Monroe—there is no record, but the significant fact that Adams was chosen as Monroe's successor would indicate that Taylor's suggestion was not wholly lost and that for a while, at least, he helped to defer the triumph of General Andrew Jackson, whom he had in mind when he spoke of supporting Calhoun and Adams, Federalists, on the principle of choosing the lesser of two evils.

Taylor's closing years were filled with suffering, but notwithstanding this fact he remained active in public life to the end, being in the United States Senate at the time of his death. He died at his plantation, "Hazelwood," in Caroline county on August 21, 1824. One hundred years after his death, the citizens of Caroline county, under the leadership of A. B. Chandler, placed a life-sized portrait of this distinguished patriot, planter, publicist and statesman, in the Court-House at Bowling Green in recognition of his distinguished services to the State and nation.

Judge Edmund Pendleton

EDMUND PENDLETON

Jurist and Statesman

The Pendletons of Virginia are descended from Philip Pendleton, who, with his brother, the Rev. Nathaniel Pendleton, came from Lancashire, England, to Virginia, in 1676, and settled in that part of the State which afterward became Caroline county.

Edmund Pendleton, whose labors had so much to do with the shaping of the life of the State and nation and who has been termed "Caroline's most distinguished son," was the fifth child of Henry Pendleton and Mary Taylor, and grandson of Philip Pendleton, the immigrant. He was born on September 9, 1721.

Before reaching the age of fourteen years he was apprenticed to Benjamin Robinson, the first clerk of the Caroline County Court, that he might learn "all things belonging to a clerk's office." The following entry made in Caroline County Court on the 14th day of March, 1735, and still preserved in the clerk's office, indicates that the custom of apprenticeship extended beyond what are commonly considered the "trades" and included the sons of families in very nearly every walk of life.

"It is ordered and considered by the court that Edmund Pendleton, son of Henry Pendleton, dec'd, be bound, and hereby is bound, unto Benjamin Robinson, clerk of this court, to serve him the full end and term of six years and six months as an apprentice, to be brought up in the said office; which time the said apprentice his master faithfully shall serve, according to the usages and customs of apprentices. In consideration whereof the said Benjamin Robinson doth agree that he will use the utmost of his endeavors to instruct his said apprentice in all things belonging to a clerk's office, and that he will provide for him sufficient meat, drink, apparell prefitting for an apprentice during ye s'd time."

After two or three years of his apprenticeship had passed, Pendleton was made Clerk of the Vestry of St. Mary's Parish in Caroline and with the small compensation received for this service he purchased law books and read them as he had opportunity and, with his master's consent, was licensed to practice law shortly before the expiration of his apprenticeship.

Pendleton's brilliant career may be briefly outlined as follows: In 1740 he was made clerk of Caroline Court-Martial; in 1741 he was licensed to practice law; in 1751 he became a justice of the peace for Caroline, which office he held until 1777; in 1752 he was elected a Burgess from Caroline; County Lieutenant of Caroline 1774; delegate to the first Continental Congress; President of the Committee of Safety in 1775 and as such was active in the control and direction of military and naval operations and was virtually Dictator of Virginia; President of the Virginia Convention upon the death of Peyton Randolph; Speaker of the House of Delegates which sat under the new Constitution; called the first Virginia Convention; head of the Judiciary Department of Virginia for fifteen years; in collaboration with Jefferson and Wythe revised laws of Virginia, when Independence was declared, in accordance with changed political situation; appointed by Washington in 1789 as Judge of the United States District Court of Virginia and leader of the Federalist party in Virginia until his death.

Judge Pendleton, while Judge of the High Court of Chancery and President of the Court of Appeals, wrote to Madison of John Marshall that "Young Mr. Marshall is elected a Councillor. He is clever, but I think too young for that department, which he should rather have earned by ten or twelve years hard service in the Assembly."

When Patrick Henry applied for a license to practice law Pendleton refused his consent, but after Henry had made many promises of further reading and study, he reconsidered and signed his license.

One of Pendleton's biographers has described him as "Spare of person, but well proportioned; with countenance serene, contemplative and benign; and with an expression of unclouded intelligence and extensive reach which seemed to denote him capable of anything that could be effected by the human mind."

Washington Irving said of him, "He was schooled in public life, a veteran in Council, with native force of intellect, and habits of deep reflection."

Wythe said of him: "His mind was clean, comprehensive and correct. He possessed a most acute and subtle faculty of discrimination. His conceptions were quick, acute and full of resource. He possessed a dexterity of address which never lost an advantage and never gave one. He was always cool, smooth and persuasive; his language flowing, chaste and embellished. As a lawyer and statesman he had few equals and no superiors. For parliamentary management he was without a rival. With these advantages of person, manners, address and intellect, he was also a speaker of distinguished eminence. He possessed a pronunciation uncommonly distinct, a perennial stream of transparent, cool and sweet elocution; and the power of presenting his arguments with great simplicity and striking effect; he could instruct and delight."

Thomas Jefferson said of him, "Taken all in all he was the ablest man in debate I have ever met."

Pendleton married Elizabeth Roy in January, 1741, who died in November following, leaving one child, a son, who died infant. He married, secondly, in June, 1743, to Sarah Pollard, by whom he had no issue. He was greatly interested in agriculture and the records in the Virginia Land Office show that grants in his name embraced nearly ten thousand acres.

The following autobiography originally appeared in the Richmond (Va.) *Enquirer*, of April 11, 1828, and was reprinted in the "Genealogy of the Page Family in Virginia," from which volume it is taken:

"I was born September 9th, 1721; my father died some time before. In February, 1734–'35, I was bound apprentice to Col. Benjamin Robinson, Clerk of Caroline Court. In 1737 I was made Clerk of the Vestry of St. Mary's Parish, in Caroline; with the profits I purchased a few books and read them very diligently. In 1740 I was made Clerk of Caroline Court-Martial. In April, 1741, with my master's consent, I was licensed to practice law as an attorney, being strictly examined by Mr. Barradell. January 21, 1741, I was married to Betty, daughter of Mr. John Roy, against my friends' consent, as also my master's, who, nevertheless, still continued his affection to me. My wife died November 17, 1742. I was married a second time the 20th of January, 1745, to Sarah, the daughter of Mr. Joseph Pollard, who was born on the 4th day of May, 1725. I practiced my profession with great approbation and success, more from my own good fortune and the kind direction of Providence than my own merit; and in October, 1745, my reputation at the County Courts prompted me to make an effort at the General Court, in which I continued until 1774, when the dispute with Great Britian commenced.

"In November, 1751, I was sworn Justice of the Peace for Caroline, and continued to November, 1777. In January, 1752, I was elected as a Burgess from Caroline. I was continued one of the representatives of that county without interruption until 1774, at which time I presided in Caroline Court and was County Lieutenant. In June of that year news arrived of inimical designs of Parliament against the town of Baltimore, on which account the Assembly voted a fast, and were dissolved by the Government. A number of members stayed in Williamsburg, to keep the fast. When news arrived of the Boston Port Bill; t hey collected, and recommended to the people to choose members for convention, to meet in August. I was chosen a member of that Convention, which voted the utility of a General Congress of the States, to meet in Philadelphia the first of September. I was chosen, and attended that Congress, and a second in May, 1775. In August, 1775, I was appointed President of the Committee of Safety, and in December following, President of the Convention, on the death of Mr. Randolph, and re-chosen President of the new one in May, 1776. In October, 1776, I was elected to the chair of the House of Delegates, which sat under the new Constitution. In March, 1777, by a fall from a horse, I had my hip dislocated, and have been unable to walk ever since, except on crutches; however, the good people of Caroline the next month chose me as a delegate, in hope of my recovery, but I could not attend the May session, and another Speaker was appointed, in which, however, I was highly honoured by all the candidates having promised to resign the chair when I should come. I attended on crutches in the October session, but meant then to take leave of all public business, and retire, but the General Court and Court of Chancery being established, I was prevailed on by some worthy members to consent to be nominated as a Chancery Judge, in which I was elected to the presidency of the whole three by a unanimous vote.

" In 1779, when the Court of Appeals was organized, and made to consist of the Judges of the General Court, Chancery and Admiralty, the Chancellors were to have the first rank, and of course I presided in that Court. In 1788, when a new arrangement was made of the Superior Court, and that of Appeals, to consist of separate Judges, I maintained my rank in that Court, and so may be considered as having been now fifteen years at the head of the Judiciary Department.

" In 1788, when a State Convention was to meet to consider of a new proposed plan of Federal government, and all the officers of the State made eligible, my good friends in Caroline again called me to their representation in convention, and that respectable body to preside over them, indulging me in sitting in all my official duties, usually performed standing. Thus, without any classical education, without patrimony, without the influence of what is called family connection, and without solicitation, I have attained the highest offices of my county.

"I have often contemplated it as a rare and extraordinary instance, and pathetically exclaimed: 'Not unto me, O Lord, but unto Thy name, be the praise.' In His providence, He was pleased to bestow on me a docile and unassuming mind, a retentive memory, a fondness for reading, clear head and upright heart, with a calm temper, benevolent to all, though particular in friendship with but few; and if I had uncommon merit in public business, it was that of superior diligence and attention.

"Under the Regal Government I was a Whig in principle, considering it as designed for the good of society, and not for the aggrandizement of its officers, and influenced in my legislative and judicial character by that principle, when the dispute with Britain began, a redress of grievances, and not a revolution of Government, was my wish; in this I was firm but temperate, and whilst I was endeavoring to raise the timid to a general united opposition by stating to the uninformed the real merits of the dispute, I opposed and endeavored to moderate the violent and fiery, who were plunging us into rash measures, and had the happiness to find a majority of all the public bodies confirming my sentiments, which, I believe, was the corner-stone of our success.   Although I so long, and to so high a degree, experienced the favour of my county, I had always some enemies; few indeed, and I had the consolation to believe that their enmity was unprovoked, as I was ever unable to guess the cause, unless it was my refusing to go lengths with them as their partisan.

" EDMUND PENDLETON."

July 20, 1793.

The Richmond (Va.) *Daily State* of May 26, 1881 said: "Judge Edmund Pendleton was the first President of the Supreme Court of Appeals of Virginia, and his autobiography will commend itself as presenting the record of a life which affords an example that ought to be cherished.   Our young men would do well to read his life and be strengthened to follow on in his slow, steady, useful and brilliant career.   Judge Pendleton died October 23, 1803, at the age of eighty-two years, in the full enjoyment of his mental faculties, and almost literally in the discharge of his official duties."

The Pendleton arms bear the following description:

"Arms: Gu. an inescutcheon arg. between D escallop shells in saltine or.

Crest: On a chapeau gu. turned up ermine a demi-dragon, wings inverted or. holding an escallop shell arg."

John Penn

JOHN PENN

PATRIOT—STATESMAN—SIGNER OF DECLARATION OF INDEPENDENCE

In the galaxy of stars which scintillate in the firmament of Caroline's history there is no luminary which burns with greater brilliancy or with steadier flame than that star which represents John Penn, patriot, statesman and signer of the Declaration of Independence.

John Penn, according to Sanderson's "Biography of the Signers," was the only child of Moses Penn and Catherine Taylor; while in Pittman's biography of Penn we are told that he had a sister. He was born in Caroline county, near Port Royal, on May 17, 1741.

John Taylor, "of Caroline" was was several years Penn's junior, is usually referred to in history as Penn's grandfather, and sometimes as his son-in-law, and it is barely possible that the latter statement is true, since the family records show that John Taylor married a Penn, but it is more likely that Taylor married a sister of Penn or some relative other than a daughter. It is no doubt quite true that Penn's mother was the daughter of one John Taylor, but certainly not of John Taylor, "of Caroline." It must be borne in mind that James Taylor, progenitor of the Taylor Family in Caroline and in Virginia, came from Carlisle, England, in 1635, and that as early as the year 1700, the family

was well established along the Rappahannock, in the territory
which in 1727, became Caroline county.

John Penn's father being possessed of a considerable fortune,
could have educated his son in the best seminaries of the time,
but, having a limited education himself and being quite indifferent
to educational matters, the son reached the age of eighteen with
only two or three years of instruction and that received in a small
inferior school which was located near his home. When Penn
was about eighteen years of age his father died and he became
his own guardian, but instead of devoting his newly-acquired
fortune to the pleasures and frivolities, such as were common to
the youth of the period, he set to work to remedy his defective
education. He became a member of the family of his uncle,
Edmund Pendleton, who, at that time had gained wide reputation
as a lawyer, and by unremitting study, aided by the atmosphere
of this cultured and intelligent family, he made rapid progress.
Having purposed to become a lawyer, he began to "read law"
in the office of his uncle in Bowling Green and so faithfully did
he labor toward the goal which he had set that, upon reaching
his majority, his unceasing application was rewarded by a license
to practice law. Possessing keen intellect, facility of expression
and great industry, he soon became widely known for his eloquence
and skill and especially efficient as a "defense lawyer." It is
recorded by Sanderson in his "Biography of the Signers" that
"he frequently drew tears from a court and jury, while his own
eyes were often suffused with tears by the sympathy of his
sensations." Another of his biographers (Lossing) says: "His
practice soon developed a native eloquence, before inert and un-
suspected, and by it, in connection with close application to
business, he rapidly soared to eminence. His eloquence was of
that sweet, persuasive kind, which excited all the tender emotions
of the soul and possessed a controlling power at times irresistible."

Penn remained in Bowling Green until he was about thirty-
three years of age, when he removed to Williamsboro, Granville
county, N. C., joining certain relatives who had preceded him to
that province. Here he found a wider field, and less competition,
for his rapidly developing legal talent and soon became a recognized
leader, legally, socially and politically, in his new home.

The attitude of Great Britain toward the colony had become
almost unbearable at this time and North Carolina was preparing
to secure redress of her grievances or else to throw off the in-

tolerable yoke, and in Penn the cause of freedom found a willing and able champion.

The year after removing to North Carolina he was chosen by the citizens of Granville county to represent them in the Provincial Congress which met in Hillsborough in August 1775.   His pleasing address and facility of expression won the instant favor of the Congress, which recognized his superior ability by placing him on many important committees, among which were the following: (1) To confer with such inhabitants as had scruples against joining the American cause and secure their co-operation; (2) to effect a temporary form of government; (3) to prepare a civil constitution; (4) to review and consider statutes and to draft such bills as might be consistent with the genius of a free people.

The Provincial Congress further honored Penn by electing him to succeed Richard Caswell as a delegate to the Continental Congress at Philadelphia.   The Provincial Congress of North Carolina did not purpose primarily a dissolution of political relations with England, but rather sought first a redress of their grievances, declaring that, "As soon as the causes of our fears and apprehensions are removed, with joy will we return these powers to their regular channels; and such institution as shall be formed from mere necessity, shall end with the necessity that created them."

The comprehensive mind of Penn was attentive to the dark political cloud which hovered over the colony, and sensing England's unrelenting and uncompromising course, he wrote from the Continental Congress in Philadelphia to his friend Thomas Person, under date of February 14, 1776, as follows: "Matters are fast drawing to a crisis.   They seem determined to persevere, and are forming alliances against us.   Must we not do something of like nature?   Can we hope to carry on a war without having trade or commerce somewhere?   Can we even pay any taxes without it?   Will not our paper money depreciate if we go on emitting?   These are serious questions and require your serious consideration.   The consequence of making alliances is, perhaps, a total separation with Britain and without something of this sort we may not be able to procure what is necessary for our defense.   My first wish is that America be free; the second, that we may be restored to peace and harmony with Britain upon just and proper terms."

Penn returned to North Carolina from the Continental Congress on April 7, 1776, and found the Provincial Congress in session. On the day following his return a committee was appointed by the Provincial Congress to consider, "The usurpations and violences attempted and committed by the King's Parliament of Britain against America and the further measures to be taken for frustrating the same, and for the better defence of the province."

This committee framed a resolution, which the congress adopted, authorizing North Carolina's delegates in the Continental Congress to join other delegates in the congress in declaring independence and forming alliances. Thus North Carolina, under Penn's wise leadership, led all other American colonies in declaring for a complete separation from Great Britain.

While in Philadelphia, in the Continental Congress, Penn did not lose touch with his people, but strove by every conceivable means to revive their languishing faith in the American cause, and to dispel the gloom which was rapidly settling over certain section of the province. His deep concern over the state of mind then prevailing in the province is revealed in a letter to his friend Person, a member of the Council, in which he urges him in the following strong language: "For God's sake, my good sir, encourage our people; animate them to dare even to die for their country!"

The overwhelming defeat of the American Army under General Gates at Camden, opened the way for Cornwallis to make his long contemplated excursion into North Carolina and so on the 8th of September following the battle of Camden he began his march from Camden to the western part of the State. The patriots at this critical period turned to Penn for leadership in a unique way, investing him with almost unlimited power. This dictatorship he exercised in seizing supplies, in disarming Tories and in animating the despairing people with hope and spurring them into action.

The expedition of Cornwallis into North Carolina was brief and disastrous to the English Army. The defeat of Ferguson at the battle of King's Mountain arrested the progress of the British and caused Cornwallis to retire into South Carolina.

Penn was successively re-elected to Congress in the years 1777, 1778, 1779 and was North Carolina's senior member during the last two years of his service. Like all the delegates, he served almost without compensation. The depreciation of currency was so great that the entire salary of sixteen hundred pounds annually proved inadequate, and a decision was reached to pay the expenses of the delegates and defer fixing compensation to a future time. Being actuated by patriotism alone, Penn disregarded the loss of salary, finding his compensation in the joy of serving his country in the hour of her supreme need. As a member of the Continental Congress he was conspicuous for his regular attendance upon the sessions and for his zeal for the cause of independence.

No legislative body in history ever faced such a staggering task as that which engaged the powers of this Congress. A government with all of its departments had to be created; a currency and credit had to be established; alliances with other powers had to be formed; an army had to be organized and the confederation of provinces had to be brought into a more compact national life. In addition to these legislative labors the Congress purchased horses, wagons, clothing and other supplies for the Continental Army, informed the Committees of Safety in the several provinces of the progress of affairs and, in general, served as financial agent, commissary general and publicist.

Of Penn and his labors in this stupendous task, Sanderson says: "Nature had formed him for the effort: indefatigable, cheerful, optimistic, conciliatory in manner, firm in political principles, and invigorated by an inextinguishable ardour, he passed through the crisis with honour to himself and satisfaction to the State."

On July 29, 1779, the General Assembly of North Carolina directed the Speaker of the House to transmit to Penn its resolution of thanks, which were, in part, as follows: "The General Assembly of North Carolina, by the unanimous resolves of both houses, have agreed that the thanks of the State be presented to you for the many great and important services you have rendered your country as a delegate in the Continental Congress. The assiduity and zeal with which you have represented our affairs in that Supreme Council of the Continent during a long and painful absence from your family, demand the respectful attention of your countrymen, whose minds are impressed with a sense of the most lively gratitude."

Upon the termination of his services as a member of the Continental Congress, Penn became a member of the Board of War of North Carolina, which Board was created by the General Assembly, at the suggestion of Governor Nash, who complained that he received no assistance from his Council in the prosecution of the war.   Mr. Penn, owing to the absence of the other members of the Board, Messrs. Martin and Davis, exercised the powers of this Board alone, until a prolonged attack of illness forced him to retire.   Shortly after his retirement, Governor Nash, feeling that the Board infringed upon the dignity of his office, asked the Assembly to disband it, which was accordingly so done.

In the year 1777 Penn was appointed judge of the court of oyer and terminer for Hillsborough District, but, questioning the legality of such a court, he declined the appointment.   He was also one of the three representatives of North Carolina who ratified the Articles of Confederation in behalf of that State.

In July, 1781, Mr. Penn was appointed by Governor Thomas Burke, his old colleague in the Continental Congress, as a member of his Council, but Penn declined in the following words: "My ill state of health will prevent my undertaking to act in the office you mention.   As I have always accepted every office to which I have been elected or appointed by my countrymen and have endeavoured to discharge the duties which have devolved upon me while in office, I expect my friends will not blame me now for declining the office you have so kindly offered me."

In March, 1784, Mr. Penn was appointed by Governor Morris as Receiver of Taxes for North Carolina, an appointment of high trust, but the position was one which involved much unpleasantness on account of the increased taxation necessary to the conduct of the affairs of the colony; and the constant solicitation on the part of the Receiver's office, which solicitation was essential to the gigantic task of collecting funds to aid the general government, made his life in this office most unhappy.

Finding himself a buffer between the taxpayers and the State legislature, in that he had to be the organ of censure and complaint to the legislature, he tendered his resignation to the Governor, stating his reasons for the same, and retired from the office.

Penn was married to Susannah Lyme, of Granville county, N. C., on July 28, 1763 and to this union were born three children, one of whom—William Penn—removed to Virginia, established his home in what afterward became Henry county and became the progenitor of the large and influential family of that name, scattered throughout Virginia and other States.   Many direct descendants of John Penn are widely known tobacconists in

Martinsville and Danville, Va., and in Reidsville, N. C.   The author recalls that he visited Reidsville, N. C., in the year 1912 and preached there, and while in the city was the guest of Mr. and Mrs. F. R. Penn, whose sons afterward became the heads of the American Tobacco Company.

Brought up in an atmosphere of refinement, Penn was quite familiar with the social usages of the most exclusive circles, and moved with ease and grace in all circles and upon all occasions. His colleagues in the Continental Congress, recognizing his superior social tastes, wrote from Philadelphia the following: "In the social life of Philadelphia we propose that Penn shall represent the whole State."

From Pittman's Biographical History of North Carolina, we learn that Penn, while in Philadelphia, became involved in a personal difficulty with the President of the Congress—Mr. Laurens, a fellow-boarder, who challenged Penn to a duel.   The "affair of honour" was arranged and when the day arrived Penn and Laurens, after breakfasting together, set out for the place of meeting which was opposite the Masonic Hall on Chestnut street.   At the crossing of Fifth street was a deep mud-hole, in approaching which Mr. Penn offered his hand to Mr. Laurens, the older of the two, to aid him in crossing over.   The hand was accepted and the magnanimity so impressed Mr. Laurens that he withdrew his challenge and the matter was amicably settled on the spot.

Penn died in September, 1788, at his home in Granville county, N. C., and was buried near Island Creek.   In 1894 his remains were reinterred in Guilford Battle Grounds, a few miles from Greensboro.   A monument twenty feet in height, crowned with a statue of an orator, holding a scroll in his hand, marks his grave.   Upon the monument is the following inscription:

IN MEMORIAM

William Hooper and John Penn, Delegates from
North Carolina, 1776, to the Continental Congress, and Signers of the Declaration of Independence.   Their remains were reinterred here
1894.   Hewesgraveislost.   HewasthethirdSigner.

James Hoge Tyler

JAMES HOGE TYLER

The name Tyler is of Norman-French origin—first Tiller, then Tyler, the same crest—a demi cat, rampant and erased—being appropriated in books on heraldry to both names. In 1202, there lived a Gilbert de Tiller, and in 1311, a Thomas le Tyler was a member of the English Parliament.

The Tylers of Virginia trace their ancestry to Wat Tyler, who, in the reign of Richard the Second, about 1381, led the commoners of England in what is known to history as the "Wat Tyler Rebellion." So successful was this rebellion against oppressive taxation and other excesses of Richard's reign, that the king sued for terms and was forced to sign a charter abolishing serfage, reducing rent rates and taxes and giving freedom of commerce in market towns. While in an interview with the king, at the king's invitation and under promise of protection, Tyler was treacherously slain and the stout resistance against oppression, having lost the leader, weakened. The royalty-worshipping historians of the fourteenth century, regarding it outrageously insolent for a plebian to make any assertion of manhood, have caused Wat Tyler to fare poorly in history.

The first member of the Tyler family to come to Virginia was Henry Tyler, of Shropshire, England, who, with his wife and family, settled on a small estate in "Middle Plantation"—near Williamsburg, which was granted him for transporting six persons to the colony.

This family has given many illustrious sons to America, among them John Tyler, Sr., Speaker of the House of Delegates, member of the Convention of 1788, Judge of the General Court of Virginia, Governor of Virginia, Founder of the "Literary Fund" in Virginia and Judge of the United States District Court.

John Tyler, President of the United States, and his son Lyon Gardiner Tyler, author, scholar and for many years President of William and Mary College, added further glory to the name.

The Tyler family has been represented in Caroline from the formation of the county to the present day. The old deed books of Essex county and the records of South Farnham Parish, show that "William Tyler, of Caroline county," sold a certain tract of land, lying in Farnham Parish, to Joseph Dunn as early as 1749. This William Tyler died about 1767, and his son William was the administrator of his estate. The County Court of Caroline on November 3, 1767, appointed three commissioners to settle the accounts of William Tyler as administrator for William Tyler, deceased. The County Court record of August 8, 1767, shows that the latter William Tyler was one of Caroline's Justices of the Peace, and the Caroline county assessor's books for the year 1787 show that he was taxed with 1003 acres of land. The *Virginia Gazette* of 1771, shows that he was at that time Clerk of the County Court of Caroline. This William Tyler was of the same lineage as President Tyler, and was the great grandfather of James Hoge Tyler, Governor of Virginia 1898–1902.

James Hoge Tyler was born at "Blenheim," the beautiful estate of the Tylers, of Caroline county, on August 11, 1846. His father, the Honorable George Tyler, was a representative of Caroline in the State Legislature, both before and during the between the States. Mr. A. B. Chandler, for many years Commonwealth attorney for Caroline, in his history of Antioch Church (Disciples) of Bowling Green, which appeared in the *Chesapeake Christian* (Richmond, Va.), of June 15, 1920, says:

"Brother George Tyler was a prince among men. Of all of our brotherhood, during these fifty-two years, I think I am not departing from the truth when I say he was the most cultured of them all. His field of vision was very large, his erudition profound and his judgments liberal and charitable. Learned as he was he could discuss the Bible or the tariff with equal lucidity and hold his end of the discussion in either. He was Chesterfieldian in manners and gave you always a cordial grasp of the hand, while his heart overflowed with love for all men."

James Hoge Tyler's mothers was Eliza Hoge, the daughter of General James Hoge and Eleanor Howe of Pulaski county. His mother dying at his birth, he was taken to the home of his maternal grandparents in Pulaski county, where his early years were spent and after the General's death he returned to his father in Caroline county, who sent him to Edge Hill Academy, then under the direction of Samuel Schooler, of whom see chapter on Education and Educators. From Schooler's academy he was sent to Minor's Academy in Albemarle, where he remained until he entered the Confederate Army.

After the Civil War, Tyler decided to return to the old home of his grand-parents, where he held some property and so was soon settled in Pulaski, where he became active in public affairs. He was elected to the State Senate in 1877 and was a member of the Board of Public Buildings at Blacksburg and Marion, which committee received special mention and commendation from the Governor in a message to the State Legislature, because of the economic manner in which its work had been accomplished.

He was elected Lieutenant Governor in 1889 and in 1897 was nominated by acclamation as the candidate of the Democratic party for Governor of Virginia. His service as Governor was marked by a careful, economical policy, and by general prosperity in the State. As Governor he met all current expenses of the Commonwealth, including those of a special session of the Legislature and a Constitutional Convention; gave an increase to the public schools of the State of $21,000 and increased the Literary Fund by the addition of $68,000 and left in the State Treasury when he retired from office a sum of $800,000.

Among the beneficial measures, which received his support and which were passed during his administration, were the Labor Bureau and the Conditional Pardon System. The boundary line dispute between Virginia and Tennessee was also settled during his administration.

Mr. Tyler was married to Miss Sue Montgomery Hammett in 1868 and to this union were born four sons and three daughters.

His biography may be summed up in the words of the gentleman who nominated him for Governor: "A man whose personal character cannot be assailed, whose political integrity requires no defense, whose record is clear, whose purpose is high, whose bravery and love of country have been amply proven on many a hard fought field, whose fidelity to his party is an inspiration, whose public career has illustrated the Jeffersonian virtues of honesty, capacity and fitness, and whose private life is a benediction."

THE TYLER ARMS

Sable, on a fesse invected or, between three cats a mountain passant guardant argent, a fasces in bend, surmounting a sword in bend sinister proper, between two crescents gules, in the centre chief point a rose of the third.

Crest: A demi cat rampant and erased.

Motto: Solo des Solus.

GENERAL JO LANE STERN

General Jo Lane Stern, son of Levi Stern and Elizabeth Hall, was born at Ruther Glen, in Caroline county, Va., on December 23, 1848. He received his preparatory education in the public schools of his native county and served for a brief period as telegrapher near General Lee's temporary headquarters on the Virginia Central Railroad. He afterward entered Washington and Lee University, from which he graduated in 1870 with the degree of bachelor of law. Locating in Richmond soon after his graduation he became active in the legal profession and prominent in military affairs.

General Orders No. 13, in the Adjutant-General's office of the Commonwealth of Virginia, dated March 16, 1922, sets forth General Stern's military record as follows:

Private, Company "C," First Virginia Infantry, April 12, 1871; appointed Regimental Sergeant-Major, First Infanry, 1876; Captain and Adjutant, First Infantry, April 12, 1877; Major, July 21, 1879; Lieut.-Colonel April 17, 1882; elected Lieutenant-Colonel and Assistant Inspector-General, Virginia

Volunteers April 12, 1884; appointed Acting Adjutant General of Virginia May 26, 1898, per General Orders No. 12, Adjutant General's office, relieved as Acting Adjutant General of Virginia December 1, 1898, per General Orders No. 18, Adjutant General's office.

Detailed for duty as Inspector, State Mobilization Camp, Richmond, Va., per General Orders No. 12, Adjutant General's office, June 18, 1916, and served until abandonment of Camp, October 31, 1916.

Detailed for duty as Assistant to Adjutant General in organizing companies to replace State organizations drafted into Federal service, and also as Inspector of troops on duty in aid of civil authorities, per Special Orders No. 147, Adjutant General's office, May 16, 1917.

Detailed as Acting Adjutant General of Virginia January 29, 1918, per General Orders No. 1, Adjutant General's office, in addition to duties as Lieutenant-Colonel and Assistant Inspector-General; appointed Brigadier General, Virginia Volunteers and the Adjutant-General of Virginia, May 2, 1918, and directed to perform duties of Inspector-General until further Orders, per General Orders No. 12, May 2, 1918, Adjutant General's office of Virginia. Commission vacated by tenure of office of Governor Davis.

Re-appointed The Adjutant General of Virginia February 23, 1922, with rank of Brigadier-General, February 1, 1922.

Resigned March 15, 1922, per General Orders No. 11, Adjutant General's office, March 15, 1922.

Early in 1922 General Stern retired from military service. The story of his retirement is told in the records of the Adjutant General's office of Virginia, in the following words:

CommonWealth of Virginia

Adjutant General's Office

Richmond, March 16, 1922.

General Orders No. 13

1. Upon his own application and satisfactory evidence he has served the required number of years in the military service of the Confederate States Army and the State of Virginia, Brigadier General Jo Lane Stern, formerly the Adjutant-General of

Virginia, is placed on the Retired List of the Virginia Volunteers, with rank of Major General, as of this date.

Upon General Stern's retirement *The News Leader* of Richmond commented editorially, under date of March 16, 1922, as follows:

TOO YOUNG FOR A FAREWELL

"Arbitrary as a rule, classifications sometimes are absurd.

"Witness General Jo Lane Stern. Yesterday, with due formality, he turned over his office to his successor and took his place on the 'retired' list of the National Guard of Virginia. He will have the rank of Major-General and he will merit by the character and the length of his service that exalted title. But it is nonsensical to regard General Stern as 'retired.' He will not even be 'inactive,' as the term is used, either in the army or colloquially. As he transfers official duties to General Sale he plunges into the vast detail of preparation for the reunion of the United Confederate Veterans, of whose local committee he is general chairman. 'Retired?' He never was doing more public service! 'Inactive?' Never was he busier!

"For these reasons *The News Leader* cannot bring itself to review a military record that runs back to the days when Jo Lane Stern was a youthful telegrapher near General Lee's temporary headquarters on the Virginia Central railroad. All that can be said is that when the militia of the Commonwealth most needed prestige in the eyes of indifferent youth, General Stern did much to establish it. When the National Guard lacked vigor, General Stern helped to infuse it. Soldier as well as telegrapher in the War Between the States, student at Washington College under General Lee, one of the few men now living that ever rode 'Traveler,' in the service of the Commonwealth during the Spanish-American War, with the National Guard during the whole period of reorganization, thrice Adjutant-General, kept from the army in 1917–18 solely because he was indispensable to the State, at one time in *propria persona* the National Guard of Virginia because all the units had been mustered into the service— with this remarkable career General Stern would be a tempting subject of comment were it not certain that a man as young in spirit as he is certainly will add more chapters to a picturesque record."

Colonel H. L. Opie, President of The Leader Publishing

Company, of Staunton, and distinguished soldier of the World War, wrote to General Stern as follows:

March 23, 1922.

General Jo Lane Stern,
  Westmoreland Club,
    Richmond, Va.

My dear General Stern:

I cannot note your passing from the high office of Adjutant-General of the State of Virginia, without feelings of the deepest regret. In one capacity or another, I have looked to you for military administration and guidance for upwards of twenty years. I gained my first ideas and ideals of military thoroughness and efficiency from you as inspector general when in the old days you inspected my company with eyes that seemed to search out every defect, but always with the spirit of kindliness and helpfulness.

And when you assumed command of the active military affairs of the State as Adjutant-General, that same spirit prevailed, with a determination to give to Virginia the best Guard units it was possible to have. To your efforts is largely due the spirit and determination which carried our old Guard units through the war to their credit.

You have always shown a realization of the difficulties confronting the various unit commanders and have helped them overcome these in the spirit of true co-operation.

The ending of the late war found Virginia without any National Guard troops whatever, by reason of the fact that the war destroyed the Guard in toto. But hardly had the first troops been mustered out when you set about reorganizing the Guard from the veteran officers and men. In this you were eminently successful and the present Virginia Infantry brigade and auxiliary units must stand as the highest testimonial of your services rendered the Commonwealth.

In bidding God-speed to your passing into civilian life, may I bespeak new activities for your indomitable spirit.

Most sincerely,

(Signed) H. L. Opie.

Brigadier-General Samuel G. Waller, of the Virginia National Guard, writing to General Stern from Front Royal, Va., under date of March 20, 1922, says in part:

"I am delighted that the Brigade was completed before the expiration of your service, and join with you in the pleasure and gratification that so much was accomplished during your unusually fine administration. Personally I am very grateful to you for your constant courtesies to me and your unfailing help at all times. Yours has always been a strong and safe arm to lean upon, and I shall miss your wise counsel and intimate friendship. I sincerely trust that there may be much yet to bring us together in companionship and effort and that you may never fail to realize that as one of your old friends I shall always be with you."

R. L. Purdon, Major, C. A. C., Virginia National Guard, writing from Chatham, Va., under date of April 13, 1922, says in part:

"Congratulations on the signal token of esteem and affection conferred on you recently in naming our C. A. C. regiment the 'Jo Lane Stern Artillery.' This makes me prouder than ever of my association with it. I don't know whether or not I am letting a secret our when I tell you that all the officers in the State are joining in the purchase of a suitable token of our esteem and gratitude for your services to the Virginia National Guard. If I am, please keep 'mum' and endeavor to register joyful surprise when the presentation committee calls on you."

LeRoy Hodges, Major Ordnance Department, Virginia National Guards, and Aide to Governor Westmoreland Davis, wrote under date of March 22, 1922, as follows:
Dear General Stern:

"I wish to express my deep appreciation of your many courtesies to me since my appointment as State Ordnance Officer in September, 1920, which I owe very largely to you. I regret very much, as I am going on in the State service, that I shall not have the pleasant association with you during the new administration that I had during the four years of the administration of Governor Davis.

The Virginia National Guard owes you a great debt of gratitude for your untiring efforts in reorganizing the various units, creating a new interest and developing the splendid morale now found among the officers and men."

The *Index-Appeal* of Petersburg carried the following editorial concerning the resignation of General Stern:

"The retirement of General Jo Lane Stern from the military service of the State is an incident in Virginia history of more than passing interest.   General Stern has been a Virginia military officer since 1871.   In 1870 he graduated from Washington and Lee University, just a few months prior to the death of the immortal head of that institution.   General Stern has served three years in the Confederate army under General Lee, although but a boy.   It was not long after he left college and entered upon the practice of his profession of the law that he entered the volunteer service, seeing in it an opportunity to serve the State in the time of peace.   For many years he was Assistant Inspector General of volunteers, and for several years was Adjutant-General, a position which he now gives up to go on the retired list.

It is probable that General Stern is the most accomplished military man in the State.   Officers of the regular establishment have frequently paid tribute to the extent and accuracy of his knowledge of military subjects.   He has done a great work for the Virginia Military and he deserves the honor conferred upon him by Governor Trinkle in placing him on the retired list with the rank of major general.   In addition to the high position which General Stern has had in the Virginia military for many years, he has long been known as a lawyer of great ability, enjoying a lucrative position.   Socially, General Stern is delightful and advancing years have accomplished nothing in the way of subduing his spirits or dimming his *savoir faire*.

We salute the retired veteran and wish for him many years of life which he has the knack of enjoying so thoroughly."

The *Daily Press* of Newport News, Va., carried an editorial under the caption "General Stern's Service," which reads as follows:

"The announcement that Major General Jo Lane Stern is about to retire from the military service of the Nation and State after a distinguished career of fifty-one years, is of more than passing interest.   It is no disparagement to others to say that General Stern has done more for the militia of Virginia than any other man in the service, and with him it has been a labor of love and duty; not of emolument.   For many years General Stern has had a lucrative practice at the law in Richmond, and ample income for all his needs.   So with him military service was not an occupation, nor was it merely a diversion, but a means of doing something for the public safety and the public welfare. Right well does he deserve the honors that have been bestowed upon him; and he deserves, also, the gratitude of the public."

Many other Virginia newspapers carried editorials and articles concerning General Stern's retirement, indicating the esteem in which he was held by the entire State, and expressing profound gratitude for his untiring services.

In a letter to the author, dated November 16, 1923, General Stern says: "My mother's great grandfather was David Ussery, a Revolutionary soldier of Virginia, and his wife was Eunice Barrett, daughter of Dominick Barrett, of Ireland. I think I must have gotten my liking for military life from these old fighters."

General Stern is a member of Centenary Methodist Church, of Richmond; is connected with his brother, Cary Ellis Stern, in the practice of law; is a bachelor and resides at the Westmoreland Club. He is also a member of the Commonwealth and University Clubs of Richmond and of the Country Club of Virginia.

LEWIS MELVILLE GEORGE BAKER

The first paternal ancestor of L. M. G. Baker, of whom we have an exact record, was Jacob Baker. He had a son, Joseph Baker, who married Catherine Todd, of Caroline, and who established the first female academy in the Valley of Virginia. This school was located at Winchester.

Cecil Baker, son of Professor Joseph Baker, married Pauline Jane George, daughter of Lewis Melville George and Sarah Elizabeth Samuel, granddaughter of Lewis George and Agnes Wilson, and great granddaughter of John Dudley George, Revolutionary soldier, who married Lucy Dickinson. Colonel Archibald Samuel, grandfather of Cecil Baker, on the maternal side, was a soldier in the war of 1812, a member of the General Assembly of Virginia, Sheriff of Caroline and prominent in the social life of the county. Cecil Baker was lieutenant in the Ninth Virginia Cavalry in the Civil War and was killed in action when but little over twenty-one years of age. He left two children, Cecil and Lewis Melville George. Cecil married Mary Linda Allen, of Bowling Green, a half sister to Thomas C., and Aubrey Valentine, and conducted a mercantile business at Athens, Tenn., for some time.   He died in 1920.

Lewis Melville George Baker was born in Caroline in 1864 and was educated in the University of Virginia, from which he received the degrees of Bachelor of Science, Bachelor of Arts, Bachelor of Philosophy and Master of Arts.   He founded the Baker-Himel school in Knoxville which ranked as one of the finest preparatory schools in the South and he presided with distinction over this school for some time.   He entered upon the practice of law in 1900, entering into partnership with Webb and McClung in 1902 and later became one of the firm of Webb, Baker and Egerton.   He ranks among the strong lawyers of the South and is a member of Knox County Bar Association, Tennessee State Bar Association and American Bar Association.   Mr. Baker married Blanche McClung Tomeny and has issue : (1) L. M. G., Jr., (2) William Cecil, (3) Douglas Dudley and (4) Catherine Blanche.   The eldest son served in Battery 3, 114th Field Artillery in World War and his second son, William Cecil, in the aviation department.

The Baker arms are thus described:

Ar on a fesse nublee betw. three keys, sa., a tower triple towered of the first.

BIOGRAPHICAL NOTES

JAMES B. WOOD

James B. Wood, son of Colonel Fleming Wood and Lucy Tompkins, was born near St. Margaret's Church in Caroline county about 1850. His father and mother and his grandparents, both paternal and maternal, were active in the life of St. Margaret's.

Mr. Wood's first public service was in the capacity of deputy Sheriff of Caroline county, under Sheriff T. D. Coghill. He later removed to Richmond where he became prominent in the life of the city, serving on the Board of Alderman for ten years. During this period Mr. Wood was Chairman of the Finance Committee and also President of the City Council. He was connected with the Virginia State Penitentiary nearly twenty years, much of this time as Superintendent of the institution. His son, Jesse F. Wood, is a prominent banker of Richmond.

NICHOLAS WARE

Nicholas Ware was born in Caroline county, Va., in 1769. He received a classical education, and afterward studied law and was admitted to the bar. After a few years of practice he entered the political arena and became United States Senator from Georgia. He was elected and served from December 11, 1821 to September 7, 1824. He died in New York City in 1824. For fuller biography see the Biographical Congressional Dictionary.

FRANCIS JOHNSON

Francis Johnson was born in Caroline county, Va., during the latter years of the eighteenth century. He removed to Kentucky in early manhood, settled in Bowling Green, which had been named for the county-seat of his native county, and practiced law. He was delegate to the Kentucky Legislature, and was afterward elected a member of the Sixteenth, Seventeenth and Eighteenth Congresses of the United States. He died in Louisville. Ky., December 14, 1851.

ANTHONY THORNTON

Anthony Thornton was born November 9, 1819 in Bourbon county, Ky., whither his parents had gone from "Ormesby" in Caroline. He graduated from Miama College in Ohio and settled at Shelbyville, Illinois, where he engaged in the practice of law. He was a Delegate to the Illinois Constitutional Conventions of 1847 and 1862, a member of the State Legislature in 1850, and a member of the Thirty-Ninth United States Congress.

RICHARD HAWES

Richard Hawes was born in Caroline county on February 6, 1797, and, with his parents, removed to Kentucky when he was fifteen years of age. He was educated in Transylvania University and about the time he reached his majority was admitted to the bar. He began to practice law in Winchester and represented the State in the legislature for several years. He represented Kentucky in the Twenty-Fifth and Twenty-Sixth Congresses of the United States as a Whig. He afterward became a member of the Democratic party and an advocate of the Southern Cause. He was installed Provisional Governor of Kentucky on October 4, 1862. He was elected County Judge in 1866 and served until his death, which occurred in Bourbon County May 25, 1877. For more complete biography see Biographical Congressional Dictionary.

SAMUEL AMERY SWANN

Colonel Samuel A. Swann

The Swann Arms

Samuel Swann was born in Caroline county about 1828. He was educated in old Concord Academy and in the University of Virginia. His first work was that of teaching. To him belongs the distinction of having taught the first "free school" ever established in Caroline county.

When the Civil War broke out Mr. Swann became a lieutenant in Company B, Ninth Virginia Cavalry, and in 1862 was promoted to a captaincy. Shortly afterward he was made Colonel of the regiment and served in this capacity to the close of the war.

After the war Colonel Swann became Sheriff of Caroline and representative in the House of Delegates. He was later Superintendent of the Virginia State Penitentiary. He died while attending the marriage of his niece, Miss Shelton, in Goochland county, and was buried there.

Colonel Swann was never married. One of his sisters, Lydia A. Swann, married Cyrus Carson and had issue several children, one of whom, Carrie Lee Swann, married Lewis Dudley George, of Penola, Caroline county, Va.

COLONEL ARCHIBALD SAMUEL

Colonel Samuel was one of the most prominent men of Caroline in his time. He served as adjutant in the War of 1812 and also represented his county in the House of Delegates. He married Nancy Woolfolk and lived at "Bath" his beautiful estate nine miles north of Bowling Green. His descendants are in Caroline county, Va., Tennessee and elsewhere.

L. HAZELWOOD KEMP

L. Hazelwood Kemp was born at "Greenwood" in Caroline county, Va., on September 20, 1851. He was the son of Leroy Hazelwood Kemp. He served as Sheriff of Henrico country for several years and Treasurer of the same county for a longer period probably than any other man. He died in 1924, leaving a son, L. H., Jr., a daughter, Mrs. Miles Selden, and a brother, Walter L. Kemp. He was buried in Hollywood, Richmond.

J. B. LIGHTFOOT

John Bernard Lightfoot was born at Port Royal in Caroline March 29, 1851. He was the son of John Bernard Lightfoot. He removed to Richmond in 1871 and shortly afterward entered upon the tobacco business. He founded the firm of J. B. Lightfoot and Company from which he retired in 1917. He died in 1924 leaving a widow, Mary Washington Minor Lightfoot, two brothers William B., and Lewis H., and one nephew, J. B. Lightfoot, Jr. He was buried in Hollywood.

H. C,.15

REVOLUTIONARY SOLDIERS FROM CAROLINE COUNTY

NOTE.—The following list is not complete. It is probable that a number of names of Caroline soldiers in the War of· the Revolution may hereafter be found.

LEGEND.—A. A.—Indicates that name is found in Auditor's Account. B. W.—Bounty Warrants. C. S. P.—Calendar State Papers. L. P.—Legislative Petition. M. L. W.—Military Land Warrants (in State Land Office). W. D.—Report of War Department, V. R. P.—Virginia Pension Roll, Saf.— Saffell's List. H. D.—Home Delegates. S. W.—Report of Secretary of War. H.—Manuscript Volume. R. A.—Revolutionary Army Muster Rolls. K. S. S. R.—Kentucky Society Sons Revolution. I. P. D.—Illinois Papers. C. J.— Council Journals. (These abbreviations obtain in the Virginia State Library).

Anderson, Richard	Saf.	Boulware, Musco	R. A.
Armistead, William	Saf.	Brown, Wm	S. W.
Athey, John	Saf.	Buchanan, Capt.	S. W.
Atkins, Thos. B.	V. P. R.	Barlow, Joseph	W. D.
Allen, Wm.	V. P. R.	Baylor, Thos.	M. L. W.
Allen, John	A. A.	Baynham, John	W. D.
Anderson, Chas.	A. A.	Beazley, Ephraim	M. L. W.
Anderson, Jno.	A. A.	Beasley, Reuben	W. D.
		Bernard, Thos.	W. D.
Barber, Gray	V. P. R.	Bledsoe, Miller	W. D.
Baylor, Walker	V. P. R.	Boulware, Mark	W. D.
Burk, Matthew	V. P. R.	Boulware, Obediah	A. A.
Beazley, Edmund	V. P. R.	Boulware, Samuel	W. D.
Beadles, Edmund	V. P. R.	Boutwell, James	H. 12
Bradley, James	V. P. R.	Bowers, Thos.	W. D.
Brown, William	V. P. R.	Bowers, John	W. D.
Baylor, George	Saf.	Broaddus, Robt.	W. D.
Bernard, Wm.	Saf.	Burk, Cornelius	W. D.
Boutwell, Sam'l.	Saf.	Burk, John	W. D.
Broaddus, Edw.	Saf.	Burk, James	W. D.
Broaddus, James	Saf.	Burruss, John	W. D.
Broaddus, Rich'd	Saf.	Butler, Samuel	R. A.
Broaddus, Wm.	Saf.	Butler, James	W. D.
Bruce, Jno.	Saf.	Barksdale, Dan'l.	C. J.
Buckner, Thos.	Saf.	Baylor, John	W. D.
Buckner, Sam'l.	Saf.	Baylor, James	W. D.
Bullock, Obadiah	Saf.	Baylor, Wm.	W. D.
Barlow, Joshua	Saf.	Buckner, Philip	A. A.
Barlow, Ephraim	Saf.	Buckner, Sam'l.	A. A.
Bartlett, Henry	C. J.	Buckner, Wm.	A. A.
Beazley, Cornelius	S. W.	Buckner, Thos.	A. A.
Bernard, John	H. D.		
Blanton, John	A. A.	Campbell, James	W. D.
Boulware, Samuel	B. W.	Campbell, Hugh	W. D.

List of Revolutionary Soldiesrs from Caroline County

Campbell, John.........W. D.
Carr, Wm..............W. D.
Carson, Thos...........W. D.
Carter, Joseph..........W. D.
Chandler, Thos..........W. D.
Chapman, Wm...........W. D.
Chapman, Benj..........W. D.
Coleman, Wyatt.........W. D.
Collins, Geo............W. D.
Collins, Joseph..........W. D.
Conway, Wm...........W. D.
Cook, Wm.............R. A.
Cosby, Hicks...........W. D.
Cosby, Thos............W. D.
Coghill, Fred'k..........W. D.
Coghill, James..........W. D.
Coghill, Robt...........W. D.
Cox, John.............W. D.
Cox, Jeremiah..........W. D.
Cox, Thomas...........A. A.
Clark, Robert..........V. P. R.
Coleman, James........V. P. R.
Carter, John...........V. P. R.
Coates, Wm...........V. P. R.
Campbell, Sam'l........S.
Campbell, Rich'd.......Saf.
Carson, John...........Saf.
Carson, Daniel.........Saf.
Carter, Wm............Saf.
Carter, Thos...........Saf.
Carter, Sam'l..........Saf.
Catlett, Thos...........Saf.
Chandler, Robt.........Saf.
Chapman, John.........Saf.
Chapman, Thos.........Saf.
Clark, Wm.............Saf.
Clark, John............Saf.
Coates, James..........Saf.
Coleman, Nathan'l......Saf.
Coleman, Rich'd........Saf.
Corbin, Isaiah..........Saf.
Conway, Joseph........Saf.
Chandler, Jesse.........B. W.
Chandler, Rich'd........B. W.
Chandler, Wm..........B. W.
Chapman, Reuben......B. W.
Chewning, Robt........A. A.
Chewning, Chr..........B. W.

Chiles, Thos............H. D.
Cross, Wm.............A. A.

Dixon, Thos............W. B.
Dixon, James...........W. B.
Dickinson, Martin.......I. P.
Dickinson, Wm.........W. D.
Durrett, James..........B. W.
Durrett, Claiborne.......V. P. R.
Daniels, Joseph.........Saf.
Dickinson, E. B.........Saf.
Dickinson, Edm.........Saf.

Elliott, Wyatt...........W. D.
Elliott, Martin..........W. D.
Eubank, Royal..........V. P. R.
Elliott, Sam'l...........Saf.
Eubank, Wm...........W. D.
Eubank, Ambrose.......A. A.

Fitzhugh, Wm..........Saf.
Farmer, James..........A. A.
Farish, Rich'd..........W. D.
Flippo, Joseph..........B. W.

Gatewood, Rich'd.......A. A.
George, Wm...........H. D.
George, Jesse...........B. W.
Goodwin, Ennis.........I. P.
Goodwin, Toler.........W. D.
Gouldin, Jesse..........A. A.
Goulding, Wm. T........H. D.
Gray, Wm.............A. A.
Green, James...........A. A.
Green, Wm............A. A.
Green Saml............W. D.
Gray, Francis..........V. P. R.
Graves, John...........V. P. R.
Gatewood, Edmund.....V. P. R.
Gatewood, Wm.........V. P. R.
Gordon, James.........Saf.
Gravatt, John..........Saf.
Gray, George..........Saf.
Green, Gabriel..........Saf.
Guy, Samuel...........Saf.
Guy, William...........Saf.
Guy, Joseph............Saf.
Garrett, Wm...........W. D.

List of Revolutionary Soldiers from Caroline County

Garrett, Rich'd..........W. D.
George, Reuben..........W. D.
George, John............W. D.
Gilchrist, Geo...........W. D.
Green, Moses............W. D.
Green, Rich'd...........W. D.

Harris, Wm..............S. W.
Harris, John............S. W.
Harris, James...........A. A.
Hill, Gideon............B. W.
Hill, Martin............A. A.
Hoomes, Benj...........V. P. R.
Hurt, Benj..............V. P. R.
Harris, Wm.............V. P. R.
Hoomes, Isaac..........V. P. R.
Hoomes, James.........V. P. R.
Hoomes, David.........V. P. R.
Hoomes, Thos. C........V. P. R.
Hord, Thos.............V. P. R.
Hill, George...........V. P. R.
Hill, Baylor...........V. P. R.
Hay, John..............W. D.
Hay, Morning...........W. D.
Hewlett, John..........W. D.
Hoomes, John..........W. D.
Hord, James............W. D.

Innis, Robt.............W. D.
Innis, John.............W. D.
Innis, Hugh............H. D.

Jordan, Mark...........W. D.
Jordan, John...........W. D.
Jesse, Turner..........W. D.
Jones, Jesse...........V. P. R.
Jones, John...........V. P. R.

Kay, James.............W. D.
Kay, John..............W. D.
Kidd, Benj.............Saf.
Kemp, James...........B. W.
Kemp, Wm.............B. W.

Long, Benj.............V. P. R.
Loving, Christopher......V. P. R.
Long, James............V. P. R.
Luck, James............V. P. R.

Munday, Thos..........W. D.
Motley, Wm............W. D.
Martin, Robt...........W. D.
Martin, Reuben.........W. D.
Martin, Farish.........W. D.
Martin, Moses..........W. D.
Martin, James..........W. D.
Martin, Gideon.........W. D.
Martin, John...........W. D.
Minor, Peter...........A. A.
Minor, John............W. D.
Minor, Vivian..........C. J.
Minor, Wm.............A. A.
Motley, David..........B. W.
Motley, Joseph.........W. D.
Morgan, John..........V. P. R.
Madison, Wm...........V. P. R.
May, Thomas...........V. P. R.
Marshall, George........V. P. R.
Miller, Thomas.........V. P. R.

Napier, Wm. P..........V. P. R.
Nixon, Andrew.........Saf.
Norment, John.........Saf.
New, Jacobs............W. D.

Oliver, John...........V. P. R.
Overton, Thos..........B. W.

Parker, Thos...........W. D.
Parker, James..........W. D.
Pitts, David...........W. D.
Pitts, Wm.............W. D.
Pratt, Wm.............W. D.
Plunkett, Reuben.......V. P. R.
Perry, Simon...........V. P. R.
Parker, Wm. H.........Saf.
Parker, John...........Saf.
Pendleton, James.......Saf.
Pendleton, Nathaniel....Saf.
Pratt, John............Saf.
Powers, Robert.........Saf.
Pendleton, John........K.S.S.R.
Parker, Richard........B. W.
Penn, Abraham.........A. A.
Penn, Wm.............A. A.

List of Revolutionary Soldiers from Caroline County

Quarles, John...........Saf.
Quarles, James.........Saf.
Quarles, Wm. P.........Saf.

Rogers, Bernard........A. A.
Reynolds, Wm...........V. P. R.
Rains, James...........Saf.
Reynolds, Robt.........Saf.
Richeson, Geo...........Saf.
Row, Joseph............Saf.
Roy, Beverly...........Saf.
Roy, Jacob.............A. A.
Rogers, John...........A. A.

Samuel, Henry.........W. D.
Samuel, James..........W. D.
Samuel, Wm............W. D.
Singleton, John.........A. A.
Swan, Charles..........B. W.
Shackelford, John.......V. P. R.
Satterwhite, Robt.......V. P. R.
Southworth, Wm.........V. P. R.
Saunders, Geo...........V. P. R.
Sutton, John...........V. P. R.
Samuel, Gray...:.......V. P. R.
Saunders, Rich'd........V. P. R.
Stanley, Moses..........V. P. R.
Sale, Leonard..........Saf.
Saunders, John.........Saf.
Saunders, Joseph........Saf.
Saunders, Wm..........Saf.
Scott, Robert..........Saf.
Scott, Joseph..........Saf.
Sorrell, Richard........W. B.
Sorrell, William........W. B.
Sorrell, John...........W. B.
Sorrell, Elisha.........W. B.
Smith, Saunders........W. B.
Smith, Reuben..........W. B.
Smith, Wm.............W. B.
Smith, James..........W. B.
Shepherd, Wm..........W. B.
Shackelford, George.....W. B.
Saunders, Daniel........W. B.
Saunders, Presley.......W. B.
Swann, John...........Saf.
Sutton, Martin.........Saf.
Sutton, Benjamin.......Saf.

Thomas, John..........R. A.
Thomas, Reuben........W. D.
Thornton, Anthony......W. D.
Thornton, James........W. D.
Thornton, John.........W. D.
Thornton, Reuben.......W. D.
Todd, Matthew.........W. D.
Todd, Wm.............W. D.
Turner, Francis.........W. D.
Turner, Joseph.........W. D.
Tyler, Wm.............W. D.
Tyler, Joseph..........W. D.
Tyler, Charles.........W. D.
Torrent, Rich'd.........V. P. R.
Taylor, Bartholomew.....V. P. R.
Tucker, Wm...........V. P. R.
Thomas, Catlett........V. P. R.
Toombs, Wm...........V. P. R.
Taylor, John...........Saf.
Taliaferro, Benj.........Saf.
Taylor, Reuben.........Saf.
Taylor, James..........Saf.
Thomas, Elijah..........Saf.
Thomas, James.........Saf.
Todd, Robert...........Saf.
Tompkins, Christopher...Saf.
Tompkins, Henry........Saf.
Travis, Edward.........Saf.
Taliaferro, John.........C. J.
Taliaferro, Rich'd.......W. D.
Taliaferro, Francis.......C. J.
Taliaferro, Walker.......A. A.
Taylor, Thornton........A. A.
Temple, Samuel.........A. A.
Tennant, Rich'd.........C. J.
Tennant, James.........C. J.
Terrell, Sam'l..........A. A.
Thomas, Buckner........W. D.
Todd, John.............A. A.
Todd, Bernard..........A. A.
Tompkins, Wm.........A. A.
Tompkins, Robt.........Heitman
Tribble, Joseph.........W. D.
Tyler, John.............A. A.
Thornton, Patrick.......Saf.
Thornton, Joseph.......Saf.

Whitaker, John.........W. D.

List of Revolutionary Soldiers from Caroline County

Whitaker, James.........W. D.
White, Joseph...........W. D.
White, John.............W. D.
Wyatt, Elisha...........W. D.
Wyatt, Edmund..........W. D.
Wyatt, Pitman..........W. D.
Washington, John........W. D.
Walden, George.........V. P. R.
Wright, Robt...........V. P. R.
Walden, Charles........V. P. R.
Waller, Wm.............Saf.
Washington, Wm.........Saf.

Welch, Benj. A..........Saf.
Woodford, Wm..........Saf.
Wood, Robt.............Saf.
Wright, Wm.............Saf.
Waller, Edmund.........B. W.
Waugh, Rev. Abner......R. A.

Yarbrough, James........V. P. R.
Yarbrough, Joel.........V. P. R.
Young, John............W. D.
Young, Lewis...........W. D.
Young, Robert..........W. D.

ROLL OF CAROLINE MEN WHO QUALIFIED AS OFFICERS IN THE MILITIA DURING THE WAR OF THE REVOLUTION 1776–1783

Thomas Alcock, Lt. Dec., 1777.

Gregory Baynham, Lt. Mch., 1778.
Thomas Beazley, Ens. May 1781.
John Boutwell, Lt. May, 1778.
John Brame, Ens. Feb., 1778.
Thomas Broaddus, Lt. Nov., 1779.
Richard Buckner, Maj. Feb, 1778..
Philip Buckner, Capt. Dec., 1777.
William Buckner, Capt. Nov., 1777.

Daniel Coleman, Lt. May, 1779.
Julius Coleman, Lt. May, 1779.
Samuel Coleman, Capt. Jan., 1779.
William Collins, Lt. June, 1779.
William Connor, Lt. May, 1779.
Francis Connor, Ens. Nov., 1777.

James Daniel, Ens. Nov., 1779.
Joseph DeJarnette, Lt. May, 1781
John Downer, Lt. Nov., 1777.
William Durritt, Capt. June, 1778.
Richard Durritt, Lt. June, 1778.

Thomas Ellis, Ens. March, 1779.
Johnson Faulkner, Lt. Nov., 1777.
John Fitzhugh, Lt. Dec., 1777.
——— Fletcher, Capt. Dec., 1779.
Duncan Graham, Jr., Lt. March, 1779.
William Graham, Lt. Dec., 1777.
Robert Graham, Capt. Mch, 1778.
John Gravatt, Ens. January, 1779.
William F. Gray, Lt. May, 1781.
Thomas F. Guy, Lt. May, 1781.

George Guy, Capt. Nov., 1777.
John Hall, Ens. January, 1779.
Thomas Hawes, Ens. May, 1779.
Joel Higgen, Ens. May, 1779.
Thomas Hord, Lt. August, 1778.
James Hord, Lt. August, 1778.
John Hord, Lt. May, 1778.
David Jameson, Ens. Dec., 1777.
Ambrose Jeter, Ens. May, 1778.
Philip Johnson, Maj. Jan., 1779.
Thomas Jones, Lt. Nov., 1778.
John Jones, Capt. Nov., 1777.
James Kay, Ens., January, 1778.
William Long, Lt. January, 1779.
John Long, Capt. Feb., 1778.
Thomas Lowry, Col. June, 1778.
George Madison, Capt. May, 1779.
John Marshall, Capt. Dec., 1777.
William Mitchell, Ens., Nov., 1779.
Anthony New, Capt. Dec., 1777.
Samuel Norment, Ens. Dec., 1777.
John Norment, Lt. Dec., 1777.
Roger Quarles, Capt. May, 1779.
Samuel Rawlins, Ens. Feb., 1778.
James Rennolds, Lt. Nov., 1779.
Joseph Richeson, Capt. Jan., 1779–May, 1781.
Mungo Roy, Ens. Nov., 1777.
Samuel Sale, Lt. Nov., 1779.
William Samuel, Ens. May, 1779.
Reuben Samuel, Lt. Jan., 1778.
William Streshly, Capt. 1779.

Peyton Sterns, Capt.   1778.

James Sutton, Capt.   May, 1781.

Samuel Temple, Capt.   Nov., 1777.

George Terrell, Ens.   Dec., 1777.

John Thilman, Capt.   Nov., 1777.

John Thompson, Lt.   Dec., 1777.

Anthony Thornton, Jr., Lt. Col.   Nov., 1777.

George Thornton, Lt.   Dec., 1777.

Lewis Timberlake, Lt.   Dec., 1777.

Francis Tompkins, Capt.   May, 1779.

Robert Tompkins, Capt.   May, 1779.

Daniel Turner, Lt.   Feb., 1778.

Daniel Twiner, Lt.   Nov., 1777.

Richard Tyler, Lt.   Oct., 1779.

John Tyler, Lt.   Dec., 1777.

George Tyler, Lt.   May, 1779.

Jeremiah Upshur, Lt.   Nov., 1779.

James Upshur, Lt. Col. Mch., 1778.

Ambrose White, Ens.   Nov., 1778.

Chilion White, Lt.   Dec., 1777.

Benjamin Winn, Lt.   July, 1779.

John Woolfolk, Lt.   Jan., 1779.

Charles Woolfolk, Lt.   May, 1778.

Richard Wyatt, Ens.   Feb., 1778.

THE MILITIA OF 1812

From June 18, 1812, when a declaration of war with Great Britain was made by the United States, the County Militia was frequently called out in Caroline and surrounding counties to meet and expel the British, who were landing on the banks of the Rappahannock river, making incursions into the county, destroying private property and carrying off negroes.   These were dark days.   The United States forces were crippled by the bitter controversies raging between opposing political parties and, as a result, lost many battles.   The spirit of '76 was only a memory.   The gloom only began to lift when Andrew Jackson won the splendid victory at New Orleans, which made him the National hero and elected him President.   When peace was restored corn sold at ten dollars per barrel, wheat at three dollars per bushel and other necessities accordingly.   Speculation became rife and capital reckless and when production exceeded the demand and the loans, made on the basis of high prices were called in, there was failure all over the country.

PAY ROLL

Of Captain Armistead Hoomes Company, Virginia Militia, stationed at Camp Holly, &c., first under the command of Major William Armistead, and afterwards under Colonel John H. Cocke, from the 24th of March to the 16th of August, 1813.   (See

Virginia Militia Pay Roll, page 172).   All Caroline men with possible exception of Thos. and James Jarrett.

Armistead Hoomes, Capt.	George Hord.
John Battaile, 1st Lieut.	George Hughes.
Richard Hoomes, 2nd Lt.	John Hackett.
Rufus Downing, Cornet.	William Harrison.
George Tompkins, Sgt.	James Jones.
Patrick C. Robb, Sgt.	Charles S. Jones.
Edmund Pendleton, Sgt.	Thomas Jarrett.
Lewis Battaile, Sgt.	James Jarrett.
Richard P. Camp, Cpl.	Wm. J. Murray.
Richard Davenport, Cpl.	James R. Miller.
John B. Valentine, Cpl.	Samuel Norment.
Philip Fitzhugh, Cpl.	John Norment.
Ben Anderson.	Wm. B. Pope.
Henry B. Alsop.	James Parker.
Thomas Brooks.	John T. Rawlins.
Richard Berry.	Norborne E. Sutton.
John Burke.	John Sutton, Jr.
Peter Bullard.	Wilson Swann.
Robert Camp.	Humphrey Sale.
Thomas Carter.	Louis W. Taliaferro.
John Conway.	George Taylor.
John Dickenson.	William P. Taylor.
William Dishman.	Paul Ulgate.
Robert Goodloe.	George Winn.
Thomas Guthrie.	Ben Wright.
William Gray.	Thomas Woodford.

MUSTER ROLL

Of the Field and Staff of a Squadron of Dragoons, commanded by Major John T. Woodford, in the Service of the United States during the years 1814 and 1815.   Majority of these were Caroline men.   (See Virginia Muster Rolls).

John T. Woodford, Major.	Joseph B. Anderson, Serg. Major.
Armistead Hoomes, Adjutant.	Augustine Leftwich, Serg. Major.
James Henderson, Surgeon.	Charles Whitley, Q. M. Serg.
William Leftwich, P. Master.	William Woodford, Serg. Major.
Fabius Lawson, Q. M. Serg.	

MUSTER ROLL

Of Captain Elliott DeJarnett's Company of Infantry, of the Thirteenth Regiment, in the Service of the State of Virginia in 1814.   (See Virginia Militia Muster Rolls, page 35).

List of Members of Elliott DeJarnett's Company

Elliott DeJarnett, Capt.
William Kidd, Lt.
Lewis Madison, Ensign.
Wm. G. Pemberton, Sgt.
John P. Walden, Sgt.
Thomas Berry, Sgt.
John M. Gray, Sgt.
William Dillard, Cpl.
William Robinson, Cpl.
Henry Clift, Cpl.
Theophilus Green, Cpl.
Dudley Hall, Musician.
William Taylor, Musician.
Allen Beazley.
Arculas Beckan.
Robert Brooks.
John Baylor.
Washington Beazley.
Philip Brooks.
John Cecil.

John Donahoe.
Jesse Dillard.
James Elliott.
Edmund Fortune.
Chany Gatewood.
Bloxham Hord.
Joel Hill.
John Jones.
Diggs Luck.
Robert L. Parker.
James Pare.
John Scantland.
James Southworth.
John Searls.
John Seal.
David Seal.
Thomas Taylor, Sr.
Thomas Taylor, Jr.
Henry Taylor.
Major Taylor, Jr.

MUSTER ROLL

Of Captain William F. Gray's Company, from the Thirtieth Regiment, Virginia Militia, Caroline county, in the Service in 1813; also from Sixteenth Regiment commanded by Lt. Colonel Aylett Waller in the service of the U. S. A. in 1814. (See Virginia Militia Muster Rolls, page 48).

William F. Gray, Capt.,
C. L. Johnson, Lt.,
Benjamin Clark, Lt.,
Claiborne Wiglesworth, Lt.,
Peter Lucas, Lt.
Robert Hildrup, Sgt.,
John Summerson, Sgt.,
Richard Sale, Jr., Sgt.,
Watts Parker, Sgt.,
James W. Blair, Sgt.,
James Williams, Sgt.,
John Ledwidge, Sgt.,
Thomas N. Berkley, Sgt.,
John Harrison, Sgt.,
Richard B. Thornton, Cpl.
Charles Jones, Cpl.,
George P. Shepard, Cpl.,
Reuben Stevens, Cpl.,
Henry W. Ashton,

John Alsop,
Vivian Ashby,
James Atchison,
Lewis Andrews,
John Banks,
Gray Boulware,
Walter Bowie,
Linsey Boulware,
Baylor Banks,
Richard T. Banks,
George Baggott,
George Brent,
Thomas Ball,
Nathaniel Brown,
William Burton,
Thomas Bloxton,
John W. Beedle,
Benj. Bramhull,
John Brown, Jr.,

List of Members of William F. Gray's Company

Waller L. Brightwell,
Seth Barton,
Spencer N. Carter,
Wm. Carrack,
Chas. Carter,
Smallwood Coghill,
James Cooke,
Viomany Carter,
Daniel Curtis,
Munen Curtis,
Stiles P. Curtis,
Jeremiah Covert,
P. E. Cady,
Spencer S. Doggett,
Robert Dearman,
Thomas J. Denison,
John Duerson,
Alsop Y. Daniel,
Joseph Dennis,
John Dearson,
Thomas Douglass,
Geo. Doggett,
Thos. Edmondson,
Robert French,
Jacob Gore,
Chas. Goodwin,

David Goldsby,
John Green,
Benj. Gilbert,
James Gray,
Joseph Gatewood,
John Goldsmith,
Peter Hord,
Henry Hill,
James Long,
Ralph Lomax,
John H. Micou,
William Miller,
Thomas Minor,
John Minor,
William Martin,
Hugh Nelson,
William Proctor,
John Pitman,
Benjamin Rollins,
Charles Thornton,
Philemon Samuel,
Nicholas Thornton,
Charles Sanders,
Benjamin Pendleton,
John Young.

MUSTER ROLL

Captain Robert Hill's Company in the Sixth Regiment, Virginia Militia, in service in 1813. Nearly all Caroline men in this company. (See Muster Roll of Virginia Militia, page 426).

Robert Hill, Capt.,
Wm. C. Latane, Lt.,
Johnson Munday, Ens.,
Edmond Jones,
Lewis Hord,
Richard Coghill,
William Clark,
Goldman Carter,
William Coleman,
William Burfoot,
Churchill Ball,
Robert Ball,
Carter Ball,
Wm. B. Boulware,
Alexander Elliott,

John S. Garrett,
Lewis Gatewood,
Reuben Garrett,
Philip Gatewood,
William Gatewood,
William Garrett,
John T. Hill,
Joseph Hill,
John Mahon,
Paul Micou,
Moscoe Noel,
Edmond Noel,
Devald Noel,
Samuel Parker,
Warren Parker,

List of Members of Robert Hill's Company

Andrew Runolds,	Robert Samuel,
Walker Roy,	Streshley Taylor,
David Roper,	Thomas Taylor,
Fielding Sale,	Thomas Turner,
Streshley Stokes,	Boulware Vauter.

MUSTER ROLL

Of Captain Thomas D. Pitt's Company of the Sixth Regiment, Virginia Militia, most of whom were Caroline men.   The Company was made up from Caroline and Essex, and was in Service in 1814.   (See Virginia Muster Rolls, page 641).

Thomas D. Pitts, Capt.,	Thomas Coghill,
William Gray, Lt.,	Brooking Clark,
Thomas W. Hill,	David Dishman,
Lewis Hord,	Lewis Fisher,
Lewis Ward,	Reuben Garrett,
Edward Parker,	Philip Gatewood,
Richard Coghill,	Lewis Hord,
Reuben Pitts,	Thomas Kay,
Benjamin Coghill,	Coleman Minor,
Robert Samuel,	Nathaniel J. Mothershead,
John Thomas,	Mereday Munday,
Asee Gouldman,	John B. Micou,
Linsay Reynolds,	Pan. C. Micou,
William Parker,	Achilles Noell, Sr.,
Leonard Sale,	Muscoe Noell,
Richard Beazley,	Younger Pitts,
John Mahon,	Andrew Rennolds,
John Atkinson,	Daniel Rennolds,
Wm. T. Brooks,	Anthony Samuel.
Thomas Boulware,	

CAROLINE MEN

Of Captain Smith P. Bankhead's Company, in the First Regiment of Virginia Volunteers, called into the Service of the United States by the Secretary of War, under the Act of Congress approved May 13, 1846, for the term of " during the War with Mexico, unless sooner discharged."   Date of this Muster Roll December 31, 1846.   (See Virginia Militia Muster Roll, pages 63–64).

List of Members of Smith P. Bankhead's Company

Smith P. Bankhead, Capt.,
Robert F. Coleman, 1st Lt.,
Thomas B. Coghill, Sgt.,
James Bullard,
Lawrence Battaile,
John S. Burruss,
Albert G. Collins,

John W. Carter,
John L. Hart,
John R. Taliaferro,
John Taylor,
Thomas Taylor,
Francis L. Turner.

Roll of Company G, Thirtieth Regiment, Virginia Infantry, which entered the service on the 21st day of May, 1861, at the Fair Grounds in Fredericksburg, Va. The remnant that survived the four bloody years surrendered with the Army of Northern Virginia at Appomattox, Va., April 9, 1865. Compiled by G. Allensworth, who commanded the Company during the greater part of the conflict. Also see Roster of Virginia Infantry C. S. A. (Volume 3), in Archives of State Library.

Thos. B. Coghill, Captain. Resigned early in '62, because of ill health.

S. E. Swann, 1st Lieut. Served unexpired term of Capt. Coghill.

W. J. Hancock, 2nd Lt. Promoted to 1st Lt., latter part of '62.

G. Allensworth, 2nd Lt. Promoted to Capt. upon retirement of Capt. Swann in '62.

Genette Anderson, 1st Sgt. Promoted to 1st Lt., in '62. Mortally wounded September 17, '62.

W. A. Gatewood, 2nd Sgt. Promoted to 2nd Lt. in '62.

Other non-commissioned officers as follows:

M. L. Young,
John K. Sizer,
R. H. Sizer,
J. M. Terrell,
Jas. S. Terrell,
P. H. Lowry,
Thos. L. Luck,
J. H. Winn,
Jas. H. Sharp,

John M. Tompkins,
R. H. Tompkins,
Ben. B. Tompkins,
Robt. Tompkins,
John W. Noel,
J. S. Smith,
John K. Luck,
H. R. White.

PRIVATES

Arnold, W. O.,
Adams, J. A.,
Acors, Paul,
Acors, Jas. B.,
Armstrong, W. F.,
Anderson, B. J.,
Allen, R. T.,
Allen, W. L.,
Allen, J. O.,

Campbell, A. E.,
Carter, W. P.,
Carter, W. M.,
Carter, John M.,
Chiles, John H.,
Carneal, H. M.,
Carneal, A. T.,
Carneal, E. I.,
Carneal, John L.,

List of Members of Company G

Carneal, J. H.,
Cannon, Jas H.,

Dickerson, Geo. W.,
Durrett, Albert,
Durrett, Woodson,
Durrett, Wm. B.,
Durrett, E. A.,
Durrett, Cicero,
Durrett, J. W.,
Durrett, Lucian,
Durrett, R. A.,
Durrett, Thos. W.,
Dulaney, Morris,
Dabney, Jas. B.,
Douglass, John,
Dunn, Ed. S.,

Farish, R. S.,
Farish, F. W.,
Farish, W. H.,
Faulkner, W. H.,

Gatewood, W. C.,
Grymes, Jas. E.,
Grymes, R. C.,

Howard, Thos. H.,
Haines, Geo. L.,
Hackett, Robt.,
Harriss, O. D.,

Kelley, W. Matt.,

Luck, Wm. F.,
Luck, Geo. P.,
Luck, W. T.,
Luck, Robt.,
Long, A. J.,
Lowry, Frank,

Marshall, Henry,
Murphy, Pat.,

Mitchell, L. R.

Nuckols, James,
Newton, J. F.,

Philips, E. L.,
Penney, Cornelius,
Parr, H. B.,

Quisenberry, Thos..

Spicer, W. T.,
Spicer, J. L.,
Smith, W. W., ·
Smith, Richard W.,
Smith, Geo. W.,
Smith, Sterling M.,
Smith, R. S.,
Sutton, Richard,
Satterwhite, Frank,
Satterwhite, Wm. T.,
Sharp, Jas. H.,
Smith, L. H.,
Smith, John T.,
Shelton, J. B.,
Simpson, Geo.,
Shackleford, John L.,

Tompkins, Jas. G.,
Taylor, Wm. L.,
Taylor, John W.,
Taliaferro, W. H.,

Vaughan, Joseph,

Willard, A. J.,
Willoughby, J. R.,
Wiltshire, C. E.,
Watkins, J. W.,

Young, Leroy,
Yarbrough, Jas. J.

MUSTER ROLL OF THE "SPARTA GRAYS" OF CAROLINE COUNTY,
VA., BEING COMPANY H, THIRTIETH REGIMENT VIRGINIA
INFANTRY, CORSE'S BRIGADE, PICKETT'S DIVISION,
LONGSTREET'S CORPS.   ROLL AS OF MAY, 1861

. Milton Gouldin, Capt.,
Julian Broaddus, 1st Lieut.,
Wm. M. Kelly, 2nd Lieut.,
Richard F. Broaddus, 3rd Lieut.,
Wm. B. Kidd, Sgt.,
H. N. Broaddus, Sgt.,
Thos. G. Bagby, Sgt.,
Thos. H. Brooks, Sgt.,
Ira E. White, Corporal,
Wm. Geo. Taliaferro, Cpl.,
A. J. Pitts, Cpl.,
W. L. Andrews, Cpl.,
Geo. B. Baldwin, Musician,
W. N. Covington, Ms.,

Anderson, Walter B.,
Andrews, Edwin,

Beazley, Robt. H.,
Broaddus, J. W.,
Broaddus, Preston, Lieut.,
Broaddus, R. T.,
Broaddus, A. T.,
Beazley, Madison,

Carter, Wm.,
Croley, Jno.,
Covington, Joseph H.,
Carter, James D.,
Cole, M. W.,
Croley, Edw.,
Conduit, Wm. H.,
Conduit, Thos.,

Froner, Geo.,

Gatewood, Wm. L.,
Gravatt, A. C.,
Goodwin, Thomas,
Gravatt, Wm. B.,
Gravatt, A. G.,
Greer, Thos. W.,
Garrett, Edw.,
Greer, R. W.,

Gray, Geo. W.,
Goodwin, Littleton,

Houston, Columbus,
Houston, Alston,
Houston, W. C.,
Houston, A. B.,

Jordan, W. A.,

Jones, Robt. W.,

Kay, Wm. W., Sr.,

Loving, R. S.,
Loving, C. O.,

Marmaduke, E. S.,
Mahon, Alex.,
Motley, Thomas, J.

Newman, J. O.,

Pitts, Wm. S.,
Pitts, S. J.,
Pitts, J. H.,
Pitts, O. D.,
Pitts, Dan.,
Pavey, J. H.,
Pullen, J. T.,
Pullen, M. E.,
Pullen, Jno. M.,
Pullen, Wm. W.,
Pullen, R. T.,

Quisenberry, Wm.,
Quisenberry, John.,

Sale, M. Sedden,
Smoot, L. H.,
Streshley, J. M.,
Self, John Jr.,
Samuel, H. B.,

Terrell, R. F.,
Terrill, Jno. M.,

Vaughan, James,

Wright, O. H.,

Yates, B. C.

ROLL OF COMPANY E (CAROLINE GRAYS) THIRTIETH VIRGINIA INFANTRY

Compiled by E. R. Coghill, Clerk of Circuit Court of Caroline.

OFFICERS

R. O. Peatross, Capt.   Promoted to Major, 1863.   Wounded at Drewry's Bluff and at Five Forks.

John W. Scott, 1st Lieut.   Promoted to Capt.   At the Surrender.

Philip Samuel, 2nd Lieut.   Promoted to 1st Lieut.   Wounded at Drewry's Bluff.

Wm. E. Norment, 3rd Lieut.   Died 1862.

Henry A. Ware, 1st Sergt.   Present at Surrender.

B. T. Trevillian, 2nd Sergt.   Honourably discharged 1862, re-entered service in cavalry.

John W. Hutchinson, 3rd Sergt.   Honourably discharged 1862, re-entered service in cavalry.

Lewis A. George, 4th Sergt.   Promoted to 3rd Lieut.   Mortally wounded March 31, '65.

John P. Samuel, 1st Corporal.   Promoted to Sergt.   Mortally wounded May 16, '64.

I. M. Wyatt, 2nd Corporal.   Promoted to Ordnance Sergt., 1862.

Wm. H. Samuel, 3rd Corporal.

E. F. Flagg, 4th Corporal.   Honourably discharged, 1862.   Re-entered in cavalry.

PRIVATES

Atkins, Henry C.   At Surrender.

Atkins, Philip B.

Beazley, P. A.   Promoted to Sergt., 1862.

Beazley, O. T.

Beazley, Arch S.   Present at Surrender.

Beazley, Wm L.   Died, 1861.

Branan, John.   Died, 1862.

Branan, Thos. C.   Died, 1864.

Bendall, Albert L.   Wounded at Drewry's Bluff.

Blanton, Augustus.   Killed at Dinwiddie Court House, March 31, '65.

Blanton, Ro. W.

Brewer, James A.   Promoted to Corporal, 1862.   Killed at Drewry's Bluff.

Brewer, Wm. S.

Bowers, Wm. S.   At Surrender.

Blaydes, Hugh T.   Killed at Dinwiddie Court House, March 31. '65.

Blunt, Thos. W.   Killed at Sharpsburg, Md., September 17, '62.

Burruss, James W.   Killed at Sharpsburg, Md., September 17, '62.

Burruss, Wm. H. N.   Wounded at Sharpsburg, Md., September 17, '62.

Campbell, James T.

Campbell, John W.   Mortally wounded at Sharpsburg, Md., Sept. 17, '62.

Chandler, Rufus K.

Coates, John B.

Cobb, Montgomery.

Coghill, E. R. Promoted to Cpl., '62, to Sergt., '63, wounded '62, at Surrender.

Coghill, T. D. Severely wounded at Five Forks, April 1, '65.

Collins, Geo. R. At Surrender.

Coleman, Ed. W. Died of disease, '61.

Coleman, Robt.

Coleman, Wm C.

Courtney, L. S.

Dimue, Albert C. Killed at Sharpsburg, Md., September 17, '62.

Doggett, Booth P. Wounded at Sharpsburg, Md., September 17, '62. At Surrender.

Donahoe, Reuben.

Donahoe, Arch. Severely wounded at Drewry's Bluff, May 16, '64.

Donovan, James.

Dyson, John M. Died of disease, '61.

Elliott, James. At Surrender.

Eubank, Isaac L. At Surrender.

Farish, James P.

Flippo, John G. Wounded at Sharpsburg, Md., September 17, '62.

Flippo, Samuel W.

Freeman, William. Wounded at Sharpsburg, Md., September 17, '62.

George, H. H.

Goldsby, Lewis G. Killed at Sharpsburg, Md., September 17, '62.

Goldsby, James. Wounded at Sharpsburg, Md., September 17, '62.

Hewlett, Joseph M. Promoted to Corporal, 1862. Mortally wounded April 1, '65.

Hargrave, John T.

Henderson, James T.

Hill, James H. Died of disease, September 25, '64.

Hill, Henry M. Died of disease, April 11, '62.

Hopkins, Erasmus.

Hutchinson, Richard W. Honourably discharged, '62. Re-entered service, cavalry.

Nutchinson, Chas E. Promoted to Cpl., '62. Died suddenly on picket line in '63.

Jackson, Thomas P. Promoted to Corporal. Killed March 15, '65.

Jackson, Edwin. Killed at Sharpsburg, Md., September 17, '62.

Jackson, John.

King, George W. At Surrender.

Kerr, Charles.

Lewis, Arthur.

Luck, Napoleon P.

Luck, Samuel A. Severely wounded, battle of Sharpsburg, Md., 1862.

Luck, John S.

Luck, Thomas B.

Lyell, James. Wounded.

Mason, Camillus A. Killed at Sharpsburg, Md., September 17, '62.

Mason, Frank M. Mortally wounded at Sharpsburg, Md., September 17, '62.

McLaughlin, James A. Transferred to 9th Virginia Cavalry in '62.
Mitchell, Wm. T.
Mitchell, James P.
Napier, Richard.
Norment, Thomas N.
Oliver, Oscar. Died of disease, '61.
Parr, Henry F. Died of disease, '62.
Parr, John H.
Parr, Robt. S.
Peatross, James. Promoted to Cpl., thence to Sgt., 1863.
Peatross, R. W. Promoted to Sgt. in '63 and afterward transferred to Eng. Cps.
Peatross, Walter S. Wounded at Sharpsburg, Md., '62. Present at Surrender.
Pemberton, Wm.
Pemberton, Charles.
Pemberton, John F. Promoted Cpl. Mortally wounded at Dinwiddie Court House, March 31, '65.
Pemberton, Richard B.
Pemberton, Alonzo.
Pemberton, George M.
Quarles, John W. Died of disease, '62.
Ramsey, W. P. C. Died, '61.
Richerson, Thos. W.
Richeson, John W. Died of disease, '62.
Richeson, Wm. Transferred to 47th Virginia Regiment, '62.
Richerson, Wm. Jr.
Samuel, Ro. G. Wounded at Drewry's Bluff, '64.
Samuel, Alman. At Surrender.
Samuel, Arch.
Samuel, Wm. N.
Scott, Ro. S. Present at Surrender.
Stern, Lewis H. Discharged honorably in '62, re-entered army (cavalry).
Swann, Thos. C. Transferred to 47th Virginia Regiment.
Sutton, Page T. Transferred to 9th Virginia Cavalry, '62.
Taliaferro, Philip.
Tunstall, Lewis H. Promoted to Sgt. Taken prisoner at Sharpsburg, Md., '62.
Turner, Reuben D.
Turner, William.
Turner, Wm. T. Killed at Sharpsburg, Md., '62.
Turner, Geo. T. Wounded at Sharpsburg, Md., '62.
Turner, Joshua. Died of disease, '61.
West, Joseph E. Died of disease, '62.
Wiltshire, Chas. E.
Wiltshire, William T.
Woolfolk, Wm. A. Promoted to Cpl., '63.
Woolfolk, George.
Yarbrough, John T.
Yarbrough, Henry M. Made prisoner, April 6, '65. Died in prison.

ROLL OF COMPANY B, NINTH VIRGINIA CALVARY

"CAROLINE LIGHT DRAGOONS"

The following roll of Company B, Ninth Virginia Calvalry, was made up by the late Judge E. C. Moncure, of Bowling Green, Va., who was Second Lieutenant of the Company:

COMMISSIONED OFFICERS

S. A. Swann, Captain (promoted).   James Boulware, 1st Lt.,
John Ware, Captain,   Charles Wright, 2nd Lt.,
*Cecil Baker, 1st Lt.,   E. C. Moncure, 2nd Lt.,

NON COMMISSIONED OFFICERS

Moncure, T. G.,   Broaddus, John W.,
Chandler, S. T.,   Puller, J. E.,
Waller, D. J.,   Shaddock, M. E.,
Rollins, A. B.,   Faust, Thos.,
Toombs, W. H.,   Gravatt, James D.,
Kidd, John W.,

PRIVATES

Ambold, Ernest A.,   Chandler, W. S.,
Andrews, John J.,   Chandler, W. T.,
Andrews, Charles H.,   Chandler, R. W.,
Andrews, W. S.,   Chandler, Henry,
Anderson, Alfred A.,   Cullen, W. P.,
    *Callis, R. T.,
Boutwell, A.,   Callis, W. S.,
Broaddus, James A.,   Carter, L. H.,
Broaddus, S. B.,   Cash, D. S.,
Broaddus, H. O.,   *Cash, W. S.,
Broaddus, Woodford,   Carneal, L. J.,
Broaddus, H. N.,   Collawn, J. W. S.,
Broaddus, A. T.,   Collins, J. C.,
*Broaddus, Eugene,   Collins, James T.,
*Buckner, R. H. W.,   Conway, Catlett,
Books, R. L.,   Conway, A. H.,
Burke, Thomas,   Conway, P. H.,
Burruss, J. G.,   Coleman, J. L.,
Burruss, A.,   Chapman, W. S.,
Battaile, John,   Crutchfield, G.,
Boulware, W. J.,
Boulware, Muscoe,   Dickinson, J. C.,
Branham, J. H.,   Digges, W. C.,
Burke, J. W.,   Dickinson, W. B.,
    Dade, H. T.,
    Duffee, Geo. G.,
Campbell, M.,
Campbell, F. D.,   England, John W.,
Campbell, C. R. D.,   *Edwards, J. T.,

*Indicates killed or died in service.

Monument to Confederate Soldiers of Caroline County.
Unveiled in 1906.   County Court-House in Back Ground

*Farish, Charles H.,
Farish, K. R.,
Farish, Joseph,
Farish, W. D.,
*Farish, Charles T.,
Farish, W. P. T.,
Forbes, A. T.,
*Faulkner, John W.,
Fitzhugh, Henry.,
Gatewood, J. T.,
Gouldin, W. S.,
Gray, E.,
Gray, R. A.,
Gravatt, R. A.,
Gravatt, T. E.,
Gravatt, G. C.,
*Goodwin, Clarence,
Greenstreet, A. J.,
Goodloe, Geo.,

Gwathmey, J.,
Hull, R. G.,
*Hull, J. M.,
*Harris, John T.,
Hove, J. T.,
Jesse, James M.,
Jesse, W. G.,
Jones, S. C.,
*Jordan, Alexander,
*Jordan, B. A.,
*Jeter, James A.,
Jones, W. E.,
*Jerrell, Luther,
*Kidd, B. W.,
Kidd, H. S.,
Kidd, B. F.,
Landrum, H. L.,
Long, Geo. W.,
Lewis, Thos. F.,

* Indicates killed or died in service.

List of Members of Company B

Loving, W. H.,
Lightfoot, W. B.,
Luck, W. S.,
McLaughlin, Jas. A.,
Moncure, R. C. L.,
Moncure, M. A.,
Moncure, J. D.,
*Martin, A. H.,
Mason, John G.,
McKenney, Edgar,
McKenney, James L.,
Moncure, R. C. L., Jr.,
Martin, John H.,
Norment, T. N.,
Oliver, Wm. M.,
Oliver, R. B.,
Powers, D. B.,
*Powers, Thomas,
*Powers, Willie,
Pitts, O. D.,
Penny, J. L.,
Parrish, J. G., (M. D.),
Pave, Sample,
Rowe, H. C.,
*Rowe, Charleton,
Rose, James W.,
Richardson, J. R.,
*Richardson, W. A.,
Richardson, Geo. G.,
Robb, P. L.,
Samuel, P. T.,
Scott, F. W.,
Sutton, F. K.,

Sutton, Archibald,
Sutton, Page T.,
Slaughter, J. A.,
Sale, J. J.,
Satterwhite, Benj.,
Taylor, W. R.,
Taylor, Temple,
Taylor, R. J.,
Temple, M. D.,
Temple, W. S.,
Temple, Charles,
Temple, L.,
Terrell, A. B.,
Terrell, John M.,
Thomas, J. W.,
Thomas, R. N.,
Thomas, W. W.,
Thornton, T. C.,
*Todd, George T.,
Upshur, R. H.,
Wright, R. S.,
Wright, Wesley,
Wright, W. B.,
Wright, W. S.,
Wright, B. B.,
Wright, J. C.,
Wright, B. M.,
Wright, J. F.,
Woolfolk, W. W.,
Willis, Charles,
Warwick, C.,
*White, Columbus,
*Wigglesworth, J. S.,
Waite, Charles.

*Indicates killed or died in service.

COMPANY F, THIRTIETH REGIMENT, VIRGINIA INFANTRY, CORSE'S
BRIGADE

"BOWLING GREEN GUARDS"

Jacob Currance, Capt.,
W. D. Quesenberry, Capt.,
John M. Hudgin, Capt.,
G. Allensworth, Capt.,
J. L. Burruss, Lieut.,
John H. James, Lieut.,
R. T. Hudgins, Sgt.,
P. J. McWaits, Sgt.,

———— Kell, Sgt.,
Geo. W. Broaddus,
M. W. B. Allport,
W. J. Bates,
Woodson C. Burruss,
J. B. Barlow,
E. Blondell,
G. W. Broaddus,

List of Members of Bowling Green Guards

T. S. Bullock,
B. W. Chiles,
John S. Chiles,
W. Roy Coleman,
L. Cardwell,
T. H. Chandler,
Thos. L. Cridlin,
M. W. Cole,
John Donahoe,
C. H. Dickinson,
G. L. Frazier,
James E. Garrett,
W. R. W. Garrett,
Henry Gunst,
A. J. Grimes,
W. Galaspy,
W. Gravatt,
Isaac Hessburg,
J. H. Holloway,
John H. James,
John T. Motley,
W. G. McWhirt,

James McCauley,
S. C. Madison,
L. L. Poats,
W. C. Pitman,
Edm. Pegg,
T. E. Richardson,
B. Rowe,
W. G. Ross,
Wm. Self,
W. W. Saunders,
W. J. Selph,
Wm. M. Shackelford,
J. M. Shelton,
James W. Tucker,
T. C. Thornton,
F. B. Wagner,
O. H. Wright,
G. W. Wright,
H. Whitaker,
Henry D. Willis,
W. F. Wright,
Wm. T. Wright,

CAPTAIN THOMAS R. THORNTON'S BATTERY, LIGHTFOOT'S BATTALION

"CAROLINE LIGHT ARTILLERY"

Thomas R. Thornton, Capt.,
Walter G. Hudgins, 1st Lt.,
J. D. Powers, 1st Lt.,
Wilson Dickinson, 1st Lt.,
Thomas F. Lewis, 2nd Lt.,
Robert C. Thornton, 2nd Lt.,
James S. Bowie, 2nd Lt.,
J. Coalter, Sgt.,

John J. Atkinson,
Henry Acors,
Wm. J. Allport,
S. C. Anderson,
Van Allport,
R. M. Brooks,
R. D. Barlow,
E. D. Barlow,
J. L. Barlow,
David Beasley,
Wm. Bennett,
Samuel Beasley,

Festus Brooks,
J. Collins,
C. E. Bowers,
John E. Chiles,
J. T. Carlton,
W. T. Chiles,
P. Chinault,
G. L. Dillard,
T. S. Dillard,
Thos. Donahoe,
L. M. Dyson,
A. J. Dyson,
R. L. Dillard,
George R. Edwards,
T. P. Farmer,
S. D. Fisher,
John Fisher,
Wm. H. Farmer,
W. H. Garrett,
P. P. Greenstreet,
Reuben (Ro.) Garrett,

List of Members of Caroline Light Artillery

James T. Gatewood.
W. H. Hamner,
Nicholas Jones,
L. H. Jeter,
William Johnson,
P. T. Lucord,
Thomas D. Lumpkin,
Wm. C. Moore,
J. H. Marron,
R. H. Pitts,
R. W. Pitts,
H. C. Purvis,
W. H. Perry,
G. G. Prince,
William Proctor,
Joseph B. Robinson,

C. S. Sutton,
Parkinson Spinett,
B. Saunders,
J. M. Sirles,
T. Schooler,
Ira Suthard (Southworth),
Thomas Toombs,
H. P. Turner,
I. Toombs,
J. M. Upshaw,
John W. Vaughan,
John Wharton,
Wm. Wheeley,
A. B. Wharton,
J. G. White,
F. B. Wharton.

COMPANY F, TWENTY-FOURTH REGIMENT VIRGINIA CAVALRY

L. W. Allen, Capt.,
Thos. B. Anderson, 1st Lt.,
J. E. Broaddus, 2nd Lt.,
H. B. Catlett, 2nd Lt.,
J. H. F. Tompkins, Sgt.,
Alexander Chewning, Sgt.,
Charles Smith, Sgt.,
Cornelius Carlton, Sgt.,
Lewis H. Stern, Sgt.,
Joseph Terrell, Sgt.,
John Anderson, Cpl.,
Jacob Stevens, Cpl.,
Wm. H. Goodwin, Cpl.,
William Campbell, Cpl.,
G. A. Atherton,
Theodore Allen,
Fuller Anderson,
Robert Anderson,
Spott. Byrd,
Preston Byrd,
Joseph Bareley,
C. C. Blanton,
John Blanton,
Robert Beadles,
G. W. Beadles,
Luther Broaddus,
R. F. Broaddus,
B. Bryan,
F. C. S. Bromwell,

G. W. Blanton,
Henderson Carneal,
William Carneal,
William Chewning,
Price Campbell,
F. D. Campbell,
H. N. Dickinson,
Peyton Dudley,
A. P. Davis,
Henry DuVal,
Theodore DuVal,
J. W. Flippo,
Henry Flippo,
Tulla Goodwin,
Joseph Gale,
Ben Guthrie,
Hiter Goodwin,
Dick Hutcherson,
Stapleton Hicks,
J. H. Harris,
Robert Harris,
Joe Hooper,
Robert C. Hart,
Benj. J. Hart,
J. H. Hall,
Joe Hackett,
W. (or J. W.) Haskins,
J. P. Jackson,
T. N. Jones,

List of Members of Company F

W. T. Jones,
William Jones,
W. C. Jones,
Napoleon Luck,
Virgil Luck,
Apollos Luck,
R. Lusby,
W. S. Long,
C. M. D. Mitchell,
Joseph Myers,
Robert McCray,
Thomas B. Martin,
R. Norriss,
Julian Pettus,
Andrew Pitts,
Robert Puller,
John Perdue,
F. Roby,
J. R. Redd,
R. Riggs,
Dick Sutton,
Wren Saunders (or J. W.)
James E. Smith,
Preston Smith,
Leonidas Smith,
Robert Spencer,
George F. Swann,
Ed. Seaman,
Herman Schmidt,
C. S. Shafer (or Shuler),
Wesley J. Sadler,
C. W. Tompkins,
W. T. Tompkins,
T. B. Trevillian,
B. L. Trevillian,
James E. Terrell,
Wilton Wright,
John Wright,
Warner Wilkinson,
J. B. Weisel,
LaFayette Young,
J. T. Yarbrough.

MUSTER ROLL OF COMPANY "E" OF THE FORTY-SEVENTH REGIMENT VIRGINIA VOLUNTEERS

Robt. W. Eubank, Capt.,
John W. Rollins, 1st Lt.,
Chas. P. Powers, 2nd Lt.,
Stephen B. Rollins, 3rd Lt.,
W. W. Humphries, 1st Sgt.,
W. C. Askins, 2nd Sgt.,
Robt. Farinholt, 3rd Sgt.,
R. N. Humphries, 4th Sgt.,
Richard C. Brooks, 5th Sgt.,
Kyle Farr, Sgt.,
Nelson N. Hawlor, Cpl.,
Edward Powers, Corpl.,
Eugene Farinholt, Corpl.,
Francis G. Sterne, Corpl.,
Anderson, E. D.,
Anderson, W. S.,
Brooks, Robt.,
Brooks, R. M.,
Busby, Jas. R.,
Burrows, Thos. O.,
Bruce, Dallas,
Bullock, Jno. W.,
Bullock, David,
Bullock, Cammack,
Carter, Robt. A.,
Carter, Wm. M.,
Carneal, John,
Delaney, Geo.,
England, Wm. C.,
Fitzhugh, E.,
Gravatt, Peter A.,
Garrett, H. S.,
Garrett, Geo. W.,
Gouldman, T. B.,
Gouldman, A.,
Howard, Harrison,
Howard, Thomas,
Howard, Richard,
Jones, Nicholas,
Johnston, Robt.,
Jordan, Wm. C.,
Kelley, Wm. P.,
Kay, Edward,
Kay, Wm.,
Loving, Henry,
Loving, Woodford,

List of Members of Company E

Lafoe, Jno. F.,
Mason, Wm. H.,
Martin, Henry,
Noel, Franklin,
Powers, Lucius S.,
Purks, Jno. L.,
Rose, Cornelius C.,
Rose, Philip M.,
Riddle, John,
Shaddock, M. E.,
Shaddock, J. M.,
Sterne, David,
Saunders, John,
Sylva, Jas. M.,
Thompson, James W.,
Taylor, Thomas,
Vaughan, Henry,
Wright, Robt.,
Wallace, Henry,
Whittico, Henry.

MUSTER ROLL COMPANY "K" FORTY-SEVENTH REGIMENT OF VIRGINIA VOLUNTEERS AS OF JULY 31, '62

Jordan, P. Ware, Capt.,
James R. Dickinson, 1st Lt.,
Joseph T. Terrell, 2nd Lt.,
Thomas C. Chandler, 2nd Lt.,
Jessie S. Ellyson, 1st Sgt.,
Henry C. Sutton, 2nd Sgt.,
James H. Terrell, 3rd Sgt.,
Thomas S. Burruss, 4th Sgt.,
William W. Ware, 5th Sgt.,
Richard W. Chandler, 1st Corpl.,
William W. Goodwin, 2nd Corpl.,
Julian E. Dickinson, 3rd Corpl.,
Joseph W. Swann, 4th Corpl.,
Atkins, Henry C.,
Bendall, Woodford,
Bendall, Cornelius,
Bendall, Wm. T.,
Baughan, Armistead,
Beazley, Chas.,
Barlow, John D.,
Barlow, Wm. K.,
Barker, Andrew,
Burruss, F. M.,
Burruss, W. M.,
Broaddus, S. W.,
Broaddus, Jas. J.,
Brooks, Wm.,
Burruss, Thos. P.,
Cobb, Addison T.,
Carrington, John F.,
Chiles, John G.,
Carpenter, J. S.,
Canfield, John J.,
Carter, James J.,
Cox, James W.,
Cox, John B.,
Collins, Wm.,
Carneal, Caswell,
Carneal, Jas. B.,
Carneal, Thos. W.,
Carneal, James J.,
Carneal, E.,
Carneal, Joseph B.,
Carneal, Wesley,
Chinault, Gray,
Darcy, Henry,
Dickinson, P. J.,
Dickens, Wm. N.,
Dickinson, John T.,
Evans, John T.,
Evans, R. K.,
Edwards, Thos.,
Eubank, Jas. T.,
Evans, Peter,
Goodwin, John T.,
Haines, Robt. D.,
Hargrove, Thos.,
Isbell, Henry,
Jones, J. T.,
Jones, Thos. H.,
Jones, James T.,
Jones, N. R.,
Jackson, Wm. R.,
Kelly, Rich'd H.,
Kelly, Jas. F.,

List of Members of Comyany K

Mills, Benj. F.,
Mills, Geo. W.,
Madison, R. C.,
Madison, Geo. W.,
Madison, Lewis,
Madison, Thos.,
Mason, John W.,
Martin, John,
Minor, Reuben,
Moore, Lewis T.,
Pugh, A. J.,
Perkins, Wm. C.,
Richardson, Austin,
Rosson, Wilson B.,
Satterwhite, John,
Satterwhite, Wm.,
Self, John,
Self, Paul,
Sacra, Jas. T.,

Southworth, L.,
Sutton, R. E.,
Sutton, Oscar,
Saunders, C. W.,
Sears, Geo. W.,
Small, Wm. W.,
Terry, Stephen,
Terry, Thos. F.,
Terry, Edward W.,
Thomas, Jno. F.,
Thomas, Silas,
Thomas, Wm.,
Tribble, Thos. J.,
Taylor, M.,
Thacker, Edward,
Thacker, Elijah,
Vaughan, John,
Wood, Andrew J.,
Yarbrough, Jas. H.

MUSTER ROLL OF COMPANY G, FORTY-SEVENTH REGIMENT VIR-
GINIA VOLUNTEERS, JUNE 3, '62 TO DECEMBER 30, '62

Luther Wright, Capt.,
Clarence L. Woolfolk, 1st Lt.,
Andrew M. Frayser, 2nd Lt.,
Geo. W. Marshall, 2nd Lt.,
John W. Chapman, Sgt.,
Geo. W. Cobb, Sgt.,
Summerfield Fitzhugh, Sgt.,
John S. Purks, Sgt.,
Thos. Farrar, Sgt.,
Benj. F. Childs, Corpl.,
Andrew J. Gravatt, Corpl.,
Robt. A. Andrews, Corpl.,
Geo. H. Chapman, Corpl.,

Andrews, Robt. F.,
Anderson, Samuel C.,
Alport, Josiah,
Anderson, John,

Barlow, John,
Beazley, Thos. H.,
Beazley, Spencer,
Brooks, Hyter,
Brooks, Foster W.,
Bullock, Jeff. M.,

Barlow, B. F.,
Carter, Jas. B.,
Carter, Ruffin,
Carter, Thos.,
Chandler, Rich'd F.,

Dollins, Lewis,
Donahoe, John,
Donahoe, L. B.,

Ennis, Rufus,
England, Ro. E.,
Eubank, Royal,

Farmer, Sam'l. L.,
Farmer, Ro. B.,
Farmer, Jas. S.,
Farrar, Thos. I.,
Farrar, Geo. M.,
Farmer, Thos.,

Gray, McKenzie,
Gray, Silas,
Grymes, Thos.,
Hawkins, Alex. B.,
Houston, Wm. W.,
Holt, John F.,

List of Members of Company G

Jones, Theo. F.,
Loving, Benj. F.,
Martin, Geo.,
Martin, John,
Martin, Luther,
Martin, Humphrey,
McMullen, Ed. J.,
Miller, J. J.,
Parrish, Jno. G., Jr..
Pavey, J. J.,
Phillips, F. C.,
Pitts, W. W.,
Purks, Jno. J.,
Reynolds, Henry,
Reynolds, Wm. E.,
Rouss, F. L.,
Rouss, Hayden,
Rowe, Jas. M.,

Saunders, Richard,
Seymour, Jacob,
Skinner, J. H.,
Stevens, T. J.,
Sullivan, J. R.,
Smith, Thos. G.,
Smith, John,

Tennant, John J.,
Tignor, Albert B.,
Tignor, Robt.,

Vaughan, Austin,
Withers, Joseph E.,
Withers, Jas. E.,
Withers, Douglas,
Wright, Henry,
Wright, Wiley,
White, John J.

MUSTER ROLL OF COMPANY H, FORTY-SEVENTH REGIMENT VIR-
GINIA VOLUNTEERS, AS OF AUGUST 30, '62

Thomas R. Dew, Captain,
Eugene G. DeJarnette, 1st Lt.,
Jos. F. DeJarnette, 2nd Lt.,
Theodore S. Clarke, Sgt.,
Spencer Coleman, Sgt.,
Jno. W. Wright, Sgt.,
Chas. L. Flippo, Sgt.,
Wm. J. O. Smith, Sgt.,
James W. Anderson, Sgt.,
Samuel B. Andrews, Corpl.,
Wm. T. Noel, Corpl.,
Thos. R. Jeter, Corpl.,
Reuben T. Jeter, Corpl.,
John T. Brann, Corpl.,

Anderson, Esli,
Acors, John B.,

Beazley, Bev. C.,
Bruce, Wm.,
Burrows, Wm.,

Curtis, Wm.,
Chinault, A. C.,
Chinault, Wm.,
Carlton, Jas.,
Carpenter, Joseph,

Carneal, Wm.,
Coleman, Robt.,
Coleman, Wm.,

Dervin, Jas. F.,
Dillard, Edmund,

Elliott, L. P.,

Flippo, Chas. L.,
Flippo, Major,
Fields, Wm.,
Fogg, Jas. H.,
Fugett, Walter R.,

Garnett, R. M.,
Gayle, Lewis M.,
Gayle, Geo. M.,
Gouldin, R. S.,
Gouldin, Simon,
Gouldman, G. T.,
Greenstreet, Eldred,

Hart, John L.,
Hart, Wm. T.,
Hanna, Jas. L.,
Henshaw, Geo.,
Hockaday, Robt.,
Hockaday, Richd.,

List of Members of Company H

Jones, Andrew J.,
Jones, Wm. B.,
Jones, Geo.,
James, Wm. G.,
King, Thos. S.,
Lee, Baldwin,
Lee, James,
Lewis, Wm. F.,
Long, Jno. M.,
Loving, Thos.,
Martin, Geo.,
Marshall, James,
McKenney, Oscar,
Mills, H. C.,
Moore, Lunsford,
Page, Jas. W.,
Parker, R. H.,
Payne, Elijah,
Payne, Geo. W.,
Payne, Joseph,
Payne, Thos. E.,
Pitts, Richard,
Purks, Henry,
Prewitt, John,
Proctor, Thos.,
Robinson, Joseph B.,
Robinson, A. W.,

Rosson, Franklin,
Sacra, Benjamin,
Samuel, James,
Samuel, Henry,
Saunders, Richard,
Snelson, John,
Sirls, Wm. L.,
Skinner, Wm.,
Smith, W. J. O.,
Stanley, Geo.,
Stanley, John,
Stone, Garland,
Sarthan, Pichegru,
Taylor, Thos. E.
Taylor, Henry
Taylor, Wm. T.
Thomas, Alex.
Thomas, Robt.
Thomas, Wm.
Tinder, Wm. H.
Toombs, Gabriel
Toombs, Wm.
Turner, Leland
Whittaker, Edmund
Wilkinson, T. J.
Yates, C. Y.
Yeamans, J. K.

SOLDIERS AND SAILORS OF CAROLINE COUNTY IN THE WORLD WAR 1914–1918

James Roderick Allen,
H. Broaddus Allen,
Edward Carroll Allen,
Roland Andrews,
†Hamilton F. Andrews,
James Floyd Anderson,
John William Atkins,
J. R. Ancarrow,
George M. Ancarrow,
*John Alsop,
*Daniel Anderson,
*John Armstead,
Taylor Boyd Allen,
Joseph Addison Allen,

Lawrence B. Alien,
Eustace C. Allen,
Morris Andrews,
Uly Atkinson,
William R. Arnold,
Carl Andrews,
*Addie Alsop,
*Herman Armstead,
*Clarence P. Anderson,
Kirk Broaddus,
Luther B. Broaddus,
Andrew Boulware,
Roland H. Brooks,
Thos. Benj. Blatt,

EXPLANATORY NOTE: *Indicates Negro.   †..Indicates made supreme sacrifice.

Soldiers and Sailors in World War

Frank Barlow,
Willard Barlow,
E. E. Butler, Jr.,
Harold Borkey,
Malcolm Borkey,
Warner Brown,
John Andrew Brooks,
David L. Bruce,
Peter Blanton,
Edward Bailey Blanton,
Oscar Wright Blanton,
Clement Snead Bell,
John G. Bruce,
Gilchrist G. Burrows,
*Philip Baylor,
*Melvern Baylor,
*Thomas H. Burruss,
*Wilsie John Brown,
*James Banks,
*Fletcher S. Beasley,
*James Boss,
*Tazewell Brown,
*James Brown,
*Munford Bates,
*Ulman B. Byrd,
*Morris E. Burruss,
* †Maxie Berry,
Frank Broaddus,
Mell C. Baseler,
Wm. Henry Beasley,
Otho Beasley,
Roland Jennings Beasley,
Charles M. Beasley,
Bernie Beasley,
Everette Beasley,
Frank B. Beasley,
Wm. B. Bruce,
Edw. Shepherd Barlow,
Ernest Linwood Brooks,
Eugene H. Brooks,
Milton F. Black,
Frank C. Butler,
Overton Brooks,
Alfred E. Bowers,
Wm. Robt. Brown,
John S. Buchanan,

Walter G. Beasley,
*Andrew Thos. Beasley,
*Frank Brown,
*Thomas T. Baylor,
*Willie D. Byrd,
*Willie Carroll Baylor,
*Richard N. Berry,
*Lonnie Bundy,
*Curley Lee Beverly,
*Ledger Buckner,
* †Everette L. Byrd,
*Bennie Byrd,
* †Lewis M. Baylor,
Wm. U. Campbell,
H. C. Carter,
James Collison,
†Robert F. Cooper,
Chassie D. Carneal,
Wm. R. Chinault,
Edgar H. Claytor,
James C. Collins,
Richard Bagby Chinault,
William B. Cluverius,
*John W. Carter,
*Major Chambers,
*George B. Cook,
*Shirley Commodore,
*William Chandler,
*Thomas Coleman,
*Jessie Carter,
*Dennis Childs,
*Charles Coleman,
*Samuel C. Clarke,
*Robt. Lewis Childs,
*Harvey Clark,
*Wm. Thos. Clory,
*Samuel Christian,
*Nathaniel Carter,
C. B. Conway, Jr.,
Frank Chinault,
Clary Carter, D. S. O.,
Julian B. Catlett,
Emmett C. Carter,
Perry Carter,
Charles C. Chiles,
Archie Hilton Carneal,

EXPLANATORY NOTE: *Indicates Negro.   †Indicates made supreme sacrifice.

Soldiers and Sailors in World War

Julian H. Coleman,
Joseph Benj. Carter,
†Herrell Carneal,
*Alfred B. Carter,
*Robert Courtney,
*Jas. Leslie Carter,
*Otho Clark,
*Willis C. Childs,
*George Coleman,
*Stanley Childs,
*Cary Crutchfield,
*Maxie Coleman,
*Carl Childs,
*John Geo. Carter,
*Mansfield Coleman,
*James C. Carter,
John J. Dratt,
John G. Durrett,
Joe Willis DeJarnette,
Frank Woodford Dyson,
Stephen W. Donahoe,
Stephen C. Dabney,
Herndon Davis,
*Wilbur Davis,
*Otho P. Darling,
*Cobb Davis,
*Herbert Davis,
Woodford Dillard,
Frederick Y. Denson,
†Armstead L. Davis,
*Dodson Davis,
*Arthur Dennis,
*James Davis,
Edward J. Eubank,
L. Bransford Elliott,
John W. Elliott, Jr.,
*Cosmo Epps,
*Robert Evans,
Ashby D. Elliott,
Eddie Elliott,
Wm. H. Edwards,
*Wirt Evans,
*Thornton Evans,
Nelson Moffett Fox,
Floyd Farmer,
John S. Farish,

James E. Farmer,
*Harrison Fox,
*Charlie Fox,
*William Fox,
*Richard Fox,
*Matthew Frye,
*Cliff. E. Flippo,
*Caleb Freeman,
*Roy French,
Robert Vivian Farish,
John F. Flagg,
Percy R. Fox,
Royston A. Farish,
*Ernest D. Fortune,
*Winkley A. Freeman,
*Melvin W. Fortune,
*Allen Mack Fortune,
*Elmer E. Fortune,
*George E. Fortune,
*Harvey Fells,
* †Lawless P. Fortune,
Wilbur Gray,
Robert H. Gouldin,
William E. Garrett,
Berry Gray,
Brook W. Gray,
Leslie E. Garrison,
Alfred W. Garrett,
Stephen E. Garrett,
Lewis E. Gouldman,
Richard P. Garrett,
*Robert Garnett,
*Prince A. Garnett,
*Willie B. Garnett,
*Frank Gatewood,
*Joseph Gregory,
*Frank Green,
Dal Gayle,
Maynard O. Gibbs,
Earle C. Garnett,
*William N. Garnett,
*John Douglass Garnett,
*Dolly Gouldman,
*Jenette Gouldin,
* †Alexander Green,
*Robert Gibbs,

EXPLANATORY NOTE: *Indicates Negro.   †Indicates made supreme sacrifice.

Soldiers and Sailors in World War

Winston D. Gravatt,
William B. Gravatt,
Henry J. Garnett,
Lewis E. Gouldman,
Clarence E. Gouldin,

Thomas Hiram Henderson,
Edmund Lee Henshaw,
John M. Henderson,
James Wm. Hayden,
Thomas L. Hunter,
Homer Clyde Hayden,
Wm. Benjamin Hayden,
Scott W. Henderson,
Jos. Minor Holloway,
John T. Hearn,
*James J. Harris,
*Geo. Alfred Harris,
*Edward Hill,
*John Hopkins,
*Emory Holmes,
*William Harrison,
* †Geo. Daniel Howard,
Clement M. Harris,
John A. Holloway,
Garland M. Hale,
Robert Hughes,
†Geo. Clarence Haynes,
Ashton B. Hart,
L. H. Hicks,
*Isaac Hill,
*Rennie Harris,
*Ernest Harris,
*Samuel W. Hailstalk,
*Walter Hicks,
*Harold Hill,
*Lawson W. Hill,

†Henry E. Johnson, Jr.,
Rennie Jones,
William A. Jones,
James Jones,
*Luther Jones,
*Roy James,
*James E. Johnson,
*Samuel Johnson,
*Joseph Jones,
*Clyde Jones,

*Charles Johnson,
George Jones,
Clifton Jones,
Andrew B. Jones,
Angel T. Jennings,
*Peter Johnson,
*George E. James,
*Robert F. Johnson,
*James Jackson,
*Jasper Jackson,
*Beverly Jones,
*James Jefferson,

Richard Kay,
Ashley Weldon Kay,
*Oda Knuckols,
Snowden Kay,
Stanley B. Kay,
*Welford Kay,

James Woody Loving,
Richard G. Liverman,
Jesse Lumpkin,
*Willie Lewis,
*Davis Tally Lindsay,
*Geo. Wm. Lonesome,
*Oliver W. H. Latney,
Dory Loving,
John C. Liverman,
*Garnett Lee,
*Eddie Lawson,
*Albert Lipscomb,
*David Lucas,

John Lewis Motley,
Thomas J. Mundie,
Melchoir Mundie,
Bernard W. Mahon,
Frank Motley,
*Robert Mont,
*Bonnie Miller,
*George Wormley,
*George Butler Moore.
*Esau Mines,
*George Mines,
*Wade Myers,
* †Conway Otis Myers,
*John Lewis Minor,
*Garnett H. Mont,

EXPLANATORY NOTE: *Indicates Negro.   †Indicates made supreme sacrifice.

Soldiers and Sailors in World War

*Jas. Irvin Moore,
*Moses W. Mines,
*Otis Minor,
*Preston M. Morton,
*Richard Mines,
Charles C. Madison,
Joseph E. Middlebrook,
Edward Lee Mills,
Emmett Moss,
*Granville Mosby,
*Herman Minor,
*Roddie Minor,
*John H. Minor,
*Rollen Myers,
*Vivian C. Nelson,
*Clarence Norman,
Jake Morton Newton,
Charles Osburn,

Charles H. Pitts,
Aubrey D. Pickett,
Erin B. Peatross,
Joseph Pickett,
John Lee Parker,
Samuel I. Pitts,
†Henry Motley Pitts,
Floyd Carroll Pitts,
*Junius Page,
*Clifton Parker,
*Weavely T. Parker,
*Thomas Pryor,
*Grover C. Parker,
Roy W. Pickett,
†Ernest C. Purks,
Seth C. Peatross,
Robert L. Pickett,
Bennie B. Purks,
John B. Pugh,
Robert A. Pugh,
*James A. Pitts,
*Samuel Parker,
*Alfred Pendleton,
*Thomas Parker,
*Philip I. Peyton,
*John Pratt,
*Charles H. Pitts,
Wm. T. Ross,

Jas Edgar Richards,
Aubrey D. Reynolds,
Edgar H. Rowe, Jr.,
*Robt. Gordon Ross,
*Joseph Robb,
*John Reynolds,
* †Carlton Redd,
*James H. Robinson,
*Russell E. Ross,
*Charles S. Rollins,
Joseph W. Robinson,
*Eugene Roots,
*Clarence Ross,
*Willie Lee Roane,
*Flandreal T. Rich,
*Ernest L. Rollins,
*Nelson Ross, Jr.,
*Jesse J. Roots,

Willie Frank Southworth,
Guy Harrison Sumner,
Abram Satterwhite,
Leonard Street Southworth,
Wilbur Lee Sacre,
Mason Ryland Sale,
Eugene L. Smith,
Stanley T. Self,
Julian D. Snell,
Adoniram G. Smith,
Fred G. Sirles,
Frank P. Smoot,
Aubrey Southworth,
Henry Saunders,
Lawrence E. Southworth,
*Benjamin Samuel,
†James Reuben Samuel,
Clarence F. Satterwhite,
Oscar Satterwhite,
Allie Sacre,
Howard Alvin Sirles,
Wilbur E. Sale,
Andrew B. Seal,
James A. Skinner,
T. B. Snell,
Worth Shuman,
Frank Samuel,
*John Smith,

EXPLANATORY NOTE: *Indicates Negro.   †Indicates made supreme sacrifice.

Soldiers and Sailors in World War

†L. D. Satterwhite,
Clyde Southworth,
Lee Goodwin Scripture,
*John H. Scott,
*Virgil A. Stern,
*Percy Wm. Sayles,
*Charles Samuel,
*Penny Shields,
*Austin J. Saunders,
*Ernest Saunders,
Walter P. Skinker,
*Larry Sale,
*James Shakespeare,
*James Lyle Sirles,
*Joseph Shepherd,
*Albert Simms,
*John Seymour,
*Clarence Samuel,
*Benjamin Samuel,
*William Starke,
*Wilson Shepherd,
Ryan G. Smith,

Dr. J. R. Travis,
Caldwell M. Tate,
Walter C. Thomas,
Arthur L. Taliaferro,
Geo. Welford Taylor,
*Harrison Towson,
*Charles Taylor,
* †John H. Taylor,
*Clarence Taylor,
* †Alfonso Taylor
Richard Thomas,
†Harry M. Taylor,
Ernest P. Thomas,
Herman Thomas,
Roscoe C. Travis,
*Henry Taylor,
*Wilbur M. Thompson,
*Casper Terrell,
*Woody Thompson,
*Robert Upshaw, Jr.,
Ernest Linwood Upshaw,

Wm. A. Vaughan,
*Chas. Vaughan,
Clem Vaughan,

Charles S. Wharton,
Robert R. Wright,
John Butler Wright,
Henry J. Warrington,
George Williams,
Floyd Wright,
Otis Wright,
†Reuben Wright,
*Luther Wright,
*Grant Wright,
*Spencer Whiting,
*Minor Wingfield,
'Harry Wilson,
*Clem A. Woolfolk,
*Willie A. Ware,
*Henry Wright,
*Eddie Julian Waller,
E. May Wright,
Harold Wright,
Julian B. Wright,
*James Washington,
*Clarence Washington,
*Burton Washington,
*Dennis Weathers,
*Leonard White,
*Silas Washington,
*Taylor Wright,
*Major Wright,
*Frederick A. Wilbur,
Thomas B. Washington,
Fred Whittaker,
Patrick H. Wright,
Edw. Glassel Wright,

Henry S. Young,
*John Wm. Young,
*Luther L. Young,
*Chester Yates,
*Jesse Edw. Young,
* †Stephen R. Young,

EXPLANATORY NOTE: *Indicates Negro.   †Indicates made supreme sacrifice.

NOTE.—Soon after the Armistice, November 11, 1918, the citizens of the county erected a bronze tablet at the court house on which are the names of the twenty-three men who made the supreme sacrifice.

THE CAROLINE HOME GUARD OF 1917–18

Shortly after America's entrance into the World War many citizens of Caroline who, became of age or other hindrance, could not enter the regular army, but who desired to express their loyalty to the nation, came together and organized a company known as the Home Guard of Caroline County. Led by a distinguished veteran of the Civil War this company drilled and practiced regularly and thus became prepared to maintain law and order at home and, if it came to the worst, were also prepared to defend hearth and home against any invasion of the enemy.   A roster of the Caroline Home Guard follows:

T. D. Coghill, Captain,
H. T. Louthan, 1st Lieut.,
B. P. Noland, 1st Sergt.,
J. W. Allport, 3rd Sgt.,
R. B. Covington, Corpl.,
J. R. Houston, Corpl.,
Dr. J. R. Allen,
G. D. Allport,
R. W. Allen,
A. H. Allen,
B. F. Allen,
R. B. Andrews,
A. F. Turner, 2nd Lieut.,
O. W. Southworth, 2nd Sgt.,
C. F. Hicks, 4th Sgt.,
T. K. Boulware, Corpl.,
G. R. Dorsey, Corpl.,
J. L. Bullock,
Geo. Burruss,
J. R. Blanton,
Lewis Brooks,
C. L. Bullard,
Corbin Bowie,
Geo. W. Boulware,
J. D. Coghill,
E. S. Coghill,
R. A. Coghill,
E. B. Collins,
W. L. Campbell,
O. M. Cass,
Le Roy Dunn,
J. F. Davis,
S. H. Evans,
R. D. Flagg,
T. R. Gibson,
J. H. Gatewood,
T. B. Gill,
Dr. L. J. Head,

R. F. Holberton,
H. L. Isbell,
R. L. Jones,
M. H. Jones,
J. L. Jordan,
Geo. R. Jeter,
Eugene Jeter,
Benjamin Jeter,
L. E. Martin,
W. L. McAlister,
W. G. Motley,
Dr. A. C. Monroe,
J. B. Meyers,
R. B. Parr,
Roper Rains,
J. T. Richards,
F. B. Richerson,
W. B. Seaman,
H. B. Shuman,
J. W. Simpkins,
W. T. Satterwhite,
Wm. B. Smith,
A. L. Smith,
D. C. Smith,
F. Y. Sirles,
W. G. Taliaferro,
John M. Taylor,
C. H. Taylor,
Willie Thomas,
T. B. Trevillian,
R. L. Upshaw,
T. C. Valentine,
A. F. Wright,
Clarence Williams,
R. M. Waller,
Jourdan Woolfolk,
J. D. Williams,
R. J. Wright.

CIVIL WAR STORIES

REMINISCENCES OF JUDGE E. C. MONCURE

"I rode by the side of General Lee from Guiney Station in Caroline to within a few miles of Spotsylvania Court House. We were being pressed closely by the enemy, and the soldiers who had preceded us were almost worn out and were lying by the roadside resting and sleeping. General Lee rode up to them and said very gently, " I know you are tired and sleepy, but you do not want to be taken prisoners. The enemy is advancing on us and will be along before daybreak, and it is better for you to move on."

Some of the men were in bad humour and replied, "It is easy for you to tell us to move on. You are mounted and have all the rations you want." Then some one recognized General Lee and whispered "Marse Robert." In an instant every man was on his feet while there went up a shout, "Yes, Marse Robert, we will move on and go anywhere you say—even to hell itself."

REMINISCENCES OF A. B. CHANDLER, SR.

On October 1, 1858, having completed my course at the old-field school, my father sent me to Hanover Academy then owned by Lewis M. Coleman. Here I spent two sessions and a half, leaving in 1861 for the army. Mr. Coleman managed the school until 1859, when he was elected professor of Latin in the University of Virginia. He was afterwards colonel of artillery in the C. S. A., and was killed in battle. Mr. Hilary P. Jones succeeded Mr. Coleman as owner and principal of the Academy, and so continued until 1861, when the school was disbanded for the war. Mr. Jones also became Colonel of Artillery and survived the war. At this school were gathered about eighty young men from Virginia and all over the South. We had students from Mississippi, Alabama, Louisiana and Texas. These were all splendid young men, the flower of Southern culture. In the spring of 1861 the war broke up the school. Grant's army came through Bowling Green and Caroline in May, 1864. My grandmother was still living at Woodlawn, and also my father and mother. The Northern soldier laid waste everything that he could reach. They filled my grandmother's residence, stole everything they could carry off, and what they could not carry away they destroyed. My father was sick and died while his bed-chamber was full of these soldiers. After they had appropriated everything on the place that could be eaten, my grandmother asked them what she was to live on, and they told her to "eat grass," and this she had almost to do. On April 2, 1865, I was taken prisoner at Hatcher's run, south of Petersburg, and spent ten weeks a prisoner at Point Lookout, Maryland, and released from there in June. Our rations there were a small piece of raw cod fish, a half a loaf of bread and a small tin cup full of bean water slightly seasoned with meat. This was a day's ration. The water was sweet and very scarce. The prisoners suffered greatly for want of water. The pumps in the prison enclosure would give out about 10:00 A. M. and then there was no more water that day. I have seen prisoners jammed around these pumps for a hundred yards fighting to get to them for water. I was more fortunate than the soldiers generally because I met an old friend named Vinson, a fellow student from Louisiana, at Hanover Academy. The prisoner camp was laid out in streets, and the prisoners were divided into companies and a corporal put in charge of each company. This corporal was a Confederate soldier, and his duty was, at dinner time, to collect and march his company to the dining room to get their bean water, and for this service he was given a paddle which entitled him to get his water at the commissary pump. Vinson, being a friend of mine, invited me to come to his tent whenever I wanted water, and I availed myself of this privilege and thus never suffered for water. The prison consisted of many acres enclosed by a high plank fence with a parapet on which negro soldiers walked guarding the prisoners, and if you happened to step beyond the dead line you were shot down.

REMINISCENCES OF T. B. WYATT

The section of the country from the Wilderness, Fredericksburg, Guines Station, Louisa, etc., was famous for Yankee scouting and some big battles. The roads and land were generally level and the roads composed of sand mixed with clay. Many wattle fences were to be seen in this neighborhood. These fences were made with split cedar stakes driven down about two feet apart and cedar brush wattled in, which made a tight and almost impregnable fence. These fences were renewed annually with new cedar brush. The roads were built with reference to saving distance, but necessarily there were a good many angles.

One evening in early spring, 1863 I heard that the Yankees were in our section. I started on a voyage of discovery down the Needwood Road by the Hunters, Vaughan, Grubbs, Peatross, Moores, Hurts, Seays, Concord Church, Needwood, Bowers Store and Bethel Church. Then I came into the main road from Mangohick to Hanover Court House, and there I saw a Yankee cavalryman going toward Hanover Court House at full speed. I could have captured him with his fine horse and accoutrements.

I went back to Taliaferro Hunter's and, firing him with zeal and enthusiasm at my lost opportunity, he decided to go back with me and try his luck the next morning. Early the next day I fixed up my Sharpe's carbine or army gun, from which, owing to an explosion, eight or ten inches had been taken off. After pocketing half a dozen home made cartridges of brown paper and G. D. caps, Hunter and I started out looking for the Yankees and hoping that we might find a straggler and take him in. We had not ridden very far before people along the road stopped us, asked us what we meant by facing in battle array a Yankee army, and begged us to go back home.

When we had gotten six miles from home, three hundred yards from Dr. R. T. Wortham's home, "The Grove," we had come to the end of these wattle fence angles (not "the bloody angle.") At the front end, within fifty yards of us, were four Yankees moving in a slow, quiet walk. On account of the wattle fence we were unable to escape and hastily I threw the old carbine over the fence, hoping it would escape notice. However, one of the sharp-eyed Yanks saw it going over and immediately went after it, while the other three took possession of us and our horses. They laughed heartily upon seeing my old dilapidated weapon and its crude worn out condition when compared with fine arms of the Yanks. When we reached Dr. Wortham's house, the ladies were sitting on the piazza, and on approaching I hollered "The Yanks have me."

Our captors then took us to Pamunkey bridge, where their command had made camp. After loitering there for several hours, we marched leisurely down the river to Mr. Geo. Taylor's home, an old time, colonial, fine brick mansion. The Yanks camped in front of the house and in the midst of a magnificient wheatfield the extent or size of the field being easily two or three hundred acres, and the wheat not ripe but in full flower, headhigh, and the stake so strong that a tin plate would easily be held up by the stalks.   Soon after getting there, Captain Ward, Company F, 9th or 11th Pennsylvania Cavalry, an exceptionally nice man, took us up to Mr. Taylor's to get lunch.   Mr. Taylor received us, Taliaferro and me, but showed no friendliness for the Yank. On getting back to the camp one of the four Yanks who captured us, came up, pulled out his pistol, pointed it at me and said he was going to shoot me.   He had been drinking and I was very much frightened indeed.   Fortunately, another Yank came along and made him put his gun up and leave.   We were then taken before Colonel Spears.   He asked us what we were doing there. I told him I heard the Yankees were in the neighborhood and had come to find the best way to get out of their reach.   He said, "You are a spy.   We will have you shot."   Hunter said that I then commenced praying.   That night we slept in the woods with only the sky and the stars for covering, Yankees on all sides of us.

STORY OF DR. JOSEPH W. EGGLESTON

During the years the manuscript of this work was in preparation, the author frequently visited Dr. Joseph W. Eggleston at his office in the Masonic Temple in Richmond.   Dr. Eggleston was Grand Master of Masons in Virginia in 1908, and since has served for many years as Treasurer of the Grand Lodge of Virginia.   One of his brothers, George Cary Eggleston, became famous as editor of the New York *World*, and another brother, Edward Eggleston, became famous as author of "The Hoosier Schoolmaster" and other novels.   Dr. Joseph W. Eggleston himself has written and published several books, among them "Tuckahoe"—an old fashioned story of an old fashioned people; but those who have known him personally will remember him best as a raconteur.   Following is a story he once told the author of his experience as a soldier in the Confederate Army.   It is included in this work because the scene of it is laid in Caroline:

"When Grant moved to Lee's left and tried to beat him to Richmond, it so happened that Lamkin's Battery of Haskell's Battalion, of which I was a member, was the very last to leave encampment on the Po river not far from Spotsylvania.   We were to have drawn rations that morning but they only came up in the wagons at about five o'clock in the afternoon, almost the very moment we were ordered to march.   We started hungry and did not pause till sometime the next day.

"I was fortunate in that when we had last drawn rations I got a triple ration of fat bacon by accepting a piece that was bruised black before the hog was killed, but perfectly sound.

"All night the only order we got was "close up," often repeated because Grant was close behind. When we got water at all it was by dipping our canteens in a creek or pond as we waded through. What wells there were on the line of march were drawn dry before we got to them. The dust was a cloud of impalpable powder which, I was afterwards told, was seen ten miles away. The men were a funny sight. A pile of dust over eyebrows and mustaches, and streams of sweat running down every face.

"As we trudged along, we were somewhat silent as a rule. This was uncommon in that army, for a laugh was the common condition, even in the deadliest fight. Indeed the famous "Rebel Yell" was as much a laugh as anything else. It was a mixture the like of which has never been known since and never will be again.

"About midday I came up with my brother, George Cary Eggleston, later editor of the *New York World* for twenty years and he was all but dead. All his life he boasted that he never knew he had a stomach except by being hungry, and as he had nothing for thirty-six hours he must have been hungry indeed. Somehow it had not occurred to me that he was worse off than I who had been munching that dirty black pork without bread. I heard him exclaim "If I had a million dollars I give give it all for a piece of meat as big as two fingers." Of course I hauled out my pork, covered with dirt and offered it to him. He refused it and I told him I was no longer hungry and that we must soon halt from exhaustion, if from nothing else, and that plenty was in the wagons right in front of us. He still refused to take it till I told him I would throw it over the fence unless he took it. Many years later, after he had lived in New York clubs for years, I was there on a visit. He gave a dinner in my honor in the Reform Club. After a luxurious meal, while we were still at the table, he asked each one to give an account of the most enjoyable meal they could recall. One of the guests was a son of General O. O. Howard. After each had spun his yarn, he described the above and said that it had always remained in his memory as the most luxurious food he could remember.

"When we crossed the North Anna the enemy opened on us, the rear of the army, but we met Pickett's Division there fresh and ready for them.   There was no time to tear down the bridge but the Artillery shot it away.   As soon as we stopped we drew rations and I saw a man fall asleep with food in his hand.   I also saw a chaplain of Corse's Brigade preaching in a piece of woods, with shells tearing the trees, and he preached a long sermon too."

DABNEY JORDAN WALLER'S EXPERIENCE

Dabney Jordan Waller, when past four score years, related the following Civil War experience to the author:

"I was a member of Company B., Ninth Virginia Cavalry, S. A. Swann was Captain when the war began and John H. Ware was captain of this company when the war closed.   Our first Colonel was W. H. F. Lee, and when the war closed Thomas W. Waller, of Stafford was Colonel.   General Beale commanded the Brigade and W. H. F. Lee the division.

"I have no war record worth noting, save that I conscientiously performed the duties which devolved upon me.   About the middle of June, 1861, I returned home from college, and after a few days spent in fitting myself out for service I set out for the army, accompanied by my servant John.   The army was then near Manassas awaiting battle.   I was mustered into the company known as the Caroline Light Dragoons, and shortly after we went into battle.   Our regiment acquitted itself so well here that we won the title, "The Fighting Ninth."

"I had a thrilling experience near Brandy Station, Culpeper, Va., during the cavalry engagement there.   I was unhorsed, through my mount rearing and falling back on me, and though surrounded by the enemy I managed to regain my saddle and ride through the enemy lines and back to my command.

"Again at Ashland, Va., I was in a charge and was near our flag-bearer when he was shot down.   I caught the flag and carried it through the day.   We defeated the enemy that day and I came out without a scratch, but with two bullet holes through my hat and two in my coat.   The old flag had several.

"I was on detail service at the time of the surrender, and returned home about three weeks afterward.   When I joined my company I was the youngest member of it and received the nickname "Baby" which clung to me through the war.   When the conflict ended I was sergeant of Company B, Ninth Virginia Cavalry."

GENERAL JACKSON'S LAST WINTER IN CAROLINE

From a very remarkable paper read before the Military Historical Society of Massachusetts by the late James Power Smith, Captain and A. D. C. to Stonewall Jackson, we learn that the General spent his last winter in an office building adjacent to the residence of James Parke Corbin at Moss Neck, Caroline county.

" Moss Neck," Where Jackson Spent His Last Winter—House to Right

Colonel Corbin was a man of large estate, and generous heart, and so when Jackson decided to go into winter quarters at Moss Neck the Corbin mansion was placed at the disposal of the famous General. The courtesy was declined on the grounds that Jackson was unwilling to enjoy the comforts of a mansion when his men were poorly clad and living in tents, and so he and his men went into tents together.

Owing to the severity of the weather the General contracted a serious cold which caused his friend and Medical Director, Dr. Hunter McGuire, to insist that he seek better shelter and, reluctantly consenting, he compromised by occupying the office building which stood in the yard of the mansion.

During the winter at Moss Neck many famous men visited Jackson's Headquarters, among them Generals Lee and Stuart; Colonel Leslie, of England; Colonel Freemantle, of the famous Cold Stream Guards; Lord Wolsley, afterward British Commander-in-Chief; John Esten Cooke the famous novelist; Mr. Lawley, editor of *The London Times;* and the Marquis of Hartington, afterward the Duke of Devonshire.

Some time in March General Jackson broke up headquarters at Moss Neck and pitched his tents at Yerby's place in the Massaponax Valley, a short distance from General Headquarters and here made preparations for what proved to be one of the most remarkable series of battles in all history, and which were fought at Fredericksburg, Salem Church, Chancellorsville and the Wilderness.

James Power Smith related that, "Generals Lee and Jackson spent the night before the battle of Chancellorsville sleeping on the pine straw at a point about one mile and a half east of Chancellorsville, where the Catherine Furnace road leaves the old Orange Plank road and sometime during that night I was awakened by the chill and saw the two generals seated on cracker boxes, leaning forward, warming their hands over a scant fire of twigs." Captain Smith further relates that 3:00 P. M. of the following day he saw Jackson seated on a stump, on the old Brock Road, writing what proved to be his last dispatch to General Lee, the original of which is now in the Virginia State Library. A part of this stump for many years had an honoured place in the home of Mr. Smith.

Probably the most accurate story of the wounding of Jackson is to be found in the paper above referred to, the substance of which is as follows: On the evening of May 2nd, after a day of signal victories, General Jackson, in his eagerness to press his front lines on to Chancellorsville, consented that the reserve division of General A. P. Hill should be brought up and placed in the front, and, while the new line was forming, Jackson rode forward with two of his staff and a number of signal sergeants and couriers.

He had not gone very far when he came upon a detachment of Federal infantry, lying on their arms, who fired upon him causing him to turn back toward his line. As he approached the the Confederate line he and his horseman were mistaken for a party of the enemy and fired upon, the volley disabling several of his companions. Spurring his horse across the road he was met by a second volley from a company of Lane's North Carolina Brigade, from which he received a ball through the palm of his right hand, a ball through his left wrist, and a third through the left arm, half-way between the shoulder and the elbow. The latter bullet splintered the bone and severed an artery.

Litter bearers were brought and, under a galling fire, started with the wounded to the rear, but before reaching an ambulance the stretcher bearers were twice shot down, and once the fainting General fell to the ground.

At a field hospital in the wilderness, after midnight, Dr. Hunter McGuire amputated the left arm near the shoulder, and removed a bullet from the right hand.

"The Office" at Fairfield, in which Stonewall Jackson Died—House on Left

On the following day General Jackson was removed to Guiney Station in Caroline county, on the Richmond, Fredericksburg and Potomac Railroad, and there on Sunday, May 9, 1863, in "The Office"—a building which stood near the manor house on the estate of "Fairfield," established at the beginning of the eighteenth century by John Thornton, of the famous Thornton family of "Ormesby," but owned at the time by Thomas Coleman Chandler, whose descendants still occupy a prominent place in the life of the Guinea community, the great general passed over the river to "rest under the shade of the trees."

The house in which the great strategist died, a picture of which appears in this volume, was purchased many years after the Civil War, by the Richmond Fredericksburg and Potomac Railroad Company, and is kept as a shrine for the lovers of the Lost Cause.

THE KILLING OF BOOTH IN CAROLINE

Many historians have stated that John Wilkes Booth killed Abraham Lincoln to rid his country of a tyrant. But the south was not his (Booth's) country for he was never at any time a citizen or a resident of the Confederacy. The true motive of the assassination was to avenge the death of Captain John Y. Beall, Booth's bosom friend, whom he thought had been unjustly executed.

Beall, a Virginian of good birth, liberal education, attractive personality and remarkable courage, undertook a hazardous enterprise on Lake Erie in the fall of 1864, and was captured and sentenced to death as a pirate. Booth interested himself in Beall's behalf, procured documents to prove that his friend was a commissioned officer of the Confederate Navy, presented the evidence to Lincoln, and secured from him the promise that Beall should not be executed, but should be treated as a prisoner of war. This promise gave offense to Secretary Seward, who induced the President to sanction the execution and Beall was hanged at Governor's Island on February 24, 1865.

Booth, immediately upon the execution of Beall, organized a conspiracy for the assassination of both Lincoln and Seward, and on April 14, 1865 seven weeks after the hanging of the gallant Confederate captain, the plot was executed.

On April 24th, just ten days after the assassination, Booth and Herold, his accomplice, entered Caroline, being ferried across the Rappahannock river, from Port Conway to Port Royal, by a negro fisherman named Rollins. On the same ferry boat were three Confederate cavalrymen—Jett, Ruggles and Bainbridge—and it is said that Booth sat on one of their horses while crossing the river.

Three or four miles farther on Booth was left at the residence of Richard H. Garrett, under the guise of a wounded Confederate soldier by the name of Boyd, and Herold went on with the three soldiers to the town of Bowling Green, thirteen miles distant.

The next day Herold came back to the Garrett farm and joined Booth, and that same afternoon a troop of Federal cavalry in search of the assassins passed the Garrett home (Booth lying in the yard at the time) and aroused so much suspicion on the part of Mr. Garrett that he urged the departure of his questionable guests, who thereupon sought refuge in a woods back of the plantation. After nightfall the assassins returned and pleaded so earnestly for shelter that "Jack" Garrett, one of Mr. R. H. Garrett's sons, consented that they might occupy a large tobacco barn which stood near the house; but becoming apprenhensive that the men might try to make off with his father's horses, the son stationed himself in an adjacent corn-crib and remained on watch that night.

The Garrett House, in Which John Wilkes Booth Died

The Federal cavalrymen came on to Bowling Green, where they found Jett, one of the soldiers with whom Booth had journeyed as far as Garrett's, and seizing him in bed at midnight, they compelled him, at the point of a revolver, to guide them to the Garrett plantation where Booth had been left the previous day. The cavalrymen reached Mr. Garrett's home at 2:00 o'clock Wednesday morning, April 26th, and demanded that he disclose the whereabouts of the assassins. Mr. Garrett insisted that the two strangers had gone to the woods, whereupon Lieutenant Baker, thinking that he was being foiled in his effort to capture the men, called for a rope to hang Mr. Garrett to one of the trees on the lawn. To save his father, the son came forward and pointed out the tobacco barn as the hiding place of the fugitives. (Garrett's Testimony—*Surratt Trial*—page 302). The boy was pushed inside the dark building by Lieutenant Baker, but was ordered out by Booth who threatened to take his life. Baker then called to Booth saying, "We have fifty armed men around this barn, and unless you surrender we will set fire to the building." Out of the darkness came the voice of Booth, saying, "Captain, give a lame man a chance. Draw your men up before the door and I will come out and fight the whole command." Baker replied to this challenge saying, "We came to arrest you, not to fight you," to which the voice in the darkness responded, "Well then, my brave boys, you may prepare a stretcher for me."

Herold broke under the strain and surrendered his arms, and was pulled out empty-handed and turned over to one Doherty, one of the cavalrymen, who tied him to a tree. Conger, another member of the troop, then set fire to the barn, and, as the flames lit up the interior, Baker caught sight of Booth as he was about to make his exit. He had just arisen from his bed of straw, with a crutch under his left arm and a carbine in his right hand, and was in the act of starting toward the fire. He caught up an old table as if to smother out the blaze, but, looking up he saw the flames mounting to the rafters. "Then," Baker relates, "he seemed to abandon hope, and his countenance fell. Dropping his crutch and passing the carbine to his left hand, with a kind of limping, halting, jump, he advanced toward the door where Baker, unseen by him, was awaiting his approach. When within about twelve feet of the door he paused for a moment, as if trying to make some decision, when a shot rang out, and, with an upward spring, Booth fell on his back, a ball having passed entirely through his neck.

Baker was upon the fallen man in an instant, wrenching the revolver from his clenched hand. Garrett next entered the barn calling for help to put out the fire. Conger rushed in, exclaiming, "he shot himself," to which Baker replied, "He did not, you shot him." Conger rejoined, "I did not," and Baker persisted in saying, "He did not shoot himself, for I saw him the whole time; and the man who shot him goes back to Washington under arrest."

The fire continued to gain headway, and the apparently lifeless body was removed from the danger of the flames and laid under a tree. Signs of life reappeared, and he was carried to Mr. Garrett's porch and a messenger was sent to Port Royal for a physician, Doctor Urquhart, who, on his arrival, gave it as his opinion that Booth could not live more than one hour.

Conger, eager to be off to Washington with the momentous news, began to rifle the pockets of the dying man, who murmured all the while, "Kill me, please kill me," until he lapsed into unconsciousness which at seven o'clock deepened into death.

The first sergeant of the company from which the detachment of cavalry was drawn—Boston Corbett by name—soon claimed that he fired the shot which killed Booth, and when called to account by his superior officer, said "Colonel, Providence directed me." Corbett afterward toured the North lecturing on the pursuit and capture of the assassins, and was everywhere acclamed and welcomed as an avenger of blood. His story was not corroborated by the testimony of a single witness out of the thirty-four men who were his comrades on the expedition.

In after years Corbett received an appointment as door keeper of the Kansas House of Representatives, and, while serving in that capacity, tried to exterminate that body with a revolver, in consequence of which he finished his days in a lunatic asylum.

The question as to whether Booth was shot by one of his captors, or whether he killed himself, has never been, and never can be, definitely answered.

Booth's body was sewn up in an army blanket and conveyed by a market wagon to Belle Plain where it was put on board a boat and sent to Washington. A post mortem examination, for the purpose of identification, revealed that the bullet which caused his death passed through the neck bone, and this section of the perforated vertebrae was removed by the surgeon-general for preservation as a national memento. His remains were placed in a gun box and buried beneath a cell of the Old Penitentiary.

Herold, Mrs. Surratt, Payne and Atzerodt were tried as accomplices in the conspiracy, and were convicted and hanged. Miss Rita Gray, of Upper Zion owns a charred section of Booth's crutch which was taken from the barn.

UNITED DAUGHTERS OF THE CONFEDERACY

CAROLINE CHAPTER

The Caroline Chapter, U. D. C., was chartered and organized on May 4, 1896. The first officers were as follows: Sallie Collins Smith, president; Mary M. Wallace, vice-president; Margaret Wallace, secretary and M . Lydia Luck, treasurer.

The present membership is as follows: Miss Elizabeth Boxley, Richmond; Mrs. C. C. Chewning, Chilesburg; Mrs. A. W. Davis, Blantons; Mrs. R. T. Dillard, Fredericksburg; Mrs. C. R. Dickinson, Florida; Mrs. G. K. Coleman, Ruther Glen; Miss Fanny Ellyson, Richmond; Mrs. W. C. Flagg, Houston, Texas; Mrs. Gertrude Coleman Hart, Chicago; Miss Annie Hall, Fredericksburg; Mrs. M. E. Luck, Ashland; Mrs. M. Luck Grove, Richmond; Mrs. Lydia Luck Quarles, Ashland; Miss Grace Moncure, Ruther Glen; Miss Elizabeth Moncure, Ruther Glen; Mrs. M. D. Parr, Paige; Miss Susie Parker, Suffolk; Mrs. J. M. Quisenberry, Richmond; Mrs. J. S. Ryland, Cedon; Mrs. Charles Semff, New York; Mrs. Cornelius T. Smith, Croxton; Mrs. C. T. Smith, Jr., Charlottesville; Mrs. W. W. Smith, Golansville; Mrs. A. G. Smith, Golansville; Mrs. C. A. Smith, Richmond; Miss Clara L. Smith, Croxton; Mrs. Edna Wallace, Warren; Miss Lizzie White, Chilesburg; Mrs. C. J. Wright, Bowling Green; Miss Maggie R. Wallace, New York; Mrs. S. W. Ware, Croxton. The officers are: Mrs. C. T. Smith, president; Mrs. R. T. Dillard, first vice-president; Mrs. A. W. Davis, second vice-president; Mrs. M. D. Parr, secretary; Miss Lizzie White, treasurer.

BOWLING GREEN CHAPTER

The Bowling Green Chapter was chartered on June 18, 1904, with the following members: Mrs. Lina J. Baker, (President), Mrs. W. L. Broaddus, Mrs. A. B. Chandler, Mrs. G. R. Collins, Mrs. Charles W. Collins, Miss Blanche Coghill, Mrs. Ellen W. Downing, Mrs. T. B. Gill, Miss Louisa Brown Glassell, Mrs. R. T. Glassell, Mrs. J. L. Jordan, Mrs. E. C. Moncure, Miss Annie McCaulay, Mrs. R. O. Peatross, Mrs. L. M. Robinson, (Secretary), Miss Julia Lindsey Samuel, Miss Frances O. White and Mrs. John L. White.

The present membership is as follows: Mrs. Kate Broaddus, Mrs. Blanche Broaddus, Miss Mary Buckner, Mrs. Frances Glassel Beale, Mrs. Nettie Blank, Miss Minnie Broaddus, Miss

Lois Broaddus, Mrs. Susie Broaddus, Mrs. W. L. Burruss, Mrs. A. S. Crouch, Miss Blanche Coghill, Mrs. A. B. Chandler, Miss Bertha Ennis, Mrs. Alice McKinney Finch, Mrs. L. D. George, Miss Louisa Glassel, Mrs. Lucy Moncure Gill, Miss Sue Gouldman, Miss Louisa B. Glassel, Mrs. Florence Hoskins, Mrs. Frances Miller Haynes, Mrs. J. L. Jordan, Mrs. A. L. Martin, Mrs. Andrew Marshall, Mrs. W. P. Miller, Miss Helen Miller, Mrs. Susan Martin, Mrs. Kate Mayo, Mrs. Richard T. Pratt, Mrs. B. M. Skinker, Mrs. O. P. Smoot, Mrs. Eugene Travis, Mrs. O. E. D. Warner, Miss Lucy Marshall Woolfolk, Miss Mary M. Woolfolk, Mrs. J. Boyd Washington.

CLERKS OF CAROLINE COUNTY COURTS

Benjamin Robinson, from 1727 to 1763.

Joseph Robinson, (son of Benjamin) 1763 to 1780.

William Nelson, 1780 to 1799.

John Pendleton, 1799 to 1814.

John L. Pendleton, 1814 to 1845.

Robert Hudgin (Circuit Court), 1831 to 1845.

George W. Marshall (County Court), 1845 to 1863.

George Keith Taylor (Circuit Court), 1845 to 1863.

Robert Hudgin (County Court), 1863 to 1892.

T. C. Valentine (Circuit Court), 1892–93.

Thomas W. Valentine (Circuit Court), 1893 to 1901.

T. C. Valentine (Circuit Court), 1901 to consolidation of the two offices.

E. R. Coghill (County Court), 1893 to consolidation of the two offices.

E. R. Coghill (Circuit Court), 1904 to the present (1924).

During the Reconstruction Period following the Civil War it was necessary to subscribe to the "Test Oath" in order to hold office. This Mr. Hudgin declined to do, upon which General Canby, then in charge of the military district in which Caroline was located, appointed Mr. John Dratt, of Woodford. Mr. Dratt held the office until after the election which ratified the new constitution which had been adopted by the Reconstruction or Underwood Convention. Mr. Dratt, very magnanimously, insisted that Mr. Hudgin discharge the duties of the office as before, and draw the salary for the same, which was done.

EXTRACT FROM THE AUTOBIOGRAPHY OF ROBERT
HUDGIN WHICH WAS PUBLISHED IN "MEMORIALS
OF OLD VIRGINIA CLERKS" BY F. JOHNSTON
(LYNCHBURG) 1888.

"In 1817 my mother placed me in the office of John T. Ford,
Clerk of Fredericksburg District Chancery Court, to remain until
I was twenty-one years old. I was then fifteen. I served out the
time and remained in Mr. Ford's employ until his death. I then
entered the employment of his successor, the venerable Isaac H.
Williams and remained with him until 1827.

"At the instance of several leading lawyers of Fredericksburg
I came to Caroline county in 1827 and arranged with John L.
Pendleton, Clerk of the County Court, to take sole charge of the
Clerk's Office for a term of years, and entered upon the duties of
the office at once. I soon put in order and rearranged all of the
old books and papers, which had been entrusted to deputies whose
neglect had caused much complaint, and for this work I received
from the justices of the county, sitting as a court, a vote of thanks.

" In 1831 I was appointed Clerk of the Circuit Court by Judge
John Tayloe Lomax and discharged the duties of this office, in
connection with my duties as Mr. Pendleton's deputy, until 1845,
when I resigned both offices to take up the practice of law.

" In 1860 I moved to Fauquier county and took charge of the
Fauquier White Sulphur Springs, which I had bought, and remained there until 1863, when my entire property was destroyed
by the Northern Army. From sheer destitution I was compelled
to return to my old home in Caroline and upon my return George
K. Taylor, Clerk of the Circuit, (now Clerk of the Court of
Appeals at Richmond) and George W. Marshall, Clerk of the
County Court, resigned their offices and I was appointed in their
stead and have held the offices ever since. In the last election of
county officers I received, out of a voting list of three thousand,
every vote but three and have good reason to know that two
of these were scratched by mistake.

"I am now eighty-four and a half years old and have been
blessed with good health all my life and am now able to walk to
and from the office, half mile from my house and to discharge
its varied duties."

(Signed) ROBERT HUDGIN."

February 4, 1887."

TREASURERS OF CAROLINE

The office of Treasurer dates to 1869. Prior to that time the county Sheriff collected the taxes and was sheriff-treasurer. George Marshall was the first treasurer under the new system and was succeeded by Reuben Richerson. Together these two men served fourteen years. They, in turn, were succeeded by the following men: Cornelius T. Smith, show served eight years; S. J. R. White, two years; W. R. W. Garrett, two years; W. G. Coghill, one year; Cornelius T. Smith, twenty-eight years. Captain Smith retired in 1923 and George Ridgley Dorsey was elected to succeed him.

COMMONWEALTH'S ATTORNEYS FOR CAROLINE

The office became elective in 1851. Since that time the following men have served the county in this capacity. Randolph Peyton, Eustace Conway Moncure, Algernon Bertrand Chandler, William E. Ennis, Willing Bowie and Thomas H. Blanton. The latter was elected in 1923.

SHERIFFS OF CAROLINE

This office dates back to 1634. Became an elective office with the Constitution of 1851. Prior to that time the office was usually held by the presiding Justice of the County Court. The following men have served since the office became elective: Alexander Scott, Samuel Swann, T. D. Coghill, W. J. Collawn and T. B. Gill

JUDGES OF THE CIRCUIT COURT OF CAROLINE

The Circuit Court was established in Virginia in 1819. Since that time the following Judges have presided over the Caroline Circuit Court: John Taylor Lomax, Richard H. Coleman, John Critcher, J. M. Chapman, W. S. Barton, J. E. Mason and R. H. L. Chichester.

SOME CAROLINE MERCHANTS IN 1924

C. L. Allen, Balty; E. C. Allen, Guinea; J. W. Barlow, Bowling Green; L. W. Baylor, Bowling Green; John W. Basley, Milford; Mrs. O. B. Blanton, Cedon; Mrs. Cora L. Blanton, McDuff; R. L. Blanton, McDuff; W. E. Blair, Cedon; Frank Bowie, Mica; S. W. Broaddus' Sons, Bowling Green; R. F. Broaddus, Newtown; J. I. Broaddus, Gether; M. W. Byrd, Central Point; T. E. Campbell, Milford; O. H. Carneal, Knopf; E. M. Coleman, Penola;

G. K. Coleman, Ruther Glen; R. A. Coghill, Bowling Green; J. W. Gill, Bowling Green; R. M. Gray, Bowling Green; L. D. Vincent, Bowling Green; Peyton Davis, Bowling Green; Leroy Pugh, Bowling Green; Mrs. Maggie Collins, Ideal; H. E. Covington, Kidd's Fork; C. W. Colbert, Guinea; J. F. Davis, Blantons; Joe Willis DeJarnette, Bowling Green; W. H. DeShields, Milford; J. W. Elliott, Bowling Green; Mrs. Ada Fraunaugh, Smoots; A. Farmer, Whites; Flagg Brothers, Ruther Glenn; J. H. Frazier, Bowling Green; George W. Gray, Upper Zion; Mrs. C. M. Harris, Whites; B. C. Harding, Woodford; P. S. Hart, Balty; J. E. Howerton, Bowling Green; O. E. James, Gether; T. B. Jeter, Penola; John W. Clark, Milford; Mills and Blaydes, Guinea; Farmers Exchange Corp., R. F. Holberton, Manager, Milford; C. M. Pitts, Alps; W. B. Pitts, Bowling Green; S. E. Pitts, Sparta; G. H. Pitts, Upper Zion; James Pleasants, Milford; W. P. Pugh, Woodford; Rains and Co., Druggists, Bowling Green; R. C. Richardson, Penola; H. L. Richardson, Bagby; F. B. Richerson, Bagby; J. A. Sanford, McDuff; Silas Sale, Corbin; J. A. Shuman, Shumansville; F. E. Shuman, Guide; J. E. Silvae, Lauraville; J. D. Smithers, Delos; Snell and Thomas, Woodford; E. G. Thornton, Milford; F. M. Travis, New London; J. H. Wright, Naulakla; James H. Wright, Brandywine; W. H. Carter, Port Royal; W. T. Powers, Port Royal; Latane Sale, Port Royal; and B. A. Dratt, Woodford. All of the above merchants are on the Caroline County Telephone System.

JUSTICES OF THE PEACE IN COLONIAL CAROLINE

(1758–1772)

Edmund Pendleton, Robert Gilchrist, Anthony Thornton, William Tyler, James Jameson, James Tyler, Benjamin Robinson, Robert Taliaferro, William Parker, John Taylor, John Baynham, Gabriel Throckmorton, Lunsford Lomax, William Buckner, Walker Taliaferro, James Miller, William Woodford, Thomas Lowry, William Jones, Thomas Slaughter, Samuel Hawes, John Armistead, William Buckner, Jr., George Taylor, James Taylor, John Buckner, Jeremiah Rawlings, John Minor, James Upshaw, Gawin Corbin, William Harrison, Roger Quarles, George Guy, Anthony New, Robert Taliaferro, Jr.

INDEX TO ENROLLED BILLS OF THE GENERAL AS-
SEMBLY OF VIRGINIA, 1776–1910, WHICH
PERTAIN TO CAROLINE COUNTY

SOME CAROLINE ITEMS IN ACTS OF ASSEMBLY

In Acts of 1884 (extra session), page 176, is recorded an Act
to incorporate The Bowling Green Tobacco Association. The
purpose of the Association was "to promote the sale and trade

of tobacco in the county." The capital stock was to be not less than $1,000 nor more than $10,000. The incorporators were James E. Ennis, William T. Chandler, R. Vincent, William Murray, James A. Chapman, S. P. Trewalla, G. T. Swift, C. L. Bullard, K. R. Farish and J. M. Hudgin.

Acts of 1887, page 207, records an Act to incorporate the town of Milford in Caroline. The trustees named are John W. Gill, W. S. Stone, James E. Grimes, T. B. Gill, Arthur Lyell, J. W. Knight and W. N. Blatt.

Acts of 1889–90, page 625, records an Act to incorporate the Bowling Green Cemetery Company. The capital stock was not to be less than $200 nor more than $2,000 and shares were to sell for $10.00 each. Dr. C. S. Webb, John G. Rowe, George R. Collins, A. B. Chandler and William T. Chandler were the incorporators.

Acts of 1889–90, page 231, records an Act to incorporate the Caroline Railway Company, for the purpose of building a railroad from Milford to Port Royal via Bowling Green. Minimum capital stock $200,00 and maximum $2,000,000. W. D. Quesenberry, John R. Baylor, J. P. Carson, Otway Warwick, Wm. T. Chandler, W. E. Ennis, D. B. Powers, R. G. Holloway, and S. J. R. White incorporators.

Acts of 1883–84, page 190, records the establishment of thirteen voting precincts and defining boundaries of same. These were Gouldmans, Sparta, Moss Neck, Guiney's, Shumansville, Bowling Green, Whites, Port Royal, Needwood, Bowers, Cedar Fork, Flippo and Gray's Mill.

MANUSCRIPT PAPERS IN STATE LIBRARY OF VIRGINIA

In the State Library are thousands of Executive and other papers recommending men for militia officers and other appointive offices. From these may be learned the names of Caroline officers from year to year. The following is taken from the collection and shows names of men recommended for militia officers by the county court of July, 1793, Captains: James Sutton, Geo. Terrell, Henry Chiles, Thos. Miller, John White, Wm. Saunders, Sam'l Norment, Daniel Turner, Reuben Chapman, Thos. Guy. Lieutenants: Joseph Timberlake, Richard Willson, Reuben Broaddus, Fred'k Phillips, Wm. Conner, John Carter, George Hampton, Wm. Coghill, Thos. Burk, Joseph Sutton. Ensigns: Wm. Walker, Thos. Kidd, Benj. Carter, James Samuel, Reuben Saunders, James Coates, George Guy, Wm. Ellis, James Collins and James Higgins.

ARTS AND LETTERS

There were few artists in Virginia prior to 1750. Those who desired portraits sat to English artists in England. There were a few exceptions to this rule, however, one of these being associated with Caroline county is worthy of mention here. An artist named Bridges came over from England as early as 1737 and rented a house in Williamsburg and painted a number of portraits of prominent colonists. In 1740 he was employed to paint the King's Arms for the Court-house of Caroline county at the price of sixteen hundred pounds of tobacco. This painting adorned the court house for many years. The author has not been able to find any clue as to what became of this ancient painting. Reference is made to it in Mary Newton Stanard's *Colonial Virginia.*

John Baylor, of "Newmarket," in Caroline, in the year 1770 bequeathed to his son John, all his books, and directed that he should pay to his brothers, George and Robert, 25 pounds sterling each, to assist them in establishing libraries, "Which," he concludes, "I highly recommend to be yearly added to."

Thomas P. Westendorf was born in Bowling Green, Va., February 23, 1848. His family lived at the place now owned by Miss Linda Anderson on Anderson Avenue. He married in Caroline and shortly thereafter removed to Germany. It is said that the homesickness of his wife prompted him to write the ballad, "*I'll Take You Home Again, Kathleen,*" which has become popular both in this country and Europe. The words are:

> "I'll take you home again, Kathleen,
> Across the ocean wild and wide,
> To where your heart has ever been,
> Since first you were my bonny bride.
> The roses all have left your cheek,
> I've watched them fade away and die;
> Your voice is sad whene'er you speak,
> And tears bedim your loving eyes.
>
> I know you love me, Kathleen, dear,
> Your heart was ever fond and true;
> I always feel when you are near,
> That life holds nothing dear but you;

The smiles that once you gave to me,
I scarcely ever see them now,
Tho, many, many times I see,
A darkning shadow on your brow.

To that dear home beyond the sea,
My Kathleen shall again return,
And when thy old friends welcome thee,
Thy loving heart will cease to yearn;
Where laughs the little silver stream,
Beside your mother's humble cot,
And brightest rays of sunshine gleam,
There all your grief will be forgot.

CHORUS—

Oh! I will take you back, Kathleen,
Where your heart will feel no pain,
And when the fields are fresh and green,
I'll take you to your home again.

The original draft of this song, or a copy of the original issue (the author is not sure which), was presented to Mrs. J. T. Richards, of Bowling Green.

Mrs. Stanard in her very fine book—*Colonial Virginia*—says: "It was not unusual for parents to have several children in school in England at the same time. One such family was Col. John Baylor, of Caroline who had received his own education at Putney Grammar School and Caius College, Cambridge. In 1762 he sent his 12 year-old son, John, to Putney, and later entered him at Caius College, where he was friend and class-mate of William Wilberforce. He also sent his daughters, Courtney, Lucy, Frances and Elizabeth abroad to boarding school, placing them at Croyden in Kent."

In 1906, Mr. J. P. Babington, who was then publishing a weekly newspaper in Bowling Green, known as *The Caroline Echo*, published and copyrighted a small book entitled *The Biography of Mrs. Catherine Babington, the Only Woman Mason In the World*. In this work, a copy of which is in the hands of the author, Mr. Babington relates how that his mother, Catherine Sweet, when a girl in Greenup county, Ky. (afterward Boyd county), secreted herself under the pulpit of an old church, which was used as a Masonic Lodge room, and heard and saw and inwardly digested the ritual and ceremony of Blue Lodge Masonry. Her uncles, the Ulen brothers, finding that she knew Blue Lodge Masonry, attempted, through many traps set for her, to intimidate her into revealing the secrets of the fraternity; but, finding her faithful, the Lodge obligated her in the usual manner, and she remained faithful to the end of her days. The book is of interest to Caroline people chiefly because it bears a Bowling Green imprint.

George Fitzhugh, son of Dr. George Fitzhugh and Lucinda Stuart, and descendant of William Fitzhugh, of England and Stafford county, Va., was born July 2, 1807. He was educated in the University of Virginia and admitted to the bar upon graduation. He married Mary Metcalf Brockenbrough, of Port Royal, Caroline county, and had issue R. H. Fitzhugh, Captain of Engineers under Lee; George Stuart Fitzhugh, who was ordered an Episcopal clergyman in 1873 and who at the age of eighty still survives; Champe, Lucinda, Augusta, Mary Ella, Harriett and Emily.

George Fitzhugh spent all of his life save the closing years at Port Royal and at one time presided over a noted male academy located at that place. He wrote and published the following books and papers and was a frequent contributor to DeBow's Review. "Cannibals All" (1857); "What Shall We Do With Free Negroes?" (1851); "Sociology for the South" (1854); "The Valleys of Virginia" (1859); "The Northern Neck of Virginia" (1859); "Ancient Families of Virginia and Maryland" (1859); and "The Revolutions of 1776 and 1861 Compared."

John Taylor was known as "The Publicist of the Revolutionary Period," and was a strong and voluminous writer. For list of his works see his biography elsewhere in this volume.

CAROLINE COUNTY ESTATES

Name	Original Owner	Present Owner
Aspen Hill	Campbell	Henderson
Auburn	Moncure	Moncure
Airy Hill	Broaddus	Broaddus
Bath	Samuel	
Belvidere		Levering
Belleville	Miller	Garrett
Blenheim	Tyler	
Brandywine	Boutwell	Farmer
Burton Hall	Chandler	Flippo
Berry Grove	Lewis	Haynes
Broomfield	Chandler	
Camden	Pratt	Pratt
Clay Hill	Martin	Martin
Cedar Creek	Lightfoot	Powers
Chestnut Valley	Dickinson	
Cedar Vale	Redd	
Clifton	Martin	Smith
Edgewood	Wyatt	
Ellerslie	Moncure	Moncure
Edge Hill	Schooler	
Eastern View	Skinker	Skinker
Elson Green	Chandler	
Eldorado	Coleman	Jeter
Fairford	George	
Fairfield	Chandler	
Flintshire		
Fontaine Hill		Burruss
Gaymont	Bernard	Robb
Green Fall	Wright	Wright
Greenwood	Seay	
Hayfield	Taylor	Berger
Hampton	DeJarnette	Poyner
Hazelwood	Taylor	Turner
Holly Hill	Woolfolk	Rowe
Hillford	Motley	
Hard Bargain		
Haymont		
Ingleside	Chandler	Chandler
Idlewild	Chandler	Chandler
Ivy Hill		Battaile
Jack's Hill	Smith	Smith
Landora	Anderson	
Locust Hill	Catlett	Cosby

Lake Farm.................Buckner......................Ayers
Liberty Hill
Mill Hill....................Taylor
Moss Neck..................Corbin.....................Skinker
Mulberry Place..............Woolfolk...................Woolfolk
Maple Swamp...............Tompkins
Marl Hill...................Coleman.......................Dew
Marengo...................Martin.....................Martin
Milwood..................Lewis....................Bowie
Melrose...................Quesenberry.................Washington
Mt. Gideon....................Hill
Mt. Zephyr...................White...................Brooks
Midway.....................Taylor
Newmarket.................Baylor.....................Baylor
Nyland....................Chandler....................Claiborne
North Wales................Carter.....................Usinger
Normandy.................Boutwell.....................Smith
North Garden..............Thornton...................Vaughan
Ormesby...................Thornton...................Tompkins
Old Mansion...............Hoomes.......................White
Oakley......................Goodwin
Oak Ridge..................Hoomes....................Jordan
Port Tobago................Corbin.....................White
Providence..................Anderson
Poplar Grove................Campbell
Palestine...................Wright.....................Wright
Row's Hill..................Row.....................Conway
Rosedale...................George.....................George
Springfield..................Minor
Shepherd's Hill..............Woolfolk...................Brookes
Spring Hill.................Buckner...................Washington
Spring Grove...............DeJarnette.................DeJarnette
Santee....................Gordon....................Gordon
Sunnyside..................Buckner
Thornhill...................Hurt
Topping Castle..............Minor
Thornberry.................George.....................George
The Neck...................Buckner
The Hill...................Bowie
The Grove..................Wortham
Vernon....................Thomas
Windsor...................Woodford......................Dew
Woodlawn.................Coleman....................Cobb
Woodpecker...............Washington.................Washington
Walden's Towers............Walden
Walnut Hill................Waller.....................Waller
White Plains................Pendleton..................Broaddus
Waverly...................Lightfoot
Yew Spring.................Corbin

VILLAGES OF CAROLINE

PORT ROYAL

It is recorded in the Legislative Journals of the Council of Colonial Virginia, Volume 2, page 941, that on October 3, 1744, the Council received a message from the House of Burgesses stating that the House had passed "A Bill entitled an Act for establishing a town near Roy's Warehouse in the County of Caroline etc." This message was read the first time when it was presented, and the second and third times on the following day, whereupon it was resolved by the Council "That the Bill do pass." Thus begins the history of Port Royal. This documentary evidence substantiates the statement of Hayden that Thomas Roy founded Port Royal, and that the town was called Port Roy for several years.

Thomas Roy married Judith Beverly Kenner prior to 1740. She was the widow of Rev. Rodham Kenner, an Episcopal minister. A daughter of Thomas Roy and Judith Beverly Kenner, Elizabeth by name, married James Miller whose name frequently appears in the ancient minutes of Kilwinning-Crosse Lodge of Masons. Mr. Miller was a Scot and remained loyal to the crown, although his son was an officer in the Revolutionary Army. James Miller's portrait was painted by Copely and photographic copies of the same are now in the possession of his descendants, Mrs. J. E. Warren, of Newport News, and Mrs. J. H. Rives, of Richmond.

The town of Port Royal is situated on the Rappahannock River, 22 miles below Fredericksburg and 15 miles east of Bowling Green, the county seat. It once had an excellent harbor and enjoyed a large tobacco trade direct with England. Before the advent of the railroad, when the county relied chiefly on the river for transportation, it was a place of no small importance. Tradition has it that Port Royal was considered for the site of the National Government.

Many famous families and persons have had residence in Port Royal. Here lived Rev. Jonathan Boucher, George Fitzhugh, author and professor, Captain Sally Tompkins, of Civil War fame, and many others. Nearby lived the eminent John Taylor, James Taylor, John Penn, Colonel Butler, William Bernard, the Lightfoot, Robb, Magruder, Gravatt, Pratt, Micou, Farish, Catlett, Gilchrist and other equally prominent families. On the opposite bank of the Rappahannock, at Port Conway, President

Madison was born and brought up. There were several old
academies nearby at different periods which gave a cultural
atmosphere to the community not surpassed elsewhere in Virginia. Indeed no part of the South had a more brilliant social
life than this town and its environs.

With the coming of the railroad and the lessened importance
of the river as a channel of commerce, Port Royal, like many
other river towns in the South, dwindled in importance and today
it is but the ghost of its former glory. There are now a few stores,
a bank, a hotel, a garage, and possibly a half hundred residences.
The bank has resources of approximately $75,000 and is conducted
by Dr. J. M. Holloway, R. F. Tankard, W. H. Carter, Latane
Sale, C. K. Hearn, W. T. Powers and A. F. Turner. Many of
these are descendants of men and women who lived in Port Royal
in the days of its prosperity.

BOWLING GREEN

This, the county seat town of Caroline, was established shortly
after the formation of the county, as will appear from the Legislative Petitions elsewhere in this volume, and received its name
from the estate of Major Hoomes on which it was built, the said
estate taking the name "Old Mansion," by which it is still known.

The Bowling Green, as it was originally called, was once quite
a social centre. The races of the American Jockey Association
were frequently held here in the latter years of the eighteenth
century. Preparatory to these occasions temporary hotels were
erected and the town during the week of the races was wholly
given over to merriment. The sporting journals of the period,
many of which have been preserved, tell the story.

Bowling Green is situated on the old State Road—one of the
first roads to be surveyed in Virginia—and is forty miles north
of Richmond and twenty-two miles south of Fredericksburg.
The railroad station for Bowling Green is Milford, and is two
miles west of the town and connected therewith by two bus lines.
The Richmond, Washington and Baltimore papers may be read
by the residents at breakfast of the day of issue, and the New
York papers at noon. In addition to the public buildings there
are a number of stores, a mill, two hotels, newspaper office (*The
Caroline Progress*) light and power plant, ice plant, high school,
five churches, a bank, and many of the most attractive residences

in eastern Virginia.   The lawns are commented on far and wide because of their spaciousness and beauty.

An Avenue of Old Cedars at Bowling Green.

The old Stage Road over which passed the through traffic from North to South in colonial times, is now the main thoroughfare for automobile traffic between these two sections and in the spring and autumn approximately a thousand cars daily pass the village en route to or from Florida and other points. The Union Bank and Trust Company, of Bowling Green, originally Caroline County Bank, operated by L. E. Martin, Leroy Dunn, F. H. Borkey, Richard Barlow, John Cox, George P. Lyon, J. T. Richards and T. C. Valentine, does a business of one million

The Lawn Hotel at Bowling Green on Site of Old New Hope Tavern

dollars annually. The automobile business of J. W. Elliott and Sons is the next most important business establishment in town.

An old and pleasant custom, which grew out of the old county court, is the "Social Court" in Bowling Green on the second Monday of every month. On this day one may see nearly all of the citizens of the county in town. Buying, selling, "swapping," and speech-making, in political season, and social intercourse, make it a great day for the county and the county seat. On this day one may buy anything from puppies to plantations without leaving the street.

MILFORD

Milford is situated on the Richmond, Fredericksburg and

Broaddus Lake at Bowling Green

Potomac Railroad, 40 miles north of Richmond and 22 miles south of Fredericksburg. The town dates back to November

2, 1792, at which time an Act was passed by the Virginia Assembly
"To establish a town and inspection of tobacco on the lands of

An Avenue in Bowling Green

John Hoomes, in the county of Caroline."   See Hening's Statutes
Volume 3, page 576.

This town was once the head of navigation on the Mattaponi,

as will appear from the Legislative Petitions elsewhere in this book, and had a large tobacco inspection or tobacco warehouse.

Lawn of the Rains Home in Bowling Green

Today there stands farther back from the river and on the east side of the railroad a large tobacco warehouse erected by the Co-operative Tobacco Growers Association for the receiving and

H. C.-19

grading of Caroline tobacco which was formerly sold at auction on the open market in Richmond. Here also are located the plants of the Wilson Lumber Company, the Miller Sumac Extract Company. The mercantile establishments operated by T. E. Campbell, W. N. Blatt and Sons, R. Lewis Gravatt, E. G. Thornton, Farmers Co-operative Exchange and Milford Produce Company, are among the most prosperous in the county.

The Milford State Bank, organized in 1912, and operated by Dr. E. C. Cobb, H. D. McWhirt, Walter Wilson, C. W. Colbert, G. K. Coleman, W. P. Miller and L. E. Martin, is a flourishing institution and serves a large territory.

GUINEA

Guinea is situated on the Richmond, Fredericksburg and Potomac Railroad, about 50 miles north of Richmond and 12 miles south of Fredericksburg. The name was originally spelled Guiney, and was always spoken of in the plural—Guiney's The name is supposed to have been derived from a family of the name which once lived nearby. Here are stores operated by E. C. Allen, C. W. Colbert, Mills and Blaydes; the grist mill of D. L. Cook, and the plant of the Dill Lumber Company, of Baltimore of which Mr. E. V. Russell is the local manager. There are many beautiful old homes around Guinea, among them "Ormesby," old estate of the Thorntons; "Hillford," old estate of the Motleys; "Idlewild," home of the Chandlers and birthplace of Dr. J. A. C. Chandler, President of William and Mary; "Burton Hall," home of Mr. and Mrs. Clarence Flippo; "Mill Hill," birthplace of John Taylor; "Nyland," an old Chandler estate and now the home of the Claibornes; "Spring Grove," home of Mr. and Mrs. Cutler Beasley; "North Garden," home of the Thorntorns; "Braynefield," old Buckner home; "Fairfield," old home of the Chandlers, and many others.   David Lloyd George, Prime Minister of Great Britain, visited the old house at "Fairfield," in which Stonewall Jackson died, and standing by the old house in the presence of Admiral Cary T. Grayson, Mayor Ainslie, of Richmond, Editor Douglas Freeman and other notables, remarked: "That old house witnessed the downfall of the Southern Confederacy." Strawberries are shipped by the carload from Guinea every year.

WOODFORD

Woodford is situated between Guinea and Milford, about two miles from the former and seven miles from the latter, and was named in honor of General William Woodford, who was born and brought up near the place. For many years the railroad station was called Woodslane and the post-office about one hundred feet away was called Woodford. Here are several stores operated by Dratt, Washington, Southworth and others and on the ridge lying above the village are many beautiful old homes. At Woodford are the headquarters of the George P. Lyon Excelsior Company, the largest industrial concern in the county.

PENOLA

Penola, situated on the Richmond, Fredericksburg and Potomac Railroad, five miles south of Milford, was named in honor of John Penn, of Caroline and as nearly the name Penn as possible without confusing it with an existing name in Virginia at that time. The original name of the station was Polecat, so called from Polecat creek which runs nearby.

Here are stores operated by T. B. Jeter, E. M. Coleman and R. C. Richardson, and excelsior mills operated by W. R. Jeter, Caroline's largest land owner, and Lyon and Smith. Here also are the Rose Hill Lumber Company, operated by L. D. George and John W. Clark, and a flour mill, operated by George R. Jeter.

There are several well-known estates, among them "Marl Hill," of the Coleman family, and now owned by the Dews, "Thornberry," of the George family, "Fairford," of the George family, and others. It is quite probable that as much mail is distributed from this office as from any other of similar classification in the State.

RUTHER GLEN

When the Richmond, Fredericksburg and Potomac Railroad was built through Caroline county, the place now known as Ruther Glen was called Chesterfield Station, from the old Chesterfield Inn on the Stage Road nearby. But confusion was often caused by mail and freight being sent to Chesterfield Court House, and, so, shortly after the Civil War, Major Myers, then Superintendent of the railroad, renamed the place for an ancient Scottish town on the river Clyde near Glasgow. The Scottish

Ruther Glen is associated with the Scotch heroes, Wallace and Bruce, and was made a royal burgh in 1125. It was here that Sir John Monteith agreed to betray Sir William Wallace into the hands of the English. Here also stands an old castle taken by Robert Bruce from the English in 1313.

Near Ruther Glen in Caroline is "Ellerslie" the old home of the Moncures so named from the home of Wallace in Scotland. There are a number of well known old estates nearby. Here were born General Jo Lane Stern and his brother Cary Ellis Stern who became so prominent in the life of Richmond. Here also is St. Margaret's Church. The mercantile establishments of G. K. Coleman and the Flagg Brothers and the excelsior plant of Mr. Coleman constitute the greater part of the business life of Ruther Glen.

CHURCHES AND CHURCHMEN

THE EPISCOPALIANS

In the Legislative Journals of the Council of Colonial Virginia, Volume III, page 1279, it is recorded that at a session of the Council held on April 3, 1762, there was presented:

"A message from the House of Burgesses by Mr. Pendleton that they had passed a Bill entitled, An Act to Impower the Vestries of the Parishes of Drysdale in the counties of Caroline and King and Queen, and of St. Stephen in said county of King and Queen to sell their glebes and lay out the money in purchasing more convenient glebes, to which they desired the concurrence of the Council. The Bill was read the first time, and ordered to be read a second and third time immediately. The said Bill was accordingly read and second and third time. Resolved, that the Bill do pass."

The Parish of Drysdale, referred to in this Bill, was established in 1723 and named for Lieutenant Governor Hugh Drysdale. It was originally a long, ill-shaped parish, extending from Spotsylvania county on the north, to very nearly the central part of King William on the south. It was divided in February, 1780, as follows:

"By a line to begin at the lower corner of the land of John Page, Esq., upon the Mattaponi river, and run along his lower line, and those of Christopher Smith, Anthony Seale, and

Frederick Phillips, to the corner of the lands of Edmund Pendleton, the elder, Esq., and Edmund Jones; thence along the lines between them to Morococick creek; thence up the creek to the mouth of Phillips run; thence up the said run to Digges upper line; thence along that line and the course thereof continued to the line of Essex county; and all that part of the said parish which lies to the eastward of the said line, shall be one distinct parish, and retain the name of Drysdale; and all that other part thereof shall be one other distinct parish, and shall be called and known by the name of St. Asaph."—Hening's Statutes at Large, Volume X, page 209.

This parish—St. Asaph—was the last parish erected by the General Assembly in Virginia before the disestablishment.

The first churches built in these parishes, like the first homes, were rude and unpretentious structures, but these were replaced by substantial and attractive buildings, and later still by large and massive brick structures, such as may still be seen in many sections of eastern Virginia. Several massive brick church-houses were erected in Caroline before the Revolution—but they have all been destroyed, and only the bare sites of two or three are now to be found. Near Rappahannock Academy post office may be seen the beautiful site of old Mount church, which was one of the largest and most beautiful churches in Virginia in that day, and which contained a fine organ imported from England, an unusual thing in Virginia at that time. Just when Mount church was erected, or what churches preceded it cannot be definitely ascertained, but it is quite certain that it was one of the first, if not the first church established in St. Mary's Parish and it was undoubtedly intended to serve the whole of St. Mary's since it stood near the center of the parish. After the Revolutionary War, with the social, political and religious revolution which followed it, Mount church fell into disuse and was afterward appropriated by the State and given over to school purposes, becoming the Rappahannock Academy.

W. W. Scott, in his History of Orange County, Virginia, says: "One of the first effects of the 'freedom of worship' and the practical confiscation of the glebes and church properties was, that the people's consciences became very 'free' also to do as they pleased with the church belongings. * * * Churches were actually and literally destroyed, the very bricks carried off and the altar pieces torn from the altar and attached to pieces of household furniture. * * * Communion plate came to be regarded as common property. * * * Nor did the despoilers overlook the churchyards when the work of destruction began. Tombstones were broken down and carried off to be appropriated to unhallowed uses. * * * The slab which marked the grave of the Rev. Mungo Marshall was taken away and used first to grind paints upon, and afterward in a tannery on which to dress hides."

Dr. J. B. Baylor says: "With the rise of Jefferson and his party and the disestablishment of the Episcopal church, many of the old Colonial houses of worship were desecrated, or confiscated by the State; many beautiful marble monuments in the church yards were wrecked; glebes were confiscated; and many pious ministers were driven out of their homes."

From the Rev. L. E. Goodwin, Historiographer of the Diocese of Virginia, we learn that the first minister of record in St. Mary's Parish was the Rev. Owen Jones who came over from England and served the church from 1704 to 1724 and was succeeded by the Rev. Musgrave Dawson and the Rev. Jonathan Boucher, respectively. The latter, we are told, was a very brilliant man and a close personal friend of George Washington, who intrusted him with the education of his stepson, young Custis. With the approach of the Revolution he proved himself such a staunch Tory that he was banished from the country. On returning to England he published a pamphlet which discredited the ability of his friend, General Washington, but later atoned for this slight by dedicating to Washington a volume of his Sermons which he had preached in Caroline. Washington gracefully acknowledged the dedication and they remained warm personal friends and equally warm political enemies. The Rev. Abner Waugh succeeded the Rev. Mr. Boucher in St. Mary's Parish and remained in this charge until his death in 1806.

There were two large brick churches in St. Margaret's Parish; Reedy church, situated not very far from the present site of Edmund Pendleton High School and Bull church, or St. Margaret's, a few miles west of Penola. A magisterial district of the county bears the name of the old Reedy church. Both of these old churches have long since disappeared, but the sites may still be found. The Rev. Francis Fontaine was rector of this parish before the formation of Caroline county and the Rev. John Brunskill, Sr., and the Rev. Archibald Dick, served the parish from 1748 to very nearly the end of the century.   When the old St. Margaret's church was destroyed an unpretentious frame building was erected near Ruther Glen to take its place.   In addition to the three clergymen above named, St. Margaret's has been served in succession by the Rev. Messrs. H. C. Boggs, William Friend, C. J. Good, L. H. Johns, W. N. Ward, D. M. Wharton, W. W. Greene, W. B. Williams, J. K. M. Lee and Morris Eagle.   St. Margaret's Parish was established in 1720 and originally lay partly in King William and partly in Caroline, but it was divided in 1744 and all below the Caroline county line was made a part of St. David's Parish, King William, while all that lay in Caroline remained as St. Margaret's.

James B. Wood, Superintendent of the Virginia State Penitentiary, once wrote the author concerning Bull church in the following words:

"My father, Col. Fleming Wood bought the old home place of his father, which was one mile from the church.   At the time of his death my grandfather, Robert Wood, was a lay reader in the church and had been from my earliest recollection.   My mother's father, Bailey Tompkins, lived three miles from the church.   He was a member of the vestry.   I do not recollect him.   The first rector I recollect was Rev. Dabney Wharton, who preached at St. Margarets on the third Sunday of each month.   He had other churches and lived near Spotsylvania Courthouse fourteen miles from the church.   He was a large portly man, but had a throat affection that kept him from filling his appointments at times and those were the times that my grandfather Wood conducted the services.   In those days besides my two grandfathers' families, the following families were members of the church.   John V. Kean, Samuel Amery Swan, George Tompkins, Curtis W. Durrett, Frank Tompkins, Thomas Goodwyn, William B. Harris, Edmund Tompkins, Mrs. Lucy Temple, Mrs. Judy Swan, James L. Ball and Cyrus Carson.   There were probably others that I do not recall.   Just before the Civil War Mr. Wharton left and Rev. William Green from Fredericksburg became pastor.   During my early boyhood days Bishop Meade visited the church, next was Bishop Johns and then later Bishop Whittle.   All three visited my home.

"The old church was in the shape of an 'L,' the bottom of the 'L' was not used and was left to go to ruin when I first recollect the church.   Some said it was the newest part of the church.

It had the figures 1755 in the brick over the door. It was said the workmen who built this addition lived on bull meat during the time of construction and that they named it Bull church. The skull and horns of the bull were placed in the fork of one of the large oaks in the church yard and in time the oak grew over them. The points of the horns could just be seen in 1858, I having seen them myself."

Drysdale Parish, as before stated was formed in 1723 and contained one large church, known as Joy Creek, situated on the eastern side of the county. This parish was served by the Rev. Messrs. Robert Innis, Andrew Moreton and Samuel Shield respectively, from about 1750 to 1780, when the parish was divided and Rev. Mr. Shield became the first rector of the new parish of St. Asaph. He was succeeded in Drysdale Parish by the Rev. Jesse Carter.

St. Mary's Parish was established prior to the year 1700 and as before stated was served from 1704 to 1806 by the Rev. Messrs. Jones, Dawson, Boucher and Waugh. After the confiscation of Mount church by the State at the close of the Revolution, St. Mary's Parish declined, but was revived through the heroic labors of the Rev. J. P. McGuire, of Essex. Grace church at Corbin was built in 1833 and St. Peter's church at Port Royal about 1835. In 1835 the Rev. William Friend removed from St. Margaret's to Port Royal and was rector of St. Mary's Parish until his death in 1870.

The Rev. Mr. Friend was succeeded in St. Mary's by the Rev. James E. Poindexter who resigned in 1888 and was succeeded by the Rev. S. S. Ware who served the parish until 1918; so for eighty-three years St. Mary's parish was served by three rectors. The Rev. Messrs. J. K. M. Lee and Morris Eagle have served the parish since 1918. The county of Caroline has given several of her sons to the ministry of the Gospel in the Episcopal church, among them the Rev. George Fitzhugh, of Spotsylvania, the Rev. Austin Mitchell, of West Virginia, the Rev. J. J. Gravatt, Rector of Holy Trinity church, Richmond, Va., and the Rt. Rev. Wm. Loyall Gravatt, Bishop of West Virginia. The latter two are sons of St. Peter's church, Port Royal.

St. Asaph's Parish was formed from Drysdale in 1780 and the parish church which was built before the division of Drysdale was situated a short distance north of the town of Bowling Green. The Rev. Samuel Sheild, one of the most prominent clergymen in Virginia in his day, retired from the pastorate of Drysdale Parish to become the first rector of St. Asaph's. He afterward removed to York county and was succeeded in St. Asaph's by the Rev. Messrs. James Taylor and George Speirin. A commodious brick church was erected in Bowling Green about 1832, but St. Asaph's parish becoming too weak to support a minister, the members usually attended St. Margaret's. After the war between the States the church house in Bowling Green was sold to the Methodist church by consent of the Bishop of the Diocese and since that time services have been held, with some degree of regularity in a hall or chapel, chiefly by the rector of St. Mary's.

The parish registers and the record books of the vestries of the parishes of Caroline have been lost. Had they been preserved we should have a list of the families of the county for nearly a century and many other valuable historical incidents besides. Other records have preserved the names of many of the families of first rank who, before and after the Revolution, were Episcopalians.   To name but a few, they include the Thorntons, Baylors, Pages, Pendletons, Woodfords, Woolfolks, Battailes Taliaferros, Taylors, Corbins, Fitzhughs, Tompkins, Temples, Minors, Fontaines, Hoomes, Robbs, Washingtons, Bernards, Buckners, Upshaws, Colemans, Wyatts, Clarks and others of equal standing.

THE METHODISTS

The Rev. D. G. C. Butts, who spent over one-half century in the Methodist itineracy and whose first service as a Methodist minister was in Caroline county, writes in his autobiography as follows:

"The fathers who laid the foundations of Methodism in Caroline, laid them broad and deep and strong. Notwithstanding the Baptists had been in the county for years before the pioneers of Methodism arrived and had their congregations comfortably housed in commodious brick buildings at central points, yet these early circuit riders succeeded in reaching some of the finest material in all that region, and brought into the Methodist fold as fine a band of converts, socially, intellectually and spiritually as could be found anywhere in the commonwealth of Virginia. Swann, Hancock, DeJarnette, Waller, Wright, Smith, Carneal, Stern, Doggett, Jarrell, Burruss, Catlett, Chandler and Broaddus and a host of others, were names which stood for a high grade of intellectuality, incorruptible morality and social prestige, which under the lead of Methodist teaching now took first place in the county for spiritual power and devotion. "The Church of the Regenerate Heart," as Dr. Gilbert C. Kelly aptly calls our Methodism, had none who more consistently and beautifully illustrated the worth of experimental religion than the men and women from the families above named."

The Rev. Samuel Wesley Day, a grandson of the late Rev. Luther Wright, of Caroline, contributes the following information relative to the planting of Methodism in the county:

"In the latter part of the eighteenth century the Methodists were holding a camp meeting at Fork church (Episcopal) in Hanover county. A number of people from Caroline attended, among the number being William Wright, who became so much interested in the way the Methodists conducted the meetings that he invited them to visit Caroline county and to hold meetings in his house.

"The invitation was accepted and the Rev. Charles Hopkins was sent over to hold the meetings. When these meetings closed William Wright offered his house for a regular meeting place for the Methodists, thus turning his own home into a Methodist chapel or meeting house as it was then called.

"This arrangement continued for a number of years and then William Wright gave an acre of ground and built upon it, at his own expense, a small chapel or meeting house. That was the first Methodist meeting house in Caroline county. Thus the Methodists of Caroline can look back at "Wright's Chapel" and exclaim: "She is the mother of us all!"

"What is more remarkable is that William Wright, through all these years was not a member of the church, but united with the church on his deathbed and received the sacrament of the Lord's Supper. Caroline Circuit in 1870 was composed of seven appointments as follows: Rehoboth, Wright's Chapel, Bowling Green, Hopewell, St. Paul's, Vernon and Shiloh. The people had preaching twice monthly."

Rev. John G. Rowe served the Caroline circuit as pastor three terms of several years each. It is related that when he came back to the circuit for the third time he preached his opening sermon from the first verse of the thirteenth chapter of Second Corinthians: "This is the third time I am coming to you, etc."

Rev. E. H. Rowe, well-known educator and son of Rev. John G. Rowe, records it as " a dim recollection" that he heard his father say that the first Woman's Foreign Missionary Society ever organized in Methodism was in St. Paul's church on Caroline Circuit. This church has a long established custom of setting apart every fifth Sunday for special services under the auspices of this Woman's Foreign Missionary Society.

At a session of the Virginia Sunday School Association held in Bowling Green in 1921 the author heard the Rev. Andrew Broaddus, D. D., remark that "The Methodist church in Bowling Green has more wealth than any other church in Caroline;" to which Rev. E. H. Rowe replied, "I hope that it may be as truly said that our church is equally rich in faith and good works." And it may be stated as a matter of impartial history that Mr. Rowe's hope has not only been realized in the Bowling Green church, of which he is member, but in the world at large, for Methodism has had a salutary effect wherever it has gone.

David Lloyd George, when Prime Minister of Great Britain, said: "I personally cannot boast of being a Methodist (the Prime Minister was originally a member of the Disciple church and afterward a Baptist), but I have this qualification to speak to Methodists: I come from the country (Wales) that owes more to Methodism than to any other movement in its history * * * Like the Reformation the indirect influence of the Wesleyan movement was even greater, if possible, than its direct influence * * * It revived every religious community in the Anglo Saxon world * * * It put new blood into the veins of the older communions * * * Therefore one can imagine that its influence has been not only on the British Empire and America, but on the destiny of the whole world."

The then Prime Minister of Great Britain further said, in this London address, that "John Wesley was unquestionably the greatest religious leader the Anglo-Saxon race ever produced. His spirit, working through the movement he inaugurated, gripped the soul of England, deepened her spiritual instincts and trained and uplifted them with the result that when a great appeal is made to England there is always a generous response."

Woodrow Wilson, in his admirable monograph on John Wesley, makes an appraisal of Wesley's influence on the Anglo-Saxon race very similar to that given by Lloyd George. Thus from the strong and the great, as well as from an unnumbered host of the meek and lowly, come overwhelming testimonies of the potent and salutary influence of John Wesley and the child of his flaming spirit, the Methodist Episcopal communion.

The *Richmond Christian Advocate* of April 12, 1894 contains an article written by Mrs. Rachael Wright Jerrell, then eighty-four years of age, which is in part as follows:

"My grandfather Wright, who was an Episcopalian, heard that the Methodists were preaching in Hanover county, Va., and resolved that he would go and hear them. He heard them and was so much pleased that he invited them to Caroline to preach at his house. They accepted his invitation and came over. So the first Methodist sermon preached in Caroline was preached in his house in 1774. That house still stands, about a quarter of a mile from Wright's Chapel and about nine miles west of Bowling Green. My father, William Wright, was nine years of age at that time and the house was used as a regular preaching place until 1835. My grandfather died and my father fell heir to the old house. Before father died he said a chapel must be built; so he donated the land and started the subscription with ten dollars. The chapel was built and named Wright's Chapel after him. This Chapel was replaced by the present building a few years ago. Quarterly meetings were held at my father's and also protracted meetings. At the latter there were great revivals and many conversions. At one of these meetings there were two conversions; one young lady named Rachael Harris laughed incessantly and seemed unable to restrain herself ("then was our mouth filled with laughter and our tongue with singing," Psalm 126:2); the other was Josiah Carneal, now eighty-three years old and preaching in Kentucky. * * * * At another protracted meeting held in my father's house as late as 1825, by Peyton and Wilkerson, who then traveled the circuit, there was a great revival and among the large number of conversions were five of my father's children: Annie (Mrs. Haley), Jane (Mrs. Anderson), Rebecca (Mrs. Parr), Wesley (Dr. Wright), and myself, Rachael Jerrell. All these except me have "passed over the river." "They died in the faith." On one occasion a regular service was continued from 11:00 A. M. until 4:00 P. M. There was a great outpouring of the Spirit and a great many souls were converted. In those days the preachers preached every day. Rest day came sometimes once in three weeks.

"I can remember when Jacob Hill preached at my father's. I remember also that John Wesley White preached his first sermon there. His text was, "Prepare to Meet Thy God." But he did not get through. He lost his subject and went

upstairs and wept.   Stephen W. Jones also preached his
first sermon there and William Rowzie preached his first sermon there.   Peyton and Wilkerson traveled the circuit in
1825 and 1826 and preached at father's.   Skidmore was Presiding Elder and had a collection of hymns called "Skidmore's
Collection."   I acted as agent for him and sold his hymn books
and a number of other books on Baptism.   In 1828 there was a
camp meeting on this circuit not more than three miles from
where I now live.   My father had a tent there and I with a sister,
and quite a number of other friends, started in the night for the
camp and reached there just at daybreak.   Sykes and Wood
traveled the circuit that year.   One spring afforded abundance
of water for man and beast.   It was there I saw and heard the
famous colored preacher, David Payne.   I also heard him sing
"The Old Ship of Zion."   I was then seventeen years of age
and took great delight in this meeting.

"Nearby the old Wright home is the Wright burying ground
and in it sleep the remains of three preachers of the name—my
brother Luther, my brother Durrett, who died in his thirty-fifth
year, and who was said to have been an eloquent preacher.   The
third one died much younger and was my father's great grandson,
James Wright, son of James D. Wright, of this county.   He was
a Baptist preacher, but preached his first sermon in St. Paul's
church in Caroline."

THE ROMAN CATHOLIC CHURCH

In the year 1908 a number of Slovaks removed from the
States of New Jersey and Pennsylvania to Caroline county, Va.,
and settled around the villages of Guinea, Woodford and Milford.
These first families proved to be the vanguard of a considerable
colony.   Being an energetic and industrious people and naturally
inclined to agricultural pursuits they soon brought the abandoned
and supposedly worn-out farms on which they settled to a high
state of cultivation; thus adding materially to the economic life
of the county.

When the colony was of sufficient strength a meeting was held
for the purpose of devising ways and means of securing the
establishment of a church of their faith (Roman Catholic) near
Woodford, the central point of the settlement.   A petition was
presented to Rt. Rev. D. J. O'Connell, Bishop of Richmond,

requesting his aid and co-operation in the building of a church, which petition met with an encouraging response.

The Rev. J. M. Perrig, resident pastor of St. Mary's church, Fredericksburg, was secured to visit the colony semi-monthly and so faithfully did he discharge the duties of his office that in the year 1913, a beautiful chapel was erected near Woodford and dedicated in honor of the "Annunication of Mary the Mother of our Saviour." Present at the consecration were Bishop O'Connell, and many of the clergy and laity from Richmond and Fredericksburg.

Shortly after the consecration of the chapel Rev. Mr. Perrig died, beloved and respected by all who knew him, and was succeeded in the Caroline county parish by Rev. William Jan, of Richmond, and later by Rev. Thomas B. Martin, the successor of Rev. Mr. Perrig at St. Mary's church, Fredericksburg.

In 1918, Rev. John F. Kociela was appointed resident pastor of the Chapel of the Annunication and soon after entering upon his duties, a rectory was erected for him opposite the chapel, which he now occupies. Being a gentleman of genial manner and unfailing courtesy he has the respect of all who know him and under his administration the church prospers.

On July 6, 1924, the Rt. Rev. D. J. O'Connell consecrated Sts. Cyril and Metlodious Catholic church at Welch, Caroline county, and also confirmed a class of thirty-five children and adults. The Rev. Mr. Kociela, pastor, assisted with the ceremonies and celebrated the mass.

THE PRESBYTERIANS

The first record of the Presbyterian church in Caroline county is given in the Manual of East Hanover Presbytery, in which is recorded the fact that as early as 1855, an organization was effected at Bowling Green and the congregation so formed called the Caroline Presbyterian church.

No definite information of this congregation can be found in the Minutes of the East Hanover Presbytery of that year, nor of the year 1885, at which time the church first appears on the minutes of the General Assembly; but such a congregation did exist and was ministered to, in part at least, by the Rev. Dr. James Power Smith, who for many years was pastor of the Presbyterian church at Fredericksburg.

This work which for some reason was abandoned was revived in 1909 by an evangelist of the Synod of Virginia, who conducted a series of meetings and inaugurated a movement to secure a lot at Milford and to erect a chapel thereon.   This movement was successful.   A lot was secured and a building erected immediately following the meetings.

A commission of the East Hanover Presbytery met in the new church building on March 7, 1909 and re-organized the church, changing the name from the 'Caroline Presbyterian church to Milford Presbyterian church and dedicating the new building.

Since that time the congregation has been served by ministers from Richmond and Fredericksburg and by students from Union Theological Seminary at Richmond.

THE DISCIPLES

About the close of the eighteenth century the Reverend Thomas Campbell, a Presbyterian minister came from Scotland to America and located in Pennsylvania, where he became pastor of a parish covering a large and sparsely settled territory.   The people were neglected in spiritual ministrations and Mr. Campbell determined to be a shepherd of all regardless of creed or party. Accordingly he administered the Lord's Supper to all Christians, in consequence of which a charge of irregularity was brought resulting in his retirement from the Presbyterian fold.   Mr. Campbell then issued his famous "Declaration and Address," which has been called "America's Declaration of Religious Independence" and with his son, Alexander, who had come over from Glasgow University, set about to "restore Primitive apostolic Christianity in its doctrines, ordinances and its fruits."   For a time they worked in and through the Baptist Church, but finding their views were not welcomed here any more than they had been in the Presbyterian fold they withdrew and decided to continue their restoration movement independently of all organized religious bodies.

While still a member of the Baptist Church, Alexander Campbell made a tour of eastern Virginia which brought him into Caroline county.   Here he met the Reverend Andrew Broaddus—a man of highly cultivated intellect and liberal spirit. Mr. Broaddus had sent a communication for the *Christian Baptist*, which Mr. Campbell was then publishing at Bethany, Va., (now

West Virginia) in which he expressed his approval of Mr. Campbell's views of the Christian religion as a dispensation and also of his views on the two Covenants—Law and Grace. In regard to the *Christian Baptist*, Mr. Broaddus wrote: "I find much in it to approve and much to admire and some things from which I must dissent. I am greatly pleased with your aim to clear the religion of Jesus of all the adventitious lumber with which it has been encumbered and to bring back the Christian Church to its primitive simplicity and beauty."

This letter elegantly written and breathing the utmost Christian courtesy and candour was commented on by Mr. Campbell, who said that there had not appeared in the *Christian Baptist* a letter "more evangelical in scope; more clear and luminous in its object; more exceptional in its style; or more perfect in its body, soul and spirit." The correspondence between Mr. Campbell and Mr. Broaddus appears at length in the Memoirs of Alexander Campbell by Robert Richardson and for the most part breathe an exceptional spirit, coming as it does from an age in which religious discussions were generally acrimonious. Mr. Campbell's views were sometimes expressed harshly and it was of this mainly that Mr. Broaddus complained, and justly. In his zeal to purge the church of those things which he regarded as divisive and evil Mr. Campbell frequently wrote harsh things which caused the *Christian Baptist* to be regarded in many quarters as a bitter-spirited paper.

In eastern Virginia Mr. Campbell's discussions with Dr. Andrew Broaddus and Bishop Semple had excited much interest among Baptists. Prominent among these were Thomas M. Henley, of Essex; Dr. John DuVal, of King and Queen; Peter Ainslie I, M. W. Webber, John Richards and Dudley Atkinson.

It was not the idea or purpose of Campbell, Stone, Scott or those adhering to their views, to establish another religious organization, but rather it was their purpose to work out their proposed reforms within the then existing religious bodies, even as John Wesley proposed to work out certain reforms in the Church of England. Finding the same opposition with which Wesley met, Campbell and his adherents decided that these reforms could be wrought out more quickly through the organization of those of like belief, by which a greater impact could be made on the mind of the Christian world.

Accordingly a number of organizations were formed in Eastern Virginia in the early years of the nineteenth century and in some instances Baptist churches came over bodily into this restoration

movement. These bands of Christians were not known by any
one name and were not intended to make a party. Frequently
they were known as Christians only; sometimes as Christian
Baptists, by which name they are now frequently called in southwestern Virginia. Sometimes they banded themselves together
as a "gospel church." They were often called "Campbellites"
by their opponents, but owing to the improvement in courtesy
over the days of Luther and Wesley the name did not stick and
one only hears it now in those remote sections where preachers
wear long whiskers and celluloid collars. The name by which
this communion, embracing over one and one-half million souls,
is now known, is Disciples of Christ.

The first of these organizations in Caroline county was effected
about 1826, near the place now called Penola and the organization
was known as Emmaus church. Many prominent men and
women held membership during the first half century of its
existence, among whom may be named: H. H George, L. M.
George, Ellen W. George, M. M. George, Luther Wright, Susan
Wright, Burton B. Wright, Marius H. Wright, Dr. Charles Wright,
Francis E. Wright, Betty Sutton, Robert C. Sutton, O. W. Sutton,
Clayton Sutton, John H. Ware, Mary Z. Ware, Dr. Philip Dew,
P. Samuel, Jr., L. J. Baker, L. M. G. Baker, Charles C. Blanton,
Richard Blanton, Mary J. Blanton, Isla S. Blanton, Alphonso
Blanton, Nannie Blanton, John T. Blanton, Tazewell Blanton,
Charles Blanton, Archibald Blanton, George G. Blanton, John
J. Blanton, John T. Blanton, Sally Burke, Thomas Buke, Belle
G. Burke, Emmett Collins, Catherine Collins, Eugenia Collins,
Emuella Collins, E. E. Collins, George R. Collins, E. B. Coleman,
James L. Coleman, J. G. Coleman, E. D. Coleman, Louisa
Chiles, Richard H. Chiles, J. A. Chisholm, James Chapman,
Henrietta Campbell, George Cobb, Cornelia Cobb, A. E. Camp,
George Camp, Nannie B. Coghill, Cecil L. Baker, James Jesse,
E. J. Lumpkin, Paul T. Samuel, Rachael T. Terrell, Garland
Taylor, Waller Shepherd, Columbia Trice, John Sutton, Robert
Terrell, Emma Snow, Ida Samuel, A. G. Samuel, Susan W. Cox,
George O. Luck, William Hutcheson, J. W. Hutcheson, Lee
Hutcheson, Lucy Richerson, Mildred Beazley, C. A. H. Goodwin,
Frances Saunders, S. C. Goodwin, A. N. McChesney, Fanny
Peatross, Lucy A. Saunders, Eva Saunders, Sally Campbell,
James F. Campbell, R. S. Hargrave, Louisa Turner and G. W.
Blanton.

Antioch Church (Disciples) in Bowling Green, Showing Residence of the Hon. A. B. Chandler

The second organization in Caroline, known as Antioch church, was formed near Bowling Green on January 1, 1832.   On this day "Hill Jones, Thomas Jones, Clayton Coleman, Charles B. Tennent, Angelina Woolfolk, Elizabeth P. Woolfolk, Mary Jones, Ellen Taliaferro and Ellen Maury, who upon a profession of their faith in the Lord Jesus Christ have been baptized into His name, met at the house of Mrs. Jane Jones for the purpose of associating themselves together in a church capacity."   At this meeting it was *"Resolved*, That the above named persons, considering it our duty to God and believing it will tend to the mutual edification of each other, have agreed and do hereby agree and bind ourselves as a Gospel church, to live together as brothers and sister in the Lord, to love each other and as far as in us lyeth, to do and perform all the duties required of us as Disciples of the Lord Jesus Christ. *Resolved*, further, That discarding all human opinions, such as creeds and confessions of faith, we look upon the Scriptures of the Old and the New Testaments to be equally of divine authority, but as the Old Testament was the rule and guide of the Jewish Church before Christ, so we regard the New Testament as being the sole and only guide of the Christian Church and that we bind ourselves to each other and to God, that through His strength we will make it our only directory in all matters of Faith and Practice."

The first house of worship of Antioch was located two miles south of Bowling Green, was constructed of wood and destroyed by fire.   The second house was built of brick on the same site and was subsequently sold upon the removal of the church to Bowling Green.   It was converted into a handsome dwelling house and is now owned and occupied by Mr. Melville Broaddus. The third dwelling at Bowling Green was destroyed by fire on February 21, 1886, and the fourth building, a splendid house roofed with slate, was burned in the spring of 1892.   A fifth building was erected on the same site and was struck by lightning and burned on June 9, 1917.   A sixth building, more modest than all the others save the first, was erected and dedicated in 1920.   J. T. T. Hundley, President of Lynchburg College, delivered the dedicatory sermon and the pastor, Marshall Wingfield, performed the ceremony of dedication.

Alexander Campbell visited Antioch church first in 1838.   He came from Bethany, Va., by way of Baltimore and Washington, D. C., accompanied by his daughter, Lavinia, and Joseph Henley.

From Baltimore and Fredericksburg he was accompanied by William Carman, a member of the church in Baltimore. From Fredericksburg to Caroline Mr. Campbell sat with Bishop Meade in the stage coach and records in his journal that he was much pleased with the Bishop's good nature and liberal views. Mr. Campbell further records in his diary that "R. L. Coleman met us at Fredericksburg and continued with us the whole time in Virginia, much to our gratification and comfort. We found our brethren, Bagby, of Louisa, and Henshall, of Richmond, waiting for our arrival at our old friend Woolfolk's in Caroline. We met our much esteemed brethren, Henley, DuVal and Pendleton with many others at Antioch church. At Newtown, King and Queen county, we had a very pleasing visit with our old friend, Andrew Broaddus. He attended our meeting and favored us with friendly conversation on incidental topics. He enjoys good health, but like most men in the environs of seventy, is evidently descending the hill of life. It would be a consummation devoutly to be wished could he, before he passes the Jordan of Time, induce his brethren to rescind their 'Orders in Council,' and to open their ears to a candid consideration of the points at issue between them and us. It would do no harm to move forward a few paces toward the primitive simplicity of the Gospel and to the practice of the ancient institutions of Christ. They would not have to give up any truth in admitting all we contend for, as many of them now concede. We only ask for a renunciation of human traditions and wherever they are found they ought to be abandoned."

Mr. Campbell visited Charlottesville in 1840 and while there met Dr. Chester Bullard, of southwestern Virginia, who had journeyed thence to see him and whom Mr. Campbell found in complete agreement with his views. In his notice of the Charlottesville visit Mr. Campbell made an allusion to the "Dover Decrees" and a friendly reference to Andrew Broaddus, which elicited from the latter a kindly communication (see page 476, Volume II, Memoirs), stating that "I have seen in the 'Harbinger' (successor to Christian Baptist) for several years past much to approve and I have met with nothing for which my fellowship in the Gospel would be forfeited. I cannot say the same for some things which you have put forth in former times. I regret, my dear sir, that you should be separated from us and much would I rejoice in seeing your talents enlisted in the one great Cause.

That the Church needs a progressive reformation, I have no doubt, and to all efforts for this object on a scriptural basis I would say 'God-speed.' "

To this kindly and fraternal letter Mr. Campbell replied, reciprocating the good feelings Mr. Broaddus had expressed and disclaimed any desire or intention of forming a new party. Mr. Campbell also stated that in his opinion the "Beaver Decrees" of 1829 "were occasion by some violent movements on the part of our brethren in the Western Reserve, Ohio, in the height of a great excitement." He also added that "The Dover Decrees and similar acts of exclusion and proscription from other quarters, probably had their rise in the indiscretions and unguarded expressions of our over-zealous brethren."

Mr. Campbell visited Antioch church a second time during his tour of May, 1853, in the interest of Bethany College and a third time in the fall of 1855. During this latter visit he also preached at Corinth church in King William, Smyrna in King and Queen, Acquinton in King William, Rappahannock in Essex, and addressed the Athenaeum Literary Society of Richmond. After another trip to Caroline he returned to Richmond, where he was called on by Doctors Burroughs, Jeter, Ryland and Gwathmey, with all of whom he had pleasant visits. From Richmond he went to Washington where he visited his son-in-law, Dr. J. J. Barclay, who having returned from his missionary labors in Jerusalem was preparing his book, "The City of the Great King."

Many of Mr. Campbell's warmest personal friends were members of Antioch church and of these he names in his journals Pichegru Woolfolk, Jourdan Woolfolk, Elizabeth Woolfolk, William G. Maury, Daniel C. DeJarnette, Francis V. Sutton, Ann H. Maury, Mildred Crump, Joseph Jesse, John Hampton DeJarnette, George Tyler (father of Governor Tyler), Benjamin Anderson, H. T. Anderson, James Taylor White and Elizabeth Coleman.

Mr. A. B. Chandler writing of Antioch church in the *Chesapeake Christian* (Richmond) of April, 1920, says:

"Fifty-two years ago when I became a member of Antioch church, Brother Benjamin Anderson was the leading and teaching elder. A large, portly gentleman, a gentleman—'*intus et in cute*'—learned in Biblical lore, coming from Guiney's to church, ten miles, every Sunday morning and rarely failing to be present, never when energy was equal to the task. The courtliest of the courtly and yet absolutely frank and sincere, with no superfluous embellishments. Well do I remember when shortly after I joined the church he came to me, then just twenty-six years old and insisted that I should lead the congregation in prayer and how I rebelled and finally, after many entreaties, consented and wrote out and read my first public prayer. He thereafter insisted that I should take his place as elder, as he was growing old, which I tried to do. Dr. Anderson was a grand old man. He never forgot the patriarchs and whether in prayer or in the blessing of the emblems at the Communion table, he always concluded by asking that we all might finally be gathered with Abraham, Isaac and Jacob in our Father's Kingdom. I do not propose to recall in sequence the men and women of the older Antioch church, because memory fails me in accuracy of time. I mention, however, secondly, Brother John Taliaferro, one of our most enthusiastic and fervid elders, a man of firm convictions, to whom every thing he saw at all was "clear and unmistakable"—a phrase he never failed to use in his exposition of the scriptures in the Sunday school class and in the morning worship which he frequently conducted. Next, I recall Brother John Hampton DeJarnette, who was never especially active in Church work in any official capacity, but his constancy and fidelity to the church and his unfailing attendance were greatly to be admired. Another staunch member of Antioch was Deacon John Woolfolk, a name most honored and venerable, one of the most sociable and agreeable of men, as impervious to blandishments as steel, a man who had the courage of his convictions and who never wavered in his friendships. With Brother Woolfolk stood another deacon, W. R. W. Garrett, a man of a great, warm heart who had the love and confidence of every member of the congregation. Brother Woolfolk was tall and Brother Garrett was short in statue and the contrast between them as they distributed the emblems was marked. No truer man to his friends, neighbors and mankind ever lived.

"Another light in the watch tower was Elder Thomas W. Valentine, clerk of our circuit court for a great number of years. He was an elder of our church and superintendent of our Sunday school until called home by the Master. Brother Valentine was always at his post of duty on Sunday and always rendered an acceptable service to the church. He was as honest as the days were long and one of the most honorable of men. And while Brother Anderson never lost his desire for association with

Abraham, Isaac and Jacob, Brother Valentine in his prayers never forgot the warm and pathetic appeal of David in the fifty-first Psalm, 'Create within me a clean heart and renew a right spirit within me.'

"There was no man with a larger heart or who walked nearer to God than Elder John Dratt.   He came to us from the other side of the Mason and Dixon line, but was a sincere friend of his adopted people.   Mr. Robert Hudgin, our County Clerk, could not take the 'Test Oath' in order to hold his office after the Civil War and Brother Dratt qualified as Clerk and let Mr. Hudgin hold the office and receive all the emoluments of the same.   Where shall we find a purer unselfishness?   He was always present at our church services and we greatly loved him.

"Deacon George Boulware was another faithful member of Antioch and although he had to ride horseback or drive in ten miles or more he was rarely absent.

"And now the last of our brethren of a former day that I shall specifically recall, but by no means the least, is Brother George Tyler, father of Governor Hoge Tyler, and a prince among men.   Of all our members during these fifty odd years of my service in the church he was the most cultured.   His vision was broad, his erudition profound, his judgments liberal and charitable. He could discuss the Bible or the tariff with equal lucidity and hold his end of the discussion in either.   He was Chesterfieldian in manners and always gave a cordial grasp of the hand while his heart overflowed with love for all men.

"And now I turn to the companion page of the book and speak of our women, whose souls were so beautiful that they could not fail to cast a rare fragrance along any path they trod.   They adorned any circle they entered and drew one to them not only by the charms of their personality, but also by their Christian life and conversation and by their unceasing good works.   Let me call the roll of these immortelles: Sisters Saunders, Robert Hudgin, James Ennis, Pitman, Bettie Roper, Lucy Woolfolk, Fenella White, Fannie White, Ellen Downing, Sallie Sutton and Sister Valentine.   This coterie of women in my judgment have never been excelled."

Mr. Campbell's admiration for Bishop Semple was no less than that for Dr. Broaddus.   He tells us in his journal, of preaching in Upper Essex church on which occasion the venerable Mr. Semple came to hear him.   They spent the evening together in the home of Thomas M. Henley and after prayer and praise reposed that night upon the same bed. The following morning after Mr. Campbell had baptized a young disciple from King William, they parted with mutual good wishes.

"What I admired most of all," wrote Mr. Campbell, "was the good temper and Christian courtesy of this venerable disciple * * * who did not lose sight of the meekness and mildness, the candor and complaisance which the religion of Jesus teaches and without which, though a man's head were as clear as an angel's intellect, his religion is vain."

The fact that the Disciples have not been aggressive in Caroline in recent years may be explained by the very genius of the movement, which holds it as fundamental that no organization should be established where others are already standing for the faith set forth by the pioneers of the movement. No better statement of this faith may be found than that given to a lady inquirer by the martyred President, James A. Garfield, a life-long member and for some time a preacher in the Disciple fold. His statement was as follows:

(1) We call ourselves Disciples or Christians.

(2) We believe in God the Father.

(3) We believe that Jesus is the Christ, the son of the living God and our Savior. We regard the divinity of Christ as the fundamental truth of the Christian system.

(4) We believe in the Holy Spirit, both as to his agency in conversion and as a dweller in the heart of the Christian.

(5) We accept the Old and New Testaments as the inspired word of God.

(6) We believe in the future reward of the righteous and the future punishment of the wicked.

(7) We believe that Deity is a prayer-hearing and prayer-answering God.

(8) We observe the institution of the Lord's Supper on every Lord's Day. To this table we neither invite nor debar. We say it is the Lord's table for all the Lord's children.

(9) We plead for the unity of God's people.

(10) The Bible is our only discipline.

(11) We maintain that all ordinances should be observed as they were in the days of the Apostles.

Among the pastors who have served Antioch church may be named: J. G. Parrish, who is buried in the church yard;

Robert C. Cave, John L. Brandt, I. J. Spencer, Peter Ainslie, II, Landon A. Cutler, C. S. Ehlers, Preston A. Cave, Richard Bagby, W. M. Forrest, F. A. Hodge, C. M. Kreidler, D. E. Motley and Marshall Wingfield.

HOPEWELL CHURCH (DISCIPLES)

On September 30, 1876, B. C. Burnett, Sr., Pan Burnett, B. C. Burnett, Jr., Angelina Burnett, Mignonette Burnette, John J. Blanton, Sarah E. Diggs, Ellen Ophelia Diggs, Josie Lumpkin, Sallie Lumpkin, Archibald Blanton, John T. Blanton, Ann Blanton, Sallie Haley, Ada Burruss, Ann Marmaduke, Hause Marmaduke, Willie Marmaduke, Richard Marmaduke, George Marmaduke, Mary Marmaduke and Atwill Cannon, members of Emmas church, petitioned their mother church for authority to band themselves together as a separate and distinct congregation and to meet for worship in Hopewell meeting-house. The petition was granted and the petitioners became the charter members. The charter members added to their number rapidly and was soon a thriving congregation with a regular pastor. After more than twenty-five years of service the congregation fell on evil days, owing to the burning of their house of worship and removals and so disbanded. For names of other acquisitions from Emmas church see Emmaus Church Records, Volume 1864–1888 in possession of Mr. L. D. George, Penola, Va. Athens, the location of this church, was originally Athey.

LEBANON CHURCH (DISCIPLES)

Lebanon church was established in 1840. The Rev. Albert R. Flippo gave one acre of land on which the house was erected with the provision that if the land should cease to be used for religious purposes it would revert to his estate.

Dr. Joseph A. Chandler, Mr. and Mrs. Thomas K. Chandler, Mr. William Chandler, Mrs. George B. Washington, Dr. William Seaman and Miss Sammie Williams were members of this church and out of this congregation came two ministers of the Gospel— namely, Rev. Albert R. Flippo and Rev. Hervey J. Seaman, of whom see elsewhere in this volume.

Many eminent ministers of the Disciples communion preached in Lebanon church, among them Rev. Messrs. Peter Ainslie, Anderson, Dangerfield, DuVal, Henley, Abell, Cutler and Pendleton.

The congregation on the death of the above named members

began to decline and about the year 1900 ceased to meet altogether. The house was subsequently used for about three years by a religious body known as "Apostolics," under the leadership of Mr. M. T. Beasley, agent of the Richmond, Fredericksburg and Potomac Railroad at Woodford. After this the building was taken for a school-house and is used for school purposes to this day.

BITHYNIA CHURCH (DISCIPLES)

Bithynia Christian church (Disciples) was established near Guinea, Caroline county, about 1868 by several of the members of Lebanon church who lived in the vicinity of Guinea. These members continued to hold membership with the Lebanon church, but conducted Sunday school at Bithynia and had ministers come and preach at every opportunity, with the hope of establishing a strong congregation there in the course of the years. Among those who led in this work were Dr. Joseph A. Chandler, M. D., father of J. A. C. Chandler, President of the College of William and Mary, and of the late Campbell Chandler, whom he named for Alexander Campbell; Mr. and Mrs. Thomas K. Chandler, parents of Boyd D. Chandler, of Spotsylvania, and of Mrs. J. E. Warren, of Newport News; Mr. William Chandler, Dr. William Seaman and Mrs. Mildred Chandler Washington, wife of George B. Washington and mother of Messrs. Henry, Thomas and John Washington, who are well known in Caroline at this day (1923). On the death and removal of the founders of this congregation interest waned and after about thirty or forty years of existence the property was sold to the colored people and is now used by them, under the name of First Baptist church, as a place of worship.

REV. ALBERT R. FLIPPO

Rev. Albert R. Flippo, a minister of the Christian Church (Disciples), was born in Caroline county near a place now called Welch in the year 1816. During his active ministry he served at various periods Zion, Slash, Independence and Ground Squirrel churches in Hanover county; Enon church in Louisa county and Corinth church in King William county. He was ordained in Lebanon church in Caroline. He married Miss Susan Key Burruss. Having no children of their own Rev. Mr. Flippo and his wife adopted a niece of Mrs. Flippo's—Miss "Sammie" Williams—whom they brought up as tenderly as if she had been their own daughter. Miss "Sammie" taught school in Caroline for nearly half century and many eminent men and women came up through her school room. Rev. Mr. Flippo died in 1888, having been terribly afflicted during his last years.

REV. HERVEY J. SEAMAN

The subject of this sketch was the second of three sons of the late Dr. William Seaman, of "Medway," near Welch, in Caroline county. He was born March 21, 1859, and when quite young attended a school taught by Miss Sammie Williams, of Welch. He later attended an academy at Dunnsville, Essex county conducted by Prof. Hundley, father of J. T. T. Hundley, present head of Lynchburg College. From Hundley's Academy Mr. Seaman went to Richmond College, thence to Transylvania University at Lexington, Ky. At the Bible College of the last named institution he studied for the ministry of the Gospel in the Disciples Church. After graduation and ordination he served the churches in Martinsville, Va., Danville, Va., Charlottesville, Va., Ronceverte, W. Va., and also churches in the States of California, Washington and Kentucky. Mr. Seaman married Miss Lucy Walters, of Charlottesville, Va., and had issue: Forest, who married Howard Wester, lawyer; Geraldine, who married J. Jaeger, of New York State, and Stacy, who married a lady from Kentucky. The Rev. Mr. Seaman has lived in Charlottesville for the last quarter of a century where he is highly esteemed. His brothers, J. P. and C. H. Seaman, live in Caroline, where they are highly respected and useful citizens.

THE OLD QUAKER CHURCH AT GOLANSVILLE

S. B. Weeks, in *Southern Quakers and Slavery*, states that the Golansville or Caroline Meeting was established in 1739 and discontinued in 1853. On page 211 it is recorded that, "At a Monthly Meeting held in Caroline county, Virginia, on eighth day of the fifth month, 1773, by a report from Camp Creek Preparative it appears the Friends of that Meeting are desirous there should be prohibition of Friends hiring negroes; believing that practice to be attended with the same covetous disposition as the purchasing of them." Weeks, on page 106, names Joseph Hoggatt, Stringman, Nathan Stanley, Robert, John and William Johnson as members of the Caroline Monthly Meeting who have removed to North Carolina.

In *Our Quaker Friends of Ye Olden Time*, published by J. P. Bell Book Co., appear the names of several members of the Caroline Meeting, but little or none of the history of the same. All of the old books and records of this old Caroline Meeting are in the possession of Mr. John C. Thomas, 1333 Bolton street, Baltimore, Md.

THE BAPTISTS

The people called Baptists were well established in Caroline within the first half century of the county's existence. There is no definite record of the first preaching in the county by Baptists, but it is certain that ministers of this faith preached in the county prior to 1760. In the Clerk's office of the county may be seen court records of the imprisonment of several Baptist ministers, one of which reads as follows:

Monument to Imprisoned Baptist Preachers at Bowling Green

"July Court MDCCLXXI, 1771

"Bartholomew Chewning, James Goodrich and Edward Herndon being brought before the court for teaching and preaching the Gospel, without having Episcopal ordination, or a license from the General Court: *Ordered*, that they be remanded back to gaol of this county, & there remain till they give security, each in the sum of twenty pounds & two securities each in the sum of two pounds, for their good behaviour twelve months and a daye."

Records of similar charges and punishments are found in the same book against John Burruss, John Young and Lewis Craig, and upon one occasion Patrick Henry came to Caroline to defend the liberties of these ministers when they were charged with preaching without the proper authority.

At the present time there are sixteen white Baptist churches in Caroline with a membership of approximately four thousand, and nearly a score of colored churches with a membership equally as large as that of the white churches. It is conservative to say that the membership of the white Baptist churches will out-number the combined membership of all other denominations in the county. Following are sketches of nearly all of the Baptist churches in the county:

BETHEL BAPTIST CHURCH

Bethel church, which is located about five miles west of Bowling Green, was organized in the year 1800. Rev. Andrew Broaddus I, was the first pastor, and Messrs. Charles Woolfolk and Thomas Jones were the first deacons.

In the minutes of Goshen Association of 1802, as preserved in Semple's History of Baptists in Virginia, it is recorded that Bethel church had, by a majority vote, passed a resolution compelling each member to contribute to the expenses of the congregation according to their ability, under the penalty of the displeasure of the church. This rule offended many members of Bethel and also several churches in the Association. The question was put before the Association as to the attitude of that body toward such a ruling and the following reply was given: "We do not approbate the method of raising money by assessments, upon the principle of its not being sanctioned by New Testament examples and the general principles of the Baptists and because of the unhappy consequences which may result from such a practice." Thus was demonstarated, over a century ago, the loyalty of the Baptists to the spirit of the New Testament and to principles of individual liberty. They knew full well that where the love of Christ does not constrain the ruling of a congregation cannot compel.

This church has been unusually peaceful and prosperous. Among the pastors who have served Bethel in the last century may be mentioned the following: The Rev. Messrs. Andrew Broaddus I, Spilsby Woolfolk, H. W. Montague, James D. Coleman, R. H. W. Buckner, A. B. Dunaway, C. W. Trainham, James T. Eubank, James Long, J. W. McCown, C. R. Cruickshank and S. B. Overton. Among the deacons of the past fifty years may be named J. B. Washington, S. G. Coghill, W. A. Woolfolk, P. A. Gravatt, J. C. Chandler, Robert Woolfolk, E. S. Coghill and T. C. Thomas.

MT. HERMON BAPTIST CHURCH

Mt. Hermon Baptist church had its origin in a Union Sunday school organized June 11, 1869, by C. A. Shuman, of Mt. Horeb Baptist church and Mrs. Martha Sirles, of Shiloh Methodist church. On the 11th of the following October there were 61 students, and officers and teachers as follows: C. A. Shuman, Mrs. C. A. Shuman, W. S. Cecil, W. S. Moore, A. Judson Blanton, J. H. Covington, Mrs. Martha Sirles, Mrs. Emeline Blanton, Mrs. L. J. Vaughan, Miss Lelia Page, T. W. Green and T. G. Burke.

In November of the same year a series of meetings were held by the Rev. Messrs. J. W. Hart and N. Short, during which W. P. Sirles, James Vaughan, Lucy J. Vaughan and Lucy Pavy became members of the church. Thomas R. Dew, of King and Queen county gave one acre of land to the new congregation in 1870, which was cleared of the pine growth, leaving the young oak shrubs to grow into the present beautiful shade trees. In 1871 26 united with the church during a meeting held by the Rev. Messrs. Hart, Short and Broaddus. The church was formally organized in 1872 with 14 male and 13 female members from Mt. Horeb and 1 male and 9 female members from Providence, making a total of 37 members. Dr. Andrew Broaddus preached the organization sermon.

The origin of the name of Mt. Hermon is interesting. A colored congregation had been organized nearby and a committee from the same called on Mr. C. A. Shuman for a name for their new church. Mr. Shuman read to them Psalm 89:12, "The North and South thou hast created them; Tabor and Hermon shall rejoice in thy name." Then he said, "You can take Mt. Tabor or Mt. Hermon, as you may prefer, and we will take the name you leave for our church which we now call Mt. Horeb Mission." Thus the names of the two congregations were fixed at once. The Mt. Hermon Baptist Association is named for this church.

Mt. Hermon church has been served by the following ministers: Rev. Messrs. J. W. Hart, 1872; I. T. Wallace, 1877–78; W. T. Derieux, J. R. Land, Alexander H. Sands, Howard Montague, James Mitchell, S. U. Grimsley, 1879; P. J. M. Osborne, 1884; Rev. J. R. Moffett, 1887; J. T. Lynch, 1888; J. J. Wicker, H. H. Street, F. E. Beale, E. E. Northern, Jacob Sallade, 1895; Andrew Broaddus II, 1896; H. T. Musselman, J. F. Billingsley, George M. Donahoe and W. D. Bremner, 1921–24.

CARMEL BAPTIST CHURCH

Carmel church, situated about twelve miles southwest of Bowling Green, "was planted by S. Harris and J. Reed" in 1773. The first name of the church was Polecat, so called from its proximity to Polecat Creek. This name was changed to Burruss's church, in honor of Rev. John Burruss, the first pastor. Upon the erection of a new house of worship in 1838, on the present site, a new church constitution was adopted opening with these words: "This church is called and shall be known by the name of Burruss's Baptist Church of Christ at Mt. Carmel." The house erected in 1838 was burned in 1874. During the interval between these dates the name Mt. Carmel gradually took precedence over Burruss's and Mt. Carmel was finally adopted as the name. Later the "Mt." was dropped by a formal vote and Carmel became the name of the congregation.

Among the families represented in the church during the first century of its existence may be named the following: Adams, Anderson, Allen, Abrams, Atkins, Acres, Brown, Burruss, Butzner, Boxley, Bibb, Broaddus, Butler, Blunt, Chiles, Cleere, Carter, Coleman, Chandler, Cobb, Carneal, Cannon, Davenport, Day, Dickenson, Dunn, DeJarnette, Estes, Enroughty, England, Flippo, Fletcher, Fox, Flagg, Gatewood, Goland, Goulding, Goodwin, Hewlett, Harris, Hargrave, Hackett, Holloway, Isbell, Kelly, Knote, Long, Luck, Middlebrook, Mills, Malone, McLaughlin, Matthews, Minor, Moncure, Montgomery, Madison, Miller, Mitchell, Newson, News, Patterson, Price, Pemberton, Peatross, Quarles, Reynolds, Redd, Richardson, Smith, Spearman, Stevens, Sacra, Swann, Southworth, Temple, Tisdale, Terrell,

Trevilian, Tyler, Terry, Tinsley, Turner, Valentine, Wyatt, Woolfolk, Winston, Woodson, Waddey, Wright, Yarbrough. These names largely represent the membership of Carmel up to the beginning of the twentieth century. In the list are all the names of all the deacons, trustees, clerks, treasurers of the first 125 years. Nor does this list give the names of the colored members who out-numbered the white members three to one at times. For instance in 1809 there were 162 white and 342 colored members. There is no record of the slightest friction between the races.

The first pastor was John Burruss who had associated with him John Waller. This pastorate continued twenty years and was followed by that of Dr. Andrew Broaddus who served as pastor for thirty years. Dr. Broaddus was followed by M. L. Jones, Rufus Chandler and Warren Woodson, in the order named. M. L. Jones returned in 1837 and served as pastor until 1841 and was succeeded by Samuel Harris. Samuel Harris was succeeded by the Rev. Messrs. Andrew Broaddus, James D. Coleman and Joseph Baker in the order named. In the sketch of Baker which appears in Taylor's Virginia Baptist Ministers it is recorded that he left "the upper country" (Winchester) and went down to "the lower country and assumed the pastorate of Burruss's Church in Caroline county." Both Baker and Jones died during their pastorates at Carmel. The Rev. Mr. Baker was succeeded in turn by W. D. Thomas, A. M. Poindexter, Charles H. Ryland, J. B. T. Patterson, P. B. Rennolds, E. G. Baptist, G. W. Reggan, E. W. Winfrey, Edmund Harrison, J. T. Betts, T. R. Carr, J. W. McCown, Hugh Goodwin, Hugh Musselman, L. D. Craddock, L. L. Gwaltney and W. D. Bremner, W. B. Carter and G. T. Terrell. During Mr. Ryland's pastorate the Federal troops riddled the church inside and turned it into a slaughter pen. A. M. Poindexter was a great orator and G. W. Reggan was a great scholar. L. L. Gwaltney became editor of the *Alabama Baptist*. The longest pastorates were those of Burruss, Waller and Broaddus. W. D. Bremner and M. L. Jones were pastors on two different occasions. Mr. Bremner served from 1905 to 1913 and from 1917 to 1924, when he removed to Gloucester.

The following men have been ordained to the ministry from the membership of Carmel: Robert Tisdale, Rufus Chandler, John M. Waddy, Archibald Dick, William I. Chiles, Thomas H. Fox, John W. Walsh and Henry Wise Tribble.

The minutes show that in the late sixties colored deacons were ordained, and that in 1868, "Elmore E. Taylor was granted a license to preach the gospel to persons of his own colour." When the building burned in 1874 the colored members erected a church of their own. The new house had no gallery for colored people. Practically all country churches with galleries were built prior to the Civil War.

Carmel once owned an adjacent building, called Temperance Hall. It was the outgrowth of a organization known as the Temperance Society. By an irony of fate it was removed to Ruther Glen in the seventies and used for a saloon.

In 1923 Carmel spent $5,000.00 in improvements on the building preparatory to the celebration of the 150th anniversary held that year. The location on the Telegraph road and at the fork of the Milford and Chilesburg roads is very desirable and the church prospers. The present membership is approximately 300.

CONCORD BAPTIST CHURCH

This church is situated near Dawn in the southern part of Caroline and was organized on July 10, 1841, with the following charter members: Albert S. Hundley, William Mallory, Edmund C. Chiles, John Thompson, Wm. R. Peatross, Thomas Hurt, Benjamin Hurt, Samuel C. Peatross, Andrew Long, Richard Baughn, John T. Harris, John S. Blanton, John W. Hundley, James F. Chiles, John Lucord, John E. Bowers, Mary J. Hundley, Frances O. Harris, A. V. Harris, F. E. Harris, M. E. Harris, Nancy Shipp, Parmelia Mallory, Elizabeth Burruss, Sarah P. Peatross, Elizabeth Seay, Angelina W. Seay, Frances Peatross, Sarah P. Kelly, Jonah Peatross, Lucy Hundley, Frances Stuart, Jane Thompson, Elizabeth Chiles, Lucy Ann Chiles, Frances Bowers, Lucy A. Bowers, Mary D. Peatross, Lucy Blanton, Eliza A. Blanton, Jane E. Duval, Ann R. Peatross.

The larger part of these members came by letter from the Reed's Baptist church. Their first pastor was the Rev. George W. Trice. Descendants of many of the charter members still reside in Caroline and hold membership with Concord.

The first house of worship of this congregation stood across the road from the present site. Mr. Joseph Brame, a great uncle of Mrs. Sarah Peatross Saunders, who united with the church in 1855 and is still a member, donated the land and had the first house erected at his own expense.

H. C,.21

A Sunday school was organized in 1856 with John T. Harris as superintendent. The report of the following year shows eight teachers and thirty scholars. In 1858, W. C. P. Ramsey became superintendent.

In 1842 Concord reported 74 white and 12 colored members, in 1847 it had 114 white and 102 colored members and in 1859 there 86 white and 262 colored members. In September, 1857, the present building was erected and dedicated. The fact that the church constitution stated that, "The government of the church shall be in the hands of the free white male members" probably kept the property from passing into the hands of the colored membership after the Civil War.

Among the church clerks from 1859 to the present time have been: A. S. Hundley, Thomas R. Haywood, Joseph M. Seay, Wm. T. Blank, Wm. S. Bowers, W. H. Bowers, R. N. Allen, Wm. W. Carter and Claude Hutcheson.

Among the moderators who presided over the business meetings of the church from 1868 to the present were: James T. Hurt, Isaac H. Bullock, Obediah Atkinson, Aldred Blanton, W. R. Peatross, John E. Chiles, Wm. T. Chiles, A. M. Hundley, W. B. Garnett, Wm. C. Moore, Dr. L. C. Pollard, James Garnett, J. J. Atkinson and Alfred E. Bowers.

John B. Gathright was chosen superintendent of the Sunday school in 1880, George H. Saunders in 1866 and later John T. Terrell and Samuel L. Chiles filled this office.

Rev. A. B. Smith was chosen pastor of the church in 1849, again in 1854 and still again in 1875, serving about seven years all told. Rev. Thos. H. Fox was chosen pastor in 1851, and served a short time. After 1859 no records can be found of the affairs of the church until 1866, when the church reported 67 white members. Rev. A. R. Fox was pastor in 1867–69, then follow the pastorates of Rev. P. B. Reynolds,:Rev. J. H. Newbill, Rev. Geo. W. Reggan, Rev. Chas. P. Scott and Rev. J. B. Wright. At the age of 80, Rev. Robert Ryland, D. D., first President of Richmond College and the first Baptist Chaplain of the University of Virginia, became pastor and served one year. Among the later pastors of the church are Rev. Messrs. W. T. T. Noland, W. E. Robertson, Wm. Owen Carver, Melvin A. Martin, James Quarles, Geo. Tyler Terrell and W. D. Bremner.

Among the women who wrought in Concord church between 1850 and 1880 may be named Mesdames Mary Croughton Hurt,

Elizabeth Hurt Seay, Lucy Kidd Hundley, Sarah Hundley Kelly, Lucy Johnson Peatross, Mary Peatross Moore, Jane Seay Duval, Lucy Duval Martin and Miss Marie Etta Peatross.

In more recent times we find among the prominent workers in the church Mesdames Etta Saunders Duval, Emma Dabney Freeman, Louise Terrell Campbell, Georgianna Hill Andrews, Mary Heywood Campbell, Mary Atkinson Barlow, Anna Young Dimue, Ruth Bowers Martin, Margaret Pollard Bowers and Misses Kate Garnett, Otera A. Campbell, Mabel Chiles, Gertrude Saunders and Ruth Hutcheson.

UPPER ZION BAPTIST CHURCH

Upper Zion Baptist church, six miles northeast of Bowling

Upper Zion Baptist Church

Green, was organized in 1774 and was originally known as Tuckahoe church. The first Baptist preacher to visit the community where the church was subsequently established was the Rev. John Corbley who came to Virginia from Ireland. He was imprisoned in Culpeper for preaching the Gospel and later was imprisoned in Pennsylvania on the charge of complicity in the "Whiskey Insurrection." He died in 1805 and his wife and children were murdered by the Indians.

The Rev. Messrs. Lewis Craig and John Waller preached in the vicinity of this church in 1771 and 1772. It was here that a warrant was issued for the arrest of Mr. Craig on the charge of preaching the Gospel without proper ordination. He was carried before a magistrate to whom he gave bond not to preach in the county within a certain number of days, but reconsidering what he had done and feeling the injustice of the measure, he decided to violate his bond and incur the penalty. Accordingly he preached for some time on Reuben Catlett's plantation for which he was again arrested and committed to jail in Bowling Green where he remained for three months. He found in the jail Edward Herndon and B. Chewning who had been committed on the same charge, but being "exhorters" only they were soon released. In 1773 James Ware and James Pitman were im-

Rev. William A. Baynham

prisoned sixteen days each for having preached in their houses. They offered to give bond for their good behavior, but not for preaching in their houses in particular, which offer was at first refused and acceded to afterward. It is recorded in Semple's History of Baptists in Virginia that when Waller and Craig were imprisoned in Fredericksburg the minister of the established church, who had preached a sermon in Caroline against the Baptists, paid them a visit, conversed with them on religion and on taking leave of them, offered to be their security if they chose to give bond. In 1775 the Rev. Younger Pitts and his companion, one Mr. Pickett, were arrested and threatened with being brought before a magistrate, but after some abuse were released.

In 1819 the name of the church was changed from Tuckahoe

to Upper Zion. The Rev. Messrs. John Shackleford, John Sorrel, John Micou, Mordecai W. Broaddus, Robert W. Cole, George W. Trice, William A. Baynham, A. J. Ramsey, Andrew W. Broaddus, II, R. L. Gay, E. M. Dowley, John Pollard, J. M. McManaway, R. E. Vellines and L. M. Ritter have served this church in a pastoral capacity.

Among the deacons of Upper Zion in former years may be named Younger Martin, George Marshall, Sr., John Cherbury Gravatt, Dr. Lunsford, Thomas Broaddus, James H. Broaddus, James U. Carneal, Philip H. Carter, Andrew J. Gravatt, William L. Andrews, John F. Wright and Thomas J. Motley.

More recently and of the present day may be named Deacons Luther B. Brooks, Calvin N. Houston, A. F. Wright, R. H. Eager, M. H. Jones, T. J. Carter, D. L. Cook, J. W. Guerrant and Andrew B. Marshall.

Among the Clerks of the church may be named Robert S. Wright, Sr., George W. Marshall, Sr., Robert S. Wright, Jr., George W. Marshall, Jr., Benj. F. Smoot, Sr., G. H. Pitts, J. C. Sale and A. B. Marshall.

SALEM BAPTIST CHURCH

Salem Baptist church which is located at Sparta, about ten miles east of Bowling Green, was formed from Upper King and Queen church in 1802. The "Great Revival" which spread over Virginia in 1788 stirred Tuckahoe and Upper King and Queen churches mightily, causing these two congregations to meet upon the site of old Salem church, which was half-way ground, under an arbor in a great series of revival meetings. These meetings were attended by multitudes and great numbers were baptized, most of whom united with Upper King and Queen church, then under the pastoral care of the Rev. Theodrick Noel. The arbor, which had been the scence of the remarkable revival, continued to be a regular preaching point, served largely by Rev. Mr. Noel, and many citizens of the community came into the church under his preaching. The large number of Baptists living in the community, who found it inconvenient to attend Upper King and Queen and Tuckahoe churches, made the establishment of new congregation necessary, hence Salem church was constituted on July 10, 1802.

The first house of worship erected by this new congregation was a frame building without ceiling of any kind and was situated

Andrew Broaddus I.

Andrew Broaddus II.

Andrew Broaddus III.

Salem Church at Sparta

in Caroline about six miles from the spot where the present Salem church stands. A second house was erected on the same site which was used until the erection of the splendid brick structure which now stands in the village of Sparta.

The first pastor of Salem was the Rev. Mr. Noel through whose efforts the church had come into being. After the resignation of Mr. Noel, in 1809, the church was served by the Rev. Messrs. John Sorrel and Spilsby Woolfolk, both natives of Caroline county. Following the pastorate of Mr. Woolfolk there began a series of the most remarkable pastorates in the history of the Baptist church, if not the most remarkable in the history of Christendom. The Rev. Andrew Broaddus, whose biography appears elsewhere in this chapter, who had been born and brought up in the vicinity of the church was called to the pastorate of Salem in 1820 and accepting he served the church for twenty-eight years. Immediately upon his death his son, Rev. Andrew Broaddus II, became pastor and served continuously for forty-eight years, retiring December 31, 1896 on account of failing health. Immediately upon his retirement his son, Rev. Andrew Broaddus III, entered upon the pastorate of this church and continues in that capacity to this day.

Salem church has given many of her sons to the Gospel ministry, among whom may be mentioned the Rev. Messrs. John Sorrel, Spilsby Woolfolk, Andrew Broaddus I, Andrew Broaddus II, Andrew Broaddus III, Julian Broaddus, Luther Broaddus, Maurice Broaddus, Mordecai W. Broaddus, Henry G. Segar, Albert Anderson, Robert W. Cole and Joseph W. Atkinson.

COUNTY LINE CHURCH

This church, organized in 1784, is situated near the dividing line between Caroline and Spotsylvania counties, the house of worship being in Caroline about one-half mile from Chilesburg and about three miles from the North Anna River. The site of the original house of worship was about one mile from the present house and nearer the Spotsylvania line. This congregation was constituted by those who withdrew from Waller's church at the time Waller's was excluded from the Association on account of the Arminian tendencies of the pastor, Rev. John Waller. When Mr. Waller was reinstated in the Association, County Line church was received also.

Probably no man of his time contributed more to the establishment and growth of the Baptist church in Virginia than John Waller. He was born in Spotsylvania in 1741 and was noted in his early life for his recklessness and profanity. His nicknames were "Swearing Jack" and "Devil's Adjutant." He was one of the jury that punished Rev. Lewis Craig for preaching. He was remarkably converted in 1767 and was baptized by Rev. James Read. A church was constituted and committed to his pastoral care in 1769, subsequently becoming known as "Waller's church," and being one of nine which he planted within the Goshen Association. He removed to Abbeville, S. C., in 1793 and died there in 1802.

William Edmund Waller, brother of John, was the first pastor of County Line church. He removed to Kentucky in 1784 and was succeeded by Absalom Waller.

In 1841 the old church property near the Caroline-Spotsylvania line was sold to the Rehoboth Methodist church and County Line moved to its present location. The church house was rebuilt in 1894 on the opposite of the road in a grove of fifteen acres. The site across the road was taken for a cemetery.

The following pastors have served this congregation: John Waller, Wm. Edmund Waller, 1784; A. M. Lewis, 1829; J. A. Billingsley, 1831; W. R. Powell, 1837; J. M. Roane, 1866; L. W. Allen, 1866; C. B. Dickenson, 1872; J. L. Lawless, 1881; J. T. Dickenson, 1886; T. R. Corr, 1890; E. G. Baptist, 1894; J. S. Ryland, 1896; E. W. Robinson, 1924.

The following Clerks have served County Line: Fleming Terrell, 1829; Thomas D. Smith, 1831; Genett Anderson, 1833; John K. Luck, 1842; W. D. Waller, 1866; A. G. Smith, 1886. Captain Cornelius T. Smith, who represented Caroline in the Legislature, and who served the county as treasurer for many years, has been very active in this church and for many years moderator of the Association of which the church is a part.

BOWLING GREEN BAPTIST CHURCH

This church, located on Main Street of Bowling Green, was constituted September 18, 1878, with a membership of thirty-nine, of whom twenty-two were men and seventeen were women. The church was admitted into the Goshen Association in 1879 and in 1902 regularly withdrew with other churches to form a new association, now known as the Hermon.

For about three years after its organization this church was regularly supplied by various ministers, among them being Dr. A. E. Dickinson, Rev. George W. Reggan, Dr. A. B. Dunaway and Professor John Hart.

The following ministers have served the church as pastors: Rev. J. L. Lawless, April, 1881, to February, 1884; Rev. Dr. Andrew Broaddus, April, 1885, to January, 1893; Rev. R. L. Gay, April, 1893, to 1898; Rev. E. M. Dowley, 1899 to 1901; Rev. Dr. John Pollard, July, 1901, to October, 1904; Rev. Dr.

Bowling Green Baptist Church

J. M. McManaway, January, 1905, to January, 1910; Rev. R. E. Vellines, November, 1910, to January, 1915; Rev. L. M. Ritter, October, 1915, to present.

The present house of worship, a picture of which appears herein, was dedicated on Thanksgiving Day, 1899. The Rev. J. B. Hawthorne preached the dedicatory sermon. The church owns a comfortable parsonage adjoining the church grounds.

The present officiary of the church is as follows: Pastor, Rev. L. M. Ritter. Deacons: Dr. E. E. Butler, O. P. Smoot, E. G. Smoot, M. G. Garrett, C. R. Dickinson, R. B. Broaddus and Col. R. L. Beale.   Trustees: Dr. R. T. Glassell, C. R. Dickinson, Dr. C. S. Webb, M. G. Garrett and L. D. Vincent.   Treasurer, H. D. McWhirt; Mission Treasurer, George Dorsey; Auditor, Arthur H. Allen.

MT. HOREB BAPTIST CHURCH

Mt. Horeb church was organized as Reed's church in 1773 by Elders Samuel Harris and R. Ford. John Young was then ordained elder and installed as pastor of this congregation and continued to serve in this capacity until his removal to Amherst in 1799. During his ministry at Reed's church he was imprisoned for six months in the county jail for preaching. He baptized seventy persons while pastor of Reed's. Upon the retirement of Elder Young, John Selph was ordained elder and set over the congregation as pastor. Thos. Kidd and Wm. Kelley were ordained deacons and Wm. Rawlins clerk.

After a lapse of years Joel Mason, Chas. Atkinson and Joseph Norment were ordained deacons and in 1835 John D. Hargrave and Wm. Mason were added to these. The church was served by Elders Selph, Woolfolk and Hatchett until 1834 when Geo. W. Trice became pastor and J. D. Hargrave clerk. From 1834 to 1839 there were twenty-seven white persons added to the membership.

In September, 1839, a series of revival meetings was held in which Elders M. W. Broaddus, Henry Segar, George W. Trice, Andrew Broaddus, and Philip Taliaferro of the Baptist church were assisted by two Methodist ministers with the result that about one hundred persons dedicated their lives to Christ, sixty of whom were baptized.

In the year 1840 the church decided to build a brick meeting house on the old site. The contract was let to Joseph Norment for the sum of $1,093.00. Shortly after this action another meeting was held near Concord and by another vote the building enterprise was defeated.

In April, 1840, W. M. Mason was elected clerk to succeed J. D. Hargrave. In June of the same year the members of Reed's church living near Concord desiring to organize themselves into a separate and distinct congregation were given permission to do so in a resolution which commended them to God and the Word of His grace. Elder Trice resigned the pastorate of Reed's in 1842 and was succeeded by Elder Cole who served the church two years after, which Elder Trice was chosen pastor for the second time. Mr. Ed. West was ordained deacon in 1842.

At a meeting of Reed's church in April, 1845 the weak state of the church was discussed and the matter of disbanding was.

put forward for consideration until the next monthly meeting. In May, after one month's deliberation, the church came together and decided to disband and unite with neighboring church, but after a short period, becoming dissatisfied with this decision, rescinded their action and engaged Elder Hatchett to serve as pastor.

In September following the church was reorganized and Thos. Woolard and Winston Atkinson were ordained deacons by Elders Hatchett and Trice.   Elder Hatchett resigned as pastor in 1847 and the congregation was pastorless until 1850 when Elder J. W. Atkinson was engaged to serve in this capacity.   He died in 1851.

In 1851 the erection of a meeting house on a site more conveniently situated to the members was proposed and a committee, composed of W. M. Mason, Winston Atkinson and J. R. Mason, was appointed to dispose of the old property and to take such measures for the procuring of a new house as they might deem best.   Owing to a defect in the deed to the old property it could not be sold and the church decided to build without this assistance.   J. R. Mason gave one acre of land on which to build and agreed to erect the house for $800.00.   The house was built and dedicated on Friday, September 30, 1853.   Dr. R. B. C. Howell preached the dedicatory sermon.   The name was changed from Reed's church to Mt. Horeb and Elder A. Eubank chosen as pastor.   He resigned in 1854 to continue his studies in the University of Virginia and Elder R. W. Cole was chosen pastor with R. A. Fox as co-pastor.

On the second Sunday of November 1860, J. E. West and Wm. Young were ordained deacons by Elders Cole and Fox.   In March 1863, Elder Cole resigned and was succeeded by R. A. Fox. Obedian Atkinson, C. A. Shuman and Wm. T. Taliaferro were ordained deacons in 1866 and W. R. Peatross and L. M. Hart in 1867.   R. A. Fox resigned as pastor in 1869 and was succeeded by Elder J. W. Hart.   During the pastorate of R. W. Cole, 1854–1863, forty-one white and one hundred and fifteen colored persons were added to the membership; during that of R. A. Fox, 1863–69, fifty-seven whites and five colored and during that of J. W. Hart, 1869–72, eighty-six whites were added.   The colored members of this church, at their own request, were given letters and constituted themselves into a church, known as Mt. Tabor, on January 20, 1872.   The pastor and deacons of Mt. Horeb officiated at the organization.

In 1869 a mission Sunday school was established by Mt. Horeb at Shumansville with a view to establishing a church there. Mr. C. A. Shuman was made superintendent. On July 13, 1872, twenty-seven members of Mt. Horeb were given letters for the purpose of entering upon the formation of a new church. Upon the constitution of the new church Mr. E. Trice was made deacon. A building was erected near Oakley, the site of the mission Sunday school, and was dedicated on September 22, 1872, by Rev. Andrew Broaddus and Rev. N. Short.

Mt. Horeb celebrated its centennial April 13, 1873 and its one hundred and fiftieth anniversary in 1923. On the former occasion Rev. A. H. Sands preached the sermon and on the latter occasion sermons and addresses were delivered by Rev. Messrs. W. E. Warren, L. M. Ritter, Tyler Terrell and Andrew Broaddus III.

Pastor J. W. Hart resigned in 1873 and was succeeded by Rev. Wm. E. Talley. Richard Baughan was made clerk in 1874 and Messrs. J. W. Young, W. Long and M. W. Head were made deacons in 1877. Mr. W. M. Mason was ordained to the ministry in 1877, Rev. Messrs. A. B. Smith, H. Satterwhite and J. O. Turpin acting as presbytery.

The pastoral succession in Horeb church from the time of Rev. J. W. Hart is as follows: Rev. W. E. Talley, 1877–78; Rev. S. U. Grimsley, 1878–80; Rev. A. W. Graves, 1881–83; Rev. A. C. Pugh, 1884; Rev. Mr. Noland, 1885–87; Rev. J. J. Wicker, 1889–90; Rev. R. L. Gay, 1890; Rev. W. O. Carner, 1891; Rev. H. H. Street, 1892–93; Rev. J. W. Hart, 1893–95; Rev. W. C. Foster, 1895–96; Rev. H. T. Musselman, 1896–98; Rev. H. A. Willis, 1898–03; Rev. J. C. Quarles, 1903–04; Rev. J. F. Billingsley, 1905–10; Rev. W. B. Carter, 1911–13; Rev. G. Tyler Terrell, 1913–17; Rev. George Donahoe, 1917–19; Rev. W. D. Bremner, 1920–21, and Rev. W. E. Warren, 1922.

The present building of Mt. Horeb church was dedicated on December 23, 1890, by Dr. Wm. E. Hatcher, of Richmond, assisted by Rev. Messrs. R. L. Gay, W. O. Carter and Andrew Broaddus, III.

GUINEY'S BRIDGE BAPTIST CHURCH

Guiney's Bridge church was organized about 1783 and named for a bridge over the Mattaponi near Guiney. The house of worship stood near the place which was later made historic by the death of Stonewall Jackson. The first pastor of this church was one Rev. Mr. Holloway. Upon his removal to Halifax county the congregation was served by the Rev. John Waller and Rev. Absalom Waller in succession. About 1840 this church disbanded, its members going into Round Oak church. R. B. Semple, in his History of Virginia Baptists, relates that at Guiney's Bridge church several preachers were arrested on a warrant from a magistrate on the charge of preaching without proper authority. Among these were Rev. Joseph Craig, brother of the Rev. Messrs. Lewis and Elijah Craig. On their way to the magistrate Mr. Craig, thinking it no dishonor to cheat *injustice*, slipped from his horse and escaped in the swamps. The officers, says Mr. Semple, hunted him with dogs, but he was not apprehended.

LIBERTY BAPTIST CHURCH

Liberty church appears for the first time in the minutes of the Goshen Association in 1813 where it is recorded as a new church. Its pastor, Rev. Hipkins Pittman and P. Merriman, were its messengers and these with R. Long, Reuben Rose, Charles Taliaferro and Stanfield Jones represented it until 1822, at which time the church reported 123 members.

From 1822 to 1827 the church was pastorless. Lawrence Battaile became pastor in 1827, although the church did not "set him apart for the ministry" until 1830.

In 1832 Liberty reported 277 members, two Sunday schools and "a large Temperance Society still gaining ground." In 1833 the church "recommended that each member furnish a bench for the people of colour." In 1834 Woolfolk Estes, "who had moved to the Western country," was succeeded as clerk by Richard Buckner, Sr., and he in turn was succeeded two years later by R. H. Washington Buckner. In 1836 Charles A. Lewis "was set apart to the work of an evangelist" and in 1837 Thomas Royster was chosen deacon.

Fifteen members were dismissed in 1840 "for the purpose of constituting a church at Round Oak" and among the number was the treasurer, Robert Jesse, in whose place W. Bates was chosen.

In 1847 when "The Test" was an issue in this section the church passed resolutions condemning the making and selling of liquor, but by a majority of one vote refused to make compliance with this sentiment a test of church membership, where-upon 36 of the members who believed in "The Test" withdrew and organized Bethesda church, carrying with them the clerk, Addison L. Long and the pastor, Rev. Lawrence Battaile, who had served Liberty nearly twenty years. Aaron Thornley was then elected clerk and Rev. George W. Trice pastor. Mr. Trice served the church until his death in 1867.

In 1848, R. H. Washington Buckner was ordained to the ministry and George B. Samuels became clerk. He was followed by Charles T. Jesse in 1854, A. H. Conway in 1867 and S. Fitzhugh in 1878.

The church reached its largest numerical strength in 1861, reporting 163 white and 546 colored members. In 1867 letters were granted the colored members who wished to organize a church of their own, leaving a white membership of 181.

Rev. James D. Coleman died in 1878 after serving the church for ten years. His successors in the pastorate have been the Rev. Messrs. A. B. Dunaway, A. G. Loving, C. W. Trainham, J. W. McCown, J. T. Eubank and S. B. Overton. The present (1924) clerk is W. H. Collawn, of New London, Caroline county. The foregoing facts were obtained for the author from the old records by Dr. Garnett Ryland of the University of Richmond.

BETHESDA BAPTIST CHURCH

This church was formed in 1847 by members of Liberty church who were defeated in their advocacy of a measure, "prohibiting the manufacture and sale of ardent spirits for ordinary use by members of the church on pain of excommunication."

The organization was effected in May, 1847. On this occasion Rev. Edward Kingsford delivered the sermon from a text in the book of Numbers, "Lo, the people shall dwell alone and shall not be reckoned among the nations." Rev. R. W. Cole delivered the charge to the church and Rev. Andrew Broaddus, II, gave the hand of fellowship. The charter members were: Samuel Battaile, John Gouldin, Samuel Coghill, John Rose, James F. Gouldin, Thomas I. West, Addison L. Long, Henry A. Jones, Thomas W. Gouldin, John Massey, Aaron Thornley, William Collawn, Ann Coghill, Lucy A. Roane, Ann Shaddock, Louisa Gouldin, Ann Rose, Mary Farish, Clementine Farish, Sarah Collawn, Frances A. Goodloe and Lettie W. Long.

Bethesda adopted as one of its fundamental laws that "No member of this Church will be permitted to manufacture, sell, use, or furnish to his guests, or labourers, intoxicating liquor as a beverage."

The church has had eleven pastors as follows: Lawrence Battaile, 1847–52; Andrew Broaddus, II, 1853–58; James D. Coleman, 1859–78; A. B. Dunaway, 1879–86; A. G. Loving, 1887–89; C. W. Trainham, 1890–93; J. W. McCown, 1894–95; J. T. Eubank, 1895–03; James Long, 1904–05; B. C. Jones, 1906–10; Rev. Norman Luck, 1911. Rev. B. C. Jones was ordained to the ministry by this church upon accepting the pastorate. The Rev. Messrs. T. S. Dunaway, Ryland Knight, E. L. Grace and Andrew Broaddus III, officiated on this occasion.

The first deacons of Bethesda were Dr. T. W. Gouldin and A. L. Long. Dr. Gouldin was Sunday school superintendent for many years. Among the early deacons and prominent members may be named, Wm. I. Broaddus, Wm. A. Collawn, Benj. F. Kidd, John Gouldin, Thos. R. Dew, K. R. Farish, Lewis Gouldin, John Lefoe, Wm. R. Sale, Judson J. Sale and John W. Broaddus. R. H. W. Buckner was a very useful and conspicuous member and often occupied the pulpit. He was at one time employed by Round Oak, Liberty and Bethesda churches to hold special services for the instruction of the colored members. Dr. R. G. Holloway and David T. Bullock were leading members from the beginning and later deacons Anthony J. Sale and James Bullock were prominent in the church. Bethesda prospers and now has 180 members.

CALVARY BAPTIST CHURCH

This church, located on Milford Street in Bowling Green, was constituted on June 6, 1897, upon the advice of W. E. Hatcher, T. S. Dunaway, L. R. Thornhill, L. J. Haley, J. B. Winston, S. J. Quinn and C. T. Smith, who had been called to confer with a number of persons not then in fellowship with the Bowling Green Baptist church on account of conflicting sentiments regarding the pastor of the Bowling Green church.

The charter members were: W. W. Rains, Webb Rains, D. W. Beazley, Mrs. Lizzie Beazley, Mrs. Rebecca J. Collins, Miss Floyd Smith, R. M. Gray, Gus Throm, W. G. Coghill, Mrs. Lou Coghill, Miss Bessie Coghill, Harry Coghill, Mrs. C. J.

Wright, J. L. Jordan, James R. Collins, Mrs. Louisa Jordan, Mrs. Fanny S. Campbell, Miss Emma S. Campbell, E. B. Kay, John Selph, Milton Selph, Callie Selph, Miss Addie Irby, Mrs. Fanny Irby Moncure, Mrs. Molly R. Coghill, Miss Blanche Coghill, Miss Mary Dallas Coghill, A. P. Gouldman, Mrs. M. E. Gouldman, Miss Henrietta Gouldman, Miss Sue Gouldman, Miss Virginia Byrd Todd, Miss Sallie Bullard, Miss Mattie Throm, Clem Jordan, Mrs. Kate S. Broaddus, Miss Annie W. Broaddus, Miss May M. Broaddus, Miss Caroline Broaddus, Mrs. Lucy Moncure Gill, T. B. Gill, Mrs. Annie B. Wright, R. S. Wright, Jr., Charles H. Wright, Miss Ethel Wright, Robert A. Coghill, K. R. Farish, Cecil Farish, Lewis Farish, Mrs. Fanny Taliaferro, Mrs. Sallie Pollard, R. S. Wright, E. C. Moncure, T. D. Coghill, Dr. W. L. Broaddus and Geo. R. Collins.

Dr. W. L. Broaddus and Judge E. C. Moncure were the first deacons and R. S. Wright was the first clerk. G. R. Collins and John Selph were added to the diaconate a few weeks after organization. Judge Moncure and Major T. D. Coghill were appointed the first trustees. The church was unanimously received into the Goshen Association, at New Hope church in Spotsylvania in the year of its organization, despite the opposition of the pastor over whom the division had occurred. A lot was purchased from C. L. Bullard in 1898 and a substantial building erected thereon and dedicated on June 16, 1899. Dr. W. E. Hatcher preached the dedicatory sermon. Dr. J. W. McCown became the first pastor and served until 1901 when he was succeeded by Rev. H. L. Quarles. Mr. Quarles was succeeded by Rev. C. R. Cruikshank, of Singer's Glen, Va., who served until 1912. Rev. S. B. Overton served from 1912 to 1923.

The clerks of Calvary church have been as follows: R. S. Wright, J. R. Collins, K. R. Farish, R. A. Coghill and E. A. White. The following have served as deacons: Dr. W. L. Broaddus, Judge E. C. Moncure, G. R. Collins, John Selph, William B. Broaddus, J. J. Wright, W. G. Coghill, W. W. Green, J. W. Beazley. The church has had only two treasurers—namely, W. W. Rains and R. A. Coghill. Major T. D. Coghill, Judge Moncure, Joseph Baker and H. B. Smithers have served as trustees.

Calvary church has a membership of nearly two hundred and is a vital religious force in the community.

PROVIDENCE CHURCH

Providence Baptist church which is located four miles east of the county seat of Caroline was founded in 1837. The late Dr. George W. Beale in his Historical Sermon before the Baptist General Association in 1898 said: "The earliest Sunday school of which we have any knowledge in Virginia was gathered where Providence church in Caroline later built its meeting house."

ROUND OAK BAPTIST CHURCH

Mrs. Robert Gordon, of "Santee'," relates that John Battaile, of "Belle Park" had one son who wanted to go to Africa as a missionary. In order to keep the son at home Mr. Battaile volunteered to build him a church on the estate and thus gratify his desire to do missionary work among the negroes. The chapel was erected and the work flourished until there were many white persons interested in and connected with it. Grace Episcopal church nearby engaged the services of one Rev. Mr. Walls, who was considered an "high churchman," and on this account many white persons adhered to the mission. These constituted Round Oak Baptist church about 1840. Lawrence Battaile became the first pastor of this church and was succeeded in turn by the Rev. Messrs. Trice, James D. Coleman, A. B. Dunaway, A. B. Loving and J. W. Reynolds. The last named has served the church for thirty-three years.

Round Oak church, prior to the Civil War and for some time afterward, had a large colored membership and it is probable that this church has done more for the negroes than any other church in the county. For many years Round Oak co-operated with Liberty church in employing R. H. W. Buckner to preach for the colored people. It is interesting to note that the church at its regular monthly meetings always appointed four of the officers to attend the Buckner meetings.

Robert Jesse, Richard Pittman, K. Rowe, Wm. Farish, Hyter Farish, Joseph Skinner, Henry Skinner were among the charter members.

The clerks of Round Oak have been as follows: ————— Marshall, W. H. Farish, James Rowe, James M. Dillard, Arthur Skinner and W. H. Purks. Thus it will be seen that this church has had only six pastors and six clerks in its long history.

The present deacons of Round Oak are: W. H. Purks, Wm. Hayden, J. B. Flippo and James M. Dillard.

H. C.-22

Among the leading families in the church may be named the Yates, Purks, Flippo, Skinner, Sale, Cash, Denson, Dillard, Thomas, Brown and Jones families.

John Goodwin organized the first Sunday school in Round Oak church and drafted the rules for the government of the same.

The main building was erected in 1852 at a cost of $2,250 and the wings were added in 1915 at a cost of $4,000. The cornerstone was laid by the Masonic Lodge at Fredericksburg. The splendid brick structure, although erected at low cost, is one of the best in the county. The church is located at Corbin, in the northern end of the county and is only a few hundred yards from Grace church.

CAROLINE'S CONTRIBUTION TO THE BAPTIST MINISTRY

ANDREW BROADDUS I

The twelfth child of John Broaddus and Frances Pryor, was born November 4, 1770. His eldest brother, William, was educated for the ministry in the Protestant Episcopal church, but died before entering upon the calling. His father cherished the hope that his youngest son, Andrew, would follow in the steps of his eldest, but this was not to be, for he preferred the Baptists, toward whom his father was antagonistic, and united with them on May 28, 1789, being baptized by Elder Theodrick Noel. He preached his first sermon at the home of a Mrs. Lowrie in Caroline on December 24, 1789 and was ordained at Upper King and Queen church on October 16, 1791, by Elders R. S. Semple and Theodrick Noel. In 1817 he made a trip to Kentucky, where he was offered the presidency of Hopkinsville Academy, which he declined, and returned to Virginia. He was married, first to Miss Fanny Temple, daughter of Col. John Temple, of Caroline and had issue: (1) John Wickliffe, (2) William Temple, (3) Eliza S., (4) Maria, (5) Fanny Temple. Second, he married Lucy, daughter of Dr. Robert Honeyman, of Hanover, by whom he had no issue. Third, he married Mrs. Jane C. Broaddus, widow of Christopher Broaddus and sister of his second wife. By this marriage he had three children, Wilton H., Andrew and Columbia. Fourth, he married Miss Caroline W. Boulware, of Newtown, King and

Queen, by whom he had one child, William Lee Broaddus, who practiced medicine in Caroline for many years and whose son, Dr. John G. Broaddus, is at present (1924) a practicing physician in the county.

Rev. Andrew Broaddus, I, was the most widely known Baptist minister Caroline county has ever given to the church, and while he devoted his life for the most part to the churches in Caroline, he was constantly called to the greatest city churches of his time. He was moderator of Dover Association, succeeding R. B. Semple, for many years. In 1843 Columbian College of Washington conferred on him the Degree of Doctor of Divinity. He was an author of prominence and among other works published a History of the Bible, a Catechism for Children, A Form of Church Discipline, A Reply to Thomas Paine's Age of Reason, Dover Selection of Hymns, Virginia Selection of Hymns, Sermons, Essays, Poems, Notes on Texts, etc.

Following are some lines written by Dr. Andrew Broaddus, I, for his friend Rufus Chandler on his (Mr. Broaddus's) departure northward in 1827 in quest of health:

Companion of my life, once more we receive the sad farewell;
The parting pangs my spirit feels, these lines but feebly tell:
To leave the dear domestic group, and far away to roam—
What objects shall supply the place of well-beloved home?

But while to distant Northern climes I trace the lengthening road,
And waters rise and rivers roll 'twixt me and my abode,—
Untravel'd still my heart remains, through all the lonely way,
And, lingering round my own abode, my best affections stay.

There, to fancy's eye portrayed, your image I shall view,
And, flying swift on fancy's wings, shall place myself with you:
How sweetly smile these little ones, while seated on my knees!
How pleasant are these sounds I hear upon the evening breeze!

The carefree laugh, the mingled words—I catch a distant noise,
And see, returning home from school, my much-loved little boys:
They rush along with prattling glee, and mount with hasty feet,
And enter with joyous, carefree, smiles and make the scene complete.

Thus fond imagination dreams; but ah! the vision flies!
Reality obtrusive comes, and other objects rise;
In vain those dear domestic scenes around my fancy play—
My wife, my little ones are there, and I am far away.

Then, if a sigh my bosom heave and if a tear should fall,
As on the distant place I think which holds my earthly all,
I'll blush not as I wipe the tear, but make my just appeal,
To every soft indulgent heart—the hearts that know and feel.

But why despond? and why resign this aching heart to woe?
Since God—the God in whom I trust—will be where'er I go:
To Him myself I would commend, as all I leave behind;
For in His power and grace I know I shall my portion find.

When Time, some tedious months around, has wing'd his silent flight,
Perchance we all shall meet again—God grant the welcome sight;
Meanwhile my best remembrances wait on these at home, and you:
The parting hour draws on apace!   Adieu! dear friend, Adieu—

Dr. Andrew Broaddus died December 1, 1848 and was buried
at Old Salem church near Sparta, which he served so long and so
well.   His son, Andrew Broaddus, II, succeeded him in the
pastorate.   His picture appears on page 326.

ANDREW BROADDUS II

was born in Caroline county, Va., about 1815 and upon the
death of his distinguished father, Rev. Andrew Broaddus, I,
was chosen to succeed in the pastorate of Salem and Upper King
and Queen churches.   The pastoral relation thus formed continued for over forty years.   In December 1838, Andrew Broaddus
II, was married to Martha Jane Pitts, of Caroline and to this
union there were born eight children, only five of whom lived to
maturity.   These five were: (1) Rev. Julian Broaddus, (2) Rev.
Luther Broaddus, (3) Florence, (4) Rev. Andrew Broaddus, III,
(5) Mignonette.   He lived a long and useful life and was a worthy
successor to a noble father.   He died about the close of the
nineteenth century.   His picture appears on page 326.

ANDREW BROADDUS III

was born in Caroline county shortly before the outbreak of
the Civil War and after receiving an excellent education entered
upon the high calling of his ancestors.   He succeeded his father
in the pastorate of Salem church and the relationship continues
to this day (1924).   Thus three of the same name, father, son and
grandson, have served one church for over one hundred years.
Rev. Andrew Broaddus has been twice married and has several
children among whom is Kirk Broaddus, who as yet has

not entered the ministry. A few years ago Richmond College conferred the Degree of Doctor of Divinity upon him. His picture appears on page 326.

MORDECAI W. BROADDUS

was born in Caroline county, Va., January, 1798. He united with Salem church at Sparta in his native county and appears as a delegate from that church to the Dover Association for a number of years following 1828. In 1835 he was chosen pastor of Upper Zion church and at the constitution of Providence church he was chosen its first pastor. His labours were short, for he died on November 26, 1840.

REV. M. E. BROADDUS

the subject of this sketch, was the son of Richard Franklin Broaddus and Virginia Mercer Henshaw and was born near Sparta, Caroline county in 1853. He was educated in the Southern Baptist Theological Seminary and has held pastorates at Newberry and Abbeville, S. C., Bristol and Mill Swamp, Va., and Clinton and elsewhere in Missouri. He is now (1924) pastor at Donna, Texas.

Dr. Broaddus has four brothers and one sister: Wm. Richard, Manley, Maxie Gregg, Richard Franklin and Mrs. Effie Virginia Brownley.

JULIAN BROADDUS

the oldest son of Rev. Andrew Broaddus II, and Martha Jane Pitts was born in Caroline county, Va., in 1840. He married Miss Hallie Terrell and had nine children. For a number of years he was pastor of the Baptist church at Berryville, Va., where, as a preacher, pastor and citizen, he exercised a wide influence.

LUTHER BROADDUS

the second son of Rev. Andrew Broaddus II, and Martha Jane Pitts, was born in Caroline county, Va., about 1843. He became a "full graduate" of the Southern Baptist Theological Seminary in three years, though beginning without any previous knowledge of theology or Greek. He was pastor of the Baptist church at Newberry, S. C., for nine years. He was one of the strongest and most original preachers of the Baptist denomination in his day. He died at Newberry, S. C., October 21, 1885.

HENRY G. SEGAR

was born near Salem church in Caroline county, Va., in the year 1796 and united with Salem about the year 1820, under the preaching of Rev. Andrew Broaddus, I.   In 1824 he appeared as a delegate from Salem to the Dover Association and again in 1828 and then successively for seven years.   In March 1836 he was ordained to the ministry and assumed the pastorate of Enon church.   His career as a minister was brief.   He died in the year 1840.

SPILSBY WOOLFOLK

was born in Caroline county, Va., in 1765 and united with the Baptist church in 1800.   He became a minister in 1814 and devoted the early part of his ministerial work to Burruss's, Concord, Providence, Reedy Mill, and Bethel churches in Caroline.   His later years were devoted especially to the last named church.   It is said that he was a good man, of cheerful and sociable disposition and very popular.   His name is frequently found in the county records as a celebrant of matrimony.   He died July 23, 1841, in his native county.

THOMAS CONDUIT

was born in Caroline county, Va., about 1805 and united with Enon Baptist church in Caroline sometime in 1831 and was baptized by Elder Micou.   He then entered Rappahannock Academy in Caroline county to prepare himself for the ministry. He entered upon his ministry in Charles and St. Mary's counties, Maryland and here laboured with great success.   He visited Dover Association in 1836 and in September of that year died at the home of Mrs. Lucy Gravatt at Port Royal, Va.

ROBERT T. DANIEL,

the son of Samuel Daniel and Eliza Thomas, of Caroline, was born on the 10th of June 1773.   At the close of the Revolutionary War his family removed to Orange county, N. C., and settled near Hillsboro.   Here Robert Daniel was united in marriage to Miss Penelope Cain Flowers, of Chatham county, N. C., on March 1, 1796.   His ministry extended over the States of North Carolina, Virginia, Tennessee and Mississippi.   During the forty years of his ministry he traveled over sixty thousand miles, preached five thousand sermons and baptized more than fifteen hundred people. He was often connected with the mission board of his church and served acceptably as a home missionary. He died in 1838.

SIMEON U. GRIMSLEY

There is a tradition that Mr. Grimsley was born in Richmond, but his entire life was so intimately connected with Caroline (if he wasn't born in the county, which is a mooted question) that this county may well claim him among her sons. He was ordained to the ministry in Horeb Baptist church on January 16, 1879, three years after he had been licensed to preach by the Smyrna Baptist church. His first charge was Mt. Horeb, Mt. Hermon and Providence churches in Caroline county. It is said that his salary did not warrant him in keeping a horse, but he always kept his appointments, going on foot when some friendly traveler did not "give him a lift" on the road. After leaving Caroline he went to Chincoteague Island, off the coast of Accomac county and here did a splendid work. He died on November 29, 1906.

JOHN YOUNG

was a native of Caroline, having been born in the southeastern part of the county on January 11, 1739. He was baptized by Elder J. Reed about 1770 and soon began to preach. He was ordained to the ministry in 1773, at which time Reed's church in Caroline was constituted and became the first pastor of this congregation. Here he labored for about twenty-five years. He was once imprisoned in the jail of Caroline county for preaching without the sanction of the General Court, but was soon released. He was prominent in the civic life of the county. There is in the Archives of the State Library of Virginia, a petition protesting against the payment of religious teachers from the public funds of the county and the first name on this significant religious document is that of John Young (See page 52). He died on April 16, 1817.

JOHN SHACKLEFORD

was born in Caroline county in 1750. When twenty-two years old he became a minister of the Gospel. He was ordained in 1774 and immediately became pastor of Tuckahoe church in Caroline. Here a great revival was experienced in 1788 and that year he baptized over 300 persons. The Rev. Andrew Broaddus,

I, paid a splendid tribute to his work, which tribute may be found in the First Series of Taylor's Virginia Baptist Ministers. He died in Kentucky in 1829.

THEODRICK NOEL

was born in Caroline county about 1745 and was baptized in August 1773. He shortly afterward began to preach and with such power that he was soon formally set apart to the work of the ministry. The Rev. Andrew Broaddus, I, says that few men were more successful in the ministry than Mr. Noel. He baptized as many persons as any other preacher of his day. The first person baptized by Mr. Noel after his ordination was a young lady. Her brother had threatened to dip any minister who should attempt to immerse her. True to his threat he made the attempt on Mr. Noel but did not succeed. Being pursued by some who resented his attempted treatment of the preacher, the young man was forced to flee the community. He died a few weeks afterward, having first sent a messenger to Mr. Noel asking his pardon. As minister in Salem, Upper King and Queen and Upper Essex churches, Mr. Noel was eminently successful. Mr. Semple in his History of Baptist Churches in Virginia says that it was " usual for him to baptize at every monthly meeting," and that for many months there were seldon fewer than twenty baptized. A great revival was experienced in Upper Essex church in 1812 at the close of which he baptized about three hundred and twenty persons. Mr. Noel died on August 27, 1813.

JEREMIAH CHANDLER

was born in Caroline county in the year 1749. From Caroline he removed to Orange county where he had the care of North Pamunky church. At the same time he ministered to Piney Branch church in Spotsylvania county. These two churches he served for nearly forty years. The place and date of his death are unknown to the author.

RUFUS CHANDLER

was born in Windham county, Conn., May 26, 1785, and was educated in Plainfield Academy and Yale College. In 1806 he was invited to take charge of Wingfield Academy in Hanover county and accepted, labouring here many years. He was baptized in 1812 by the Rev. Andrew Broaddus, I, and preached his first sermon at the baptismal waters. He married Miss Nancy

Trevillian, daughter of Thomas Trevillian, of Caroline, in 1815 and the same year located permanently in the county. He was ordained by Elders Woolfolk, Keeling and Ball in 1830 and died at Little Yale, Caroline county, July 18, 1837. He was probably the best scholar of the Baptist church in his day.

LITTLEBURY W. ALLEN

Caroline and Henrico both claim the honor of having been the birthplace of this distinguished minister, but the claim of Henrico is probably better sustained than that of Caroline, although it is an undisputed fact that practically all of his life was spent in Caroline. He was born March 26, 1803 and as a young man he was gay and dashing and aspired to military honors. He first was known as Captain and later as Colonel Allen. He was an officer in the Confederate Army and a prisoner at one time on Johnson's Island. He was married three three times; his first wife being Miss Bradley; his second, Miss Ann Martin and his third Miss Lucy Martin, of Spotsylvania. His ministry began in 1835 and the greater part of it was spent with County Line and Bethany churches in Caroline, two Sundays monthly with each. After filling a large and influential place in the Baptist denomination in Virginia he died at "Applewood" in Caroline county in 1872.

WARREN G. ROANE

was born in Caroline county, Va., December 31, 1852. He united with Massaponax Baptist church, Spotsylvania county, in his youth and was ordained to the ministry by Elders James D. Coleman, L. J. Haley, E. G. Baptist and T. S. Dunaway in September, 1875, and at once became pastor of Waller's church, not far from Massaponax. Here he remained several years. He was subsequently pastor of Upper Essex and Mt. Zion churches in Essex and of Louisa (Court House) church, in Louisa, Cedar Run in Culpeper and Beulah church in Fluvanna. The exact date of his death is unknown to the author.

ELLIOTT ESTES

was born in Caroline county, Va., July 23, 1795, and baptized by the Rev. Andrew, Broaddus, I, at Burruss's church, now Carmel, in 1810. He entered a high grade school then under the direction of Rev. Mr. Broaddus and at the age of twenty-two went to New Orleans to preside over a Lancasterian school. He had a degree of success in this undertaking and accumulated enough means to complete his own education. He was ordained in 1820, returned to Virginia in 1827, settled in South Carolina in 1829, married Mrs. E. A. McPeherson in 1830, went to Europe in 1835, preached frequently in London, again took up the pastorate in South Carolina upon his return and died on June 9, 1849, having given about thirty years to the gospel ministry.

WILLIAM BAYNHAM, M. D., F. R. S. L.

Doctor William Baynham was born in Caroline county about 1750. His father was an eminent physician and was also prominent in the church and political life of the county, serving as magistrate and vestryman for many years.

William Baynham studied medicine under his father several years, after which he went to England and studied under the celebrated Doctor William Hunter. He became an eminent anatomist and made several important discoveries in this department of medicine. He was chosen assistant to the celebrated Doctor Calignon, of Cambridge, and afterward assistant at St. Thomas' Hospital and in both of these positions sustained his splendid reputation. On the retirement of Doctor Else, he would have been appointed Chief Surgeon of St. Thomas' Hospital, but Dr. Else died suddenly and thus Doctor Baynham was deprived of the support which had been promised him, and in the election of Dr. Else's successor Baynham was defeated by one vote. During his sojourn in England he became Fellow of the Royal College of Surgeons of London. He returned to Virginia in 1785 and settled near the Caroline-Essex line where he died in 1814. He preached frequentedly.

WILLIAM A. BAYNHAM, M. D.

William A. Baynham, M. D., son of the celebrated Dr. Wm. Baynham, was born October 19, 1813, and at the age of eight years was placed in Concord Academy in Caroline county, where he remained until he was fourteen. At the age of fifteen he entered the University of Virginia, from which he was graduated at the age of twenty-one, with the degree of Doctor of Medicine. He subsequently attended the University of Pennsylvania from which institution he was graduated after two years of study. Being a rich man he did not find it necessary to practice his profession for a livelihood, and so after a few months he retired from the activities of the profession and devoted the remainder of his life with "singleness of purpose and rare consecration" to the preaching of the Gospel, being an honored minister in the Baptist church. Dr. Baynham boarded for thirty-five years in the home of John Henry Martin, father of the wife of Dr. A. L. Martin, of Naulakla, Caroline county.

CHARLES A. LEWIS

The son of Charles A. and Catherine Lewis was born in Caroline county about the close of the eighteenth century. He acquired a splendid English and classical education, being for a time a student in the University of Virginia. Upon the completion of his education, he married the widow of his cousin Colonel William Woodford, of Caroline and accepted the headmastership of Rappahannock Academy, which position he filled with distinction for three years. After he had been absent for four years he was prevailed upon to again head the school, and during the two years of his second term he raised it from a declining to a prosperous condition and during his second term at the Academy he united with the Liberty Baptist church and was baptized by the pastor, Elder Lawrence Battaile. Not long afterward he decided to preach and so gave himself to the study of the Scriptures and being able to read the language in which they were originally written he became remarkably proficient in the Sacred writings. It is said that for a time after uniting with the Baptist church he used the Prayer Book of the church in which he had been brought up and that he was always remarkably charitable to all religious bodies regardless of theological differences. He was a warm hearted and generous natured man and had profound sympathy for the unfortunate. His messages were marked by a great tenderness and had a profound effect upon those who heard them.

He preached extensively in Eastern Virginia and served Providence, County Line and Waller's churches as pastor. During his last years he preached for Zoar and Flat Run churches in Orange county and for Crooked Run church in Culpeper county. He was in advance of his generation in many things, one of these being his conviction that abstinence from intoxicating liquors as a beverage should be made a test of fellowship in the church. His wife died during his second term at Rappahannock Academy and he placed his six year old daughter with her maternal grandmother and aunt, and he remained a widower to the end of his life. His last sermon was preached at Liberty church in Caroline. He contracted a cold from over-exertion, hemorrhage followed and he died early in the spring of 1847.

REV. JAMES D. COLEMAN

James D. Coleman, son of Thomas B. Coleman and Elizabeth Coghill, was born at "Concord," Caroline county, Va., about the year 1800. The foundations of his education were laid in Concord Academy, a school founded by his grandfather, Daniel Coleman, and made famous in after years by his distinguished brother Frederick William Coleman, of whom see chapter on Education and Educators. His later training was received in the University of Virginia.

The plantation known as "Concord," upon which stood the famous academy, was an estate of nearly two thousand acres and here James D. Coleman lived for many years the life of the old-time southern planter, owning many slaves and cultivating an extensive acreage. From here he went to the churches in Caroline, which he served as pastor.

His work as a minister was confined largely to his native county and to Carmel, Bethel, Bethesda, Liberty and Round Oak churches. He was pastor of Carmel as early as 1855. At this early date Carmel was a strong church having over five hundred members. He was pastor of Bethel for more than a quarter of a century and of Bethesda, Liberty and Round Oak many years.

The Rev. Mr. Coleman was born of the best English blood in Virginia, from an ancestry noted for intellectuality, and is described by the Rev. T. S. Dunaway, a friend and associate of many years, as "a man of fine physique, tall and well-proportioned and looked like one of nature's noblemen who was born for a leader and ruler. His deportment was dignified and courteous, impressing one as a gentleman of the highest culture. He was a minister of the deepest consecration and during the last years of his life neglected his plantation and all material interests to devote himself wholly to his calling. His sermons were methodically arranged and gave evidence of great thought and of familiarity with the best literature of the time. He was a true pastor of the churches he served and was devoted to every member of his flock, visiting them in sickness and distress and encouraging them in their Christian life."

The Rev. Mr. Coleman married Miss Hulda DeJarnette and had issue: James Coleman, Jr., Alice Coleman and Lucy Coleman. Among his descendants are the following grandchildren: Hampton Coleman, Belle Coleman, James Coleman, James Daniel Coleman DeJarnette, Elliott DeJarnette, Burbage DeJarnette. There is one great grandchild, Edmund T. DeJarnette.

The Rev. Mr. Coleman was at the bedside of a sick parishioner when stricken with the disease from which he never recovered. He preached his last sermon on the day after he was stricken, the fourth Sunday of December 1877 and died on November 21, 1878.

REV. ANDREW TRIBBLE

The Rev. Andrew Tribble, son of George Tribble and Betty Clark, was born in Caroline county in March 1741. He removed to Louisa county when a young man and united with Goldmine Baptist church. In 1777 he was called to the pastorate of Albemarle church and on receiving the call was ordained to the ministry by a presbytery of which Lewis Craig was a member. He removed to Kentucky whither some of his mother's people had gone and became prominent in the Baptist denomination of that State. He died in Clark county, Ky., December 22, 1822.

REV. ROBERT HUNTER BEAZLEY

Robert Hunter Beazley was born at Sparta, in Caroline county, April 1, 1841. He was the son of John Beazley. At the outbreak of the Civil War he enlisted in the Sparta Grays and saw service under R. M. T. Hunter for whom he was named.

After the Civil War Mr. Beazley settled in Manchester, now South Richmond and engaged in the mercantile business under the firm name of Beazley, Ogden and Chiles. Upon the dissolution of this firm he engaged in the shoe business in which he was successful. He was Clerk of the Hustings Court of Manchester during his business career in that city. He was also teacher of the Men's Bible class in Bainbridge Baptist church and deacon in the church until his removal to Halifax in 1876.

Upon removing to South Boston in Halifax county, Mr. Beazley organized a Baptist Sunday school and superintended it for several years. He was licensed to preach in the eighties by the Dan River Association and served as pastor of several churches, one of them being Musterfield, now Scottsburg church. He was instrumental in organizing the church of South Boston, now one of the strongest Baptist churches in that section of the State.

Mr. Beazley became the editor of *The News* in 1890 and remained editor until 1913. He died of apoplexy in 1914. There are many interesting articles on Caroline, in the files of *The Free-Lance* of Fredericksburg and *The News* of South Boston, written by Mr. Beazley during his newspaper career. Mr. R. C. Beazley, eldest son of Mr. R. H. Beazley, now publishes *The News*.

REV. M. E. SHADDOCK

The subject of this sketch was born near Upper Zion in Caroline county on November 23, 1840. He married Miss Sallie Jennings, of Lynchburg, on August 12, 1871 and removed to Tennessee where he taught and preached for eight years. In 1879 he located in Avoyelles parish in Louisiana where he lived a number of years, during which time he was Baptist State Sunday school organizer. He removed to Lake Charles in 1890 and was principal of Lake Charles College for some time. He was a member of Company B., Ninth Virginia Cavalry and served throughout the Civil War being wounded at Gettysburg. He died at Lake Charles on December 27, 1920 and was survived by the following sons and daughters: E. J. Shaddock, W. B. Shaddock and Mrs. R. P. Howell, of Lake Charles; Mrs. F. W. Wilcox, Beaumont; Mrs. Isaac Derouen, Bell City; Mrs. H. W..Evans, Alexandria; Mrs. Archie Cameron, Lake Charles; C. B. Shaddock, Beaumont; R. M. Shaddock, of Eola and a number of grand children and great grandchildren. A more detailed biographical sketch of Mr. Shaddock may be seen in the Lake Charles American Press of December 27, 1920.

REV. RICHARD BAYNHAM GARRETT

Richard Baynham Garrett, son of Richard Henry Garrett and Fanny Holloway, was born in 1854 near Port Royal in Caroline county. He was the oldest of the five children of the second marriage of his father. There were six children of his father's first marriage. He united with old Enon church when nine years old and grew up with the consciousness that he would be a minister of the Gospel. In his young manhood he taught school for a brief period and then entered the Southern Baptist Theological Seminary, from which he was graduated in 1882.   Upon graduation he supplied the Fulton church, Richmond and later was called to the Baptist churches of Flemingsburg and Carlisle Kentucky. He subsequently served the Baptist church, Maysville, Ky.; First church, Austin, Texas; First church, Chattanooga, Tenn.; Court-Street church, Portsmouth, Va.; and Tappahannock and Ephesus churches in Essex county.   The latter two churches he served after failing health had caused him to retire to his plantation on the Rappahannock.   The Carson-Newman College conferred the degree of Doctor of Divinity on him in recognition of his work in Chattanooga.

Dr. Garrett was married in 1883 to Miss Annie Laurie Howe, of Mount Stirling, Ky., and had issue four children.   Two of these died in childhood and two, R. H. Garrett, of the S. A. L. Railway and Mrs. Felix Wilson, of Caret, Va., survived him. He was also survived by one brother and one sister.   A picture of the house in which Dr. Garrett was born appears in chapter on The Killing of Booth in Caroline.   He was a lad of eleven years when John Wilkes Booth was killed in his father's barn. Dr. Garrett died in July 1922, after forty years in the ministry of the Gospel.

REV. ROBERT WALKER COLE

The subject of this sketch, the son of John G. Cole and Nancy Broaddus was born in Caroline county in September 1812.   He united with the Baptist church under the ministry of the Rev. Andrew Broaddus, I, was baptized by him and in 1840 licensed by Salem church to preach.   The following year he was ordained by a presbytery consisting of the Rev. Messrs. Andrew Broaddus, Philip Montague and Lawrence Battaile.   His first charge was the Reedy Mill church in Caroline and he was subsequently pastor of Upper Zion, Providence, Concord, Mt. Horeb and Bethel churches in the same county.   He was pastor of Upper Essex, Bethlehem and Providence churches at the time of his death on September 16, 1868.   Mr. Cole is described as "a man of commanding figure, black hair, blue eyes, jovial, good conversationalist, splendid singer, beloved as a pastor and highly esteemed as a preacher."   He devoted much time to work among the soldiers during the Civil War.

The Rev. Mr. Cole, married Lucy F. Broaddus, daugther of

William Temple Broaddus and Fannie Robinson, on April 12, 1849. William Temple Broaddus was a son of Dr. Andrew Broaddus, I., of whom see elsewhere in this chapter. Of this marriage there were the following children: Maria Louise, who died in youth; Elton F., who married George Winfree, of Chesterfield county; Robert W., who died in childhood; Nannie R., who married Beaufort S. Ragland, of Richmond; Robert T., who m. 1st Claribel Terry and 2d Hattie Heckman, and John Harry, who m. Lillian Haskins. Mrs. Ragland alone survives at this time (1924).

REV. GEORGE M. DONAHOE

The subject of this sketch, the son of Reuben and Martha Donahoe, was born near Bowling Green September 20, 1848. His Sunday school teacher, Judge E. C. Moncure, taught him to read and beyond this he was self-educated. At the age of seventeen he united with Antioch church under the preaching of one Rev. Mr. Arnold, of Kentucky and shortly thereafter decided to enter the ministry. He then united with the Methodist church and was licensed to preach by the Bowling Green Quarterly Conference. After six or seven years service as an "exhorter" he united with the Baptist church and was ordained to the ministry by the Rev. Messrs. Broaddus, Cruikshank and Eubank. Following this ordination he served Mt. Horeb, Mt. Hermon and Providence churches for about three years. He also served Providence and Traveler's Rest churches in Spotsylvania county. There are several chapels standing in neglected communities as monuments to his faithfulness.

Mr. Donahoe married Maria L. Weedon, of King George county in 1872 and had issue four children: Lillian M., Mary L., Frederick T., and Rosie M. The daughters are all married. The son died in his twenty-fourth year.

REV. JOHN HERNDON WRIGHT

The subject of this sketch, the son of Robert and Martha S. Wright, was born near Upper Zion, in Caroline county, on April 17, 1852. The first building of Upper Zion Baptist church was erected on the land of his ancestors. Ne was educated in the schools of Caroline county, Va., Fulton, Ky., Jackson University, Jackson, Tenn., and Baptist Theological Seminary at Louisville, Ky. Ne was ordained to the ministry in 1874 and has held pastorates in Olivet, Fulton, Oak Woods and Adairsville, Ky., and at Union City, Milan, Nashville and Memphis, Tenn., the last named city being the present scene of his labours.   In recent years Jackson University conferred on him the degree of Doctor of Divinity.

Doctor Wright was married in 1888 to Miss Laura Wilhelm of Paducah, Ky., by the Rev. Lewis Hall Shuck, son of Dr. J. Lewis Shuck and Henriette Hall Shuck, the latter being the first American woman missionary to China.   She was a daughter of the Rev. Addison Hall, of Lancaster county, Va.   Of this marriage there were the following children: Irene, who married Edward Hill, of Nashville, Tenn., and John Herndon, Jr., who married a Miss Stephens, of Nashville and now lives in Birmingham.   Dr. Wright had one brother and one sister, Fuller Wright and Miss Allie Wright and five half brothers, James, William, Robert and Albert Wright and Rev. M. E. Shaddock, of whom see elsewhere in this chapter.

REV. ANDREW V. BORKEY

Rev. Andrew V. Borkey, second son of B. F. Borkey and Sarah Jane Selph, was born July 19, 1889.   His maternal ancestors, the Selphs and Pavys, were from England and France respectively. His grandfather, John Anderson Selph, III, married Sarah Ann Pavy (originally Pave') and had issue: Edgar William, Mary Frances, Virginia Ann, George W., Emma Ellen, Sarah Jane, (Dr. Borkey's mother) Eva Lillian, John Anderson, IV, Milton Linwood, Carrie Floyd, Collins McRae and Arthur Byrum.   His great grandfather, John G. Pavy, was born in 1815 and was the son of John G. Pave who served eleven years with Napoleon. He crossed the Alps with the renowned warrior and was in the shivering, starving, dying army in its disastrous retreat from Moscow.   He was finally captured by the English and with 180 others sent to America to fight the colonists.   The ship was wrecked coming into the American port and Pave, with 24 of his companions, swam ashore.   He then enlisted in the army of the Revolution which he had been sent to fight, and so was once more arrayed against the ancient enemy.

The Rev. Mr. Borkey was privately tutored in Bowling Green after which he entered the College of William and Mary.   Upon graduation he became principal of the high school at Surry Court-house where he remained four years. He then entered Crozer Theological Seminary from which he was graduated after four years. During this time he also did some advanced work in the University of Pennsylvania. He served as chaplain in the United States Army during the latter days of the World War, and afterward was Secretary of the Industrial Y. M. C. A. at Jewel Ridge, Va. He married Miss Irene Hunter of Polk, Pa., and became pastor of North Chester Baptist church in 1922. In 1924 he became the associate of Dr. Russell Conwell at the Baptist Temple of Philadelphia. Mr. Borkey has ten brothers and one sister: Benjamin F., Malcolm R., Cecil E., John Earl, Floyd H., Harold V., Edgar Clyde, Wm. Ervin, Guy Ollie, Richard L. and Sarah Frances.

REV. WILLIAM OSWALD BEAZLEY

The subject of this sketch was the son of Wm. F. and Emma J. Beazley and was born in Caroline January 27, 1882. He was educated in the Shenandoah Collegiate Institute (1903), Richmond College (1906), Crozer Theological Seminary (1911) and the University of Pennsylvania (1912). He held the degrees of A. B., A. M., and Ph. D. He taught at Singer's Glen, Rockingham county, Va., Newport News Academy and at Wakefield, N. C. He was ordained at Salem church in Caroline county on July 7, 1910. His first pastorate was at Wayne, Pa., during the years 1910–13. He was professor of Philosophy and Biology at Hampden-Sidney College 1913–15. and pastor of the Baptist church in Lexington, Va., from 1915 until his death on October 22, 1918.

Dr. Beazley was a man of fine personality and endowed with many gifts. When he died he was mourned by a great host of friends and admirers. He was survived by his wife, who before marriage was Miss Norma Beatrice Funk, of Singer's Glen, Va., one son Wm. O. Beazley, Jr., his parents, two brothers and two sisters. His dust reposes at Singer's Glen, Va. A more detailed biography may be found in the *Virginia Baptist Annual* for 1918.

REV. ROLAND J. BEAZLEY

Roland J. Beazley, son of O. Z. Beazley and Almyra Virginia Jenkins, was born at Upper Zion on February 7, 1894. He was educated in the Upper Zion grammar school, Sparta High school,

Richmond College, Crozer Theological Seminary and University of Pennsylvania and holds degrees from the three last named. For the past four years Dr. Beazley has been pastor of a community church at Jobstown, N. J.   Dr. Beazley has one brother, Latimer, and one sister, Eva.

REV. JAMES H. MARSHALL

The subject of this sketch was the son of George Marshall and Theresa Broaddus and was born near Upper Zion on January 28, 1829.   He was for the most part self educated.   He served as lieutenant in Company H, Thirtieth Virginia Infantry, during the Civil War.   Mr. Marshall's ministerial labours were chiefly in Upper Zion church, where, in the capacity of assistant and supply, he rendered great service to the church and community.   He married Miss Mary E. Kay, of Caroline and had issue two sons and two daughters, namely: Thomas Roper Marshall, of Neenah, Va.; James Glassell Marshall, of Caroline; Mrs. Lucy Gravatt, of Caroline and Mrs. Maria Theresa Vaughan, of Caroline. Andrew Marshall, of Upper Zion, a prominent citizen and churchman, is a nephew of Rev. J. H. Marshall and a son of George Marshall, who was once sheriff of Caroline.

OLD HOMES AND FAMILIES

THE OLD MANSION

"Old Mansion" has the distinction of being the oldest house in Caroline. Just when it was erected cannot be definitely stated

The Old Mansion

but it is quite certain that it was not later than 1675. The house stands just to the south of the corporate limits of Bowling Green and is probably in or about the center of that large tract of land granted to Major Hoomes by the British Crown in 1670.

The structure is of the early colonial "one and a half story" type and is said to have been built of bricks brought from England. It is also said that this particular style of architecture prevailed in the earliest colonial period because of the higher tax levied by England on two story, or three story houses.

Little is known of Major Hoomes, grantee of this estate, save that he had one son, Col. John Waller Hoomes, who was a great sportsman and an importer of thorough-bred horses.

A race track circled the lawn, on either side of which cherry trees were planted. There was also a fine bowling green before the house, from which the estate was named. The giant cedars which for more than a century bordered the avenue leading to the house were brought, as tiny switches, from Gloucester county in the saddle bags of Major Hoomes. Avenues of elms—old English prides—graced the south side of the house, while on the north were avenues of aspens. Box-bordered plots to the front of the house and a succession of terraces on the west, or rear, added to the natural beauty of the site.

When the county seat was removed from the original site Col. Hoomes donated to the county sufficient land for the Court House and other public buildings and also gave the name of his estate—"Bowling Green"—to be the name of the county seat, taking the name "The Mansion" for his place instead. This name was changed, in the course of the years, to "Old Mansion."

Col. John Waller Hoomes had one daughter, Sophia, who married one Major Allen and for whom a frame addition was added to the house. Later Col. Hoomes built his daughter a home a short distance below "The Mansion" which was called "Oak Ridge." There is a tradition that after removing to "Oak Ridge" the daughter never again visited the old home by daylight, but, according to stories accredited to her coachman, she made long visits to by night.

Many ghost stories are associated with "Old Mansion"—as with all old places—chief among these being the story that the "ghost" of Col. Hoomes always appeared to each member of the family before their death, walking out in full view, dressed as when in the flesh and not in grave clothes. The appearance of his "ghost" is said to have been an unfailing warning of the approach of death to some member of the family. Another equally hair-raising ghost story connected with this old place is, that a headless horseman, riding furiously around the old race track, always heralded the approaching death of an eldest son.

There is a tradition that here an invalid wife was frightened to death by her husband placing a hideous mask at the window of her sick room, and that this husband, while enamoured of his housekeeper, affected great grief at his wife's funeral, sitting his horse backward and demanding a sheet for his tears. Growing out of this tradition is another ghost story to the effect that the spirit of this woman haunted the house for many years and that groans, screams, stealthy footsteps and other fearful sounds, drove tenant after tenant away from the place.

Still another tradition—this colored with a little historical support—has it that on the spacious lawn Washington and his weary soldiers, camped and rested en route to Yorktown; while of more authentic historicity is the story that Washington, returning from Yorktown, after the surrender of Cornwallis, made a great banquet on the lawn in honor of LaFayette, which was spread on three great tables extending almost across the lawn, at one of which were seated the guests of honor, Washington and the officers of his army and at the other two the private soldiers.

In 1842, Mr. William Grymes Maury purchased "Old Mansion" and here brought up his large family of twelve children. In 1862 the place passed into the possession of Mr. James Thomas White, who married Fenella Strachan Maury, second daughter of Wm. Grymes Maury and remains in possession of the White family to this day, being owned by Mrs. J. L. White, her son, John Cary White, and her daughter, Anne Maury White, of Richmond.

A strange coincidence in connection with the recent ownership is the fact that the late J. L. White, whose widow and children now own the place, was a nephew—thrice removed—of Col. John Waller Hoomes; and Mrs. J. L. White (*nee* Cary) was a niece—thrice removed—of Mrs. John Waller Hoomes, who graced the "Old Mansion" so long ago.

GAY MONT

The following description of this interesting old estate is taken from Mrs. Sale's remarkable book Historic Gardens of Virginia. "Gay Mont lies on a high hill overlooking the Rappahannock River and Valley, twenty miles below Fredericksburg. The estate was originally a part of the Miller grant and comprised about two thousand acres. It later became a part of the Catlett estate and was purchased from this family in 1790 by John Hipkins, of "Belle Grove," on the opposite bank of the Rappahannock in King George county. At his death the place was left to John Hipkins Bernard, grandson of John Hipkins.

The original house comprised only the central, or two-story portion of the present building and was erected about 1725. Two wings, one at either end, were added in 1798, and the octagonal music room at the back in 1830. The latter opens on a small porch, from the steps of which one can look down the central garden walk to the sun dial.

John Hipkins Bernard was born January 10, 1890 and was educated at Charlotte Hall, St. Mary's county, Md. He was a grandson of William Bernard who was a nephew of Sir John Bernard who married the granddaughter of Shakespeare. Upon reaching his majority he went abroad for several years and on his return brought with him many things for his home, including landscape wallpaper—then a novelty in France—for the Gay Mont hall, parlor and dining room. The paper in the hall shows brightly colored Italian scences, that in the parlor represents the Bay of Naples in soft grey tones, while that for the dining room pictures mythological characters in sepia. He also brought over two English gardeners who remodeled the grounds and garden into their present form. That a rose garden antedated their arrival and was a feature of the place from its beginning is apparent from the original name "Rose Hill" which Mr. Bernard changed to "Gay Mont" in honor of his bride, Miss Jane Gay Robertson, daughter of William Robertson and Elizabeth Bolling. John Hipkins Bernard and Jane Gay Robertson were the parents of six children, the youngest of whom, Helen Struan, married Philip Lightfoot Robb in 1865, and had issue whose descendants own Gay Mont to this day. The founder of Gay Mont also owned lands in Alabama, Arkansas and Texas, and was a wealthy man for his time. He was prominent politically and represented Caroline, King and Queen, King William, Hanover and Essex counties in the State Senate in 1828–30. He died in 1858, and with his wife is buried at Gay Mont.

The portico at Gay Mont is supported by six large pillars with balustrades between, and is enclosed at each end by the wings.

Between the windows opening on the portico and at either end
are plaster busts of Washington, Franklin, Shakespeare, Milton,
Scott, Byron, Napoleon and LaFayette.

In front of the portico is the driveway, and beyond are three
terraces, each three hundred feet in length. The last terrace,
twice the depth of the first two, broadens out at its base into a
semi-circle at either end and has a border of roses its entire length.

Between the second and third terrace there is a small formal
garden, in the shape of a circle, consisting of four plots separated
by gravel walks, with a fountain in the center surrounded by
conch shells and ivy. This little garden was christened "The
Beauty Spot" by which name it is still known. Water supplying
the fountain was brought in lead pipes from a reservoir in the
rear of the house and after the War between the States, when
ammunition was scarce, the lead from the pipe was made into
"slugs," and used instead of shot by the huntsmen of the family.

In connection with the fountain there is an amusing story
told of a small dog which had been trained to turn the wheel
which supplied the water. He would sit on the lower terrace
overlooking the avenue, intently watching for visitors, and on
seeing them approach would dash to the wheel and work violently
in order to have the fountain spraying freely by the time the host
greeted his guests at the front door.

At either end of the house there is a circular rose garden
surrounded by box bushes. Formerly this box was kept neatly
trimmed, but it has long been allowed to grow at random and
has now assumed the form of great, round masses, higher than a
man's head.

At the back of the house, separated from the lawn by trees
and shrubs, is the garden proper, consisting of a gravel walk,
three hundred feet long, parallel to the lawn, the three lateral
walks, ending in a wide terrace. Mr. Bernard is said to have
brought shiploads of gravel from Bermuda for these walks, as
well as conch shell for the fountain. The walks were bordered
with shrubs—pyrus, japonica, forsythia, spirea, in all varieties,
lilac, snowball, weigela, althea, syringa, mock-orange and others.
These were trimmed to form arches over the paths. Between
the walks were formal gardens laid out in shape of diamonds
and filled with many old-fashioned flowers. Peonies seemed to
have been the favorite centerpiece. On either side of this flower
garden, separated by walks, were two large squares devoted to

small fruits and vegetables. A hedge, formerly of roses but now of althea, encloses the whole garden.

In addition to the lawns and gardens, a large part of the estate of Gay Mont was given over to what might be called pleasure grounds. On the north side of the hill was a deer park of eight acres, with clumps of beautiful holly and enormous tulip poplars. Mr. Bernard had a great love of trees and imported many kinds, not only for the immediate grounds but also for the hill-sides. Some years ago fifty varieties were counted within a comparatively short distance of the house, among them a variety of French chestnut, still vigorous and bearing nuts.

To the south of the hill ran "Golden Vale Creek" the name given it on an old atlas printed before the city of Washington was founded. Its waters were dammed to form a pond, and stocked with fish. Here Mr. Bernard loved to entertain his friends and it was no doubt, the scene of many gay parties. A large, round stone table, and a spring enclosed by stone slabs are all that now remain to mark the spot.

As horseback riding was the favorite pastime of Mr. Bernard's daughters, he built for them a private road through the woods and "the long meadows." This road crossed a small creek seven or eight times by rustic bridges; the upkeep of both road and bridges was given over to "Uncle Roly" a faithful slave. "Uncle Roly" loved to tell stories of the past and always ended by saying, "He had more recollections than he could remember." He loved to boast that "Ole Missis' flowers was so sweet you could smell 'em a mile away—just as soon as you turned into de abenue."

During the War between the States, Gay Mont, from its commanding position, narrowly escaped having a battery placed on the hill. This would have made it a target for the gunboats which shelled Port Royal and vicinity. The officers sent to place the battery desisted at the earnest entreaties of the women of the family.

Two of Mr. Bernard's daughters remained at Gay Mont with their faithful servants during the entire war, thus, no doubt, saving the place from entire destruction. General Abercrombie, the Union Commander stationed in Port Royal, showed them great courtesy and kindness. Many nights these young ladies sat in a low window holding by the bridle their favorite horses, "Ariel" and "Empress," to prevent them from being stolen.

These horses were finally taken, however, but were instantly released when the owners appeared next day at headquarters and begged their return. General Abercrombie then sent a special guard to protect Gay Mont from further interference while the Northern troops remained in the neighborhood.

The Confederate officers encamped around Fredericksburg, General J. E. B. Stuart and his staff among them, were frequent visitors at Gay Mont. General Stuart was very fond of a music box in the library and would often enter the house unobserved and announce his arrival by playing some familiar air. A chair much scratched by his buttons was long kept as a souvenir of his visit.

Major Duncan McKim, "the Gallant Pelham," and other officers were dining at Gay Mont the evening before the Battle of Fredericksburg, when a courier arrived summoning them to headquarters. So furious was cannonading in that battle that the big bell over the kitchen and the smaller servants bells which hung outside the several windows, all rang while the battle was in progress. Several of the guests of the preceding day were killed in this battle.

The servants bells attached to the windows at Gay Mont deserve mention only as relics of by-gone days. Each room had its bell, rung by means of a cord within, to summon a servant whenever wanted. One wonders how many servants were required and where stationed to catch and locate the sounds of these bells, hung into space from any window in the rambling old house.

Like many Virginia homes, Gay Mont suffered severely during the War between the States and the years following, when the labor necessary for its upkeep could not be obtained. But so well had the original plans been carried out and moulded into terraces and other enduring landmarks that today Gay Mont reflects honor on those who planned and those who carried the plans to completion.

General Dabney Herndon Maury in his "Recollections of a Virginian" said: "It was once my delightful privilege to pass the Christmas holidays with Judge Butler and a company of bright ladies and gentlemen, old and young, at "Hazelwood" that old Virginia home of the Taylors, of Caroline. We had a dinner party every day and every night had its delightful close in a dance at Gay Mont, or at Port Royal or at Hazelwood.

The house, big as it was, had no vacant bed, or empty places at
the table and we young people greatly enjoyed the older people.
I remember a dinner of twenty or more seats, when we young men
and maidens listened with delight to the witty and wise conversation sustained by Judge Butler, William P. Taylor, of "Hayfield"
and John H. Bernard, of Gay Mont, that cultured trio of gentlemen of the old school."

PROSPECT HILL

About ten miles south of Fredericksburg on the Tidewater
Trail is a slightly traveled road leading off on the right in a
southeasterly direction to Prospect Hill, one of the most beautiful
estates in Caroline county.   The present house, a substantial
brick structure, occupies the site of the old Battaile mansion,
and was erected by Basil Gordon, whose daughter, Mrs. Charles
Herndon, of Fredericksburg, remembers that when but a little
child a workman held her up so she might have a part in placing
a brick in the walls.

The house itself, without the lovely natural beauty surrounding,
is most attractive.   Its spacious rooms, wide halls, beautiful
woodwork, remarkable pillars all speak of a past of wealth and
splendor.

The driveway to this old home is over-arched with great
branches of oak, sycamore, maple and elm and the brick walkways
around the house are overgrown with moss, which adds the
charming touch of age.   The vines clinging close to the walls
and the great shade trees on the lawn remind one of the beautiful
old homes in "Merrie England."   The adjacent woods are also
interesting aside from their natural beauty, for here are old gun
pits and breastworks, relics of the War between the States.

The location of Prospect Hill, which, by the way, suggested
the name of the place, leaves nothing to be desired.   The old
Virginian not only had in mind the practical side when he chose
a site for his house, but the aesthetic as well.   Here may be seen
miles of gently swelling hills, beautiful Rappahannock Valleys
and the Rappahannock itself, like a silvery ribbon, as it courses
to the sea.

It was here that Colonel Henry Fitzhugh, of "Bedford" ·
across the Rappahannock, married Sarah Battaile in October

1748. The place is now owned by Mr. and Mrs. C. L. Gage. For further description, especially for a description of the beautiful flower garden, see *Historic Gardens of Virginia*, by Edith Tunis Sale, from which the foregoing is largely taken.

SANTEE

Santee, familiarly known as "The Gordon Place" was originally one of the many Fitzhugh country seats and is one of the most interesting places in Caroline. The house was built by Battaile Fitzhugh in 1807 and is about one-half mile distant from Prospect Hill. Here, as at Prospect Hill, are the same masses of boxwood, locust, poplar linden and walnut trees and the same symmetrical hollies guarding the entrace. Here too are the bridal wreath, honeysuckle, summer lilacs, phlox, clematis, calycanthus, wild roses, mimosa, flowering quince, euonymus and privet hedge. The old rose garden and the grape vine arbor are haunted with that indefinable something which cannot be put in words or set to music. Dora C. Jett in *Historic Gardens of Virginia*, from which the foregoing is taken, says: "It was in the grape vine dell probably that Patsy, the beautiful daughter and only child of Battaile Fitzhugh, plighted her troth to Samuel Gordon, of historic Kenmore. 'I love you,' said Patsy, 'but I cannot leave Santee' and ever since that time the place has been owned and occupied by members of the Gordon family. Today the grandson of the late Robert V. Gordon holds sway over the old homestead."

Present House on The Neck Plantation

THE NECK

This estate was founded by William Buckner who married Judith Aylett Hawes, widow of————Hawes, and daughter of Wm. Aylett, of King William county.   William Buckner was a Justice in Caroline in 1768 and was succeeded in that office by his son, William, Jr.   There is a tradition, recorded in the History of the Buckners of Virginia, by Crozier, that Judith Aylett Hawes Buckner was a lady of ungovernable temper and great family pride, and that she did not hesitate to horsewhip her coachman when she thought the occasion demanded such treatment. She was known as "Lady Buckner."   Her dying request was that she be buried beneath the pavement of the aisle of Rappahannock church, which was occupied by the poor, "that those whom she had regarded with contempt in life might walk over her dust." The house shown in the accompanying picture occupies the site of the old Buckner residence which was destroyed by Federal gunboats in the Rappahannock.

Braynefield

BRAYNEFIELD

By his marriage to Dorothea Brayne McWilliams, widow of Col. Wm. McWilliams, of Fredericksburg, Captain George Buckner became the owner of "Braynefield" one of the finest estates in Caroline. Captain George Buckner, son of George Buckner, was born in 1750 and served in the War of the Revolution.

Lake Farm

LAKE FARM

This was originally the estate of Thomas Buckner (1771) and was inherited by his son Thomas who married Lucy Fitzhugh, daughter of Henry Fitzhugh and Elizabeth Stith, in the year 1800. See *"The Buckners of Virginia"* by William Armstrong Crozier.   The estate is now owned by Mr. J. W. Ayers.

THE ATHEY FAMILY

The family name of this ancient house has been spelled in various ways—"Athy," "Athey," "Atha," "Athol," and "Athil." From all these variations "Athey" has come to be the accepted spelling of the name of the American branch of the house.   The family had its origin in Ireland where the name was originally spelled "Daitha."   Green in his history, *"The Making of Ireland,"* says: "The family of Athy, officials of the town (Galway) from father to son, were doubtless Irishmen who, in obedience to the statute about taking English names, had taken the name of a town."   The family is of record in Ireland as early as 1313. John de Athy was Marshall of Ireland in 1326.   Many members of this family were officials in the town of Galway early in the fourteenth century.

The first of the family to come to America was George Athy who was born in Galway, Ireland, in 1642 and came to Maryland in 1674. He received from Lord Baltimore patents to lands in Charles county. John Athy, Sr., son of George Athy, Jr., and grandson of George Athy, the immigrant, was born in 1730 and being early orphaned, was, with his brother Robert, brought up by an uncle in Caroline county. When forty-seven years of age he enlisted in Captain Philip Richard Francis Lee's company, Third Virginia Regiment, Continental Line and served the cause of American Independence. He was with Washington at Valley Forge. After the revolution he settled with his wife, Sarah Foster, in Fairfax county, but, within a short time, removed to Caroline county where his son, Elisha Athy was born July 23, 1782.

Elisha Athey was educated in the schools of Caroline and afterward took commercial training in Baltimore. He emigrated to Kentucky in early manhood and settled in Middletown. In 1825 he removed to Louisville and opened the first wholesale drygoods house in that city. In 1840 he was reputed to be one of the largest landed proprietors and slaveholders in the State. He lost much of his fortune by endorsing for his friends. Elisha Athey married Anne Roley White, daughter of William White, of Westmoreland county, Va., who emigrated to Kentucky and laid out the town of Middletown.

John William Athey, son of Elisha Athey and Anne White, was born in 1812 and married Phoebe Yarnall, sister of Mordecai Yarnall who was the first Signal Service officer of the United States Government. He was secretary of the Jones McElway Foundry Company at Holly Springs, Miss., which made the first guns used by the Confederate Army. The Confederate Government bought the foundry in 1862 and employed Athey as chemist during the course of the war.

The Athey family is not now represented in Caroline county but is well established and prominent in other parts of Virginia, in Kentucky, Maryland, West Virginia, Ohio, Iowa, Wisconsin and other mid-western States. Among the many descendants of this ancient Caroline family may be named Alexander Athey, Attorney-at-law, Prairie Du Chien, Wisconsin; Dr. Caleb Athey, Baltimore, Md.; Raymond B. Dickey, attorney-at-law, Washington, D. C.; Rev. S. M. Athey, Orleans, Va.; his son Rev. S. M. Athey, Jr., Paris, Ky.; and C. W. Bransford, Owensboro, Ky.

The Athey coat of arms is described as follows:

Arms: Checky; argent and gules, on chevron of the last three etoiles or.

Crest: Demi lion rampant.

Motto: *Ductus non coactus.*

THE ARMISTEAD FAMILY

The name Armistead is derived from the name Darmstadt. The family was originally of Teutonic origin, but were Englishmen for many generations before coming to America in 1635.

William Armistead received a patent in 1636 from Captain John West, Governor of Virginia, for 450 acres in Elizabeth City county and here the seat of the elder line in Virginia was established and called "Hesse." The family early became prominent in Middlesex, Matthews, New Kent and surrounding counties.

The first member of this family to come to Caroline, so far as authentic history records, was Henry Armistead, who was the first representative of the county in the House of Burgesses 1727–35 and who was sworn county lieutenant in 1733.

John Armistead inherited much property in Caroline by the will of Henry Armistead, and married Lucy Baylor, of "New Market"—the ancient estate of the Baylors in Caroline. Lucy Baylor was the daughter of John and Fanny (Walker) Baylor and the sister of Col. George Baylor, Washington's chief of staff and of Walker Baylor, who commanded the "Washington Life Guards" at Germantown, Pa.

To John Armistead and Lucy Baylor his wife, were born seven children—six sons and one daughter—one of whom, George Armistead, may be numbered among the most noted men of America.

George Armistead was born at "New Market," Caroline county, April 10, 1780 and was appointed county lieutenant January 8, 1799 and First Lieutenant in the Continental Army in May 1800. He was promoted to the rank of Captain in November 1806 and was made Major of Third Artillery in 1813. He distinguished himself at the capture of Fort George, Upper Canada, May, 1813, and became known as one of the bravest and most resourceful men in the American Army. He was in command at Fort McHenry, Baltimore, in 1814, and successfully defended the city against the British attack under Admiral Cochrane.

Colonel George Armistead

For his gallant defence of Fort McHenry and the city of Baltimore, he was brevetted Lieutenant Colonel and was hailed throughout the country as "The Hero of Fort McHenry."

It was during his gallant defence of Fort McHenry that Francis Scott Key was inspired to write "The Star Spangled Banner" which has since become the national anthem. The flag which flew over the fort and which Key saw "by the dawn's early light," was presented to Colonel Armistead by the Government, who in turn presented it to his son-in-law, Mr. William Somner Appleton, of Boston, as a wedding gift. The flag which inspired the national anthem remained in the Appleton family for many years, during which time Baltimore and Boston contended with each other for its possession. Finally, at the suggestion of of Mr. James B. Baylor, of "New Market," Caroline county, Va., the flag was presented by Mr. Appleton to the National Museum at Washington, where the same is now preserved in a glass case built especially for its keeping. In the same case with the flag is the beautiful silver service which was presented to Colonel Armistead by the city of Baltimore in recognition of his service as savior of the city.

Colonel Armistead's five brothers served in the War of 1812, three of them in the regular army and two in the militia.

THE BAYLOR FAMILY OF NEWMARKET

According to family records in the possession of James B. Baylor, of "Newmarket" plantation and Washington, D. C.,

Newmarket as it Appeared in 1768

the first members of the Baylor family to settle permanently in America were John and Robert Baylor who came to Virginia toward the close of the seventeenth century. They were born in Tiverton, Devonshire, England, John Baylor's birth date being 1650. Shortly after their emigration to Virginia they were followed by their father, John Baylor, I, who had lived in Virginia or owned property in the colony as early as 1650. The Lancaster county records show that he was assessed in 1854 with three tithables.

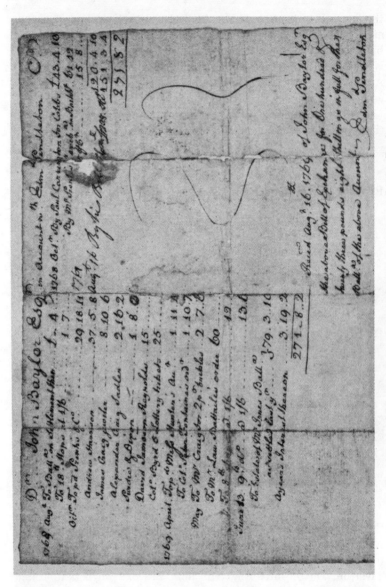

Fac simile of Statement of Account Between John Baylor and Edm. Pendleton

John Baylor, II, was married in 1696 to a widow, Mrs. O'Brien, of New Kent, whose maiden name was Lucy Todd. He lived first in Gloucester, which he represented in the House of Burgesses, and afterward removed to King and Queen which he represented in the House of Burgesses in 1718. He was a merchant as well as a planter and employed a number of ships to bring in goods for his stores in Gloucester, King and Queen and New Kent. His principal warehouses were at a placed called "Baylor" on the Mattaponi, between Walkerton and King and Queen Courthouse.

John Baylor, III, son of John and Lucy Todd O'Brien Baylor, was born at Walkerton May 12, 1705 and was educated in England at Putney Grammar School and Caius College, Cambridge. He was granted lands in King and Queen in 1726, upon which he established his home calling the same "Newmarket." The County of Caroline was formed the following year and the plantation of "Newmarket" fell in the new county. John Baylor III was Colonel in the Caroline Militia and was a Burgess for Caroline from 1742 to 1765. He was also County Lieutenant for Orange where he had been granted a vast tract of land upon which he lived during the summer months. His commission as Lieutenant is still preserved. He died April 16, 1772. Colonel Baylor was noted as an importer and breeder of thoroughbred horses. Among the famous horses which he brought to the colony may be mentioned "Fearnaught" who cost him one thousand guineas as the bill of sale, still in possession of the Baylor family, will testify. In the *New York Herald*, of February 12, 1922, appeared the following:

"FEARNAUGHT'S IMPORTANCE AS A SIRE"

"The importance of the English horse Fearnaught, whose offspring included Apollo and Regulus, two of the five topnotchers of the Colonial turf mentioned by Judge DuVal, is thus asserted by Patrick Nisbett Edgar in a footnote in his pioneer stud book:

"Until the days of Fearnaught no other than quarter races were run in Virginia. Speed had been the only quality sought for. But his progeny were remarkable for their fine figure and lasting bottom and introduced a taste (in imitation of the English) for course racing, which led the Virginians to seek for race horses of size and bottom."

Col. John Baylor, of Newmarket, in Caroline county, who imported this great sire in 1764 and kept him until the turfman's death in 1772, rivaled Col. John Tayloe, of Mt. Airy, as a breeder of race horses. His stud included nearly one hundred horses

when his executor came to sell it.   He was a man of wealth and
prominence in the colony and a personal friend of Washington.
Born in 1705, his name appears among the students at Cambridge
University in 1722.   He was a Burgess from 1742 to 1765, and
was the father of Col. George Baylor, aid to Washington at the

Colonel George Baylor

outbreak of the Revolution, and later a cavalry leader to whom
Congress gave a charger in appreciation of his services at the
battle of Trenton.

While he was with Washington's Army at Tappan, N. Y.,
Col. George Baylor was shot through the lungs and captured by
the British.   He afterward re-entered the service, but this wound
caused his death in 1784.   In his *"Blooded Horses of Colonial
Days"* Francis Barnum Culver says the elder Baylor bequeathed

to his son George "his own riding mare, Jenny Dismal's colt Godolphin, his gray mare Sprightly, and the young brown English-begotten mare Stella," showing pretty clearly that the Revolutionary hero inherited his father's love of blooded horses.

The importer of Fearnaught must have been on very intimate terms with Washington, judging from an order sent to London in 1759, just after the Colonel married the widow Custis and made her mistress of Mount Vernon. This order was addressed to Robert Cary & Co., and it directed them to procure for him one-half dozen pairs of shoes, "*to be made by one Didsbury, on Col. Baylor's Last—but a little larger than his—and to have high heels.*"

To Col. John Baylor, III and Frances (Walker) Baylor were born eight children: Courtney, Lucy, Frances, Elizabeth, John IV, George, Walker and Robert. All of the daughters and several of the sons were educated in England. Lucy married John Armistead and became the mother of Colonel George Armistead, "The Hero of Fort McHenry." (See Armistead Family).

George Baylor was born at "Newmarket" January 12, 1752, and was educated by private tutors at Newmarket plantation and in England. He was a member of the Caroline Committee of Safety 1775–76 and entered the military service at the beginning of the Revolution. He was Lieutenant-Colonel and Aide-de-Camp to General Washington from August 15, 1775, to January 9, 1777. He participated in several battles and carried the news of the victory over the Hessians to Congress then sitting in Baltimore. By order of Congress of January 1, 1777, it was "*Resolved,* That a horse, properly caparisoned for service, be presented to Lieutenant Colonel Baylor." He was also Colonel of Third Continental Dragoons from January 9, 1777, to end of year. In September 1777, his command was surprised near Tappan, N. Y., at midnight, by a British force under General Grey, with the loss of sixty-seven killed and the remainder captured. Colonel Baylor himself received a bayonet thrust through the lungs from which he never fully recovered,—although he later returned to the service and commanded the First Continental Dragoons to the close of the war. He was commissioned Brevet Brigadier-General September 30, 1783. The wound which he received in his lungs near Tappan brought on pulmonary trouble and he sought relief in the balmy climate of the West Indies, but in vain. He died at Bridgetown, Barbadoes, W. I., in March, 1784, and was buried in the church yard of St. Michael's Cathedral.

Walker Baylor was Lieutenant in Third Light Dragoons in 1777 and was promoted to a captaincy in February 1780. He was disabled at Germantown by a ball which shattered his foot. He married Jane, daughter of Joseph Bledsoe, of Caroline, and a sister of Jesse Bledsoe who was United States Senator from Kentucky.

Major Walker Baylor

Walker Baylor was the progenitor of the Baylor families of Kentucky and Texas. One of his sons, Robert Emmett Bledsoe Baylor, served in the War of 1812 under Colonel Boswell and was in the battle which was fought near Fort Meigs. In 1819 he was elected to the Kentucky Legislature and the following year he removed to Alabama where he became prominent in politics, representing that State in the twenty-first Congress. During the Creek War he commanded a regiment of Alabama volunteers which rendered notable service. He removed to the Republic of Texas in 1839 and was, almost immediately, elected a Judge of the Supreme Court of the Republic. He was a member of the Convention which framed the Constitution for the State of Texas and was District Judge in the State for more than a quarter of a century. In 1845, just before the State was admitted into the Union, a charter for a Baptist college, to be located at Independence, was granted by the Congress of Texas and to this institution, which was named Baylor University, Judge Baylor made large gifts of land and money. A county in Texas was also named for him. Judge Baylor was the father of General J. R. Baylor, C. S. A.

James Bowen Baylor, son of Dr. John Roy Baylor V, and Anne Bowen, was born at "Mirador" the home of his maternal grandfather, James Marshall Bowen, on May 30, 1849, and was brought up at Newmarket plantation which he now owns. Mirador later became the home of the Langhorne family and here Lady Astor and her famous sisters were brought up. James Bowen Baylor graduated with honors from Virginia Military Institute in 1865 and won B. S., and C. E. Degrees from the University of Virginia in 1872. Baylor University conferred the degree of Doctor of Laws on him in 1903, at which time he delivered before the University a remarkable address on "Education in its Relation to Production." He was married on January 5, 1881 to Miss Ellen C. Bruce, of "Staunton Hill" Charlotte county, who was a sister of William Cabell Bruce, author of "Life of Benjamin Franklin," "Life of John Randolph, of Roanoke," and who is now U. S. Senator from Maryland. She had one sister who became the wife of the famous author, Thomas Nelson Page.

Dr. Baylor was appointed aid in U. S. Coast and Geodetic Survey of 1874, after a competitive examination, and has been Field Officer of this department since. He has determined the elements of earth's magnetism from Canada to Mexico in almost every State and has done hydrographic, astronomical and geodetic work for surveys in various sections of the United States. The "Baylor Survey" of the oyster grounds in Virginia is too well known to Virginians to need comment here.

In 1900 the United States Supreme Court appointed Dr. Baylor, Professor Buchanan, of Tennessee and W. C. Hotchkins, of Massachusetts as Commissioners to settle the Virginia-Tennessee boundary line dispute which had been in court for nearly one

hundred years. Dr. Baylor made the minority report defining
the boundary line along the middle of Main Street, Bristol, which
report the Supreme Court confirmed. He also served as boundary
engineer in establishing the Virginia-Maryland, New York–
Pennsylvania and United States-Canadian boundaries.

Having served with the cadet corps of Virginia Military
Institute during the last year of the Civil War, Dr. Baylor is a
member of the Confederate Veterans organization and frequently
attends the reunions of the men in grey. He is also a member
of the Society of the Cincinnati, the Philosophical Society of
Washington, The Cosmos, Metropolitan and Army and Navy
Clubs of Washington and of the Westmoreland Club of Richmond. For a more detailed account of his life and activities
see *Who's Who in America*, issue of 1923.

JOHN ROY BAYLOR

John Roy Baylor, a brother of Captain James Bowen Baylor
and the seventh of the family to bear this name, was born in
1851 and began his education under the Rev. William Dinwiddie
at the Bookland School, Greenwood, Va.   On completing his work
there he turned his steps toward the University of Virginia.
Here he remained several years, graduating with the degrees of
bachelor of arts and bachelor of literature.

Upon graduation he chose the profession of teaching as his
life work and entered upon the calling at the Mountain Spring
School at Trinity, Ala.   He next served in the Miller Manual
Labor School, Albemarle, Va., which was an endowed institution
for the purpose of preparing orphans for vocational work.   Prof.
Baylor's service at this school extended over a period of ten
years, from 1878 to 1888.

In 1889 Prof. Baylor moved to Savannah, Ga., and taught
in a school for boys in that city for two years, when he went
to Anniston, Ala., and took charge of the Noble Institute.

After this long service as a teacher of young men, Prof. Baylor
went to Chattanooga, Tenn., at the solicitation of Dr. Charles
W. Dabney, and there in May 1893, in conference with Messrs.
Robert Pritchard, Theodore Montague, H. S. Chamberlain and
L. M. Coleman in the home of Dr. J. W Bachman, he organized
The Baylor School which has become nationally known as one
of the greatest preparatory schools for young men in the entire
country.

The first location of the school was in the old McCallie homestead, a landmark in the city.   After six years here it was moved to the corner of Vine and Palmetto Street where it remained until 1915.

In 1915, through the interest of J. T. Lupton and the alumni, the school was removed to Baylor Station, its present site, and the group of buildings which house the institution at present will compare favorably with the best in the country.

Prof. Baylor is well known as a Greek and Latin scholar, but he modestly gives the credit for his interest in the classics to his old professors, who are nationally known figures.   Colonel Venable, one of his instructors, was chief of General Lee's Staff; Dr. Gildersleeve, his professor of Greek, was considered the greatest Greek scholar in the world; Col. William E. Peters, his instructor in Latin, was a cavalry leader under General Jubal Early; and Dr. Frank Smith, his teacher of Natural Philosophy, was considered one of America's leading scientists.

Prof. Baylor married Miss Julia Howard, a lady of splendid ancestry and active in the Society of Colonial Dames and other similar organizations, and to this union was born a daughter—Miss Eloise Baylor—who is regarded as one of the most talented musicians in the entire South.

In June 1923, the University of the South bestowed upon Prof. Baylor the honorary degree of Doctor of Literature in recognition of his services to the educational world.   He has also been included in *Who' Who In America.*   For a more complete biography the reader is referred to *The Chattanooga Times,* of September 19, 1923, from which the foregoing has largely been taken.

Blanton Arms

THE BLANTONS OF CAROLINE

It is supposed upon good authority that the Blantons are French Hugenots who fled to England before the year 1600.

A legal search of the records in England resulted i   the following statement: "In consideration of this matter a thorough and exhaustive search has been made of all the available printed and manuscript records of the County of Lancashire together with a portion of the Counties of Cheshire and Yorkshire, but without any discovery of the existence of the family, other than the record of the arms about the middle of the sixteenth century. Robert Grover, Somerset Herald, from 1571 to 1588 includes in his ordinary of arms two coats for Blanton of Lancashire, and the simplicity of the first coat points to great antiquity and it may be assumed that the second coat is of later date and adopted by a descendent of the family bearing the first coat.

Description of arms: Blanton (Lancashire) silver or white on a bend sable three lions rampant out of the field.

The bearing of such coats of such a period clearly denotes that the family then occupied a position of some consequence, as the heralds of the day exercised great vigilance in preventing unauthorized bearing of arms and possessed considerable powers which they did not hesitate to employ as occasion required.

In the face of this, however, the name is not contained in any of the miscellaneous records affording the only means of identification, leading to the conclusion that the surviving members left the county during the late sixteenth or early seventeenth century leaving no trace. A long list of authorities then given as being 'consultant,' shows that no other possible conclusion, other than extinction, can be made."

There are two coats of arms, the first exactly like the second except for the lions. It is believed that with the emigration from Lancashire, England, the Blantons came to Stafford county, Va., thence to Caroline. From the records in the land office at Richmond we find that one Thomas Blanton received grants of land in old Rappahannock county, and that he also received other grants in Caroline in 1682 and 1687. In 1783 William Blanton received a grant of 400 acres (see page 228 book 14, 1775 and 1781.) In 1785 Thomas Blanton received 1,050 acres. See book "O" pages 556 and 618. He married Jane Moore, of Spotsylvania county. In 1749 William Blanton's name is again mentioned. In 1742 John Blanton's name appears. In 1778 James Blanton's. In 1807 and 1816 James W. Blanton and William Blanton are mentioned. In 1749 John Blanton who married Hannah Anderson, both of Caroline, removed to Cumberland county and settled near Brown's church. He was the progenitor of the Cumberland Blantons.

The geneaology of the Caroline Blantons as known today is as follows: There was a family, probably the children or grand-children of the above mentioned Thomas Blanton, whose several names were John Blanton, Richard Blanton, William ·Blanton and Polly Blanton.

The descendants of John Blanton were: James, Charles, John, Eldridge, Richard, Augustus, Robert, Milton, Lewis, Lucyella, Bettie, Sallie, Lina and Eliza Ann.

The descendants of James Blanton were: Judson, James, Nannie and Jennie.

The descendants of Charles Blanton were: Etta, Ida, Mollie and Alley.

John Blanton died without issue.

Eldridge Blanton had issue: Aubrey, Sallie, Asa, and Lee.

Richard Blanton had issue: Eugene, Julia and Ethel.

Augustus Blanton died without issue.

Robert Blanton had issue: Daisy and Grafton.

Milton Blanton died without issue.

Lewis Blanton had issue: Weldon, Lewis and Steward.

The descendants of Richard Blanton were: Charles, John George, James and Mary.

Charles Blanton had issue: Nannie.

John Blanton had issue: Richard, Sallie, Mary, Archibald, Tazewell, Ada and John.

Richard Blanton had issue: Emmett, Alfred, Arthur, Cecil, William, Elizabeth, Lula, Ruth and Harry.

Archibald Blanton had issue: John, Herbert, Clarence, Thomas, Linwood, Maud and Julia.

Tazewell Blanton had issue: Edwina and Ernest.

George W. Blanton had issue: George G., James, Betty, Laura, Sallie, Isla, Mollie and Nettie.

George G. Blanton had issue: Clifton, Lonnie, Oscar, Lyn-wood, George and Mellen.

James Blanton had issue: Clarice, Evelyn, Kate, Carrie, James, Thomas, Louise and Christine.

Thomas Blanton was graduated from the Law Department of the University of Virginia, m. Blanche Broaddus, dau. of Eugene Broaddus and Blanche Ennis and has issue one daughter, Jean Dulaney. He was elected Commonwealth's Attorney for

Caroline in 1923. This office was held by his wife's uncle, W. E. Ennis, for several years.

James Blanton died without issue.

William Blanton had issue: John, Betty, Thomas, Letitia, Jennie, Mollie, Lucy, Lawrence, Robert and Charles.

John Blanton had issue: Julian and Bettie Roy.

Julian Blanton had issue: Hampton, John, Leonard and Allie Blanton.

Thomas Blanton had issue: Cora, Kate, Carrie, Robert, Cedon, Wallie, Lula and Mamie.

Robert L. Blanton: No issue.

Cedon Blanton had issue: Audrey, Earl, Franklin, Reid and Loise.

Lawrence Blanton died without issue.

Robert Blanton had issue: Annie, Grace, Eliza, Robbie, Charles and Alvin.

Charles Blanton: No issue.

Alvin Blanton: No issue.

Earl Blanton married Lawrence Durrett.

Emmett m. Grace Blanton.   Arthur m. Mrs. Massey. Wiliam m. Miss Evans.

George G., m. Miss Sutton.   James, m. Cora Blanton.

Bettie m. John Allen.   Sallie m. W. L. Allen.   Isla m. John Arnold.   Mollie m. R. E. Smith   Nettie m. C. O. Allen.

Lawrence m. Miss Mattie Winn.   Robert m. Miss Flippo.

Julian m. Miss Allen.   Bettie Roy m. Broaddus Allen.

Cora m. James Blanton.   Kate m. E. E. Burruss.   Robert L. m. Maud Hargrave.   Cedon m. Ora Haley.   Wallie m. J. W. Allen.   Lula m. A. J. Haley.

Grace m. Emmett Blanton.   Eliza m. Harvey Durrett.   Robbie m. J. F. Davis and has issue: William Franklin.

THE BOUTWELL AND SMITH FAMILIES

The name Boutwell is derived from Bouteilles, a village near Doeppe in Normandy.   The first of the name to come to America were three brothers who arrived at Port Royal, on the Rappahannock, at the very beginning of the eighteenth century.   One of them settled on a large tract of land here in the Rappahannock valley, which is still owned by a descendant, John Boutwell Smith and the other two moved on farther North, where they became the progenitors of large and influential families and among whose descendants are Senators and Governors and other makers and moulders of the Republic.

Birkenhead Hawkins Boutwell, descendant of the original Boutwell settler, married Catherine Harrison Smith, daughter of William Smith, of Revolutionary fame, granddaughter of Capt. Joseph Smith and great-granddaughter of Sir William Sidney Smith of England. A daughter of Capt. Joseph Smith m. a Mr. Keith. She was an aunt of Chief Justice Marshall (See *W. and M. Quarterly, Mead's Old Virginia Families, Buck's Eminent Virginians, Hardesty's Historical Encyclopaedia*, &c.)

Birkenhead Hawkins Boutwell and his wife had issue: Dr. Wm. S. Boutwell, Birkenhead H. Boutwell, Apollos Boutwell, Walter J. Boutwell, Martha Smith Boutwell, Catherine Anne, Elizabeth and Doniphan Boutwell. The last named daughter

Arms of Smith Family of Caroline and Essex

was born April 27, 1823 and was married to William Chowning, of Middlesex. Martha Smith Boutwell married James Madison Smith, brother of Governor William Smith "(Extra Billy)" and her cousin. Only one son of Birkenhead Boutwell ever married. He was the eldest son, John F., who married Mary Smith Blackford. They had issue three daughters. The last member of the Boutwell name in Caroline was Apollos Boutwell who was born in 1828 and died in 1917. He was the son of Birkenhead H. Boutwell, who was considered a very rich man in his day and is said to have kept his money in shot bags in the locker room of his residence. He is also said to have kept three or four barrels of whiskey and brandy in his cellar "for family use" and for his friends.

James Madison Smith was twice married: First, to Mary Bell by whom he had four children; Second, to Martha Smith Boutwell by whom he had five children, John Boutwell, Kate Harrison, Ida Birkenhead, Wm. Apollos, Camille Pauline. He died in

New Mexico while serving as Government Agent to the Indians. He was a prominent lawyer in Washington.

John F. Boutwell, brother of Birkenhead H. Boutwell, was a captain in the Confederate Army.

Miss Ida Birkenhead Smith wrote the author of this work as follows: "During the Civil War my grandmother, Mrs. Birkenhead Boutwell, lived at "Shady Grove" between Supply and Brandywine. She turned her house into a hospital for wounded and disabled soldiers until the fall of Richmond. Dr. Urquhart, of Port Royal gave them medical attention. There were seven left with her at the fall of Richmond, all of whom soon left save one, whose health was so bad that he was unable to travel. She fitted up the family school house which stood in the yard and placed him in it that she might be able to look after him. We children liked to go to his door to talk with him and hear him sing. One morning he decided to leave and, of course, we gathered around him. He fastened his little pack on his back and said, "Good bye, purty gals, I am sorry to left you, but I am 'bliged to went." We ran after him a little way then went back and told grandma of his going. She was sorry she did not see him to say "goodbye" and to give him some money as she had given the other six who had gone some weeks before."

The Smith family aforementioned claim several Spanish ancestors, the first being Don Iphan (afterward corrupted into Doniphan by running the title and name together) who was knighted by Isabella, of Spain, for gallantry during the war with the Moors. When the Inquisition was introduced he was exiled from Spain to save his life and so came to America. He married a wealthy lady, a Miss Mott, and by this marriage had a daughter, who married a member of the Sidney Smith family. A son married into the Anderson family, later renowned in Caroline. A descendant of these families is said to have passed through the British lines at Charleston and returned with her skirts filled with powder for the use of the Colonial troops.

THE BOULWARE FAMILY

There are several branches of this family in Caroline, all of whom, according to family tradition, similarity of names, etc., came from the same ancestor, who came over from England and settled at the place now known as Boulware's Wharf in Essex county.

The first member of the family to come to Caroline was Richard Boulware who, a few years prior to the Revolution, purchased a section of Beverley's Chase from Robert Beverley, of "Blandfield," in Essex, and established his home thereon. This place became known as Boulware's Chase and a part of the estate is now owned by the descendants of Richard Boulware.

Two sons of Richard Boulware and Frances, his wife—namely: William and Mark, also settled in Caroline. ' Among the des-- cendants of William may be named Mrs. Mary Eliza Flippo, wife of Dr. Flippo, a prominent physician of the county, and Mrs. Maria Allensworth, wife of Captain Gibbons Allensworth who represented Caroline in the Legislature. Mark Boulware inherited Boulware's Chase and was twice married. By his first marriage to Milly——————, he had issue: Frank, b. 1780, d. 1870; Molly, b. 1781; Richard, b. 1783; Dorothy, b. 1785; Elizabeth, b. 1788. By his second marriage to Agatha Saunders he had issue: Turner, b. 1792; Lucy, b. 1793; Elliott, b. 1795; Judith, b. 1797; James, b. 1799; Ophelia, b. 1801; Battaile, b. 1802. Mark Boulware d. February 22, 1811 and his widow d. 1836.

The children of Mark Boulware married as follows: Lucy m. ——————Long and among her descendants may be named John C. Howlett, of South Boston; Mrs. Solon B. Woodfin, of Ashland; Mrs. James W. Jeffries, of Warrenton and Miss Maude Woodfin, of the faculty of the University of Richmond.

Judith m. David Evans, of Caroline, and removed to Shelby- ville, Tenn. She had issue a son, Dr. Robert Evans, who died a few years since at an advanced age. Among her descendants are David Evans Miller, prominent railway official of Atlanta, Ga.; Mrs. Margaret Lyle, of Johnson City, Tenn., and Mrs. Margaret Cooper, of Thomasville, Ga.

Ophelia m. James Harwood Broaddus and had issue: Caroline, George and Agnes. These are named in the History of the Broaddus Family. Of the descendants of Ophelia Boulware and J. H. Broaddus may be named Mrs. Lillian Chockley, of Rock- ford, Ill., and Mrs. Irene Fuller, of Bradford, Penn.

Turner Boulware, son of Mark, removed to Wood county, Va., now W. Va., in 1810 and settled where Parkersburg now stands. It was only a trading post then. Young Boulware helped to erect the court house and the old Bell tavern, the first

brick houses in Parkersburg.   He enlisted in the American Army
in 1812 under Col. John McConnell, of the First Virginia regiment
and marched to Sandusky, O., thence to Delaware, Ohio, thence
to Ft. Meigs on the Maumee river, which fort he helped to defend
against the British under General Proctor.   For further details
see *History of Wood County* by A. F. Gibbons.   After peace was
made Turner Boulware was discharged with the rank of sergeant
and returned to Parkersburg.   He kept a journal while in the
army which is now deposited with other war relics in the Pioneers
Cabin in the city park of Parkersburg.

Turner Boulware
Born October 4, 1792.   Died while visiting his old home in Caroline in 1872.

Turner Boulware m. Mary Ann Creel, dau. of George Creel
and Clara Buckner and had issue: Mark, James, Elizabeth, Agnes,
John, Maria, George, Lucy, and Clara.

Mark, son of Turner, removed to Kansas in 1862 and married
Paulina Brockman, of Illinois.   He died in 1902 leaving three
daughters, namely: Mrs. Mary Atkisson and Mrs. Nannie Waddel,
of Blue Mound, Kans., and Mrs. Calista Atkisson, of Coalinga,
Cal., and one son, George Boulware, of Kansas.   Two of Mark
Boulware's grandsons, John Atkisson and Mark Atkisson served
in the World War.

James Boulware, son of Turner, b. 1832, came to Caroline
after the death of his bachelor uncle, Elliott Boulware and resided
with three of his father's maiden sisters.   He enlisted in the

Confederate Army in 1861 and was made first lieutenant of Company B; 9th Virginia Cavalry. He was in many engagements, and he and a soldier named ————Martin were the last ten men to cross Falmouth bridge after firing it to keep the Northern troops from crossing the Rappahannock. When peace came he returned to Caroline from prison at Fort Delaware and on December 14, 1865, married Caroline Broaddus, daughter of James H. Broaddus. Four children were born to this union: Eugene, b. 1866, d. 1872; Clara, who m. Harry J. Motley; Allie, who m. T. S. Jones, of Orange; and Linwood, who now lives in the old home. Mrs. Caroline Broaddus Boulware died on August 21, 1913 and her husband, James Boulware, died on March 15, 1915, being the third member of his family to die on March 15th.

Elizabeth Boulware died unmarried at Freeport, W. Va., March 18, 1912.

Agnes Boulware m. Thomas Gilmer, lawyer, and had issue eleven children of whom four are now living, namely: Mrs. Benton Jackson, of Parkersburg, W. Va.; A. L. Gilmer, of W. Va.; Mrs. Bessie McClintock, of Ardmore, Okla., and Miss Barbara Gilmer, of W. Va.

John Boulware, fifth child of Turner Boulware, removed to California where he was killed in a skirmish in 1862.

Maria Boulware m. Edwin Dean and died in 1906, survived by two sons: Julius and James, and one daughter, Mrs. Mary Cooper, of Harrisburg, W. Va.

George Boulware married Miss Malana Cain and died at Parkersburg without issue.

Lucy F. Boulware, b. 1846, m. Levi Morgan in 1874. He died in 1919.

Clara, youngest child of Turner Boulware, m. George Lockhart and had issue six children, five of whom are now living, namely: Mrs. Laura Smith, of Spencer, W. Va.; Mrs. Lena Pribble, of Parkersburg; Cleveland, Garland and Benjamin, all of Wirt county, W. Va. Mrs. Lockhart died in 1915 and her husband in 1917. In addition to five children, twenty-one grand children survived them.

Turner Boulware was a charter member of the first Masonic Lodge chartered in Parkersburg, W. Va. Of his nine children Mrs. Lucy Morgan, of Parkersburg is the sole survivor. Turner Boulware died while visiting his only surviving sister Mrs. Lucy

Long at the home of her son-in-law, Robert B. Wright, and was buried on the old family estate on his 80th birthday. See *History of Wood County, W. Va.*

THE BOWIE FAMILY

In the year 1742, or thereabout, two brothers—Scots—bearing the names of John and James Bowie, obtained a grant of land in Caroline county, near Port Royal, on the Rappahannock, and here settled. The estate of James Bowie, who was never married, was named "Braehead," and the estate of John Bowie was called "The Hill."

Bowie Arms

John Bowie married Judith Catlett, daughter of Col. John Catlett and Mary Grayson and had issue (1) James Bowie who m. Catherine Miller; (2) Catherine Bowie who m. James Pendleton; (3) Elizabeth Bowie who m. James Smith; (4) Judith Bowie who m. a Mr. Noel; (5) Eleanor Bowie who died unmarried; (6) Mary Bowie who m. a Mr. Timberlake; (7) Janette Bowie who m. Joseph Duerson.

James Bowie, only son of John Bowie and Judith Catlett, married, first, Catherine Miller, a niece of the wife of Robert Gilchrist and had issue: (1) John Catlett Bowie who served in the War of 1812.

John Catlett Bowie m. first, Jane Timberlake and had issue:

(1) Lucy Anne Bowie, who m. John L. Quesenberry. John L. Quesenberry and Lucy Anne Bowie had issue: (1) John James Quesenberry; (2) William Bowie Quesenberry. William Bowie Quesenberry m. Emma Fitzhugh and had issue: (1) Mary Brockenbrough Quesenberry and (2) William Fitzhugh Quesenberry. John Catlett Bowie m. second, Sarah Cox and had issue: (1) Allen Brockenbrough Bowie; (2) James Livingstone Bowie;(3) Catherine Miller Bowie.

Allen Brockenbrough Bowie enlisted in the Caroline Artillery, commanded by Captain T. R. Thornton, but on account of ill health was transferred to the Commissary Department and served in South Carolina under General Drayten. Allen Brockenbrough Bowie married Elizabeth Lovell Duncanson, a descendant of Col. James Duncanson, of Revolutionary fame and had issue: (1) Mary Alphonsa Bowie; (2) John William Bowie; (3) Allen H. Bowie; (4) James G. Bowie.

Julia Duncanson Bowie married Capelle H. Archer, a prominent real estate dealer of Richmond and had issue: (1) Elsie V. Archer; (2) Allene B. Archer; (3) Mary Randolph Archer; (4) Katherine Bowie Archer.

John Wm. Bowie settled in Covington, Va., operating a drug establishment.

Allen H. Bowie served in the Spanish-American War and was hospital sergeant in the McGuire Unit during the World War, being stationed at Toul, France. He married Ella Mae Womble and has issue: (1) John W. Bowie, (2) Allen Morris Bowie and (3) Robert Duncanson Bowie.

James Livingstone Bowie, second son of John Catlett Bowie and Sarah Cox, served as Lieutenant in the Caroline Artillery during the Civil War and afterward settled in Louisville, Ky., where he became auditor for the Louisville and Nashville Railroad. He married Alice Duncanson and had issue: (1) Catherine Bowie, (2) Livingstone Bowie, a broker; (3) Alice M. Bowie, an attorney and (4) James L. Bowie, business man of Louisville, Ky.

Catherine Miller Bowie, only daughter of John Catlett Bowie by his second wife, Sarah Cox, and an unusually brilliant woman, married John Henry Martin, a descendant of Colonel John Martin who was prominent in the life of Caroline from its very beginning as a county and who represented the county in the House of Burgesses 1738–1741. A large section of the county now known as "The Chase" was originally owned by this Colonel

John Martin of pre-Revolutionary fame. Many of his descendants are now to be found in Orange county, seven or eight miles east of the courthouse, where they first settled upon removing from Caroline.

John Henry Martin and Catherine Miller Bowie had issue: (1) Julian Bowie Martin, well known educator, who m. Ruby Snead, of Fluvanna county and had issue: Julian Bowie Martin II, and Catherine Isabel Martin.

(2) Sallie Martin who married Dr. Arthur Lewis Martin, of Naulakla, Caroline county, descendant of Warner Lewis, and who has three daughters, Pattie Livingstone Martin, Mary Bowie Martin and Garnett Lewis Martin.

(3) Henry Miller Martin, A. B., A. M., Ph. D., is Professor of Spanish in the University of Illinois. He was a Fellow of John Hopkins University, from which he received his Ph. D. He studied abroad for several years.

(4) Judith H. Martin, of "Clay Hill" Caroline county.

Walter Bowie, son of James Bowie and Catherine Miller, was twice married: First, to Julia A. Spindle by whom he had issue: (1) Catherine N. Bowie, who m. a Mr. Chewning; (2) James Barbour Bowie, who m. Anna Forbes; (3) Walter Bowie, C. S. A. veteran and Professor of Mathematics in V. M. I., and who married First a Mrs. Miller and Second, Eugenia Miller, of Caroline. Walter Bowie lived on his estate—"Kernan"—in Westmoreland. His grandson, Gordon Forbes Bowie, was a prominent physician. His second wife was Mary S. Todd by whom he had the following children: (4) Walter Bowie, II, who m. Gillie Jones; (5) Sarah, who m. T. M. Murphy; (6) Mary; (7) Margaret, who m. Col. R. S. Lawrence; (8) Edwin, (9) Ella who m. Judge J. T. Pendleton.

Walter Bowie, II, married Gillie Jones and had issue: (1) Walter Russell Bowie, III. Walter Russell Bowie, III, married Elizabeth Branch, of Richmond and had issue: (1) The Rev. Dr. Walter Russell Bowie, IV, former Rector of St. Paul's church (Episcopal) Richmond and at present (1923) Rector of Grace church, New York City; (2) Martha S. P. Bowie, who married her cousin Melville Campbell Branch, well known banker of Richmond.

William Miller Bowie, son of Robert Bowie and Catherine Miller, was married first, to Elizabeth Farrish, no issue and, second, to Nannie Jessie by whom he had issue: (1) Charles Bowie, (2) Eugene Bowie

Charles Bowie, son of William Bowie and Nannie Jessie, married First, Sarah Jones, no issue; Second, to Fannie Catlett by whom he had issue: (1) William D. Bowie, (2) Nannie Bowie, (3) Walter Nelson Bowie and (4) Frank E. Bowie. Charles Bowie lives at "Midway" near Woodford in Caroline county. "Midway" is named for its geographical location in the county. The water from one side of the roof flows to the Mattaponi and from the other side it flows to the Rappahannock. The town of Midway, Ky., was named for this old Catlett estate. Charles Bowie was married a third time to Miss Boulware, daughter of George Boulware.

Eugene Bowie, son of William Bowie and Nannie Jessie, married First, Julia White, of "Mt. Zephyr" in Caroline, now owned by Mr. R. L. Brooks and had issue: (1) Eugene Bowie, II, (2) Margaret Anne (Madge) Bowie, who married Dr. W. A. Shepherd, a prominent physician of Richmond, by whom she has three sons, William, Bowie and Daniel. Eugene Bowie married Second, Sophia Corbin, of Caroline and had issue: (3) Willing Bowie, lawyer and commonwealth's attorney for Caroline for eight years; (4) Eugene Bowie, named for deceased half brother; (5) Charles Bowie, who m. Elizabeth Wirt Washington; (6) Lulie, died infant; (7) Mary Jessie Bowie m. Ira Muse, of "Oak Grove" Westmoreland county; (8) Catherine Nelson Bowie; (9) Garnett Bowie and (10) Corbin Bowie, who m. O'Neal Broaddus.

The *Times-Dispatch*, of Richmond, of January 8, 1911, carried an obituary notice of the death of Eugene Bowie, which is, in part, as follows:

"On December 3, 1910, Eugene Bowie, aged fifty-six years, died at his home, "Mica," in Caroline county, Va. Mr. Bowie was twice married, his first wife being Julia Campbell White, of Caroline, from which union there was one son Eugene, who died in his seventh year, and one daughter, Margaret B. Shepherd, wife of Dr. Wm. A. Shepherd, of Richmond. His second wife was Sophia Corbin, of Caroline, to whom he was married in August 1888. From this marriage seven children and the widow survive.

"Mr. Bowie possessed such qualities of character and exerted such influences in his county that his death deserves more than a passing notice. He was of the true type of old Virginia gentle-

man. Open hospitality held sway in his home. Friend and
stranger were welcomed and his generosity extended to all. Perhaps
he helped more of his friends to succeed thar did any other man
in the community.   His success in business ano the means resulting
from his industry enabled him to gratify his desire to help others.
Deep sorrow throughout the community is felt on his passing,
for he will be greatly missed."

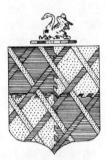

Broaddus Arms

THE BROADDUS FAMILY

The name Broaddus is a contraction of Broadhurst and corre-
sponds to Whitehurst, Deerhurst, Penhurst and many other
kindred names, the "hurst," denoting a knoll or wooded hill.
The family is of Anglo-Saxon origin and for centuries has been
prominent in British life, having given to the Empire many statesmen, among whom may be mentioned Henry Broadhurst, a member of Gladstone's government and for many years a member of
Parliament.   The family name in America is written by a few
with one "d" but by the majority with two.   The arms of the
family are thus described:

Arms: Quarterly, az. and or, fretty, raguly counterchanged.

Crest: A swan erm. swimming, charged on the breast with an
estoile sa. wings expanded or, fretty, raguly az.

Edward Broaddus, the first of the family in America of whom
anything is definitely known, emigrated from Wales and settled
on Gwynn's Island in Virginia. From Gwynn's Island he removed to the lower part of Caroline—then King and Queen—
in 1715, where he resided till his death at about seventy years
of age. He was twice married and had by his first wife two
sons and two daughters and by his second marriage five sons.

His eldest son, Thomas, married Ann Redd by whom he had seven sons. He was a soldier in the War of the Revolution and died in Caroline at an advanced age. The *History of the Broaddus Family*, by Rev. Andrew Broaddus, II, of Sparta, Va., (Central Baptist Print, St. Louis 1888) traces the descent of various branches of the family through Thomas Broaddus, son of Edward the emigrant and his daughter Catherine who m. Edwin Motley and through Robin Broaddus, seventh son of Edward the emigrant.

Edwin Broaddus, son of Thomas, I, and grandson of Edward the emigrant, removed to Kentucky at an early day, being the first member of the family to leave Virginia. He became the progenitor of the Broaddus family in Kentucky and other midwestern States. His youngest son, Andrew Broaddus, removed to Missouri and married there. While living in Missouri he made a trip to Santa Fe with Kit Carson, and while on this trip accidently shot himself in the hand making an amputation of the arm necessary. This operation was performed by his companions with a butcher knife, using the instrument first to cut through the flesh and afterwards converting it into a saw, by hacking the edge, for cutting the bone. The wound was cauterized by a red hot king-bolt from one of the wagons. He returned to Kentucky where he died at an advanced age, leaving forty-two grandchildren and fifty-five great grandchildren.

Eldridge J. Broaddus, son of Andrew of Missouri and Kentucky, was elected Circuit Judge of the Seventeenth Judicial District of Missouri in 1874 and served six years. He was for many years attorney for the Chicago, Milwaukee and St. Paul Railroad.

The Broaddus family has been prominent in the life of Caroline from the formation of the county to the present. Hardly a Legislative Petition from Caroline is to be found without the Broaddus name. The family has been no less prominent in the history of the Baptist church, having given more ministers to that denomination than any other one family in America.

Burke Arms

THE BURKE FAMILY

The name Burke, Burk, Bourke or Bourck, as it is variously spelt, was originally written De Burgh and under that form is an ancient name, traceable back to the fourteenth century. The family is of Norman origin and is prominent in Irish and English history. The first person of the name, of record, in America was Richard Burke, of Sudbury, Mass., of whom nothing is known previous to his marriage in Sudbury in 1670. Connecting his appearance with the fact that less than twenty years prior to 1670, Michael de Burgh, Earl of Clauricarde, was driven from his country, his estate sequestered and his home broken up, we are led to wonder whether in the consequent dispersion of his retainers, one of his relatives, or possibly himself, did not find passage to the new world to start life anew, under less oppressive circumstances. Major John Burke was born at Hatfield, Mass., November 28, 1717 and died at Deerfield, October 27, 1786. Richard Burke, a descendant of the Burkes of Massachusetts, came to Virginia, it is supposed, about 1775. He had issue: John, Henry and William. John Muse Burke, his son, married Frances Sophia Woolfolk, of "Shepherd's Hill," in Caroline, May 31, 1817 and had issue: Thos. George, John, Jourdan, Bettie Ann,. Cordelia, Maria Louise, Margaret, Fanny and Mary Ellen. Thomas George Burke m. Isabella Garnett and had issue: Betty W., John Muse, Thos. George, Robt. Hampton, Sallie M., Belle Garnett. John Muse m. Sarah Grineck and had issue: Daniel G. Burke. Thos. George m. Nannie Beazley and had issue: Charles, Leslie, Harry, Mabel, Earle, Thomas, Grace. Robert Hampton m. Agnes Lowe and had issue: James, Isabella and Robert. Bettie W., m. James M. Jesse and had issue: Fannie, Corra and Annie. Sallie M. died unmarried.

Belle Garnett m. Robt. Emmett Collins, son of Capt. Charles Collins of War of 1812 and had issue: Mary Lou, Emmett Burke, Sarah Muse, George Waverly, Thomas Maury, Belle Hampton, Margaret Catherine, Samuel Dickinson and Ione Bertrand Mary Lou m. Wm. A. Beazley and had issue: Robert Hampton, William Ashby, Thos. Collins and Emmett Garnett. Emmett Burke, unmarried. George Waverly, unmarried. Thomas Maury, unmarried. Sam'l Dickinson, unmarried. Sarah Muse m. Thos. Orin Hyatt, no issue. Belle Hampton m. Elwood Dunn Davies and has issue: Elwood Dunn, Jr., Dickinson Maury and Lou Belle. Ione Bertrand m. David C. Glascock, no issue. For further Burke genealogy see History of Burke Family, 239 pages, and also Woolfolk genealogy elsewhere in this volume.

Campbell Arms

THE CAMPBELL FAMILY

The Campbell family received the name de Campo Bello during the period of the Norman Conquest, which name was soon anglicised to Campbell. Among those knighted by the

Conquerer was one of the name Campo Bello, who received as a reward for his services that territory in Scotland known as Argylshire. The Campbells of Argylshire have always been regarded as the head of all the several branches of the family scattered throughout the English speaking world. The Argyle Campbells were early among the nobility, among the first, if not the very first, being Baron Campbell, whose son was made Duke of Argyle and married Isabella Stuart, Princess of Scotland. Title after title has been added to this dukedom until the present Duke of Argyle holds almost as many titles as the King of England.

When Mary Stuart was in prison she naturally expected aid from her cousin, the Duke of Argyle, who was in a number of conspiracies to effect her release. When Elizabeth signed the bill permitting the execution of Mary she also signed another banishing certain noblemen, among them the Duke of Argyle. He took up residence in France and was here many years before he was permitted to return to Scotland. While in France one of his sons fought a duel with a Frenchman and, killing his antagonist, was compelled to flee the country. England being closed to him, he came to the Colony of Virginia, arriving at Jamestown about 1650. He married and removed from Jamestown to a settlement in Accomack thence recrossed the bay to Gloucester where he died. His family later came to King and Queen and of this family one son, James, came to Caroline and established himself at "Poplar Grove" near Golansville. Later the Caroline family acquired Aspen Hill near Milford, now owned by Mr. and Mrs. John U. Henderson, and are now strongly established in both Caroline and Hanover counties.

THE CHANDLER FAMILY

The Order Books of Caroline county show that the Chandler family was prominent in the life of the county as early as 1734. In Order Book, No. 1, (1732–1740) page 149, mention is made of the deeds of lands of Timothy Chandler and Justin, his wife. On page 518 of the same book is recorded an order "That Robert Woolfolk, Timothy Chandler and Moses Hart (or Hurt) lay off the most convenient road from the Mattaponi River across Polecat Swamp to Chesterfield church."

There is a tradition, with much historical color, that three men of the name Chandler came from Essex, England to Roxbury,

Mass., in 1637 and one of these, William Chandler, settled at Roxbury; one, Timothy Chandler, came to Maryland; and one, Robert Chandler, came still farther south and settled in Virginia.

Chandler Arms

It is significant that the Massachusetts, Maryland and Virginia families bear the same arms, of which the following is a description:

Arms: Chequy argent and azure, on a bend engrailed sable, three lions passant or.

Crest: A pelican sable, in her piety, vert.

Motto: *Ad mortem fidelis.*

Robert Chandler died *circa* 1803 and his will, according to Caroline Order Books, was probated that year. He left four sons and four daughter. (1) Henry, (2) William, (3) Edmund, (4) Robert, (5) Molly who m. —— Bibb, (6) Fanny who m. ——Hackett, (7) Sally who m. —— Jones and (8) Lucy.

Robert Chandler was evidently a churchman for his name is found on one of the early Legislative Petitions from Caroline, praying that body to continue the establishment. The petition was drawn by Edmund Pendleton whose name heads the list, and the name of Chandler is second.

William Chandler, second son of Robert, I, married Ann (sometimes called Nancy) Coleman and had issue: (1) Lucy who m. James Smith, (2) Elizabeth who m. Benjamin Coleman, (3) Rebecca who m. John Smith, (4) Thomas Coleman who m. Clemantine Alsop, of Spotsylvania county.

Clemantine Alsop was the daughter of Samuel Alsop, a wealthy planter of Spotsylvania, whose will is of record in that county and was probated in 1859. This will names his old and infirm slaves and provides that they must not be sold, but cared for "at the expense of my estate."

The mother of Clementine Alsop was Dorothea Campbell of Caroline. This Campbell family has its seat at "Poplar Grove" near Golansville. Dorothea Campbell had brothers, Matthew, Elliott and William; and one sister, Mary, who married a Mr. Henderson. These Campbells were of the Duke of Argyle clan. Mr. and Mrs. Henderson had a daughter who married one Mr. Reynolds and whose descendants live in Richmond.

Members of the foregoing branch of the Chandler family have intermarried with members of the Kay, Campbell, Tompkins, Coleman and other families and have numerous descendants in Virginia and elsewhere. Thomas Kay Chandler, who died in Newport News in 1920, was a son of Thomas Coleman Chandler who married Miss Alsop. He (Thomas Kay Chandler) married the daughter of Dr. Benjamin Anderson, who was a brother of Henry Tompkins Anderson, the famous educator and translator. Thos. K. Chandler and his wife had issue: (1) Boyd D. Chandler, who m. Miss Jennie Frazer, of "Coventry" in Spotsylvania and had issue one daughter, Anne Boyd, who m. J. H. Rives, attorney of Richmond; (2) Roberta, who m. J. E. Warren, of Newport News and had issue one son, Bankhead Warren.

One of Thomas Coleman Chandler's brothers, Dr. Joseph A. Chandler, married Emuella Josephine White by whom he had several children, among them two sons, Julian Alvin Carroll Chandler and Campbell Chandler. J. A. C. Chandler, m. Lenore Burton Duke, of Churchlands, Va., and had issue three sons. Campbell Chandler, m. Annie Beasley, daughter of Chas. E. Beasley and Mary Jane Chandler, and had issue one son and one daughter, Charles and Jane Campbell. Campbell Chandler died in 1918 and his widow and two children reside at "Idlewild" near Guinea, which was built by Dr. Joseph Chandler. Dr. Chandler also built "Spring Grove" near Guinea which is now owned and occupied by his nephew, Cutler Beasley. Thomas Coleman Chandler, father of Dr. Joseph A. Chandler owned "Fairfield" near Guinea, when Stonewall Jackson died there.

"Burton Hall" stands on a beautiful knoll a few hundred yards from "Idlewild" and is owned and occupied by Mr. and Mrs. Clarence Flippo. Mrs. Flippo is a sister of Mrs. Campbell Chandler, who owns "Idlewild." "Burton Hall" was built by President J. A. C. Chandler, of William and Mary College, and named for his wife, Lenore Burton Duke. These two homes are among the most beautiful in Caroline, and within their walls the Old Virginia spirit and hospitality still survive in all their glory.

Rev. Richard Woolfolk Chandler was born *circa* 1730, and married Sarah Tompkins and had issue several children, among them being Timothy Chandler and Robert Chandler, who is mentioned in the foregoing as a co-petitioner with Edmund Pendleton.   Rev. Richard Woolfolk Chandler is buried at "Broomfield" in Caroline.

Timothy Chandler, son of Rev. Richard Woolfolk Chandler, was born September 29, 1761, and was married circa, 1788, to Lucy Temple, daughter of Captain Samuel Temple and Fanny Redd, of Caroline.   Captain Temple was sworn into service in the Revolutionary War in November, 1777, according to McAlister's Virginia Militia in the Revolutionary War, page 333. See also *Virginia Magazine* (published by Virginia Historical Society) Vol. 7, p. 20.   Militia section No. 223, p. 165; also No. 257 of Caroline and Virginia Library Report, vol. 1912, p. 431. Captain Samuel Temple, of Caroline, is listed in Auditor's Accounts of 1779, p. 155, and in Council Journals of 1782–3, pps. 125–209.

The children of Timothy Chandler and Lucy Temple were: Samuel Temple, Norborne E., Frances R., Leroy, John, Hugh, and Timothy, Jr.   The last named died young.   Norborne E. Chandler removed to Mobile, Ala., and there married Miss Rebecca B. Wiggins.   Hon. A. B. Chandler at one time owned portraits of this couple, representing the wife as a very beautiful woman, and the husband as a man of strong intellect and character. He was shown with the old goose quill pen in hand and full ruffled shirt bosom, and she with the quaint dress and coiffure of that period.   Samuel Temple Chandler, married a Miss Todd and settled in Rockbridge county, Va., and had two sons, Samuel Temple, Jr., a doctor of medicine, and Norborne E., and one daughter, Maria, who married Madison L. Effinger, of Rockbridge.   Both sons married daughters of one Grigsby family, of Rockbridge.

The widow of Samuel Temple Chandler and a number of his children removed to St. Louis, Mo., where they and their descendants became prominent.   The children of Norborne E. Chandler went to Chicago where they became wealthy and prominent men.   Frances R. married Fleming James, a prosperous merchant of Richmond.   Leroy Chandler removed to Missouri, where his descendants are numerous and prominent today. He was twice married. Hugh Chandler married Miss Virginia Wyatt, of Caroline, and by her had William Timothy Chandler who married Alice E. Scott, daughter of Francis W. Scott, of Caroline. Mrs. Alice Scott Chandler founded Bowling Green Female Seminary, which is now located at Beuna Vista, Va., under the name of Southern Seminary. William Timothy Chandler, her husband, practiced law in Bowling Green. John Chandler married Miss Ella Cook, of Norfolk or Portsmouth, and had no issue.

John Chandler, son of Timothy Chandler and Lucy Temple, was born in November, 1801. He was married on November 26, 1836, to Lucy Ann Coleman, the daughter of Benjamin Coleman and Elizabeth Chandler, of Caroline. To this union were born two children: Betty Ann in 1837, who married Dr. Samuel Dickenson, and Algernon Bertrand Chandler, in 1843. A very fine portrait of John Chandler is now owned by his grandson, Algernon Bertrand Chandler, Jr., President of the State Teacher's College at Fredericksburg, Va.

Algernon Bertrand Chandler, Sr., son of John Chandler and Lucy Ann Coleman, was born at "Woodlawn" in Caroline county, August 16, 1843, and educated at Washington and Lee University. He was married on September 10, 1867, to Julia Yates Callaghan, of Fincastle, Va. To this union were born nine children: (1) W. Temple, who was drowned at age of 14; (2) Algernon Bertrand, Jr., (3) John Washington, who lived and died in Houston, Tex.; (4) Ferdinand Wiley, attorney in Bowling Green; (5) Julia Yeatts, (6) Charles Guy, (7) Lucy and (8) Landon Spencer, twins; and (9) Edith Temple.

Leroy Chandler, son of Timothy Chandler and Lucy Temple, who has already been mentioned, was twice married—first, to Elvira Copeland in Richmond, Va., on October 8, 1817, and, second, to Sarah Ann Quarles, of Belmont, Louisa county, on April 21, 1825.

To Leroy Chandler and Elvira Copeland were born three daughters: (1) Frances Eliza, b. August 28, 1818; (2) Lucy Temple, b. January 20, 1820; (3) Virginia Ann, b. December 2, 1821. Frances Eliza married John W. Conner at Glen Burnie, Mo., June 6, 1838. Lucy Temple married James R. Payne at Glen Burnie, Mo., December 5, 1837. Virginia Ann married—first, Dr. John Field at Belmont, October 29, 1851; second, Jacob Keiser, of Woodlandville, Mo., on February 22, 1855.

To Leroy Chandler and Sarah Ann Quarles, his second wife,

were born thirteen children: (1) Charles Quarles, (2) Timothy, (3) Elvira Copeland, (4) Margaret Mills, (5) Mary Lewis, (6) John, (7) James (John and James twins), (8) Maria Louisa, (9) Sarah Ann, (10) Susan Henry, (11) Florence M., (12) Robert Leroy, (13) Kelly R.

Charles Quarles Chandler, eldest son of Leroy, was born January 26, 1826, at Belmont (or Belle Mont), Missouri. He married Ann Elizabeth Woods on October 10, 1861, and had issue: C. Q. Chandler, Jr., banker at Wichita, Kansas, and Mattie Leroy Chandler, who married H. J. Hammond, banker, and who for many years lived at Clayton, N. M.

Timothy Chandler, son of Leroy and Sarah Ann Quarles, married Louisa Temple, daughter of Dr. Peter Temple, and made his home at Lexington, Mo.

Elvira Copeland Chandler, dau. of Leroy, married Dr. Francis Carr in 1852 and had issue Frank E., John H., and Nannie. Frank E., a banker at Wellington, Kans., married and had four sons. John married and lived in St. Louis, Mo. He had two children. Nannie married Dr. ——— Ridgeway and removed to Seattle, Washington. They had two daughters.

Margaret Miles Chandler, dau. of Leroy, m. Augustus Goodman, of Gordonsville, Va., and had issue three daughters and two sons.

Mary Lewis Chandler, dau. of Leroy, m. Oren Tucker and had issue three daughters and two sons, all of whom live in St. Louis, Mo.

John and James Chandler were twin sons of Leroy. John was twice married and left at his death one daughter by his first wife and an infant son by his second. James left at his death one son who married and removed to Kansas City, Mo.

Mary Louisa, dau. of Leroy, m. Henry McPherson and had issue one daughter and two sons.

Sarah Ann, dau. of Leroy, m. Thomas L. Tucker and had issue ten children, all of whom reside in Cooper county, Miss.

Susan Henry, dau. of Leroy, m., first, James Wallace by whom she had a son and daughter, and, second, to a Mr. Collins, of Kansas City, Mo.

Florence M. Chandler, dau. of Leroy, m. a Mr. Ferguson and lived in Booneville, Mo.

Robert Leroy Chandler, son of Leroy, died at age of 28 unmarried.

Kelly R. Chandler, son of Leroy, m. Sarah Bowles and had issue one son. They lived in St. Louis, Mo.

At the opening of the twentieth century there were six children of Leroy Chandler living—one by his first wife and five by the last. They were: Mrs. Virginia Keiser (by the first wife), Woodlandsville, Mo.; Mrs. Mary L. Tucker, St. Louis, Mo.; Mrs. Maria L. McPherson, Booneville, Mo.; Mrs. Susan H. Collins, Kansas City, Mo.; Mrs. Florence M. Ferguson, Booneville, Mo., and Kelly R. Chandler, St. Louis, Mo.

Further light on the Chandler family and on Caroline county is given by the following:

REMINISCENSES OF A. B. CHANDLER

"About nine miles southwest of Bowling Green is Woodlawn, the present home of Dr. E. C. Cobb. This farm was owned by my grandfather, Benjamin Coleman, in 1843, and here I was born August 16, 1843, and lived her four years until my father, John Chandler, bought Elson Green, two miles north of Page's Bridge. At Elson Green I lived during my boyhood days until my father sold in 1863, and loaned the proceeds to the Confederate Government. He was a Whig and voted for Bell and Everett for President and Vice-President in 1860. He was, however, an ardent secessionist, and believing that if the United States Government could liberate the slaves contrary to the constitution, it could also confiscate our lands, and, therefore, he would risk all he had in the success of the Confederate cause. He did so and lost all.

"In my boyhood days up to 1858, I went to school in the 'old field schools,' as they were called, schools taught by a single teacher, in a log cabin of one room, built convenient for the neighborhood and by the patrons of the school, of pine logs chinked and daubed, with daubed wood chimneys, with one window and plain blank benches with no backs, generally made out of a slab from a saw-mill log. My teachers of those days, whose memory I recall with great pleasure, were Henry A. Ware, Henry C. Peatross and Wm. G. Taliaferro, father of our present W. G. Taliaferro. These were all fine men of old Virginia stock, intelligent, faithful and efficient. I wish I had space to give a short biographical sketch of each. While these schools were located as conviently as possible, I had to walk from two to five miles twice daily to reach them. Mosquitoes were superabundent in the bottoms of Caroline, and unmercifully innoculated us with malaria, though we did not know that malaria came from this source. Malaria, more than any other thing, interferred with the educational progress of that day. These schools were good schools, the teachers earnest and unremitting in their labors. The school hours were from 8:00 A. M. to 4:00 P. M., with one hour for recess at noon. The discipline was exacting, and, on occasion, the hickory was not spared. Children were taught spelling, reading, writing, arithmetic, geometry, algebra, history, and some Latin. In the fifties the weather was much more severe than in later years. It was but the usual thing to see the highways so covered with snow and ice that they were used for continuous sleighing for months at a time. In 1856 and 1857 we had two snows five or six feet deep, and in one of these years the public did not use the highways for months; not until spring weather melted the snow. In some cuts the snow was ten feet deep. The period of which I am writing was the period of slavery and the South's highest civilization. In no period of time, in no country of earth, did civilization and culture reach that of the South as it was immediately preceding our war between the States. I make no apology for African slavery; I am sorry it ever existed in Virginia. I never owned a slave, but my father owned many. This culture, I have spoken of, however, was based largely upon slavery. Every owner of a large plantation was lord of all he surveyed. He had ample leisure for reading the best literature of the day, and so had his family. The ladies of the house had only to direct the management of the household, with an ample supply of highly-trained servants. The young men spent their leisure time in neighborhood social gatherings and shooting partridges, frequently a single huntsman killing twenty or more birds a day. There were large neighborhood dinings, held first at one mansion and then at another, at which all the familes of the neighborhood gathered, and the tables groaned under the superabundance of all things tempting the appetite of man. The sons and daughters of this class of whom I am now writing were sent, after finishing their 'old field school' training, to the very best colleges and universities to properly equip them to maintain their station in life. The sons either succeeded their fathers as owners of the old homestead or filled the learned professions, generally law and medicine.

"Upon the principle of *suggestio falsi suppressio veri* (a suggestion of falsehood is suppression of truth), I trust the present generation of Caroline may not be shocked when I record that, at these neighborhood feasts not only were there abundant solids, but there were placed on the sideboards an abundance of crushed loaf sugar and ice, mint, and several varieties of old Bourbon and rye. A peculiarity of our people of that generation was that, whenever one citizen became offended with another they rarely adjusted their differences at that time, but adjourned the matter until the next court day, then when they met they would fight it out on the court green. I remember witnessing a man on the court green going up to another very upright and peaceful citizen, and putting his fist under his nose, gave the nose a very severe punch upward. The citizen punched did not resent the very severe intrusion on his nose, which brought the blood, but simply took out his large bandanna handkerchief and wiped off the blood. Thus culture and degredation, virtue and vice seem to move on together through the ages.   *   *   *   *   *

"I arrived home at my grandmother's in June, 1865, too late to do more than to sow some wild oats during the remainder of that year. The next year, 1866, I rented land and made a crop, sold the crop in the fall, sold my horse (all I had saved from the war), and borrowed $100.00 from a friend and started in the fall for Washington and Lee University to study law under Judge Brockenbrough, who had a private law school in Lexington, which was absorbed by the university that year. In June, 1867, I came home to Caroline with my diploma, certifying that I was a Bachelor of Law, and I did more than this, I also brought home with me in the same year my wife. Studying law and desperately loving at the same time do not usually run smoothly together. I succeeded in both simply because the love disease did not violently seize me until near the end of my collegiate term. This brings me to the fall of 1867, when I came to Bowling Green to live and start the battle of life.

"Before proceeding from this date I wish to go back to the fifties and call attention to the fact that, in a few of those years there were in Caroline and Virginia, literally millions of wild pigeons in the fall. They were so numerous that they went in great flocks, and darkened the sky in their flight. They fed on acrons, and thousands upon thousands of them were shot and trapped. They were a little smaller than our domestic pigeons, and of solid slate color. They have now almost disappeared, there being only a few in one county in New Jersey, and an effort is being made to protect these by law.   The robin, too, was very numerous in those days.   The highways were lined with cedars full of berries, and thousands of robins during the entire winter were in these trees, and thousands were shot.   This bird, while it continues to be with us, is now very scarce and we see but few of them, and these only in the spring of the year.   It is wonderful how various species of both animals and birds disappear altogether from age to age and other species take their place. Man yet remains, although many races have degenerated and been blotted out, while other races have advanced and developed in body and soul nearer their Creator.   It all depends upon the degree of success they attained in living up to and practising the tenets of life as laid in Christ's Sermon on the Mount.

"The period of time from 1867 into the seventies was the period of reconstructing the South.   We were fought by the North on the theory that we could not secede from the Union, but when we were 'frazzled out,' then we were considered out of the union and had to be brought back.   The negroes were given the right of suffrage by constitutional amendment, and the Southern States were forced to ratify this amendment as a condition precedent to their re-admission to the Union.   A constitutional convention was called in Virginia, while it was Military District No. 1, ruled by Gen. Canby of the Federal army.   This convention sat in Richmond, composed largely of 'gentlemen' of pure African descent, half breeds, carpetbaggers and scalawags, which framed a constitution disfranchising a very large portion of the best white people of the State for participating in the rebellion.   General Grant was President and permitted the people to vote for the constitution, and at the same time vote against the clause of the same which disfranchised our white people.   At the same time that we voted on the constitution we voted for a governor and members of the legislature.   This was in 1869, and politics were at red heat.   The whites were linked up solidly on one side and the blacks on the other.   The result of the election was that the constitution was ratified with the disfranchising clause stricken out.   Caroline elected Capt. J. M. Hudgin and Maj. R. O. Peatross to the House of Delegates by 170 majority over Tukey and Crockett, the latter colored.   Thus we got back into the union.   The political contest between the whites and blacks kept up many years, and all kinds of means and devices were employed to keep the State from negro domination.   Frederick S. Tukey, a Massachusetts Yankee, was sent to Caroline as head of the Freedmen's bureau. He was personally a kind dispositioned man, but a South hater, and while the whites tried to conciliate the blacks and induce them to vote with us, since their interests were identified with ours, Tukey invariably told them to first find out how the whites were going to vote and then they must vote directly opposite. The blacks, with their new acquired freedom, and the belief instilled into them that the South was responsible for their slavery, and that they owed their freedom to the North, were easily led and consolidated against the whites. Some few of them always voted with the whites but if it was discovered they were ostracised and otherwise ill treated by their color. The people of Virginia and the South saw that their civilization was in peril, that under no circumstances could they afford to see ignorant black men holding positions as magistrates, legislators and judges, and hence every means was resorted to to prevent these catastrophies.

"I was young and full of spizzerinktum, hence soon found myself deep in politics. Whether the end justified the means I need not at this late day discuss. It was so deemed by our people, and no means available were omitted to have the offices of the State filled by white people. The colored people on election day would choose a ticket holder, and he put all the ballots intended for the negroes in a bag folded, and each voter was instructed to get his ballot from this ticket holder. On a certain occasion two gentlemen, the night before election, met in an office in Bowling Green to determine what had better be done to make safe the election of the next day. They got hold of a colored man, whom they thought they could trust, and paid him to take $5.00 to a distant precinct, and fifty Democratic ballots, and to give both the five dollars and the fifty ballots to the negro ticket holder of that precinct for use the next day. The scheme worked and this far-off precinct, which usually gave 75 Republican majority gave 50 Democratic majority. The negroes were greatly puzzled; they knew something had happened but just how the thing was done they did not know.

"Since I am speaking of the relationship between the races I will say that I have always found the negro kind and friendly, courteous and respectful, ready to lend a helping hand to one in need, and as reliable in the performance of their engagement as other people. Many of them are among our very best citizens.

" When I located at Bowling Green, the first of October, 1867, to enter upon the practice of my profession (this was my purpose but I had no clients) I stuck up my shingle. Having a wife to support, as well as myself, I could not wait for clients. There being no common schools at that date, I rented a portion of the building now owned by Dr. Butler and secured patrons enough to give me a good school and taught this for one session and a half when I relinquished the school and gave my time to the practice of my profession.   When I came to the bar, it was a large and eminent one.   From the City of Richmond came James Lyons, Travis Daniel, Chastain White, of Holladay, Bailey and White, Mr. Griswold, and from Fredericksburg came John L. Marye, Jr., with whom was associated shortly afterwards St. Geo. R. Fitzhugh, Braxton and Wallace (Elliott M. Braxton and Wistar Wallace), A. W. Wallace, Wm. A. Little and W. S. Barton and occasionally others from that city.   Mr. John L. Marye, the father of John L. Mayre, Jr., was then an old man and retiring from the practice, though he usually came down to enjoy himself and be with the fraternity.   He was a bright and jovial man, full of anecdote and wit and could tell a good joke and enjoy it as much as any man I ever knew, expressing his joy in hearty laughter.   The Caroline resident bar embraced John Washington, Scott & Chandler, (F. W. Scott and W. T. Chandler), E. C. Moncure, Walter G. Hudgin, John M. Hudgin, T. N. Welch and R. O. Peatross.   These were practicing attorneys when the War between the States commenced.   This was the Bar when I joined it in 1867.   When the new constitution for the State became effective after the war, and the County Court was created with a single judge, Walter G. Hudgin was elected Judge and presided over the Court for several terms, being succeeded by T. N. Welch when the re-adjusters (so called) in combination with the Republicans captured the State.   Welch (as Congressman Harris said) was a 'Re-adjuster in the cool.' We lived under this motley judicial reign until this combination was overthrown when E. C. Moncure succeeded Judge Welch as Judge of the County Court and held the position until the County Court was abolished.   Judge John Critcher was Judge of the Circuit Court when I came to the bar and was succeeded by Judge Wm. S. Barton (*venerrabile et clarissimo nomen*), of Fredericksburg. This order was true, except for a short period during reconstruction when Virginia was in a military district ruled over by General

Canby, who removed Judge Critcher and appointed a man named Thompson.

"The old bar was composed of men of exalted conceptions of the dignity and honor of their profession and the most genial and sociable of men. Many of the men I have named were profound in learning and eloquent in debate. In those days the Circuit Court, which had jurisdiction in most civil and criminal cases, met only twice a year, and usually continued in session from two to three weeks. Most of the attorneys put up at the Lawn Hotel, and at nights would meet in social intercourse, and have a most enjoyable time, telling anecdotes and discussing the intricate problems of law. We had many strong men at the bar. James Lyons was tall and well proportioned, and while not quite as forceful in debate as Mr. Daniel, was one of the most suave and polished men I ever knew. Chastain White, with a large, bald head, was a good, all round, forceful man, and continued to practice law in Caroline longer than any of the Richmond lawyers. George Ridgely Dorsey, father of our present County Treasurer, came to us from Maryland. Having been a Confederate soldier he found a more congenial atmosphere in Caroline than in his native State. I would name him as the most brilliant member of the old Caroline bar. Certainly no one of equal intellectuality has succeeded him. The ethics of the profession were very high and scrupulously maintained. I am sorry I can not affirm same to be true of all men who have joined the profession since that time. Next to the ministry the bar has the power to be of the greatest good to mankind, but it all depends upon whether or not they use their great offices in allaying or fomenting strife.

"In speaking of the bar I can not omit to say a word about our most excellent sheriff of that day. A lawyer cannot prosper very much without a good sheriff. Mr. Geo. W. Marshall was sheriff and no one could possibly have discharged the duties of the office better than he did. The sheriff not only attended to the law business of the bar, but he also collected the public revenue. Having the public revenue to collect, the sheriff was thus the better enabled to collect money on executions by combining the two collections. Mr. Marshall was very fine at this and, in many instances, I have had him collect money for me when it could not have been made by forceful proceedings. He was exceedingly genial, sociable and polite, and a universal favorite with the bar and the public."

THE CHAPMAN FAMILY

The name Chapman is of Saxon origin. The Saxon word chapman means a chapman, marketman, merchant, monger or cheapner. The several American branches of this family had their origin in England where the family has long been prominent, letters of nobility having been granted as early as the fifteenth century. In 1854 it was estimated that more than twenty members of this family were clergymen in the Established Church in England.

The Royal Book of Crests (London 1863) shows the crests of ten different branches of the Chapman family. The different families have, however, the same coat of arms which is described, as follows:

Arms: Per chev. argent and gu. in the centre a crescent counterchanged.

Crest: Arm embowered in armour holding a broken spear encircled with a wreath.

Motto: *Crescit sub pondere virtus.*

The first members of this family to come to Virginia were Richard and Thomas Chapman who arrived on the ship *"Tryali"* in 1610. Other members of the family came on the ship *"Bonaventure"* April 3, 1635 and from this date to the present the family of Chapman has had unbroken representation in Virginia.

The family is not largely represented in Caroline today, but in the past has been one of the largest, wealthiest and most influential. Of the Caroline house, now residing out of the county, there are known to the author Professor William Robert Chapman, of Lois, Fairfax county, son of the late Orville Claud Chapman and Lucy Ann Green. Professor Chapman was born in 1872 and is a great nephew of Reuben Chapman who was the eleventh Governor of Alabama. Mrs. Lillian Chapman Hudson, of Alameda, California, published the genealogy of the Chapmans in 1894, and to this work the reader is referred for more complete genealogical data.

Reuben Chapman, eleventh Governor of Alabama, was born in Caroline county, near Bowling Green, and was the son of Colonel Reuben Chapman and Anne Reynolds. His father was a soldier in the Revolutionary War. His mother was a native of Essex county, Va. He was educated in Caroline and in 1824 removed to Alabama, making the journey on horseback. He settled in Huntsville and read law in the office of his brother Judge Samuel Chapman who had preceded him to Alabama by several years. On his admission to the Bar, Reuben Chapman established himself at Somerville, Morgan county. In 1832 he was elected to the State Senate, and in 1835 he was elected to Congress by a large majority over R. T. Scott, of Jackson, and William H. Glascock, of Madison. Two years later he was re-elected over Governor Gabriel Moore, his majority being six thousand three hundred.

In the four succeeding elections he had no opposition save in 1841, when the Hon. John T. Rather, of Morgan county, was a candidate on the Whig ticket. Among the questions voted on during his term of office was the issue of Treasury notes, which he favored.

He was elected Governor of Alabama in 1847, his opponent being Hon. Nicholas Davis, of Limestone county. It was said that he received the nomination entirely without solicitation, and in order to remove him from his apparently life-time contract with the people of his district to represent them in Congress. His inauguration was rendered remarkable in a social way by a public reception given by him at Montgomery on a scale of extraordinary liberality and hospitality. When he was inducted into the office of Governor, Alabama was financially embarassed because of the mismanagement of the affairs of the State Bank and its trustees. He had the good fortune to be able to remedy the difficulty and relieve the Treasury. His term was characterized by wisdom and devotion to duty, as was acknowledged by all. In the Convention which chose his successor he received a majority of votes but yielded to the "two-thirds rule," which he believed to be right. He then withdrew from political life and devoted himself to the care of a handsome estate until 1855, when, on the demand of the Democratic party, he consented to become a candidate for a seat in the State Legislature in opposition to the Hon. Jeremiah Clemens, who represented what was then known as the American Party. This was his last political experience except that he was several times a delegate in the National Conventions of his party.

Soon after retiring from official service he went with his family to Europe, and was residing in France when the Civil War began. He then came home and attended the Baltimore Convention, held in the interest of peace, doing his best to bring about reconciliation between the Northern and Southern representatives, and nearly succeeding. During the Civil War he was imprisoned, and his home and property were destroyed by Federal troops.

During the career of Mr. Chapman in Congress many questions of vital importance to the country came up for consideration, and it was said that few statesmen ever exercised more sagacity with reference to the interests of his country, or exhibited greater familiarity with its political history.

In the community where he lived it was said of him that, "his worth and weight could not be measured, for in all matters requiring manhood, judgement and honor, personal or political, he stood forth as an exemplar and a sage."

Governor ·Chapman was a man of splendid figure and proportion, erect in his carriage, handsome in feature and frank in expression. He was married in 1839 to Felicia Steptoe, daughter of Colonel Steptoe and Sarah Chilton Pickett, of Faquier county, Va., but then residing in Limestone county, Ala. They had two daughters and two sons, one of whom was killed in battle during the Civil War. Governor Chapman died in Huntsville, Ala., on May 17, 1882, at the age of nearly four score years. For a more detailed biography the reader is referred to the *National Cyclopaedia of American Biography*.

THE CARTER FAMILY

According to the Carter MSS of 1858, by Colonel Norborne Sutton, which are liberally quoted in the book—*The Descendants of Capt. Thomas Carter*—by Dr. Joseph Lyon Miller, of Thomas, W. Va., the first Carter to settle in Caroline was John Carter, son of Thomas, of Lancaster. He was married on November 21, 1798, to Frances Ball, eldest daughter of Col. Joseph Ball, and a sister of Mary, the mother of Washington. Upon his marriage to Miss Ball he settled in territory which became Caroline county in 1727, and here his youthful bride died on September 3d of the following year. He married 2d a Miss Payne, by whom he had several daughters. Upon her death he married 3d on January 4, 1714, to Miss Margaret Todd, daughter of Wm. Todd, of "Toddsbury" Gloucester county. By this third marriage he had issue: John Carter II, James, Robert and William.

John Carter II, of "Nomini Hall" was born in 1715 in that part of King and Queen which in 1727 became Caroline, and was a Captain in the Revolutionary War. He married 1st Elizabeth Armistead, b. 1716, daughter of Francis and Sarah Armistead, of Richmond county, and had issue: William, John III, Robert, Mrs. Hillman, Mrs. Nancy Bayliss, Mrs. Marshall and Mrs. Sarah Sutton, who was the grandmother of Col. Norborne Sutton. John Carter II, m. the second time to Hannah Chew, daughter of John Chew, Justice of the Peace in Spotsylvania county, and Margaret Beverly, of "Newlands" Spotsylvania. By this second marriage he had issue: Mary, Lucy, Margaret, Judith, Elizabeth and Robert. Seven of his daughters and two of his sons left descendants in Caroline, King and Queen and King William counties.

Sarah Carter, daughter of John Carter, II, by his first marriage, m. William Sutton, of Caroline and had issue: Bettie Sutton, Sarah Sutton and John Carter Sutton.

Bettie Sutton, daughter of William Sutton and Sarah Carter, m. a Mr. Chapman and had issue three sons and two daughters: James, Reuben, Robert, Martha and Lucy. Her son Reuben was the father of the eleventh Governor of Alabama, Reuben Chapman, of whom see Chapman Family. Sarah Sutton, daughter of William Sutton and Sarah Carter, m. Robert Lewis, of Spotsylvania. He was the son of Dr. John Lewis and the brother of Doctors Zachariah and John Lewis. John Carter Sutton, of "Pine Forest" on the Mattaponi, son of William Sutton and Sarah Carter, m. 1st, his cousin, Maria Chew Sutton, daughter of Joseph Sutton and Judith Carter, and by this marriage had one son, John Oliver Sutton.

John Carter Sutton m. 2d, Elizabeth Page Pendleton, only child of Edmund Pendleton III, great nephew of the famous jurist Edmund Pendleton. This Edmund Pendleton, great nephew of the jurist, m. Jane Burwell Page, daughter of John Byrd Page and lived at "Edmundton" in Caroline, which had been given to him by his great uncle, Judge Edmund Pendleton. His father, a nephew of the great jurist, was also named Edmund and lived at "White Plains" in Caroline, now owned by Rev. Andrew Broaddus III. This Edmund Pendleton II, of "White Plains" was the son of the Hon. John Pendleton, of whom Rev. Philip Slaughter wrote in his "St. Mark's Parish" as follows:

"John, 4th son of Henry Pendleton and Mary Taylor, was

born in 1719 and died in 1799. He held various offices of trust and honor in the Colony and in the Senate. He was appointed by a Convention of Delegates of the Counties and Corp. of Virginia at Richmond on Monday, July 17, 1775, to sign a large issue of Treasury notes. The issue was about 350,000 pounds, and the Ordinance read: 'Of the notes to be issued 50,000 shall be of the denomination of one shilling and shall be signed by John Pendleton, Jr., Gentleman, which notes shall be on the best paper.' Later he was appointed by the Governor of Virginia a Judge of the County Court. He was a grandson of Philip Pendleton who was born in England in 1650 and came to Virginia in 1676."

John Carter Sutton and Elizabeth Page Pendleton had issue: (1) Edmund Pendleton Sutton, (2) William Carter Sutton, (3) Hugh Carter Sutton, (4) Norborne E. Sutton, (of whom see biography elsewhere in this volume) (5) John Carter Sutton, (6) Robert W. Sutton, (7) Patrick H. Sutton, (8) Sarah Jane Sutton, (9) Lucy Carter Sutton, (10) Anne Lewis Sutton and (11) Betty Burwell Sutton.

William Carter, who was named for his grandfather William Todd, settled on the family estate in Caroline. His name appears in the old Order Books of Caroline in connection with various suits between 1745 and 1770. Norborne Sutton's MSS of the Carters of Spotsylvania states that William Carter left descendants in Caroline.

George Carter, of Christ Church Parish, Lancaster, was born in 1725, married a Miss Beale, of Westmoreland and settled in Caroline in 1750. His children were: Charles, Edward, John, Richard, Thompson, Spencer, George, Presley, Betsy, Peggy, Sally. He received grants of land in Halifax county in 1766 and 1768, and not long thereafter removed to that county with all his family save John who married in Caroline and remained in the county, where he kept a tavern. The Caroline Order Books covering the period 1795-1798 mentions his "Ordinary Bond." His children, according to the Caroline marriage register, married as follows: Thompson Carter, m. Polly Farmer, December 22, 1814; Spencer Carter, m. Sarah Fletcher, March 24, 1815; Charles Carter, m. Matilda Hans, December 18, 1818; George Carter, m. Anne Shackelford, December 18, 1818.

Owen and Griffin Carter (probably brothers) of the Essex family, settled in Caroline about 1745 and established homes and became the heads of families.

John Carter, of "Nomini Hall" inherited "North Wales" an estate of nearly ten thousand acres lying along Pamunkey and North Anna Rivers, on the southern border of Caroline. This land had been granted to one of his ancestors some time before by the British Crown, and the estate remained in possession of the Carter family for nearly two centuries, passing into other hands in 1896. The original manor house, a very imposing structure of early colonial type, was burned many years ago, but a number of the houses of the "quarters" and the overseers house, are still standing.

The Carters of "North Wales" were connected with the Todd, Chew, Bell, Sutton, Chapman, Lewis, Pendleton, Taylor and Lee families. It is said General Lee visited "North Wales" shortly before his death. The plantation is now owned by Messrs. Frederick and Adolph Usinger, of Milwaukee.

It appears that the present Carter families of Caroline are descended from William Carter, son of John Carter and Margaret Todd. Philip Carter, grandson of William Carter, m. a Miss Hackney in 1807 and had issue four sons and one daughter. His son Peter Carter married Sarah Hill and settled at "Mt. Gideon" near "North Wales," and had issue: Edward, Hill, James and Mattie.

John Carter, Armistead Carter, Captain John Carter, of Caroline, served in the War of the Revolution. And in the War of 1812 the 30th Regiment, from Caroline, had seven Carters on its roll, namely: James Carter, James B. Carter, Vicman Carter, Joseph Carter, Spencer M. Carter, Philip Carter and Charles Carter. The Voters List for 1923 shows that Caroline had forty-one white voters bearing the name Carter.

The Carter arms were granted many hundred years ago. It is said that the name, as well as the arms, was derived from their occupation as carters, indicated by the four wheels on the escutcheon. Some authorities say that the original Carter was, if we may use such an espression, Master of Transportation for one of the Kings of England. In ancient days when rivalry for the crown made violent deeds of frequent occurrence, the King, owing to the vicissitudes of war, had to move frequently and sometimes very quickly. The carter was an important man in his retinue, as the only means of transportation in those days was by cart or wagon.

THE COGHILL FAMILY

The earliest ancestors of the Coghill family had their home in York, England, and can be traced back in a direct line to Knaresborough, 1378, on the paternal side, and to 1135, on the maternal—the Slingsbys of Scriven Hall.

The origin of the name Coghill, says Playfair in his *British Family Antiquary*, volume 7, page 226, was probably derived from a place anciently called Cockle-Hall, now Coghill Hall, in Yorkshire; or perhaps from the residence of one of the family on a hill near the river Cocke, which runs through the country.

The first ancestor, according to records in the Castle of Knaresborough, was John Coghill, or Cockhill, of "Cockhill" who resided in the county of York in the reign of Henry IV (1378–1413). From John Coghill, of "Cockhill" the American branch of the family is descended. (See *The Family of Coghill*, by James Henry Coghill, which was published by The Riverside Press (Cambridge) in 1879).

The first member of the Coghill family to reside in America, so far as the record goes, was Samuel Coghill, who under date of February 20, 1662, was granted four hundred acres of land lying on the north side of the Rappahannock River in Farnham Parish in what is now Richmond county. The patent was never recorded, which fact led the family historian above mentioned to conclude that he failed to take possession. The name is not found again and it is presumed that he died in the colony soon after his arrival or else returned to England.

The progenitor of the Coghills, of Caroline, who have played so important a part in the life of the county, was James Coghill. He received three patents to land for the transportation of persons to the colony, which patents and deeds are of record in the Land Office. The first is dated March 24, 1664, and is for 246 acres lying in Essex, that part which afterward became Caroline, and is for the transportation of five persons. The second patent bears date of April 17, 1667, and is for one thousand and fifty acres lying in old Rappahannock county. The third patent is dated April 17, 1667, and is for six hundred acres in old Rappahannock county.

The Coghill family has given many great men to England, among whom may be mentioned Sir John Jocelyn Coghill, Bart. of Glen Barrahane, Castle Townsend; Marmaduke Coghill, LL. D.,

Chancellor of the Exchequer, Privy Counsellor and member of Parliament; Lieutenant Nevill J. A. Coghill; John Coghill, of London, and Sir Thomas Coghill, Knight, of Blechingdon.

Probably no family has had a larger place in the life of Caroline county during the past two hundred years than the family of Coghill. Among the many members of this family now active in the affairs of the county may be mentioned E. R. Coghill, Clerk of the Circuit Court for many years, and one of the best loved men who has ever lived in the county; his son, E. S. Coghill, Deputy Clerk, and Major T. D. Coghill, brother of E. R., and for many years Sheriff of the county and otherwise prominent in public life. R. A. Coghill, son of Major Coghill, has long been a prominent merchant in Bowling Green.

The Coghill arms are thus described:

Gules on a chevron; argent, three pellets, a chief, sable.

Crest: On a mount, vert, a cock, wings expanded or.

Motto: *Non dormit qui custodit.*

THE COLEMAN FAMILY

EXPLANATORY NOTES—A, B, C, and etc., denotes generations.; 1, 2, 3, and etc., denotes order, according to birth; X denotes one of direct line from whom descent is traced; ½ added to a number denotes person who married into the family; C C or B B mean contemporary generations of C or B of collateral lines.

(*a*) *John Coleman, 1st,* son of Sir James Coleman of Braxton, Mango, Essex county, England, settled in Fairfax county, Va., in 1640, and married a Miss Hawes of King William county, Va. ISSUE:

(*b* 1) James Coleman, 1st.

(*b* 2) Hawes Coleman, 1st.

(*b* 3) John Coleman 2d.

(*b* 4) June Coleman.

(*b* 5) Robert Coleman, 1st.

(*b* 5) *Robert Coleman,* married [Elizbeth Lindsay, and had issue as follows:

(*c* 1) Wyatt Coleman.

(*c* 2) Samuel Coleman, 1st.

(*c* 3) Robert Coleman, 2d.

(*c* 4) Thomas Coleman.

(c 5) John Coleman 3d, b. 1723, d. 1763. Married Eunice Hawes, b. 1725, d. 1807.

(c 6) Richard Coleman.

(c 7) Spilsby Coleman.

(c 5) *John Coleman, 3d*, who married Nicie Hawes, had issue as follows:

(d 1) Samuel Coleman 2d, married Sarah Coleman.

(d 2) John Coleman 4th, married Molly Coleman.

(d 3) Hawes Coleman, Jr., b. 1757, d. 1840. Married Anne Harris, b. 1756, d. 1809.

(d 4) Frances Coleman, m. Joseph Graves.

(d 5) Mary Anne Coleman, m. William Blades.

(d 6) Spencer Coleman, married Miss Goodwin. He died 1830.

(d 3) *Hawes Coleman, Jr.*, who m. Anne Harris, had issue as follows:

(e 1) William Harris Coleman, b. 1787, d. 1842; m. Anne Hawes, b. 1793, d. 1852.

(e 2) Hawes Netherland Coleman, b. 1788, d. 1876.

(e 3) Mary Coleman, b. 1790, d. 1824; m. John Warner Harris, in 1811.

(e 4) John Joy Coleman, b. 1797, d. 1869; m. in 1819, Catherine Walker Hawes, b. 1800, d. 1876.

In the Genealogical Column of the *Times-Dispatch* (Richmond), of March 29, 1908, appeared the following item concerning the Coleman family:

"In the Spotsylvania County Records of 1738 mention is made of William Coleman, of St. John's Parish in King William county, son and heir of Darby Coleman, deceased, of King and Queen county. In 1732 James Coleman is a legatee in the will of Ambrose Madison. In 1744 there is a deed of Edward Coleman and Lucrea, his wife. In 1795 is a will of Edward Coleman mentioning his wife, Sarah, and sons James and Thomas; grandson James (son of Robert Edward Coleman) and other children, Caty Waggoner, Phoebe Hutcherson, Henry, James and William.

"It appears from the will of Spilsby Coleman, 1757, that 'Robert Coleman, Gent., of Drysdale Parish' in Caroline county had five sons: Thomas, Robert, John, Richard, and the said Spilsby; and a daughter, the wife of William Daniel. In 1745 this Robert Coleman of Caroline deeded lands to his son John, of Spotsylvania, and the deed is witnessed by Leonard Wyatt,

Samuel Hawes, Thomas and Wyatt Coleman. In the same year the said Robert deeded land to his son Robert, of Spotsylvania. In 1745 Robert Coleman and Sarah, his wife, living in Spotsylvania on the land given him by his father, Robert Coleman. This second Robert Coleman had a son named Robert who lived in Orange and later in Culpeper, as appears from deeds of 1748 and 1761, in one of which he mentions lands he patented in Spotsylvania in 1744. Besides his son Robert, of Orange and Culpeper, he had sons, James, of Orange; Reuben, Lindsey, Caleb, Joseph and Clayton; and daughters: Sally and Molly, who married, respectively, their cousins Samuel and John Coleman, sons of the John aforementioned. This John Coleman's wife was Nicie Hawes whose name appears in the foregoing table.

"Reuben Coleman, son of Robert, 2d, died in Georgia in 1797, and in that year is recorded a power of attorney to John Waller, of Georgia and John Coleman, of Amherst county, to secure for the following their rights in the Reuben Coleman estate: (1) Robert, Samuel, Clayton, Rebecca, Nancy, Frances, and Nicie Coleman, children of Samuel Coleman, of Caroline county, whose late wife, Sally, was sister of Reuben Coleman deceased; (2) George, Lindsey, John and Hawes Coleman, children of John Coleman, of Caroline county, whose late wife, Molly, was also a sister of said Reuben; (3) Thomas (then of age), Wilson, James, Elizabeth, Sally, Nancy, Polly and Catherine Coleman, children of James Coleman, deceased, of Orange county and brother of said Reuben; and (4) Lindsey, Caleb, Joseph and Clayton Coleman, brothers of the said Reuben Coleman, deceased. Witnesses to this paper were Robert Coleman, Farish Coleman and Farish Coleman, Jr.

"The Rev. Mr. Slaughter in his *St. Mark's Parish* says that this Robert Coleman 3d, was the first of the name in Culpeper and that he m. Sarah Ann Saunders and had one son, Robert, and eight daughters, of whom Gilly, m. General Edward Stevens, of Revolutionary fame; Anne m. Samuel Clayton, her cousin; Lucy, m. the Hon. French Strother, of Culpeper; and the others m. respectively, Francis Slaughter, Col. John Slaughter; ——— Foster, ——— Yancey, ——— Crutcher. Philip Clayton was executor of the will of Robert Coleman of Culpeper."

John Joy Coleman, whose name is the last mentioned in the foregoing table, m. Catherine Walker Hawes on June 17, 1819, and had, among other issue, Dr. Hawes Nicholas Coleman (the

Nicholas in this name comes from the Nicholas Spencer family with which the Coleman-Hawes family was connected) who was born at Wintergreen, Nelson county, September 18, 1825, and m. Nannie Elizabeth Watson, daughter of Dr. Daniel E. Watson, of Albemarle, in 1863. Dr. Hawes Nicholas Coleman was a member of the House of Delegates 1861–63.

The children of Dr. Hawes Nicholas Coleman and Nannie Elizabeth Watson are as follows: The late J. Tinsley Coleman, of Lynchburg, lawyer and member of the House of Delegates 1889–90, died 1916; Daniel Edward Coleman, merchant of Lynchburg, died 1899; Aylett B. Coleman, Lawyer, of Roanoke, Va., and member of the House of Delegates 1904–06; Maury Joy Coleman, lawyer, of Roanoke, died 1898; Charles O. Coleman, Pennsylvania Railway official, home on Long Island, N. Y.; Mrs. Arthur T. Ewing, of "Elk Hill" Nelson county; and Mrs. J. Fulton Williams, of Charlottesville. To Mrs. Williams the author is greatly indebted for much of the foregoing material.

Other members of the Coleman family whose names merit a permanent place in this work are:

Samuel Coleman, of Caroline, Ensign 8th Virginia, 1776; 2d Lieutenant, February, 1777; 1st Lieutenant in 1st Continental Artillery, June 15, 1778; killed at Camden, August 16, 1780.

Richard Coleman, of Caroline, Ensign in 7th Virginia; transferred to 5th on September 14, 1778; 1st Lieutenant in 1780.

John Coleman, Ensign 2d Virginia, July 4, 1779.

McAllister's Virginia Militia of Revolutionary War, Section 257, page 193, shows Samuel Coleman, of Caroline county, was commissioned a captain of Militia in January, 1779.

Samuel Coleman, m. Sarah Coleman (daughter of his uncle, Robert Coleman, and Elizabeth Lindsay) and had issue, four daughters and three sons: (1) Rebecca, m. Mr. Bosher; (2) Frances, m. John Gatewood; (3) Nancy, unmarried; (4) Eunice Hawes, m. Major Wm. Harris Diggs and lived in Nelson county; (5) Robert, unmarried; (6) Clayton, m. Elizabeth Cross, of Hanover county, Va., whose mother was a Miss Harris and her mother was Miss Nelson, of Hanover county, Va.; (7) Samuel lived at "Marl Hill," near Penola, Caroline county and died in 1862 at Bowling Green. He m. first, Ann DeJarnette in 1804. His second wife, was Mary Withers (niece of first wife and daughter of Edward Withers and Mary DeJarnette). Issue by second

marriage: Charles, Robert and Edward, unmarried; Samuel, m.
Emma Jordan; Waller, m. Sallie Duerson; Rebecca, first wife of
George Keith Taylor; Cornelia, m. Arthur Lewis; Susan, m.
Luther Wright (Captain Confederate Army); Mary Z., m. John
Ware, (Captain Confederate Army); Ottawa, m. James Wright;
Huldah, m. Boyd Brooks, Washington, D. C.; Hawes second wife
of George Keith Taylor.

Corbin Arms

THE CORBIN FAMILY

The name Corbin has been associated with the history of
Virginia since the earliest colonial times. The Hon. Henry
Corbin came to the colony in 1650 and resided, first, in Stratton
Major Parish in King and Queen county, and afterward at
Buckingham House where he died in 1676. He was a member
of the King's Council and a burgess from Lancaster. His portrait,
in his robes of office as Councillor of State of England may still
be seen at "Mt. Airy" the estate of the Tayloe family in Richmond county.

Major Richard Corbin, a descendant of the Hon. Henry
Corbin, owned the estate called "Moss Neck" in Caroline county,
and commanded a company of artillery in the War of 1812.

The Hon. Francis Corbin, of "The Reeds" in Caroline county
was the son of Col. Richard Corbin and Elizabeth Tayloe. He

was born in 1760 and educated at Cambridge, England, and the Temple, London. He m. Anna Munford Beverly, daughter of Colonel Robert Beverly, of "Blandfield," in Essex.

Robert Beverly, son of Colonel Robert, of "Blandfield" came into possession of "The Reeds" in Caroline, which had been the home of his sister, Mrs. Francis Corbin. He m., first Rebecca Sims, of Philadelphia, and second, Mary Mills, of Richmond. His children assumed their mother's maiden name, and one of them, Nicholas Mills, M. D., was living unmarried at "The Reeds" as late as 1809.

The Hon. John Corbin, of "Port Tobago" in Caroline was the second son of the Hon. Gawin Corbin, of "Peckatone" and "Lanesville" in King and Queen county. He was born in 1710, educated in England, and m. his cousin, Letitia Lee, of London.

Gawin Corbin, son of the Hon. John Corbin, of "Port Tobago" inherited the estate and m. Elizabeth, daughter of Col. Thomas Jones, of Northumberland.

George Lee Corbin, son of Gawin, of "Port Tobago" was one of the most prominent men of Caroline in his day.

The Corbin arms are thus described:

Arms: Sable on a chief or, three ravens of the first, all proper. Motto: *Probitas vertus honos.*

THE DEW FAMILY

Thomas R. Dew, the son of William, who came from England and settled in King and Queen in the opening years of the eighteenth century, was born in 1765 and died in 1849. He m. Lucy Gatewood, of Caroline and had issue six sons and three daughters: Dr. William Dew, Thomas R. Dew, President of William and Mary College; Philip Dew, John W. Dew, Benjamin F. Dew, L. Calvin Dew, Mrs. Hudgins, of Mathews; Mrs. Thomas Gresham and Mrs. Temple.

He was a large land and slave owner in King and Queen, (near the Caroline line) and served with distinction as a captain in the War of 1812. Tradition has it that Captain Dew was descended from Oliver Cromwell.

Dr. William Dew, eldest son of Captain Thomas R. Dew, located in King and Queen county, m. Miss Susan Jones by whom he had issue three sons and five daughters: Thomas R. Dew, II; William Dew, Jr., Benjamin F. Dew, Mrs. Hord, Mrs.

Robert Gresham, Mrs. Hilliard, Mrs. Gregory and Miss Lucy Dew. His fame as a practitioner of medicine was not confined to King and Queen.

Of the children of Dr. William Dew many pages might be written. His son, Thomas R. Dew, II, removed to Wytheville, where he became prominent; H. W. Dew, the son of Thomas R. Dew, II, and grandson of Dr. William Dew, became a prominent physician in Lynchburg and another son, W. B. Dew, became prominent in Arizona.

Philip Dew, son of Captain Thomas R. Dew, m. Lucy De-Jarnette, of Caroline and settled at "Windsor" in the same county. This estate belonged in Colonial times to one Major Woodford, the father of General William Woodford, and here the General was born. Colonel William Byrd, of Westover, says that when visiting Major Woodford at "Windsor" he "surprised Mrs. Woodford in her housewifery in the meathouse, at which she blushed as if it had been a sin."

The children of Philip Dew and Lucy DeJarnette were Thomas Roderick Dew, III, Dr. Philip A. Dew, II, and Mrs. Welch, wife of Judge Welch, of Caroline. Dr. Philip A. Dew, m. Fannie McCoy, and settled at "Marl Hill," an old Coleman estate, near Penola, and had issue as follows: Philip A. Dew, III, who m. Miss Mary Holladay, of Spotsylvania; Roderick Dew, who m. Sallie B. Dew and settled near Welch, where he practices the profession of medicine, as did his father before him. He has one daughter, Ellen Byrd Dew.

Miss Mary Dew, who lives with her mother and brother at "Marl Hill," Fannie Dew, who m. James Swann; Gertie Dew, who m. a Mr. Reynolds, and Lucy Dew who m. Dudley Davis, of Goochland and now lives at Milford.

The children of Philip Dew, III, and Mary Holladay are Philip A., Linton M., and Sallie G. Dew.

John W. Dew, son of Capt. Thomas R. Dew, m. a Miss Pendleton, of Caroline, and had issue three children: Mary, who m. Judge A. B. Evans, of Middlesex; Roderick Dew, of Plain Dealing, and Alice, who also married Judge Evans.

Benjamin F. Dew, son of Capt. Thomas R., graduated from the College of William and Mary, taught school, practiced law and conducted the affairs of his farm. He was m. first, to Miss Mary Susan Garnett, and second, to Miss Bettie Quesenberry.

His oldest son, Dr. J. Harvie Dew, graduated from the University of Virginia and, in 1868, settled in New York City in the practice of his profession.   John G. Dew, second son of Benjamin F., graduated from the Law Department of the University of Virginia, settled in King and Queen and practiced law for a number of years.   He was Judge of the County Court for sixteen years, and for some time was Second Auditor of the State of Virginia.   He married Lelia Fauntleroy, daughter of Dr. Samuel G. Fauntleroy, of King and Queen.

L. Calvin Dew, son of Capt. Thomas. R., m a Miss Boulware, of Caroline and died while still young, leaving four children: Mrs Thomas B Henley, Mrs. A. C. Acree, Robert S. Dew and D. B. Dew, who was killed in the first engagement after joining the Ninth Virginia Cavalry during the Civil War.

Of the three daughters of Capt. Thomas R. Dew, Mrs. Hudgins was the mother of Col. Wm. P. Hudgins, who became prominent in railway circles in Texas; Mrs. Temple left no children, and Mrs. Gresham had five sons, Rev. Edward Gresham, Col. T. Robert Gresham, Wm. D. Gresham, Dr. Henry Gresham and Dr. Charles Gresham, all of whom were prominent men.

The Dew arms are thus described:

Gu. a chev. ar. betw. nine plates, five and four.

THE DEJARNETTE FAMILY

The earliest ancestors of this ancient family to come to America were Samuel and Joseph DeJarnette (originally De-Jarnatt) who were among the Hugenots that fled from LaRochelle when the Revocation of the Edict of Nantes, in 1685, banished from France so many of her most intelligent and useful citizens.

The DeJarnettes first settled in South Carolina where they intermarried with the famous Hampton family and others of the best blood of that State.   Joseph DeJarnette m. Mary Hampton, and came to Virginia and settled about the end of the seventeenth century in what afterward became Caroline.   He was the progenitor of the DeJarnette family of Virginia.   One of the most beautiful homes in Caroline is "Hampton" which was built by one of the descendants of Joseph DeJarnette and named for the family of his maternal ancestor.   The name Hampton has descended in the DeJarnette family through several generations.

"Spring Grove" which is located about six miles south of Bowling Green is another beautiful DeJarnette estate. This home was built about the middle of the nineteenth century by Daniel Coleman DeJarnette who was one of the most highly cultured men of his time. He was a scholar of the first rank, and was prominent in political life. He served in the House of De-

Spring Grove

legates and was afterward elected as an anti-Administration Democrat to the Thirty-sixth Congress. He was re-elected to the Thirty-seventh Congress of the United States but declined to take his seat and was soon thereafter elected to represent Virginia in the Confederate States Congress. He was re-elected a member of the Confederate Congress and served. He died at White Sulphur Springs, W. Va., on August 18, 1881. His son, Daniel Coleman DeJarnette who m. Miss Nancy Willis, of Richmond, Ky., owns and lives at "Spring Grove." They have one son, Joseph Willis DeJarnette, a young business man of Bowling Green, who m. Alice Richards, daughter of James T. Richards and Nettie Rowe.

THE DICKINSON (OR DICKERSON) FAMILY

In Caroline Marriage Bonds, elsewhere in this volume, is recorded the marriage of Jonathan Dickerson and Croshe Sizer which occurred on February 9, 1792. They had issue: John, Woodson, Henry, Charles, Nancy, Sizer, Elizabeth, Martha, Flower, and Lucretia. John d. young. Woodson, m. Sarah

Liggon and had residence in Salem, Va.; James Woodson, son of Woodson and Sarah Liggon, m. Elizabeth Craig and had res. in Lynchburg, Va., until his death in 1901.   Henry, m. Martha Mills and settled in Richmond where he d. in 1839, leaving three children.   Charles, no record.   Nancy, m. Benj. Howard and lived in Richmond, a dau., Belle, m. —————— Duesberry.   Elizabeth, m. Geo. Howard and had res. in Richmond.   Martha, m. —————— Bowers and lived in Roanoke, Va.   Flower, m Adam Miller and lived in Richmond.   Lucretia, m. —————— Buckner and lived at Louis C. H.

Chestnut Valley, Old Home of the Dickinson Family of Caroline
Courtesy Mr. W. D. Buckner.

James Woodson Dickerson and Elizabeth Craig had issue: Woodson W., who m. Miss Hardenberger; Julia, m. Emil Berger; Irmya, m. Geo. Palmer, of Newport News; James Warren, m. Lucile Trout, of Lynchburg; Robert, m. Miss Jones and has res. in Lynchburg; Margaret, m. Harry Mays, res. Lynchburg.

Henry Dickerson and Martha Mills had issue: John H., who m. Virginia Jacobs in 1858; Joseph Coleman, who m. Rebecca Garrison, and Virginia, who m. Joseph Heath.

John H. Dickerson and Virginia Jacobs had issue: John H., Jr., who m. Sarah DeHart; Joseph E., who m. Byrd Bennett and lives in Asheville; Charles, who d. unmarried; Mary, who is unmarried; Fanny, m. Henry Moore and had one son, Franklin; Annie, who m. James Drinard in 1896 and has res. in Richmond.

Joseph Coleman Dickerson and Rebecca Garrison had issue: Henry G., who m. Fannie Dickie in 1894; James E., who m. Florence Glenn in 1895; Camilla, unmarried; Martha, m. Rev. W. P. A. Haynes in 1917; Joseph G., m. Annie Coleman, of Charles City county, in 1905, and has res. in Richmond; Colin R., m. Margaret McGehee in 1907 and has res. in Richmond; Russell H., m. Nonia Powell, of Norfolk and has res. at Toana; Rebecca who d. unmarried 1917; and Robert who d. unmarried in 1906.

Henry G. Dickerson and Fannie Dickie have issue: Ethel L., m. J. Floyd Bradley in 1915, res. Richmond; Elizabeth, m. Hunter Wagner in 1917, res. Richmond; Henry W., unmarried, res. Richmond; Robert T., unmarried, res. Richmond.

THE DORSEY FAMILY

The Dorsey family of Caroline is descended from the Dorsey, and Ridgely families, of Maryland, than whom there are no more prominent families in that commonwealth. The complete genealogy of these two famous old families appeared in *The Sun* (Baltimore) of January 12, 1908, *et seq*, from the pen of Emily Emerson Lantz.

The first member of this ancient family to settle in Caroline was Charles Ridgely Dorsey. He was born at "Spring Hill" the ancestral estate of his family, which is located about two miles from Ellicott City, Howard county, Md. He attended school at Ellicott City and afterward was graduated from Princeton University.

At the outbreak of the War Between the States, he and his brothers, John W., and Samuel, joined the Confederate forces, enlisting in the Fifth Maryland Regiment, commanded by Colonel George R. Gaither, their brother-in-law. Later in the war they joined Mosby's command and served with it until the end of the war.

Before enlisting, Charles Ridgely Dorsey, his brothers, and two of their friends, burned the bridge over the Patapsico river, at Ellicott City, to keep back the Federal troops and upon their return home after the war they were tried by a Federal Court and sent to Cuba. Returning to Maryland, Charles Ridgely Dorsey stopped with a family named Reynolds who lived at the Union tavern about two miles from Penola, at the junction of the Penola road with the Stage road, and this family employed him to teach school.   He lodged here for a considerable period and while here married Catherine Collins, daughter of George T. Collins.   She bore him two children, Charles Ridgely and Mary Comfort, (twins) both of whom died when they were about two years old.   His wife died shortly afterward and he married Margaret Ann Collins, his first wife's sister, in 1872.   By this marriage he had issue: George Ridgely Dorsey.   Charles Ridgely Dorsey practiced law in Caroline and adjoining counties until his death in 1874.   Of him the Hon. A. B. Chandler said: "I would name him as the most brilliant of all the Caroline Bar. No one, I think, his equal intellectually has taken his place."

George Ridgely Dorsey, son of Charles Ridgely Dorsey and Margaret Ann Collins, was born, November 18, 1874.   He m. Estelle Marie Shuman on June 20, 1904 and had issue: Margaret Comfort Worthington, b. April 27, 1905 and Ridgely Corbin, b. January 15, 1907.   George Ridgely Dorsey was elected Treasurer of Caroline county in 1923.

THE GARRETT FAMILY

The Garrett family, of Caroline is sprung from ancestors who have been honored in many lands for many centuries.   The family is of Teutonic origin, "Ger," the root of the name, meaning "firm spear."   The family, or a branch of it, came over to Britain with William the Conquerer, and there the root "Ger" became "Gar." A number of this family were ennobled by the English kings and Queens from time to time and a coat of arms granted to them. Some of them became high church officials in the Church of England, and others became Quakers.   A number of the members of this family went to Ireland and purchased the sequestered lands of the Irish gentry after the Conquest.   Many of the Garretts, of England and Ireland bear noble titles to this day. The Caroline Garretts are descended from ancestors who came to Virginia from Leicestershire England in 1684.   Sir William Garrett, of London, was one of the charter members of the first Virginia colony, and it is believed that he was one of its first Chairmen.   The Garretts of Caroline have been, for the most part, planters, but several have held public office, among them W. R. W. Garrett, Treasurer of the county, and C. W. Garrett, his son, postmaster at the county seat.

The Garrett arms are thus described:

Arms: Ar. on a fesse sa. a lion pass. betw. two flanches sa.

Crest: A lion pass. erm. resting the dexter paw on a fleur-de-lis or.

THE GATEWOOD AND MONCURE FAMILIES

Three brothers by the name of Gatewood came from England to Virginia about 1745, or 1750, and received grants of land in the Colony. The Gatewood brothers were: Thomas, who never married; William, who took up land in Norfolk county, where the city now stands, and from whom descended the Kemp, Burruss, Kent, Capp and other Virginia families; James, who received a large grant of land in Caroline county extending from White Chimneys tavern on the south toward the Spotsylvania line on the north.

James Gatewood, m. Amelia Peatross, of a nearby estate and left issue: (1) John (d. unmarried); (2) Jane m. Wm. W. Dickinson, of Golansville, and left issue: (3) Maria m. —— Walden and left issue; (4) Amelia, m. Terrell, left issue. (The Terrells were Quakers); (5) Betsy, m. Richard Boulware, and left issue; (6) William m. ————; (7) James, m. Anna George, daughter of Reuben George and Mildred Rogers, who was descended from Col. Wm. Byrd, of Westover on her father's side and from John Rogers (the Martyr), on her mother's. James Gatewood fought in the War of 1812, was made captain and fitted out his own company. The old roster of his company is now in existence, and shows many names familiar to Caroline county. He m. Anna George in ˙1800 and brought her, a bride, to "Ellerslie" his home, a part of the original grant of land, which at this date (1924) is still in the family of his direct descendants. The children of James Gatewood and Anna George his wife, were (1) Thomas Jefferson, (2) Reuben George, (3) Philip, m. Catherine Gentry, and removed to Richmond, left issue; (4) Lucy Anne, m. Wm. A. Moncure. Her descendants are still in Caroline county; (5) Amelia Peatross, m. Terrell Cobb; (6) Cassandra, m. Hiram Oliver (her cousin).

The name Moncure is derived from the French words "*Mon Coeur*," meaning "my heart." The first of the family to come to Virginia was the Rev. John Moncure, who came from Kincardineshire, Scotland and settled in Stafford county at the beginning of the eighteenth century. He married Frances Brown, of Charles county, Md., June 18, 1741. He d. in 1764 and was buried under the Chancel of Aquia church in Stafford county. His will, which was probated July 9, 1764, is quoted in Du Bellet's *Prominent Virginia Families*, Vol. II, and is very interesting.

William A. Moncure, great grandson of Rev. John Moncure, was born at "Somerset" in Stafford county in 1805. He was the third son of John Moncure III, and Alcey Peachy Gascoigne. He came to Caroline county in 1825 and m. Lucy Anne Gatewood on March 4, 1827. He bought a home on the Cedar Fork road, called "Wilton." He afterward bought "Chesterfield" farm, and later "Ellerslie," the old Gatewood homestead. Soon after his marriage he became County Surveyor, later he was a member of the House of Delegates of Virginia, and State Senator for a good many terms. In 1856 or 1857 he became Second Auditor of Virginia, a position he held until his dealth in 1861. His children born and brought up in Caroline county were: (1) John James, m. Anne Deckard, and lived in Texas, left issue; (2) William Cassius, m. Allenia Cottrell, lived in Richmond; (3) Anna Gatewood, m. Daniel Norment, lived in Texas, left issue; (4) Thomas Jefferson, m. Margaret Moncure, lived in Stafford county, left issue; (5) St. Leger Landon, m. Lucy G. Oliver and lived in Caroline county, left issue; (6) Eustace Conway, m. Fanny Irby, lived in Caroline county, left issue; (7) Mary Alice, m. Samuel Burke, lived in Burkeville, Va.; (8) Rubynetta Burnes, m. Wm. Henry Glascock, lived in Burkeville, Va.; (9) Cassandra Oliver, m. William H. Lyne, has issue living in Orange county; (10) Richard Travers, m. Anna James Gascoigne, lives in Richmond.

The Moncures living in Caroline county were St. Leger Landon and Eustace Conway. Children of St. L. L. Moncure and Lucy Oliver, his wife were: (1) Frances Belle, (2) Elizabeth Cabell, (3) Anna George, (4) Philip St. Leger, (5) Alice Burke, (6) Orlando Shay, (7) Grace Eloise, (8) Clarinda Byrd. Anna G. Moncure, m. D. L. Bibb, lives in Richmond; Clarinda Byrd Moncure, m. Munson B. Conine, and removed to Hanover county. They have a daughter, Margaret Byrd; Orlanda Shay Moncure, m. Gertrude Wells and has two sons, John Philip and William Orlando, and a daughter, Mary Bush; Philip St. Leger Moncure, m. Grace Fortescue Terry and lives in Norfolk.

Philip St. L. Moncure graduated from the Medical College of Virginia in 1898, winning three prizes. He was appointed interne at St. Vincent's Hospital. Later he became house physician and head surgeon in this institution. In 1915 Dr Philip St. L. Moncure was President of the Congress of American Surgeons, which met in London. He is a member of the Board of Medical

Examiners of Virginia, and of the faculty of the Medical College of Virginia. He is a 32d Degree Mason and instructor in his Lodge in Norfolk.

Orlando Shay Moncure, graduated in Law from the University of Richmond, securing the prize for the best examination in 1900. He lives at his place "Idlewild," near Ruther Glen and is in government service.

Judge Eustace Conway Moncure

The children of Eustace Conway Moncure and Fanny Irby his wife are: (1) Anne Lilbourne, m. Pinkney Gravatt, left one son, Wm. Moncure Gravatt, (2) Eustace Conway, m. Fanny Norment, and has two sons, and a daughter, who live in Texas; (3) William Augustus, m. Margaret Tinsley, lives in Richmond has issue; Wm. A., Jr., Margaret, Tinsley, Rutherford, Eustace Conway, Martha and John. He graduated from the Virginia Military Institute, winning the Jackson Hope Medal. Returning home, he was made principal of the Bowling Green public schools. Later he took a law course at the University of Virginia, went to Richmond, and opened a law office, became a member of the law firm of Gordon, Smith and Moncure, and afterward became Judge of the Chancery Court of Richmond.

Eustace Conway Moncure, son of William A. Moncure and Lucy Gatewood, was a scout in the Civil War, on the Confederate side, and was later made Lieutenant. After the war he studied law and opened a law office at Bowling Green, Va. He was soon elected Commonwealth's Attorney for Caroline county and later became Judge of the county in which capacity he served with honor for many years. In 1905 he was elected to the House of Representatives of the State. He was a Mason and a member of the Kilwinning Crosse Lodge. His death occurred August, 1921. He is buried in Lakewood Cemetery at Bowling Green. His wife died the 26th of May, 1923 and rests by his side. **(4)** Maria Roper Moncure, m. Elmer Moore and lives in Norfolk, Va., has issue: Lucy, Ruby, Moncure, Fanny, Elmer; (5) Irby Moncure, m. Martha Eppes and has issue: Anne Lilbourne, m. ——— Nelson, Eustace C., Eppes, Fanny; (6) Lucy Alexander' m. T. B. Gill, Sheriff of Caroline and lives in Bowling Green; (7) Richard Gascoigne, m. Cordelia Lee Winston, had issue: Richard Gascoigne, Cordelia Lee and Elizabeth.

The Moncure Arms are thus described:

Gu. on a chief ar. three hearts of the first.

Motto: *Virtuti non armis fido.*

THE GEORGE FAMILY

The history of the George family in Virginia dates back almost to the beginning of the seventeenth century, when Henry George came over from England in the good ship *Assurance*. Lieutenant-Colonel John George, a son of Henry George the immigrant, was granted a large tract of land on Bagley's Creek in Isle of Wight county prior to 1640 and respresented Isle of Wight in the House of Burgesses in 1653. A grandson of Colonel George—also named John, m. Ursula Dudley, a daughter of John Dudley, of Middlesex and Ursula Beverly. Ursula Beverley was the daughter of Robert Beverly and Ursula Byrd, daughter of Colonel William Byrd, of Westover.

John Dudley George, son of John George and Ursula Dudley, died at Williamsburg about 1790, leaving one son, Lewis George, who was born in 1779. Lewis George, m. Agnes Wilson and to this union were born three sons and two daughters.

Captain Henry Hortensius George, son of Lewis George and Agnes Wilson, was born at "Fairford," near Penola, Va., in 1824, and m. Ellen Woolfolk Samuel, daughter of Colonel Archibald Samuel and Ann Woolfolk. To this union were born five sons and four daughters. Capt. George, when quite a young man, built "Thornberry" near Penola, making the bricks for the house on the premises, and sawing the timbers by the old "pit and whipsaw" method, using one man in the pit below the log, and one man on the scaffold above the pit. "Thornberry" at the

Thornberry

present time belongs to H. H. George, II., of Richmond, Va., a prominent railroad contractor. Lewis Dudley George lives at "Rose Hill" near Penola, and is engaged in the lumber business, being President of the Rose Hill Lumber Company. Ellen Maude George, the eldest sister, m. James Horace Blackley, to whom were born ten children. Mr. and Mrs. Blackley live at Thornsburg. Catherine Wilson George, a younger sister, m. Clarence E. Wright, son of James C. Wright and grandson of Dr. Wesley Wright, of Palestine, Caroline county. Archibald Samuel George died unmarried and is buried at "Fairford."

A very brief genealogical table of the George family follows:

(1) Robert George, Sr., d. 1734, Middlesex county, Va.: Children: *John*, Richard, Suzanna, Catherine and two other daughters.

(2) John George, Sr., b. 1704, d. 1784. Children: (first wife, Mary Jordan) Reuben, John, James, Ann, Elizabeth, Sarah, Mary and two other daughters. (Second wife, Ursula Dudley) *John Dudley*, Catherine, Patsy.

Ursula Dudley was the daughter of John Dudley, of Middlesex county, Va., and Ursula Beverly, who was the daughter of Robert Beverly, Jr., and Ursula Byrd, who was the daughter of Col. William Byrd, of Westover.

Robert Beverly, Jr., was the son of Robert Beverly, of Beverly, England, and Catherine Hone, of Jamestown, Va.

(3) John Dudley George d. in 1781 at Williamsburg, Va.; m. Miss Lucy Dickinson, daughter of David Dickinson. Children: *Lewis George*.

(4) Lewis George, b. 1779, d. 1847; m. Agnes Wilson, daughter of Zachariah Wilson and Catherine Pickett, daughter of John Pickett and Agnes Woolfolk, daughter of Robert Woolfolk and Ann George, who was a daughter of John George, Sr., mentioned above. Children: *Henry Hortensius George*, Lewis Melville George, Oscar, Louisa and Virginia.

(5) Henry H. George, Sr., b. at Fairford, Caroline county, Va., in 1824, d. at Thornberry, Caroline county, Va., June 26, 1902; m. Ellen Woolfolk Samuel, b. October 22, 1823, d. April 20, 1905 at Thornberry, she was a daughter of Archibald Samuel and Ann Woolfolk, daughter of Paul Woolfolk and Sarah Terry.

Archibald Samuel was the son of Phillip Samuel, Sr., and Elizabeth Pickett, the daughter of John Pickett and Agnes Woolfolk. Children: Henry, Philip Samuel, Jr., Paul, T., Arthur S., Elizabeth, Ellen and Ann.

Children of Henry H. George, Sr.: Ellen Maude, Archibald Samuel, Henry H. George, Jr., Lewis Dudley and Catharine Wilson. (Annie, Oscar, Ashby and Irene, four children that died under ten years of age.)

(6) Henry Hortensius George, Jr., b. April 15, 1858, m. Lillian Wright, daughter of Capt. Luther Wright and Susan Withers Coleman. Married on the 9th day of February, 1887. Children: Henry H. George, 3d, b. April 12, 1888, at Moss-Side, Va.; Luther Wright George, b. August 28, 1891 at Moss-Side, Henrico county,

Va., d. at Gloucester Point, Va., September 3, 1908, buried in Hollywood, Va.; Suzanne Withers Wright, b. June 24, 1895, in Richmond, d. August 28, 1898, buried in Hollywood Cemetery, Richmond, Va.; Helen Lillian George, b. in Richmond, November 28, 1901, Thanksgiving Day; Lewis Dudley George, 2d, b. in Richmond, February 14, 1905, Valentine Day; Anne Beverly George, b. in Richmond, Va., September 5, 1910, Labor Day.

Archibald Samuel George, b. June 25, 1856, d. August 1, 1913, at Thornberry, Va., and was buried at "Fairford," Caroline county, Va.

Lewis Dudley George, 1st, b. December 8, 1859, m. December 9, 1886 Carrie Lee Carson, daughter of Cyrus Carson and Lydia A. Swann, daughter of S. Amery Swann, and sister of Col. Samuel A. Swann. Lydia Swann's mother was Caroline Lowery whose whose mother was Nancy Tompkins.

Ellen Maud George was born at Thornberry, November, 1854 and was m. to James Horace Blackley, December 1, 1875. Children: Irene and Inez (twins), b. January 5, 1877; Henry George, b. January 25, 1879; James Horace, b. May, 1882, and Lillian Hortense, b. June 28, 1887. (Five other children died in infancy.)

Catherine Wilson George, b. at Thornberry, April 12, 1865, m. May 20, 1891, to Clarence E. Wright, son of James C. Wright, who was a son of Dr. Wesley Wright, of Palestine, Caroline county, Va., Catherine Wilson Wright, d. August 1, 1911, at Ashland, Va., and was buried there by the side of her son, James Calvin Wright. Children of Catherine Wilson Wright: Ellen, b. March 31, 1892; James Calvin, b. March 28, 1893, d. January 6, 1906, in Ashland, buried there; Agnes, b. June, 1895; Lillian, b. June, 189—.

Agnes Wright, m. J. Manning Potts, December 23, 1920; Lillian George Wright, m. to Arthur Price Morton, November 26, 1921.

(7) Henry H. George, 3d, m. Louise Richardson, daughter of Judge David C. Richardson, of Richmond, Va. He (Henry H. George, 3d) was a Captain of Engineers in the 105th Regiment, 30th Division, U. S. Reserves, and served in the World War. He went across to England and France, and fought against the Germans, his regiment being brigaded with the British, fighting in France and Belgium. He received his commission in 1917, went to Europe in 1918 and returned to the United States in 1919, when he was honorably discharged.

CHILDREN OF ISAAC GEORGE

John George, 1710, m. Ursula Dudley.

Robert George, 1715, m. Clara Daniel in 1746.

James George, 1730, m. Mary Swift in 1767.

Enoch George, of Staunton, m. ———— 1767.

Agatha George, m. George Payne, of Goochland county.

Susannah George, m. G. Holland.

INCOMPLETE GENEALOGICAL DATA

Isaac George, b. 1680.

Henry George came to America in ship *"Assurance."* Exact date unknown to author.

Lieutenant Colonel John George, b. 1610, m. Jane ————.

Major John George, b. 1670, m. Frances ————, in 1700.

John George, of Caroline, b. 1704, m. 1st, Mary Jordan, 2d Ursula Dudley.

Katherine George, sister of John, of Caroline, m. William Mansfield, of Louisa.

Robert Mansfield, m. Mourning Clark, dau. Micajah Clark, of Louisa and Albemarle.

Rev. Joseph Allen Mansfield, m. Susan Ann Lindsay, of Orange.

Mary Lindsay Mansfield, m. Jackson L. Thornton, of Orange and Greene.

Lelia Thornton, m. James C. Gentry, of Gordonsville. Home, Atlanta, Ga.

Arms: Ar. on a fesse gu. betw. three falcons, rising, az beaked, legged, and belled or, as many bezants, each charged with a lion's head sa.; on a canton vert a harp, gold, stringed of the first.

Crest: A falcon as in the arms.

Motto: *"Magna est veritas et prevalebit."*

THE GLASSEL FAMILY

The Glassel family is said to be of French descent. Tradition has it that the first of the name went from Poisters, France, to Scotland with Mary, Queen of Scots, on her return to her native land in 1550. The name is supposed to have been "Glassele" originally.

John and Andrew Glassel, brothers, were born in Galloway, Scotland, at the beginning of the eighteenth century and emigrated to Virginia in 1738. John settled near Fredericksburg, but later returned to Scotland, and Andrew settled in that section of Culpeper which in 1792, became Madison county. Here he built "Torthowald" after the pattern of the old home in Scotland. The workmen who erected the house were brought from Scotland.

John Glassel, son of Andrew, of "Torthowald" was born at "Torthowald" October 29, 1780, and m. (1) Louisa Richie Brown, of Prince Edward county, on September 11, 1806, and had issue as follows: Andrew McMillan, Fanny, Louisa and Marion; (2) to Mrs. Margaret Scott Lee by whom he had two children, the Rev. John Glassel and Mildred; (3) to Sarah Ashton by whom he had no children. There is a true story touching the religious life of John Glassel to the effect that he traveled from "Torthowald" to Fredericksburg—a distance of sixty miles—four times annually to attend the communion services in the Presbyterian church. He was educated in Scotland.

The Rev. John Glassel, son of John by his second marriage, was born August 16, 1828, and educated in Princeton. He received the Degrees of M. A. and M. D., and practiced medicine for a short time. He was an officer in the Confederate Army and was prominent as a clergyman. His descendants are prominent in Louisiana

Andrew McMillan Glassel, son of John Glassel, by his first marriage, was born in 1807 and was educated in the University of Pennsylvania. He removed to Bowling Green in 1834 and practiced medicine there until his death in 1888. He was m. to Miss Frances A. Downing, of Caroline county shortly after his removal to Bowling Green and had issue as follows: John, Fannie, Eugenia, Ada, Andrew, William, Robert, Louisa and Marion.

Dr. Robert T. Glassel, son of Dr. Andrew, was born in Bowling Green and educated in Baltimore, and succeeded to his father's practice. He was m. to Miss Russell Williams, of Essex, and had issue as follows: Frances, Louisa and Marion Walker. Frances was m. to Col. R. L. Beale, of Bowling Green, attorney-at-law and former representative in the House of Delegates, and has one son, R. L., Jr.

A prominent member of the Glassel family was Commander William T. Glassel, U. S. Navy, 1845–1861, C. S. N., 1861–1864. He designed and constructed the first submarine—"*The David*" and commanded it in the attack on the "*New Tromider*" Both ships were disabled—"*The David*" so seriously that the crew had to swim for safety Commander Glassell was captured after an hour in the water and held prisoner for one year, and exchanged. He commanded *"The Fredericksburg"* until he had to blow it up to prevent capture. His descendants are numerous and prominent in California.

THE GRAVATT FAMILY

The Gravatts are lineally descended from Colonel Miles Cary, of Warwick county, Va., who came over from England about 1645, and who, during Berkeley's administration, was escheator-general of Virginia.

John James Gravatt, M. D., was born at Port Royal, Caroline county, November 27, 1817. His grandfathers, Col. Larkin Smith, of King and Queen and Col. John Ambler, of Jamestown, were both distinguished soldiers in the War of the Revolution. Doctor Gravatt graduated with distinction from William and Mary College in 1838 and won the degree of M. D. from the University of Pennsylvania in 1842. Upon graduation he married Eliza Ambler Smith and settled in his home town and entered upon the practice of medicine. He so devoted himself to his profession that he soon secured the confidence of all classes of people and built up a large practice.

Shortly after the outbreak of the Civil War he gave up his practice in Caroline and assumed the responsible position of head of the large receiving hospital at Richmond, and here, as in Caroline, he soon distinguished himself as one of the most skilful surgeons in the service. Amid the trying scences of that eventful period, his skill and Christian kindness won for him not only the confidence and love of the many thousands of sufferers under his medical care, but of every subaltern and dependent under his command. At the close of the war the surgeon-general said, "I have never known Dr. Gravatt to make a mistake in diagnosis."

John James Gravatt II, son of Dr. John James Gravatt and Eliza Ambler Smith, was born at Port Royal, Caroline county, May 14, 1853. He attended schools at Port Royal conducted by George Fitzhugh and Carter Page and later went to the preparatory school conducted in connection with the Protestant Episcopal Theological Seminary at Alexandria, Va. He graduated from the Theological Seminary in 1876, and upon receiving his degree, went to Hampton as rector of St. John's, the oldest parish in the country having a continuous life dating back to 1610. While at Hampton the Rev. Dr. Gravatt, m. Miss India Wray Jones by whom he had issue: J. J. Gravatt, III, now rector of Trinity church, Staunton, Va., and Mrs. R. A. Goodwyn, whose husband was at one time rector of St. John's, Richmond, and afterward missionary to China.

The Rev. Dr. J. J. Gravatt, II, came from Hampton to Moore Memorial Episcopal church, Richmond, on October 1, 1893. Work had just been started on a new church edifice, but under the leadership of Dr. Gravatt a new architect was called in, new plans were drawn, and a building was erected wholly different from that originally planned. When completed it was called Holy Trinity instead of Moore Memorial, but was a memorial to Bishop Moore.

On September 30, 1923, J. Mark Lutz, writing in the *Times-Dispatch*, Richmond, said in part as follows: "With the close of services in Holy Trinity today will come the conclusion of thirty years of work in that church by the Rev. J. J. Gravatt, D. D. During this period the church has grown from a membership of 150 to 1,289. A new church and parish house have been built, and the building which Dr. Gravatt saw begun in 1894 he saw completed in 1901, and consecrated in 1907, on the day before the General Convention opened in the building, at which opening service the Bishop of London preached. Dr. Gravatt has been identified with a number of civic and fraternal organizations of Richmond, having served as president of the Richmond Ministerial Union, Richmond Clericus, Richmond Convocation, Deputy to General Convention, Trustee of Stuart Hall, Member of Council of Defense in World War, Chairman of Richmond Vice Commission, Chaplain of Travelers Protective Association, Master of Strict Observance Lodge of Masons, and Orator in the Scottish Rite Bodies of Richmond of which he is a Thirty-Third Degree member."

Charles Urquhart Gravatt, son of Dr. John James Gravatt I, and Eliza Ambler Smith, was born at Port Royal, June, 1849. After attending the preparatory schools of Port Royal he entered medical college in Baltimore from which he was graduated with high honors. He at once entered the U. S. Navy as Assistant Surgeon where his unusual talents were quickly recognized and rewarded. He became Full Surgeon, Fleet Surgeon and at last Medical Director. After the Spanish-American War his eyes were so affected that he was told by specialists that he would become blind unless he entered upon some mode of life which would remove him from artificial light, and so he retired; but the Navy Department, recognizing his splendid services, retired and pensioned him.   He then returned to Port Royal, settled at the old home place, and after a few years was elected to represent Caroline, Hanover, and King William counties in the State Senate. He was serving in this office at the time of his death in 1921.   He left one son, Marshall Gravatt who resides in North Carolina.

At a mass meeting held in Bowling Green on January 8, 1923, for the purpose of electing delegates to a convention to be held in Ashland, Va., on January 18th for nominating a successor to Dr. Gravatt, the Hon. J. W. Guerrant, formerly a member of the House, offered the following resolutions which were unanimously adopted, and published in *The Caroline Progress* and *The Free Lance:*

"Whereas, Dr. Charles U. Gravatt, a noble and honorable son of this county, has departed this life, and

"Whereas, he did faithfully, and with honor, represent us for nearly sixteen years in the Senate of Virginia, and

"Whereas, we meet today in connection with choosing his successor with the memories of his fine qualities of mind and heart fresh in our thoughts, now therefore be it,

"*Resolved,* by the Democrats of Caroline in mass meeting assembled, that we express our admiration for his integrity and intellect, gratitude for his valiant services, sorrow for his departure, and sympathy for his son who survives him."

William Loyall Gravatt, son of J. J. Gravatt, I, and Eliza Ambler Smith, was born at Port Royal, December 15, 1857. After attending the local schools he entered Virginia Polytechnic Institute.   He taught school a few years and then entered the Theological Seminary at Alexandria.   Upon graduation he became assistant rector to Dr. Minnigerode at St. Paul's church, Richmond.   After a year or two he accepted St. Peter's church, Norfolk, from which he went to Zion's church, Charleston, W. Va.   While rector here he was elected Bishop Coadjutor of West Virginia—1899—and became Bishop of the diocese upon the death of Bishop Peterkin.

He m. Miss Sidney Peyton, of Richmond, and has three children, one son and two daughters, William Loyall, Jr., Cary and Mary.

The Gravatt arms are thus described:

Az. a fesse embattled erm. betw. three wolves heads erased ar.

Crest: A wolf pass. per pale erminois and ar.

THE HAWES FAMILY

The Hawes family in America dates back to 1635, at which time Richard and Edward Hawes, presumably brothers, emigrated to New England and settled in the Massachusetts Bay Colony. From this point several members of the family removed to Virginia about half century later.

The name is derived from the old Saxon word "Hawe" which means thorn hedge. From this name came the names, Hawley, Haworth, Haughton, Howe and Hawes, the last two being the oldest and the most widely scattered.

The following brief and partial record of the Caroline-King and Queen family will serve to show how it was connected with other prominent families early in the eighteenth century, and also serve as a starting point for the genealogist:

Samuel Hawes 1st m. Anne Spencer about 1712, and had issue: (1) Isaac Hawes, (2) Marye Hawes, who m. Elijah Daniel; (3) Elizabeth Hawes, who m. Thomas Coghill; (4) Nicie Hawes, b. 1723, who m. John Coleman, III; Samuel Hawes, II, b. 1727, m. Anne Walker in 1751.

Samuel Hawes, II, and Anne Walker had issue: (1) Samuel Hawes III, b. 1754; (2) Walker Hawes I, b. 1755; (3) Anne Hawes, b. 1758, m. Henry Washington in 1775; (4) Elizabeth Hawes, b. 1759, m. Thomas Buckner; (5) Benjamin Hawes, b. 1782; (6) Mary Hawes, b. 1764, m. Robert Buckner; (7) Charlotte Hawes, b. 1765, m. 1st, to Richard Buckner in 1782, 2d to William Buckner in 1797; (8) Aylett Hawes, b. 1768, m. 1795; (9) Richard Hawes, b. 1772, m. Clary Walker, 1792, d. 1848; (10) Walker Hawes II, named for older brother who died, was born 1776, m. 1797 and died in 1828.

Samuel Hawes, I, was commissioned Captain 2d Virginia Regiment February 19, 1776; Major 10th Virginia Regiment, October 4, 1777; Lieutenant-Colonel, March 1, 1778; Lieutenant-Colonel, 6th Virginia Regiment, September 14, 1778; transferred to 5th Virginia Regiment, January 1, 1783, and served until November 13, 1783.. There is preserved in the State Papers of Virginia his discharge or certificate of service, with a large red wax seal attached, of which the following is a copy:

"I do certify that Sam'l Hawes was appointed an officer in the 7th Virginia Continental Regiment in the winter of 1775-

'76, and continued in service till the close of the war at which time he ranked as Lieutenant-Colonel.

"Given under my hand this 27th of June 1807.

"Th. Posey, Late Lt. Col. in the Va. Line on '
Continental Establishment."

Samuel Hawes II, or Samuel Hawes, Jr., as he is called in the records, represented Caroline county in the Virginia House of Delegates in the year 1784–5, 1785–6, 1786–7 and 1787–8.

Both Samuel Hawes and Samuel Hawes, Jr., were members of the Caroline Committee of Safety in 1774–1775. Samuel Hawes, Jr., was Clerk of that body. See chapter on Committee of Safety elsewhere in this volume.

A road branching off from the old Stage Road just a few yards north of the town limits of Bowling Green, and leading to Paige, bears the name Hawes' Lane, in honor of this ancient family.

Arms: Azure a fesse wavy between three lions rampant or.

Crest: Out of a mural coronet azure a lion's head or.

THE HURT FAMILY

Arms: Sa. a fesse betw. three cinquefoils or.

Crest: A hart pass. ppr. horned, membered and hurt in haunch with arrow or feathered ar.

Motto: *Mane-praedam vesperi spolium.*

Benjamin, Moses, and Philemon Hurt, who were brothers, came from England to America probably in the early part of the eighteenth century. They settled on the Rappahannock River in St. Margaret's Parish, near Port Royal, Caroline county, Va. Some of the descendants of Moses Hurt went to Fauquier county, Va., and a Colonel Moses Hurt was living on his plantation near the Fauquier White Sulphur Springs just prior to the Civil War. Some of the descendants of Philemon Hurt settled in Nottoway county, Va., and intermarried with the Turners of that county. Other descendants of the Caroline Hurts went early to Georgia, Alabama and Tennessee, and probably to Mississippi. Complete data of this family are not obtainable, as many of the Court records of Caroline were destroyed or lost during the Civil War.

An old deed, however, shows that Benjamin Hurt, the grandfather of Thomas Hurt, of the "Thornhill" plantation mentioned below, bought land from James Murry, in St. Margaret's Parish, on April 13, 1764. He was an officer in the commissary department of the American Army during the Revolutionary War, and the steel-yard and quinine scales used by him in this capacity are now in the possession of his great-great-granddaughter, Mrs. Elizabeth Rowland Hurt Louthan. He had two sons, Benjamin and William Hurt, the latter went south, probably to Alabama.

Benjamin Hurt, the son of the Revolutionary soldier, m. Frances Richerson about 1793, and lived on his plantation near Sparta in Caroline. They left the following children: Benjamin, Thomas, James and Jane. James and Benjamin grew to manhood, but never married. Jane, m. a Mr. Stuart, leaving one daughter, Frances, who m. a Mr. Chapman. They had two sons, Scott Chapman, who m. a Miss Sinclair, and had two sons, and a daughter named Narcissa. Scott Chapman's brother, Robert Henry Chapman, was a successful business man, but never married. These last two generations of the Chapman's lived at Ripley, Tenn.

Thomas Hurt, the second son of Benjamin Hurt and Frances Richerson, his wife, was born September 13, 1798. On December 24, 1829, Thomas Hurt, m. Mrs. Mary Margaret Croughton Peatross. She was the daughter of Charles Croughton and Margaret Hudson, his wife, who were married in Durham Parish, Charles county, Md., on July 29, 1799. Their daughter, Mary Margaret Croughton, was born at "Woodend," her father's plantation near Falmouth, Stafford county, Va., on December 30, 1804. Charles Croughton was a native of London, England, and his wife, Margaret Hudson, was born February 15, 1777 at Whitehaven in the shire of Cumberland, England. Their daughter, Mrs. Thomas Hurt, was taken from Virginia, when a girl, by her father to the home of her grandmother Croughton in England and was educated at Spark Hill, at that time a suburb of London.

Thomas Hurt and his wife, nee Mary Margaret Croughton, lived at "Thornhill," a plantation which joined "Needwood" and "White Chimneys" plantations, near the present postoffice of Lorne in Caroline. Thomas Hurt was a successful business man, and prior to the Civil War his estate consisted of fifteen hundred acres of land, about one hundrd slaves, and many real estate mortgages. His entire property is estimated to have been worth something over a half million dollars. He and his family frequently spent the summer at The Greenbrier White Sulphur Springs, the noted all-South resort in the mountains of Virginia, taking their private coach and a certain number of slaves with them. They had three children, who reached their majority: Elizabeth Young Hurt, b. December 2, 1830; Charles Benjamin Hurt, b. February 6, 1833; and James Thomas Hurt, b. December 31, 1842. Thomas Hurt died at "Thornhill" full of years and of honors, on February 16, 1870, and is buried there with his brothers, James and Benjamin, and with his wife, who died on July 10, 1888.

Elizabeth Young Hurt was m. on November 23, 1856 to Joseph M. Seay, who about this time was High Sheriff and Treasurer of Caroline county. After the Civil War they made their home on the "Greenwood" farm, a part of the "Thornhill" plantation. Here Mr. Seay engaged successfully in merchandising and farming, until his death in September, 1891. Mrs. Elizabeth Young Hurt Seay was a fine business woman and took an especial interest in Concord Baptist church, of which her father and mother, and brothers had also been members. She exercised a wide influence for good, had a large circle of friends, and dispensed a bountiful hospitality at "Greenwood." There on September 9, 1911, surrounded by relatives and friends, she passed to her reward, and was laid to rest among her dearest kin at "Thornhill." Charles Benjamin Hurt was educated by private tutors and at Richmond College. He was at the latter institution from about 1853 to 1856. He died on July 12, 1871, never having married.

James Thomas Hurt was educated at a neighboring plantation school at "Alan Gowan," under a master of arts from Harvard, and at Ellington Academy in Hanover county. The war prevented his receiving a college training. During the last months of the Civil War, he was a member of Colonel John S. Mosby's Partisan Rangers of the Confederate States Army. On July 14, 1870, he was m. to Ann Eliza Ewing Thomas, a daughter of Ira Lomax Thomas and Mary Jones Morgan Thomas, of "Vernon," Caroline county, Va. James Thomas Hurt and his wife lived for several years after their marriage at "Thornhill," where their daughter, Elizabeth Rowland Hurt, was b. on January 3, 1874. On March, 1874, he and his wife went to Detroit, Mich., where a son, Ira Thomas Hurt, was b. on August 12, 1876, but d. on December 24, 1881. Mr. Hurt was a forceful speaker and a good debater. He was in business in Detroit until his death on August 17, 1895, when his wife and daughter returned to Virginia.

Elizabeth Rowland Hurt was born in Virginia, but was reared and educated in Detroit, Mich. She visited her aunts in Caroline and King William counties, Va., practically every year of her girlhood days. On March 25, 1903, she was m. to Henry Thompson Louthan, at "Retreat," the home of her uncle and aunt, Mr. and Mrs. Rowland Greene Tyler, in the northern part of King William county, Va. Mr. Louthan at this time was pastor of the Baptist church in Williamsburg, Va., and that fall became a professor in the College of William and Mary. There in Williamsburg were born their two children, Mary Tyler Louthan, on May 9, 1904; and Carter Thomas Louthan, on July 23, 1906. The "Greenwood" farm, a part of the "Thornhill" plantation, is now owned by Mrs. Elizabeth Rowland Hurt Louthan.

Martin Arms

THE MARTIN FAMILY

The Caroline members of this ancient family are descended from Col. John Martin, of "The Park*," who represented Caroline in the House of Delegates and who late in life removed to King William and represented that county in the same body. He m. Martha Burwell, daughter of Col. Lewis Burwell, of Gloucester county. At Clifton, an old Martin estate about seven miles from Bowling Green, is an old gravestone with the following

---

* This estate was granted to the Martin family by the Crown, as a reward for chivalry, and was used for a deer park, hence the name.

inscription: "Interred beneath this stone lies the body of Mrs. Martha Martin, wife of Col John Martin, of Caroline and daughter of Lewis Burwell, Esq., of Gloucester county, who departed this life, 27th day of May, 1738, in the 36th year of her age, and left three sons and four daughters." (See Robert DeJarnette in *William and Mary Quarterly*, vol. 11). In the *William and Mary Quarterly*, Vol. 12, is reproduced an advertisement in which John and Samuel Martin offer for sale 2,700 acres of the estate of their late father, Col. John Martin. John Martin, son of Col. John, is supposed to have been the John Martin, of "The Park," in King and Queen county, who is frequently mentioned in various Colonial records. He m. Haley Jones, of King William, and has issue, of whom was Younger Martin.

Younger Martin, m. Elizabeth Boulware and had issue: John B. Martin, Thomas C. Martin, Younger Martin, Jr., Catherine and Frances.

John B. Martin, of the "Hermitage" in Caroline county, eldest son of Younger Martin, m. Mary Saunders and had issue: Samuel, Cornelius, Alex., and Ernest. Samuel, a Civil War veteran, married in Texas and had two daughter, Catherine and Ruth. His three brothers were killed in the Civil War.

Thomas C. Martin, of "The Park," in King and Queen county, and second son of Younger Martin and Elizabeth Boulware, m. Matilda Clark and had issue: (1) John Younger, m. ———— (2) Frances, m. ———— Ramsay; (3) Emma, m. ———— Hundley; (4) Elizabeth, m. Samuel; (5) Margaret, (6) Lee, (7) Hamilton. The two last named—Lee and Hamilton—were killed in the Civil War. Emma Martin, who m. Hundley and had issue Thomas M. Hundley and Mary Hundley, of Richmond.

Catherine Ann, daughter of Younger Martin and Elizabeth Boulware, m. Thomas Motley, of King and Queen county and had issue: Thomas Judson Motley, Civil War veteran and member of Pickett's Division.

Younger Martin, Jr., of Clay Hill in Caroline, m. Sarah Motley, of King and Queen and had issue: Catherine and John Henry Martin. John Henry Martin was educated at Columbian University, of Washington, D. C. He m. Catherine Miller Bowie and had issue: Julian Bowie, Sally Brockenbrough, Judith H., and Henry M.

Julian Bowie Martin, son of John Henry Martin and Sarah Motley, was educated in Richmond College, now University of

Richmond, and for many years was principal of Fork Union Academy. He m. Ruby Snead, of Fluvanna county and had issue: Julian Bowie and Isabelle.

Sally Brockenbrough, dau. of John Henry Martin and Sarah Motley, was educated in Bowling Green Female Seminary and m. Dr. Arthur Lewis Martin. Issue: Mary Bowie, Patty Livingstone, Garnett Lewis and Arthur Lewis, Jr.

Judith H., dau. of John Henry Martin and Sarah Motley, educated in Woman's College of Richmond. Unmarried and resides at "Clay Hill."

Henry M., son of John Henry Martin and Sarah Motley, educated in Richmond College, (A. B., A. M.) John Hopkins University (Ph. D.) and is Professor of Spanish in the University of Illinois. He is a Fellow of Johns Hopkins and studied abroad several years.

John Younger Martin, of "Marengo" in Caroline, eldest son of Thomas C. Martin and Matilda Clark, was educated in Richmond College and Columbian University. He m. Rebecca Warner Lewis and had issue: (1) Olive Lee, (2) Ruth Lewis, (3) Isabel M., (4) Ethel E., and (5) Arthur Lewis.

Olive Lee Martin, m. J. C. Wiltshire, of West Virginia.

Ruth Lewis Martin, m. Dr. J. T. Harris, of West Virginia, and had issue: George Hunter, lawyer of Parkersburg; Thomas Lewis, prominent surgeon of Parkersburg; and Mildred Warner, who m. Thomas Thornbury Tyler, nephew of President Tyler.

Isabel M. Martin, m. Rev. B. M. Foreman, of South Carolina and had issue one son, Arthur Ashley Foreman, who m. Mary Cassell. They have one child, Arthur Lewis Foreman.

Ethel E. Martin, m. (1st) J. B. Hare, of South Carolina; (2d) Townsend D. Wolfe. By the first marriage she had issue: one daughter, Olive Warner Hare, who m. George Timmons; and by the second marriage she had one son, Christian Townsend Wolfe, who is engaged in banking.

Arthur Lewis Martin received his medical education in the University of Maryland and is a practising physician in Caroline. He m. Sally Brockenbrough Martin and had issue: Mary Bowie, graduate University of Richmond; Patty Livingstone, graduate University of Richmond; Garnett Lewis, and one son, Arthur Lewis, Jr., who died in infancy.

John Buckler Martin, of Horatio, Arkansas, writing to Mrs. Arthur Lewis Martin under date of January 11, 1924, says:

"My grandparents were William Martin and Ann Brumley. My parents were Thomas Brumley Martin and Frances Ann Boulware. They were married in Caroline on December 23, 1834. My mother was the daughter of Muscoe Boulware and Elizabeth Spindle and was born in Caroline county on October 14, 1814. My father was born in Caroline on December 15, 1807. My parents removed to Winterham, near Acquinton church in King William county, about 1843, where they died. My father had two brothers, William and Frank, who lived in King and Queen and King William counties respectively. I was boarding with Uncle William at King and Queen Courthouse, and attending Stevensville Academy, when the town was burnt by Federal troops in 1863."

The arms of the Martin family are thus described:

Arms: A chevron betw. three crescents.

Crest: Ar. a dexter hand brandishing a sabre trenchant ppr hilt gold.

Motto: *Auxilium ab alto.*

THE MINORS OF "TOPPING CASTLE"

Doodes Minor, m. Elizabeth Cocke, issue: Garret Minor, b. 1679, d. February 20, 1720, m. Diana Vivian (October 17, 1706). She d. April 16, 1718.

Issue: John Minor, b. June 22, 1707, d. August 2, 1755, m. Sarah Carr (November 14, 1732); she was the dau. of Major Thomas Carr, of Caroline county, and Mary Dabney.

Issue: (1) Major John Minor, of "Topping Castle" Caroline county, Va., b. November 18, 1735, d. March 21, 1800, m. Elizabeth Cosby (dau. of David Cosby and Mary Garland Overton). (2) William Minor (nothing known of him); (3) Thomas Minor, b. August 5, 1740, d. February 16, 1816, m. Mary Dabney, March 10, 1763; (4) Mary Ann Minor, b. March 7, 1742, d. 1818, m. Joseph Herndon, August 15, 1765. They were the ancestors of Mrs. Mathew Maury, of Fredericksburg, Va., and Mrs. Carter Blasingame, of Ashland, Va.; (5) Col. Garret Minor, b. March 14, 1744, d. June 25, 1799; m. Mary Overton Terrell, dau. of Richmond Terrell and Nancy Overton, ancestors of Mrs. C. P. Cardwell *nee* Bessie Lee, of Hanover county, and Mrs. Laurie Smith, nee Mary H. Tyler, of Gwathmey, Va.

Issue: (1) Samuel Overton, m. Lydia L. Lewis; (2) Patsy

Minor, b. 1770, m. 1st, Robert Quarles, 2d Mr. Hall; (3) Garrett
Minor, Jr., b. December 25, 1776, d. June 30, 1832, m. Eliza
McWilliams, 1802, d. August 20, 1832; (4) Sally Minor, b. 1780,
d. 1849, m. David Watson, of Green Spring, Louisa county, 1801;
(5) Mary B. Minor, b. 1781, m. Garland Anderson; (6) Peter
Minor, b. 1730, m. Lucy Gilmer, 1806; (7) Rebecca Minor, b.
1772, m. John Quarles; (8) Dr. James Minor, b. 1785, m. Polly
Watson, 1813; (9) Elizabeth L. Minor, b. 1773, m. Col. Stapleton
Crutchfield, of Caroline county, Va.; (10) Nancy Minor, b.
1771, m. Thomas Meriwether, 1791;   (11) Louisa Minor, b. 1787,
m. Hutchinson.

(6) James Minor, b. February 18, 1745, d. June 7, 1791, m.
Mary Carr, June 20, 1773. She was b. September 14, 1756, d.
July 7, 1797; (7) Diana Minor, b. February 28, 1747, d. March
28, 1748; (8) Dabney Minor, b. June 11, 1749, d. November 7,
1799, m. Ann Anderson, October 12, 1773, she was b. January
30, 1751, d. March 27, 1831; (9) Capt. Vivian Minor, b. No-
vember 4, 1740, d. October 15, 1798, m. 1st, Barbara Overton
Cosby, June 15, 1773, she was b. February 11, 1752, d. September
21, 1778; m. 2d, Elizabeth Dick, March 31, 1780; (10) Elizabeth
Minor, b. August 3, 1752, d. 1786, m. Col. James Lewis, of "Laurel
Hill."; (11) Peter Minor, b. August 16, 1754, d. 1773, m. Miss
Jones.

Major John Minor, of "Topping Castle," Caroline county,
Va., m. Elizabeth Cosby, sister of his brother Vivian's wife. First
of the Cosby girls, m. Richard Tompkins and one m. Harry
Collis, they are the ancestors of Judge William J. Leake, of
Ashland and the Keans of Goochland and Louisa counties, also
of Mrs. Margaret Berry, of Washington.

Major John Minor of "Topping Castle" had issue: (1) Thomas
Carr Minor, m. Ann Redd, of "Cedar Vale," Caroline county,
Va., she the dau. of Samuel Redd and Lucy Rogers, m. in 1779;
(2) William Minor, of "Topping Castle," m. Mildred Gregory
Lewis, dau. of Capt. John Lewis and Lucy Thornton;(3) Gen.
John Minor, lived at "Hazel Hill," Fredericksburg, Va., m. 1st,
Mary Berkley; m. 2d, Lucy Landon Carter, December 12, 1793.
They were the ancestors of Lucius Minor, of "Edgewood,"
and Mrs. Blackford; (4) Lancelot Minor, m. his cousin, Mary
Overton Tompkins in 1792. They were the ancestors of Prof.
John B. Minor, of the University of Virginia; (5) Diana
Minor, m. Richard Maury, the father of Commodore Mathew

Fontaine Maury; (6) Sarah Minor, m. Harwood Goodwin, in 1798, of "Oakley," Caroline county, Va.; (7) Charles Minor, took his degree of M. D. at Edinburg, Scotland, d. in 1806; (8) Elizabeth Minor, m. Humphrey Hill in 1820. He lived at "Mount Airy," Caroline county, Va.; (9) Barbara Cosby Minor, d. in 1849, m. William Kemp Gatewood (March 19, 1807), of Middlesex county.

Capt. Vivian Minor, of "Springfield," Caroline county, Va., son of John Minor and Sarah Carr, m. 1st, Barbara Overton Cosby.

Issue: (a) Mary Overton Minor, m. John McLaughlin, son of John McLaughlin and Sarah Mackie, of Scotland; (b) Ann Minor; (c) George Minor.

Capt. Vivian Minor, m. 2d, Elizabeth Dick.

Issue: (a) Joseph Minor, (b) Lewis Minor, (c) Alfred Minor, (d) Archibald Minor, b. May 12, 1781, m. Ann W. Rawlins; (e) Susan B. Minor, m. Wm. Wyatt, of Caroline county, Va., November 11, 1813; (f) Matilda Minor, m. Robert Coleman, of Caroline county, Va. They were the ancestors of Col. Lewis Minor Coleman, who m. Miss Mary Ambler Marshall, of Fauquier county, Va., and Mrs. Edward Watts Morris, of Claremont, Hanover county, Va., also of Miss Willie Schooler, dau. of Prof. Samuel Schooler, who m. the Rev. Frank Page, of "Oakland," Hanover county, Va.

Mary Overton Minor, dau. of Capt. Vivian Minor and Barbara Overton Cosby, m. John McLaughlin, son of John McLaughlin. Issue: (a) Harriet McLaughlin, m. Dr. Thomas Bates Anderson; (b) Barbara McLaughlin, d. July 23, 1820; (c) John Vivian, d. in 1844, m. Miss Johnston, of Tennessee. No issue; (d) Thomas McLaughlin, d. 1838; (e) Cornelia M. McLaughlin, b. December 2, 1810, d. April 12, 1889, m. Samuel Redd, the son of Samuel and Elizabeth Taylor, of "Cedar Vale," Caroline county, Va. Their issue is given in the "Cedar Vale" Redds.

George McLaughlin, son of John McLaughlin and Mary O. Minor, m. Mildred Duke, dau. of Burnley.

Issue: James, m. his cousin, Miss Duke.

His issue: Ridgeway McLaughlin, of Huntington, W. Va., and Mrs. Harrison, of Ohio; Mary Overton McLaughlin, m. her cousin, Mr. Smith, of Kentucky, and lived in Texas.

FURTHER NOTES ON THE MINORS OF "TOPPING CASTLE"

John Minor, I, was born in 1707 and on November 14, 1732 was m. to Sarah Carr, dau. of Thomas Carr and Mary Dabney, of Caroline county. He received as a gift from his father-in-law the estate known as "Topping Castle," which was situated on the north bank of the North Anna River in Caroline. He served the county as a Justice, was a man of superior intellect, and had a prominent place in the life of colonial Caroline.

Of the eleven children of John Minor and Sarah Carr the eldest was John Minor, II, better known as "Major John, of Topping Castle." Major John Minor was b. November 13, 1735, m. Elizabeth Cosby in 1755, and d. March 21, 1800. He was one of the most prominent and successful men in Caroline in his day. Unlike his father, he never held public office of any kind. He was a successful planter, and, in addition to the care of his own extensive plantations, he managed the affairs of General Thomas Nelson while that gentleman was engaged in affairs of State. He visited the plantations of the General monthly and saw that the several overseers were properly attending to their duties. There is a story to the effect that when on these rounds which covered many miles, the plantations being widely separated, Major Minor always rode a bob tailed black cob of great endurance, and never slower than a brisk canter. If he met any one who wished to talk to him, the person had to turn, take the Major's gait, and ride on with him until the conversation was finished.

Among Major Minor's children was a daughter, Diana Minor, who m. Richard Maury and was the mother of Commodore Matthew Fontaine Maury. There is a tradition that in a bath tub at "Topping Castle" young Matthew F. Maury demonstrated that a boat could be built which would function under water, thus forecasting the submarine which came into service many years later. Other children of Major John Minor were Lancelot Minor, father of John B., and Lucian, who were professors of law at the University of Virginia and the College of William and Mary respectively; and Dr. Charles Minor, an eminent physician, of Charlottesville.

The third child of Major Minor, was John Minor, III, who, like his father, was born at "Topping Castle," in Caroline in 1761, and who, with his wife, is buried in the old Masonic burying ground in Fredericksburg, where a red marble mausoleum marks the grave. He entered the Revolutionary Army when a mere boy and was with his distinguished father, Major Minor, at the siege and surrender of Yorktown.   After peace was declared he studied law under George Wythe and settled in Fredericksburg where he achieved reputation both for his knowledge of law and his eloquence.   He was m. 1st, to Mary Berkely, of "Airwell," Hanover county, in 1790, who died a few months after their marriage; and 2d to Lucy Landon Carter, of "Cleve," King George county.   She was a dau. of Landon Carter and Mildred Washington Willis, of Fredericksburg.   When the War of 1812 broke out John Minor, III, was made a General in the Virginia line and was stationed in and around Norfolk.   At the close of the war he returned to the practice of law.   While trying a famous case at Culpeper General Minor was so impressed by the clear and intelligent testimony of a lad who appeared in court as a witness, that he afterward sought out the boy and asked him to go back to Fredericksburg with him and attend school there. The lad accepted the offer, went to Fredericksburg, lived with John Minor, received his academic training, studied law, and became famous in after years as Benjamin Botts, counsel for Aaron Burr, when Burr was tried for high treason.   Botts named his eldest son John Minor in honor of his benefactor.   General Minor also befriended William Wirt at Culpeper Court House when Wirt as a young lawyer was struggling with an adverse bench in the county court.   Wirt related the incident afterward and added, "There was never a more finished and engaging gentleman nor one of a more warm, honest and affectionate heart.   He was a most excellent lawyer, with a persuasive flow of eloquence, simple, natural, graceful and most affecting where there was room for pathos of the true sort which flows from a feeling heart and a noble mind."

General Minor was a member of the House of Delegates in 1790 and introduced two bills looking to the emancipation of slaves, the first providing for the gradual emancipation, and the second for transportation and colonization, and although both bills had the approval of Thomas Jefferson, no action was taken on them by the House.   He was an intimate friend of President Monroe and was one of the Electoral College which cast the vote of the State of Virginia for Monroe on his second election to the Presidency.   The Electoral College met as usual in Richmond and the citizens of the city tendered them a public dinner in the State Capitol. General Minor was designated to speak on this occasion, and while doing so in his usual eloquent manner, was stricken with apoplexy and was carried into one of the committee rooms where he died in a few moments, at about 11:00 P. M. At the same evening there were gathered around the parlor fire at "Cleve" in King George a number of the members of the family of General Minor's wife, among them her brother-in-law, Mr. William McFarland, a lawyer and poet. At eleven o'clock he left the company to retire, but in a moment returned in a somewhat alarmed condition and declared that he had seen General Minor in the gallery upstairs—yet he was sure it was only his ghost. He was laughed at and told that it was only his impressionable fancy, so he started up again, but soon returned with the same story, whereupon the whole company went with him, but, not being so impressionable as Mr. McFarland, the ghost was not seen. Early next day they learned that at the very moment Mr. McFarland had seen the ghost of General Minor upstairs the General had died in Richmond, and afterward Mr. McFarland's fancies were more esteemed. This story is well authenticated in the Minor family records and leads one to believe that there are minds so peculiarly sensitive that impressions may be made on them by occurrences at a distance, to which the average mind is wholly oblivious.

General Minor retained the ancestral estate, "Topping Castle," in Caroline, until his death, using it as his summer home. His town home, "Hazel Hill," at the lower end of Fredericksburg is said to have been one of the finest places in or around the city. The house was surrounded by beautiful grounds some fifty acres in extent, and here General Minor lived in grand style and dispensed hospitality with a lavish hand. "Hazel Hill" was a strategic point during the Civil War and at the battle of Fredericksburg the house was riddled by shells.

General Minor had seven children: Mary Beverly who m. William M. Blackford and became the mother of Charles M. Blackford, of Lynchburg, from whose story of the Minors in the *Virginia Magazine* the foregoing is taken: (2) Lewis Willis, who distinguished himself in the United States Navy; (3) Rev. Launcelot Byrd Minor, who was a famous missionary to Africa from the Episcopal church; (4) Charles Landon Carter Minor, of the United States Army; (5) James Monroe Minor, of the United

States Navy; (6) Lucius H. Minor, of Hanover, and (7) John Minor, IV.

The only daughter died in 1896 at the home of her son, Professor Launcelot Minor Blackford, Principal of the Episcopal High School, of Alexandria, in the ninety-third year of her age. John Minor, IV, being born at "Hazel Hill" and therefore not a native of Caroline, as were his forefathers, does not come within the scope of this work. Suffice it to say that he maintained the high standards and traditions of his family, was a man of superior education, a lawyer, a writer of ability, a lover of children and a benefactor to struggling young men. Among his many proteges were two well-known artists, Leutze who painted "Washington Crossing the Delaware," and "Westward the Star of Empire Takes its Way," and Elder who painted "The Battle of the Crater." John Minor, IV, died unmarried in Fredericksburg on January 12, 1862.

THE MOTLEY FAMILY

This family, which is of English origin, came to Virginia about the close of the seventeenth century and settled in that section of the State which was included in King and Queen, Essex, and Caroline, when these counties were formed. In the Clerk's office of Essex county is recorded a Motley will in which certain moneys are left to his son "to pay for the surveying of his land at the foot of the mountains." This son, John Motley, was the progenitor of the Motleys, of Pittsylvania and Henry counties, and it was in the former county that the "land at the foot of the mountains" was situated.

Among the early members of this family in the Rappahannock Valley was Henry Motley, who m. ———— and had issue: (1) Nathaniel, (2) Thomas Hugh, (3) Henry, (4) Sally, and (5) Elizabeth.

Nathaniel, m. Lucy Broaddus, sister of Judge Andrew Broaddus who emigrated westward, and had issue: (1) *John Leland*, m. Maria Broaddus, (2) *Elizabeth*, m. Garland Samuel, (3) *Christina*, who m. Woodson Broaddus, (4) *Sally*, who m. Richard Green, (5) *Polly*, who m. George Marshall; (6) *Louisa*, who m. John Broaddus; (7) *Alice*, who m. Dr. C. C. Broaddus; (8) *Victoria*, who m. Frank Gouldin, and (9) *Virginia*, who m. ———— Green.

Thomas Hugh Motley, m. Catherine Martin, of Caroline and

had issue: (1) Thomas Judson, who m. Martha Samuel and had issue: (1) Henry Judson, (2) Nannie, (3) Ida, (4) Govan, (5) Bowie and (6) Nellie.

Sally Motley, m. Younger Martin, of Caroline and had issue: (1) John Henry, (2) Eliza. *Eliza,* m. Philip Green and had issue: (1) Henry, (2) Elizabeth, (3) Nellie, (4) Nola, and (5) Lillie.

Elizabeth, m. Andrew Pitts and had issue: (1) Chester, (2) Eugene, (3) Jefferson, (4) George H., (5) Andrew.

Other early members of this family were Andrew Motley, Col. Thomas Motley, Harry Motley, Robert S. Motley, Lunsford Motley, Nathaniel Motley, Edward Motley, Silas Motley, Richard Motley and Polly Motley. The homes of the greater number of these were in King and Queen, although a number lived in Caroline and Essex. Polly Motley, sister of Col. Thos. Motley, m. ──── Henshaw, and was the grandmother of Rev. M. E. Broaddus, M. G. Broaddus, W. R. Broaddus, Manley Broaddus, R. F. Broaddus and Mrs. Effie Brownley.

Several members of this family emigrated to the Pittsylvania county, as heretofore noted, and established the Motley family of the South Piedmont section of the State

John Motley, son of John, one of the emigrants before named, m. Geddie Jones and had issue: (1) *Betty,* who m. Robt. Blackwell; (2) *Mary,* who m. Wm. Hall; (3) *Catherine,* who m. John Allen; (4) *Anne,* who m. Wm. Allen; (5) *Susan,* who m. William Motley; (6) *Sally,* who m. ──── Yeatts; (7) *Martha,* who m. ──── Yeatts; (8) *Amelie,* who m. Nathan Riddell; (9) *George,* who m. 1st, Martha McGuire, and 2d, Missouri Lawrence Woodall, widow of ──── Woodall.

William Motley, who m. Susan Motley, had four brothers: (1) Samuel P., (2) John (commonly called Jack); (3) James and (4) Daniel.

William Motley and *Susan Motley* had issue: (1) John A., (2) Wm. G., (3) Josiah, (4) Richard, (5) David, (6) Scroggs, (7) Daniel W., (8) Malinda, (9) Polly, (10) Ella, (11) Lucy, (12) Geddie, (13) Catherine. Richard (see 4) was a Disciple minister.

John A., m. Minnie Fowler and had issue: (1) Beatrice, (2) Leonard, (3) Carrie, (4) Mary, (5) Earle, (6) Hugh, (7) Ruth, (8) Joe, (9) Averett and (10) Lester.

William G., m. Pinckney Shelton and had issue: (1) Edna Elizabeth, (2) Ruby Frances and (3) Mary Wills.

Josiah C., m. Nellie Bennett and had issue: (1) Viola, (2) Voyls, (3) Virgil, (4) Douglas, (5) Anderson, (6) Regina, (7) Rebecca, (8) Bennett, (9) Wesley, (10) Catherine.

Richard Motley, m. Nellie Williams, of Giles county, and had issue: (1) Lucile, (2) Ruth, (3) Langhorne, (4) Richard, Jr., (5) Ralph.

Malinda Motley, m. Bedford Motley, and had issue: (1) Sally, (2) Charles, (3) Daniel, (4) George, (5) Ernest, (6) Lindsay, (7) Betty Sue. After the death of Malinda Motley, Bedford Motley, m. 2d, Lydia Atkinson and had issue: (8) Hattie, (9) Mary, (10) Reed, (11) Eloise, (12) Martin and (13) Hale. Daniel Motley (see 3) became a minister in the Church of Disciples of Christ.

Polly Motley, m J. T. Hodges; Ella Motley, m. J. W. Bradner; Lucy Motley, m. W. J. Horner, Jr., of California; Geddie Motley, m. W L. Lewis.

Anne Motley, sister of Wm. and dau. of John Motley and Geddie Jones, m. William Allen and had issue: (1) Sally, (2) Lavinia, (3) Fanny, (4) Robert, (5) Lena and (6) Emma

Sally Allen, dau. of Anne Motley and Wm. Allen, m. James Motley and had issue: (1) Rawley, (2) Edwin, (3) Ernest, and (4) Mercer. Ernest is a minister in the Disciples church, and Mercer is a tobacconist in Danville.

George Motley

George Motley, son of John Motley and Geddie Jones, m. 1st, Martha McGuire, and 2d, Missouri Lawrence Woodall, and had issue, by the first marriage: (1) Fanny, (2) Mary, (3) Martha, (4) John Fontaine, (5) Joel, (6) LaFayette; and by the second marriage he had issue: (7) Henry Clay, (8) Virginia, and (9) Benjamin.

Fanny, m. Daniel J. Motley; *Mary*, m. Ephraim Hundley; *Martha*, m. Wm Woodall; *John Fontaine*, m Nannie S. Martin, dau. of Chas. Martin, *Joel*, d. unmarried; *LaFayette*, m. Lula Gilbert; *Henry Clay*, m. Mary Fuller; *Virginia*, m. William Terry; *Benjamin*, m. Ola Brandon.

John Fontaine Motley

John Fontaine Motley and Nannie S. Martin had issue: (1) *Sally*, m. Frank Amos; (2) *Henry George*, m. 1st, Leanna Reynolds, 2d, Lou Arrington; (3) *Mary*, m. Tazewell Tarleton Wingfield; *Martha*, m. 1st, W. F. Mills, 2d, J J. Okes; (5) *John L.*, m. Kate Reynolds; (6) *Nannie*, m. John Blackwell.

George Motley, son of John and Geddie Jones, ran away to sea when a lad of thirteen and did not return until he was past thirty years of age. During his seafaring days he visited practically every country of the world and had a remarkable fund of knowledge and experience. He was an enthusiastic Mason, possibly initiated in some foreign port. He rode horseback across Turkey Cock mountain to old Snow Creek Lodge in Franklin county every month as long as he lived. His son, John Fontaine Motley, was prominent in the political life of Henry county. George Motley and his son John Fontaine, were maternal great-grandfather and grandfather respectively of the author of this volume.

The Peatross family is of Welch and Scotch descent. Robert Peatross, the first of the name in Virginia, came from Wales to Caroline during the latter part of the eighteenth century. He had five sons and three daughters. Of the sons, Robert was a local preacher in the Methodist church. He m. Ann Scott, of Caroline, by whom he had six sons and four daughters. One of the sons, Richard Peatross was the third generation in America, of his name. He resided at "The Glebe," near Needwood Precinct, in Caroline county. He was the father of nine children: M. D. Peatross, J. W. Peatross, Richard Peatross, Robert Sale Peatross, William E. Peatross, Sally E. Peatross, Frances Peatross, Clarissa Peatross and Malindia Peatross. Taking the daughters first: Sally E., m. Warner M. Mason, she being his second wife; Frances, m. Warner M. Mason, she being his first wife; Clarissa, m. Richard Turner, Matilda, m. Samuel Lawrence; Sally E., d. without issue; Frances had four children: Cornelius, Kate, Jennie, and Margaret. Cornelius was killed in the Civil War at Sharpsburg; Jennie, m. Walter Scott Peatross, and is survived by several children now living in Richmond. Margaret never married; Clarissa, wife of Richard Turner, had issue: Richard, Agnes, Daniel, Reuben, Mary, Rebecca and Sally; Matilda, wife of Samuel Lawrence, had issue: Richard, Clarissa, Mary, James, William and Samuel. Taking the sons of Richard Peatross: M. D. Peatross had a dau. named Adelaide, who m. James Munday and has descendants residing in Maryland; J. W. Peatross had children: Maria Ann, Richard, Francis and Sally. Richard Peatross had a dau. named Fanny. William E. Peatross, died without issue; Robert Sale Peatross, m. Elizabeth Scott, sister of Samuel Soctt, a prominent lawyer of Caroline county, who represented the district in Congress at one time. She had another brother, Thomas Scott, a physician, who resided near Ruther Glen. The children surviving Robert Sale Peatross were: Annie C., who m. Charles T. Wortham, of Richmond and is survived by a son, Coleman Wortham, a prominent business man of Richmond. Mary F., who m. Dr. Robert T. Wortham, who resided at "The Grove" in the lower end of Caroline county and is survived by several children, still living at the family residence. Ella, who m. Thomas C. Williams, of Richmond and is survived by three children, Thomas C., Jr.; Adolphus D., both

of Richmond and Mrs. Sue Massie, of Albemarle county. Walter
Scott, a farmer, who resided in the lower end of Caroline county,
died about 1910 and is survived by several children, living in
Richmond. He m. Jennie Mason and their descendents are referred to above. Richard Warner, who practiced law in Danville,
was prominent in legal and educational circles, was the founder
of Randolph-Macon Institute, of Danville, a member of the
Board of Trustees of Randolph-Macon College and at the time
of his death, about 1919, was judge of the Corporation Court of
Danville. He is survived by four children, Richard Warner, Jr.,
a mining engineer, of Waco, Texas; Garnett, who resides in
Danville; Hunter, who resides in New York City and Bessie Lee,
who resides in Danville. Robert Olin Peatross, resided in
Caroline county, where he practiced law up to the date of his
death in 1905. R. O. Peatross, R W Peatross and W. S.
Peatross served in the Confederate Army during the Civil War.
R. O. Peatross was Major of the Thirtieth Virginia Regiment,
Caroline Volunteers and participated in a number of the battles
of the Civil War, including Drewry's Bluff and Sharpsburg.
He was twice wounded. R. W. Peatross was a captain of
engineers. W. S. Peatross was a private in the Thirtieth Virginia
Regiment and was severely wounded in the battle of Sharpsburg.
Major Robert Olin Peatross left surviving him six children, all
of whom are now living—two daughters, Bessie and Alice, and
four sons, Cecil G. , Archibald Samuel, Louis Ashby and Richard
Warner. Cecil is a farmer in the lower end of Caroline county,
Archibald Samuel is division manager of R. G. Dunn Mercantile
Agency, with headquarters at El Paso, Texas; Louis Ashby,
an Episcopal minister, resides at 738 Bedford Place, Columbus,
O., and is assistant rector of a church there. He is married and
has two children. Robert Olin Peatross, m. Julia Archibald
Samuel, daughter of Col. Archibald Samuel, of Bath, in Caroline
county. Richard Warner Peatross was married in 1905 to Mary
Newman, daughter of C. S. Newman, of Knoxville, Tenn. Her
ancestors for several generations lived in Orange county, Va., at
"Hilton," adjoining "Montpelier." They have one daughter,
Miss Katherine Hazen Peatross, now a student at Mary Baldwin
Seminary in Staunton.

Richard Warner Peatross received his academic education at
the graded school in Bowling Green and at Randolph-Macon
College. He studied law while teaching school at the University

School, Knoxville, Tenn., an institution preparatory to the University of Tennessee, and was admitted to the bar in Tennessee in 1899 and has been practicing in Norfolk since 1900. He has been City Attorney of Norfolk since September 1, 1918. He is an elder in the Presbyterian church. He was a member of the Charter Commission in 1917, which drafted the Norfolk Charter of 1918 under which the City Manager plan of government was made effective in Norfolk.

The Peatross Arms (also Peat) are thus described:

Arms: Per pale wavy, ar. and gules barry of six counter-changed.

Crest: A deer's head ppr.

Motto: *Prospere si propere.*

THE PRATT FAMILY

The Pratt Family came to America from England. There is a tradition that a son of Charles Pratt, Earl of Camden and Chief Justice of England, had a difficulty with a fellow-student at Oxford and on account of this difficulty came to America rather than embarrass his father. He settled in King George county and was soon followed by a younger brother who decided to cast his lot in the new country. These brothers acquired estates, married and became heads of large families.

John Pratt came from King George to Caroline in 1790, married a widow, Mrs. Dixon, of Port Royal. He bought a large tract of land on the Rappahannock, below Port Royal, from the Micou and Lomax families and built the first Camden house. This house was of the long colonial type. In 1858 William Pratt razed the original Camden house and built the present structure, which is of the Italian Villa type, with very large rooms and porches.

Camden

During the Civil War, when the community was in the hands of the Confederate Army, this house was the scene of many dances and other festivities, and many are the stories told of the brilliant functions held here.   But when the tide turned and the Federal troops came in all was different and the house was as solemn and quiet as the burying ground hard by.   The Northern troops threatened to burn the house several times and once fired on it from gunboats on the Rappahannock, but did very little damage.

The house stands near the bank of the Rappahannock, on a bluff overlooking the broad expanse of the river which here resembles a lake.   It is surrounded by an unusually large lawn which is covered with many beautiful old trees.   The Camden farm consists of about 1,400 acres on which is one of the finest apple orchards in Tidewater Virginia.   The place is managed by the Hon. Richard T. Pratt, a lineal descendant of this ancient family, who for a time represented Caroline in the House of Delegates.   Mr. Pratt m. Miss Courtney Crump, daughter of Judge Beverly Crump, of Richmond   His brother William T Pratt, m 1st Miss Marshall and 2d Miss Mary Custis Lee, of Stafford, and lives in Fredericksburg, Va.

Messrs. William and Richard Pratt have two sisters: Mrs. Ida Vivian Funsten, widow of the late Bishop James Bowen Funsten, of the Protestant Episcopal Church, and Miss Maggie Pratt, who lives with her mother at "Camden."

Arms: Sa. on a fesse betw. three elephants heads erased ar. as many mullets of the first.

Crest: An elephant's head erased ar.

Supporters: Dexter, a griffin sa. beak and forelegs gu.; Sinister, a lion ramp. or, each gorged with a collar ar. charged with three mullets sa.

Motto: *Judicium parium aut lex terrae.*

THE REDDS OF "CEDAR VALE."

James Redd, m. Miss Eastham, Issue: Samuel Redd, of "Cedar Vale," Caroline county, Va., b. 1729, m. 1755, Lucy Rogers, b. 1731. She was the daughter of John Rogers, of King and Queen county, Va., and Mary Byrd and the aunt of Gen. George Rogers Clarke and Gens. William and Jonathan Clarke; also the sister of John and Byrd Rogers, of Albemarle county, Va

Their issue: seven children—

1. Fannie Redd, m. Col. Samuel Temple, of King and Queen county, Va. Issue: six children: John Temple, m. Mary Latane; Fannie, m. Rev. Andrew Broaddus, of Caroline county, Va.; Lucy, m. Timothy Chandler, of Caroline county, Va.; Mr. Hugh Davis, from Norfolk is descended from them.; Ann, m. Henry Cocke.   There were other sons.

2. William Redd, son of Samuel Redd and Lucy Rogers, of "Cedar Vale," Caroline county, Va., m. Miss Tyler, of Caroline county, Va.

(The Moncures, of Ruther Glen, Mr. Clarence Tompkins, of "Ormesby," Caroline county, Va., and Fitzgerald Tompkins, of Ind., are their descendants.)

3 Jessie Redd, son of Samuel Redd and Lucy Rogers, of "Cedar Vale," m Miss Mary Woodson, of Goochland county, Va.

4. Lucy Redd, dau. of Samuel Redd and Lucy Rogers, of "Cedar Vale," m. John Fitzhugh, of King George county, Va. Issue:

Judge Dennis Fitzhugh, of Louisville, Ky., m his cousin, the sister of Gen. George Rogers Clarke; Samuel Temple Fitzhugh, m. Miss Fitzhugh, from near Baltimore; Lucy Fitzhugh, m. Dr.

Benjamin Harrison Hall, in 1825, or '30, and lived in Louisville, Ky.; Phillip Fitzhugh, m. Mary Macon Aylett, of King William county, Va. He was the father of Maj. Patrick and Dr. Fitzhugh, Mrs. Curtis and Mrs. John Robinson Redd, of "Cedar Vale."

5. Ann Redd, dau. of Samuel Redd and Lucy Rogers, of "Cedar Vale," m. Thomas Carr Minor, of "Topping Castle," son of Major John Minor and Elizabeth Cosby.

Issue: Eleven children: Judge Henry Minor, m. Frances Throckmorton Barbour (September 14, 1809, in Petersburg, Va.); left many descendants.; Ann Redd Minor, m. her cousin, Dr. William Tompkins Minor, brother of Prof. John B. Minor, of the University of Virginia. She left issue: Dr. Minor, m. 2d, Miss Washington.

6. Samuel Redd, of "Cedar Vale," b. March 19, 1764, m. March 2, 1797, Elizabeth Taylor, of Taylorsville, Hanover county, Va. (the dau. of Edmund Taylor and Ann Day). She was b. March 31, 1776, d. at "Cedar Vale," November 5, 1858. Issue: Lucy Anne Redd, b. December 15, 1797, m. February 28, 1822, Dr. Littleton Goodwin Coleman, son of Harry Coleman of Caroline county, by his 1st wife, Miss Goodwin.

Edmund, b. November 19, 1799, m. 1825, Sophia Pleasants Burton—they were the ancestors of Crawford Redd, of Ginter Park; Mrs. James Redd, of Churchland, Va., and Paul Redd, of Highland Park and William P. Redd, of Richmond, Va.

Elizabeth Taylor Redd, of "Cedar Vale, m. Williamson Talley on October 26, 1820, the ancestors of Mary Louisa Talley who m. her cousin, Edmund Carter Taylor. (He the son of Walker Taylor, of Taylorsville and Elizabeth Berkeley, of "Edgewood," Hanover county, Va.) They left many descendants.

Samuel Redd, of "Cedar Vale," son of Samuel Redd and Elizabeth Taylor, b. March 10, 1804, m. December 12, 1827, Cornelia M. McLaughlin, (dau. of John McLaughlin and Mary Overton Minor, of "Springfield," Caroline county, Va.) d. March 5, 1889. Cornelia McLaughlin, b. December 2, 1810, d. at "Hybla," Hanover county, Va., April 12, 1889.

Issue: Addison Lewis Redd, of "Hybla," d. 1901, unmarried; Edmund Taylor Redd, m. 1st Betty Sanford, of Brunswick county, Va., m. 2d Bertha Southworth. Issue: Claudia Minor Redd, who has a large school in Lansdown, Pa.; Mary Taylor Redd, m. Charles Green Fergusson, of N. C.; Beatrice Redd, m. Mr. Gates, no issue; Dr. John T. Redd (son of Samuel Redd and Cornelia McLaughlin) m. in 1866, Miss Kate Shields, dau. of Major G. B. Shields, of Natchez, Miss. Issue: Benoist Shields Redd, of New York City. He m. in 1897 Marie Castegnier, of N. Y. City. Issue: John Redd.

Judge Samuel C. Redd, son of Samuel Redd and Cornelia McLaughlin, of "Hybla," m. Nannie Carter, of "North River," Hanover county, Va., dau. of Mr. Henry Rose Carter and Emma Coleman, dau. of Henry Coleman and his second wife, Miss Mason, of Caroline county. Issue:

1. Hill Carter Redd, m. Virginia Campbell, of "Glen Cairn," Hanover county, Va., June 26, 1901. Issue: William Hugh Redd and Emma Coleman Redd.

2. John Champe Redd, (son of Samuel Redd and Ann Carter) m. Sallie Williams, of Brunswick county, Va. Issue: Champe Carter, John Hampden and Mary Gordon Redd.

3. Samuel Coleman Redd, m. Minnie Morcatelle, of Arizona, July, 1914.

Sarah Elizabeth, (dau. of Samuel Redd and Cornelia McLaughlin) d. at "Hybla," February 21, 1917.

Clarence Meriwether Redd, son of Samuel Redd and Cornelia McLaughlin of "Hybla," d. March 21, 1922, unmarried.

Eugene M. Redd, (son of Samuel Redd and Cornelia McLaughlin, of "Hybla,") m. Jane Rose Claiborne, of "Geddes," Amherst county, Va., dau. of Charles Buller Claiborne and Sallie Coleman, s. of Mrs. Henry Carter, of "Landora," Caroline county, Va.

Issue: (a) Sallie Claiborne Redd, m. H. P. Porter, of Albemarle county, Va ; (b) Mary Minor Redd, (dau. of Eugene Redd and Jane Claiborne), d. in infancy; (c) Eugene M. Redd, (son of Eugene Redd and Jane Claiborne), m. 1st Miss Shelton, of Nelson county, Va., m. 2d his cousin, Marie Gantt, October 28, 1916, at "Roseland," Nelson county, Va.; (d) Harry Coleman Redd, (son of Eugene Redd and Jane Claiborne) of "Bellevette," Nelson county, Va., m. Carrie Brent; (e) Cornelia McLaughlin, (dau. of Eugene and Jane Claiborne Redd, of Nelson county) m. Joe Edwards; (f) Bessie Overton, (dau. of Eugene Redd and Jane Claiborne, of Nelson county), m. Harry Massie, of "Roseland"; (g) James Mason Redd (son of Eugene M. Redd and Jane Rose Claiborne), m. Ethel Tompkins, September, 1923, Arrington, Va.

Barbara M. Redd, (dau. of Samuel Redd and Cornelia Mc-Laughlin, of "Hybla," d. December 8, 1922, unmarried.

Emily H. Redd, (dau. of Samuel Redd and Cornelia Mc-Laughlin, of "Hybla,") m. Hill Carter (son of Ann Carter, who m. Judge Redd). Issue:

Dr. Henry Rose Carter, of Ashland, Va., m. Mary Washington Pendleton, of Louisa county, Va.; (b) Samuel Redd Carter, (son of Hill Carter and Emily Redd, of Ashland), m. Bessie Dozier Lee, of Sumter, S. C., on January 7, 1903; (c) Hill Carter, Jr., m. Bessie LaDew, of Cumberland, Md.; (d) Clarence Minor Carter, unmarried; (e) Charles Harrison Carter, m. Catherine Ogie Skelton, of Richmond, Va.; (f) Shirley Carter, unmarried.

James Cary Redd, (son of Samuel Redd and Cornelia Mc-Laughlin, of "Hybla," Hanover county, Va.), m. his cousin, Jane Taylor Pearce and lived at "Sligo," Hanover county, Va.

Issue: (a) Burnley Redd, m. William E. Tyler, of "Blenheim," Caroline county, Va., youngest son of Julia Minor Magruder, of Albemarle county, Va., and Henry Tyler, of "Blenheim" (William Tyler is half-brother of Gov. Hoge Tyler, of Virginia); (b) James Pearce Redd (son of Cary Redd and Jane Taylor Pearce, of "Sligo,"), m. Miss Sullivan, of Kentucky. No issue; (c) Hardenia Taylor Redd, (dau. of Cary Redd and Jane Taylor Pearce, of "Sligo"), m. her cousin, Claude Hunter (son of Taliaferro Hunter, of Ruther Glen, Caroline county, Va., and Miss Coleman, of Alabama.)

Loula C. Redd, (dau. of Samuel Redd and Cornelia Mc-Laughlin, of "Hybla," unmarried.

Charles Overton Redd, (son of Samuel Redd and Cornelia McLaughlin, of "Hybla," Hanover county, Va.) m. Virginia Dickinson, of Louisa county, Va., d. in 1890.

Issue: Clarence Overton Redd, of New Jersey.

Emily Harris Redd, (dau. of Samuel Redd and Elizabeth Taylor, of "Cedar Vale," m. February 11, 1830, Mr. S. Gouldin, lived in Goochland county.

Sarah Taylor, dau. of Samuel Redd and Elizabeth Taylor, of "Cedar Vale," d. unmarried.

John Robinson Redd (son of Samuel Redd and Elizabeth Taylor, of "Cedar Vale"), b. September 7, 1810, m 1st, April 24, 1838, to his cousin, Lucy Aylett Fitzhugh, m. 2d, Ann Hill, sister of Mr. Lewis Hill, of Richmond, Va.

Issue 1st marriage: Lucy Fitzhugh, m. Jaquelin Holliday,

Indianapolis, Ind.; their issue: Annie Holliday, m. Harry Burnett; Jacquelin, m. Florence Baker; Lucy F., m. George Hume.

Issue: 2d marriage: Ann Redd, m. Fitzgerald Tompkins

James Temple Redd, son of Samuel Redd and Elizabeth Taylor, of "Cedar Vale," m. May 10, 1838, Tomasia Anderson, dau. of Dr. Thomas Anderson, of "Providence," Caroline county and Harriet McLaughlin, of Caroline county.

Louisa Redd, dau. of Samuel Redd and Elizabeth Taylor, of "Cedar Vale," b. December 12, 1817, m. December 5, 1839, to Dr. Thomas Waring Gouldin.

Mrs. Duncan Holliday, of Ind., Mrs. Alvin Rowe, of Fredericksburg, Va., and Mr. Rob Goulding, of Caroline county, Va., are descended from Dr. Gouldin.

THE SCOTT FAMILY

The Scott family is of ancient origin. Sir Richard Le Scott, ancestor of the Virginia branch of this family, was a person of distinction in the reign of Alexander, III, of Scotland about 1280. Sir David Scott, of Brauxholm sat in the Parliament of James, III in 1487. Sir Walter Scott is described in history as a man of valour. Sir Walter's grandson of the same name was a person of rare attainments. He died in 1574. Another Walter Scott was knighted in 1590 and elevated to the peerage in 1606 as Lord Scott, of Buccleuch. His son was created Lord Whitchester and Eskdale and Earl of Buccleuch, in 1619. A related branch of this family produced Sir Walter Scott, the illustrious author.

The younger son of one of the Lairds of Scott aided the young Pretender in 1746 and was forced to seek refuge in America. He came to Virginia and married and entered upon the practice of law. His son, William, married a Miss Anna Mason and died in 1791. His grandson was the celebrated General Wingfield Scott, hero of the Mexican War.

Francis Woolfolk Scott, III, of Middlesex, writes: " My greatgrandfather emigrated with his brother from Scotland some time in the 18th century and served in the Revolutionary army." Dr. James Scott, of St. Louis, writes: "My grandfather was called Captain Jack Scott. He fitted out a company to defend Washington against the British, but saw the city burning before he reached there."

Captain Jack Scott, m. Elizabeth Brumskill, dau. of an Episcopal rector and had issue: Samuel, Robert, John, Harrod, Richard,

Emily, Anne and Francis. Francis, m. Martha Woolfolk. Robert
Scott, son of Captain Jack and Elizabeth, was the father of Dr.
Thomas Llewellyn Scott, of Caroline. Francis Woolfolk Scott,
m. 1st, Miss ———— Coles and had issue: John Walter Scott and
Willmonia; 2d, Mrs. Joel Blake, of Mathews county, sister of
Colonels Wm. B. and Robert Davis, of Millers Tavern; 3d, Miss
Ann Maria Minor, dau. of Col. Thos. Minor, of Spotsylvania
and had issue: (1) Alice Taylor, who m. W. T. Chandler; (2)
Mary Emma, who m. Rev. E. H. Rowe; (3) Maria Louise, who m.
Prof. C. B. Stuart; (4) Francis Woolfolk Scott, who m. 1st, Julia
Mann, 2d Caroline Blake.

Alice Taylor Scott and W. T. Chandler died without issue.

Mary Emma Scott and Rev. E. H. Rowe had issue one son,
Scott Rowe, who m. Miss Alle Hunter, sister of his father's third
wife, and lives at "Holly Hill." They have two children—Mary
Frances and Emma Jane.

Maria Louise Scott and Prof. C. B. Stuart had issue: (1)
Francis Woolfolk, (2) James and (3) Alice.

Francis Woolfolk Scott, m. Julia Isabel Mann in 1866 and
had issue eight children, four of whom lived to maturity. (1)
Llewellyn Davis, (2) Francis Woolfolk, (3) Emma, (4) Bessie.
Francis Woolfolk, m. his second wife, Caroline Matilda Blake
in 1882 and had issue five children: (1) Walter Carroll, (2) Minor
Blake, (3) Robert Preston, (4) Virginia Lee, (5) Alice Louise.

John Walter Scott and Gabrielle Bosher had issue: (1)
Gabrielle, (2) Mary, (3) Rosa and (4) John Walter, Jr. This
family lived in King William.

Llewellyn Davis Scott, son of F. W. Scott and Julia Mann,
m. 1st, Lelia Wyatt Lovelace, of Marion, Ala., and had issue:
(1) Llewellyn, Jr., d. in infancy; (2) Francis W., of Huttig, Ark.;
(3) Kendrick Lovelace, lawyer; L. D. Scott, m. 2d, Josephine
Lovelace, sister of his 1st wife and had issue: (1) Alice Chandler,
(2) Josephine Lovelace, (3) Mary Wyatt.

Minor Blake Scott, son of F. W. Scott and Caroline Blake,
m. Ruth Wilson and lives at Kinder, La. Robert Preston Scott
son of F. W. Scott and Caroline Blake, m. Irene Bloomfield, of
Houston, Texas, and had issue: Robert, Irene, and Virginia Lee,
who m. Laurens Cook Pierce and lives at Ft. Oglethorpe.
Alice Louise Scott, another dau. of F. W. Scott and Caroline
Blake, is associated with her half-brother, Prof. L. D. Scott,
in the Washington Female Seminary, of Atlanta.

John Scott, m. Caroline Skinker and had issue three children. They removed to Missouri and opened a boys' school there.

James Murphy Scott, son of Harrod and grandson of Captain Jack Scott, removed with his parents to Missouri when a lad and attended a private school presided over by his uncle John Scott. He was graduated from the Medical School, of St. Louis University, practiced in St. Louis and was professor in Medical College of Washington University. Married Estelle Kirker, granddaughter of Thomas Kirker, second Governor of Ohio. Their daughter, Stella, lives unmarried in Huttig, Ark.

Emily Ann Scott, dau. of Captain Jack, m. her cousin, Drury Christian, of Virginia and had issue: (1) Stephen, (2) James, (3) Sarah and (4) Ann.

Richard Scott, son of Captain Jack Scott, was a lieutenant in Col. Miller's Regiment at the Battle of Lundy's Lane. The killing of Lieutenant Scott and his party is said to have brought on the Seminole War. Reference to this will be found in Henry Clay's speech as given in *"Eloquence of the United States."*

Richard Brumskill Scott, son of Robert Scott and grandson of Captain Jack, was a Methodist minister and a member of the Virginia Conference. His son Richard is also a member of the Virginia Conference.

Ann Scott, dau. of Captain Jack Scott, m. Nathaniel Ware, of Caroline, and had issue: John H.   John H. Ware m. Mary Z., daughter of Samuel Coleman, of "Marl Hill," and had issue: (1) Nathaniel, deceased; (2) Herbert W., (3) Coleman, (4) Ottawa Ann, (5) John H., (6) Daisy Scott.

Herbert W. Ware, m. Jennie L. Henderson, of Orange county, and had issue: Virginia Irving, m. Rev. Goodwin Frazer, now of Charles Town, W. Va., and has issue, Frances Scott and Caroline H.; John H., who died at V. M. I., in 1918; Susie H., who m. David Branch, and has issue, David Ware; Henry M., of Richmond, Va.   Herbert W. Ware is now Vice-President of Trevvett, Christian & Co., the publishers of this work.

Coleman Ware, m. Dora Frickey, of Springfield, Mo., and had issue: Scott.

Ottawa Ann Ware, m. John Hundley, of Hanover county, and had issue Harrold, Byrel W., Loice, Waller, John, George, Mary, Ann.

John H. Ware, m. Lula Covington, of Covington, Va., and had issue: (1) Martha, (2) Marion.

Daisy Scott Ware, m. Albert W. Hankins, of Louisa county, Va., and had issue: Albert W., and Mary Coleman.

Elizabeth Scott, sister of Congressman Samuel Scott and Dr. Thomas Scott, m. Robert Sale Peatross. See genealogy of Peatross family elsewhere in this book.

Sarah Scott, m. Charles Farish, of Caroline.

Emily Scott resided with Francis Woolfolk Scott, I. Died unmarried.

Samuel Scott, son of Robert, m. a Miss Flippo, of Caroline, removed to a western State.

Nannie Scott, m ——— Fitzgerald, of Nottoway county and had issue Scott Fitzgerald, who with his aunt, Mary Eliza Scott, owns valuable Scott family records.

Martha Frances Scott m. the Hon. W. R. B. Wyatt, on September 5, 1832. Upon her death, her sister, Isabelle Adelaide Scott, became the second wife of Mr. Wyatt. For dates see Wyatt Genealogy eleswhere in this volume. Ellen Scott, sister of Martha and Isabelle, died unmarried.

Harrod Brumskill Scott, son of Captain Jack Scott and Elizabeth Brumskill, m. Sarah Jordan Christian and had issue: (1) Martha Elizabeth, (2) Emily Ann, (3) James Murphy, (4) John, (5) Richard, (6) Charles Robert.

Martha Scott, m. Thomas Carter Johnson and had issue: (1) Thomas Watts, who became a physician and practiced in Missouri; (2) Edward Scott Johnson, who m. Miss Gillie Orrick, a niece of Bishop Otey, of Virginia. Res. Butte, Montana. They have six children, Mrs. Samuel Griffith, of Montana; (2) Mrs. Wolcott Allison, of Chicago; (3) Mrs. Wm. Parkinson, of Montana; (4) Mrs. Patty Naff, of Los Angeles; (5) Edward Johnson, of Montana and (6) James Johnson, of Washington State. Thomas Carter Johnson, m. 2d a cousin of his first wife who bore exactly the same name. They had issue; (1) Elizabeth, who lived in St. Louis, unmarried; (2) Robert, who m. Miss Jessie W. Wells, of Mississippi. Robert Johnson and Jessie Wells had issue: (1) Ida Wells Johnson, (2) Sidney Carter Johnson. The latter lived in St Louis until his death a few years ago, and was General Auditor of the Cotton Belt Railroad. He m. Mary Waller, of Virginia, and has issue: T. C. Johnson, Jr., (3) Thomasia Carter Johnson, m. Davis Stuart, of Marshall Texas. Issue: Martha Johnson ("Patty") on faculty of Teachers' College, Albany, N. Y.

Description of Scott Arms—

Arms: Or. on a bend azure, a mullet of six points between two crescents argent.

Crest: A dexter hand proper holding a broken lance.

Motto: *Armor patria.*

THE SUTTON FAMILY

Colonel Norborne E. Sutton, son of John Carter Sutton and Elizabeth Page Pendleton, was born at the "Old Mansion," Bowling Green, Va., in the year 1798. His ancestors came to Caroline from Manor House, Oxfordshire, England, in the early years of the eighteenth century—before Caroline had been formed of Essex, King William and King and Queen.

Colonel Sutton was first m. to Dorothea Washington, dau. of George and Elizabeth Washington, of "Woodpecker," Caroline county. By this marriage there were six children: Braxton, Courts, Hugh, Daniel and Norborne and one daughter, Georgianna. The second marriage was to Mary Jane Hutchinson, of "Chantilly" Henrico county. Miss Hutchinson's mother, Mildred Woolfolk Brown, was said to have descended directly through the royal family of King George, of England. She was the granddaughter of Ursula George who was a granddaughter of William Byrd, of Westover. To Colonel Sutton and Mary Hutchinson were born four children: Ida, Mary, William and Marion

Colonel Sutton was an attorney and practiced his profession in Bowling Green. He was postmaster of the town in 1834 and in 1845 represented Caroline in the State Senate. He served as a private in the War of 1812 under Captain Armistead Hoomes, of "Old Mansion."

During the Polk-Tyler campaigns Colonel Sutton had built on his estate at Bowling Green a log cabin. It was drawn by twenty horses, each led by his own groom. In the door of the cabin sat an old colored man playing a banjo. This was the chief object of interest in the election parade in Richmond. It was afterward carried from county to county and many speeches were made from its platform. During the Mexican War Colonel Sutton was one of twelve men who volunteered to help draw the cannon up the hill to bombard the city of Montaguna. Late in life he removed to Red River Texas where he died.

Arms: Hand and arm holding dagger cutting bar.

Motto: *Fortis et firmis.*

Of all family legends and traditions none is more ancient, or more interesting, than that of the Taliaferro Family, which carries one back to Julius Caesar and his campaign in Gaul.

This tradition has it that Caesar, while inspecting camp at twilight, was surrounded by Gallic warriors who were bent upon taking his life. In the midst of this imminent peril, Caesar so bravely comported himself that he won the admiration of the leader of the band, who refused to allow him to be slain. In the course of the campaign Caesar's captors became his captives and recognizing the man who had spared his life, Caesar made him one of his personal attendants and permitted him to bear arms— a privilege not allowed to any but Roman soldiers—and thus the name Taliaferro originated from the Latin "telum"—a dart—and "ferro"—to bear.

A branch of this family wandered to Normandy, thence to England with William the Conquerer. A member of the family—Baron Taliaferro—fought with the Conquerer and became known to history as "The Hero of Hastings." After William the Conquerer won the English throne he made large grants of land to Baron Taliaferro in county Kent, and Taliaferro and his descendants who possessed these lands were known as Earls of Pinnington.

After the Revocation of the Edict of Nantes, two brothers— James and John—came to America and purchased an estate on the James. John Taliaferro afterward settled near Williamsburg and established "Powhatan" and became the progenitor of the Taliaferro family in Caroline and in Virginia. "Hay" in King George county is also an old Taliaferro estate.

The family has given many useful men to the State and nation, among whom may be mentioned John Taliaferro, (1768– 1853) member of Congress, Presidential Elector, Librarian of Treasury Department at Washington. John Wishart Taliaferro, Surgeon on the *Bon Homme Richard* under John Paul Jones. Lawrence Taliaferro, Major in the United States Army; Walker Taliaferro, member of the House of Burgesses from Caroline, 1766–1768 and James Monroe Taliaferro, god-son of President Monroe and class-mate of Robert E. Lee.

THE TAYLOR FAMILY

The Taylor family is one of historic interest and dignity and has been closely associated with the development of this country from its earliest colonial struggles. Among the English gentry who established homes in Tidewater Virginia was James Taylor, called "James the First," who was born in 1635 in Carlisle, England and in 1665 settled in that part of Virginia which became Caroline county in 1727. He m. 1st, Frances ———— and, 2d, Mary Gregory and had issue: Ann, Mary, Edmund, Elizabeth, James and John. John Taylor, the last named of the issue of James, m. Catherine Pendleton and was the father of the eminent John Taylor, of Caroline whose biography appears elsewhere in this volume.

James Taylor, II, m. Martha Thompson (or Tompkins) about the year 1800 and became the progenitor of the Taylors of Orange and of the Valley of Virginia. He was one of the first Surveyors of Virginia and established the lines between Hanover, Spotsylvania and Orange counties. In August, 1736, the House of Burgesses ordered these counties to pay to Martha Taylor, his widow, sixteen thousand pounds of tobacco for his services in establishing these lines. Of the nine children of James Taylor and Martha Thompson two became grandparents of Presidents of the United States, namely, Frances Taylor, who m. Ambrose Madison, and Zachary Taylor, who m. Elizabeth Lee. Martha Taylor, daughter of James Taylor, II, m. Thos. Chew, of Spotsylvania and James Taylor, III, m. Alice Thornton Catlett, of Caroline. James Taylor, I, was a large land owner and prominent in the colony. A seal ring which belonged to him and which bore the crest and motto of the Taylor Arms, has been handed down to the present generation, and with this seal ring has also descended a legend to the effect that on a certain occasion the King of England was enjoying a chase in one of the royal forests when a wild boar, hard driven, turned upon the royal huntsman, whereupon there sprang to his defense one of his knights who slew the boar. The king out of gratitude gave this knight a crest, the distinguishing mark of which was an uplifted arm with lance in hand, accompanied by the motto: "*Consequitur quod cunque petit.*"

Two brothers, Robert and William Thomas, emigrated from Wales to Virginia in the seventeenth century and received large grants of land in the Province. Tradition makes them of the family seated at "Pwllyrach" in Glamorganshire. William Thomas received a patent to lands in Lancaster county, Va., on July 13, 1653.

Robert Thomas received a land grant, November 20, 1654. He m. ——— Massie and had a son, Edward, b. 1643. Edward Thomas became High Sheriff of Essex county, Va., June 10, 1696; received patents for 8,880 acres of land in Essex, Middlesex and Rappahannock counties; resided at "Thomas' Neck," on the Rappahannock River in Essex and had a son William, born about 1683, who was a large contributor in 1730 to the building of St. Anne's Parish church (called Vawters) in Essex county. The bricks were stamped with the contributors' names and "Thomas" may still be read on some of them. He sold 1,000 acres of "Thomas' Neck" to a Mr. Layton. His wife's first name was Elizabeth and they had one son, William, Jr., born about 1716.

William Thomas, Jr., m. Susannah Boulware, a dau. of John Boulware and heiress in 1739, at the death of her brother John and sisters Mary and Elizabeth, of her father's estate, six hundred acres in Essex. They had six children: (1) Lewis, b. 1759, m. Margery Noel. Their son, Captain William Thomas sold "Thomas' Neck," in 1818, to R. Payne Waring for $17,300 and moved to Fall River, Mass.; (2) Edward, b. 1760, died young.; (3) Susan, b. 1761, m. Joseph Cropp, of Stafford county, Va.; (4) Catherine, b. 1763, m. Captain William White, of Hanover county, Va. She is said to have lived to the age of 105 years. Their descendants went to Kentucky; (5) James, b. at "Thomas' Neck," in Essex county, on March 2, 1765, of whom see below; (6) Elizabeth, b. 1776, m. Joseph Brame of Caroline county, Va.

James Thomas, the third son of William Thomas, Jr., and Susannah Boulware Thomas, m. January 9, 1793, Elizabeth Andrews, a daughter of Joshua Andrews and Joyce Garnett, his wife, of "Elmwood," Essex county, Va. Elizabeth Andrews, who was born November 28, 1768 and lived until May 5, 1848 had two brothers, who were Revolutionary soldiers in the Body Guard of Gen. George Washington, the purpose of which company was to give special protection to the commander-in-chief of the American Army in camp, on the march and during battle. James Thomas bought a plantation called "Low Grounds," in the northwestern part of King William county, but later moved to his "Vernon" plantation, near Point Eastern in Caroline. He donated the land upon which the present Vernon church is built. Here he had a large estate with many slaves to till it; and here he lived until his death on February 29, 1852. To him and his wife, Elizabeth Andrews Thomas, there were born nine children: (1) Nancy, b. November 3, 1793; d. July 30, 1795; (2) Archibald, b. March 28, 1796, m. Catherine Puller; (3) Susannah, b. August 12, 1798, m. Thomas Patterson. Dr. R. A. Patterson, a son of this marriage, founded the famous R. A. Patterson Tobacco Company, of Richmond, Va., and his son, Archie W. Patterson, is now President of the Board of Trustees of the University of Richmond; (4) James, b. January 1, 1800, d. in infancy; (5 and 6) Ira Lomax and Emeline, b. May 13, 1803, twins; (7 and 8) James and William, twins, b. February 8, 1806, the latter died 1827; (9) Elizabeth Garnett, b. November 11, 1811.

Ira Lomax Thomas, the third son of James Thomas and Elizabeth Andrews Thomas, m. on December 15, 1825, Mary Jones Morgan, who was b. on May 7, 1805. She was a dau. of Dr. John Morgan and Hannah Jones, his wife, both of Philadelphia. Dr. Morgan was a member of the Medical Society of Philadelphia, also of Maryland and of the Royal Society of London. His son, Dr. Daniel S. Morgan, graduated in medicine at the University of Virginia on July 17, 1830.

Ira Lomax Thomas and Mary Jones Morgan, his wife, first settled in Richmond, Va., where he conducted a classical school. He later moved to Clarksville, Mecklenburg county, Va., where he engaged in the manufacture of tobacco. About 1843, when his father had grown to be an old man, in order to care for him in his declining years, he removed with his family to "Vernon" plantation in Caroline. They had ten children: (1) James Morgan Thomas, b. October 23, 1826, received a classical education in Clarksville and Richmond, Va., being in business in the latter city for a number of years. On July 3, 1857, he m. Robertine Sterrett Hodge, of Augusta county, Va. When the Civil War came on, he served first in an artillery Company under Stonewall Jackson. Later he became a member of Company C., First

Virginia Infantry, Kemper's Brigade, Pickett's Division, Long-street's Corps. He was mortally wounded in Pickett's famous charge at Gettysburg, July 3, 1863, and died the following day. His body now rests in Hollywood cemetery, Richmond, near the tomb of General Pickett.

2. Emily Thomas, who was born January 8, 1829, m. James R. MacTyre, of Chesterfield county, Va., on March 16, 1871. After the death of her husband, she made her home with her sisters, Mrs. Rowland Greene Tyler and Miss Isabelle Morgan Thomas, at "Retreat," King William county, Va., where she died April 4, 1920.

(3) Daniel, (4) Hannah, and (5) Ira, all three died in infancy. (6) Archibald Roanoke, was b. September 25, 1836 and d. August 23, 1856.

(7) Mary Hannah Elizabeth Thomas was b. May 28, 1839. On September 27, 1870, she was m. to Rowland Greene Tyler, of Detroit, Mich., where they made their home until 1888. They then came back to Virginia and settled at their "Retreat" plantation, in the northwestern part of King William county. Mrs. Tyler died there on November 21, 1903. Mr. Tyler continued to make his home there until his death on October 13, 1915. He was a native of Griswold, Conn., and was a brother of Dr. Moses Coit Tyler, who for some time was professor at the University of Michigan and at Cornell University and author of *"A History of American Literature"* and other works.

The next three children were daughters: Isabella Morgan Thomas, Alice Virginia Thomas, and Ann Eliza Ewing Thomas, all three of whom were educated at Hollins Institute, Va. The first two of these sisters never married. Ann Eliza Ewing Thomas, m. James Thomas Hurt, of "Thornhill," Caroline county, Va., on July 14, 1870, and, after 1874, made their home in Detroit, Mich. James Thomas Hurt died in Detroit, August 17, 1895 and is buried at "Thornhill." They had one child, who grew to maturity, Elizabeth Rowland Hurt, b. at "Thornhill," Caroline county, Va., on January 3, 1874, but was reared and educated in Detroit.

Elizabeth Rowland Hurt, dau. of Ann Eliza Ewing Thomas and James Thomas Hurt, is the last surviving grandchild of Ira Lomax Thomas, of "Vernon" and of Thomas Hurt, of "Thornhill" in Caroline. Elizabeth Rowland Hurt on March 25, 1903, m. Henry Thompson Louthan, a son of Carter McKim

Louthan, of Clarke county, Va., and his wife, Mary Ella Brown, of Rappahannock county, Va. Henry Thompson Louthan and Elizabeth Rowland Hurt, his wife, have two children: Mary Tyler Louthan, b. May 9, 1904 and Carter Thomas Louthan, b. July 23, 1906.

James Thomas, Jr., son of James and Elizabeth Andrews Thomas, was born, February 8, 1806, at "Vernon," in Caroline and settled early in Richmond. By his first wife, Mary Cornick Puller, he had two children: William D Thomas, D. D., for many years Professor of Philosophy in Richmond College; and Mary Ella Thomas who m. Dr. William D. Quesenberry, of Caroline. James Thomas, Jr., m. second, Mary Woolfolk Wortham, of Richmond and died, 1882. Among the children of this marriage: Mary Wortham Thomas, m. in 1867, Dr. J. L. M. Curry, of Alabama, who was United States Minister to Spain under President Cleveland's administration; Kate Cornick Thomas, m. Calderon Carlisle, of Washington, D. C.; and Gabrielle Thomas, m. Richmond Pearson, at one time United States Minister to Persia.

Crest: A paschal lamb.

Motto: *Nil Desperandum Christo Duce.*

THE THORNTONS, OF "ORMESBY"

The Thorntons came from Yorkshire, England. and settled in York and Gloucester counties, and their descendants were soon found in Caroline, Essex and adjacent counties. York county records show that this family was represented there as early as 1646.

When Caroline was formed the Thorntons were already established within the territory of the new county. The first member of the family to become actively identified with Caroline is referred to in Slaughter's "*St. Mark's Parish,*" as "Francis Thornton, of Caroline, Gentleman." Records in the Clerk's Office of Spotsylvania dated 1736 and Orange 1737 refer to "Francis Thornton, of St. Mary's Parish in Caroline."

Francis Thornton had several daughters of whom one married William Buckner, one General William Woodford and one James Taylor who represented Caroline in the House of Burgesses for several terms.

Reuben Thornton, of Drysdale Parish in Caroline was b. ————, and d. in 1768. He m. the widow of Henry Willis, of Spotsylvania. His will which was proved in Caroline court in May, 1768, devised his property to his nieces Mary Woodford, Lucy Gilmer, Mildred Washington and his nephews, James Taylor, Richard Buckner, Thornton Washington and others. Thornton Washington was the son of Samuel Washington and the nephew of George Washington. Dr. Hugh Mercer also shared

Ormesby

in this estate. The will was witnessed by William Buckner, Matthew Gale, Anthony Thornton and George Todd. William Woodford was named one of the executors.

John Thornton, of Caroline m. Mildred Gregory, by whom he had four daughters: Mildred, Mary, Elizabeth and Lucy. Mildred, m. Samuel Washington, brother of George Washington; Mary m. General William Woodford; Elizabeth m. John Taliaferro, of "Dissington," in King George county; and Lucy m. John Lewis, of Spotsylvania.

Anthony Thornton built "Ormesby" about the year 1715. He brought to this new estate his bride who was the daughter of Colonel John Presley, of "Northumberland House" in Northumberland county. Upon the death of Anthony Thornton, I, his son Anthony, II, inherited the estate and made it his home. Anthony, II, was Sheriff of Caroline. When he died "Ormesby" passed into the hands of his son, Anthony, III, who was county lieutenant of Caroline, and who held the rank of Lieutenant-Colonel in 1777. He commanded the militia of Caroline county at the siege of Yorktown. At the close of the War of the Revolution, Colonel Thornton sold "Ormesby" to his brother, Thomas Griffin Thornton and removed to Kentucky. Thomas Griffin Thornton was probably the most famous fox-hunter of his day and files of the old sporting magazines of the period contain many stories of his hounds. He was murdered, while Sheriff, by a man against whom he had a writ.

James Bankhead Thornton was born in 1770 and died in 1843. He lived at "Mt. Zephyr," but whether it was built by him is not definitely known. He was Justice of the Peace in Caroline in 1802. He married a daughter of Colonel Anthony Thornton. "Mt. Zephyr" was advertised for sale in 1845 and passed into the hands of the White Family. It is now owned by Mr Brooks.

The *Calendar of State Papers* (Virginia) contains several letters to and from Colonel Anthony Thornton. From one of these we learn that at the time it was written there were 644 Caroline men under arms. Governor Nelson writes Colonel Thornton to have all the flour he can get in Caroline shipped from Port Royal round into the Piankatank with all possible dispatch. Col. Thornton writes Colonel Davies under date of May 1, 1782, that "clothing for the army, due from Caroline, has been ready at Bowling Green for some months."

Charles Thornton, of "North Garden," was a captain of militia in the War of 1812. He m. Sarah Fitzhugh, of "Bellair," Stafford county and removed to Oldham county, Ky.

George Thornton was born in Caroline November 18, 1752. He m. on June 9, 1774, to Margaret Stanley, the daughter of Moses Stanley and removed to that territory which afterward became Greene county, Va. He was a soldier in the War of the Revolution and afterward received a pension. He died on August 30, 1853, at the age of 101 years. Mrs. J. C. Gentry, of Atlanta is one of his many descendants.

Robert Horsley Thornton, another one of his descendants, m. Louisa, dau. of Rev. Charles Wingfield, of Albemarle.

For more complete genealogy see *Thornton Excursus* by W. G. Stanard in *The Virginia Magazine of History and Biography.*

THE TERRELL AND RICKS FAMILIES

Alfred Ricks, a native of Southampton county, Va., m. Mary Ann Terrell, of Caroline county on April 14, 1822. They lived in Southampton county for a number of years and then removed to the old Terrell home in Caroline. This place is located on the north banks of North Anna River (the house is actually about three-quarters of a miles from the river on a high hill, but the farm borders the river), and was owned by the family for over 100 years until R. A. Ricks sold it in 1905. The house was built about 1780.

Mary Ann Terrell was the daughter of Samuel Terrell and Elizabeth Harris, both of Caroline county, who were married, May 7, 1800. Her brothers and sisters were: Samuel, Walter, James P., Henry O., and George Fox Terrell. George F. was a physician. He lived at the old Terrell home and practiced medicine in Caroline and adjoining counties. He died at the early age of 37, but it is said that he had already endeared himself to the people by his devotion and skill as a physician.

Dr. Terrell, his mother and father and other members of the family are buried at Golansville, Caroline county, in the little burying ground which adjoined the Quaker Meeting House that formerly stood there.

Richard Arnold Ricks was the fifth of ten children. The others were: Joseph, Julia W., Samuel T., Elizabeth H., Robert B., Mary W., Deborah, Walter A., and Samuella, who m. John C. Winston, of the John C. Winston Publishing Company, of Philadelphia, and who is the sole survivor of her generation.

Richard A. Ricks was 1st m. in 1873, to Mary Susan Whitlock. There was one child born of this marriage, who died at birth. The mother also died at the same time.

On June 23, 1881, R. A. Ricks, m. Eliza Catherine Crenshaw, of Richmond, Va. To them were born four children: Julian W., who died in infancy; Katherine C., who is now librarian at Guilford College, N. C.; Richard A., Jr., who is now engaged in real estate business in Richmond and James Hoge Ricks, of Richmond.

James Hoge Ricks was born at the old home "Prospect Hill," in Caroline county, July 14, 1886. His mother was the dau. of John Bacon Crenshaw, of Henrico county, and Richmond, and Rachel Hoge, of Loudon county. John Bacon Crenshaw was a Friends, or Quaker minister. All his ancestors on both sides for several generations were Friends (Quakers), and the Judge is still of that religious faith.

R. A. Ricks was interested and active in the affairs of Caroline and held various offices, among others that of delegate to the General Assembly for one session. He died in Richmond, January 4, 1911.

Judge Rick's mother was very active in temperance work in Caroline and at one time was president of the county W. C. T. U. She died in Richmond, May 30, 1909.

For several years R. A. Ricks had a teacher in the home for his children. The younger children, however, attended the little one-room country school, which was located about half way between their home and the station—Ruther Glen. Miss Janie Wortham was teacher of the school at that time.

For half a session Judge Ricks, with his brother, attended Corinth Academy, a Quaker school, in Southampton county. In the fall of 1902, they entered Guilford College, N. C.   Their sister graduated at Guilford in 1904, Judge Ricks graduated in 1905, and his brother in 1906. In the summer of 1905, Judge Ricks took a stenographic course at Massey Business College and in the fall of that year took a position as a stenographer in the office of Cutchins & Cutchins, lawyers. This position he held for three years, taking the law course at Richmond College in the meantime. He graduated in law in 1908. During college days he was a member of the Fraternity of Phi Gamma Delta at Richmond College. He spent the year 1908–1909 at the University of Virginia, taking a special course in law and English. In the summer of 1909 he took the Bar examination and was admitted to the practice of law. During the years 1909–1910 he was associated with ex-Attorney General William A. Anderson, who at that time, had a law office in Richmond, but later removed to his old home at Lexington, Va.

Judge Ricks practiced law from 1909 to 1912. In April, 1912, Police Justice John J. Crutchfield appointed him as the Clerk and Probation Officer of the Juvenile Division of the Police Court which was at that time established for the hearing of children's cases. He served in this capacity for three years and a half. In the fall of 1915, the City Council provided for the establishment of a new court to be known as the Juvenile and

Domestic Relations Court. He was elected Justice of that Court and has held the office since January 1, 1915.

On September 22, 1914 he m. Anne Elizabeth Ryland, dau. of Rev. Charles Hill Ryland and Alice M. Garnett, of King and Queen county. Dr. Ryland was for many years treasurer and librarian of Richmond College. They have one child— James Hoge, Jr., b. January 1, 1916.

In 1921, Governor Westmoreland Davis named him as a member of the Children's Code Commission, which he appointed at the instance of the League of Women Voters, to codify and revise the existing laws relating to children and to suggest such legislation as the Commission might deem necessary. He was elected chairman of that Commission. In the report of this Commission 26 bills were recommended, 18 of which, with amendments, were enacted into law by the General Assembly of 1922.

From 1920, to 1922, inclusive, Judge Ricks served as a member of the Executive Committee of the National Conference of Social Work. In 1923, he was elected Third Vice-President of that Conference, which was held in Washington, D. C. At the same time he was elected President of the National Probation Association, an organization composed of judges and probation officers from practically every State in the Union.

THE WALLER FAMILY

The family of Waller is one of the most ancient and distinguished among English ancestry. There is an unbroken male line from William the Conquerer down to the present time. An English genealogist claims to have traced the name back to the sixth century.

The English speaking branch of the Wallers was founded by two brothers, John Henry David de Waller and Alfred de Waller, Normans, who came into England with William the Conquerer the year 1066 and fought with him at Hastings. John Henry David was given lands in Nottingham county, Alfred in the county of Kent. The American branch traces descent from Alfred de Waller, of Kent, who died in 1083 (Domesday Book.)

David de Waller was Master of Rolls to Edward, III, for thirty years. He dropped the "de."

Sir Richard Waller, of Speldhurst, Greenbridge, Kent, High Sheriff of Kent, distinguished himself at the battle of Agincourt 1415, and Prince Charles, Duke of Orleans, detained him at

Greenbridge, Kent for twenty-four years, a strong friendship growing up between them. He was a benefactor to the Church at Speldhurst, where his Arms still remain cut in the stone work over the entrance. The arms of this ancient family are thus described:

Arms: Sa. three walnut leaves or, betw. two bendlets ar.

Crest: On a mount vert a walnut tree, ppr.; on the sinister side an escutcheon pendent charged with the Arms of France, with a label of three points ar.

Motto: *"Hic est fructus virtutis."*

John Waller, gentleman, 1617–1688, a prominent citizen of Newport Paganel, Buckinghamshire, younger brother of the Poet. m. Mary Key, or Kay, obtained a grant of land and emigrated to Virginia in 1635. Settled in Gloucester county. "A wild young fellow packed off to the colony of Virginia, there to take his chances, rather than stay in England, where temptations surrounded him."

John Waller, b. in 1673, gent., the 2d, third son of the immigrant, m. Dorothy King. He was Sheriff of King and Queen county 1702, represented King William county in House of Burgesses, 1719–1721, first Clerk St. George's Parish, one of the founders of Fredericksburg and organizers of Spotsylvania county. He lived on his estate "Newport" in Spotsylvania, d. in 1754, both he and his wife, Dorothy King, are buried at "Newport." His tombstone bears the following inscription: "Sacred to the memory of Col. John Waller, Gentleman, third son of John Waller and Mary Key, who settled in Virginia in 1635, from Newport Paganel, Buckinghamshire, England." Silver seal, suit of horse arms, silver cap pistols, silver hilted sword and prayer book of Col. Waller are still in existence, but in possession of a family not of the name Waller (records show that all of the Wallers belonged to the Church of England).

Issue of Col. John Waller, gent., of "Newport," Spotsylvania in order of birth: Mary, who m. Zachary Lewis, a near relative of Fielding Lewis, who m. Betty Washington; Edmund, 1st son, m. Mary Pendleton of Caroline county. He was 2d clerk of Spotsylvania county, 1742–1751. He is the ancestor of the late Judge R. E. Waller, of Spotsylvania; the late Dr. Judson Cary Waller, of Albemarle; the late Samuel Gardner Waller, of Front Royal, his only son is Gen. Samuel Gardner Waller, of the Virginia National Guards. The only daughter of Edmund, 1st, m. George Mason.

William Waller, 2d son, 1714–1760, m. Ann Becker or Beuckie, 3d clerk of Spotsylvania county, 1751–1759, was a prominent lawyer and business man of his day, buried at "Newport."

Col. John Waller, 3d son, founder of "Cedar Point," on the Pamunkey, now called North Anna river, in Spotsylvania county, 4th clerk of Spotsylvania, 1760–1774, m. Agnes Carr, dau. of Thomas Carr, of "Bears Castle," Louisa county, brother of Hon. Dabney Carr, who m. sister of Thomas Jefferson. John Waller, 3d, died in 1774, buried at "Cedar Point."

Thomas Waller, 4th son of John Waller, gent., of "Newport," is the ancestor of the Wallers of Stafford county, among whom may be mentioned the late Col. Thomas Waller, of Stafford, C. S. A.; Col. 9th Virginia Cavalry at the end of the Civil war. He strongly resembled Col. John Mercer Waller, of "Cedar Point," and they were often mistaken for each other, although cousins four generations removed.

Benjamin Waller, 5th son, was a prominent lawyer, and while a young man he moved to Williamsburg and later became a celebrated Judge. He served as clerk of the Council, Burgess from James City county, 1744–1761, member of the Convention, 1775–1776, judge of the General Court, 1779 to his death, 1788, m. Martha Hall, of Bermuda, N. C. He is the ancestor of Major-General Littleton Waller, U. S. Marine Corps and Page Waller, of Norfolk, who m. a dau. of General J. E. B. Stuart.

Thomas Carr Waller, 1732–1788, son of Col. John Waller, founder of "Cedar Point, m. Sarah Dabney, lived and died at "Cedar Point." Succeeded by, Dabney Waller, 1772–1849, m. Elizabeth Minor, lived and died at "Cedar Point."

Sons of Dabney Waller in order of birth: Thomas Carr Waller, 1799–1872, lived at Woodland, one of the farms composing "Cedar Point," served as treasurer and Sheriff of Spotsylvania.

Cap. Dabney Washington Waller, 1804–1880, m. Caroline Pleasants, dau. of Jordan Pleasants and Elizabeth Tyler, who was a sister of Henry Tyler and great aunt of Ex-Governor James Hoge Tyler. Jordan Pleasants was first cousin of the late James Pleasants, Governor of Virginia, 1822, and brother of John Hampden Pleasants, Editor of the old *Richmond Whig*, who was killed in a duel by Ritchie, Editor of the *Richmond Enquirer*.

Col. John Mercer Waller, 1814–1876, lived and died at "Cedar Point," and was the last of the name of Waller to own "Cedar Point." At his death the estate was sold, and bought by Col. Bigger, of the General Assembly of Virginia.

Col. John Mercer Waller was a prominent business man and sportsman and one of the few practical farmers of his day, a large slave owner and under his management "Cedar Point" reached a high state of cultivation, was especially noted for its splendid crops of wheat and clover. He also took an active part in Spotsylvania politics, held several offices, was for a long time Colonel of the Spotsylvania Militia. Married three times and had three sons: Capt. William, C. S. A.; John Mercer, Jr., Pvt. 9th Virginia Cavalry, killed in skirmish at Lebanon church, Caroline county, age 18, buried at "Cedar Point, Spotsylvania county. Thomas Carr Waller, moved to Missouri.

Capt. Dabney Washington Waller, son of Dabney Waller and Elizabeth Minor, was born at "Cedar Point," Spotsylvania county, January, 1804, received his early education from private tutors at "Cedar Point," later graduated from Humanity Hall Academy, Hanover county, had made preparations to enter the University, when he was taken with the roving fever and decided to go West. Accompanied by a servant, he rode as far as the Mississippi River and was made several splendid offers to locate out there, but returned to Virginia and on March 6, 1827, m. Miss Caroline Pleasants. For the next nine years he rented the "Red House," on the Pamunky river, an estate then belonging to the De Jarnette family and conducted a private school for young men. In 1837, he bought from a Mr. Wright, the Walnut Hill Farm, located in Caroline county, western edge. At Walnut Hill he opened a school known as Waller's or Walnut Hill Acadmey, which he conducted for nearly fifty years and gained quite a reputation as an educator. He was known as one of the best grounded Latin and Greek scholar of his time; an expert mathematican and surveyor, large slave owner and farmer, Capt. in Caroline Militia, member of Rehoboth M. E. church, and known far and wide for his truthful and upright character. Died at Walnut Hill, Caroline county, August 16, 1880.

Capt. Dabney Washington Waller was succeeded by Dabney Jordan, who was b. at Walnut Hill, June 29, 1841, educated at Walnut Hill Academy and Randolph-Macon College, m. 1st, Ann Catherine Waddy, dau. of Garland T. Waddy and Sophia

Ann Pleasants, of "Oak Hill," Louisa county, m. 2d, Alice Caroline Lee, dau. of Robert Baker Lee, of "Laxfield Hall," Linstead Magna, Suffolk county, England.

Walnut Hill farm is situated on the extreme western edge of Caroline, lying partly in Spotsylvania, on the main road that leads from Goodloes to Blantons, about half way between the two places. Little is known of its early history. Dabney Washington Waller purchased it in 1837, from a Mr. Wright, who moved West. The old house was burned in 1880, it was a large rambling frame house of the two and a half story type, with basement, shed rooms in the rear and a large porch in front. There are signs of a very old brick settlement. An ancient Goodloe family was supposed to have lived there, the old Goodloe burying ground being near by. Also from the number of relics that are found, there must once have been an Indian village here. Arrow heads, broken pottery, etc., were found. A few years ago, in digging a ditch an Indian tomahak, stone hammer, part of a clay vessel were found.

Descendants of John Waller, gent., of "Newport," Spotsylvania, of the name Waller married into the following families: Lightfoot, Carson, Breckenridge, Bibb, Aylett, Curtis, Custis, Pritchett, Rowzie, Terrell, Waddy, Goodloe, Swann, Cowherd, Pollard, Wheeler, Pettitt, Hancock, Carter, Crump, Harrison, Carr, Marshall, Langhorne, Ware, Gresham, Alexander, Shelton, Jennings, DeJarnette, Dew, Gordon, Knowles, McGruder, Armstead, Buckner, Towles, Granville, Taylor, Page, Payne, Tazewell, Smith, Greenshaw, Montague, Barrett, Barnett, Johnson, Corbin, Griffin, Garland, DuVal, Caldwell, Coles, Rutherford, Cabell, Moore, Littleton, Tunstall, Barkley, Lee, Dabney, Minor, Tyler, Pleasants, Hart, Bently, Mann, Duerson, Anderson and many others. (Records of the Waller Family.)

Dorothy Waller, of Williamsburg, became the wife of Henry Tazewell and was the mother of Littleton Waller Tazewell, 1784–1860, U. S. Senator, Com. under Florida Treaty, Governor of Virginia, 1834–1836. Governor Tazewell writing in 1823, says of his maternal grandfather, Judge Benj. Waller, of Williamsburg, son of Col. John Waller, gent., of "Newport," Spotsylvania: "He was descended from Sir Edmund Waller, the Poet and traced his lineage to the days of William, of Normandy. He often spoke of the antiquity and respectability of his descent, saying that one of his ancestors greatly distinguished himself at the

battle of Agincourt, where he made prisoner one of the peers
of France and that, in testimony of this, Henry, V, gave as a
crest the Arms of France, suspended on an English oak with the
motto, '*Haec fructus virtutis,*' which armorial insignia was suspended in his great hall."

THE WASHINGTONS, OF "SPRING HILL" AND "WOODPECKER"

John Washington, nephew of George Washington, was m.
in 1770 to Elizabeth Buckner, sister of Captain George Buckner,
of "Braynefield." To this union were born two sons: John
Washington in 1772 and George Washington in 1775. The eldest
son died unmarried. George Washington, m. Elizabeth, dau of
Dr John Coates, of Maryland and had issue: *Catherine*, (1796),
George, (1798), *John*, (1800), *Susan Elizabeth*, (1802), *Ann*, (1802),
Selina, (1806), *Dorothea*, (1808), *William*, (1810), *E¹izabeth*, (1812),
and *Caroline* (1814).

Washington Arms

Catherine Washington, m Robert Sutton in 1811 and had
issue three sons and two daughters; George Washington died at
the age of seventeen, unmarried; John Washington, m. Ann
Hawes and had issue a son, whom they named George; Susan
Elizabeth Washington was m in 1821 to Thomas Henry Burke
and had issue three sons and one daughter; Ann Washington was
m. in 1825 to Ezekie! D. Withers and had issue two sons and
two daughters; Selina Washington, m. Daniel Payne and had
issue two daughters, the eldest of who m. Dr. William Wirt, a
son of the famous attorney William Wirt, of "Wirtland"; Dorothea
Washington, m. Norborne E. Sutton and had issue six children:
Braxton, Coutts, Hugh, Daniel, Norborne and Georgianna;

William Washington, m. a Mrs. Vass, of King William; Elizabeth Washington, m. William Taliaferro; Caroline Washington died in childhood.

George Washington, son of Colonel John Washington and Anne Hawes, m. Mildred Chandler, sister of Dr. Joseph A. Chandler and had issue: (1) Thomas, (2) John, (3) George, (4) Cora, (5) William, (6) Clement, (7) Henry.

Spring Hill

John Washington, second son of George Washington and Mildred Chandler, m. Byrd Boyd, of Essex county, and established "Spring Hill," and practiced law in partnership with A. B. Chandler until his death, which occurred suddenly in Bethel church while attending the morning worship. His children were: (1) Boyd, (2) Mary, (3) Walker Hawes, (4) Dollie Buckner, (5) Fannie Pryor, (6) Eugene and (7) Roberta Boyd.

Boyd Washington, son of John Washington and Byrd Boyd, m. Minnie Dew, of "Windsor" and has issue one son, Thomas Boyd, a physician and one daughter, Catherine.

THE WOOLFOLK FAMILY

The Woolfolk family is of Welsh extraction. Robert and Richard Woolfolk, brothers, emigrated to Virginia in the early part of the eighteenth century. Richard established "Holly Hill" and Robert "Shepherd's Hill" near Bowling Green, in Caroline county. Of the descendants of Richard but little is definitely known. Robert Woolfolk, the emigrant, is said to have married a Miss Lee, by whom he had several children.

Robert Woolfolk, II, m. Ann George and had issue eleven children, of whom eight removed to Kentucky and three remained in Virginia.

(1) John George Woolfolk was born October 1, 1750. He m. Elizabeth Powers Broadnax in 1790, and established the estate known as "Mulberry Place" which is still in the possession of his grandchildren. He was a man of considerable affairs and was granted by the State a charter to operate transportation service from points north and east of Richmond. His family Bible may still be seen at "Mulberry Place."

(2) Achilles Woolfolk, son of Robert Woolfolk and Ann George, settled near Ruther Glen. He served in the Revolutionary Army and was the ancestor of the late Robert Woolfolk, who m. Virginia White, dau. of Hugh White, by whom he had three sons, William, Richard and Lucian and one daughter, who m. ——— Stevens.

(3) Francis Woolfolk, son of Robert Woolfolk and Ann George, remained in Caroline. The obituary of his wife in an old Richmond newspaper is the only available data concerning this member of the family.

(4) William Woolfolk, m. a Miss Noden. He was an ensign in the Revolutionary Army. Emigrated to Kentucky and was the progenitor of the Kentucky Woolfolks.

(5) Robert Woolfolk, III, was born April, 1756. He m. Jane Peay and later removed to Kentucky. He was orderly sergeant under Colonel Holt Richardson in 1780–81 and died in Louisville, Ky., August 18, 1854. His son, John Allen, was the first settler at Troy, Lincoln county, Mo.

(6) Edmund Woolfolk, m. Agnes Peay and emigrated to Kentucky.

Mulberry Place

(7) Elliott Woolfolk died in 1821. His obituary appears in the *Richmond Enquirer*, of January 23, 1821.

(8) Richard Woolfolk, m. a Miss Taylor, according to tradition a sister of President Taylor. He was a member of the firm of Coleman and Woolfolk in Richmond. He died in 1820 and his obituary appears in the *Richmond Enquirer*, of May 30, 1820.

(9) Mary Woolfolk, b. in 1759, m. Thomas Coleman.

(10) Martha Woolfolk, m Francis Scott.

(11) Nancy Woolfolk, m. ———— Campbell and removed to Illinois.

John George Woolfolk, the eldest of the foregoing eleven children, m. Elizabeth Powers Broadnax and had issue seven children: (1) Maria, b. October 28, 1790; (2) Ann Hoomes, b. March 17 1793; (3) Jourdan, b. July 23, 1796; (4) Sophia Frances, b. January 12, 1799; (5) Still born boy; (6) Charles, b. September 20, 1802; (7) John, b. July 7, 1805. These married as follows: Maria, m. Hawes Coleman, January 5, 1809; Ann Hoomes, m. Wm. Grymes Maury, July 14, 1808; Jourdan, m. Elizabeth Taylor Winston, November 9, 1820; Sophia Frances, m. John M. Burke, May 21, 1817 and John, m. Louisa F. Scott, on January 10, 1850.

The obituary of John George Woolfolk appears in the

Richmond Enquirer, of April 23, 1819. He is referred to as "a sedulous and respected citizen" who had "accumulated a handsome and independent fortune," "a man of indefatigable perseverance, great integrity of soul, benevolent manners, humane feelings, generous and charitable."

Jourdan Woolfolk and Elizabeth Taylor Winston had issue: (1) Betsy Carr, (2) John Wm., (3) Ann Terrell, (4) Sarah Winston, (5) Ellen Broadnax, (6) Mary.

Betsy Carr Woolfolk, m. Dr. Wm. W. Roper and had issue: (1) Jourdan, who m. Miss ——— Gowan; (2) Sallie, who m. W. W. Rains; and (3) George who is unmarried.

John Wm. Woolfolk, m. Lucy Trevillian Winston and had issue: (1) John, who m. Miss Lucy Marshall; (2) Edmund Winston, who m. Miss Emma Blackerby, of Kentucky; (3) Sally Winston, who m. J. L. Jordan; (4) Jourdan, (5) Elizabeth Taylor, (6) William Roper, (7) Mary Morris, (8) Anne Barton and (9) Lucy Marshall.

John Woolfolk and Lucy Marshall had issue: (1) George, who m. Grace Cunningham; (2) Sallie Elizabeth, unmarried; (3) Andrew, unmarried; (4) Edmund Winston, m. Alice Ware; (5) Jourdan, (6) Barton and (7) John.

Edmund Winston Woolfolk, son of John Wm., and Lucy Trevillian Winston, m. Emma Blackerby and had issue: (1) Roper Blackerby, (2) Pearl Buckner and (3) Edmund.

Sallie Winston Woolfolk and J. L. Jordan had issue: (1) Lucy Winston, who m. B. M. Skinker and has one son, B. M., Jr., and (2) Elizabeth, who is unmarried.

Sophia Frances Woolfolk, dau. of John George Woolfolk and Elizabeth Powers Broadnax, m. John M. Burke and had issue: (1) Cordelia, who m. Robt. DeJarnette; (2) Margaret, also m. Robt. DeJarnette (his 2d wife); (3) Thomas, m. Isabelle Garnett; (4) John, m. 1st, Miss Thompson, 2d, Miss Trist; (5) Frances, m. Robert Spindle; (6) Betsy Ann, m. Paul Blackburn and (7) Maria, who m. James Maury.

Anne Ferrell Woolfolk, dau. of Jourdan and granddaughter of John George Woolfolk, m. Dr. B. W. Morris and had issue: (1) Chas. Dabney, m. Miss Willis; (2) Ellen, m. Thos. Bernard Doswell; (3) Jourdan, m. Pauline Castleman; (4) Barton, m. 1st, Miss Frances Peatross, 2d, Miss Bessie Gordon; (5) Lelia, m. John P. Downing; and (6) Edmund Taylor, m. Miss Grace Smith.

THE WYATT FAMILY

The Wyatt family of Virginia descends from the distinguished English line of Sir Thomas Wyatt, courtier and poet. Just preceding the Revolution, Richard Wyatt, (1720–1803), at his home in Caroline county, becoming incensed at the Mother Country, tore the family Coat of Arms from the wall, and, hacking it from the frame with his sword, threw it on the blazing logs in the fireplace. It was rescued by his daughter, Nancy, who later became the second wife of Colonel Anthony New. When they removed to Kentucky, the treasured painting went with them. In the year 1830, a descendant seeing the old relic in their Kentucky home made a little sketch of the design. Though blackened by fire and smoke, there were still to be plainly seen bands of boar's heads on the shield similar to the Arms of Sir Thomas Wyatt, of England. The painting was later totally destroyed by fire, but the little sketch is still in the family.

The first of the Wyatt name on record in Caroline is *John Wyatt*, called in Bible records "Captain John Wyatt." Born in 1684, he was m. in 1711 to *Jane Pamplin*. He is mentioned as Church Warden of St. Margaret's Parish in 1737. On August 30, 1740, *John Wyatt* took the oath as Member of Commission of the Peace. His will was proved in November 1750, and his wife, Jane, was also deceased at that time.

The earliest known Wyatt home in Caroline county, called "Plain Dealing," was on the North Anna River, five or six miles from its junction with the South Anna, and in old papers and letters is spoken of as the ancestral seat. No doubt earlier members of this branch lived in this locality before Caroline county was formed.

John and *Jane* (*Pamplin*) *Wyatt* had issue:

(1) *William*, b. 1713, m. *Elizabeth*, dau. of Joseph and Ann (Pettus) Eggleston. The will of William Wyatt was proved April, 1772.

(2) *John*, d. aged seventeen.

(3) *Anne*, m. John Starke on May 25, 1735. They had thirteen children.

(4) *Richard*, b. May 20, 1720, d. at "Plain Dealing" in November, 1803. His first wife was *Elizabeth Streshley*, who died at the birth of her first child. The child was born in 1744, m. John Starke, of Hanover and died in 1830. Mr. Wyatt then married on November 17, 1752, *Amy*, dau. of Walter Chiles,

a descendant of the immigrant, Walter Chiles, who respresented Charles City county in the General Assembly, was Speaker and member of the James City Council.

(5) *Mary*, m. Captain Henry Gilbert.

(6 and 7) *Thomas* and *Henry*, died unmarried.

(8) *Lucy*, m. Captain Mills of Greene county.

(9) *John*, m. 1st, *Elizabeth*, dau. of Thomas Ballard Smith, of Louisa and had issue, Francis, John and Thomas Ballard Wyatt. His second wife was Anne Stark.

Richard and *Amy* (*Chiles*) *Wyatt* lived at "Plain Dealing" and there the following children were born to them:

(1) *Mary*, m. *William Peatross*, great-uncle of the late Major R. O. Peatross, of Bowling Green. Ten children were born to them.

(2) *Sarah*, m. 1st, *Mathew Thompson*, and 2d, *Austin McGhee*. She died in Washington county, Va.

(3) *Lucy*, m. *James Hawkins*, of Kentucky.

(4) *Nancy*. On August 3, 1782, became the 2d wife of *Colonel Anthony New*. She died in 1833.

(5) *Joseph*, died in his seventh year.

(6) *Richard*, b. January 1, 1763, d. June 12, 1845. He m. *Nancy*, dau. of Captain John and Ann (Harrison) Ware, of Goochland county in 1796. He served with credit in the Revolution, leaving an Academy in Caroline to enter. He took the oath as Ensign in Caroline county, on January 8, 1778. Later he settled in Louisa county.

(7) *Walter*, m. *Elizabeth Brame* and 2d, *Mrs. Bliss*. He removed to Kentucky and later to Illinois where he died.

(8) *Major John*, b. 1769, d. September 11, 1846. He m. *Lucy Richardson* and 2d, *Mrs. Patsy Harris*, widow of *Overton Harris*, of "Cedar Hill," Hanover county. He served with Harrison in the Indian Wars.

(9) *Barbara*, (1773–1804), m. *Overton Harris*, of "Cedar Hill," Hanover county.

(10) *William Streshley*, b. August 29, 1775, d. January 24, 1839. Little can be learned of his life, though what can be gleaned from a few old letters goes to show he was a man of affairs. On November 12, 1801 he m. *Polly*, dau. of *Colonel Anthony New* and 1st wife, *Ann Anderson*, dau. of Robert Anderson, III, of "Goldmine," Hanover county, whose wife was Elizabeth Clough. Anthony New was prominent in Caroline county affairs. He

Silhouette of Colonel Anthony New.

was Colonel in the Revolution, served in the Virginia Legislature, was appointed as Trustee to clear and improve the Mattaponi River, was Congressman from Virginia, 1793–1805, and member of Congress from Kentucky, 1811, 1823.   He died at "Dunheath," his home in Kentucky, in 1833.   Anthony New was born in Gloucester county, but when an infant his mother, the widow New, m. Dr. John Baynham and came to Caroline county to live.   The quaint little house, one of the first to be built in the county, is standing today on the place now owned by Mr. Doggett, near White Chimneys.   Here Anthony New was raised and here his half-brother, Dr. William Baynham, the eminent surgeon, was born.

William Streshley Wyatt and wife, *Polly New*, had one daughter and two sons:

(1) *Virginia Anderson*, b. September 25, 1805 and m. Hugh Chandler, September 25, 1827.

(2) *William Richard Baynham Wyatt*, b. January 16, 1809 and d. May 29, 1878.   He m. *Martha Frances Scott*, September

5, 1832, and after her death m. her sister, *Isabelle Adelaide*, August 22, 1848.

(3) *Joseph Anthony New*, died in infancy.

Polly (New) Wyatt, d. December 3, 1812 and *William Streshley Wyatt*, m. *Susan Minor*, dau. of Vivian and Elizabeth Minor.

William S. and *Susan (Minor) Wyatt* had:

(1) *John Vivian*, (1816–1889), who m. *Emma Burton Doggett* in 1859 and lived at "Sunnyside" in Hanover county. Their children were: Mattie Susan, m. Douglass Doswell and lives in Ashland, Va.; John and Barton (a daughter), both unmarried and living in Washington, D. C.

(2) *Mary Elizabeth*, b. in 1814, m. *John G. Coleman* and resided at "Pebble Hill."

William Streshley Wyatt, died suddenly on January 24, 1839 at his home, "Plain Dealing," and is buried in the old Wyatt graveyard there.

William Richard Baynham Wyatt, after an education in the county schools, studied law. He was a man of fine intellect and a great student. Books and candles were always put beside his bed that he might work in the early hours. Though urged by friends, he never became a licensed lawyer, but he practiced law repeatedly throughout the county, and it was often said he knew more law than many lawyers. He was an authority on land titles and claims, and administrator of many estates. Mr. Wyatt was Notary Public, Justice of the Peace, and chosen presiding Justice of his Court. He was presiding when the news came that Stonewall Jackson had been killed, and immediately adjourned. Mr. Wyatt served in the Legislature 1865–66, 1866–67.

William Richard Baynham Wyatt and his wife, *Martha Frances*, dau. of *Robert* and *Ann (Coleman) Scott*, lived at "Edgewood," on the North Anna River, where the following children were born: Richard Watson, Joseph Marion, Ann Eliza and Thomas Barton.

Richard Watson, b. June 27, 1833, and d. at his home in Middlesex county, April 30, 1881. He m. November 14, 1865, *Elizabeth Eubank*, of Middlesex county. They had two children, a son and a daughter, both born in Caroline, but removed to Middlesex county when quite small. They were:

(1) *Charles Russell Wyatt*, who after graduating in law at the University of Virginia, practiced his profession very successfully

in Huntington, W. Va., where he located. His tragic death, which occurred there August 7, 1913, cast a gloom of sorrow over the whole city. His wife was Sarah Paisley Sloan, dau. of Colonel John and Morton (Wortham) Sloan. Their three children were: (a) *Charles Russell, Jr.,* (b) *Morton,* who m. September 19, 1923; Lieut. Ransom Kirby Davis, of San Diego, Cal.; (c) *Joseph Willard,* a student at Harvard.

Edgewood

(2) *Belle Leighton,* m. September 16, 1891 to *Joseph E. Willard,* recent Ambassador to Spain. They now reside in New York City. Their children are: (1) *Belle Wyatt,* m. June 10, 1914, to *Kermit,* second son of President Theodore Roosevelt. The children are: *Kermit, Jr., Willard* and *Belle;* (2) *Elizabeth,* m. *Merwyn Herbert,* of England, a brother of the Earl of Carnarvon, who died before completing his Egyptian explorations.

Joseph Marion, son of William R. B. Wyatt, and wife, Martha Frances, was b. April 24, 1838 at "Edgewood." He attended Emory and Henry College. Enlisting in the Confederate service, he went through the entire war. He was in Pickett's Division, but luckily was held in reserve during the Gettysburg attack. He m. his third cousin, *Ida May Wyatt,* of Albemarle county. His high traits of character and genuine, cordial manner made everyone his friend. His sudden death occurred August 20, 1891. Their four children, all born at "Edgewood," were:

(1) *Harriet James*, who m. *Henry St. Clair Washington*, of Richmond, Va. They have a daughter, *Harriet Wyatt Washington* and reside in Huntington, W. Va.

(2) *Martha Isabelle*, m. *William Edwin Williams*, Shop Engineer of the American Car and Foundry Company, Berwick, Penn., where they reside. They have one son, *Wyatt Edwin*, b. November 19, 1906, a Senior in the Berwick High School.

(3) *Ida Marion*, Assistant to the Superintendent in Huntington Public Schools.

(4) *William R. B. Wyatt, Jr.*, m. *Geneva Niles.* They have one son (*Joseph Marion, Jr.*, b. in 1916) and reside at Vidalia, Ga., where Mr. Wyatt is in the lumber business.

Ann Eliza, dau. of William R. B. Wyatt, died unmarried at her home in Huntington, W. Va., after a long and painful illness which she bore with great fortitude.

Thomas Barton, b. 1846, m. Anna Leake, of North Carolina, where he is now living. Their children are: Dr. James Augustus Leake, Ann Eliza (Mrs. Dibble), Dr. Wortham and Junius Pembroke.

William Richard Baynham Wyatt and his second wife, Isabelle Scott, beloved throughout her entire life by all with whom she came in contact, had three daughters:

Virginia Ellen, who died unmarried in April, 1916, at Huntington, W. Va., where she had endeared herself to all by her life of sweet unselfishness.

Wilhemina, died aged four years.

Margaret Baynham, living in Huntington, W. Va., where she has been prominently identified with the educational life of the city.

APPENDIX

(Virginia's First Written History by the First Governor of the Colony. Original MS. in Lambeth Library.)

"A DISCOURSE OF VIRGINIA"

*Right Worpull and more worthy:—

My due respect to yourselves, my allegiance (if I may so terme it) to the Virginean action, my good heed to my poore reputacon, thrust a penne into my handes; so iealous am I to bee missing to any of them. If it wandereth in extravagantes, yet shall they not bee idle to those physitions whose loves have undertaken the saftie and advancement of Virginia.

It is no small comfort that I speake before such gravitie, whose iudgement no forrunner can forestall with any opprobrious vntruths, whose wisedomes can easily disroabe malice out of her painted garments from the ever reverenced truth.

I did so faithfully betroth my best endeavours to this noble enterprize, as my carriage might endure no suspition. I never turned my face from daunger, or hidd my handes from labour; so watchful a sentinel stood myself to myself. I know wel, a troope of errors continually beseege men's actions; some of them ceased on by malice, some by ignorance. I doo not hoodwinck my carriage in my self love, but freely and humblie submit it to your grave censures.

I do freely and truely anatomize the governement and gouernours, that your experience may applie medicines accordinglie; and vpon the truth of this iournal do pledge my faith and life, and so do rest

Yours to command in all service,

[EDWARD MARIA WINGFIELD.]

The Wingfield Arms

---

*Preface to Edward Maria Wingfield's "Discourse of Virginia," Addressed to His Majesty's Council for Virginia in 1607.

*Here followeth what happened in James Towne, in Virginia,
after Captayne Newport's departure for Engliund.*

Captayne Newport, haueing allwayes his eyes and eares open
to the proceedings of the Collonye, 3 or 4 dayes before his departure asked the President how he thought himself settled
in the gouernment: whose answere was, that no disturbance
could indaunger him or the Collonye, but it must be wrought
eyther by Captayne Gosnold or Mr Archer; for the one was
strong wth friends and followers, and could if he would; and
the other was troubled wth an ambitious spirit, and would if he
could.

The Captayne gave them both knowledge of this, the President's opinion; and moued them, with many intreaties, to be
myndefull of their dutyes to His Matie and the Collonye.

June, 1607. — The 22th, Captayne Newport retorned for
England; for whose good passadge and safe retorne wee made
many prayers to our Almighty God.

June the 25th, an Indian came to us from the great Pough-
waton wth the word of peace; that he desired greatly our freindshipp; that the wyrounnces, Pasyaheigh and Tapahanagh, should
be our freindes; that wee should sowe and reape in peace, or els
he would make warrs vpon them wth vs. This message fell
out true; for both those wyroaunces haue ever since remayned
in peace and trade with vs. Wee rewarded the messinger wth
many tryfles wch were great wonders to him.

This Powatan dwelleth 10 myles from vs, upon the River
Pamaonche, wch lyeth North from vs. The Powatan in the
former iornall menconed (a dwellar by Captn. Newport's faults)
ys a wyroaunce, and vnder this Great Powaton, wch before wee
knew not.

July. — Th 3 of July, 7 or 8 Indians presented the President a dear from Pamaonke, a wyrouance, desiring our friend-
shipp. They enquired after our shipping; wch the President
said was gon to Croutoon. They fear much our shipps; and
therefore he would not haue them think it farr from us. Their
wyrounce had a hatchet sent him. They wear well contented
wth triffles. A little after this came a dear to the President
from the Great Powatan. He and his messingers were pleased
wth the like triffles. The President likewise bought diuers tymes
dear of the Indyans; beavers, and other flesh; wch he always
caused to be equally deuided among the Collonye.

H. C.-32

About this tyme, diuers of our men fell sick. We myssed about fforty before September did see us; amongst whom was the worthy and religious gent. Captn. Bartholomew Gosnold, vpon whose liefs stood a great part of the good succes and fortune of our gouernment and Collony. In his sicknes tyme, the President did easily foretel his owne deposing from his comaund; so much differed the President and the other Councellors in mannaging the government of the Collonye.

July. — The 7th of July, Tapahanah, a wyroaunce, dweller on Salisbery side, hayled us with the word of peace. The President, wth a shallopp well manned, went to him. He found him sytting on the ground crossed legged, as is theire custom, wh one attending on him, wch did often saie, "This is the wyroance Tapahanah;" wch he did likewise confirme wth stroaking his brest. He was well enough knowne; for the President had sene him diuse tymes before. His countynance was nothing cherefull; for we had not seen him since he was in the feild against vs: but the President would take no knowledge thereof and vsed him kindely; giving him a red wascoat, wch he did desire.

Tapahanah did enquire after our shipping. He receyued answer as before. He said his ould store was spent; that his new was not at full growth by a foote; that, as soone as any was ripe, he would bring it; wch promise he truly pformed.

The . . . of . . . Mr Kendall was put of from being of the Counsell, and comitted to prison; for that it did manyfestly appeare he did practize to sowe discord betweene the President and Councell.

Sicknes had not now left us vj able men in our towne. God's onely mercy did now watch and warde for us: but the President hidd this our weaknes carefully from the salvages; neuer suffring them, in all his tyme, to come into our towne.

Septem. — The vjth of September, Pasyaheigh sent vs a boy that was run from vs. This was the first assurance of his peace wth vs; besides, wee found them no canyballs.

The boye obserued the men & women to spend the most pt of the night in singing or howling, and that euery morning the women carryed all the litle children to the river's sides; but what they did there, he did not knowe.

The rest of the wyroaunces doe likewise send our men runnagats to vs home againe, vsing them well during their being with them; so as now, they being well rewarded at home at their retorne, they take litle ioye to trauell abroad whout pasports.

The Councell demanded some larger allowance for them-selues, and for some sick, their fauorites; wch the President would not yeeld vnto, wthout their warrants.

This matter was before ppounded by Captn. Martyn, but so nakedly as that he neyther knew the quantity of the stoare to be but for xiij weekes and a half, urder the Cape Merchaunt's hand. He prayed them further to consider the long tyme before wee expected Captn. Newport's retorne; the incertainty of his retorne, if God did not fauor his voyage; the long tyme before our haruest would bee ripe; and the doubtfull peace that wee had wth the Indyans, wch they would keepe no longer than oportunity served to doe vs mischeif.

It was then therefore ordered that euery meale of fish or fleshe should excuse the allowance for pordig, both against the sick and hole. The Councell, therefore, sitting againe upon this proposition, instructed in the former reasons and order, did not thinke fit to break the former order by enlarging their allowance, as will appeare by the most voyces reddy to be shewed vnder their handes. Now was the comon store of oyle, vinigar, sack, & aquavite all spent, saueing twoe gallons of each: the sack reserued for the Comunion Table, the rest for such extreamityes as might fall upon vs, wch the President had onely made knowne to Captn. Gosnold; of wch course he liked well. The vessells wear, therefore, boonged vpp. When Mr Gosnold was dead, the President did acquaint the rest of the Counsell wth the said remnant: but, Lord, how they then longed for to supp up that little remnant! for they had nowe emptied all their own bottles, and all other that they could smell out.

A little while after this, the Councell did againe fall vpon the President for some better allowance for themselves, and some few the sick, their privates. The President ptested he would not be partial; but, if one had any thing of him, euery man should have his portion according to their placs. Neuerthe-less, that, vpon their warrants, he would deliuer what pleased them to demand. Yf the President had at that tyme enlarged the pportion according to their request, whout doubt, in very short tyme, he had starued the whole company. He would not ioyne wth them, therefore, in such ignorant murder whout their own warrant.

The President, well seeing to what end their ympacience

would growe, desired them earnestly & often tymes to bestow
the Presidentshipp amonge themselues; that he would obey,
a private man, as well as they could comand. But they refused to discharge him of the place; sayeing they mought not
doe it, for that hee did his Matie good service in yt. In this
meane tyme, the Indians did daily relieue us wth corne and fleshe,
that, in three weekes, the President had reared vpp xx men able
to worke; for, as his stoare increased, he mended the comon
pott: he had laid vp, besides, prouision for 3 weekes' wheate
before hand.

By this tyme, the Councell had fully plotted to depose Wingfield, ther then President; and had drawne certeyne artycles
in wrighting amongst themselues, and toke their oeathes vpon
the Evangelists to obserue them: th' effect whereof was, first, —

To depose the then President;

To make Mr Ratcliffe the next President;

Not to depose the one th' other;

Not to take the deposed President into Councell againe;

Not to take Mr Archer into the Councell, or any other,
wthout the consent of euery one of them. To theis they had
subscribed; as out of their owne mouthes, at seuerall tymes,
it was easily gathered. Thus had they forsaken his Mats governmt, sett vs downe in the instruccons, & made it a Triumvirat.

It seemeth Mr Archer was nothing acquainted wth theis
artycles. Though all the rest crept out of his noats and
comentaryes that were preferred against the President, yet it
pleased God to cast him into the same disgrace and pitt that
he prepared for another, as will appeare hereafter.

Septem. — The 10 of September, Mr Ratcliff, Mr Smyth,
and Mr Martynn, came to the President's tennt with a warrant,
subscribed vnder their handes, to depose the President; sayeing they thought him very unworthy to be eyther President or
of the Councell, and therefore discharged him of bothe. He
answered them, that they had eased him of a great deale of care
and trouble; that, long since, hee had diuers tymes profered
them the place at an easier rate; and, further, that the President
ought to be remoued (as appeareth in his Mats instruccons for
our government) by the greater number of xiij voyces, Councellors; that they were but three, and therefore wished them
to proceede advisedly. But they told him, if they did him
wrong, they must answere it. Then said the deposed President,

" I ame at your pleasure: dispose of me as you will wthout further garboiles."

I will now write what followeth in my owne name, and giue the new President his title. I shall be the briefer being thus discharged. I was comytted to a Serieant, and sent to the pynnasse; but I was answered wth, "If they did me wronge, they must answere it."

The 11th of September, I was sent for to come before the President and Councell vpon their Court daie. They had now made Mr Archer, Recorder of Virginia. The President made a speeche to the Collony, that he thought it fitt to acquaint them whie I was deposed. I ame now forced to stuff my paper with frivolous trifles, that our graue and worthy Councell may the better strike those vaynes where the corrupt blood lyeth, and that they may see in what manner of governmt the hope of the Collony now travayleth.

Ffirst, Master President said that I had denyed him a penny whitle, a chickyn, a spoonfull of beere, and serued him wth foule corne; and wth that pulled some graine out of a bagg, shewing it to the company.

Then start up Mr Smyth, and said that I had told him playnly how he lied; and that I said, though we were equall heere, yet, if we were in England, I would think scorne his name should be my companyon.

Mr Martyn followed wth, "He reporteth that I doe slack the service in the Collonye, and doe nothing but tend my pott, spitt, and oven; but he hath starued my sonne, and denyed him a spoonefull of beere. I haue freinds in England shal be revenged on him, if euer he come in London."

I asked Mr President if I should answere theis complts, and whether he had ought els to charge me wthall. Wth that he pulled out a paper booke, loaded full wth artycles against me, and gaue them Mr Archer to reade.

I tould Mr President and the Councell, that, by the instruccons for our governmt, our proceedings ought to be verball, and I was there ready to answere; but they said they would proceede in that order. I desired a coppie of the articles, and tyme giuen me to answere them likewise by wrighting; but that would not be graunted. I badd them then please themselues. Mr Archer then read some of the artycles; when, on the suddaine, Mr President said, "Staie, staie! Wee know not whether he will abide our Judgment, or whether he will appeale to the King;" sayeing to me, "How saie you: Will you appeale to the King, or no?" I apprehended presently that God's mercy had opened me a waie, through their ignorance, to escape their malice; for I never knew how I might demande an appeale: besides, I had secret knowledge how they had foreiudged me to paie fiue fold for any thing that came to my handes, whereof I would not discharge myself by wrighting; and that I should lie in prison vntil I had paid it.

The Cape Marchant had deliured me our marchandize, wthout any noat of the perticularyties, vnder my hand; for himself had receyued them in grosse. I likewise, as occation moued me, spent them in trade or by guift amongst the Indians. So likewise did Captn. Newport take of them, when he went up to discouer the King's river, what he thought good, without any noate of his hand mentioning the certainty; and disposed of them as was fitt for him. Of these, likewise, I could make no accompt; onely I was well assured I had neuer bestowed the valewe of three penny whitles to my own vse, nor to the private vse of any other; for I never carryed any fauorite over wth me, or intertayned any thear. I was all to one and one to all.

Vpon theis consideracons, I answered Mr President and the Councell, that His Matys handes were full of mercy, and that I did appeale to His Mats mercy. They then comytted me prisoner againe to the master of ye pynnasse, wth theis words, "Looke to him well: he is now the King's prisoner."

Then Mr Archer pulled out of his bosome another paper book full of artycles against me, desiring that he might reade them in the name of the Collony. I said I stood there ready to answere any man's complaintt whome I had wronged; but no one man spoke one word against me. Then was he willed to reade his booke, whereof I complayned; but I was still answered, "If they doe me wrong, they must answer it." I have forgotten the most of the artycles, they were so slight (yet he glorieth much in his pennworke). I know well the last: and a speeche that he then made savoured well for a mutyny; for he desired that by no means I might lye prysoner in the towne, least boath he and others of the Collony should not giue such obedience to their comaund as they ought to doe: which goodly speech of his they easilye swallowed.

But it was vsuall and naturall to this honest gent., Mr Archer, to be allwayes hatching of some mutany in my tyme. Hee might haue appeered an author of 3 seuerall mutynies.

And hee (as Mr Pearsie sent me worde) had bought some witnesses' handes against me to diuers artycles, wth Indian cakes (wch was noe great matter to doe after my deposal, and considering their hungar), perswations, and threats. At another tyme, he feared not to saie openly, and in the presence of one of the Councell, that, if they had not deposed me when they did, he hadd gotten twenty others to himself wch should haue deposed me. But this speech of his was likewise easily disiested. Mr Crofts feared not to saie, that, if others would ioyne wth him, he would pull me out of my seate, and out of my skynn too. Others would saie (whose names I spare), that, vnless I would amend their allowance, they would be their owne caruers. For these mutinus speeches I rebuked them openly, and proceeded no further against them, considering thein of men's liues in the King's service there. One of the Councell was very earnest wth me to take a guard aboute me. I answered him, I would no guard but God's love and my own innocencie. In all theis disorders was Mr Archer a ringleader.

When Mr President and Mr Archer had made an end of their artycles aboue mentioned, I was again sent prisoner to the pynnasse; and Mr Kendall, takeinge from thence, had his liberty, but might not carry armes.

All this while, the salvages brought to the towne such corn and fflesh as they could spare. Paspaheighe, by Tapahanne's mediation, was taken into freindshipp with vs. The Councillors, Mr Smyth especially, traded vp and downe the river wth the Indyans for corne; wch releued the Collony well.

As I understand by a report, I am much charged wth staruing the Collony. I did alwaies giue eury man his allowance faithfully, both of corne, oyle, aquivite, &c., as was by the Counsell proportioned: neyther was it bettered after my tyme, untill, towards th' end of March, a bisket was allowed to euery workeing man for his breakefast, by means of the puision brought vs by Captn. Newport; as will appeare hereafter. It is further said, I did much banquit and ryot. I never had but one squirell roasted; whereof I gave part to Mr Ratcliff, then sick: yet was that squirell given me. I did never heate a flesh pott but when the comon pot was so used likewise. Yet how often Mr President's and the Councellors' spitts haue night & daye bene endaungered to break their backes, — so laden wth swanns, geese, ducks, &c! how many times their flesh potts haue swelled, many hungry eies did behold, to their great longing; and what great theeues and theeving thear hath been in the comon stoare since my tyme, I doubt not but is already made knowne to his Mats Councell for Virginia.

The 17th daie of Septembr, I was sent for to the Court to answere a complaint exhibited against me by Jehu Robinson; for that, when I was President, I did saie, hee wth others had consented to run awaye with the shallop to Newfoundland. At an other tyme, I must answere Mr Smyth for that I had said hee did conceal an intended mutany. I tould Mr Recorder, those words would beare no actions; that one of the causes was done wthout the lymits menconed in the Patent graunted to vs; and therefore prayed Mr President that I mought not be thus lugged with theis disgraces and troubles: but hee did weare no other eies or eares than grew on Mr Archer's head.

The jury gaue the one of them 100ti and the other two hundred pound damages for slaunder. Then Mr Recorder did very learnedly comfort me, that, if I had wrong, I might bring my writ of error in London; whereat I smiled.

I, seeing their law so speedie and cheape, desired justice for a copper kettle wch Mr Crofte did deteyne from me. Hee said I had giuen it him. I did bid him bring his proofe for that. Hee confessed he had no proofe. Then Mr President did aske me if I would be sworne I did not giue it him. I said I knew no cause whie to sweare for myne owne. He asked Mr Crofts if hee would make oath I did give it him; wch oathe he tooke, and wonn my kettle from me, that was in that place and tyme worth half his weight in gold. Yet I did understand afterwards that he would haue given John Capper the one half of the kettle to haue taken the oath for him; but hee would no copper on that price.

I tould Mr President I had not known the like lawe, and prayed they would be more sparing of law vntill wee had more witt or wealthe; that lawes were good spies in a populous, peaceable, and plentifull country, whear they did make the good men better, & stayed the badd from being worse; yt wee weare so poore as they did but rob us of tyme that might be better ymployed in service in the Collonye.

The . . . daie of . . . the President did beat James Read, the Smyth. The Smythe stroake him againe. For this he was condempned to be hanged; but, before he was turned of the lather, he desired to speak with the President in private, to whome he accused Mr Kendall of a mutiny, and so escaped himself. What indictment Mr Recorder framed against the Smyth, I knowe not; but I knowe it is familiar for the President, Counsellors, and other officers, to beate men at their pleasures. One lyeth sick till death, another walketh lame, the third cryeth out of all his boanes; wch myseryes they doe take vpon their consciences to come to them by this their almes of beating. Wear this whipping, lawing, beating, and hanging, in Virginia, knowne in England, I fear it would driue many well affected myndes from this honoble action of Virginia.

This Smyth comyng aboord the pynnasse wth some others, aboute some busines, 2 or 3 dayes before his arraignemt, brought me comendacons from Mr Pearsye, Mr Waller, Mr Kendall, and some others, saieing they would be glad to see me on shoare. I answered him, they were honest gent., and had carryed themselues very obediently to their gounors. I prayed God that they did not think of any ill thing vnworthie themselues. I added further, that vpon Sundaie, if the weathiar were faire, I would be at the sermon. Lastly, I said that I was so sickly, starued, lame, and did lye so could and wett in the pynnasse, as I would be dragged thithere before I would goe thither any more. Sundaie proued not faire: I went not to the sermon.

The . . . daie of . . ., Mr Kendall was executed; being shott to death for a mutiny. In th' arrest of his judgmt, he alleaged to Mr President yt his name was Sicklemore, not Ratcliff; & so had no authority to pnounce judgmt. Then Mr Martyn pnounced judgmt.

Somewhat before this tyme, the President and Councell had sent for the keyes of my coffers, supposing that I had some wrightings concerning the Collony. I requested that the Clearke of the Councell might see what they tooke out of my coffers; but they would not suffer him or any other. Vnder cullor heereof, they took my books of accompt, and all my noates that concerned the expences of the Collony, and instructions vnder Cape-Marchant's hande of the stoare of prouision, diuers other bookes & trifles of my owne proper goods, wch I could neuer receouer. Thus was I made good prize on all sides.

The . . . daie of . . ., the President comanded me to come on shore; wch I refused, as not rightfully deposed, and desired that I mought speake to him and the Councell in the pesence of 10 of the best sorte of the gent. Wth much intreaty, some of them wear sent for. Then I tould them I was determined to goe into England to acquaint our Councell there with our weaknes. I said furhter, their lawes and governmt was such as I had no ioye to liue under them any longer; that I did much myslike their triumverat haueing forsaken his Mats instruccons for our government, and therefore praied there might be more made of the Councell. I said further, I desired not to go into England, if eyther Mr President or Mr Archer would goe, but was willing to take my fortune wth the Collony; and did also proffer to furnish them wth 100ti towards the fetching home the Collonye, if the action was given ouer. They did like of none of my proffers, but made diuers shott att mee in the pynnasse. I seeing their resolucons, went ashoare to them; whear, after I had staied a while in conference, they sent me to the pynnasse againe.

Decem. — The 10th of December, Mr Smyth wenṫ vp the ryuer of the Chechohomynies to trade for corne. He was desirous to see the heade of that riuer; and, when it was not passible wth the shallop, he hired a cannow and an Indian to carry him vp further. The river the higher grew worse and worse. Then hee went on shoare wth his guide, and left Robinson & Emmery, twoe of our Men, in the cannow; wch were presently slayne by the Indians, Pamaonke's men, and hee himself taken prysoner, and, by the means of his guide, his lief was saved; and Pamaonche, haueing him prisoner, carryed him to his neybors wyroances to see if any of them knew him for one of those wch had bene, some twoe or three yeers before vs, in a river amongst them Northward, and taken awaie some Indians from them by force. At last he brought him to the great Powaton (of whome before wee had no knowledg), who sent him home to our towne the viijth of January.

During Mr Smythe's absence, the President did swear Mr Archer one of the Councell, contrary to his oath taken in the artycles agreed vpon betweene themselues (before spoken of), and contrary to the King's instruccons, and wthout Mr Martyn's consent; whereas there weare no more but the President and Mr Martyn then of the Councell.

Mr Archer, being settled in his authority, sought how to call Mr Smyth's lief in question, and had indited him vpon a chapter in Leuiticus for the death of his twoe men. He had had his tryall the same daie of his retorne, and, I believe, his hanging the same or the next daie, so speedie is our lawe there. But it pleased God to send Captn. Newport vnto us the same evening, to or vnspeakable comfort; whose arrivall saued Mr Smyth's leif and mine, because hee took me out of the pynnasse, and gaue me leave to lye in the towne. Also by his comyng was pevented a parliamt, wch ye newe Counsailor, Mr Recorder, intended thear to summon. Thus error begot error.

Captayne Newport, haueing landed, lodged, and refreshed his men, ymploied some of them about a faire stoare house, others about a stove, and his maryners aboute a church; all wch workes they finished cherefully and in short tyme.

January. — The 7 of January, our towne was almost quite burnt, with all our apparell and prouision; but Captn. Newport healed our wants, to our great comforts, out of the great plenty sent vs by the prouident and loving care of our worthie and most worthie Councell.

This vigilant Captayne, slacking no oportunity that might advaunce the prosperity of the Collony, haueing setled the company vppon the former workes, took Mr Smyth and Mr Scrivenor (another Councellor of Virginia, vpon whose discretion liveth a great hope of the action), went to discouer the River Pamaonche, on the further side whearof dwelleth the Great Powaton, and to trade wth him for corne. This River lieth North from vs, and runneth East and West. I haue nothing but by relation of that matter, and therefore dare not make any discourse thereof, lest I mought wrong the great desart wch Captn. Newport's loue to the action hath deserued; espially himself being present, and best able to giue satisfaccon thereof. I will hasten, therefore, to his retorne.

March. — The 9th of March, he retorned to James Towne wth his pynnasse well loaden wth corne, wheat, beanes, and pease, to our great comfort & his worthi comendacons.

By this tyme, the Counsell & Captayne, haueing intentiuely looked into the carryadge both of the Councellors and other officers, remoued some officers out of the stoare, and Captn. Archer, a Councellor whose insolency did looke vpon that litle himself wth great sighted spectacles, derrogating from others' merrits by spueing out his venemous libells and infamous chronicles vpon them, as doth appeare in hiw owne hand wrighting; ffor wch, and other worse tricks, he had not escaped ye halter, but that Captn. Newport interposed his advice to the contrary.

Captayne Newport, haueing now dispatched all his busines and set the clocke in a true course (if so the Councell will keep it), prepared himself for England vpon the xth of Aprill, and arryued at Blackwall on Sunday, the xxjth of Maye, 1608.

FINIS.

I humbly craue some patience to answere many scandalus imputacons wch malice, more than malice, hath scattered vpon my name, and those frivolous three names obiected against me by the President and Councell; and though *nil conscire sibi* be the onely maske that can well couer my blushes, yett doe I not doubt but this my appologie shall easily wipe them awaie.

It is noised that I combyned wth the Spanniards to the distruccon of the Collony; That I ame an atheist, because I carryed not a Bible wth me, and because I did forbid the preacher to preache; that I affected a kingdome; That I did hide of the comon prouision in the ground.

I confesse I haue alwayes admyred any noble vertue & prowesse, as well in the Spanniards (as in other nations); but naturally I haue alwayes distrusted and disliked their neighborhoode. I sorted many bookes in my house, to be sent vp to me at my goeing to Virginia; amongst them a Bible. They were sent me vp in a trunk to London, wth diuers fruite, conserues, & Peserues, wch I did sett in Mr Crofts his house in Ratcliff. In my beeing at Virginia, I did vnderstand my trunk was thear broken vp, much lost, my sweetmeates eaten at his table, some of my bookes wch I missed to be seene in his hands; and whether amongst them my Bible was so ymbeasiled or mislayed by my seruants, and not sent me, I knowe not as yet.

Two or three Sundayes mornings, the Indians gave vs allarums at our towne. By that tymes they weare answered, the place about us well discouered, and our devyne service ended, the daie was farr spent. The preacher did aske me if it were my pleasure to haue a sermon: hee said hee was prepared for it. I made answere, that our men were weary and hungry, and that he did see the time of the daie farr past (for at other tymes hee neuer made such question, but, the service finished, he began his sermon); & that, if it pleased him, wee would spare him till some other tyme. I never failed to take such noates by wrighting out of his doctrine as my capacity could comprehend, vnless some raynie day hindred my indeauor. My mynde never swelled with such ympossible mountebank humors as could make me affect any other kingdome than the kingdom of heaven.

As truly as God liueth, I gave an ould man, then the keeper of the private stoure, 2 glasses wth sallet oyle wch I brought wth me out of England for my private stoare, and willed him to bury it in the ground, for that I feared the great heate would spoile it. Whatsoeuer was more, I did never consent vnto or knewe of it; and as truly was it protested vnto me, that all the remaynder before menconed of the oyle, wyne, &c, wch the President recyued of me when I was deposed, they themselues poored into their owne bellyes.

To the President's and Councell's obiections I saie, that I doe knowe courtesey and civility became a governor. No penny whitle was asked me, but a kniffe, whereof I had none to spare. The Indyans had long before stoallen my knife. Of chickins I never did eat but one, and that in my sicknes. Mr Ratcliff had before that time tasted of 4 or 5. I had by my owne huswiferie bred aboue 37, and the most part of them of my owne poultrye; of all wch, at my comyng awaie, I did not see three liueing. I never denyed him (or any other) beare, when I had it. The corne was of the same wch wee all liued vpon.

Mr Smyth, in the tyme of our hungar, had spread a rumor in the Collony, that I did feast myself and my seruants out of the comon stoare, wth entent (as I gathered) to haue stirred the discontented company against me. I tould him privately, in Mr Gosnold's tent, that indeede I had caused half a pint of pease to be sodden wth a peese of pork, of my own prouision, for a poore old man, wch in a sicknes (whereof he died) he much desired; and said, that if out of his malice he had given it out otherwise, that hee did tell a leye. It was proued to his face that he begged in Ireland, like a rogue, wthout a lycence. To such I would not my name should be a companyon.

Mr Martin's payns, during my comaund, never stirred out of our towne tenn scoare; and how slack hee was in his watching and other dutyes, it is too well knowne. I never defrauded his sonne of any thing of his own allowance, but gaue him aboue it. I believe their disdainefull vsage and threats, which they many tymes gaue me, would have pulled some distempered speeches out of fare greater pacyence than myne. Yet shall not any revenging humor in me befoule my penn wth their base names and liues here and there. I did visit Mr Pearsie, Mr Hunt, Mr Brewster, Mr Pickasse, Mr Allicock, ould Short the bricklayer, and diuerse others, at seuerall tymes. I never miskalled at a gent. at any tyme.

Concerning my deposing from my place, I can well proue that Mr Ratcliff said, if I had vsed him well in his sicknes (wherein I find not myself guilty of the contrary), I had never bene deposed.

Mr. Smyth said, if it had not bene for Mr Archer, I hadd never bene deposed. Since his being here in the towne, he hath said that he tould the President and Councell that they were frivolous obiections tbey had collected against me, and that they had not done well to depose me. Yet, in my conscience, I doe believe him the first & onely practizer in theis practisses. Mr Archer's quarrell to me was, because hee had not the choice of the place for our plantation; because I misliked his leying out of our towne, in the pinnasse; because I would not sware him of the Councell for Virginia, wch neyther I could doe or he deserve.

Mr Smyth's quarrell, because his name was menconed in the entended & confessed mutiny by Galthropp.

Thomas Wootton, the surieon, because I would not subscribe to a warrant (wch·he had gotten drawne) to the Treasurer of Virginia, to deliuer him money to furnish him wth druggs and other necessaryes; & because I disallowed his living in the pinnasse, haueing many of our men lyeing sick & wounded in or towne, to whose dressings by that meanes he slacked his attendance.

Of the same men, also, Captn. Gosnold gaue me warning, misliking much their dispositions, and assured me they would lay hold of me if they could; and peradventure many, because I held them to watching, warding, and workeing; and the Collony generally, because I would not giue my consent to starue them. I cannot rack one word or thought from myself, touching my carryadg in Virginia, other than is herein set down.

If I may now, at the last, pesume vpon yor favors, I am an hble suitor that your owne loue of truth will vouchsafe to

releave me from all false aspertions happining since I embarked
me into this affaire of Virginia. For my first worke (wch was
to make a right choice of a spirituall pastor), I appeale to the
remembraunce of my Lo. of Caunt: his grace, who gaue me
very gracious audience in my request. And the world knoweth
whome I took wth me: truly, in my opinion, a man not any waie
to be touched wth the rebellious humors of a popish spirit, nor
blemished wth ye least suspition of a factius scismatick, whereof
I had a spiall care. For other obiections, if your worthie selues
be pleased to set me free, I haue learned to despise ye populer
verdict of ye vulgar. I ever chered up myself wth a confidence
in ye wisdome of graue, iudicious senators ; & was never dismayed,
in all my service, by any synister event: though I bethought
me of ye hard beginnings, wch, in former ages, betided those
worthy spirits that planted the greatest monarchies in Asia &
Europe; wherein I obserued rather ye troubles of Moses & Aron,
with other of like history, than that venom in the mutinous brood
of Cadmus, or that harmony in ye swete consent of Amphion.
And when, wth ye former, I had considered that even the
betheren, at their plantacon of the Romaine Empire, were not
free from mortall hatred & intestine garboile, likewise that both
ye Spanish & English records are guilty of like factions, it made
me more vigilant in the avoyding thereof: and I ptest, my
greatest contencon was to pevent contencon, and my chiefest
endeavour to peserue the liues of others, though wth great hazard
of my own; for I neuer desired to enamell my name wth bloude.
I reioice that my trauells & daungers haue done somewhat for
the behoof of Jerusalem in Virginia. If it be obiected as my
ouersight to put my self amongst such men, I can saie for myself,
thear were not any other for or consort; & I could not forsake
ye enterprise of opening so glorious a kingdom vnto ye King,
wherein I shall ever be most ready to bestow ye poore remainder
of my dayes, as in any other his heighnes' dissignes, according
to my bounden duty, wth ye vtmost of my poore tallent.

*INDEX

A

*NOTE.—Thousands of personal names appear in this work and to list all would require more time and space than the Author has at his disposal. Possibly this index, incomplete as it is, may be better than none at all. But little more than this can be claimed for it.

In the volume will be found alphabetical lists of all Soldiers, Burgesses, Delegates, Senators, Congressmen, Merchants, Physicians, Churchmen, Justices, Attorneys, Sheriffs, Clerks, Masons, Marriage bonds, Land Grants, Obituaries, Daughters of the Confederacy, etc. (See Contents.)

In addition to these the Genealogist will find hundreds of names scattered through the Legislative petitions and elsewhere in the body of the work. Many of these, however, also appear in the Genealogical section of the volume in connection with the families to which they belong.

BIBLIOGRAPHY

Legislative Journals of the Colonial Council of Virginia—*McIlwaine*
Statutes at Large—*Hening.*
Journals of the House of Burgesses.
List of the Living on February 16, 1623.
Virginia Counties—*Robinson.*
Notes and Queries—*London.*
Notes on the Virginia Colonial Clergy—*Neill.*
Ecclesiastical History of the United States—*Hawks.*
Records in Caroline County Clerk's Office.
Old Churches and Families of Virginia—*Meade.*
Colonial Virginia Register—*Stanard.*
Register of the General Assembly of Virginia—*Swem.*
Bibliograph of Conventions and Constitutions of Virginia—*Swem.*
Legislative Petitions—*Archives of State Library.*
Early Virginia Marriages—*Crozier.*
Virginia County Records—*Crozier.*
Virginia Magazine of History and Biography.
William and Mary College Quarterly.
Southern Historical Society Papers.
Files of the Richmond *Enquirer.*
Files of the Richmond *Whig.*
Files of *The Virginia Herald and Fredericksburg Advertiser.*
Files of the Fredericksburg *Free Lance.*
Files of *The Virginia Gazette.*
Proceedings of the Grand Lodge of Virginia, A. F. & A. M.
Brief Biographies of Virginia Physicians—*Anderson.*
Virginia Schools Before and After the Revolution—*McCabe.*
Biography of E. S. Joynes—*Currell.*
Southern Literary Messenger.
Comprehensive History of Disciples of Christ—*Moore.*
The Living Pulpit of the Christian Church—*Moore.*
Virginia Conference Annuals.
Who's Who in America.
Original Journals of Lewis and Clark Expedition—*Thwaites.*
Lewis and Clark Expedition—*Coue.*
Early Western Travels—*Thwaites.*
History of Clark's Conquest—*Butterfield.*
William Clark—*Thwaites.*
Virginia Historical Collections.
Pennsylvania Historical Magazine.
Revolution in Virginia—*Eckenrode.*
Woodford-Howe and Lee Letters.
Richmond College Historical Papers.
John Taylor, Prophet of Secession—*Dodd.*
Missouri Historical Society Collections.
John P. Branch Historical Papers of Randolph-Macon College.
Autobiography of Edmund Pendleton.

Biographical History of North Carolina—*Van Noppen.*
Biography of the Signers—*Sanderson.*
Life and Times of the Tylers—*Tyler.*
Men of Mark in Virginia—*Tyler.*
Records in Adjutant General's Office.
Biographical Congressional Dictionary.
List of Colonial Soldiers of Virginia—*Eckenrode.*
List of Revolutionary Soldiers of Virginia—*Eckenrode.*
List of Revolutionary Soldiers—*Saffell.*
Calendar of State Papers.
Virginia Colonial Militia—*Crozier.*
Virginia Pension Rolls.
Historical Register of United States Army—*Heitman.*
Report of War Department.
Virginia Militia Muster Rolls.
Confederate State Papers.
Life of Jackson—*Henderson.*
Surratt Trial—*Pittman.*
Conspiracy Trial—*Poore.*
Impeachment Investigation—*DeWitt.*
The Assassination of Lincoln—*DeWitt.*
History of the Secret Service—*Baker.*
Memorials of Virginia Clerks—*Johnston.*
Index to Enrolled Bills—*Williams.*
Acts of Assembly.
Colonial Virginia—*Stanard.*
Files of Richmond *Christian Advocate.*
Memoirs of Campbell—*Richardson.*
History of Virginia Baptists—*Semple.*
Virginia Baptist Ministers—*Taylor.*
Southern Quakers and Slavery—*Weeks.*
Our Quaker Friends of Ye Olden Time—*Bell.*
Index to Southern Pedigrees—*Crozier.*
Virginia Genealogies—*Hayden.*
Bristol Parish—*Slaughter.*
The Family of Armistead—*Appleton.*
History of the Baylors—*Baylor.*
The Bowies and Their Kindred—*Bowie.*
History of the Broaddus Family—*Broaddus.*
The Burke Family—*Boutelle.*
The Campbell Family—*Lewis.*
The Chandler Family—*Chandler.*
The Chapman Family—*Chapman.*
The Carter Family of Virginia—*Carter.*
The Family of Coghill—*Coghill.*
The Coleman Family—*Coleman.*
History of the Corbin Family—*Lawson.*
The Dickinson Family.
Dorsey Genealogical Table—*Evans.*

Glassell Family—*Hayden.*
Hawes Family—*Hawes.*
The Martin Family—*Martin.*
History of the Martin Family—*Martin.*
The Martin Family—*Gallaway.*
Martin Genealogy—*Hay.*
Minor Family—*Green.*
The Scotts of Buccleuch—*Fraser.*
The Sutton Family—*Twamley.*
Pedigree of Thomas Family—*Thomas.*
The Thomas Book—*Thomas.*
Thornton Excursus—*Stanard.*
The Terrells of America—*Tyrrell.*
History of the Ricks Family in America—*Ricks.*
The Pedigree of the Washington Family—*Welles.*
The Ancestry of the Wyatt Family—*Bolton.*
Colonial Families of Southern States—*Hardy.*
Virginia Cousins—*Goode.*